Sir John Gielgud

A Life in Letters

Edited and Introduced by
Richard Mangan

Arcade Publishing • New York

First published by Weidenfeld & Nicolson, Ltd., London

Arcade Publishing books may be purchased in bulk at special discounts for sales promotion, corporate gifts, fund-raising, or educational purposes. Special editions can also be created to specifications. For details, contact the Special Sales Department, Arcade Publishing, 307 West 36th Street, 11th Floor, New York, NY 10018 or arcade@skyhorsepublishing.com.

Arcade Publishing® is a registered trademark of Skyhorse Publishing, Inc.®, a Delaware corporation.

Visit our website at www.arcadepub.com.

10 9 8 7 6 5 4 3 2 1

Library of Congress Cataloging-in-Publication Data is available on file.

ISBN: 978-1-61145-472-7

Printed in the United States of America.

For my family and my friends

Contents

Illustrations

A selection of photographs from John Gielgud's own albums appears between pages 278 and 279. The albums are held in the British Library, to whom the editor and the publishers are most grateful.

Introduction

As an actor, John Gielgud was a director's delight; ideas tumbled from his inventive mind and a good director had only to help him choose the best and most appropriate. As a director, he was a nightmare to some actors, an inspiration to others; what seemed to work yesterday did not work today, moves and motivations would change almost daily, and his cast needed to be sharp of brain and even fleet of foot to keep pace.

I believe there are times when he would have hated this book, and times when he would have enjoyed the glimpses of self which it reveals. Letters are, after all, fragments of autobiography. Gielgud wrote a number of books, but his own inherent modesty, privacy, and possibly respect for the libel laws may have had an inhibiting effect. So here are his views of himself, friends and foes, plays and places given wittily, perceptively, and sometimes painfully.

The tone of the letters varies with the recipient. Those to his beloved mother are full of news of his theatrical doings and invariably expressive of his great love and concern for her, although to include them on every occasion would be tedious. Those to writers, such as Hugh Wheeler, have aspirations to literary style and humour which the reader would appreciate, and those to theatre colleagues are full of the gossip and potential which actors recognise as the stuff of their lives, even though many of the latter projects come to nothing. Letters to loved ones express the occasional joy and fulfilment of that love as well as the problems and pain that love can bring. Sometimes they contain a personal code and slang whose meaning can only be guessed at.

To practical matters. The choice of slightly less than half of 1,600 letters I read has been mine. The editing of them is also mine, with the approval of Gielgud's executors who commissioned the book. The fact of his homosexuality is well known and we have felt no need to conceal an important part of his, or indeed anybody's, life. What some of the letters show is the extent of this aspect, the subterfuges required to conceal it, and the dangers involved therein.

I have tried to keep my own comments to a minimum consistent with keeping the reader up to date with Gielgud's life and career at any point.

Those seeking more detail can read his own books or biographies by Ronald Hayman, Jonathan Croall and Sheridan Morley. I have, for the most part, excluded salutations and farewells, often affectionate, always appropriate. I have kept to a simple chronological format other than on one or two occasions where I felt that a later letter would illuminate the present subject. Round brackets are part of the letters; square brackets indicate my own interpolations. All theatres referred to are in London unless otherwise indicated. In 2004, the terms 'producer' and 'director' are clear. Put simply, and without wishing to get into debate, the producer is the person who finds the money, the artistic team and the venue, and who retains financial control over the production. The director heads the artistic team, directs the actors and retains artistic control of the production. This definition is relatively recent and, during the last century, 'producer' would often mean 'director'; the context usually makes this clear. In similar vein, the word 'gay' for most of Gielgud's life would mean 'lively, bright, sportive or merry'. The meaning of homosexual is a relative recent one.

To have provided footnotes for each familiar and not-so-familiar name in a book of this kind would, I believe, have become irritating. I have therefore tried to use footnotes mainly to explain events and circumstances, and included a 'cast list' at the end. The 'biographies' are necessarily brief but, I hope, helpful.

The search for the letters has been long, but many individuals and institutions have been immensely helpful in it. They are listed separately, but I would like to thank especially my wife and my daughters, and my friends Sebastian Graham-Jones and Trevor Ray for their encouragement and support over the last four years; the Trustees of the Raymond Mander and Joe Mitchenson Theatre Collection for their consideration and very practical help; my copy editor Jane Birkett for her meticulous reading and many valuable suggestions, my editor and his assistant at Weidenfeld & Nicolson, Ion Trewin and Victoria Webb, for their enthusiasm and patience with a neophyte, and lastly John Gielgud's executors, Ian Bradshaw and Paul Anstee, for entrusting me with such a fascinating and enjoyable task.

There will, I am sure, be errors and omissions, and I would be grateful to hear from anyone who can add to my knowledge, offer further letters, or correct my mistakes for future editions. Letters to John Perry, 'Binkie' Beaumont and professional colleagues would be especially welcome.

Richard Mangan

THE EARLY YEARS

John Gielgud was born on 14 April 1904. Acting was in the blood of both sides of his family, notably that of his mother: his grandmother was Kate Terry and his great-aunt Ellen Terry, Henry Irving's leading lady and the finest actress of her generation. John had two older brothers, Lewis and Val, and a younger sister, Eleanor, and the family lived in London. On holiday, and when he followed his two brothers to Hillside School near Farncombe in Surrey, the dutiful son wrote regularly to his mother, a habit that would continue to the end of her long life.

1912

To his mother   *27 January, Brighton*

We have not seen anyone we know here. It says on the advertisement that Aunt Nell [Ellen Terry] is coming here to lecture on the Heroines of Shakespeare's Women in February.

1914

To his mother   *No date, Hillside School*

Torquil has written to me. Twice they've been tried to be torpedoed. Please may I do dancing. There's a much decenter dancing mistress this term. I've been to watch twice and loved it. It's rather curious.

1915

To his mother   *No date, Hillside School*

Yesterday I captained the 2nd [cricket] XI and although we were beaten pretty badly, I got the noble score of 3 and also my 2nd XI colours. We beat Prior's Field (1st XI only) on Monday. I scored and had a great time with Margaret Huxley.

To his mother   *No date, Hillside School*

Yesterday was most eventful. I played for the 1st XV (Rugger) forward. We won 15–0. Needless to say I did not get a try but I got the ball quite often. In the evening we had the *Merchant.* I played Shylock, Jack Cheatle Portia and [John] Hayward the Duke. I actually introduced (being stage manager also) a little street scenery. A wall (the Humpty one of happy memory*) in the window at the back and two screens at the sides of it thus making a street along the back of the stage, also a new exit. I enjoyed myself immensely and so did the others. We did the whole thing with very few rehearsals and got off Prep. on Thursday for the dress rehearsal. I've still got piles of make-up on.

1920

A holiday in Switzerland provided a rare glimpse of his paternal grandparents, Adam and Aniela Gielgud, known as Grampé and Gaga.

To his mother   *1 April, Vevey*

Gaga is stouter and she now parts her hair on one side and brushes it back to a bun at the back in an Early Victorian, though not unattractive way. The old man walks very slow and gets fussed very easily if anything goes out of the usual course, but his brain is amazing and his appetite extraordinarily good. She complains at the food which is quite good, and eats little, but he likes *taste* and puts Bovril in all his soups (clear and thick), eats very well and flavours his sweets with the contents of his brandy flask, which is most amusing.

In the autumn of 1922, JG's second cousin, Phyllis Neilson-Terry, gave him one of his first jobs playing a small part in her tour of The Wheel *by J. B. Fagan. It was after this tour that Gielgud went to the Royal Academy of Dramatic Art. The letters of his late teens and early twenties have a natural youthful enthusiasm and also contain many of the qualities that characterise his correspondence over the years: a passionate interest in the theatre and very little outside it, politeness, gratitude for kindnesses, flashes of wit, a flowing, conversational style, an unabashed appreciation or criticism of the work of friends and colleagues, and that openness and generosity which endeared him to his friends throughout his life.*

---

* JG had played Humpty-Dumpty earlier.

1923

To Virginia Isham   *30 March, Oxford*

Thank you so much for your letter. I'm quite glad in some ways that you missed *The School for Scandal* [at RADA], as I fear I was terribly bad in it.

As to *Twelfth Night*, of course I am vastly flattered, and long to try and play Feste of all parts on earth – tho' I fear my voice is rather sketchy, to say the least of it – but I'm afraid I can't be definite about it at present – you see, after our show of *The Admirable Crichton* [by J. M. Barrie] at the Academy, Nigel Playfair offered me a very good part in the new play which is to come on at the Regent on May the third – called *And So Ad Infinitum* or *The Life of an Insect* [by the Čapek Brothers] and if that's still running in July, of course I couldn't come. Of course, if it fails, and I'm out of work by then, I should be only too delighted to play in *Twelfth Night*.

It's an enormous piece of luck for me getting the engagement, and I have a very good part in the first act, and a small one in the third – you must come and see it.

To Kate Terry   *14 April, London**

The play is fearfully difficult but fine and *most* interesting to be in. I think it is bound to make a big stir in artistic circles even if it isn't a financial success. My part is full of difficulties and I can't help beginning to have a few qualms about it. Our act is almost the hardest of all, I fancy, and we are nearly all young and inexperienced for it. However, it is all so fantastic and unlike anything else that even the old stagers seem to find the same difficulties in dealing with it. The result remains to be seen.

The Insect Play *opened at the Regent Theatre on 5 May.*

To Anne Harvey   *19 June 1984, Wotton Underwood*

I am so sorry to hear of Noël's illness. I met her a few years ago, the first time since our appearance together at the Regent and we exchanged reminiscences of that far-off time.

She acted under the name of Noël [Noëlle] Sonning.† Nigel Playfair was rather taken with her, and she was extremely pretty in a leggy way. We were *both* very unhappy in our parts. The first act, in which we were together, had apparently been very improper and erotic in the original Czech version of the

---

* At this time JG was still living in his parents' house at 7 Gledhow Gardens, South Kensington.
† Later better known as the children's author, Noël Streatfeild.

play. Clifford Bax, who adapted and translated it, substituted cocktails and fancy badinage which was quite ineffective. Perhaps we weren't experienced enough to make the best of the material. Anyway it made a very bad start to the play which, although ambitiously original and the succeeding acts very striking and well staged, the run did not last long, and on the last night Playfair sat with his back to us in his box all through the first act! Despite this, he was kind enough to engage me again for his next play, Drinkwater's *Robert E. Lee.*

Robert E. Lee *by John Drinkwater opened at the Regent Theatre on 20 June.*

To his mother   *13 August, London*

We've had only one good house this week – Wednesday night when the place was crammed with Americans who were more than enthusiastic and applauded loudly whenever 'Dixie' was played.

On leaving RADA, JG appeared in Charley's Aunt *by Brandon Thomas at the Comedy Theatre and was then invited to join J. B. Fagan's newly formed company at the Oxford Playhouse, where his contemporaries included Tyrone Guthrie and Flora Robson. He made frequent visits to London to keep up with theatrical events.*

1924

To Gwen Ffrangcon-Davies   *February 1924, London*

I must just write this line to thank you for your wonderful performance yesterday.* I can't tell you how much it moved me from beginning to end and with one kind of emotion after another. What thrilled me so much was the way you kept the character going all through with the same elements – the striving after knowledge, the primeval sense and appreciation of beauty and the alert common sense and, I would almost say, shrewishness on occasions, and that you developed it all like a lovely pattern and roughened the edges into the old woman with her amazing experiences vividly in her memory, her body hard but tired and her soul and intelligence both striving after the fine things and the dreams which she knew she could entirely wrap herself in, but for the need of work and the jarring everyday commonplaces that continually drag her back to earth against her will. Of course I have always had a weakness for old ladies on the stage, but I refuse to excuse myself for adoring you as one.

---

* As Eve in Shaw's *Back to Methuselah.*

A short time after this letter, JG found himself playing Romeo, again at the Regent Theatre, opposite the object of his adoration.

To Mr Andreae*   *12 June, Eastbourne*

How very kind of you to bother to write – and I am already your humble debtor for your first night telegram, which I appreciated so very much and never acknowledged – but I had 60 of them, and about a dozen letters, and was just beginning to get through them when I got ill. Please forgive my rudeness. I'm much better again and digesting ozone for my better invigoration – going back to the play on Monday night. You can imagine how I raged at getting ill, and they've had an awful job, as neither of my two brilliant understudies knew the part or were competent to play it, so they've had two hectic weeks, one with Ion Swinley and the other with Ernest Milton – rather hard work for poor Juliet – rehearsing and adapting herself like that! They've all been so kind, and written me such letters and telephone messages that I feel quite grand – like an expiring Cabinet Minister – but I'm simply longing to get back again, and hope you'll come and see it. Please come round afterwards for a minute when you do, and tell me the worst!

Over the next five years, JG played a wide variety of parts all over London, many of them for small theatre clubs and societies. Among those who began to notice his work were Edward (later Sir Edward) Marsh and Gabrielle Enthoven, who was a friend of his mother and whose collection of memorabilia eventually formed the nucleus of the Theatre Museum, London. They saw him play a number of these early parts, including Konstantin in Chekhov's The Seagull *at the Little Theatre.*

1925

To Eddie Marsh   *28 October, London*

It was so kind of you to take so much trouble on my behalf and to write so fully on the matter. The most interesting part of playing in plays of this kind is that one is continually learning and finding out new points and fresh things to do. The only regret one has is that the critics only see the roughest sort of performance on the first night and a fortnight's playing usually makes all the difference. I'll certainly make a more impressive scar on my head in the third act and try to get more of an effective pause or something of the sort when I tear off the bandage.

---

* Probably Otho Stuart Andreae, better known as the actor-manager Otho Stuart.

Late in 1926, JG took over from Noël Coward as Lewis Dodd in Margaret Kennedy and Basil Dean's play The Constant Nymph *and it was during its London run that he met his first serious partner, a young Irish actor called John Perry, with whom he shared a flat in St Martin's Lane. After its London run, the play went on a long regional tour. Whenever he was away from London, JG wrote regularly to his mother, Kate Terry Gielgud, and she to him.*

1927

To his mother   *23 August, Manchester*

It's a vast theatre [Palace] – fan-shaped so that you have to be on the lookout all the time for fear of blocking one another from the audience, or sitting with your back to them or out of sight – so there's a good deal to think about, and you have to yell!

To his mother   *5 September, Newcastle*

The car is going splendidly again now. I had her decarbonised and new exhaust valves last week and she is 'as new' once more. John Perry came over to Liverpool on Saturday night and is staying here for two days with Reggie [Smith] and me. They seem to have had a gloomy week at Sheffield.* Mabel [Terry-Lewis] went down a coalmine with Miss Bannerman to brighten things up (and admire the physical perfection of our British workmen).

To his mother   *11 September, Glasgow*

Edna [Best] asked us to sup with her and we went – politely but yawning – only to find sandwiches and lose at poker, and see her off by her beastly sleeper at 1.30 a.m. and take expensive taxis home. I was *very* cross. However – once bitten! Imagine her energy (and devotion to Mr Marshall†) going up to town for Sunday every weekend and playing tennis at the Du Mauriers apparently all day. These hearties!!

To his mother   *27 October, Sheffield*

This is an appalling place and just as I remembered it before – awful slums and poverty everywhere and the audiences sparse and unresponsive. Monday

---

* Perry seems to have been on the pre-London tour of *The Golden Calf* with Mabel Terry-Lewis and Margaret Bannerman, which opened at Sheffield Empire on 29 August.
† Herbert Marshall, Edna Best's husband.

was quite deadly. We are lucky in having very tolerable digs two miles from the theatre in a dinky street with a Wesleyan chapel and a shelter for lost cats close by.

To his mother   *1 November, Bradford*

This place is better than Sheffield, and very tolerable rooms and a wonderful audience again at last. Curiously enough, I always heard it was the comedians' grave, but perhaps the fact that Irving died here awakened their appreciation of the drama! Anyway, they pulled down the theatre he played in and built a cinema there, and erected a superb mixture of the Taj Mahal and a public lavatory* in which we are whitely sepulchred.

The actor Leslie Faber had taken an interest in JG's career and it was through his influence that JG made his first visit to New York. Faber, Madge Titheradge and Lyn Harding were there rehearsing The Patriot *by Alfred Neumann; the actor engaged for the Prince was deemed inadequate and Faber put forward Gielgud's name.*

1928

To his mother   *14 January, on board the* Berlin

The people on the boat are very boring, German, American or Jews or all three mixed. One insists on discussing the least known plays of Ibsen with me, and lending me Yogi theology à la Mrs Besant, and the old American at my table loads us with fables of the might of his home town – Buffalo – and the fact that he is 77 years of age. Unfortunately he let slip yesterday that his old mother was 86 – but I made no audible comment.

To his mother   *17 January, New York*

A really wonderful setting by Norman Bel Geddes, solid wooden sets with great dignity and real mouldings to all the panelling, cornices, ceilings etc. arranged on interchangeable platforms which can be changed in 15–30 seconds! Very effective lighting all from the front and top – rather too little of it, I think, but then I do like footlights, being a true actor!

I never saw such a huge staff working on any production – technicians, secretaries and three stage managers litter the stalls and coulisses, Geddes and [Gilbert] Miller yell at each other about the lighting from different parts of

* The Alhambra Theatre, Bradford, designed by Frank Matcham.

the theatre, and we still stay here till 2.30 a.m. and nothing seems to result to make things less hectic than the usual English dress rehearsal.

To his mother   *21 January, New York*

I think it stands a goodish chance of a reasonable run – about six weeks or so anyway. Many people don't care about it at all, and no-one likes Madge Titheradge, except me, everyone thinks Faber wonderful, and the spectacle very fine. The company is really awfully nice, and the three stars and Austin Trevor, whom I've known a long time – such a welcome change after the bickering on *The [Constant] Nymph*. If we should suddenly be withdrawn in less than three weeks, I fancy I could walk easily into something else – Constance [Collier] wants me for the revival of *Our Betters* [by W. Somerset Maugham], Basil Rathbone is apparently interested in *Paolo and Francesca* [by Stephen Phillips].

Miller is not a good producer to my mind – excellent on inflections and psychology but very bad on general directions as to grouping, climax and the like, which are what Faber and Harding need most.

To his mother   *25 January, New York*

The play comes off on Saturday night, which is simple, isn't it?

JG returned to London.

To Noël Coward   *15 February, London*

I can't tell you how much pleasure you gave me last night, nor how much I enjoyed the play [*The Second Man* by S. N. Behrman], but I did think your performance quite superb, and such as no-one else could possibly have equalled, in America or anywhere else. The two moments of sincerity make the most wonderful 'setoff' to the rest of the character, and that scene with the pistol in the last act is simply brilliantly done. How envious you made me of your ease and unselfconsciousness, and the way you make use of any mannerisms you have in such a way as to illuminate your character without losing it for a moment – and you manage, too, to talk at a tremendous rate without losing any words or any appearance of spontaneity, which to me would be the hardest of all.

This letter is great nonsense, but I am so glad of your tremendous success – heaven knows you deserve it. Don't bother to answer, I'll come in and see you some time if I may.

Back in London, he appeared in a number of short runs, one of which saw him playing Oswald to Mrs Patrick Campbell's Mrs Alving in Ibsen's **Ghosts,** *an acquaintance which would be renewed some years later.*

THE THIRTIES

JG's growing reputation led to an invitation in 1929 from Lilian Baylis to join the Old Vic under its then director, Harcourt Williams. It was there that he played the leading roles which consolidated that reputation: Romeo, Richard II, Oberon, Mark Antony, Macbeth and Hamlet, Antony, Malvolio, Benedick and his first King Lear.

1930

To his mother   *14 April, London*

I am sure you know how very much we all rely on you and if you have spoilt us all rather, and we do not always express properly the gratitude and devotion we feel, it is only because you have shamelessly led us on to expect you to be incredibly devoted and generous, and you always live up to it and a bit over. However, I think if you had been at home last Sunday, you would have seen from our expressions something of what we all feel towards you, and for that you are entirely responsible. If it makes you as happy as it makes us all to know you are getting well again, you will understand why you are the world's best mother to a sometimes very selfish son.

His Hamlet was particularly successful and transferred for a short season to the Queen's Theatre under the auspices of the actor-manager Maurice Browne.

To Maurice Browne   *22 June, London*

It certainly seems a pity that *Hamlet* should come to an end with such a wonderful improvement in the business – but I honestly do not feel that I could anyhow have gone on doing justice to the part for eight shows a week and it is hateful to have to save oneself and not go 'all out' for fear of being too tired. I think the change of work will do me good for a few weeks, and that I shall be better with a short rest before another eight months of Shakespeare. However I hope you will appreciate how very grateful I shall always be to you for giving me such a fine chance, and trust that next year I may perhaps be able to be of more permanent use to you as an actor.

1931

I have been unable to date the next letter accurately, but believe it must have been written early in 1931. With other members of the Old Vic Company, JG went to Harrow School to read Hamlet *with boys playing the minor parts.*

To his mother　　　　　　　　　　　　　　　　　　　　*1931, London*

The climax came when in the play scene, I looked up to say 'Begin murderer, leave thy damnable faces' to be greeted by a minute Siamese boy – coal black – very small with enormous spectacles and an Eton collar, I hadn't noticed him before. It appeared afterwards that he is a Prince and the leading light of the Shakespeare Society – but I nearly died of inward laughter, and interpolated hysterical chuckles for a whole page after. Also we were very pleased at pushing in all the bawdy lines fortissimo which had been removed from the school edition. Can you imagine? 'Vixen like' for 'like a whore'!!!

His achievements and box-office appeal made JG much sought after by West End managements and on leaving the Old Vic he was offered the part of Inigo Jollifant in J. B. Priestley's The Good Companions *at His Majesty's Theatre.*

To Richard Addinsell*　　　　　　　　　　　　　　　*11 August, London*

I've had a marvellous week's holiday in the South of France, and am feeling so infinitely better. The play is doing very well still, though the stalls and boxes are naturally less full during August – but all this bad weather is good for the theatres I imagine. We now have a jazz orchestra (cheaper) which commits the strangest perversions of your work, but sounds good I think, except at the end, where valiant efforts are made to imitate three times the number of instruments. The result sounds rather like the Entrance of All Nations music in a provincial pantomime.

To Richard Addinsell　　　　　　　　　　　　　　　*20 August, London*

There is talk of my doing Inigo in the film [of *The Good Companions*], which appals my soul but appeals to my pocket. I'm hoping however that somebody will ask me to produce a play instead, and then I shall have the courage and excuse to refuse.

---

* Addinsell, whom JG had known at Oxford, had written the music for *The Good Companions*.

To Harcourt Williams   *September 1931, London*

It was wonderful to see the play [*King John*] today and enjoy it so much. I felt I had never given you enough tribute in my domineering carping ways in the past. This had such an air of distinction, and I was so refreshed and moved by it. Ralph [Richardson] is wonderful – how he has developed and really strides the play like a god – but I've no need to tell you that. Bobbie Speaight I can't make up my mind about – he speaks beautifully, but at times obscures the broad effects of character and prevents us knowing what his intellect is doing. I told him something of what I felt – costume and make-up, things he's not clever about yet.

It was such a joy to be there and see a lovely bit of work of yours untrammelled by my own egoistical view of it for a change. I haven't seen a Shakespeare play from the front since *Othello* (at the Savoy) – so lovely, the simpleness and sincerity and absence of all the flummery of the old productions I used to see.

To Hugh Walpole   *24 November, London*

I shall be rather busy for the next two months, for I am doing (producing) a little play called *Romeo and Juliet* for the O.U.D.S. [Oxford University Dramatic Society] on February the ninth. I had hoped *The* [*Good*] *Companions* would be over, and I might hold court at Oxford and enjoy myself and work properly. Now it looks as if I shall live in the train for a month, with a deputy to stay down there and do most of the work o' nights. Very trying.

His production of Romeo and Juliet, which included Peggy Ashcroft as Juliet and Edith Evans as the Nurse, was successful enough to transfer to the New (now the Albery) Theatre later in the year.

To Richard Addinsell   *18 December, London*

Thank you so very much for the lovely birds. It seemed a shame to pluck them. I wanted to put them in my hat and walk on in *Cavalcade*! You were a dear to think of it, and I shall remember you in every mouthful.

I wish you could see Harcourt [Williams] as Oakroyd [in *The Good Companions*]. Just like something out of Alice! He's frightfully good except in the emotional bits, where he doesn't touch [Edward] Chapman. [Frank] Pettingell said to me acidly, 'Such a pity he lets it down so. The trouble is he's exactly like me – same lovable old darling!'

I also wish you had heard Mr Justice Langton on Sunday night, who finished his eulogy of my character by 'I understand Mr Gielgud is still unmarried.' (Dramatic pause while everyone looked uncomfortable.) 'May I hope that he will soon meet with not only a Good Nymph but a Constant Companion.' La, la, Sir Percy.*

1932

Musical Chairs was an unsolicited play sent to JG by an old primary-school friend, Ronald Mackenzie. After try-out performances at the Arts Theatre in 1931, it opened at the Criterion Theatre on 1 April 1932.

To Noël Coward   *May 1932, London*

Thank you very much for writing as you did. I was very upset at the time, because as you know I had always admired you and your work so very much and also because in a way I have always thought my success in the theatre only began after the *Vortex* time – this play was my own discovery and I had much to do with the casting and getting it produced, so naturally I was very anxious you of all people should like it. But you are quite right, of course. I act very badly in it sometimes, more especially I think when I know people who matter are in front. And such a small theatre as the Criterion is difficult for me, who am used to the wastes of the Old Vic and His Majesty's. If I play down, they write and say I'm inaudible and if I act too much, the effect is dire. Now and again one can strike the happy mien [*sic*] and give a good performance. But then, it is no use trying to excuse oneself. I played ever so much better today after reading your letter, and I am really glad when I get honest criticism, though sometimes it's a bit hard to decide whom to listen to and whom to ignore. One day you must produce me in a play, and I believe I might do you credit. Anyway, I think it was like you to write like that, and I do appreciate it.

After seeing him as Richard II at the Old Vic, the author Gordon Daviot was inspired to write another play on the same subject with JG in mind. The play was Richard of Bordeaux. *Earlier in his career, JG had worked with the Russian director Theodore Komisarjevsky and greatly admired his approach. He asked Komis (as he was usually known) to direct the new play.*

To Theodore Komisarjevsky   *2 May, London*

I am so happy you like the Richard play. I have suggested to [Bronson] Albery that it should be done at the *New* – as it has a better stage – under the auspices

---

* I presume that this incident took place at a dinner, perhaps given in JG's honour. In January the next year he wrote a magazine article entitled 'Girls Who Make Good Companions'. Among those who qualified were Mrs Patrick Campbell, Martita Hunt and Lilian Braithwaite.

of the Arts Theatre Club for two Sundays in June. I do hope he will agree to spend enough on it to stage it as you think best, and I am sure we can get a good cast if you are free to produce it. My idea for Anne is Gwen Ffrangcon-Davies – if you agree, I am sure she will be pleased to play it.

Komis did not direct the play, but it had two performances in June and July 1932, directed by J G himself and Harcourt Williams. His success with Romeo and Juliet *led to further invitations. Charles (C. B.) Cochran was the leading impresario of the time, and a powerful figure in the theatre.*

To C. B. Cochran   *6 November, London*

I have read *The Winter's Tale* twice since I saw you, and think I would like very much to have a shot at it. If you are still willing for me to do so, and if my ideas coincide at all with yours, and I am free at the time you want.

I wonder if Cedric Hardwicke would not perhaps be available by then if you could not get Charles Laughton, and how you would like the idea of Frederick Ranalow for Autolycus. Also I should very much like actors like Leon Quartermaine (Polixenes), Abraham Sofaer (Camillo) and Ernest Thesiger (Time, as Chorus). I believe men who speak verse so well as these and yet are good modern actors would be the types to get.

I also feel that the richest manner for the play would be Renaissance classical dresses and decorations – a great terrace and Veronese colouring in rich dark and tawny materials for the court scenes, then the pastoral could be light and delicate in contrast. I certainly do not believe in any kind of Greek or Roman décor in the classical manner, as it would milk the play and ruin all its passion and sixteenth century character.

Regrettably this plan did not come to fruition, but just before Christmas JG directed The Merchant of Venice *at the Old Vic, in which Peggy Ashcroft played Portia.*

1933

Richard of Bordeaux received a full production at the New Theatre in February 1933, this time with only J G credited as the producer. It was a triumphant success.

To Hugh Walpole   *18 May, London*

I was so glad you were not disappointed. After 100 nights it is dangerous sometimes to see a play that is well spoken of, and it is difficult always to me to play a part for a long time and keep the proportions right. This one seemed to grow for a while, and one has to be so careful not to elaborate overmuch in order to try and keep fresh. I am so happy it appealed to you, for it is my most complicated work yet in the theatre, and I was very daring to produce it and act such a big part as well. I don't think I shall ever risk such a dangerous mixture again – it's such an anxiety, having no one to tell one about one's own performance, as well as being responsible for all the others.

JG was now the idol of London theatregoers and after a fourteen-month run in London, he took Richard of Bordeaux, *with a number of cast changes, on a six-week regional tour.*

1934

To his mother   *24 April, Manchester*

We spent the night at Morecambe, the pet watering place of Bradford and the other grim towns. It must be frightful in the summer, but at present it's empty and there is a wonderful view across the bay to the lake mountains. A marvellous new hotel built by the L.M.S.* – every modern gadget. Friezes by Eric Gill and rugs by Marion Dorn, all very BBC and smart, but I don't believe any of it will wear well as it's only been open six months and everything's cracking and chipping already. Very expensive, of course, and the food pretentious and really bad, but perhaps the chef goes to Gleneagles out of season.

To his mother   *27 April, Manchester*

I have had a hectic week of telegrams and telephones, trying to arrange about 'Mary'† with Bronnie [Bronson Albery] before he (typically) leaves for a three week cruise today on a Dutch boat to Genoa! I have remodelled all [E. McKnight] Kauffer's sets, which were all quite useless as they were, and the Motleys‡ are to do Gwen's dresses. Daviot is coming, I hope, to stay with us next week to work on the alterations in the script, which will be useful.

In November 1934, at the New Theatre, JG played his second professional Hamlet and directed the play himself. The critics, the public and many leading figures in the arts acclaimed both performance and production.

---

* The Midland Hotel built by the railway company London, Midland & Scottish.
† JG would direct Gordon Daviot's play, *Queen of Scots*, at the New Theatre in June 1934 with Gwen Ffrangcon-Davies in the title role.
‡ Margaret and Sophia Harris, and Elizabeth Montgomery, young designers who worked under the name of Motley and had designed *Richard of Bordeaux*.

To W. Graham Robertson   *6 December, London*

Thank you so much for your very nice letter. I am so delighted that you enjoyed the performance. People do seem to find it stimulating and controversial, and that is very important. I am apt to be swayed in my views about many details, both by outside criticism and my own judgement, and I suppose one cannot hope ever to play the part entirely to one's own satisfaction or anyone else's either, which gives one impossible ideals to strive for, and is very exciting.

I did so enjoy lunching with you the other day and seeing your lovely pictures, and shall greatly hope to renew my acquaintanceship at a not too distant period. Siegfried Sassoon, the poet, whom I met the other evening, was so enthusiastic about you both as a writer and a conversationalist, and I felt very proud to say I had the pleasure of knowing you.

Following the enormous success of Hamlet, *JG made a short regional tour, visiting Manchester, Glasgow, Edinburgh and Leeds. Franklin Dyall took over from Frank Vosper as Claudius.*

1935

To his mother   *April 1935, Manchester*

We had a hectic first night – the production is almost impossible to set up, light, rehearse changes and do supers and orchestra as well, all in a few hours. The staff did wonders really, but it was rather a garbled performance as you can imagine. No room on the apron at all, music all over the place, Dyall frightful, nervous, fluffy and inaudible, and soldiers of minute size – Mancunian dwarfs, I imagine, doing everything wrong conceivable and almost eclipsed (fortunately) under those large hats.

To his mother   *16 April, Glasgow*

We had a nice drive at the weekend – picnicked in Cumberland at lunchtime on Sunday, and then rather a dull run to Turnberry in Ayrshire, where there is a large, vulgar L.M.S. golf hotel, quite comfortable, where we stayed, four of us. Extraordinary storms of violent rain and the most vivid rainbows I ever saw. Ailsa Craig is not very impressive, except as Edy [Edith Craig]'s namesake!

We did a marvellous week at Manchester, £2,600 as opposed to £1,600 and £2,000 in the two weeks of [*Richard of*] *Bordeaux* there, which is rather gratifying in the shorter time and with Shakespeare – and here we opened last night to £278, nearly £100 more than the first night of Manchester. Very nice.

A huge auditorium and extremely noisy programme girls and staff. I said to one of the stagehands 'Does this ever stop?' He said, 'Oh sometimes, but you know, if this was an ordinary show you wouldn't notice it!' Musical comedy with long act waits to change the scenery is not a good training, but Dyall has improved and the play went very well on the whole. Tonight, gym shoes will be provided for the hands, which may soften their outline a little.

To his mother   *Probably May 1935, Leeds*

I hear now that [Guthrie] McClintic only liked *me* and found the production shabby and amateurish – silly man, he made no allowance for first night drawbacks, over-lighting and very tired scenery and costumes which were not designed for travelling or a long run. Americans can never see an idea unless it's got up like a million dollars, and he probably doesn't know the play well enough to realise that our treatment of it is original or how much the general style contributes and is necessary to my own performance.

After touring with **Hamlet**, *JG appeared as Noah in the play of that name by André Obey, directed by Michel Saint-Denis.*

To his mother   *July 1935, London*

Phyllis [Neilson-Terry] came to the matinée yesterday looking lovely, and also, she says, longing to do character work – she says she is definitely 43 by sunlight and refuses to play damsels at matinées opposite unfledged youths.

To his mother   *July 1935, London*

I'm thinking of doing Romeo once more to follow this, while I have a few remaining hairs – it would be undoubtedly popular as it hasn't been done in the West End since 1919 with Doris Keane.

The Cochran Cabaret* was rather fun. I had Mary Ellis for partner, who drowned my hoarse croaking with her peacock voice, and the song and dance were tremendously received. I must say we all rehearsed hours, and old [George] Robey and Ronald Squire, to say nothing of [Owen] Nares, [Nicholas] Hannen, Yvonne Arnaud and Gladys Cooper – none of them quite in the first blush – must have been pretty exhausted by the time we'd finished. Our turn didn't come on till 1.45 a.m. and most of us had two shows that day beforehand. I was lucky enough to get asked to Ivor [Novello]'s flat first for supper where were Noël, Fay [Compton] and Mary Ellis, and so I wasn't so

---

* C. B. Cochran's Mammoth Cabaret at the Grosvenor House Hotel on 10 July in aid of the Jubilee Appeal of the Actors' Benevolent Fund.

tired and bored – and the whole show was a miracle of organisation and efficiency.

The production of Noah *was not a success, but in October, again at the New Theatre, J G mounted his own hugely successful production of* Romeo *and* Juliet. *He played Mercutio with Laurence Olivier as Romeo, Peggy Ashcroft, Juliet, and Edith Evans, the Nurse.*

I cannot date the following letter with total accuracy, other than to say that it was written between 1935 and 1940; the tone is intriguing.

To Noël Coward   193–, London*

I can't tell you how enormously I enjoyed being with you and being at your lovely house, nor would I have missed our railway carriage confidences for the world. It is so very pleasant when one achieves long cherished ambitions, and to know you a little has always been one of mine. I shall look forward to seeing you on Thursday – I trust we shall neither of us promise more than we are able to perform.

Following the successful run at the New Theatre, Romeo *and* Juliet *went on a short tour.*

1936

To his mother   *Monday 13 April, Buxton*

Edith [Evans] fell last Tuesday skating and broke her wrist – she has it in plaster and it must be most unpleasant, but she plays with a little black sling and her sleeve cut and tied and nobody is any the wiser.

After the tour, J G played Trigorin in Komisarjevsky's production of The Seagull, *which opened at the New Theatre in May. He was already making plans for his appearance in Guthrie McClintic's production of* Hamlet *in the United States.*

To Theodore Komisarjevsky   *July 1936, London*

I am more sorry than I can say to have to leave this beautiful play – you know, don't you, that if I hadn't got to sail on August 26th I would have stayed, but I do need a few weeks holiday badly before tackling Hamlet again.

---

* It was during the run of *Romeo and Juliet* that J G moved from the flat in Upper St Martin's Lane to Avenue Close in St John's Wood.

But I do hope to work again with you on another play soon when I come back. I have loved Trigorin and shall be very sad to leave the part. You have helped me so much to get more reality and subtlety again – big theatres and too much Shakespeare make me tired and then I get so cheap and declamatory. I'm sure what I have learned in this part should be invaluable in working at Hamlet again.

To Peggy Ashcroft   *1 August, Vence*

We are very gay here, but think much of you and wish the nicest members of the New Theatre could be transported here by magic. On Thursday we found a very gay bar in Cannes with a good nigger band and a marvellous patronne like the mother of Mistinguett, with a minute hat covered with enormous ostrich feathers about 3 ft. high, bright red, such as only real French music hall girls can get away with, very high-heeled white sandals, and a skin-tight check dress. She danced (marvellously) with everyone in turn, and though very gay, drank nothing but orange juice. We stayed till 4 a.m. and Dick [Addinsell?] mixed brandy and Cointreau and was in bed all day yesterday as a result. We dined at Antibes with the Mielziners and Dennis Coen, then they all came here to dinner, and we lunched with them again another day. I like them so much and Dick said immediately 'Peggy's friends! Then of course they must be nice.' And so they are.

To his mother   *August 1936, Vence*

[Jo] Mielziner told us an amazing account of going to see Ted [Edward Gordon Craig] at Rapallo when he was a student – he was let in by one of the children, after much ado, and then cross-questioned at length by the boy sitting on a couch which concealed a staircase behind a curtain – Ted hidden behind it listening to the conversation and revealing himself with dramatic effect in the middle. He also told him that [Henry] Irving was his father!!!

After his French holiday, JG travelled to the USA for McClintic's production of Hamlet. Lillian Gish played Ophelia, Judith Anderson, Gertrude, and Malcolm Keen, Claudius.

To Peggy Ashcroft   *21 September, New York*

Last night I saw, at long last, the film of *Romeo [and Juliet]*.* That is, I stayed up to the meeting at the ball, which was only about ten minutes in all, and then emotion got very much the better of me and I retired from the scene of

---

* The 1936 film with Leslie Howard and Norma Shearer, directed by George Cukor.

carnage. For unspeakable vulgarity, appalling hammery and utter silliness, I have seen nothing worse, except the ten minutes of the film of *The Dream** which I also failed to survive for long. This epic is, I imagine, highly reminiscent of the worst excesses of the golden Edwardian Tree régime at His Majesty's, and, as Lady Bracknell says, you know what that unfortunate movement led to! I should not dream of jeering at the acting of [Leslie] Howard and [Norma] Shearer, for I didn't wait for them to begin, but Edna May Oliver and [John] Barrymore, who is like a monstrous old male impersonator jumping through a hoop, should really have been shot – and the cuts, and the squandering of idiotic money and the whole damned thing – well, I wait to see *As You Like It*† now, but it's really like having an operation to see anything you really love like a superb play butchered in such an unspeakable way – or am I prejudiced – you must go for yourself and see if you don't agree with me.

It's really very enjoyable in this town, I find, except that I don't like being away from my friends, or living in an hotel, or eating the rather obscene American food – and last week it was appallingly and damply hot, which made working very tiring. Everybody is very nice to me, and I get on extremely well with Guthrie. I like his production very much, especially the middle of the play, from the play scene to the graveyard, which was, in my opinion, the least satisfactory part of mine. The Polonius [Arthur Byron] is a dear old man, but he doesn't remember his lines and is far too benevolent and sympathetic, and Rosencrantz [John Cromwell] and Guildenstern [William Roehrick] are not only babies who might have been my fags at Wittenberg at the extreme limit of possibility, but also very indifferent actors, very stiff and amateurish. Apart from these, the cast is really very good – the women both excellent, as well as being dears. Malcolm [Keen] is sometimes excellent, more often not, but he will give an effective if inaccurate performance. He reads the lines of the Ghost offstage and there is to be another man walking on the stage and the voice coming out of the air per microphone, which may be good if it comes off. We have a very difficult fight which is exhausting to learn but should be effective when we know it. The American accents do not seem bad, one gets used to them so quickly. I have not yet seen the clothes and scenery, but the designs were beautiful, and some preliminary photos they took of me and Anderson and Gish were very good indeed.

The plays and many films I have been to have been nearly all most interesting, particularly *Dead End* [by Sidney Kingsley], which has marvellous children in it, little East Side wharf ragamuffins of 12–15 who really act amazingly. It's a good melodrama of the *Street Scene* [by Elmer Rice] type, only far more exciting as a production – wonderful settings and effects. Helen

---

* The Max Reinhardt version of *A Midsummer Night's Dream*.

† The 1935 film directed by Paul Czinner with Elisabeth Bergner as Rosalind and Laurence Olivier as Orlando.

Hayes is really grand in *Victoria* [*Regina* by Laurence Housman], and [Vincent] Price very good as the Prince, but [Abraham] Sofaer very poor as Disraeli (which cries out for [Ernest] Milton, *I* think) and the small parts are abominably played. The Lunts' play [*Idiot's Delight* by Robert E. Sherwood] is great entertainment and he is very good in it – she looks staggering but gives a rather sham performance in a very bogus part. The whole thing is rather pretentious and vulgar, but awfully cunningly produced, and skilfully worked theatrically so that one enjoys it. *On Your Toes* [by George Abbott, Lorenz Hart and Richard Rodgers] is really the best of all – really satiric, rather highbrow musical show, with two brilliant ballets, a first class score and three or four excellent actors and dancers. I went with Jeanne de Casalis and Maurice Evans, and we couldn't have enjoyed it more, especially as it's so typically the best sort of thing they do here that we can't do at all. I can't believe it will be a success if it's done in London, or that they'll get a good production of it there. Also it is very improper in a deliciously grand way which would, I'm sure, be all spoilt in England.

The city is marvellously fine to see, the latest buildings, Radio City and the Rockefeller Center, which has an entire street of huge shops in the basement with moving staircases up and down, are amazingly well designed, and the cheap restaurants and cinemas are not a bit sordid like London, but clean and smart, buses and taxis curiously old and unsmart, with radios playing all the time!

To his mother   *26 September, New York*

I got my arm cut in the fight, and had to have gas and four stitches put in, which made me rather sick at the time, but I am quite all right again now. I only tell you in case you see some report of it in a paper or something. We had much too sharp and heavy swords, now we are using much lighter ones and all will be well. Also, it was a hot day, and I was rehearsing with bare arms in a sports shirt – silly but it's all over now, and has healed perfectly. We saw the dresses last night. They are very magnificent – I hope not too Cochran – but I don't think so when the scenery and lights are with them. Anderson has five beautiful dresses and Keen a wonderful Charles get-up. Mine is very simple and fine with a big drape of black watered silk, like in the Lely portraits. Rosencrantz and Guildenstern like the pictures of Charles and Buckingham, in blue and pink satin – gorgeous lace and plush and velvet on everybody. Ophelia has a soft yellow dress in the mad scene with her very fair hair – sort of chiffon stuff – and a red silk stocking round her neck and another on her arm like a glove. Sounds a bit Ballets Russes, but it's good because you don't realise what they are at first, and then it suddenly strikes you and is rather weird. The ghost effect is very good, with microphones – the 'swear' spoken in a whisper under the stage really fine – it's usually funny – and a good effect of disembodiedness in the voice when it comes out of the air and I answer.

The figure on the stage in a high mask stands with his back [to the audience] and doesn't speak at all. He makes me do my death scene standing up. I rebelled rather at first, but now I like the idea very much. With three corpses on the stage it is hard to hold with the rather operatic 'Kiss me Hardy' business, or sitting up in a throne, which has been done to death. This will, I think, have a surprising effect, and after 'the rest is silence', I suddenly fall right to the ground (via Horatio) and they say it looks very fine. The gravedigger is a dear, and I give him snuff! which I am sure has never been done before! I hear the scenery is fine, with huge tapestries in the Council chamber, but we don't see that till Toronto. Jimmy* arrived yesterday, none the worse for a very bad crossing, and quite at home in New York, and he is packing for me to move into the flat I have found. It belongs to a photographer, is on the fifth floor and has a very nice sitting room and big bedroom, two bathrooms (!) and a kitchenette, extremely prettily furnished, with nice books – all for 150 dollars a month (£30) which is not bad. Jimmy will have to live out, and I have to live up to a cloth of gold bedspread!

Emlyn [Williams] and his wife [Molly] and the Ben Websters and Angela [Baddeley] all arrived yesterday. They open on Monday,† having cancelled their tryout to forestall Frank Vosper, who opens in his murder play [*Love from a Stranger*‡] on Tuesday – rather a pity, all this frenzied competition.

To his mother   *2 October, Toronto*

Pretty exhausting time – the scenery was not ready so we had to have two dress rehearsals on Tuesday, one at 2 and the other at 10 – right through the play with usual hitches and disasters. However they accomplished things remarkably well on the opening performance – it was the second one last night that was really trying – bad anti-climax and exhausting in consequence. I played abominably. It's very difficult to judge the production till it is finished. Of course I hate a lot of it – they have no music at all and though the waits are very short and will be shorter in N.Y., the lack of it depressed me and makes dead gaps in the play. The Polonius is poor and the Rosencrantz and Guildenstern rotten. Horatio [Harry Andrews] so-so and the sentinels and Fortinbras [Reed Herring] etc. terrible. This makes it all the harder work for me and it's the more maddening as I know I could bully them all into giving me something of what I want if I had them for a few hours to rehearse. But this I will not do, and I remain enthusiastic about everything and everybody so that when I want my own way desperately about some point they all agree with a good grace. I got the last scene completely rearranged to my satisfaction on the afternoon of the first night, and today I am going to

---

* Jimmy (surname unknown), J G's manservant.
† In Emlyn Williams' play *Night Must Fall.*
‡ A dramatisation by Vosper of an Agatha Christie story.

get some more altered gradually. It's much the best way to work, and McClintic takes it very well – all his lighting and mise-en-scène is well arranged, and when he has good actors, Gish, Anderson, the gravedigger and even Keen, he does very well by them. But of course the rest are cheap and inexperienced and he hasn't the knowledge or experience to teach them how to speak Shakespeare. The scenery is very fine and dignified, though they alternate between a very Craig-like permanent set of golden brown screens and steps and a very Cochran council chamber, with blue velvet doors bound in silver braid with tasselled handles and walls done in a (very beautiful) petit point tapestry design of fruit and flowers – chairs, tablecloths etc. all to match in blue-grey velvet and silver. All a bit too much of a good thing, though fine in its own way. The front cloths are lovely though, all painted on velvet, with a silver tone in the Fortinbras plain, and the Queen's bedroom has panelled grey walls – also on velvet – then a screen top with urn-shaped pinnacles and a huge bed in grey velvet and orange with a gold and orange canopy scalloped above. I should think this looks lovely and they change it very quickly and it's a pleasure to play in.

This is a one-horse town but of course we haven't seen much of it. Very big audiences, but you don't see many people about at any other time, rather like those small towns in early films, when the rustlers rode in to a square with low houses, a church, four telegraph wires and a brothel bar, and shot all their revolvers in the air and rode off again! The hotel comfortable, but a dreary caravanserai.

Emlyn's play is a success I think and Vosper's not. *St Helena* [by Jeanne de Casalis and R. C. Sherriff] opened out of town this week (with Maurice Evans). They say it needs rearrangement before New York.

Hamlet *opened in New York on 8 October. The English actor and film star Leslie Howard was preparing his own production of* **Hamlet**, *which was due to play in New York at the same time.*

To his mother   *12 October, New York*

The first night was quite extraordinary. I had 130 telegrams and huge applause on my entrance, which was unexpected and rather unnerving – and at the end nobody would leave and we took 12 or 15 curtains. I had three or four to myself with the cast applauding in the wings, and then people rushing round, headed by Noël in great emotion, and even a couple of telegrams sent by unknown members of the audience after they left the theatre.

To his mother   *19 October, New York*

Here are some more cuttings – you see how mixed they are, but of course *Hamlet* will always arouse controversy – it was the same in London. They stay at the end and shout every night and the stage door is beset by fans almost as in London, so really I don't think we've much to worry about for a bit anyway. Howard opens in Boston tonight. They got rid of Gertrude Elliott at the dress rehearsal, and a woman called Mary Servoss who played the Queen with [Raymond] Massey has been rushed to take her place.

Maxwell Anderson, who is one of their most important authors here, has sent me his play on Rudolph of Austria, but although it has fine stuff in it, it is mostly in rather ponderous blank verse, which jumps about from Elizabethan phrases like 'rout of bitchery' to modernisms like 'Q.E.D.'. The part of Franz Josef is finer, I think, than the prince, and anyway the part is so like Hamlet that I wouldn't dream of doing it immediately afterwards. I still think Emlyn's is the one to do next.* He talks of doing it with me, each putting up some money and playing himself a very important part in the last act.

St Helena is a failure, despite Maurice Evans' wonderful personal notices – they are all on cuts and likely to end on Saturday. They have also been brutally cruel to Frank Vosper. One notice said 'We are so grateful to England for sending us Evans and Gielgud that we must forgive them Vosper too', and I think his play cannot last long. Emlyn's is not a riotous success but will go for 10 weeks or so they think.

To Maxwell Anderson   *October 1936, New York*

I have enjoyed reading your fine play more than I can say. I admire the drama of it and the beautiful verse enormously and I am sure it could not fail to be a success if it is well done. But I'm afraid I think it would not be a good plan for me to play a part so temperamentally similar to Hamlet immediately following this production. You will say that all young romantic heroes with an inherent weakness are bound to be of the same class to some extent when they are played by the same actor. This is true, of course, but I still think I shall not play again this season in New York after *Hamlet* is over. It is such a part to follow, whatever one may choose.

To his mother   *1 November, New York*

[Leslie] Howard comes in next week, which will probably affect us one way or another. It would be nice to beat the N.Y. record of 101 performances for the play – [John] Barrymore's. I have suggested doing *Richard II* for a limited season to follow. McClintic likes the idea and it seems to me an ideal way of (a) following up the past success of *Hamlet* here, and trying to top it and (b) of opening a management in London with a safe card like *Richard*, which should be almost certain to make money, so that I had some capital of my own to put in to Emlyn's play to follow.

---

* Williams' play, *He Was Born Gay*, was written expressly for J G.

The Lunts and Helen Hayes came to the Wednesday matinée and were wonderful about it, which of course thrilled me very much. I lunch today with the Duveens and last weekend went to Long Island to a Mrs Doubleday of the publishing firm, who was very nice and had a charming lunch party.

I also went to *Stage Door* the new [George] Kaufman–[Edna] Ferber play (authors of *Dinner at Eight* and *Theatre Royal*). Very funny lines and scenes brilliantly produced by Kaufman himself, and a lovely performance by Margaret Sullavan. I laughed and cried and enjoyed myself no end. Amusing to see that kind of production first hand so very well done, whereas in England we always get the imitation.

Have found a beautiful apartment flat where Judith [Anderson] is – a sort of hotel really, but right down in Greenwich Village, on the 24th floor with three windows in each room, marvellous view, huge sitting room – and service. There is a small slip room next door with a separate bathroom that Harry Andrews is going to take.

To his mother   *7 November, New York*

This has been a strange week. On Monday [Alexander] Woollcott, who is the retired James Agate of America with an enormous following, broadcast about us in his hour. Then came the [Leslie] Howard débâcle on Tuesday – we simultaneously announced last weeks – with the amazing result that Wednesday matinée was sold out with 62 people standing. The box office is besieged and we have had three other sold out performances since, with the business for the week up 3,000 dollars. It shows how many people must have been waiting to see which production they would rather see, and also that a sensational failure in the theatre is always more thrilling to the public than a success. The bon mot for the unfortunate Howard came from one of the critics, who said I could now drop the GIEL out of my name, and be known simply as the GUD Hamlet, and one of our company who said his (Howard's) performance was 'more an antique Romeo than a Dane'! So many English friends in his company that will, I fear, get short stay here, as I do not think it can possibly run long. I hear his setting is beautiful, but little else. It must be a terrible blow for him, and the uncompromising cruelty of the notices has been a little embarrassing, though of course it is all very gratifying in a way, and my telephone never stopped ringing the morning after their opening. It's the first time I think I've realised that one doesn't often have really evenly balanced competition in the theatre, and though it's wonderful to have won, it is also embarrassing when people discuss it wherever one goes. However, I have had a foul throat all the week and been miserable at two performances at least, so perhaps that will modify my conceit. Better today, thanks to giving up smoking for four days, which I did not enjoy.

I am entranced with Stanislavsky's new book [*An Actor Prepares*], just out here. It is very technical, but I find it fascinating, especially the part about relaxing, which I would give my eyes to learn to do. The principle is, of course, much the same as that of Komis and Michel [Saint-Denis]. Michel is the first person in England to attempt to teach it, and I feel very proud of being associated with the scheme.

Mrs Pat [Campbell] came and I am lunching with her tomorrow. She looks well, but is very mad – has been alone in a cottage up at Arrowhead, above Hollywood, for six months, till her heart was affected by the height and she had fainting fits. She was told to come down and rest, and stays in bed here a great deal – is writing another bad book – no maid or companion but the eternal Pekingese – but she is grand and majestic as ever. Woollcott told me she was like a sinking ship firing on her rescuers, which I thought good.

To Peggy Ashcroft   *14 November, New York*

I spend the days by myself mostly, and then go out every night, which is lovely as long as one isn't too tired. Have been to some lovely parties – the Cotton Club last week where there is the most marvellous coloured show – you would go mad about it. I have made a lot of friends and it is the most charming theatre atmosphere, nearly as nice as at home. Judith and Lillian are pets – everyone in the company except a revolting boy who plays Rosencrantz abominably and drives me mad every night. The production is pretty bad really, and so is a lot of the acting, lighting, décor etc., none of them good or helpful, and that makes it much harder work. To do Mielziner justice, it was designed for a much bigger stage, and in cutting it all down he's spoilt the proportions and cramped the actors. Then the clothes are badly carried out and the Queen looks Empire, not Charles at all – Malcolm [Keen] has a very elaborate grey velvet affair with lacy frills at the knees which look idiotic in the praying scene – he is like Charles the Second in a bad temper. The ghost 'effect' I have at last got rid of after much cajolery and he speaks from the wings, only his first 'Mark me' and the 'Swears' done with the mike which is a very great improvement. My principal joys are the scenes with the two women and the Gravedigger [George Nash] who is a pet and a beautiful old actor who was once quite a star, and even when he is a bit tight he acts beautifully. Otherwise it's a pretty unsatisfactory production to be in when one knows the play so well.

I miss my friends and Foulslough* most and the weather keeps on changing and the food is horrid and the steam heat trying – otherwise it's lots of fun and I'm sure in retrospect will be delicious, over the long autumn evenings when we're playing Lotto.

---

* Foulslough Farm near Finchingfield in Essex, the country retreat that JG and John Perry, his partner of nearly a decade, bought in 1934.

To his mother   *17 November, New York*

I hate all the bars and restaurants being artificially lit (and decorated accordingly) all day long, one can hardly lunch anywhere without diving in to a welter of chromium, black walls, low ceilings, crystal chandeliers etc., and closely drawn shutters and curtains, like Hollywood versions of the boites in Paris.

I went to *As You Like It* and was agreeably surprised, being prepared to be irritated to death. I enjoyed most of the production, thought Leo [Leon Quartermaine] and [Henry] Ainley, [John] Laurie, Sophie Stewart and [Felix] Aylmer all first class, and didn't mind many of the cuts. I agree that she [Elisabeth Bergner] bores one badly half way through, but her accomplishment of diction and execution, though mannered and exaggerated as the film proceeds, attracted and interested me a good deal. It certainly is the first tolerable attempt on Shakespeare, and miles better than *Romeo*.*

Frank [Vosper] went home on Friday to do a film. Emlyn goes on but is very depressed at their business and very much opposed to my *Richard* plan, as he thinks I owe it to him to do his play next. I suppose I shall have to, but it's so difficult Bronnie not liking it, and I hate to come back to another management. We shall see.

A woman [Agnes Yarnall] is trying to sculpt me in the dressing room in my spare moments. I have refused 1000 dollars to appear on the radio in the Rudy Vallee hour at 8 o'clock (made up and dressed, before a large studio audience) to be interviewed and do a speech from *Hamlet*. No thank you.

To Douglas Fairbanks Jr.   *24 November, New York*

It is certainly very exciting over here and wonderful that people seem to like *Hamlet* so much, but I have always refused to consider it for pictures – [Alexander] Korda spoke to me about it some time ago. And certainly the Shakespeare films so far, with the possible exception of *As You Like It*, have done nothing to further my desire to see any of his plays filmed, for the essential need of the cinema demands an entire reconstruction of the dialogue and scene form on which Shakespeare based his entire craftsmanship – and with so many good stories in the world I see little excuse for re-shaping perfect masterpieces.

But I am still very keen on the idea of *Richard* [*of Bordeaux*], and would gladly make an arrangement with you to do it. I believe Gordon Daviot would be agreeable to working on the scenario. Perhaps she and I could both work with some person or persons skilled in the making of film scripts. It strikes me that Lillian Gish, who is playing with me here, would be a very ideal choice for the part of Anne – particularly as regards appearance for that

---

* A reference to the Leslie Howard–Norma Shearer film.

period. I imagine her name is still a big one in the film world, and she looks amazingly young and has cinematically much of the quality that Gwen had so perfectly in the play.

I think the part of Robert is also very important, and there should be considerably more of him than there was in the play. I don't know who could play him except you, but that would be asking a little too much, unless you want to have a 4 star film, like *Romeo and Juliet*. Perhaps Larry [Olivier] would think of doing it.

To his mother   *30 November, New York*

Dearest Mother

I am disturbed to hear you have not been well. Do please take it easy or you will have to lie up, which would bore you as much as it would upset everyone else. You must walk less, take more taxis, and eat calmly, and not be put to too much trouble by all the people you love to wear yourself out for. But I suppose it's too much to ask of you.

Last night you would have been very pleased, for the Players Club dinner was quite wonderful, and I was so much touched by the welcome they gave me and the extraordinarily generous things they said, that I could only make a very emotional and stammering speech of thanks. They had the biggest attendance they could remember, 300 men overflowing three small rooms into the conservatory on one side and the writing room on the other. I sat with [Walter] Hampden, the President, a charming, gentle man of between 50 and 60, who is a famous Hamlet and Cyrano. He was a great friend of Otho Stuart's, and played a good deal in England with [Sir Frank] Benson – understudied A. E. Matthews in *Peter's Mother* with Marion [Terry]. He is now more or less 'hors concours' and obviously feels it considerably. All the more charming of him, therefore, to be so nice to me – he lacks humour, like many actors, but he is quite a generous and courtly figurehead, like a histrionic headmaster. Otis Skinner (79) made a really charming speech, the British consul a witty one, and there were delightful telegrams from Barrymore and [Johnston] Forbes-Robertson, and all who couldn't come sent charming messages – Noël [Coward], [Alfred] Lunt, [David] Warfield and one or two others. [Cedric] Hardwicke and Maurice Evans were also guests, and I was very proud to be so honoured in front of them. It really was all most moving, and I wish you could have been there to see – the love and respect in which they all hold your family is very wonderful, and has endured through all this time as strongly, in the world of the theatre at any rate, as it has in England. It is touching to see this club, with [Edwin] Booth's room kept as it was on the day he died; they are all very English in their sentiment about the theatre, and such a place as this club is rare in America, so it was really an evening to remember.

Howard is doing badly, but continues to advertise and attempt to bluff the public with quotations praising him from Gilbert Miller, Hugh Walpole and [Leopold] Stokowski! They say he will soon take it off and go on tour – we shall see. I wouldn't go to the Colony Club when they gave a dinner last Sunday in the hope of getting us both together in public, but sent a wire and stayed away. Noël came to Emlyn's farewell party here, which was a great success. His one act plays [*Tonight at 8.30*] are very well received and booked, though the critics are not wildly enthusiastic. I heard a fine concert yesterday, a French pianist Robert Casadesus played the Franck Symphonic Variations magnificently, and also a rather pretentious but amusing programme piece of Weber, in which his handling of the piano part was masterly – a nice Mozart symphony too. On Friday there is the Beaux Arts ball at the Hotel Astor.

To his mother   *7 December, New York*

I send you the design for the dress I had at the Ball on Friday. Gertie Lawrence as Day and I as Night appeared, she on a white horse and I on a black, at the climax of the pageant. The dress looked very well and the horses behaved excellently, and it was a fine sight as all these affairs are, only too many people drink, and we didn't stay long after as we had a matinée next day.

We continue to do excellent business, and our move is arranged though not yet officially announced. Howard announces his last week, but I hear he is to stage a great reprieve on Saturday and run for yet another. They do that kind of thing a good deal here to keep in the papers all the time.

Of course the King and Mrs Simpson is the only topic at the moment in the press and everywhere else. It is a most unhappy situation, and even the Spanish war pales before it and everybody from hovel to palace is delighted with such a juicy opportunity for scandal and surmise.

Today Mrs Pat [Campbell], Joyce Carey and Ruth Gordon came here to lunch – very amusing indeed. The old lady in great form, though she complains of her head and says she thinks she has heart disease! I like Ruth Gordon so much, and hope to go to the play* next week, though it must be a shadow of the London show without [Ernest] Thesiger or Edith [Evans]. I also hope to go to Noël's plays again – they have a midnight matinée on Thursday – and to *Rembrandt* – what a notice for Laughton in *The Tatler* by Agate.

I bought a charming watercolour for myself by Dufy for 300 dollars in a fit of extravagance. It is the square at Versailles with the Roi Soleil on his horse in the foreground, and looks so well in my room here. He is thought a lot of just now, and his pictures are a good investment, besides being very attractive. McClintic is doing a fantastic blank verse play called *High Tor* by Maxwell Anderson, and has offered Peggy Ashcroft a fine part in it, which I have urged her to accept. It will be fun if she comes over, and I think she

---

* She had recently played Margery Pinchwife in *The Country Wife* at the Old Vic with great success and was now about to play it in New York.

might be glad of the chance. Burgess Meredith is playing the hero, a very brilliant young actor much thought of here. Bobbie Harris is here to play Keats, in a bad play,* he says, which they rewrite all the time at rehearsal.

To his mother   *14 December, New York*

Many thanks for your letters and the cuttings about the crisis. Everybody here was very hysterical and the 'tabloid' papers more shamelessly vulgar than ever. I took Mrs Pat to see *Rembrandt*, in which Laughton impressed us very much, on Friday and afterwards we went in to the Plaza and heard the abdication broadcast very distinctly. Of course the old lady is delighted by the Antony and Cleopatra side of the affair, and has strong sympathy for the obstinacy and rebellion from officialdom which is so marked a characteristic in her own career. Certainly one cannot help feeling sorry for the man and wondering what kind of life he will be able to lead. I imagine, too, that his frankness and obvious sincerity must have made an admirable impression. It is a pity that the old men in the Church must now crow over their triumph, for I am sure the fact of the country's ministers, both in Church and State, being all so very much in the sere and yellow makes the younger generation inclined to distrust them as old fogies – and the men of middle age like Edward are even more bitter and cynical after being through the war, and anxious to make hay while the sun shines whatever the result. The fact that the Church has had a triumph will not, I think, make the people any more likely to return to it in this age of ours, tho' I am sure the Archbishops imagine this business will send everyone flocking back to religion!

Howard gave a final performance of *Hamlet* last night in aid of the Stage Relief Fund – clever of him – with his usual 20-minute speech at the end denouncing the critics. He has bluffed cleverly, and appeared a great deal at clubs, lectures and on the radio – now goes over to the coast for a tour, but I do not think he has taken anyone in, or been particularly dignified over his failure. I am glad to have avoided meeting him. I believe he came to one of our matinées, but no one seems to be quite sure.

The weather is lovely just now, very fine and fresh, one feels very well, and I have found a good barber who massages my face and neck and washes my head and gives me sunray once a week, which is restful and refreshing after the Wednesday performances.

Maurice Evans announces *Richard II* here for mid-January, Peggy Webster to come over and produce it, so I suppose he really means to do it. I am slightly jealous, but cannot complain – after all there is no copyright! Just as well I dissuaded Bronnie, who was so keen for me to do it in London for the Coronation! By the way, I hear they have lifted the ban on *Victoria Regina* provided it is played by an English actress, so Helen Hayes won't go over in

---

* *Aged 26* by Anne Crawford Flexner.

it. How much I wish they would give it to Gwen [Ffrangcon-Davies]. She would be ideal, and it would be the part of her life. I hope Edith [Evans] won't do the Shaw play [*The Millionairess*] now. I didn't like the notices at all of the Bexhill production,* and, though it read well, I thought the play obviously falls down on the old-fashioned comedy and horseplay which he can never resist nowadays.

To his mother   *20 December, New York*

I shall hope to ring you up for a minute on Christmas morning and pass the time of day. Kit [Katherine Cornell] and her husband [Guthrie McClintic] have asked me to lunch there on Christmas Day. Peggy arrived safely on Monday by the *Queen Mary*. I got her rooms here and have taken her around a bit. She likes the play, thank heaven, and her part and the company. Everyone is enchanted with her, needless to say. She and I had supper with the Lunts last night, very delightful, and Lillian and Judith have taken such trouble to make her welcome too – they are such nice, kind people.

Tomorrow we move to the St James' Theatre on 44th Street. Harry Andrews has been threatened with appendicitis, but the doctor hopes to keep it under control with diet and treatment till he can finish out the run and have it done in England – nasty and worrying for him, however.

I lunched with Mrs Otto Kahn whom I liked very much – a beautiful flat with exquisite Chinese pottery and a lovely English Canaletto of Greenwich Hospital. Her husband lived with Lennie Messel when they were bachelors, she told me. Oliver [Messel] is here, having an exhibition. I thought his sets and costumes lovely for *The Country Wife*, but the play bored me consumedly. Ruth Gordon is brilliant, but a superimposed kind of 'turn', I thought. I should like somebody to do a version of Beerbohm's *Zuleika Dobson* for her and me – perhaps A. P. Herbert or [A. A.] Milne could concoct one. I believe it might be very good.

Galli-Curci came round the other night – a hideous woman but with great personal magnetism and extremely amiable.

To his mother   *27 December, New York*

I had an extraordinary time this afternoon. Edward Sheldon, who wrote *Romance* and other successful plays, has been stricken with some appalling petrifying paralysis† for fourteen years, and is blind too. All the well-known stage people go and see him, talk to him, and act scenes from their plays, and

---

* The first English production of Shaw's play was at the De La Warre Pavilion, Bexhill, on 17 November 1936.
† At the age of twenty-nine, Sheldon was struck down by a rheumatic disease, probably ankylosing spondylitis.

ask his advice. Mrs Pat [Campbell], who is one of his best and oldest friends, took me to see him – the most amazing thing. There he lies on a bed like a catafalque, his head bent right back, and unable to move his limbs, a black bandage across his eyes – in a gay room with flowers, books and photographs – he is beautifully shaved, a coat, collar, and tie – and he talks with consummate ease and charm, as if he had known you all your life. He has all the papers read to him, and is informed of every subject that is current, particularly about the theatre – he seems quite removed in some marvellous way from everything but the mind, and you feel after a time that he is entirely composed, alive and yet removed from life, like some extraordinary human oracle. Though the spectacle is so painful and appalling when you think of the incredible courage of it afterwards, the man himself is so magnificently powerful in his conquest that one can only long to give him all the life and vitality he craves for and accept his philosophy and wisdom with wonder and awe – I hope to go again while I am here and read some Shakespeare to him. I can well understand that people like Mrs Pat, Helen Hayes, Kit Cornell, and others feel that they are at their very best and humblest before such a tragedy, and love to go and visit him whenever they can. It is really one of the most impressive hours I ever spent in my life.

I dashed round the big galleries at the Metropolitan – which is an amazing collection. I principally remember a wonderful room of Goya and Greco – a superb view of Toledo with vast clouds threatening over it by the latter. The Whistler of Irving as Philip [in Tennyson's *Queen Mary*] – which I always wanted to see – a lovely Berthe Morisot of a woman in a garden – three heavenly Vermeers – several fine Rembrandts – and a fine modern room with Monets, Renoirs, Van Gogh etc. One needs a whole afternoon to enjoy it properly.

Woollcott gave a dinner for me last Sunday – Ruth Gordon, a man called Gerald Murphy, and Thornton Wilder, who is a funny little nervous man like a dentist turned professor – shy and suddenly incoherently explosive with expressive hands when he suddenly speaks of something he knows about.

1937

To his mother   *4 January, New York*

I was delighted to have your New Year cable, and to know you are really better again. Boats have been few and far between these last few days, but this will go on the *Europa* which J. P. [John Perry] catches tomorrow night. He had hoped to see Peggy's opening performance in *High Tor*, but unfortunately the tryout at Cleveland last week has made them decide to postpone until Saturday. Peggy says it needs incidental music badly, but Guthrie [McClintic] has no idea of the value of music, and never uses it. Of course it is horribly expensive here to have an orchestra, and nearly all straight plays dispense with it altogether. I went with John to three matinées last week – the Beatrice Lillie revue [*The Show Is On*], in which there is a fairly funny skit about *Hamlet*, in which Reggie Gardiner imitates me, and Lillie plays the latecomer in the stalls who interrupts the performance continually with loud conversation and inappropriate comments to her friends. Quite amusing and a very good advertisement for us – the jokes about [Leslie] Howard, however, go rather flat as the subject is now vieux jeu, like the jokes about Mrs Simpson, which don't 'go' any more here.

New Year's night was perfectly awful. Our theatre is on the main street, and the hooters and penny whistles began almost as soon as we were under way, and never stopped all the evening – not a pleasant accompaniment for *Hamlet*. We went out in Lillian Gish's car to Helen Hayes' country place yesterday at Nyack – a charming party and she has an amusing Victorian house with gold encrusted pelmets and mirrors, marble fireplaces and red plush curtains. Very amusing and not overdone, and some excellent pictures – Renoir, Chirico, mostly modern – that look surprisingly well in it. Noël and Beatrice Lillie, Judith, Joyce Carey and Alan Webb were of the party, and it was very nice. John [Perry] took Mrs Pat to a play on Friday, and I gave her grouse for supper which encouraged her to considerable flights of fancy. She was in great form and amused us all a great deal. We break the Barrymore record* tonight, and tomorrow another they have dug up – some quite obscure American actor who did 102† – and on Wednesday I am 'undisputed champion'. According to our press agent I have played it 400 times altogether by Saturday, including the two different runs in London, so I ought to know it by now.

To his mother   *10 January, New York*

We have been nursing Peggy through a week of crises de nerfs over her play. They opened last night and we were all rather dubious about the chances as we saw the dress rehearsal on Thursday, and it has very bad patches of weakness, especially the last act. Only three notices out yet, but they are all excellent, so I believe they may have a success which is a great relief for everybody. Peggy is perfectly charming and of great value to the play which does not play, I think, as well as it reads, but her poetic love scenes are beautiful, and the ghost effects very well lighted and arranged. Burgess Meredith very good indeed as the hero – a most interesting and unusual actor.

Walter Huston and Brian Aherne opened in *Othello* this week. Aherne as Iago got superb notices, Huston very bad ones. I hear the production and sets are wonderful. [Max] Reinhardt's monster production at the Manhattan Opera House [*The Eternal Road*], on the other hand, has rave notices, and I

---

* The longest-running Broadway production of *Hamlet*.
† John E. Kellerd (1862–1929) was actually born in England.

shall go and see it next Sunday when they give a charity matinée. It is a saga Old Testament spectacle, beginning in a Jewish synagogue, and scenes of Abraham, Isaac, Moses, Joseph, Ruth, Solomon etc. – staged on a great mountain apparently in different arrangements of stage with heaven and choirs of angels above – quite amazing, they say. The libretto by Franz Werfel, music by Kurt Weill, so all the Jews and Germans are well occupied, and apparently the result is very fine – anyhow, I am keen to see it.

I am writing this at the country house of the McClintics where Peggy and I are staying for the weekend – in front of a large fire with the rain pouring down outside – very pleasant. Guthrie just rang up from N.Y. to say notices wonderful and unanimous for *High Tor* – splendid.

To his mother   *17 January, New York*

I have just returned from an Actors Fund Benefit Sunday night performance. The usual endless affair with a programme that was not anything like over when I left at 11.45. I was there at 9.45 myself and didn't go on to recite till 11.30 – some sonnets etc. which seemed to go well. I saw an act of the Huston–Aherne *Othello* which seemed quite good to me from the wings – beautifully mounted and sincerely played, though rather pedestrian and lacking in inspiration. The critics, however, were bored and slashed it soundly and it ends next week – rather sad. As they also said it was a dull and silly play, I was out of patience with them.

Perhaps if I get a few days at Foulslough when I get back before starting rehearsals you could come down there with me and stay quietly. I hear we have a new Esso stove and shall be very grand. Elsa Maxwell, the famous cosmopolitan party queen, gave an enormous party at the Waldorf Astoria last night, but I could not go as the manager of the Empire gave one for the three McClintic companies at that theatre, and I went there and played jazz till 2.30 a.m. till my thumbs were nearly scraped off! The Maxwell affair was a 'barnyard' party – fancy dress, and real animals in pens surrounded the room – cows, sheep, goats etc. (washed and permed!). A real 'hog caller' was imported from a farm, who cried aloud (and was so dignified in simplicity that everybody felt ashamed who wasn't blind, apparently) and six hogs answered by rushing into the room with snouts raised – very biblical and odd! So do the idle rich recreate themselves!

The Barker *Hamlet** is very interesting, and I have been reading a good but typically incoherent and badly translated book on the Moscow Art Theatre, Chekhov, Gorky etc. by Nemirovitch-Danchenko, who was Stanislavsky's co-director – interesting, particularly about *The Seagull* production! I am still waiting to get Emlyn's revised version of our play and Bronnie's O.K. on the business arrangements, details of dates and so on.

---

* One of Harley Granville-Barker's *Prefaces to Shakespeare*.

A Rosamond Gilder, who writes for the *Theatre Arts Monthly*, has done a very detailed account of my performance, and I have suggested to her to offer it to Methuen who were anxious in London for me to write producer's notes for a de luxe edition of a *Hamlet* text. I thought that her notes, and reproductions of Motley's and Mielziner's designs with a few photographs – some of other famous Hamlets, some selected criticisms and a chapter of notes by me on costume and scenic traditions and general usages connected with the play, might make quite a good gift book in the style of Olivier's *Romeo and Juliet* publication (which is very dull). Anyway, it's an idea and something to play about with.*

I went to *The Wingless Victory* [by Maxwell Anderson] on Thursday. Katherine Cornell is a striking and glamorous figure, but not a great actress to my thinking. This is a stupid and pretentious play, and Anderson tries to lift its banality to a Shakespearean grandeur by rather dull verse. She looks wonderful in her Malay costumes and at the opening of the last act she crouches on the cabin floor, having had a great scene of rage against her husband and his people who cast her out. She has to raise her head with her black hair all over her eyes, and decide to murder her two children. In this she looks like a fine Japanese print and is very powerful and pictorial. Not so successful in the big scene when she strains her voice – beautiful in her walk and manner when carrying the dead child in her arms. I should like to see her have a shot at Cleopatra, but fear she is a little too voice conscious and 'the first lady of the American stage' to be really fine or great in any way. Of course, Guthrie [McClintic] has built this legend round her and arranges everything to set off the impression – she herself is so enchantingly modest and wildly enthusiastic – lives for her work, and devotes all energies to it – that perhaps she might do better away from him – one can't tell. They have certainly built up some distinction and graciousness on the management side, but without much real creative talent to follow it up – more flair for business, a certain standard of performance and very admirable publicity and administration.

They can none of them see anything in Emlyn's play [*He Was Born Gay*] or understand how I can possibly stick to my idea of going home, when a few more weeks would bring so much kudos and money with *Hamlet* in a few more towns. But I am quite determined not to play the part a moment longer. I cannot let them realise naturally how little I care for the production and the other performances, charming as they all are personally, and it is really a great burden and seldom a pleasure to play, learning more and more about the part and getting no support and even hindrance in all one's surroundings. It will be such a relief to be my own master again and to work with first class actors once more, if we can get them.

I have voluminous correspondence from Emlyn and Bronnie who have

---

* Rosamond Gilder's book *John Gielgud's Hamlet* was published by Methuen in 1937.

been having a high old time with their own and each other's amour propre but I seem to have done my bit as a linchpin and kept them from breaking altogether, though barely so. I only hope they may come to like each other better later on.

I lunched today at a nice house in Long Island and then spent several hours at [Edward] Sheldon's. We talked a lot about the theatre and I did some scenes from *Hamlet* and *Romeo* and Prospero – not very well in a room where one feels emotional and unable to 'let go' but he seemed to enjoy it very much. He is a fascinating and wise man, perhaps partly through his tragic fate, so maybe there's some meaning to it after all.

To his mother   *1 February, Washington*

Well, here we are at Washington. Peggy came down with me in Lillian's car and we had a restful and easy drive and picnic lunch in spite of pouring rain and were here by seven o'clock – then a very good dinner in Lillian's sitting room and a comparatively early night. Last week was very exhausting, though immensely gratifying in many ways. We played to 21,000 dollars and had a record house at the matinée yesterday, 300 people standing, and 150 at least at night. Sold out too on Friday night and the Thursday matinée, so really we wound up in a blaze of glory. Numerous parties were given for me, but I was too tired to stay long at either of the ones last night and on Friday. Met Stravinsky, Ina Claire, Gloria Swanson and a strange assortment of stars. Mrs Pat said in a low voice 'Look at those three frightful faces (Sibyl Colefax, Dorothy Parker and Elsa Maxwell). I bet they're discussing Mrs Simpson.'

A Negro* has done a brilliant bust of me in the play. I have bought a copy of it, and shall be interested to see if you think it as good as I do. I never sat until it was all but finished, and then only for ten minutes – he only saw the play once, but has exactly caught the expression I like to think I have in the part – perhaps you won't think so!

To his mother   *17 February, Philadelphia*

On the Monday last week they begged me to give an extra performance and after much demur I finally consented, and we gave an extra matinée on Friday, and we four stars gave our salaries to the Red Cross for the Flood relief – about 800 dollars, which wasn't so bad. The Saturday matinée we played to 4000 dollars, and on the week to 32,776 in a house whose capacity is supposed to be 29,000. Really extraordinary, and such a pleasure too, playing to such audiences, but of course I caught a cold on the

---

* Raymond Barthé.

Thursday, practically lost my voice, and spent a miserable Saturday grunting through the last two performances with no equipment and people hanging from the chandeliers to see me. Too bad, and much spoilt my enjoyment of the week as a whole.

I was supposed to go to a big dinner in New York for Woollcott last night, but got as far as the door, made gruntings and excuses and slunk away to a large plate of onion soup and bed. Consequently my cold is nearly gone and the others tell me I was well out of it as the noise, speeches and autographing of menus was endless and interminable, so I was wise to be firm. I spent hours composing wires about our new play last week. At any rate we have already Gwen, Carol Goodner, Emlyn, Glen [Byam Shaw], George Devine and self. The old ladies are not yet fixed.

Great waving of clubs in New York over the notices of *Richard* – the *Tribune* critic who said Maurice [Evans] was worth two John Gielguds came out yesterday with a further article withdrawing the remark in favour of 'six' – so he is evidently determined to be definite in his preference. [Brooks] Atkinson, who also was not too keen on me, is inclined to compare us to Maurice's advantage. The funny thing is that they are all so impressed with the beauty of the play – 'what we considered on reading a minor work is now shown by the genius' etc. etc. And of course they have seen Evans in Romeo, the Dauphin and Napoleon, all very effective by contrast. Anyway I now begin to understand a little how [Leslie] Howard must have felt! And my friends all assure me that this is not more remarkable than the best Old Vic standard! Vanity of vanities!

To Edward Sheldon   *27 February,* Queen Mary

So many thanks for the books, which I am reading with great enjoyment, and also for your generous letter of friendship and good wishes. It was indeed a privilege to make your acquaintance and to meet you alone so that in a few hours it was possible to reach an understanding that, at any kind of gathering, or with anyone less responsive and concentrated than yourself, might have taken months to arrive at. Your room is a haven in the cordial but sometimes overexciting atmosphere of New York, and I shall always think of it with pleasure and hope to come there again before very long. Meanwhile be assured I shall often think of you and will do my best, though I fear I am a poor correspondent, to let you know occasionally how things are going with me. Please do the same if you ever have the time and inclination – and thank you for so much pleasure in knowing you.

On his return to London, JG plunged almost immediately into preparations for Emlyn Williams' new play, He Was Born Gay.

To Lillian Gish   *15 March, Foulslough*

Here I am in the country getting a few days rest before we begin rehearsals. The week before last was chaotic: that friend of Bobby Harris that I told you about died after four operations, and then Frank Vosper's death;* and on top of those two disasters Albery quarrelled with Emlyn and disassociated himself from the play altogether, and so I spent all last week getting John [Perry] over from Ireland to arrange all my business, and finally Emlyn and I are going into management together in the play.

It has been pouring with rain the last two days – snow, slush, and mud everywhere – but it is lovely to be back in the cottage all the same, and today it is gloriously fine though there is a biting wind. I do so hope you will be able to come over some time this year. I miss you so much and think with great affection of our happy times together.

To his mother   *March 1937, London*

Doubts and fears about the play – the theatrical quality of it is strong and it is charmingly written – but I fear the worst if the critics should take it into their heads to find fault with the logic or the construction. However if we can make them believe in such frankly romantic melodrama it will be one up to us.

He Was Born Gay *had its first performance in Manchester, the first date on a five-week pre-London tour.*

To his mother   *21 April, Manchester*

The notices here were marvellous and we have changed a great deal for the better this week. Today we have changed the dagger at the end into poison, and I hope that may be better too, and I do a real mad scene at the end, in a very much cut version of the original speech.

To his mother   *3 May (?), Edinburgh*

Mr [Donald] Wolfit† wished to be photographed with me – Hamlets past and present – for the local press, but I was not to be drawn and was in my

---

* Vosper died in mysterious circumstances during the transatlantic crossing.
† Wolfit first played Hamlet at Stratford in 1936 and received a very good review from James Agate. Basil Langton, his understudy, told this anecdote following Wolfit's first night. 'The next day, after our morning coffee, Wolfit and I walked up Sheep Street. As we passed the Post Office he said, "Just a minute, old boy. I want to send a telegram." I stood at his side while he wrote it out. Then he handed it to me, asking, "Is that all right?" The telegram was addressed to John Gielgud in London: "In view of Agate's review of my Hamlet, I suggest we share the role in your London production. I will play Claudius to your Hamlet, and you will play Claudius to my Hamlet every other night." Gielgud made no reply.'

bath! We had a charming luncheon at Mary Anderson's on Friday – she is old now and no longer strong or very much on the spot, but even so extraordinarily gracious and dominating in the most charming way. She talked much of Nell [Ellen Terry] and [Johnston] Forbes-Robertson, but now is keener on music, and only goes out to Stratford, which however she disapproves of strongly – and to Toscanini etc.

To Lillian Gish   *4 May, Edinburgh*

Since I wrote last, the spring has come, to say nothing of your sweet letters, and the combination has cheered me somewhat. Also Guthrie [McClintic] turned up unexpectedly last Friday and was delighted with the play, to my great surprise. He of course realises its faults, but he thinks it is 100 per cent entertainment, which after all is the best I can hope for it. He also gave me one or two most valuable tips about my own performance. I tried to play the part much too straight to begin with, as the lines seem to suggest that one must not bother much about logic or character, and play each scene for all it is worth; but I found, after the first week and after a long talk with Emlyn that one has to play against the lines, particularly the first two acts, and try to create the impression of a haunted, immature youth – almost a pathological case – so that when he breaks down in the last act and goes mad, the audience realises that he was almost on the borderline from the moment he appeared on the stage. All this is quite interesting to do, and it goes very well when the houses are warm and friendly. The difficulty is that all the comedy and drawing of the other characters are crude and rather cheap. Nobody's motives bear investigation, and there is not a part in it that is really easy to make convincing, as none of them are carried out and developed in their logical sequence, but left in the manner of Dickens, as set types, to remain the same throughout the play.

Whatever may be the result, it is interesting to try to work at the sort of thing that the old actors played on their heads by the sheer force of histrionics and the romantic gusto which carried the audience away. If the press is kind to the play and gives me good notices, I think we may have a run. But it is rather strange to play a vehicle part of this kind, which is intended to show one off at one's best, doing all the things that are supposed to come easy, and to find them very hard to do because they are not backed by real truth and logic. Pray for us on the 26th.

To Peggy Ashcroft   *13 May, Foulslough*

How wonderful that you have become such friends with [Edward] Sheldon. The more one thinks of New York, the more strongly one feels he is the deep and arresting personality one met there, with amazing sympathy, wisdom and understanding.

Guthrie will have told you of the play far better than I can judge of it. If it fails, I shall go for a holiday and plan a season of plays – classics with a permanent company for the autumn. Glen [Byam Shaw], Gwen [Ffrangcon-Davies] and I have endless discussions and make vast plans continually. It's really a simply charming company. Carol [Goodner] is a bit boring but works frightfully hard at her difficult part. I think she will end by being very good, and is really splendid to act with as always. Emlyn has been extraordinarily reasonable and nice, as well as most sensible about cuts and alterations. For his sake, if not for mine, I do hope it may go for a while.

He Was Born Gay *opened at the Queen's Theatre on 26 May 1937.*

To Lillian Gish   *29 May, London*

Well, our worst fears were justified, and although on the opening night the emotional scenes went very well, the critics were embarrassed by them and puzzled by the play. Personally I had a very warm and loving reception and my own parts in the play seemed to go very well, but the comedy did not, except with the cheap parts of the house, and the general verdict all around seems to be pretty bad. It may go on for a few weeks if the audiences continue numerous, but if the Sunday notices are as bad as the dailies, I hardly think people will venture. I often think of you and wish you would suddenly land in England.

He Was Born Gay *lasted for only two weeks and after his holiday JG began to prepare for his season of classical repertory at the Queen's Theatre. The company included Peggy Ashcroft, Alec Guinness, Anthony Quayle, Michael Redgrave and many others whose work JG admired. The season –* Richard II, The School for Scandal, Three Sisters *and* The Merchant of Venice *– was to become something of a legend and had a great influence on those who were to run the Royal Shakespeare and National Theatre companies in future years.*

To Lillian Gish   *14 August, London*

We are in the throes of rehearsal [for *Richard II*] again, and it all seems to be going as well as can be expected. I am very enthusiastic about the cast, and the Motleys have done beautiful designs.

Peggy [Ashcroft] has had a holiday in Austria with Stephen Haggard and came back full of the Reinhardt *Faust* which she had seen at Salzburg.

I wonder how things are going with you. I thought of *Hamlet* last year and wished you were in these rehearsals too. Did I tell you Judith [Anderson] and her husband came down to stay at the cottage and seemed so happy and were very charming. I have heard rumours that she was to be offered Lady Macbeth at the Old Vic with Laurence Olivier.

Richard II *opened at the Queen's Theatre on 6 September 1937.*

To his mother   *September 1937, London*

I went in to Drury Lane this afternoon for an hour to see a rehearsal* – such drivel you cannot believe – but amusing to watch the organising of it all – shoals of chorines, stagehands, telephones and executive staff of all kinds, presided over by Ivor [Novello] with his touchingly sincere enthusiasm, showing off his fabulous toy with pardonable pride since he gives boundless pleasure to thousands and employment to hundreds more – our little venture seems a flea in comparison.

To Lillian Gish   *9 October, London*

Richard II is going very well, without being the 'smash hit' that *Hamlet* and *Romeo* were. The public prefer *Richard of Bordeaux* with its more attractive appeal from the humorous and sentimental point of view, but the people who one wants to please seem to like it, and we are able to pay off the production this week.

Tyrone Guthrie is producing *The School for Scandal* very amusingly, and I am delighted to be in a comedy again – the first time for five or six years! Peggy will be enchanting as Lady Teazle. We are playing it with a false proscenium and perspective drop scenes, very swiftly, without any of the traditional gags or business. In the opening scene, Lady Sneerwell is in her bedroom, putting on an elaborate make-up and being laced into her stays by a sluttish maid, while Snake sits on the other side of a screen, and peers through occasionally with a slightly prurient disgust!

The School for Scandal, *in which JG played Joseph Surface, opened at the Queen's Theatre on 25 November 1937.*

To Lillian Gish   *4 December, London*

People are divided about it, as they are about *Macbeth*,† which I saw yesterday. I thought the latter uneven, though it is quite the best production of the play I've seen yet, and it is, of course, notoriously difficult and tricky to produce at all.

Judith [Anderson] is very good, especially in her scenes with Larry, and the

---

* Ivor Novello's new show, *Crest of the Wave.*
† Old Vic production with Laurence Olivier as Macbeth and Judith Anderson as Lady Macbeth.

whole of her performance is finely conceived in a continuous line. She managed the sleep-walking scene, I thought, astonishingly well – never put down her lamp, as they always do, but used one hand for all the business, which I thought very clever and effective. Olivier is awfully unequal, and his performance continually slipped from the classical style in which he conceived it, to ranting and modernism with the murderers and in the emotional passages. It is a violent, strained performance which is exhausting to watch, and must be more so to play, but his scenes with her are beautifully produced, and carried out with real harmony and moving tragic intention.

They had an appalling time before they opened – illness, postponement and finally the death of Lilian Baylis [aged 63] the very night before. In spite of a dreadful press, the theatre was packed yesterday afternoon, when I went, and they are moving to the West End for four weeks at Christmas.

I am sure Judith must feel that it is a distinguished thing to have done, and worth all the agony she must have suffered, and though people are divided about her performance, it is a very distinguished debut for her in this country.

As for this play, Guthrie has done a very charming job and so have the Motleys, but the scenery is either rather pale or rather dark, for they are too fond of secondary colours and shadowy scenes in their decoration, and the result is like a beautiful and glowing series of French prints, instead of the solid English atmosphere that most people expect for this play. They were anxious to get away from the red plush and gold which Rex Whistler has used so successfully in *Victoria* and other productions, and Guthrie conceived the whole play as slightly satiric, and wanted to convey the squalor of the eighteenth century as well as its graces – and for this we have been soundly abused.

From the actors' point of view, it is very difficult to play light comedy in dark scenes, and there is no doubt that towards the end of the play, when they are lighter, the play goes much better – but it is so easy to be wise after the event.

Ruth [Gordon] will, I know, be very saddened over Lilian Baylis's death, but she had been fighting illness for some years and died of a heart attack without suffering, knowing that the Vic had made a profit for the first time, so I think she must almost have reached her goal before she went.

To Gabrielle Enthoven   *18 December, London*

I am so delighted to know that you enjoyed your afternoon. Funny you should mention my hands, as a lady wrote a day or two ago (a palmist) to complain that I did not 'carry my thumbs' in a way suitable to Joseph's character. I don't know what she meant!

1938

Three Sisters, *directed by Michel Saint-Denis, in which JG played Vershinin, opened on 28 January 1938.*

To Lillian Gish   *8 February, London** *

It has been really a sensation, and we are full every night. I haven't a big part and am beginning to enjoy playing it at last. It was so very difficult – patchy and a character so absolutely different from mine, though that made it more interesting, of course, and I was so afraid I should be the only blot on a perfect company, and that, in one's own show, was rather terrifying!

The School for Scandal finished up on the right side, thanks to an excellent last week, and we already have a nice little profit on the first two plays, and this being a real hit, we are bound to make some more money and be safe for the season – for which I am devoutly thankful.

To Baliol Holloway   *21 April, London*

How very nice of you to write me that charming letter; I greatly appreciate it. I am sorry you are unhappy about the *As You Like It* at Stratford. I think it is one of the most difficult plays to produce, and without an absolute genius as Rosalind I think it is fearfully difficult to give it a fresh and exciting appeal.

I certainly didn't resent anything you said about *The School for Scandal*. I wasn't at all satisfied with the production myself, but my feeling is that when you engage a producer like Tony [Guthrie] you must give him a free hand. As a matter of fact he arranged the play very well so far as I was concerned myself, but his ideas of scenery and lighting and much of the characterisation were entirely his, and the Motleys, who got the blame, were only carrying out his rather odd ideas. I didn't think the play stood much chance, and there were, of course, some very bad cases of miscasting in it.

The thing that I rebel at most in the Stratford arrangements is the ridiculous business of five rehearsals, so that people like Komis, who make their maximum effect with music, scenery and pictorial tableaux, do so at the expense of any play they are asked to produce. No company can give a good performance with ten days between the dress rehearsal and the first night. I have only seen half of Komis' *Macbeth* at that theatre, but I loathed it so much that I came out before the end. I am sure that the shape of the stage is absolute hell to work with, and it will be really a wonderful thing if you can persuade them to alter the apron. I should like to work there one day, but it

---

* At some time during 1938 JG moved from Avenue Close round the corner to St Stephen's Close, off Avenue Road.

seems to me that the essential point of a theatre in the country should be that you have a first class company and three or four weeks to rehearse at leisure. Why poor Shakespeare should be flung on with a quarter of the respect a modern author would have as regards casting and rehearsal is quite beyond my comprehension, and the difficulty is today that our few actors with fine Shakespearean tradition don't get a chance to really work in with those who have played Shakespeare for the first time during the last few years. Managers never pay enough money to the small parts, and we have no great Shake-spearean producer, like [Granville-]Barker must have been, with the unique talent for welding together actors of different schools into a comprehensive whole.

The Merchant of Venice *opened on 21 April 1938.*

To Laurence Olivier   *22 April, London*

I was so touched and pleased by those lovely flowers and your so generous wire. They don't care much for my performance on the whole, but I'm determined to stay the course and not be tempted to tear a cat as J.G. instead of trying to play Shylock! I wish I had Edith's [Evans] strength of mind not to read the notices! Hope to come to *Coriolanus** next week. Dick [Addinsell] was very much impressed by it, and I think the press was stinking to you. I thought better of [Charles] Morgan – he was very kind to us, thank God, but they're a rum lot anyway.

Advice was often sought, even by the very young, and generously given.

To Mervyn Jones-Evans   *2 June, London*

All good luck to you with Portia; it should be some help to you to remember that Shakespeare wrote the part to be played by a boy. I shouldn't worry too much about your voice, but certainly pitch it as low as you can naturally.

To Lillian Gish   *16 June, London*

A line to tell you that the season has closed and I am just off on my holiday. *The Merchant* was not really a great success, but the people that I mind about seemed to love it, and I like to think that it was another part in whiskers and the Nazi business that kept the big public away. Granville-Barker, whose preface I had founded the whole production on so much, seemed immensely pleased with it and with my performance.

---

* Olivier was playing at the Old Vic.

Binkie [Beaumont]* suddenly offered me a part in Dodie Smith's new play [*Dear Octopus*] and I jumped at it as it is a nice, modern, ordinary young man and has comedy and nice love scenes, not a big star part by any means, but sharing the honours with the old lady, which Marie Tempest is going to play, and her companion – with whom I fall in love – to be played by Celia Johnson or Diana Wynyard. It is the story of a family reunion, four generations meeting in a country house in England for the golden wedding of the old people (Tempest and [Leon] Quartermaine), and I think it has all her usual charm of dialogue and comedy, with a certain Chekhovian originality, and the sentiment is really delightfully worked in. Anyway it will be a great change for me and no responsibility, and I shall have a little while to think over plans for another season in management, which I am determined to do at some future date.

John [Perry]'s Irish play,† which I produced at the Ambassadors about a fortnight ago, is a really great success – lovely for us both – and it is really beautifully acted and very amusing. I do wish you could see it. It looks as if it will be making a nice little sum for me while I am away on holiday, which has never happened before! A woman called Margaret Rutherford is enchanting as the spinster aunt.

To his mother   *7 July, Vence*

Larry Olivier and Vivien Leigh came for a meal and Jill Esmond for another – these ex-married couples playing Box and Cox need much tact and discrimination in the handling.‡

To his mother   *14 August, Foulslough*

The play [*Dear Octopus*] seems fairly well set now, and Marie [Tempest] seems sure of her lines, though not always the order in which they come.

To Gabrielle Enthoven   *7 September, Manchester*

I wonder what you thought of our play. Mother was rather disappointed, but then she knows so much more about mammas than M. T. [Marie Tempest] ever could if she lived to 1000.

Dear Octopus *opened at the Queen's Theatre on 14 September.*

---

* Beaumont had taken over the West End management, H. M. Tennent. Around this time he displaced J G as John Perry's lover.
† *Spring Meeting* by M. J. Farrell and John Perry. M. J. Farrell was the pseudonym of Mollie Keane.
‡ Although Olivier's affair with Vivien Leigh had been current for some time, he was not divorced from Jill Esmond until 1940.

To E. Martin Browne   *23 September, London*

Now that this play is safely launched, I am very anxious to see the [T. S.] Eliot script [*The Family Reunion*] if it is ready. Perhaps you could come and see me one day during a performance, or have supper with me after the play one night. I'm sorry to hurry you but the BBC have approached me about doing a Shakespeare play in November and I have been asked to appear for one or two charities.

To E. Martin Browne   *30 September, London*

I am enormously interested in the Eliot play. I do certainly think the thing needs a good deal of clearing up and I am very troubled about the Furies, as I cannot quite see them, as he has conceived them, making anything but a comic effect. But as soon as you have talked again with him and have the revised script, do let me have it and we can talk in detail about the play. From my own point of view it would amuse me very much to do it for matinées while this present play is running because (a) I should love the interest of the extra work and (b) I am sure it would be fun to point the contrast between the two plays: this one of Dodie's has so many of the same main characteristics – the family theme and the return of the prodigal – but how differently treated. I think this would intrigue people very much.

To Mrs Patrick Campbell   *11 October, London*

It was lovely to hear from you. I heard from somebody that you had landed in France seedy, and I was distressed to think that you might be by yourself and ill all through that beastly crisis time.

I am playing in a big success by Dodie Smith called *Dear Octopus*, not under my own management. The season came out on the right side and I hadn't any more classical plays I wanted to do just yet. *Macbeth*, *The Tempest* perhaps in a few years time, but after Shylock and Vershinin last season I felt I wanted a change, so I am playing a shadowy but innocuous juvenile part in this play with Marie Tempest. It isn't much fun except as an exercise, but very well cast and just what the public wants.

Saint-Denis, who did *Three Sisters* for me last season, has just opened with *The White Guard* in which Peggy plays the leading part. He is doing a season of classics on the lines of my season – *Twelfth Night*, *The Wild Duck*, *Cherry [Orchard]* etc. and most of my old company is working with him. I can't help wishing a little that I was there too, but I suppose filthy lucre and a big commercial success are not to be despised. There are not many interesting plays to see, but I have a play by T. S. Eliot which I am hoping to do for matinées after Christmas, very original and lovely poetry, I think.* Quite a modern setting almost in the manner of Aldous Huxley, but with choruses and a sort of Greek tragedy analogy, only much better than [Eugene] O'Neill's. I saw *Mourning Becomes Electra* last year and thought it very pretentious and unreal.

I'd love to see you and talk about everything. Meanwhile keep well and have a lovely holiday. I hope Moonbeam† is well; I still carry her picture about with me.

To Leon M. Lion   *15 October, London*

I'm so sorry but I can't possibly read your play for a fortnight or so, as I have already a pile of manuscripts on hand and in addition I have to finish my autobiography [*Early Stages*] by the end of the month. If you care to send it back to me then of course I shall be pleased to read it.

Mr Lion did *send it back* – it was a play about Franz Liszt.

To Leon M. Lion   *November 1938, London*

Alas, I have an unreasoning hatred for biographical plays about musical geniuses. I think their music is so much more interesting than their idio-syncrasies, and one can never convince an audience of the talent, only of the tiresomeness. So I must send you back your play – anyway I am bound to *Dear Octopus* until June, and have two alternative schemes for next autumn. Thank you all the same for thinking of me.

1939

The approach of war rendered long-term planning difficult, but early in 1939 JG directed Oscar Wilde's The Importance of Being Earnest. *His production opened at the Globe Theatre, which, in 1994, would be renamed the Gielgud Theatre.*

To Julia Wood   *January 1994, Wotton Underwood*

I did meet Lord Alfred Douglas on two occasions. He came to see me in my dressing room after a performance of *The Importance of Being Earnest* during

---

* JG's interesting idea did not come to fruition; E. Martin Browne directed the first production of the play at the Westminster Theatre the following year.
† Mrs Pat's Pekingese.

the early years of the war, but I was very disappointed, finding him quite without charm – and when I asked him to give me some details about the way the play had been originally produced and acted, he merely insisted that most of the best lines in it were his, and that he had stood over Wilde when he was writing it.

Of course Douglas had quite lost his looks and I thought that must have been a great tragedy for him. (I felt the same when I met Mary Anderson in her old age. She was of course one of the most beautiful women of her day.)

He was invited to play Hamlet in Denmark. Prior to the visit, his new production played for two weeks at the Lyceum Theatre.

To his mother   *June? 1939, London*

I am simply delighted to have the sword* from you. Today I found an account of the presentation of it by Chippendale in the Percy Fitzgerald book on [Henry] Irving. After the Lyceum performances are over I shall have the engraving added to, putting your name and mine. Then it will be a nice thing to be handed on again to another young hopeful† when I am too old to play Hamlet any more – which won't be long now.

To his mother   *July 1939, Elsinore*

The performance has been a great success – good weather for two nights, then the third stormy and it rained so hard that we packed up after the Mad Scene.

The entertainment en masse is very badly arranged and the proprietor of this hotel obviously a rogue. We had an appalling 'night out' on Saturday – driven twenty miles in taxis not, as we hoped, to supper and a gay nightclub, but to a charity music hall performance lasting three hours in Danish in a tent in a park, crowded to suffocation with people and cigar smoke and not even a drink till 2.30 a.m.

The other night I was amused and flattered when a gentleman six or seven rows back jumped out into the aisle during the 'rogue and peasant slave' and literally snatched the umbrella from the offending hand of the poor lady sitting in the row in front.

The hotel is swarming with 'fans' and I am going tonight to Copenhagen after an hour's visit from one of my well-meaning English virgins who called on me as I wrote in my room defenceless yesterday afternoon and spent an hour discussing my soul and art! One is at their mercy here. Rosamond Gilder

---

* The sword worn by Edmund Kean as Richard III.
† In 1944 Laurence Olivier had a huge success with his performance of Richard III at the New Theatre; Gielgud gave him the sword, suitably inscribed. It remains part of the Olivier estate.

and Phyllis Hartnoll eye each other like angry codfish, and all the ladies attach themselves to other unfortunate and helpless members of the company as a first step towards Olympus. Very trying.

However, Regent's Park can hold no terrors for me now and there is always a chance of doing *King Lear* in a real storm when I am suitably hoary – perhaps declaimed from the Mappin Terraces* from a bath chair with scythed wheels!

Returning to London, JG's revived and substantially re-cast production of The Importance of Being Earnest *opened at the Globe Theatre on 16 August for a scheduled six-week run. The production was regarded by many as definitive.*

On 1 September 1939, Hitler invaded Poland.

---

* At London Zoo.

THE WAR YEARS

1939

I am sorry to worry you when you are busy, but am anxious to know if you think anything could be done about [Michel] Saint-Denis. He left yesterday for France where he has been called back for mobilisation, and it seems to me he is too important to the theatre to be allowed to go straight off to the army again if it can possibly be avoided. I wondered if you could possibly use your influence to get him transferred to some kind of liaison work, in which his knowledge of English and French might be useful, and where he might be doing some sort of job that was worthy of his abilities. I hope you'll forgive my suggesting this, but I do feel Michel is one of the few people who have something important to give in the theatre, and who ought to be looked after a bit if it is in any way possible.

Glyn [Byam Shaw] and I are supposed to join a Scottish regiment (!) eventually, but I believe they've no use for us yet for some time. I hope the theatres may open again somewhere, sometime, in a week or so, and we can perhaps be allowed to exhibit ourselves to an admiring few once more for a little while.

The London theatres having been closed, JG took his production of The Importance of Being Earnest **on a long regional tour.**

To Noël Coward   *16 October, Bristol*

Many thanks for your kindness in enquiring for Michel. I hear now that [Jean] Giraudoux is trying to pull strings for him, and if anybody can get him transferred, I imagine he is the person. We are packing out everywhere with *The Importance*, which is extremely gratifying, everyone earning about half salary – the smaller people full – and these smaller towns, which are crammed with evacuees of various kinds, and do not as a rule see good London companies, crowd the theatre, so all that is very satisfactory. Ivor Brown has written me a Shakespeare lecture about S.'s attitude to War which is very good I think. I'm trying it out here next Sunday for the Red Cross, and hope to do it every Sunday afternoon in all the towns we go to, and make a bit of money.

Harry [Tennent] saw Ian Hay in the War Office about me – it seems they don't want me to go into the army – at least for the next six months – and are anxious that if possible I should do a season again in London. If I'm not to fight, I feel it's important to do the very best plays with as good a cast as possible, and cut down production costs so as to have prices down to 7/6d top at the most, and make everyone play for minimums and a percentage, which has answered so well with this play (though in this case the production was already paid off beforehand). Perhaps I will do *The Tempest* and possibly *The Relapse* by Vanbrugh, which has a wonderful part for me of Lord Foppington, and two naughty ladies for Edith and perhaps Yvonne Arnaud. [Lord] Lloyd is coming to see me at Streatham next week. I hear he has some scheme for a propaganda tour in Spain, Portugal and Italy next year, but I suppose they would want *Hamlet* and *Romeo and Juliet*, so I should have to unearth the old toupets [*sic*] and tights again and bat out in those. Anything to be useful.

To his mother   *28 November, Glasgow*

I have definitely said I won't do the six months plan including Africa – they offer nothing but expenses and a small salary and take all the profits expecting us to provide the productions complete. As I am not a millionaire, this is hardly practicable.

After the 'phoney war' The Importance *returned to the Globe Theatre on 26 December.*

1940

At the beginning of 1940, JG directed The Beggar's Opera *at the Theatre Royal, Haymarket with Michael Redgrave as Macheath.*

To John Warner   *26 January, London*

Thank you for your letter. I'm so glad you enjoyed the lecture. Good luck with your stage career if you should take it up – though I advise you not to!

John Warner became a successful actor.
    In the spring of 1940, JG returned to the Old Vic to play King Lear and Prospero. The production of King Lear, *which opened on 15 April, was based on Harley Granville-Barker's Preface to the play and although Lewis Casson was credited as the producer, Barker himself did much of the work.*

To his father   *12 April, London*

So many thanks for the cigars – they are greatly appreciated and will be smoked to your good health.
    I am in the usual chaotic despair before a first night. Barker has tried us hard – and still demands further ideals – but his work is fine. I have learnt much this week, and everyone has struggled bravely and uncomplainingly,

though I am very disgusted with the Vic people who have foundered badly with all the stage organisation – wringing their hands and making excuses – the war, etc. – instead of putting their backs into it and getting things in order to give us the light and confidence we need. But such is the birth agony of the theatre – was in the beginning, is now and ever shall be, I suppose.

Nothing but such a master as Barker and a mighty work like *Lear* could have kept one so concentrated these ten days with such a holocaust going on around us. One must be very grateful for such work at a time like this.

To Hugh Walpole   *April 1940, London*

Your charming letter has given me so much pleasure – thank you for all the lovely things you say. You can imagine how much I wanted to do well after the wonderful help I had from Barker, a relentless but amazingly brilliant taskmaster. I have never before had so much care taken with a performance by someone on whose critical judgement I could absolutely rely, and he showed me all the gradations and subtleties of climax which enable me to husband my resources and spread my voice out so that it does not exhaust itself in the course of a performance. I hope to do better yet when I am a bit rested and in greater control of myself. It was an emotional first night and one never does oneself justice until things settle down. The audiences are wonderful and the company very helpful and responsive, though I'm afraid I agree with you about [Stephen] Haggard.* None of the critics, however, seem to be so percipient, which is lucky for him.

After King Lear *and* The Tempest *at the Old Vic, JG spent the next six months leading a small company around the country under the Entertainments National Service Association (ENSA) banner, entertaining many different audiences in a programme of short plays and sketches. Particularly in the larger cities, performances were frequently interrupted by air-raid warnings.*

To his mother   *August 1940, Edinburgh*

We had a warning on Saturday but luckily not till the show had been over for ten minutes. We had a magnificent house, which would not have been the case if the raid had been an hour or two sooner – and about 100 people were caught in the theatre as they were leaving, so we went in front with them and played the pianos and kept things going for an hour until the 'all clear' went.

I have had an offer to play Disraeli in a big film [*The Prime Minister*] when I come back. The script reads fairly well, but I wonder if the public is not sick of Victoria now! It is a very long and effective part and they want Diana Wynyard for Lady B[eaconsfield]. If the make-up test should seem satisfactory,

---

* Haggard played the Fool. The comment remains a mystery.

I am inclined to do it – a character costume part with patriotic speeches and some comedy might be interesting and they offer big money. It would take about six weeks but I shan't decide anything without seeing tests, as the likeness is really the most important thing, and [George] Arliss is well remembered for an admirable make-up and performance in the early days of talkies – it will be hard to beat him at it but it might be fun to try.

To Rosamond Gilder   *27 September, London*

Well, the bombing is very unpleasant and the results make an ugly and sad sight – but people behave magnificently – many have had wonderful escapes.

We did the nine weeks tour – six round the camps and aerodromes, playing *Fumed Oak, Hands Across the Sea* [by Noël Coward] and my fixed-up version of *Swan Song* [by Anton Chekhov], which I arranged to include four purple patches from Shakespeare. Then we went to Manchester, Glasgow and Edinburgh with the same bill, adding the Darnley murder scene from Daviot's play about Mary Stuart [*Queen of Scots*], and Shaw's *Dark Lady of the Sonnets*.

We were supposed to finish at Streatham and Golders Green, but when we got back from Scotland after ten hours in the train, the big bangs began.

We had one bomb very close to us one night – the backs of houses in Park Lane were blown out, and all the plate-glass windows on the ground floor came hurtling down into our little courtyard where all the windows broke too – a fine clatter.

Of course, traffic is rather disorganised. People walk to and from their work in long processions through the parks and back streets in this lovely autumn weather, and the shops board up and open again with amazing cheerfulness. Telephones, trains and posts are the most irritating, but will no doubt improve with time. The tubes are rather dreadful to see, with families queuing up to sleep there at five in the afternoon with bedding, food etc., children and old women all along the passages and platforms, but they seem fantastically gay and even hilarious sometimes, in that real Cockney way which is so endearing. They will get it all better organised before the winter no doubt.

Mayfair looks very dramatic – we walked round the other night before the raid began, about 6.30, and it needed a painter to do it justice – the big houses with windows blown out and torn white curtains still streaming out, and trees and railings down here and there – then whole streets quite untouched, and suddenly round a corner a big lump of devastation – with rooms gaping open to the sky, yet mirrors and pictures often still hanging on the side walls quite untouched.

There were incendiary bombs on the Globe one night, and B[inkie] and I went dashing up Piccadilly with the barrage going on all around us, feeling very heroic and terrified, to find the fire out and the stage deep in water – a lot of glass lying about and scenery soaked and damaged but no one hurt and no real damage.

1941

In 1941 JG directed and played Mr Dearth in J. M. Barrie's Dear Brutus, *which also toured the country after a five-month London run.*

During the tour he began to make plans for a new production of Macbeth. *As the designer he engaged Michael Ayrton, one of the country's leading young painters and sculptors who had been recommended to him by Hugh Walpole.*

To his mother   *27 May, Manchester*

How amazing English people are! I said in my speech last night 'I'm sorry to see your beautiful city laid waste,' the biggest laugh of the evening! One of the papers today said it was the first time anyone had called Manchester a beautiful city since the 18th century!

To his mother   *3 June, Llandudno*

Typical Whitsuntide crowds, drab looking girls like Lilian Baylis in turbans and beach pyjamas – a hideously ugly Edwardian town in wonderful natural country – a 'Happy Valley' behind this hotel – really a boarding house but quite adequate, with rock gardens laid out in vulgar bursts of purple and yellow shrubs and an open air entertainment – the shops crammed with bun-eaters and filled with the strains of radio crooners and the clatter of tins on empty counters!

To Michael Ayrton   *6 June, Llandudno*

I know you will have been deeply grieved by Hugh Walpole's death. I felt so much the same about Leslie Faber, who died unexpectedly at the same age* just when I was most relying on him to guide my faltering footsteps on the ladder, but he had already given me confidence and encouragement and good advice, and Hugh has done the same for you, I know.

To his mother   *8 June, Penrhyndeudraeth*

Had a cheerful letter from Peggy [Ashcroft]. She is at Tring but goes to Oxford to have her baby in two weeks time, so I hope to see her there, safely delivered. Her husband [Jeremy Hutchinson] was on the *Kelly* at Crete, one of the twelve officers saved, thank God. She must have had some terribly anxious days but has now heard he is at Alexandria.

---

* JG had his facts slightly wrong; Faber was fifty when he died, Walpole fifty-seven.

To Kitty Black   *13 June, Liverpool*

I am living in a house where the food and drink are completely pre-war –
rather shaming but incredibly luxurious – I feel the prunes and sago were not
totally in vain last week.

I hear you have struck up a friendship with my papa – isn't he a pet?

To Peggy Ashcroft   *7 July, Edinburgh*

I am so happy that you are all right, and that the kiddywee* is flourishing
and your husband coming home soon – how lovely for you. Alberta Holford,
who followed me to Oxford, seemed rather snotty when I told her your news!
I suppose she can't forgive my not being the father! I nearly told her that I
was, just to see her face which was more pig-like than ever.

Time passes extremely quickly and business is wonderful and the days are long
and light and I work at *Macbeth*. This is a delightful company, though [Margaret]
Rawlings is rather odd girl out. She travels a girl friend called Monica Stirling
and they keep to themselves and discuss French poetry. I hear Edith [Evans] has
had a great success with the troops in [*The Late*] *Christopher Bean* [adapted
by Emlyn Williams from a play by René Fauchois] – dead silence in her big
speeches, and an ovation after each performance. I am so glad for the old girl.

Poor Johnnie P. [Perry] has had to have a beastly operation – an abscess in
his fanny. He is in hospital for three weeks – I'm sure he'd be simply enchanted
if you found time to write him a word of consolation.

To Noël Coward   *July 1941, Foulslough*

I never wired you, thinking such extravagance unsuitable to the moment, but
I do congratulate you on the wonderful success.† You were very sweet to ask
us all to the rehearsal, and more than patient with my impertinent comments
in all of which, I understand, I have been proved to have been in total error.
I did really enjoy myself so much, and am really delighted to hear you have
such a smash hit.

I hear you have the press in your trouser pocket and I hope Leeds and the
Piccadilly will heap further laurels on your cloudless brow. More power to
your clever little elbow, and don't forget to invent a really nice *Design for
Living* offering in which I can (personally) appear with you for positively
three weeks only prior to our respective Antipodean tours at the end of the
war. We could always arrange to stop off at some outpost of the Empire every
three months, and give a few special performances just to keep our hand in –
met, of course, by bevies of ex-servicemen from all the forces, and carried,

---

* Her daughter Eliza.
† Coward's production of his own play, *Blithe Spirit*, had just opened in Manchester.

slightly hysterical, to neighbouring hotels in garlanded rickshaws. My quill runs away with me – I fear it is the heat!

To Kitty Black   *4 September, Cheltenham*

I'm glad to hear *Lear* [a version for radio] came over well – personally I thought it vilely under-rehearsed and pretty crudely acted and the cutting, of course, abominable. Why can't they do a big play like that in two sections – half each Sunday – then it could be given uncut and the listeners have some faint idea of dear Mr S's text.

I am thoroughly bored by the whole BBC set-up since doing those three broadcasts, and I shan't do another for a long time if I can help it. It's all very well with something one has studied, rehearsed and acted in the theatre, but a new play, inefficiently cast and prepared and flung over so carelessly – no, I think it really isn't worth the trouble. It's the same trouble as the cinema, they buy your name and time and don't attempt to reach your standard because they won't take the trouble and patience to work properly and consult you about the obvious details which should be considered.

To Michael Ayrton   *4 September, Cheltenham*

The casting of *Macbeth* goes slowly but steadily. I have, I hope, a terrifying, one-eyed Cyclops of a man with huge legs and arms to play the Porter – he should have just the right mixture of joviality and terror – played the convict in *Great Expectations*.*

To his mother   *September 1941, Salisbury*

A sergeant-major begged for admission for a third time, saying 'We get plenty of margarine here, but it isn't often we get butter!'

To Michael Ayrton   *13 October, London†*

We are sending you another £25, but it must be on account of royalties. I quite appreciate what you say about the extra work and your assistants, but on the other hand I can't go back on our original business contract. I know perfectly well how maddening it is to be hard up and, worse still, to have liabilities, but supposing Walton‡ and Eileen§ and other heads all started asking for more after they were engaged, where should we be with our budgets?

---

* This must have been the Scottish actor, Finlay Currie, but in the event the part was played by George Woodbridge.
† When his Avenue Close flat was commandeered by the War Office, JG moved into a flat in Park Lane, Mayfair.
‡ William Walton composed the incidental music for *Macbeth*.
§ Eileen Culshaw made the costumes.

The production is, as always, going to cost at least £2,000 more than we originally planned and you know yourself how expensive everything is, even with the care and economy which I know you have been considering. All the money I have, I have earned with the sweat of my brow, and it all goes back into the theatre except what I keep to live on and pay away in taxes. As I told you originally, if the production is a great success, I will see you have some more then, but that will be a private bonus from me and I very much hope our joint labours may provide it.

*To Alec Guinness**   *25 October, London*

Many thanks for yours, with the sad picture of you on your lonely watch, and no Horatio to your Bernardo! Why did somebody tell me yesterday you were going to become a monk? Surely a façon de parler, pis aller, or permis de séjour! London is full of people and plays and films in comparative abundance, rather a joy after being away for so many weeks. Glen [Byam Shaw] and Terry Rattigan are both on embarkation leave, alas! But it is nice to see them again. *Citizen Kane* is quite unimaginably good, and an amazing feat all round on the part of Welles and his really brilliant cast. You must not fail to see it.

Gwen [Ffrangcon-Davies] is coming back from South Africa to play Lady Macbeth. The only other people I have so far are [Leon] Quartermaine (Banquo and Old Siward), H. R. Hignett (Duncan), Jean Cadell (1st Witch and Gentlewoman) and some young (very young) hopefuls – Barry Morse, Emrys Jones, Alan Badel, Terence Alexander – mostly collected from reps. on my travels.

Arthur Macrae made me laugh last night by saying Michael Redgrave's theme song ought to be

'Some day I'll bind you,
Both hands behind you!'

I had a gay hour with that old fribble [?] Alexander Woollcott today. He was saying Ethel Barrymore had made a wonderful comeback in *The Corn is Green* in America after (like Martita [Hunt]) 'a long sojourn in the valley of the menopause'. Also a very funny description of the Lunts working out their dream production of *Macbeth*. Lady M. was to pass along the gallery to murder Duncan stark naked! 'How?' I asked. 'Oh,' said Woollcott, 'behind a high balustrade, so that her pudenda were still kept strictly for Alfred's edification!'

Binkie gravid with plans. Willie Armstrong is to direct *Auld Acquaintance* [by John Van Druten] for Edith [Evans], with Marian Spencer opposite her. I do not predict a success for this, but was still quite relieved when she turned down Lady M. which I only offered her as a kind of amende honorable,

---

* Like many other actors, Alec Guinness had joined up at the beginning of the war and was serving with the Royal Navy.

though I don't quite know for what! Emlyn's new play* is said to be very moving and well written, though I don't know how the public will react to an air raid on the stage and bodies being carried out.

No more gossip now – I must go back to reading Arthur Koestler who couldn't be more depressing. Do you want books or anything, by the way? I will try and find some chocs to send you.

His production of Macbeth *began a six-month tour in Manchester and throughout the tour JG was rehearsing and revising it.*

1942

To Michael Ayrton   *22 January, Manchester*

Have had my last tunic made longer and abandoned the boots in favour of chain mail for the last act as Alan Dent says my knees are not suited to the exhibition of high tragedy and I fancy he speaks some truth.

To Michael Ayrton   *6 February, Glasgow*

I think your points are very sound. As to the baby, I agree that it may be good to have it all, but suggest a loincloth, or Birmingham Watch Committee will probably ban us. Would swaddled bands look too much like the famous Della Robbia medallion? Anyway, let us see the eyes and nose. Perhaps it would be more impressive to have a swathing over mouth, breast and loins – wound around, as it were – and the hands outstretched towards Macbeth? I don't much like the whole face concealed. If the swathing bands were *red*, perhaps the bloody effect would be good? Or should they be grey or white, with blood on hands, head and throat?

This week has been hell. Not one light right, panatropes† breaking down, sparse audiences, stupid, giggling schoolchildren, vile weather etc., etc. But tonight at last it begins to come together and greatly improve. The play itself begins to be much better played, and I am no longer terribly overtired. But it's a big strain with these awful moves, and old switchboards managed by still older gentlemen with not a thing to be depended on, and all our hard work in Manchester to be done again because equipment is different in every theatre.

How I loathe touring – but what would you do?

---

* *The Morning Star* opened at the Globe Theatre on 10 December 1941.
† A machine that enabled recorded sound effects (on disc) to be played on cue.

To Marda Vanne   *8 February, Glasgow*

I have been meaning for ever so long to write and tell you how much I appreciate the gesture you made in not persuading Gwen against returning. I know she misses you all the time and I am sure you miss her greatly too. She has been enormously helpful and sweet to me as always, and I am only distressed that she does not feel, so far, that she has really made a success. Of course, her performance is against tradition but she has already corrected her first reading very greatly and will, I know, grow in depth and stature every week she plays.

Unfortunately, if one is not the obvious casting for Lady Macbeth one has to put over an original reading 200 per cent in order to convince the audience, whereas a booming contralto like [Margaret] Rawlings or Edith [Evans] would be far more easily accepted and perhaps have an easy success on conventional lines without any great struggle. But all the more because I am not physically ideal (mentally or intellectually either, really) for Macbeth, it is so very helpful to have a Lady who works in my way, and I know that already we have very effective moments in our scenes together.

To James Agate   *15 March, Leeds*

I cannot resist entering into your argument à propos of the time problem in Shakespeare – for Granville-Barker once gave me a magnificent disquisition on the subject. I cannot quote his brilliantly lucid words with certainty, but this is the gist of them.

We were rehearsing the great scene in *Lear*, and after the cursing of Goneril, 'Hear, Nature, hear,' Lear leaves the stage, to return a few lines later with the words 'What, fifty of my followers at a clap, within a fortnight?' I asked (like Lady Bracknell, merely for information) 'Who has told Lear about the sacking of his followers? Oswald, perhaps, off stage?' 'That,' said Barker, 'is the kind of mistake you actors make, worrying about such realistic off-stage happenings. Shakespeare never wrote in this convention. The absence and reappearance, with time and action meticulously accounted for both by actors and audience, of characters in plays was not used by dramatists until the school of Ibsen. Shakespeare wishes to show the audience that Lear, though capable of the mighty curse, leaves Goneril's house already shaken and mentally weakened by the scene he has gone through, and so he brings him back on to the stage with a weaker tearful speech before his final exit.' I'll warrant the old actors cut the return altogether, and waited for a big hand and an exit after the curse. Someone has, of course, told Lear and no matter who.

Similarly, we discussed whether Lear had decided to ask for the test of the daughters' loves before his first entrance in the play or as a sudden impulse of vanity when seated on his throne before the court. Again Barker said, 'Decide for yourself. But whichever way you play it, the audience will not have time to take in that detail. They are interested in the story as it unfolds before their eyes – the actors have enough to do to set forth the fable in that first act, and put over the story and the character of each personage that is represented.'

The same applies to *Macbeth*. Exactly *when* the two of them planned the murder, *how long* before the play opens they had talked about it ('What beast was't then that made you break this enterprise to me?') – these points will not be important except to the actors' peace of mind and the student's speculation. It is easy enough for the players to show by their manner and make-up (and Shakespeare was there to tell them just how much to show) that *some time* has gone by between the murder and their entrance as King and Queen. Similarly, time must pass to allow Macduff to get to England and return with Malcolm. Again, the Macbeths have time (in their dressing rooms) to get older before the audience sees them again. These things are pure theatre, Shakespeare always wrote for swift performance, and what the audience saw before their eyes he knew they would accept. If we had not studied the plays for three hundred years in such detail these things would not trouble us.

To his mother   *7 April, Blackpool*

The best thing about this place is the potted shrimps one can buy for succour between performances! Not really a holiday attraction, of course, and the wonder is that as many people (hideous and common as they all seem to be) come in at all. They are obviously impressed and possibly edified in their moronic Lancashire way, but it's not much fun.

To James Agate   *17 April, Liverpool*

Many thanks for your gay letter. To reply to your questions categorically, I make up my hands light brown – as Ellen says H[enry] I[rving] always did for a costume part (except 18th century) and I never wash them again in *Macbeth* after I have done them again after getting rid of the blood – so that you may take it they are grubby enough for the last act. But don't imagine that the time off the stage is very long – about twelve to fifteen minutes by the clock, though the boredom of Malcolm's self-accusation scene may give an impression of longer time. And none too much either to change wig and make-up – about two years is right, I should say. On this tour I've had to play at two and six on matinée days, murder indeed, and I should like to know what Messrs [W. C.] Macready, Irving and [Tommaso] Salvini (to put myself in no more distinguished company) would have said to such an effort.

There was a very nice misprint in the *Liverpool Echo* on Wednesday, paying tribute to our broad comedian George Woodbridge, who plays the Porter, as an 'engaging Portia'. I could not forbear to murmur that the quality of Mersey is not strained.

To his mother   *8 May, Nottingham*

More disaster here – Marcus Barron, the Duncan, had a sudden attack of angina and has been stopped work altogether. Bromley Davenport went on last night, could not remember one word or read the lines without his glasses, making havoc of his three important scenes. Another old gent tries it tonight – he is also senile, nervous and undependable, but I hope a bit more certain.

To his mother   *22 May, Birmingham*

As you will see from the enclosed, we were not greatly liked here at the opening. It was a frigid audience tempered with schoolchildren who laughed gaily when I kissed Gwen in the first act.

[Francis] Lister* getting to be very good now, and I am trying to persuade Ross [Alec Mango] to give up and let us employ a decent actor.

The panatropes on the wrong current for this place and went mad on Tuesday – one caught fire and the other played in double time – not helpful.

To Michael Ayrton   *23 May, Birmingham*

Many thanks for your reasonable letter. I don't think you can have realised what an enormously bad impression of goodwill you have engendered over the production, chiefly by ungraciousness of manner, and lack of charm and generosity towards the workpeople in every department – also by flinging up your hands at intervals and announcing bitterly either that things have been done which you don't approve of and so you wash your hands of the whole thing, or else savagely resenting that there can possibly be any improvements or adjustments still to be made. The tour has been a godsend in every way, both to us actors and to you, for your first production has been able to be tried out like our performances and worked on with every possible advantage of time and many people's criticism and opinion. The fact that you haven't made a lot of money out of it should be nothing to you compared with what you have gained in practical experience and knowledge of working conditions, and if only you would appear more modest, you'd find everyone ready to co-operate rather than oppose, to the great easing of every situation. I have found you pretty reasonable as far as I am concerned, but as I am responsible for you to the other people who have to work with you, I feel I must emphasise the general feeling and ask you to think over what I say for your own sake, quite as much as for theirs – and for future work you may want to do.

---

* Lister took over Macduff from Milton Rosmer.

To his mother   *26 May, Birmingham*

I have persuaded Ross to leave and we hope to get [Abraham] Sofaer for London. I am wangling madly to transfer Lennox [Tarver Penna] into the First Murderer and put [Alan] Badel, the clever boy, into Lennox.

To Lillian Gish   *18 June, Foulslough*

I was so greatly touched by your sweet thought of me after three long years of mad upheaval and troublous anxieties. I have thought of you very often and remembered with so much happiness all our times together in New York, your loving sweetness in and out of the theatre, our talks and laughs and motor drives. I shall never forget it all, though it does seem an awfully long time ago.

I won't begin to tell you all that has happened here since the War began – it's been an extraordinary timeless kind of nightmare – all one's friends scattered and turning up again at odd times in uniform and gone again before one can have time to settle down and enjoy their company. I've been working almost unceasingly – *Importance of Being Earnest, Dear Brutus, Lear, The Tempest,* two tours for the troops, one with Bea Lillie which was great fun, and now *Macbeth.* We've just finished a 20-week tour and now I have a fortnight's blissful rest before we rehearse ten days and open in London in July.

The production is elaborate scenically, and the cast being almost entirely men, it was no joke assembling it. I've never stopped rehearsing and improving details every week, so I hope by now it's fit to make a show in London. Gwen Ffrangcon-Davies came all the way from South Africa to be my Lady Macbeth, and she is grand in it, besides being a dear friend and wonderfully helpful companion on the tour. Leon Quartermaine is superb as Banquo, and especially in the banquet scene, into which he stalks like a murdered Christ by El Greco and really electrifies the audience. I was so delighted to read of Judith [Anderson]'s huge success as Lady M. but feel it is somewhat presumptuous of Master Maurice [Evans] to announce in cold print that Macbeth is a singularly unrewarding part written in monotonous rhythms!! The verse is about ten times as varied as that of *Richard the Second,* and the scenes. I should say, more 'jammy' than in any play except *Hamlet.* What he really means is that the *character* is not so likeable to an audience – but then I'm always surprised that Richard gets as much sympathy as he does. I'd rather meet Macbeth any day myself, for he's imagined this mighty, heroic scale, while Richard for all his enchanting mind and glorious imagery, is a bit of a fool and shallow to a degree.

I wonder what you are doing? I heard you had become a nurse. Jimmy Agate and I started on you the other night at Bournemouth, while we were watching a distant raid, and decided we couldn't go on without exhausting all our superlatives. So you see you are much in the thoughts of all those you have ever blessed with your friendship.

Macbeth *opened at the Piccadilly Theatre on 8 July 1942.*

To J. R. Ackerley   *10 August, London*

I cannot tell you how pleased I was to hear you approved of my *Macbeth*, especially as Michael Ayrton had informed me some weeks ago that you were greatly
prejudiced against the idea of seeing me in the part. I think there are various
aspects of the character that I cannot hope to achieve – the streak of coarseness
and the ruthless energetic quality which ought to pervade the opening scenes
before the murder as well as the more imaginative passages later on – but, like
all the great Shakespearean parts, there are things that I ought to be able to make
alive in the character, because I feel greatly sympathetic towards it, and I have
loved working on the production which I do think succeeds, in some of the
difficult and most technically bothersome places, in being moderately coherent.
But people are very divided about it and that is good for both sides, I think. I
hope to see you again one day. Thank you again for troubling to write, and I
much appreciate [E. M.] Forster's opinion too.

Bobbie Speaight, in a very intelligent notice in *The Tablet*, says I make
Macbeth an obvious narcissist! Very likely, but I never thought of it myself!

To Michael Ayrton   *2 October, London*

I'm sorry *Macbeth* was such a stormy passage – wartime of course made it worse,
and I have been tired and over-worked nearly all the time. The technical side of
a big production depends greatly on too many different people, and the handling of all the different departments is always a tricky and full-time job, quite
apart from the more personal agonies of seeing the finished work, judging it,
lighting it, bearing criticism and then becoming so familiar and stale with all
that one loses all sense of judgement or knowledge of the final work.

Macbeth *played until 10 October, after which J G revived* **The Importance of Being
Earnest** *for a brief season at the Phoenix Theatre. In December he again assembled
a small troupe that travelled to Gibraltar to entertain British forces there.*

1943

To his mother   *10 January, Gibraltar*

It is extraordinarily pleasant, though hectic. We have done three or four
concerts on ships, which has been a moving and exciting experience, besides
twice nightly in the theatre seven nights a week and we calculate we shall have
appeared before audiences of about 40,000 people by the time we finish. Not
a seat to be had for any performance, and they are extraordinarily well-
mannered, and never fail to listen quietly to the next 'turn', however much

they may have been shouting and whistling at the end of the one before. Of course there are criticisms in some quarters. Some say not enough straight stuff, and too many blue jokes (how oddly hypocritical Englishmen are, for the house falls down at the time the story is told – one man explained this away by saying that if his neighbour laughed, he had to, to cover his embarrassment!). We never stop going to messes, lunches on the ships, New Year's Eve party at Government House, etc. etc. The Governor took us up to the top of the Rock to see the barrage defence exercise the other night. Masses of guns let off from every nook and cranny and shivers of tracer bullets, rockets etc. flying out over the sea – an extraordinary sight – not so very much noise compared to an average London blitz, though the ground shook under our feet. It really looked much like the miniature naval battle which they used to stage in the old days in the tank at the White City.

John [Perry] has taken us twice to Algeciras, which is about 20 miles by road, through several villages – most picturesque, and a great relief to the eye after a week of these narrow, crowded streets, but of course we are lucky in this hotel having a continual and magnificent view over the Bay. The Spanish country looks very romantic and much as I expected – richer and more full of character than Provence, with beautiful avenues of eucalyptus trees, donkeys, tickbirds and ragged looking soldiers stringing along with a mule cart in their midst covered with sacks and luggage, like a war drawing by Goya. La Linea, the first town across the border, is pretty sordid and poverty stricken but Algeciras is quite an attractive provincial town with a pretty square and characteristic churches and cobbled streets – an excellent hotel with superb food, typical kind of Riviera resort in peacetime – and we had sherry and delicious slices of smoked ham at a little wayside inn on the way – hardly any cars of course, but we went in the Government House barouche and sailed through in great comfort.

The curfew is at 11, so we are not able to go out after the show – though we did go on a ship one night for drinks for half an hour – so late nights are restricted, though most of the rooms in this hotel become sitting rooms after midnight, and we continue to have some quite gay parties here in consequence. Tony Quayle's batman dresses us and presses our clothes so that we look quite imposing among the smart officers of the H.Q. staff!

In April 1943 JG's production of Love for Love, *in which he played Valentine, opened at the Phoenix Theatre. During the run, he prepared his production of* The Cradle Song *by Gregorio and Maria Martinez Sierra.*

To Bernard Shaw   *29 August, London*

I am most delighted and honoured to receive your letter, and to know that you would approve of my undertaking Caesar,* for it is indeed a great part,

---

* Gabriel Pascal was planning to film Shaw's *Caesar and Cleopatra* with Vivien Leigh as Cleopatra. Caesar was eventually played by Claude Rains.

and one that I should greatly like to try and play. But I do not like filming and should be terrified of risking giving an indifferent performance. The technique is so different, and one would need a good six months concentration with nothing else to distract. To try and act in the theatre at the same time is, I am sure, impossible, especially now with transport and blackout complications, and *Love for Love* can hardly fail to run until the spring of next year. So I must reluctantly say no to the film, and hope that you will let me do the *play* some time not too far distant.* Then if I were to please you in it (and not dislike myself in the part as well) perhaps the film could be undertaken with mutual confidence. If, however, you should think of somebody else – and of course I hope you won't – you will naturally please yourself in the arrangement of the plans for the film. I do long to play in something of yours, and soon. Did anybody tell you that I dashed on at 24 hours notice and played Dubedat [in *The Doctor's Dilemma*] for a few performances in January, when the actor [Peter Glenville] and his understudy were both ill. I greatly enjoyed myself when I knew the words, which wasn't until about the fourth performance. The earlier nights I held the book under my blanket in the death scene, and, as I believe old actors say, 'winged' the lines as best I could. I am told my conception of the part was superior to my execution of it, and of course I am far too old. But it is a part.

To Alec Guinness   *25 October, London*

I'm awfully glad to hear you're safe but sorry you are bored. I read some Keats on the air the other night for Eddie Sackville-West, and we talked at some length about your Hamlet.† I hope your ears burnt. How nice and intelligent and highly-strung he is. I think you might see *Love for Love* with any luck – it looks like going on for another six months at least. The Lunts came and were really wonderful about it – I went home on air – and then Alfred took the trouble to sit down and write me a four page letter appreciating every detail. The only two people who have not liked it very much are Edith and Peggy which naturally disappointed me somewhat, but perhaps they know me too well or something. I'm disgracefully happy at the Haymarket, installed in the big dressing room which is like Mrs Darling's Nursery.

Martita [Hunt] is to be the Vicaress in *The Cradle Song* at which, like Christian, I rejoice and tremble – never, surely, shall I persuade her to take the varnish off those famous claws. She is in a great pickle already about it, and I am invited to tea on Sunday to go into it all.‡ By the tone, I expected to be asked to lend her £1000 at least. What a pity she is so impossible over work. I do *Cradle Song* after Xmas, with Wendy Hiller, and Lilli Kann, who

---

* He would play Caesar in 1971 at Chichester Festival Theatre.
† Old Vic, 1938.
‡ In fact Muriel Aked played the part, so presumably Martita Hunt's reservations were insuperable.

is a wonderful Viennese Jewess à la Sara Allgood. After that I'm supposed to do the new [Eric] Linklater play *Crisis in Heaven* which is a delightful satire on the lines of his recent broadcasts, *Socrates Asks Why, Cornerstones* and *The Raft.*

So you see I am full of interesting plans and whirling with casting, scenic designers et alia, just like the old days, while you and so many of the stars are having a dreary, endless time working your guts out at things that don't really interest you at all. But you must go on with your writing if you possibly can.

Terry [Rattigan]'s new play [*While the Sun Shines*] has opened in Manchester with great success, despite a terrible job of direction by Puffin [Anthony] Asquith, and the Lunts open at Liverpool next week. Peggy gives a most lovely performance in [Rodney] Ackland's play *The Dark River.* Rodney's production is good, and a lot of the acting too, and the play is full of quality like all his work. But it is gloomy, painful and one is irritated by the use of the Chekhov technique of a completely second rate theme. The press have torn it to shreds and I'm sure there is no hope for it, which is sad for them all. But I *knew* it could not succeed, especially at a time like this.

JG and 'Binkie' Beaumont were looking for a young actress to play Teresa in The Cradle Song. *A wealthy lady named Gertrude Jefferson was one of Beaumont's backers and invited him and JG to a school performance in Hastings. The headmistress, Dorothy Catt, had a promising pupil called Gwendoline Watford.*

To Dorothy Catt   *18 November, London*

I have talked to Mr Beaumont about Gwendoline Watford, but we both feel that while she is undoubtedly talented, it would not be fair to persuade her to leave school at the moment, as all we could offer her in *The Cradle Song* would be a walk-on part and understudy, as she is not really suited to the part of Teresa, for which we came down to see her. If, when she has completed her schooling, she still wishes to go on the stage, I will do everything I can to help her, and give her an introduction to one of the dramatic academies, but I do not feel that I would like to take on the responsibility of persuading her to leave school at the moment.

When Gwen Watford left school, JG helped her to get her first job and took a great interest in her long and distinguished career.

Love for Love played until June 1944, during which time JG directed four plays – Landslide *by Dorothy Albertyn and David Peel,* The Cradle Song, Crisis in Heaven *and* The Last of Summer *by Kate O'Brien and John Perry. By July of that year, he was in Manchester preparing to open* Hamlet, *directed this time by the Cambridge don and Shakespeare scholar, George 'Dadie' Rylands.*

1944

JG celebrated his fortieth birthday on 14 April.

To Dadie Rylands   *17 April, London*

Indeed you are far too modest. I know your advice and help will be invaluable and I think you will find it a good lot of people to work with. I am simply delighted that you favour the idea. I long for a fresh eye to look at the play with, and a shoulder to lean on for confirmation, opposition and general debate. We are shrewd old things, the pair of us, and we ought to be able to put our heads together to good purpose.

To his mother   *13 July, Manchester*

It pours with rain here, but as weather doesn't make much difference to the beauties of Manchester, that is no matter. We had a great reception here, and are sold out for every performance. Three and a half hours solid playing, but nobody budges, enthusiastic press, so I am really very glad. So many thanks for your sweet letter and the beautiful handkerchiefs which went on to the stage to give me courage. My clothes are very successful – also the new wig! Thank God for paint when golden youth is on the wane at last!

To Alec Guinness   *14 July, Manchester*

I was so pleased to get your letter yesterday. J. P. is home and already gave me news of you. He says you and B. [Robert] Flemyng are the only ones he has seen who look better and younger for the war and seem to have made a great success of it! Here we are not without our excitements. We rehearsed the new *Hamlet* to the accompaniment of showers of flying bombs, and one morning when we were at the Lyric, one came down on the Regent Palace Hotel. The musical comedy company who were rehearsing at the Piccadilly Theatre were miraculously unhurt. But the unfortunate Peg [Ashcroft] who had just left us and was in the street, dived into a hairdresser's shop and got a $1\frac{1}{2}$ inch glass cut in her thigh just above the knee and another in her instep which has put her out of commission for the moment. The production, by George Rylands of Cambridge, is far the best I have been in yet, I think – a very long version – $3\frac{1}{2}$ hours, but they sit like mice to the end. [Leslie] Banks excellent as the King and [Miles] Malleson and Leo [Quartermaine] splendid as Polonius and the Ghost. [Francis] Lister not right as Horatio, but it was hard to find anyone with the right stolidity and distinction. Marian Spencer v. good as the Queen, Hazel Terry puts up quite a passable Ophelia till Peggy can join us. Early Henry VII clothes and a very simple semi-Elizabethan set with only a few steps. I wish you could see it. If we get it established in our repertory, perhaps you will by the time year is over. It's awfully exciting to have found a new producer of real integrity and taste – no stunts and tactful with the actors, but quite firm in ideas and clear in understanding of rhythm and drama too. He helped me more than I can tell you, and John and Binkie both think I play with more power and relaxation than ever before, which is gratifying.

This hotel is shocked this morning to its foundations, as a poor old man, who was asleep in bed with his key left on the outside of the door, was attacked by two G.I. deserters last night and slashed about the head with razors. We heard the screams, and saw the aftermath, but the culprits got away somehow. I was in that room till yesterday and only moved because Binkie had gone back to London, and I decided to take over his sitting room for supper, so what an escape I had! Really, the times one lives in, one way and another.

This bomb business in London is hell for the theatres, nearly everything has closed except Blithers [*Blithe Spirit*], Terry's comedy [*While the Sun Shines*], the *Ambassadors Revue* and gallant old *Arsenic Lil.** I feel rather a rat playing to huge business in the provinces, but it seems the only thing to do under the present conditions. Take care of your dear self – my love to you as ever.

After the Manchester opening, Hamlet *embarked on a long regional tour.*

To his mother   *19 July, Glasgow*

We had a fine audience and reception last night, despite a noisy staff and trams clanging by at inopportune moments of suspense! I felt much rested after the two clear days, despite a very hot and crowded journey on Monday. Here it is Holiday Week – half the shops shut, no drink left anywhere and vast crowds of hideous people thronging the streets and bus queues.

To Alec Guinness   *14 August, Bristol*

We had a week out last week and London was as empty and sad as the provinces are crammed, ill mannered and noisy. The papers are wild with optimism about the battle in France, and the possible threat of V2 is the only fly in the ointment. I expect you saw that Rex Whistler was killed in Normandy – that's a major tragedy, it seems to me, and makes me very ashamed, for he was only a year younger than I am, and went in to the Welsh Guards – all that frightful training – and took an ordinary commission, disdaining all offers of special service, camouflage etc. which he could have so easily been switched to, as he knew all the top people. He wanted to prove that 'artists can be tough' and alas, he has done so – but the world is greatly the poorer for his sacrifice.

---

* *Arsenic and Old Lace* with Lilian Braithwaite.

Your ideas about Prince Hal are v. good. I wanted to do the Henriad –
Richard II–Henry V – at the beginning of this year and tried to inveigle Ralph
[Richardson] in for Falstaff, but I imagine Tony [Guthrie] and Larry [Olivier]
had already begun planning with him their own scheme which now they are
preparing. Anyway, he turned it down, so it is there to do perhaps after
the war. They have opened with *Arms and the Man* [by Bernard Shaw] at
Manchester, and add *Peer Gynt* [by Henrik Ibsen] and *Richard III* coming to
the New at the end of August. We hope to bring in *Hamlet, Love for Love* and
The Circle [by W. Somerset Maugham] soon afterwards, so that would make
a tolerable contribution to the more intelligent theatre if and when London
is possible again.

I rang Martita [Hunt], but she cooed mildly and did not bother to turn
off her gramophone, so presumably was not in the mood for a chat that
evening, or had other and more congenial company sitting or lying with her.
She wouldn't go on tour in *An Ideal Husband* [by Oscar Wilde], which was I
suppose a relief for the company, though I think stupid of her, and is now
waiting for a film, and crouching over her frocks and furniture in Wimpole
Street, with, I imagine, the faithful Winnie in attendance.

We are going to play at Cambridge in two weeks time as an especial
compliment to Mr Rylands, who is high in all our favour at the moment. It
will be fun to act in a really small theatre again, and in *Hamlet* too. Vivien
Leigh is with child, and Claude Rains has to leave in a month or pay thousands
of pounds income tax, so I imagine Pascal's *Caesar and Cleo* will not be
finished at all. They have only made about four minutes of it so far in so
many months. Serve them right.

My parents went to Foulslough for a fortnight but couldn't stand the planes
and food difficulties, so back they have come to London which makes me
very uneasy as they are now very old and tired and difficult and get terribly
on each other's nerves and won't do anything one asks them to. It's rather
tragic to see them and I dread another bomb falling anywhere near them, for
they are much too gallant, and then pay for it with delayed shock and reaction
weeks afterwards.

Christopher Hassall was at Leeds, writing yet another book about Stephen
Haggard. What a dark horse that one turned out to be, but as I told C. I think
it a pity to write again about him until the whole story can be truly told, for it
was his potentialities that were far more interesting than his achievements.

To his mother   *16 August, Bristol*

Wonderful weather here, but the theatre [Bristol Hippodrome] is like the
Coliseum – dirty, noisy staff, and crossing the stage is like doing the quarter
mile – I run in my exits out of sheer panic! However, it goes wonderfully,
despite a few drunks in the gallery who are expecting Evelyn Laye or a Negro
Band! I don't exactly dote on music halls for acting straight plays in.

To his mother   *22 August, Bournemouth*

We have huge houses, but I don't think they understand it much – typical holiday vulgarians.

To his mother   *29 August, Cambridge*

Very moving and exciting playing in the tiny theatre last night. Pin-drop silence and attention, and wonderful appreciation from everyone one meets. Luncheon today at the Rothschilds* who have an enchanting 12th century house nearby, with lovely oak beams. Quite small cottages originally, only knocked into big rooms, with Renoirs on the wall, a Scotch nannie and two small children, one Peggy's Eliza who is now 3 and quite talkative.

To Dadie Rylands   *6 September, Derby*

The conventional bread and butter letter is hardly suitable to this occasion. I do hope you know how delightfully you entertained and cosseted me and put up my friends and made yourself generally agreeable, diverting and sympathetic. I really believe, too, that with a triple alliance of yourself, me and that arch sphinx Binkie, great possibilities for the future are conceivable, especially as we can each contribute something different to the general welfare – and then, besides, we are all dears – and there is Arthur [Marshall], and Noël too, no doubt, to stir the gravy and add the pepper to the brew! It really was a memorable time for me, both in the theatre and out of it – and never an impure thought, either – yet I was content.

To Gwen Ffrangcon-Davies   *15 September, London*

The troupe had a wonderful time at Gibraltar and in the Middle East – they all lost weight and gained sunburn – Binkie came back quite an Adonis! – and laden with frankincense and myrrh from the Cairo bazaars. Alec Guinness and Alan Webb are both in Sicily – extraordinary to think of little Alec commanding an invasion craft!

To Dadie Rylands   *24 September, Oxford*

I have had my wig considerably darkened. Alan Dent and many others thought it much too golden, and I *don't* want to be strikingly beautiful in appearance as much as *real*. I do not think Hamlet should have the same remarkable beauty as Richard II should have.

I hear Larry's Richard III is absolutely terrific – even Binkie and John

---

* Victor, Lord Rothschild was at this time working for MI5 as Head of Counter-sabotage.

raved – so I would like to play my best and am so anxious that you and the company should get the appreciation which you deserve.

During the tour, JG had been rehearsing The Circle, *which opened in Glasgow.*

To his mother   *26 September, Glasgow*

The play went very well last night, though it was so cold on the stage that one wanted to close the French windows, and the autumn barrage of coughers in front made our witty remarks sound rather explosive at times. I was glad for once that the ladies of the company were in full décolleté instead of me.

To his mother   *4 October, Edinburgh*

All thanks for the jam and your letter and wire. I was very glad of the former, as this hotel is worse than ever, and one gets nothing whatever to eat at tea or breakfast except stale bread and butter! However, we have a terrific week booked, and they eat the play, the only snag being Yvonne [Arnaud] who has a laryngitic cold and is almost speechless. Poor old Annie Esmond, who understudies her, is in very bad health, has no proper clothes and would not be at all right. Poor thing, she is naturally in a flat spin and it's all a bit nerve-racking. Also, Yvonne wants to scrap her last dress, which she thinks too outrageous and comic, and as it cost £120 Binkie does not fancy the idea. No one dares to have a row with her over it, as she will undoubtedly take finally to her bed if she is crossed. Ah, these coups de théâtre – they never fail, especially if everything else seems to be fairly favourable.

The repertoire of Hamlet, Love for Love *and* The Circle *opened at the Theatre Royal, Haymarket, on 11, 12 and 13 October.*

To Dadie Rylands   *22 October, London*

The first tone of the press seemed slightly grudging to my tired old eyes, but one is always hypersensitive after those awful opening nights. They appear to be making up for it in the later notices. I hope you saw *Time and Tide*, which is really appreciative in an intelligent way all round. [Desmond] McCarthy helped me a lot, especially about what our dear Allies call my tendency to become piss-elegant. I am curbing my unfortunate tendency to 'hold the pose' and sit down with my knees together à la Marie Tempest and I believe this gives a certain strength to my performance in both plays. If one has a meticulous and accurate method as I have by nature, I think it is right to roughen the edges and play with apparent casualness at times – perhaps you should have told me this – but those accursed provincial theatres, whose size forces one to hold one's effects so that they may carry further, are largely to blame.

To Frith Banbury   *23 October, London*

Agate has a bee in his bonnet that Wolfit is an unappreciated genius and
thinks he should be publicly supported and have a better theatre than the
Scala. He will probably get it, all in good time, for the critics and public
appear to be giving him all the support he wants and, if he could control his
actor-managerial arrogance, he would probably get a good company himself
one day.

Alfred Lunt and Lynn Fontanne were playing in London at the time in There
Shall Be No Night *by Robert Sherwood and came to see* Love for Love.

To Alfred Lunt   *October 1944, London*

Your sweetness and generosity has given me so much joy – you can never
imagine how anxious we all were that you should both have a happy evening,
and that the play should seem fresh and real to you. But I do believe your
being in the audience gave everybody the most wonderful fillip, and whenever
we give bad, repetitive performances in future, I shall put firecrackers under
all the seats on the stage labelled 'The Lunts ARE IN FRONT AGAIN!'. I
shall keep that letter of yours amongst my most prized possessions, for nobody
knows better than you two how seldom the 'right night' comes for play and
audience, and if it ever does once in a while, it's something to thank the Gods
for. My love to you both, and again thank you for all your own personal
enthusiasm and brilliance for all you stand for in your own theatre which we
love so much and long to emulate. Surely you are the only successful pair
whom no one ever dares to be catty about in this highly-strung profession.

To Alfred Lunt and Lynn Fontanne   *October–November? 1944, London*

Such an inspiration to be at your performance tonight – such a lesson to
watch you, such a pleasure to forget about being an actor and yet to mentally
pocket one by one, first, the impression of the scenes and acting, then to
consider, almost in terror of forgetting, the faultless precision and exquisite
sensitiveness and detail which informed your playing in every single scene.

    The direction fascinated me, of course. The arrangement of the moves, the
lovely flow of the home atmosphere which is so skilfully suggested, Lynn's
two exits to the hall and the despairing 'cooking' one sees through the doors
at the back, the timing of words and movement in there and the divine way
her movements seem to make the exact balance to the angular agony of the
farewell scene after the boy's departure – the way you both enfolded the girl
on the sofa with hands and arms and bodies – the way you, Lynn, clung to
your mask of grace and poise and chic without any more taking pleasure in
them in the last two scenes – Alfred's comedy touches, laughing at the

engagement and trying on the uniform – and the superb handling of those difficult scenes – the broadcast at the beginning and the reading of the letter at the end with that marvellously controlled break in the voice at the mention of the son, and the pause and rush of recollection at the memory of the broadcast. Oh yes, it was all fine and touching and absorbing, and no less your beautiful handling of those not always properly cast actors and your generosity in bringing them out to the best of their abilities – and indeed it is a test for any company to appear with you, for so few actors know what hard work means as you do. What they must learn about acting with you all the time, and how gracious and fine of you to come here in this fifth year and warm London with real glamour and pity and excitement in the theatre again after so much that has been pedestrian and 'rubbing along'. It is indeed something one longs for – two artists of such calibre to talk to and look up to, with a standard of perfection, reached and accomplished, that would make any nation in the world proud to own them, and particularly England and America. Please don't think me fulsome, but I couldn't say any of this to you, and shall not try. But I do mean it from my heart, and thank you both most deeply.

To Dadie Rylands   *31 December, London*

And pray how dare you sir, ensconced amid your Kingly* pinnacles, presume to compare my art with those two posturing mountebanks Messrs Wolfit and Olivier? It is curious that you can find leisure to watch and criticise the efforts of these gentlemen and yet cannot spare the necessary modicum of time to look after your own poor fluttering pigeons. Are you aware, sir, that M. de Diaghilev never missed a single performance of his troupe – at least I never went to a performance without seeing him come through the pass door just before the curtain rose – woe to the girl who added so much as a ring or a brooch to her costume in *Sylphides!*

As you most justly observe, it is after the production that the rot begins to set in, and that is why, in my own small way, I have always kept my own productions – but not often my own role, naturally, in decent shape for a longer time than most, because I am always there to keep noting and improving the details and general standard. But when the cast is altered or too much time elapsed (as in *Love for Love* now), the task becomes well nigh impossible.

Picture me then, trampling through the second performance of *Hamlet* yesterday, with [Abraham] Sofaer, Dorothy Lane as the Queen, and a raw amateur as Guildenstern (Marian [Spencer] and [John] Blatchley both 'flu victims) to an audience of would-be pantomime visitors – overflow from His Majesty's – afflicted with the final paroxysms of fogbound laryngitis and stuffed with an excess of farinaceous wartime Christmas food – myself raw in

* Rylands was bursar of King's College, Cambridge.

voice, depressed and full of apprehension and cumbersome details about *The Dream* – and then you ask if I am still acting well?

Oh this curse of the theatre – to continue and continue – to improve a little and slip back again, to find the precise formula and not to be able to pin it down – that is our cross, we wretched mummers.

1945

A Midsummer Night's Dream *directed by the Oxford don Nevill Coghill was due to join the repertoire in January 1945. JG was also planning his own production of* Lady Windermere's Fan, *with décor by Cecil Beaton.*

To W. Graham Robertson   *8 January, London*

Thank you for your kind and generous note of greeting which I much appreciated. Alfred and Lynn were at dinner also, looking much younger and gayer under the influence of their new comedy and great success [Terence Rattigan's *Love in Idleness*], than they did when they were bowed down with the cares and tragedies of *There Shall Be No Night*. I am off to rehearse Oberon, which is a good exercise on a chilly morning. The designer has made me the most beautiful Leonardo da Vinci helmet in cellophane, with a transparent visor for 'I am invisible', worn over dark green hair and a Greek kilt à la Inigo Jones, that has already gone quite to my head – as the saying is. What an entrancing play it is.

To Cecil Beaton   *23 February, London*

I have been thinking a great deal about *Lady Windermere's Fan* since our talk the other night, and I have come to the conclusion that we shall make a great mistake if we alter the period of the play by more than a very little. The play is so very definitely a Victorian story, that I think we should be much blamed if we take it out of its proper setting and, in any case, it is a procedure that has never brought me luck when I have tried it before. I am quite sure that with your distinctive ideas, and very special colour sense, you will not invite invidious comparison with Rex [Whistler]'s work, and it would be a great mistake to do the play other than with an 1890 setting.

I think the décor must be pretty realistic, but also witty. Maybe your composite period may work, but I do think the general style of both clothes and scenery should be ninetyish to match the dialogue and general manners of the text. Marie Löhr is being approached about the Duchess – she could carry off elaborate dresses well.

To the Editor of The Times   *April 1945, London*

I shall be shortly removing from 55 Park Lane to 16 Cowley Street and am very anxious to continue receiving *The Times* daily. My newsagent up to date has been P. Andrey of 8 Trebeck St, Mayfair, but I am wondering if you could suggest a stationer or newsagent near Cowley Street who could supply me with *The Times* once I have moved?

Lady Windermere's Fan *opened at the Theatre Royal, Haymarket, on 21 August 1945.*

To Dadie Rylands   *20 September, London**

Will you be kind and read *The Assassin* by Peter Yates if you have half an hour to spare? I have bought a year's option on it and like it myself, but John and Binkie are frightened because it is in verse and they don't know if it is good verse. Nor don't I but I believe it would speak well, and one should encourage a new English writer. Also it is comparatively cheap to do as it is a simple play with no important parts except mine.

I hope we will work again together one day under more ideal conditions – a nice summer season at the Arts [Cambridge] with rehearsals under the trees, I think, don't you? – and Peggy and a lot of nobodies!

After the successful season at the Haymarket, JG embarked on an ENSA tour of the Middle and Far East with Hamlet *and* Blithe Spirit.

To his mother   *20 October, Bombay*

When we got to Karachi early yesterday morning, I was whisked off to stay with the Governor in a fine car. Such a lovely house – huge rooms, tiled passages with lattices and big saloons – modern Lutyens furniture and architecture but extremely good of its kind – empty and comfortable. I was given a palatial bedroom and bathroom and velvet-footed bearded servants crept hither and thither to carry out my slightest wish. The Governor an intelligent, capable man with a very ugly Cockney accent and the wife a fussy little suburban pouter pigeon of about 60, full of WVS and glee clubs. She apparently obliges with a song a good deal herself – 'Senta's Ballad' and 'O sole mio' with 'Caller Herrin' as the pièce de résistance.

Lunch consisted of 'boiled hump' which I took to be camel but tasted just like beef, and blackcurrant suet roll with treacle, which I must say made me feel there was no place like home!

---

* JG had by now moved to 16 Cowley Street, Westminster, where he would remain for the next thirty-one years.

To his mother   *28 October, Bombay*

Went to a frightful Indian party on Wednesday night. Decadent and snobbish Indian Princes, educated at Sandhurst and Oxford, who were pockmarked and degenerate and asked after Tom Walls and Ralph Lynn* – and hen-like women sitting round the walls with no conversation whatever.

To his mother   *7 November, Deolali*

I have a little private jeep which buckets me around wherever I want to go with a coal black driver with very white teeth, who doesn't speak a word of English and goes fast asleep over the wheel the moment we get back to the house!

The theatre is a big hut – quite good for sound, holding about 1000 and we have wonderful audiences for *Blithe Spirit*. Irene [Browne] sprained a ligament in her foot and missed one performance, and Marian [Spencer] has an ulcerated throat which threatens to lay her off at any minute. Fortunately the fuzzy-haired Jewess [Nancy Nevinson] who plays Mrs Bradman is an excellent understudy and has already played Gertrude and Arcati admirably, only it's a bore having to rehearse continually.

The natives are idiotic and everything is cold, late, badly organised and slovenly, and yet there is a certain leisureliness and decorative elegance about it that is not wholly unattractive.

I had a fantastic lunch party in Bombay with a Mrs Sabewala, the local Lady Colefax-cum-Susan Birch. A huge, fat woman in a brilliant scarlet saree, the house red sandstone with the hardest teak furniture I ever sat on, divans and cushions à la Bakst – low windows you had to kneel down to look through, and ornamental pools with lotus flowers in the middle of the floors. The unbelievable coloured photos of relations stuck on nails in corners – cheap Madonnas in plaster and reproductions of Italian saints jostling Indian gods and Billiekins from Birmingham – an appalling modern bathroom in L.M.S. pink marble and more dreadful portraits and photographs of adored sons and mothers pinned up in corners against bits of exquisite Indian silk – a fantastic muddle of tastes – and there were beautiful Parsee ladies and a frightfully boring fuzzy-haired Indian poet with glasses and a face like a chimpanzee who recited lyrics at me in bell-like tones – and two young students of Shakespeare who goggled at me and said they would cut off their right hands to meet me and why couldn't they come to England and act Shakespeare in my company! The hostess who is a Parsee also, and thinks herself a great character, obliged throughout with an obbligato of heavy bromides like 'You like the colour of this room Mr Gielgud? I live for colour. It means everything to me' and 'People

---

* English actors famous for their appearances in the Aldwych farces in the 1920s.

think me rude. I am. I live for Truth. At all costs. Truth. It is all that matters in life.' I must say I wish I could put the whole thing into a short story.

To Cecil Beaton   *5 December, Ceylon*

Someone just out from England whom I met at Trincomalee last week lent me your new book [*Far East*], which I am reading with great amusement and delight – also with undiminished admiration, for I am, in my own small way, dismayed to find how difficult it is to record impressions even in letters, and you manage it with such vivid ease, apparently. I must say some of the parties in India made me long for a photographer, diarist or playwright, preferably Rodney Ackland or Peter Ustinov to record them. Ram Gopal, who spoke enthusiastically of you, was very nice to us in Bangalore. I found him excessively glamorous and thought I had had some mild success, with a present arriving of a dressing gown, scented joss sticks and an Indian battle in miniature – painting. My face fell somewhat when I discovered that John P. (despite violent sciatica which appeared to be keeping him in purdah) had received a parcel of moonstone cufflinks! Gopal took us to Mysore where the elephants all got violent erections, and we had to shroud our ladies in cloaks and admire the surrounding scenery to conceal our fascinated amazement at the prodigy.

Do you see Binkie? And are you busy with *Our Betters* [by W. Somerset Maugham] and the concertina cushions and cloche hats? Have you found another country house yet? You see from this questionnaire that I should like an answer. We've had very few letters and this old timer of the Avenue is homesick for news – even after seven weeks.

Your Gov. House description is masterly. We have madly enjoyable times what with food, bathing, hot weather and the colour of the native clothes which ravishes me. On the other hand I think sightseeing rather boring – temples etc. – and there are hours of exquisite boredom in messes, diabolical acting in *Hamlet* from my C3 supporting cast (Marian and George Howe excepted) and occasional bouts of exhaustion and general irritation when organisation fails or too many stupid strangers hem one in. Alan Moorehead has been here – en route for Australia where he is going to write a life of Montgomery – told me fascinating tales of his wicked old mother (Monty's) and a three handed interview between Montgomery, Augustus John and G.B.S. How is the Chips [Channon]–Terry [Rattigan]–Peter [Coats] triangle? Nobody writes me any gossip, and you know it's the only thing I really enjoy. I am mad about the flowered sarongs worn by all the men here and mean to borrow some coupons from my hostess to buy a few to wear in the evenings on my return – and the peons in the house wear wonderful semicircular tortoiseshell combs – very nice if you have the hair to stick them into.

To Kitty Black *22 December, Raffles Hotel, Singapore*

We are all well despite the sticky heat, but have not a great deal of energy during the day – just as well, really, as there is nothing to do. Prices impossibly high unless one has whisky or cigarettes to barter, and then mostly for indifferent goods (though there are masses of things like jewellery, watches, cameras, torches and suchlike), and all one does is search for the odd restaurant where one can eat. We are supposed to be on rations in this hotel (at 20 dollars a day – £2) but find ourselves low and hungry if we eat in. Fortunately there is a certain amount of hospitality – we lunched with the Supremo and General Dempsey on different days and had an unforgettable Chinese dinner with a local plutocrat – *twelve* courses, including birds' nest, shark fin, fried oysters and roast sucking pig! Something really worth waiting for, I must say. But his house was utterly boring and hideous – like a set for one of the Hulberts'* musical comedies. Wonderful box spring beds, exquisite tiled bathrooms and spacious verandahs and balconies overlooking a lovely view, but awful Waring and Gillow furniture, modern covers, carpets and bric-à-brac of conventional Maple dreariness, and even the chinoiserie – cabinets, ornaments etc. all spick and span, expensive but utterly ugly – and those awful imitation electric candlesticks with modelled wax dripping from them, and Lalique bowls and 'bunny' ashtrays!

Their culture too, like that of the Indians, is an extraordinary mixture of ignorance and pretentiousness, and you feel that under the surface of Western amiability they are secretly primitive and superstitious and Oriental, though outwardly so impassive and intelligent.

The plays go wonderfully well everywhere, and here we play to 1000 every night in a theatre that really holds 600 – but have some difficulty making ourselves heard, as there are curtained doorways instead of doors at the back, opening to one of the noisiest squares I ever saw – lorries, children, planes and traffic, with an occasional conjuror, with a pipe or army band thrown in for good measure, and inside the theatre there are electric fans and several hundred swifts which come out as soon as the orchestra begin, and twitter and swoop in and out round the lights making a considerable row. But the men sit like mice and seem to enjoy themselves immensely though I don't suppose they get a drink outside their ration, and food and cigarettes anything but plentiful.

We go to a naval mess to lunch on Christmas Day and have a party at the ENSA Hostel in the evening, where I gather there is to be an entertainment in my honour with a kind of topical revue written and produced by the company. The material has, however, been somewhat rigorously censored by George Howe and John P. and I trust we shall avoid too many blushes. Joe Davis has been a tower of strength, Jack Wood is hard working though somewhat hysterical, and the company is, as usual on these occasions, somewhat divided into a series of cliques and factions. However, we all manage

* Jack Hulbert and his wife Cicely Courtneidge.

pretty well on the whole, and best when things are not going so well, as usual in the theatre. It is when they have a few days off or nothing to do that they all get bad-tempered and fractious, and fortunately that isn't often.

London sounds very grim with prices still higher than when we left, and coal, gas and electric light shortage, and I fear you will not have a gay time. The theatres, however, don't seem to have changed their programmes at all, and that must mean good business – anyway, I hope so.

To his mother   *28 December, Saigon*

Christmas Day quite amusing, though everybody drinks too much everywhere on the slightest excuse, and I do get so bored with drunks. Then on Boxing Night there was a huge party given by the Admiral in a bungalow, with Cameron Highlanders marching up and down on the lawn playing the bagpipes which was a pretty and pre-war sight, and about 400 people danced on the verandah to quite a good band and there were even a few hysterical attempts at reels inspired by the pipers.

1946

To his mother   *2 January, Hong Kong*

The ENSA officer is an ex-stage manager of mine who was with me at the Queen's in 1938 and he had re-equipped an old theatre in a few weeks – spick and span, clean paint everywhere, a small stage and cosy auditorium with boxes, lavatories, single dressing rooms and even two small Chinese boys to fetch and carry, and women for the girls. Last night a gala audience – Air Marshal Keith Park, Sir Bruce Fraser and a galaxy of staff officers, governors etc. The play was a riot and we were besieged with invitations, almost as exciting a night as the first opening at Gibraltar in 1942, and we all enjoyed ourselves immensely.

JG played his last stage Hamlet in Cairo.

To his mother   *8 February, Cairo*

Ralph [Richardson] wired me the day before yesterday – would I think of joining him and Larry at the Vic – I suppose for the autumn, but have cabled asking for details and particulars. I should like nothing better if it is an equal partnership and plays and parts that I like. I am longing to hear what they suggest. It is an exciting thing that the Stratford and Old Vic should amalgamate. I have always thought it the only possible and sensible solution.

THE POST-WAR YEARS

1946

Now, young Randall, it's no good buttering me up with all that pretty speech-making. Did I or did I not see you last Thursday week, nudging your way among the crowds at the Earl's Court Exhibition, elbowing your course towards the Big Wheel with your hands stuck disgracefully far into the pockets of your shorts, and clinging feverishly to Bulstrode Minor as you emerged shrieking from the Tunnel of Love. These pranks, out of school hours, are only a further proof of your unfailingly mischievous behaviour during class time, which I have had frequent occasion to reprove. I have ordered Matron to sew up the linings of your pockets, all of which, I under-stand, are torn and stained in a most offensive manner, and to dose you with a sedative which I think may help to calm your unduly feverish disposition. Let me see no more of those lines under your eyes, sir, or lines may have to be written, not only on paper, but on a more substantial and resilient part of your anatomy.

Yours more in anger than in sorrow,
Augustus Lingerstroke

P.S. If you care to call on me to give an account of yourself, I usually find half an hour after school – between six and seven o'clock, when I take a warm bath and change into more informal attire – riding breeches or velvet cords, before the evening meal. Pray do not smoke cigarettes or eat peppermints before you come.

I am rehearsing next week in the daytime. How about dining with me one evening, say Tuesday next week, or tomorrow (Saturday). Ring up if you can WHI1618.

To Julian Randall   *London, 1946*

The March of Time (1911–1946)
(issued by the Trouser Press, Cock Yard, Cripplegate, E.C.)

Development (not yet arrested) or Plus Corduroyaliste que le roi.

At school I loved to watch, with furtive greed,
Young masters part their coats of Harris Tweed,
Jingling and thrusting in their trousers' pockets
While youthful eyes popped from their pupils' sockets.
Grey flannels were the then prevailing fashion,
And for these garments I conceived a passion.
Masters and boys, in tempting shades of greys
Disturbed my nights and dramatised my days.

The First Great War was quite an education,
In uniforms and mutual masturbation,
In riding breeches, boots and spurs, peaked caps,
And streamlined whipcords bulging at the flaps.

The Twenties blossomed – boys in peacock hues,
Whose Oxford trousers quite concealed their shoes,
Fawn, pink, cerise, in serge or gaberdine,
The hearty looked as garish as the Queen.

The Thirties ushered in a compromise,
Discreet zip-fasteners took the place of flies.
The width decreased, but looseness still remained,
And corduroys were Paradise Regained.
Breeches, alas, now shunned by the nobility,
Resumed a strict equestrian utility.
Plus fours waxed gross in hideous baggy tiers
And velvet vanished with the Cavaliers.
Grey flannels, shaved [?] in worsted, off the peg,
Lost all distinction on the common leg.

Then, in the Second War's most hideous year,
With siren suits for every wear and tear,
With women breeched in shameless imitation,
And blackout time the crudest compensation,
The gloomy curtain rose an inch or so,
Official sanction played the gigolo.
Austerity decreed that men and boys
Should help the war by wearing corduroys.
The British citizens complied with pleasure,
Gave their five coupons, donned for work and leisure,
Squeaking and rustling, grey and pink and brown,
Creased for the country, pressed and washed for town.
The Desert Rats took them for battle dress,
And Monty's 'cords' made headlines in the Press,
When suddenly, without a word of warning,
Once more the knell to masculine adorning.

The government announced in accents cultural,
'No corduroy, save for the Agricultural.'

Prince, you and I have noted predilictions [*sic*],
Britons shall not be slaves to such restrictions.
We'll crave indulgence, by the country's pardon,
Dress in fresh cords and cultivate our garden.

After the Middle and Far Eastern tour, JG prepared to play Raskolnikov in Rodney Ackland's adaptation of Crime and Punishment.

To Edith Evans   *25 March, London*

I must respect your frankness about the Dostoyevsky play, and though naturally I am disappointed that you do not want to work under my direction I am not altogether surprised, as I know you did not care for either *Love for Love* or [*Lady*] *Windermere*['*s Fan*]. I told Binkie when he asked me to do this play that I thought it likely you would not care to do it with me, and I have told him since that I will gladly give it up if you have someone else in mind. As you know, I had not meant to do any work for a few months, but it appears they are not able to get the producers they originally wished for and have therefore offered it to me.

I like the play immensely, but I will definitely not direct it with you if you feel so strongly about it, for obviously we should not work in harmony.* I hope, however, that this will not make any difference to our personal relationship, and that we may be at one over *The Importance*, even though you may find it rather a bore to work at it again.

To Howard Turner   *6 May, London*

I have you very much on my conscience, for I have never answered two long letters from you, and I feel sure that at least one rich parcel of goodies that I received last week came from New York and from you. Thank you so very much for keeping me so much in your thoughts.

We are in the thick of rehearsals for *Crime and Punishment* which opens in Manchester on May 20th – only two weeks away – and it is a fearfully complicated play with a cast of 40 people popping on and off all the time, so that one's own part is not in long consecutive scenes but broken up into snippets which have somehow to fit together and make a series of climaxes and gradations – a very hysterical, neurotic and altogether miserable young man who needs a great deal of attention – from me as well as, I hope eventually, the audience. I am really too old for the part, but it has an

---

* The play was eventually directed by Anthony Quayle.

immature, would-be superman weakness which I understand easily and should be within my range if I *arrange* it all properly and don't over or under act. Fortunately I find the director very helpful and sympathetic – an old friend of mine who has been at the war – never directed before, but often acted with me in the old days – Anthony Quayle – nice and clever, I think. Edith Evans will be wonderful in her part, but we scarcely meet in the play and have no scenes together. I don't much like the girl [Audrey Fildes], who is very important, and some of the others are not too good and need a terrible lot of work, so the going is slow and a bit wearing, but I hope it may all come out well in the end.

Dear Howard – my love to you – take care of yourself and be happy in your work and become a good actor – amen.

Crime and Punishment *opened at the New Theatre on 26 June.*

To Kerrison Preston   *27 July, London*

I am so glad to hear you came up to see the play, and I am so delighted that it interested and moved you. It is a strenuous and difficult part, too much on one note for ease of accomplishment, but it is interesting to have no memorable dialogue to speak after so many finely written characters that I have had the luck to play before, so that here one has to 'throw away' the words and try and make the emotions and crude violence of the action express what the author had in mind. The greatness of the conception (of the novel) and the extreme skill and ingenuity of the stage arrangement and incidents give distinction and psychological significance to the melodrama which might otherwise seem ordinarily sensational. But, as with Dickens, the sweep and compassion of the original is well sustained and supports the background of the play.

I am sad to hear Graham [Robertson] is so weak, but I am glad he received the greeting we all sent. Lady C. [Sibyl Colefax] kindly sent me a copy and I thought it enchantingly phrased. I am so glad it gave him pleasure. He is often in the affectionate remembrance of so many people and talked of continually whenever they meet.

To Cecil Beaton   *25 August, London*

I was simply delighted to get your long letter with all the *Windermere* news. Now I hear you are playing Cecil Gray [Graham] yourself* – and your English style will no doubt put all the other gentlemen to bed – I speak figuratively of course. How I should love to see you do it. I shall be fascinated to hear of

---

* Beaton played the part in San Francisco.

the reception – I'm glad Penelope [Dudley Ward] is so good. Noël always believed in her and Binkie too – they said she was good in *Blithe Spirit* but I've never seen her myself.

I took some Americans to the Haymarket [*Lady Windermere's Fan*] yesterday afternoon – a packed house – they are still doing £1800 a week. A very good performance except for Dorothy [Hyson], who tweets more like a canary than ever. Athene [Seyler] does one or two naughty mandarin nods for fear the audience mightn't see the joke, and Isabel's [Jeans] walk (who am I to cast a stone), splays outwards with a strange totter that suggests the cab horse about to slip on an icy paving stone saving itself by a valiant effort – but it all looks splendid still, and old ladies were being unpacked by the dozen into the dress circle – one of them having her neck massaged by two antique females who were escorting her. I never saw her face, only these large arthritic hands on each side massaging the neck and holding the head on, I suppose. I fully expected the corpse to be carried out during the course of the afternoon, but I think the play probably gave her another year!

Crime and Punishment does well too. I shan't be sorry when Edith retires to her barge on the Nile next week,* as she is a rather depressing influence upon a none too gay atmosphere. I also hope Rosalind Atkinson [taking over from Edith Evans] may make a success, as we are hoping to run on until the end of November. Then I want to do *Importance* in Canada and N.Y. followed in April by *Love for Love*. Much depends on casts and possible doubling, but I trust we may get an interesting company together. I am thinking of Marie Löhr for Bracknell, if she will not be tempted to play for sympathy which I hear is her Achilles heel.

London is not particularly gay – the Gish girls a welcome exception – and the American ballet boys† do not appear to be stepping out, despite one or two exploratory invitations. The women in it are pretty unattractive, though Nora Kaye has a certain Disney charm. I think Jerome Robbins has the only talent as choreographer, and then his ballets are really only Cochran Revue stuff. I'm a little disappointed in the music of *Annie Get Your Gun* which was sent me the other day. But I gather one has to see the production to appreciate it to the full.

[Robert] Helpmann has been very bitter, I gather, about *C & P*‡ He's been awfully ill, and walking with a stick, has now retired to Portugal for three months with Michael Benthall. They came to see the play but scrupulously avoided coming round – and distant bows in the Ivy have been vouchsafed since, which all seems very silly to me. He has taken up the American option, and I wonder if he will really play it there. I believe Garson Kanin wants to

---

* Edith Evans was about to start rehearsals for *Antony and Cleopatra*.
† The New York City Ballet was appearing at the Royal Opera House, Covent Garden.
‡ Helpmann had been announced for Raskolnikov.

direct it, and Lillian Gish wants to play Edith's part?! Anyway B. was determined *I* shouldn't do it in America, and I am rather glad to have the temptation to do so taken out of my hands, as I am not sure of the play for N.Y. and it is such a tiring, hardworking part to play. I shall certainly enjoy being there far more if we do the comedies, and I might have some fun in my leisure hours. Terry hopes to have his new opus for me to see by Christmas.

To Cecil Beaton   *7 October, London*

How are you? I hear you have had a great success as Cecil Gray [Graham] and I am sure you must be splendid in it. I only hope your production won't swamp the pitch before we get to New York with *The Importance*! Will you be so very kind as to do something for me. Binkie says you stay at the Plaza, and like it very much. Could you make inquiries for me as to whether they would let me have rooms there from about Feb. 20th until the end of May – 16 weeks or a little more – and on what terms. Everybody alarms me somewhat about the expense of everything, and I cannot even travel my dresser, but if it's not too wildly dear I think I must stay somewhere fairly smart. But possibly you know of some other hotel less expensive than the Plaza, or even of someone whose flat I could rent – or are servants impossible and utterly ruinous? I am very silly about money and feel I should budget it all a bit carefully before I start. It always takes me about a month to get used to the exchange and so on!

We have, I think, a wonderful cast for *Importance*. I had a reading last week – [Margaret] Rutherford really wonderful in her own way as Bracknell – Bobby Flemyng, Pamela Brown, Jane Baxter. Prism not settled yet* but what we have I am delighted with. Am hoping to persuade Isabel [Jeans] to come for *Love for Love* if only *Windermere* will fall off, which at present seems extremely unlikely! We have moved *C & P* to the Globe, where it goes well enough – still another 8 weeks to play it. Rosalind Atkinson has replaced Edith, and George Hayes Ustinov – both very good – the former better than Edith in my opinion.

Bobby Helpmann is back from Portugal and is, I hear, to play Oberon to [Margaret] Rawlings' Titania (should it not be in reverse order?) at Covent Garden (Purcell's *Fairie Queene*) and intends to follow it with *The White Devil*! What is the dirt on [*The Duchess of*] *Malfi*?† I hear Canada Lee is playing Bosola and that Dadie [Rylands] deputised at Hartford and Boston while he was learning his words. I know nothing of the young man who plays my part.

---

* Miss Prism would be played by Jean Cadell.
† Dadie Ryland's production with Elisabeth Bergner in the title role.

*Lear** is not a bit good, except for a miraculous Fool by Alec Guinness – played like a sad little Cairoli Brother sacked from the circus, intensely real and moving. Larry is brilliantly *clever* and absolutely complete in his characterisation, but it is a little doddering King without majesty or awesomeness – and the production is vile and also the rest of the acting. Roger Furse has come a heavy cropper with Bayeux Tapestry scenery and dresses – all bits and pieces, blackouts and waits – no drive or speed, and curtains, flats, cyclorama, ground rows and painted bits jostling one another in unsatisfactory juxtaposition. However, the critics were lyrical, and I hope I am not jealous. Sibyl Colefax still in hospital but unflaggingly directing operations from her Heath Robinson-bestrewn couch, with telephone at one arm's length and the 'whole of London' at the other.

To Theodore Komisarjevsky   *13 October, London*

Do you remember years ago suggesting I might play Raskolnikov? Well, I'm doing it now in a good adaptation by Rodney Ackland, but unfortunately I have not got the rights for America ... I wish you would come back and do some work here. We all miss you – the actors – and long for your stimulating direction and artistry. Peggy has two babies now, the last a son [Nicholas], of which she is very proud. I wonder if you saw the Vic shows – they were not well directed, but I loved Olivier's Hotspur (though not his Oedipus at all) and Richardson's Falstaff.

To Howard Turner   *28 October, London*

I'm horrified to find a letter from you on my table dated July 27th. Could I have been all this while without answering it – I hope not, but I fear so, for I have been lazy about writing letters and very busy all summer, and this last month I've been awfully exhausted – really had a minor nervous breakdown – broke out in rashes, could not eat, got into rages on slight provocation etc. Finally I had to get the matinées taken off altogether, and a week off the run to fly to Portugal for a fortnight's real holiday – and pray God some sunshine – before we start rehearsing the American production of *Importance*. We sail on the *Q.E.* Jan. 9th, which isn't far off really. Larry Olivier and Vivien Leigh are going on the same ship, and I hope to make the grade on arrival by hanging firmly on Mrs O's other arm as soon as the photographers get on board and refusing to be shaken off on the slightest pretext whatsoever.

We are collecting, gradually, really first rate casts for both plays [*The Importance* would be followed by *Love for Love*], and I have great hope of their quality all round – and it will be good to have three weeks in Canada first, to

---

* The Old Vic Company production at the New Theatre with Olivier as King Lear.

get the first one really played in. I went to Hampton Court today – did you ever see it – marvellous in the autumn sunshine. Have you read Edith Sitwell's *Fanfare for Elizabeth* – you would love it, I'm sure – and I think it so like Lear and his daughters. The Vic production is rather disappointing by the way, but I believe the *Cyrano* [*de Bergerac*] is better – I'm going next week to see it.

1947

In January 1947 JG took his own production of The Importance of Being Earnest *to North America.*

To his mother   *20 January, Ontario*

We had a very hectic three days in New York – saw three magnificent musicals and met a host of people we knew and didn't know. [Alfred] Lunt has had an emergency operation and they've had to close the play [*O Mistress Mine* by Terence Rattigan] for a month, but I went to tea with Lynn [Fontanne] who seems to think he is now out of danger (stone in the kidney). [Lillian] Gish and Judith Anderson and many others welcomed us at a big reception given by the Theatre Guild – it was surprisingly pleasant and informal – the McClintics as ever welcoming and hospitable. This town rather miserable and one-horse, what one can see of it through the blizzard of sleet – and the hotel distinctly utility – but there appears to be wild enthusiasm and interest in our playing here, and it is good enough for a trial and dress rehearsals which we begin this evening. The night journey from New York very comfortable but one is chiefly concerned in keeping cool in the frightfully over steam-heated rooms, theatres and restaurants, and in not eating and drinking too much rich food and drink, which is pressed on one everywhere.

I do hope things are easing up with you – that Father is getting better and you less tired, and the servant problem nearer to solution. I must say the latter seems to be a difficulty even in American homes, but of course with lots of provisions it's so easy to drop in to a delicatessen or restaurant. They are open until very late and one can get a good meal at any hour of the day or night it seems.

To his mother   *7 February, Toronto*

It has been icy here all week, real arctic blizzards that cut one's face off if one tries to walk in it, but our houses have been full and I haven't minded it at all. It is a horrid shack-like kind of town, and I'm getting tired of lunches and parties and polite speeches, both from me and Canadians, but this is the last of that for the present.

The theatre in New York is still a problem. Now we have to do a week in Baltimore after Boston and open at the Plymouth March 3rd. I'm rather cross about this as I had no wish to tour this play for weeks, but it can't be helped, it seems. However, I am quite determined to carry through my original schedule. I get so annoyed when I always keep to my promises and business people try to cheat on theirs, but even Binkie is sometimes fallible in that respect when big profits are involved. But there can't be big profits on this tour anyway for the management and they might just as well allow me to run the thing as I originally wanted to. We shall no doubt have some arguments but I hope I shall get my way in the end.

To his mother   *12 February, Boston*

We have had a really wonderful press here – and the first night reception was something remarkable, they tell me, for Boston. At the end after we had taken a lot of curtains and the house lights had gone up they wouldn't go home and we had to put them out again (the lights) and take another call with speeches.

The shops are lovely here and packed with good things. I will send you soap and olive oil in a day or two. I simply can't bear to think of you all in such a wretched crisis in London – the cold and discomfort must be simply appalling to say nothing of the general atmosphere of rage and depression. I do really feel a pig to be away from it all and living in such luxury and ease. Do let me know if there is anything urgent I can send you back by Binkie – clothes, warm things, hot water bottles or the like – when he comes.

Donald Wolfit was making his first transatlantic tour at the same time. After a brief visit to Canada, he took his company and its Shakespeare repertoire to New York.

To his mother   *21 February, Boston*

I sent Father the *Lear* notices yesterday. Here is one for *As You Like It*. The New York critics have torn him [Wolfit] to shreds and I can't say I'm sorry – except for the company – as he went out of his way to write me two very foolish and jealous letters when we were in Canada. I answered the first with some coldness but without rancour, and received a second, condoling with me on not getting a theatre in New York and bragging about the season which had been offered him there quite unsolicited! So I cannot but feel he deserves all he gets. I have always been amazed at the way Agate and the London critics have praised his work, but his rage at this failure will know no bounds, and both Olivier and I have been the object of his rancour for some time. This should really take him down a peg, and he will have a busy time if he starts writing protests to the critics as he does in England whenever he gets a bad notice.

We are doing capacity business and they say the Baltimore advance is wonderful, and that mail orders in New York are so big that they do not dare to open the window sale. I went again to Harvard to a cocktail party (at 3.30 in the afternoon) and they got me into a corner and made me read them Shakespeare for an hour and a half which was exhausting but flattering. The thirst for good dramatic speaking and the longing for advice and encouragement on theatrical matters is really remarkable, and whenever I speak, the young people are so wonderfully responsive and well mannered. Terry Rattigan has arrived in New York with the new scripts for me, and I hope to see him at Baltimore and read them for the first time. I am very keen to find out what sort of plays they are.*

Wonderful museum here – superb pictures both classical and post-impressionist, and a corridor of lovely panelled French rooms, lifted wholesale with exquisite furniture from chateaux! Lotte Lehmann sang beautifully last Sunday and I saw a painful but excellent American film about post-war reunion, *The Best Years of Our Lives*. New novels by James Cain [either *The Butterfly* or *Past All Dishonour*] and Steinbeck [*The Wayward Bus*] have a certain slick readableness but really too disgustingly scatological even for my fairly strong palate.

Donald Wolfit's Hamlet *was described by one critic as 'incredibly bad'.*

To Vivien Leigh   *February 1947, Baltimore*

The play [*Importance*] a great success and Don [Wolfit] the Baptist who wrote me two typically humourless and impertinent letters in Toronto has a bee in his knickers the like of which no onion will assuage. He must be incredibly cross but I have not the slightest compunction in being delighted.

To his mother   *26 February, Baltimore*

A horrid barn of a theatre with a huge apron which divides us by ten feet from the audience, hopelessly bad for light comedy, and tiny, overheated dressing rooms. Everyone but me fries under the stage. My room is above, but a sardine tin at that.

To his father   *2 March, New York*

I was very delighted to know you were a bit better after this appalling winter and all the discomforts and acts of God which seem to have assailed you in addition to the tedium of being laid up. The only consolation you may give

---

* They were *High Summer* and *The Browning Version*.

yourself is that your own bed and Mother's tender solicitude were probably a good deal more agreeable than going about in London would have been in such an impossible winter.

I have renewed many former acquaintances and made a lot of new ones. Mrs Otto Kahn is still sprightly and charming despite the ten years since I saw her last, and her exquisite pictures and Chinese bronzes look wonderful in a new flat she has looking over the East River in a fine panorama. I met there General Sir Jock Balfour, who is in the Embassy at Washington. He amazed me by reeling off a whole poem of Alfred Douglas – the only good one, he said, that Douglas had ever written – what erudition! The musical plays are miracles of efficiency and they sing, dance and present them far better than in England – less noisy too, strangely enough, for the orchestras play much better too.

Take care of yourselves and I do hope you will continue to improve so that you can go to Scotland later on – the change of atmosphere would surely do you all the good in the world and make a break for Mother too. There will be sadness at Smallhythe over Edy's [Edith Craig] death. I hope she did not suffer. It must have pleased her that the memorial service to her mother [Ellen Terry] was well attended.

The Importance of Being Earnest *opened at the Royale Theatre, New York, on 3 March 1947.*

To Cecil Beaton   *1 April, New York*

Yes, how lucky I am – the success and heavenly life of this town was more than I dared to hope for. [Margaret] Rutherford is not a patch on Edith, but how much nicer to work with, so it cuts both ways, and fortunately most of the audience did not see Edith in the part. The girls are wonderful, and Pamela Brown should make a great difference to *Love for Love* – Cyril [Ritchard] will be good too. Adrianne [Allen] has been studying with Athene [Seyler], and is a terrific worker, so I hope she may not let down the side. They are fond of her here, and she had a success in *Pride and Prejudice*.

I have not ventured to see *Windermere* – feel I would hardly view it fairly, and it would be embarrassing going round and being insincere. I'm afraid I didn't sit out *Joan of Lorraine* [by Maxwell Anderson]. My two favourite performances are [Ethel] Merman and Judy Holliday, and the musicals, though whimsy and patchy, have such wonderful liveliness, orchestration and skill in presentation that I loved them all, save *Street Scene*, which I find pretentious and boring, music and all.

I am so glad you want to do *High Summer*. No one who has read it here seems to think much of it, and I agree that it is thin and a bit inconclusive, but I hope to get Terry to work on it a bit when he returns from Florida. The atmosphere and construction are both admirable, and I believe it will do for

England – but do tell me what *you* really think. I want him to develop the characters of the Mother and her lover to give more point to my character in attitude to both of them.* The other short play is really excellent, but that is only a dull little set and would give you no scope. *High Summer* is obviously your dish, but I fear lest your work may prove to be the best thing about it, which may be one thing for *Windermere* but not so good for a new play, and it is so difficult to find a new script that really gives one scope for acting – people expect me to do something spectacular in some way or other, I suppose.

There are a whirl of nice people and pleasant things to see, wear, eat, drink and do. It is like a dream, and I couldn't be happier, but I do feel a bit of a truant from time to time. Poor bloody old England – yet I *hate* it when Miss Desmond and Mr Buckmaster† toss their heads and say they really can't go back and fight in a queue for a cake of soap – as if they have ever done such a thing! Suddenly one feels intensely patriotic and resentful.

To his mother   *4 April, New York*

I'm glad to hear Edy had a peaceful death, but the others will miss her sadly and there is sure to be a lot to arrange and clear up. I was shown in the N.Y. Public Library yesterday a fascinating mss. copy of *The Importance* – first act only unfortunately – a stage manager's brown paper bound typed version with masses of corrections, emendations and notes in Wilde's own pencilled handwriting. I only got a short glimpse of it and hope to read it right through one day later on. The play was called *Lady Lancing*, was in four acts, and several other characters in the cast that were evidently omitted afterwards. As I had spent the previous day wrestling with the radio people to prevent them ruining the play in the broadcast version which we are doing on Sunday week (they want to add frightful American slang lines to make the 'visual plot' clearer to the Middle West listeners), it was especially fascinating to see this different version almost in early rehearsal form.

[Katherine] Cornell gave a party last night before leaving for a West Coast tour of *The Barretts [of Wimpole Street]* – her eternal standby. Rebecca West was there, also Ruth Gordon and the Robert Sherwoods. She has brought Wilfrid Lawson over, against all our advice, to play the father, and he is already going on the bat and being unable to rehearse, which is nerve-racking for her with an opening on Monday. He is a sad case of hopeless drunk, like [Henry] Ainley used to be, but a fine actor in between times.

A kind friend offered me his ration card and I shall send you some white flour and sugar, probably by Rattigan who goes home next week. You might be able to make some jam with it.

---

* *High Summer* never had a stage production but a television version was shown in 1972.
† Florence Desmond had been appearing in *If the Shoe Fits* and John Buckmaster in *Lady Windermere's Fan*.

To his mother   *9 April, New York*

I had a box at the Metropolitan to hear Marian Anderson, the Negro singer. She had a crammed house, many Negroes, of course, amongst them. She and Paul Robeson are the foremost singers in America and I must say her range and personality are most striking. She sang Handel, Massenet, Schubert, Old English, Peter Warlock and finally some spirituals, with only a piano accompaniment, and controlled the enormous audience without the slightest sense of effort and with a great beauty of style and diction. Only her French is not good, though I believe she was principally trained in Paris. I enjoyed the concert very much.

The Lunts gave a dinner on Sunday to say goodbye to Rattigan who sailed today. Wonderful food at the Lunts, though he is on a strict diet and looks very tired. She [Lynn Fontanne] wore an amazing white crinoline dress she had designed herself, made of some sort of white holland material with a huge berthe and apron which looked like the cut out paper which men used to do in the theatre queues. Very effective when she appeared in the doorway, with orchids over one ear and down one side of the corsage – not bad at her age – about 58! But when she had sat in the dress all the evening it looked very crushed and peculiar, I thought!

To his mother   *15 April, New York*

I went to a big Russian Easter party at the dressmaker's Valentina [Schlee]. All the élite, masses of champagne, and beautiful pictures and flowers in a lovely house. Had a long talk with Garbo who is the most extraordinary individual – little girl face and now quite short, straight hair tied with an Alice ribbon, hideously cut dress of beautiful printed cotton to her calves, and then huge feet in heel-less black pumps. Lovely childlike expression and great sweetness. She never stopped talking, but absolutely to no purpose – said her life was empty, aimless, but the time passed so quickly that there was never time to do anything one wanted to do! All this with twinkling eyes and great animation, not at all the mournful tones of her imitators – charming slight accent. But I couldn't make out whether her whole attitude was a terrific pose or just plain stupidity – perhaps a mixture of the two!

To Harry McHugh   *20 April, New York*

I was delighted to hear from you and to know that the parcel had arrived safely. I sent another a little while ago, which I hope will turn up in due course – but I'm afraid they take rather a long time to travel. I am extremely well and having a wonderful time here. We have not had an empty seat since we opened in New York, and Canada was a great success also – and I spoke and lectured at the Universities and found the response very gratifying and enthusiastic. We are hard at work rehearsing *Love for Love*, and I think it is going very well, though some of the performances will be rather different, though good in another way. But I shall miss Miss Arnaud and Mr [Max] Adrian. I have thought very much about you all at home while I have been here living such a comfortable and luxurious life. I have a young student dressing me who was in an amateur society at London, Ontario – he wanted to work in the theatre in any way, so I took him on, and he has done quite well in a rough and ready way.

I'm glad to learn you are in a good job for the moment, though of course, I hope you will be free to come back to me eventually when I do begin playing again in England.

To his mother   *29 April, New York*

Sunday night I had to go to a deadly Shakespearean dinner in honour of the [Shakespeare] birthday, usual endlessly boring function with pointless compliments and speeches interspersed with a baritone who sang appalling pseudo-English ballads. We sat down at seven and did not rise till eleven, natural inclinations quite ignored! But the queues afterwards for the four available comfort stations delayed our getting away for another half hour after that. Really!

I have signed to come back here for a few weeks in September to direct a new version of the *Medea* by an American poet [Robinson Jeffers] for Judith Anderson. I think it is a fine thing and am very anxious to have a stab at it. But I have arranged to come back to London for a fortnight anyway at the end of August, so you will see me then and perhaps before if *Love for Love* does not go as well as *Earnest*.

To his mother   *14 May, Washington D.C.*

The play went well last night, though the theatre is very big and the usual apron puts us too far back from the audience to be good for comedy – the older members very nervous and the rest of us inclined to overplay to encourage laughs which were very few and far between. We were all frightened of going too fast and not being understood, but the reception was very good indeed and the notices this morning excellent.

There was quite a wonderful dinner at the Players Club for Alfred Lunt, the best, they said, since the one they gave for me in '37. Paul Robeson sang and there were other excellent turns and speeches, and I was able to speak of the affection for the Lunts on behalf of the English Theatre which seemed to be very much appreciated.

I also went to a charming party at Ruth Draper's where we heard her do several monologues right in our midst in a smallish room – very fascinating. One brilliant one in a completely invented foreign language, sort of Polish-

Serbian, a woman nagging with her husband, then playing a bantering scene with her lover and finally telling the servant to clear the table and tidy the room – all remarkably clear in her tones and looks without a word being understood. Also, she did a young peasant in Brittany waiting on the beach to bid goodbye to her lover who is leaving to join the resistance. She has brought the old mother with her and sits with a shawl round her head, nervously scooping the sand in her fingers. Then she stands aside while he says goodbye to the mother, and they both cling together while his boat is lost in the mist. Suddenly, she hears planes and realises it is the British flying over and cries out 'Vivent les Anglais!' waving wildly to the sky. Very upsetting and beautifully done. She is such a charming and simple person, and I loved meeting her again.

J.P. has sold Foulslough. He had a good offer for it and has been playing with the idea of getting rid of it for some time. It does seem too expensive to try and run two establishments with the appalling difficulties of domestic arrangements as they are today, coupled with postal restrictions and taxation, so there it is. Now that one can go abroad for holidays it is probably more of a break to do so and settle in London when one is in England.

To Vivien Leigh   *23 May, Washington*

Washington is rather a nightmare – steam heat mugginess and the Daughters of the American Revolution, hundreds of middle aged monsters in full make-up, gardenias, orchids and rimless glasses, to say nothing of deep evening dress from morning till night, through the elevators and lobbies with overwhelming scents and hideous accents.

George Hayes [is] a pain in the neck – his old-fashioned mannerisms and personal conceit of almost Wolfitesque dimensions make him a trial and tribulation to us all.

I met Garbo in New York the other day – what an extraordinary little creature, without a brain in her head, I thought – but such beauty of feature though she had all her hair cut off and what was left tied up in a little blue ribbon like a tweeny. She was very amiable, but her conversation smiling but utterly negative.

To Isabel Wilder   *25 May, Washington*

So many thanks for your sweet letter and to Thornton too for troubling to write. Curiously enough, vain though I am, his criticisms did not at all make me despair. Indeed, from someone so obviously fastidious as he is and without a trace of malice, I would much prefer the truth, however unpleasant it might be to hear. And there is much in what he says – *only* one would need a more perfect cast of actors to carry it out. Edith too (Evans) thought the production too 'busy' and restless and said she was muddled by the plethora of realistic business and background. But I still think the only way to sell the play to the general public as entertainment is to attract them by colour and action, and lead them to imagine they are seeing *The Loves of Charles the Second*, which of course they would greatly prefer.

Anyway, I sent out on Wednesday and bought a large supply of brown gauze which has been upholstered over the whole of the big sofa. It now blends into the set without entirely obliterating the pattern – the piece looks a sort of brownish lavender, old and a bit dowdy, and is certainly a far better background both for faces and costumes than it was before. So you see Thornton did me a good turn in telling me of it. One's own eye becomes unduly blind after looking at the stage for many weeks, and I think he did me a great service.

Apart from this, we have had several days' excellent rehearsal. I have cleaned up and simplified groupings and timing wherever they seemed to be muddled or obscure, and judging by the playing time and the really attentive silence with which they listen now, I feel certain it is a different thing to the performance you saw on the opening night. At least I greatly hope so.

Love for Love *opened at the Royale Theatre, New York on 26 May 1947.*

To his mother   *27 May, New York*

Here are the daily notices, and very indifferent they are. The play went so wonderfully last night – far better than *The Importance* did – that these are something of a cold douche, but perhaps I have been spoilt by the panegyrics in the earlier production. It is annoying that [Brooks] Atkinson blames me for doing exactly what the author seems to have intended.*

But I hope *Love for Love* will not prove a real failure, for they might lose a great deal of money, including any profits from *The Importance*. One never ceases to be surprised at anything that happens in the theatre.

To his mother   *28 May, New York*

I was very tired after the opening and rather disappointed, but I'm glad to say that the general tone of the press, though all of them have reservations and say it is not as good as *The Importance*, is really pretty good. We have had two wonderful houses with cheers at the end and rounds on every exit, so I think we may do a good short season with the play.

I was asked by the United Nations to record a preamble to the Charter,

---

* JG may have been complaining about Atkinson's comment: 'Despite the licentiousness of Restoration manners, Congreve wrote *Love for Love* with wit and elegance. Mr Gielgud has taken it too much at face value. He plays Valentine as though he believed in the essential high-mindedness of the character.'

which I did yesterday at Lake Success where they have fabulous headquarters in a converted factory. The speech only runs 1 min. 35 seconds and is said to have been composed by Smuts* – most difficult Macaulay-like prose – 14 lines of parentheses without a full stop! They said I was better in it than Charles Boyer who made the French recording, but it was rather interesting trying to make it impressive, smooth, comprehensible and impersonal all at once! I dare say it will be heard over the air in London some time and you may recognise my voice.

To his mother   *10 June, New York*

I saw *Alice in Wonderland* on Sunday night with Peggy Webster and Eva le Gallienne as the Red and White Queens. They have both become rather grim and suffragette in manner, and I fear their intensity mars their good intentions. The world is too gloomy today to allow the theatre to lack a sense of humour, and when things do not go well one needs it more than ever. Peggy has great drive and efficiency, but I think she is rather oppressed by the personality of le Gallienne, who is a disappointed, bitter woman, though also an actress of considerable talents.

I hope Agate did not suffer.† He was a wicked old man in many ways but sometimes a fine critic and enthusiast, only he went on too long and became very cruel and mischievous at times in later years. Still, he is a figure missing.

To his mother   *27 June, New York*

I had the most enchanting letter from Larry Olivier and also one from Ralph. They are both touchingly sincere and generous in saying they feel embarrassment in being recognised over me‡ – and I must say the fact that they should feel that way towards me and the knowledge that I have so many good friends in the theatre is a great satisfaction to me. I should like to have the honour because I know how much it would please *you* – but otherwise I think it is the standard of work more than actual achievement in terms of spectacular success that counts, though indeed I've had my share of the latter too, one way and another. But I used to be rather jealous – and should still be indeed if someone like Wolfit was put over me – but I am not at all so when it concerns Ralph and Larry, whom I genuinely admire and respect and whose quality I know from working with them.

---

* Jan Smuts, Prime Minister of South Africa.
† James Agate had died on 6 June.
‡ Richardson was knighted in January 1947 and Olivier in May the same year.

To his mother   *Sunday 6 July, New York*

Our final week has been enlivened by a typical theatrical upheaval. Judith Anderson, who has been in a very odd state since a bad marital fiasco in the spring, saw fit to ring me up from California where she has been lurking all this while, find fault and disagree with everything I and the management had been planning for the *Medea*, and the net result is that I have resigned from the production. It is typical Mrs Pat, Edith Evans behaviour – injured vanity at not being consulted on every detail, yet a canny instinct not to really be responsible herself. We are all very disappointed, and I resent the effort and waste of time.

On the other hand I have had the opportunity of meeting this new young firm of presenters [Robert Whitehead and Oliver Rea], who are rich and enthusiastic and would be so much nicer to work with than the Theatre Guild. The latter have been very mercenary and mean over *Love for Love*, and only carried out such obligations as were in the letter of the contracts, and I really shouldn't want to play for them again. It would be fun to help these people have a first success in New York.

To his mother   *21 July, Ottawa*

We play here in a large cinema with what they call a Public Address System! This lack of decent theatres will always deter me from a long tour in Canada or America – one would simply hack oneself to pieces and give ineffective and stagey performances. The provincial theatres in England are bad enough. It is the shape I resent – one would not mind discomforts or shabbiness provided the audience can hear and see properly – and then the unions are so ridiculous. Last week a violinist at the head of the band, getting 100 dollars a week and not one note in tune or time. Simply excruciating and ruined the dance at the end and the songs.

Now here we may not have them in the pit in front of the stage, otherwise we have to have (and pay for) twelve musicians! So they are to be crammed somehow into the very narrow wings and then a loudspeaker will relay the music to the audience through loudspeakers at each side of the proscenium. Poor Congreve!

The rift with Judith Anderson over Medea *seems to have been temporarily healed;* some three weeks later J G is writing to the poet who made the adaptation.

To Robinson Jeffers   *26 July, Ontario*

I have been meaning for many weeks to write to you to express my admiration for your fine *Medea*, and to say how privileged I feel in being selected to undertake the direction of its stage presentation. There are many details and points which I should like to have discussed personally with you about the play, but I gather you do not feel inclined to come East. Perhaps, when rehearsals are begun, I may write to you from time to time if it seems necessary to tamper with the text in any way. I do not want to do so if I can help it, but it is just possible that when spoken and acted there may appear to be lines or phrases – speeches even – which seem to need cutting or reshaping, and I hope you will not think me impertinent if I ask your consent or advice on these matters when the time comes. I believe Whitehead has told you of my idea about the scenery – to bring it forward, so that the second act may be more static and concentrated in grouping and tension – whereas I plan to have greater freedom to move the characters to and fro in the first act, and to try and give the feeling of the seashore and the Mediterranean mountains at the early moments of the play. Judith Anderson is not too happy about this question of two scenes, but I hope to convince her when she sees the plans I am developing. Also, I am troubled about the children being brought on on stretchers as you direct. I feel it might be more dramatic, when the doors swing open, to have some sort of altar, on a raised dais, with Medea crouching at the foot of it, her hair streaming over her shoulder and, one on her lap and one beside her, covered with some great embroidered material, the bodies of the murdered children, which she can uncover with a single gesture as she rises to her feet and advances in to the doorway. Does this idea carry out your intention? Judith, I know, feels that she should never leave the bodies or allow them to be touched by anyone else after the murder. I must say this seems to me a fine notion, and in the spirit of the text.

I should be more than grateful if you would, at your convenience, write me any ideas or very strong views on character, detail or stage arrangements which may have seemed important to you in writing the play, and I shall only be too anxious to fall in with them, and they would help me in my work with the actors. This also applies, of course, to the question of the treatment of the verse and things appertaining to it.

I do hope I may have the privilege of meeting you and talking to you one day, either before or after the production. I am deeply conscious of the task you have set me, and will do my best to interpret your work with dignity and truth.

London, Ontario, was the final date for Love for Love *in North America. After his much-needed August holiday, JG returned to New York to rehearse* Medea.

To Robert Flemyng   *Probably August 1947, New York*

You were a pet to write and I did appreciate it. You know how I loved your being with me and how enchanted I was not only by your sympathy and sweetness but also by your two successes. I know how difficult you found the work and how impatient and fussing I frequently was. I do so hope things will turn out well and happily for you both at home and in the various work you have before you and that it won't be long before we are together again.

Just back from Terry's. He showed me the Lunt opus* and I am rather relieved to say I didn't like it a bit after the first few pages, so that temptation is removed! Emlyn and Bobby Helpmann came over and I felt on plough-shares, blindfold, waiting to plunge if I missed an inch, into a very kiln of bricks – the tact was rather a strain to keep up, and on Friday at Harold's I said a great deal too much to Alan Webb and no doubt the Lisbon wires are humming this very minute.

To Harry McHugh   *31 August, R.M.S.* Queen Elizabeth

I asked Mr Corbett to ask you if you would kindly go round to Nathan's at your convenience and try and trace my *Crime and Punishment* clothes, so that they can be put aside to send over to me if I decide to do the play in America. They produced the blouse and trousers, but not the dark blue frock coat, hat or Inverness cape. I think you would be the person who could best identify them for me.

To his mother   *4 September, New York*

I was so delighted to get your letters telling me that Father had been able to go out. The relief of change of scene is bound to be beneficial and even if it tires him and shortens his life in the end, anything must surely be better than interminable armchair apathy. I dare say to have him out of the flat again, even for an hour, makes a lighter day for you and one less anxious time with your ear permanently cocked towards the drawing-room door even when you are out in the passage. There should be many fine days between now and the autumn and perhaps you might even find it possible to get him away for a day or two in to a country garden, and above all have a little holiday yourself. I do beg you, however, not to make this new improvement an excuse for not getting the extra woman to help and spend time to save you and Eleanor,† as we talked about before I left. It is doubly important if Father is going to live that you and she should shift the burden as often as you possibly can to make your tasks less onerous and exhausting.

Judith is all graciousness and charm, and is now trying to persuade me to play Jason for the first four weeks. It is not a good part, nor very much up my street, but I am rather tempted to agree, as I think it would be quite a popular gesture from me to her and also I cannot get a really suitable actor. If I could get a really striking make-up, wig and clothes and

---

* Probably *Perdita*, which later became *Harlequinade*. The acting couple in the play was based on the Lunts.

† JG's sister, Mrs Ducker, known to family and friends as Nell but not, apparently, to JG.

play it as a character part – a sort of young Macbeth – I think the strength of the character would be very effective for me. I am hearing someone else read the part today and shall probably decide definitely before the end of the week. My only fear is that it really is rather a poor and unsympathetic part and it would be rather humiliating to make a failure of it! However it is something a bit different from anything I've done and that always tempts me, especially as I am very deep in the play itself and might as well be in that much deeper!

To his mother   *12 September, New York*

Things are going along pretty smoothly so far, I'm glad to say. We have had to change one man but I think the others will pass. Judith is rather slow to get under way but is quite co-operative and agreeable and if she can find variety in voice I believe she'll give a fine performance. My part is not very interesting but I believe the last scene can be made striking. I am going to have armour and a tawny fair wig, a white tunic in the second act, and then at the end the whole thing burnt and scorched, my face and arms and hair blackened with the fire, so that I am a dark, broken figure sprawling on the steps when she comes out in a light dress stained with blood, and goes down a rocky decline towards the sea carrying the bodies of the children – something like my exit in the gallery scene of *Bordeaux*.

I have an excellent old actress [Grace Mills] as leader of the three women, an experienced player who was with Ben Greet, and has real power and poetic imagination. Aline MacMahon, who plays the Nurse, does not arrive till next week. I believe she is fine and a very nice woman – an unusual combination of talents! Komis has drastic ideas of revising the *Crime and Punishment* script. I am delighted with his ideas but fear we shall have a struggle to persuade [Rodney] Ackland, especially after the success of the play in London, but I have written him a long, preparatory, soothing letter, and I hope they will both work on the script, and that Ackland will come over in a few weeks time and complete it working together. I have not yet heard if Binkie will sell us the set.

Dined with Constance Collier, who is in great form, with her appearance considerably renovated by the arts of Hollywood! She was six months in London recently, horrified by conditions there, and is suffering from a bad foot which, her doctor tells her, is due to malnutrition – at Claridges!!

To his mother   *19 September, New York*

There is trouble over the costumes which are being designed by a friend of mine who seems to have let us down pretty badly, but they may come out all right in the end, though Judith is kicking up hell about hers and trying to bring in a new designer. No production can be achieved, it seems, without a

certain amount of chaos and emotional friction – it was always the same with
the dear Motleys.

To Lawrence Langner   *19 September, New York*

I am very glad you wrote me about *Crime and Punishment*, for I feel that both
you and Binkie think I have behaved rather shabbily and ungratefully in
doing the play with another management and I welcome the opportunity to
explain my behaviour, at the risk of boring you with rather a long letter.

The situation came about entirely through a series of critical conversations
with Judith just before I left New York for Boston. I was so despairing of
making her see reason over *Medea* and certain circumstances in connection with
it that I told Whitehead and Rea – and Judith also – that I would not do the
play, though I had already signed my contract. They felt so strongly that I was
right in my stipulations that they said they would also abandon it, and it was
then, really with the thought of helping them out and trying to honour my
obligation to them that I said, 'Well, we might do *Crime and Punishment*
instead.' I know that you had bought an option early in the year and had no idea
that you had let it lapse – but they quickly ascertained that the rights of the play
were free and bought an option on it. We then became reconciled with Judith
after the usual theatrical impasse, and I thought no more about it. They did
ask me if I might not do it after *Medea* and I said I thought my London
commitments made that impossible. Besides, I had had numerous cables from
John and Binkie, when I told them I was toying with the idea of doing the play
again, begging me for various reasons not to dream of doing it. They do not like
the part for me – play would not be a success and so on.

I then went home, and talked to Terry Rattigan and to Rodney [Ackland]
and discussed the possibilities of postponing the Rattigan plays and revising
the script of *Crime*. Also I got Komisarjevsky to read the play and give his
honest opinion both on the script and its weaknesses and on his views as to
my suitability for it.

It was not until this was settled to my satisfaction that I told Whitehead I
would agree to do the play here – and I was further influenced by the sterling
block, which has made it impossible to get out of England the money I have
put aside there for my Income Tax. This second engagement in America has
made me liable for taxation on my whole season's earnings with you, so I have
got to work here for four months at least to collect enough money to pay it
off.

The weakness of this explanation, I am well aware, lies in the fact that I
should not have suggested doing the play with Whitehead knowing you had
already bought it for me. I can only say that in the excitement of the row with
Judith, the fact did not enter my head – and though I must say it crossed my
mind when I heard the rights were free that you had been previously holding
them, it did not honestly occur to me that you would have wished to renew

the option if I were willing to play it. I am sorry you did not tell me when you proposed dropping your rights, for by that time I might have been willing to say 'Well, perhaps I will do it after all.' I have changed my mind so often about the play, and none of the people whose judgements I most value are quite in agreement with me about it.

I was extremely happy working with you, and I so hope this contretemps will not mar our friendship or future relationship and that I may have the pleasure of being with you again at some future time.

To his mother   *26 September, New York*

We are at the usual critical state of rehearsal, one or two obstinately weak performances and the question arising of whether to make changes or not before the opening, and a rather disappointing Dress Parade, which means a lot of redesigning and changes done in a hurry; as they are by a great friend of mine, it is naturally an unpleasant task telling him he has done a bad job. Anderson has been in bed with a cold and the actress who plays the nurse is very intellectual and decorative where she ought to be earthy and powerful. However, much may happen in a week, I hope.

To his mother   *6 October, Philadelphia*

Our scenery is magnificent and my trick of showing it from a closer viewpoint in the second act is, I think, extremely successful as it varies the grouping possibilities and concentrates the action for the climax. But we had a ghastly post-mortem on lighting and costume, with the final result that I re-lit the whole thing myself in five hours. It had been done by a so-called lady expert from New York, whose ideas were excellent for musical comedy, but made our set look like a cheap picture postcard of the Riviera – and we are scrapping all the clothes. Judith fortunately rebelled ten days ago and hers are brilliant, designed by a French-Italian [Castillo] who works for Elizabeth Arden, so we have now asked him to do all the others, and hope we may get them early next week to get used to them before New York. Of course this has meant endless conferences, heartbreaks and difficulties of all kinds, which I found rather trying coming on top of having to get rid of the actress who was engaged to play the Nurse. Fortunately she is an exceedingly nice person in herself and took it in admirable part. The old girl who replaces her [Florence Reed] is a clever but rowdy character who followed Edith [Evans] here as the Nurse in *Romeo and Juliet*, played Paulina in *The Winter's Tale* and the fortune-teller in *[The] Skin of Our Teeth* [by Thornton Wilder]. A bit slow and old-fashioned, a cross between Haidee Wright and Ada Reeve – but of great value to the play and will be better still when she is more sure of her words and business. In four days she did a remarkably fine job for an elderly woman, and she is a great trouper.

The play had tremendous ovations at all three performances at Princeton. However, I am not allowing this to blind us to the manifold weaknesses and faults which I hope to correct to some extent during the two weeks here. Unfortunately the stage here is horribly cramped – no room for backings or place for the orchestra behind the scenes and I fear it will all be a bit makeshift and disagreeable.

My own appearance is not at all good yet, the wig too fair and the dress far too pretty and fairy tale. All the clothes are picture book-y and operatic. Judith's alone has style and barbaric authenticity. I *must* look vulgar, over-bearing and violently masculine on my first appearance. We now talk of black armour, leather and a scarlet cloak and short, brown hair. Judith is very fine, but shoots her bolt too soon. She needs more vocal variety and range and a stiller, more deadly grandeur in the final scenes.

Ackland has refused to sail on reading Komis' new version of the first act of *C and P,* so we have more complications to persuade them both to compromise. I'm sure if he arrives and *talks* to Komis it can all be sorted, but naturally he is jealous of his rights as author and suspicious that he [Komis] is trying to rewrite the play completely and muscle in on the rights after-wards! No doubt his English friends here persuaded him that we are all plotting to destroy his work, but I believe we shall reach some final solution soon – I hope so. I won't do the play at all unless it is altered considerably, for I never felt in London my part was good enough.

To his mother   *16 October, Philadelphia*

Incredibly beautiful weather here – midsummer sunshine and warmth. We had a final dress rehearsal yesterday with the new clothes, improved lighting and effects and so on. It was a long session, but we were rewarded by a greatly improved performance at night. The new costumes are quite lovely against the grey scenery, grey porticoes and walls, pearly grey sea and mountains in the background, and costumes in every shade of pale beige, lavender, pink (Creon) leading up to Aegeus who wears two shades of red. Judith is in grey with first a black, then a wine-red drapery, the Nurse in purple and grey. I am beige with a leather breastplate (grey-brown) and boots and a very dark green cloak – huge helmet in my hand – curly brown hair and quite a full curly beard. The three women of the chorus in shades of purple, brown and grey, most beautifully draped and the colours blended very cleverly so that they look a unity, yet each has its individual character. How I wish you could see it yourself. I also had a three hour session with Judith on her own character the night before last, and she took it all very well, and I thought last night her performance was 100 per cent improved.

Medea *opened at the National Theatre, New York, on 20 October 1947.*

To his mother   *21 October, New York*

A pretty mixed bunch of notices as you will see from the enclosed – a bit disappointing after the quite sensational ovation we had last night – but her [Judith's] own personal success is, I imagine, a pretty sure sign of a box office hit, for a while anyway, and I know the work I did was responsible for a lot of the best things in her performance, which is some satisfaction. I am very tired and need a few days relaxation to recover myself, which I think I have fairly earned. Florence Reed came up trumps last night having driven us all mad at Philadelphia with her inaccuracy and ineffectiveness!

To his mother   *27 October, New York*

Little news save that Binkie has arrived for the opening of *The Winslow Boy* [by Terence Rattigan] on Wednesday here, so he will be in New York all this week. The play is really a smash hit, but of course I am disappointed that the press do not like my work either as actor or director. If they knew the play better they might realise that I have done a good job for the author in both capacities, but they are, as usual, blinded by the size and range of the part of Medea and give Judith all the praise. Well, that brings the public in and will do me no harm once my vanity is under control. The theatre people here, both American and English, and the cast themselves are all conscious of the service I have done the play and that should be satisfaction enough, though it is always something of a blow when one reads unfavourable things in print. Judith gave me the most lovely present – an edition of *Little Dorrit* in the original parts, weekly magazine form as published in 1855 with all the drawings, wrappers and advertisements complete. I shudder to think what it must have cost her, but it is a lovely thing to have.

We are busy trying to cast *C and P.* Rodney is staying here with me and working with Komisarjevsky. I think Lillian Gish is going to do Edith's part. I only hope she won't be too sentimental for it. I am, of course, delighted at the prospect of working with her again.

To his mother   *4 November, New York*

The play continues to be a big draw. Toscanini has been twice to see it. Dennis King has been engaged to follow me in Jason and I shall be delighted to pass it on to him, I need hardly say. It is very easy work, however, except that I have to paint my arms and legs and take hours washing them clean again.

We are beginning to collect a cast for *C & P.* Yesterday Dolly Haas, a tiny little thing with red hair like a young Bergner read very well for Sonya and I think we shall have her. She has hardly any accent though originally German! [Alexis] Minotis, the husband of [Katina] Paxinou, is to play the detective.

I went on Sunday to see Edith Piaf. Very badly presented little vaudeville show with awful turns in the first part, then nine young men called 'Les Compagnons [de la Chanson]', who sing delightful songs with mimed accompaniment and comedy business – extremely original and amusing and beautiful teamwork. They brought the house down, especially in a skit on an American dance band singing 'Au Clair de la Lune' and then a Cossack choir singing the same song. Piaf herself is a tiny creature of the street – reddish-brown, tousled hair on a very short, thick neck, almost a dwarf but with really wonderful hands and eyes, a great simplicity of pathos and gesture and a foghorn voice that can rasp or plead with equal power.

To his mother   *17 November, New York*

Not much news save that our casting seems to be going well and we had a pretty good reading of the play last week. I think Lillian Gish will be very good, on much more fragile lines than Edith, and the new Sonya seems to be charming – also lots of good character actors in the bit parts. *Medea* continues to play to enormous business and they will soon have paid off the production and be able to give the whole cast a rise in salary! Amazing!! Mrs Roosevelt was round the other night to see Judith and was very agreeable to me. She has aged considerably but has great dignity and charm, since I saw her in 1937 at the White House.

Komis and Ackland are getting on extremely well now, after a certain amount of mutual distrust and skirmishing, and I think their joint skill will make a far better balanced play, and a more varied and consistent character for me to play.

To his mother   *2 December, Massachusetts*

I drove up here by car with some friends on Sunday morning, and it is a most pleasant change. The quiet of the snow-covered country, no-one about at all except a few deer stalkers in red hunting caps, sunny and cold. I am staying in a sort of bungalow about 100 miles from New York, very lazy existence – breakfast when one wakes, books, big fires and a few amiable but engaging guests.

The rehearsals last week promised exceedingly well I thought. Only one drama so far, we had to get rid of one actor [Alexis Minotis], the Greek husband of Madame Paxinou, who was to have played the detective. Unfortunately his English is very bad, and he gave no indication after ten days work of any comedy or lightness – played the whole thing with heavy solemnity, making the scenes utterly dull. So we decided against him and he took it very ill – all the usual embarrassing scenes of protestation and recrimination – but I am becoming hardened now when the whole play is at stake, and as Komis entirely agreed with me, I feel sure we are right to change. Vladimir Sokolow is to replace him, and comes in from Hollywood by the end of the week. He also has an accent, but has been in America for longer than Minotis, and I have seen him give fine performances in films. He should get on well with Komis, being Russian, and also understands what we want in eccentricity and comedy for that part. The changes in the script are all great improvements, and the rest of the cast very good. In fact, Rodney thinks the whole company better than in London and the play very much better. I am certain of the latter fact.

The last night of *Medea* was very nice. The company embarrassed and touched me by singing 'Auld Lang Syne' at the end of the performance in which the stagehands, orchestra and electricians joined. I was given a beautiful Cartier cigarette case by the management.

I laze and relax and then think of you and Eleanor at your gruelling and inexorable routine, day after day, week after week, with all the worries and petty inconveniences of that endless responsibility and anxiety. How I wish you could be here to have a few days of forgetfulness and relief and be looked after by others for a change.

To his mother   *8 December, New York*

I feel so much better for my few days in the country, and I'm delighted to say the play seems to be going very well. Sokolow, who now plays the detective, is a great artist, and I am simply enchanted with him. Those scenes which were always a strain to me to hold in London even with Ustinov, seem to go so easily with this man, who is a brilliant actor, as finished and exquisite as Quartermaine, only with a far wider range. He must be sixty, or nearly so, but he is elegant, small, neat, with fascinating cat-like smile and very curious slanting eyes with very high white lids, and black eyebrows crookedly set. He has played in Russian, German and French and must be fantastically versatile. Puck, Robespierre, villains and comedy are all equally in his scope, and his accent is not worrying. Gish is really splendid and, of course, a darling to have in the cast.

I saw an interesting play called *The* [*sic*] *Streetcar Named Desire* in which Jessica Tandy has made a great success. Very fine direction with an imaginative set – three rooms and a staircase also but quite different from ours, with transparent backings that occasionally show the street behind the walls – subtle noises and music. Very unpleasant and brutal, but awfully well acted, and the direction and writing, in a kind of counterpoint of violence contrasts with nostalgic tenderness, very effective and original. Without the subtle handling they give it, it would be merely pathological gloom and ugliness, but it has a kind of weird beauty and pathos, like Debussy's or Poulenc's music.

Crime and Punishment *opened at the National Theatre, New York, on 22 December 1947.*

To his mother   *28 December, New York*

It has been a mad rush all week. After the two dress rehearsals with audiences on Friday and Saturday nights last week, we worked till 4 a.m. Sunday night and had another dress rehearsal from two till five on the day of the performance. A good deal of hysteria and unpleasantness between Komis and the lighting director and the management which I had, as usual, to bridge with as much tact as possible. But, as usual, I was dead tired and despairing by the time the curtain went up on the first night, and did not play the first act at all well in consequence. However, the reception was tremendous, and I have great hopes of at least a 12-week run.

1948

To his mother   *6 January, New York*

I think Komis never really liked the play itself and secretly resented that we would not let him rewrite it altogether in his own version. He is a curious creature and very enraging to a management – this one thinks him a fascist and of course now the play is on he does not come near it and everyone has suggestions of what ought to be altered and tightened up, so that there is no proper development and solidifying of the production as there ought to be after a few performances.

To his mother   *20 January, New York*

The benefit on Sunday was quite exciting and my Hamlet speech really got the biggest hand of the evening, as well as at the rehearsal, which was a bit nerve-racking with about 200 actors and actresses sitting in the stalls.

JG decided not to do the two plays which Rattigan had written for him.

To Terence Rattigan   *21 January, New York*

I am really very touched that you should have written me that most charming and sympathetic letter and understood my feelings about the plays. You know my childish and impetuous nature – if I don't start in to something right away in the first flush of enthusiasm, it is liable to go cold on me and then I am beset by doubts and fears. I think the fiasco of [*He Was*] *Born Gay* following my last American visit has haunted me ever since – it was the only time I've really made a spectacular personal failure both as director and actor, and in a much-publicised and disappointing way in a play by a modern author 'written specially for me'. I've been very uncertain for the last year or so as to what I really want to do next and am afraid of being pushed towards something I don't particularly like myself either by a fear of being eclipsed by the Vic boys and other rivals in the classic field or by the habit of always being in the theatre. You are forgiving and sweet and believe me I do appreciate it and rejoice that our much valued friendship has not been touched, for I should regret that more than having a failure in the theatre.

To his mother   *15 February, New York*

We finished *C & P* last night, doing much better business in the final week, so I made a bit of money to carry me over my holiday. Next week I am going to the musicals and to see Martha Graham dance. Many people think she is the one genius of America – she is 50, I believe, and very 'modern'. She makes no money and has only a couple of short seasons every year in N.Y. but has a great cult among the intellectuals. I met her and she is interesting and striking looking – a great friend of Kit Cornell.

I hope to have next Saturday with two friends, one of them the designer for *Medea* [Ben Edwards]. I hope to plan with him designs and plans for a *King Lear* production, so that if I want to do it again any time I will have it all worked out. We are going to a little place in Florida, Key West, where Ernest Hemingway, the author, lives. I gather it is tropical, peaceful, cheap and not smart. After that I shall come back here and motor to Mexico City via New Orleans, which I have always wanted to see. It is lucky that *Medea* is likely to run till June, as I get a nice little cheque every week without doing any work, which is a rare pleasure!

To Hugh Wheeler   *19 February, New York*

Thank you for your delightful letter and kind invitation. I was ashamed of having been rather Mistress Tantrum the last night you came to see me at the National and I do hope I wasn't disgustingly rude.

I hope you are enjoying the Californian Poppies and Mandragola, and that you have not heard mysterious music in the night proceeding from a musical box of strangely phallic shape and design stuffed nicely down the front of a pair of Christopher [Isherwood]'s silver grey flannel trousers, with an antique key sticking out of the fly! If you meet Dodie Smith give her my love and tell her that her piano is still intact and much enjoyed,* and goose that horrid Alec [Beesley] of hers which is more than he deserves.

---

* Dodie Smith had lent J G her baby grand piano and it remained at Cowley Street for many years.

To Isabel Wilder   *29 March, Acapulco*

I adored Thornton's book [*The Ides of March*], and what a huge success it is, Only wish he could find it in his heart to adapt it as a play for me! I really could look very like Julius – baldness, big nose and all! And I would be delighted, tell him, to play without any scenery whatever!!! I so long to play in something written to be directed in a new style – and he is the only author for years who has had the brilliant notion of using the stage in a different way.

To his mother   *6 April, New Orleans*

Four or five delightful letters from you were awaiting me at Cook's on Friday when we got back to Mexico City. I am so very glad you made the decision about the nursing home, and trust you managed the move without undue difficulties. I feel sure you have done the very best possible thing to give yourself and Eleanor a chance of some kind of relaxation from the impossible tension you have both been living under for so many months and I do not believe Father, in his present condition, will care greatly, provided he can see you constantly and is given all the thought and attention which you so unfailingly remember to provide, and indeed he will have your visits to look forward to every day – an event for him instead of something taken for granted. He may be sad at being separated from his books and pictures and the familiar details, but I fancy even those must have begun to pall and bore him over such a long period of frustration and inactivity. I do hope you are feeling confident about it all and beginning to sleep and take a little thought for yourself again in the new conditions.

On his return from holiday, JG began preparations for Tennessee Williams' The Glass Menagerie *in which he would direct Helen Hayes.*

To Vivien Leigh and Laurence Olivier   *17 May, Brill, Buckinghamshire*

I hope you are pleased with the reception of the film.* Everyone in London talks of nothing else. I thought it both noble and impressive and only quarrelled with certain details which one would argue in any production of the play. The achievement is a very fine one and will undoubtedly bring you laurels wherever it is shown and enhance not only your own prestige but that of the whole English film industry.

The London theatre is very dull without you. Poor old Ralph had a really horrid play† – he is on the stage from beginning to end, but with neither conflict, character nor situation to keep one interested or give him any chance

---

* Laurence Olivier's film of *Hamlet* opened in London in May 1948.
† *Royal Circle* by Romilly Cavan.

to be amusing. Mu [Meriel Forbes] is quite good in a poor part. In fact it is quite well played by everyone. Even Lilian [Braithwaite], who staggered on occasionally like a terrifying scarecrow, manages to waft a few faint laughs out of the air, but there simply isn't a play.

It is wonderful here this weekend – blazing summer weather and Ena [Burrill] up at 6.30 to milk her cows with the most improper looking machine.

To Hugh Wheeler   *16 June, New York*

Thank you both for a heavenly and relaxing time – and I was so happy to have the chance of knowing you, and all our gossip and witchery just couldn't have been more delicious, to say nothing of the maiding, feeding and flattery which you both served at the most timely intervals. Even Olivia and the Moated Grange fitted marvellously into the scheme of things, and the mad family next door added a frisson that was only equalled by the charm of waking up in your house not knowing whether one would see a vista, gazebo, pergola or pleasaunce from the bedroom window – herd of deer or a flight of ortolans! My sincerest thanks and love to you both.

Even before The Glass Menagerie *opened at the Theatre Royal, Haymarket, on 28 July, JG started on his next project which was the British production of* Medea, *with Eileen Herlie in the title role.*

To Robinson Jeffers   *20 July, London*

It is interesting to be working on the play again with a fresh cast, and I am hoping the general balance and level will be better than it was in New York.

Miss Herlie is extremely agreeable to work with, and is a girl of remarkable power and magnetism, and youthfulness should be an asset in some ways, but I hardly imagine she will be so successful in the 'tigress' passages as Judith was, but I do not know her work well, and it is early days to judge her yet. She is wildly excited about the part, and well she may be. The Nurse [Cathleen Nesbitt] and Jason [Ralph Michael] are both excellent and the Chorus shaping well.

To Mrs Robinson Jeffers   *12 September, Antibes*

All thanks for your kind letter and to your husband my best wishes for his speedy recovery and thanks for the new lines which I will try out when I go to see the play in Newcastle after next week. We return on Wednesday after a beautiful holiday. I'm glad you were pleased with the production on the whole. I was distressed for Eileen that she had to face the London critics in Edinburgh as I am sure she will gain greater variety and a more distinct line when she has played in for a while and is less anxious and nervy. The chorus are rather disappointing I'm afraid – and I have thought of changing 2nd and 3rd if they are not improved by the time I see it again. I only hope they have found a style and more impressive certainty in the interim. We shall change the bigger of the children and find one who is more attractive and smaller.

I so much appreciated your understanding of the whole situation as regards Judith. She and I will, I fear, never be friends again, which I much regret, for I have a real admiration of her talents and we always seemed to get on well together. She was *most* kind to me in '36 when we did *Hamlet* but it really was not possible to side with her against Bob [Whitehead] and Oliver [Rea], who are the last possible men to do a mean trick to anybody, and who were always only too anxious to do anything possible to help and further the success of the play. I am sure you too appreciated this. I do hope you will both be able to see it again before we open in London.

To Lawrence Langner and Theresa Helburn   *30 September, London*

I have had a baffling year. The Rattigan plays which I let go are the most enormous success, and I fear it was a great error of judgement on my part not to do them. I am waiting for Pamela Brown to come out of *The Gioconda Smile* [by Aldous Huxley] before essaying a tricky but fascinating verse play by Christopher Fry called *The Lady's Not for Burning*. This we shall do together in February, and before that I am going to do a short revival of *The Return of the Prodigal* by St John Hankin.

I wonder if both, or either of you will be over here in the next few months? The *Menagerie* was a very happy experience for me, and my love and admiration for Helen [Hayes] is unbounded. It is such a pity the critics were so hard on the play, for it is enormously liked by many people, and with a better press would have been a real success I'm sure.

The Return of the Prodigal, *in which J G played Eustace Jackson, opened at the Globe Theatre on 24 November, but did not grip the town.*

To Christopher Fry   *6 December, London*

My mind is going on about *The Lady* like a squirrel in a cage, and I read it at odd moments in my dressing room and everywhere else with increasing pleasure. But I have taken on three weeks' broadcasting of a four hour *Hamlet* and a *Tempest*, for which I have had to work for several days with the boy who is playing Ariel. I have not had a minute for anything else since we opened in *The Prodigal*. However, I am going to see Oliver [Messel] on Wednesday night and discuss the set, of which I gather he has done a rough model, and as soon as we are through with Xmas I am most anxious you should come up and spend the night here so that we can have a more detailed talk and agree on the casting.

I would like you to see *The Prodigal* because it seems to me that Audrey Fildes would be awfully good as Alizon.* She gives a brilliant performance in a very sketchy part and is quite beautiful to look at as well as speaking excellently. It's exciting to think that Pamela is free at last and we can get down to business. I'm not at all sure we oughtn't to do three weeks on the road before we come into London so as to be really comfortable by the time we open in town. The one week we had in this play was barely sufficient, and I didn't really feel at ease on the first night, and that too we can discuss when we meet.

To Christopher Fry   *11 December, London*

I wondered if Esmé Percy might do Skipps. He is wonderful vocally, has a rich imagination and made a great success some years ago in a drunken tramp part, in *Distant Point* [by Afinogenev].

Oliver has done a very original and delightful rough model, but I don't judge it until it is painted and finished. We talked at length about lines of sight, furniture disposal and mundane exigencies.

After the opening of The Return of the Prodigal, *JG took over (from John Burrell) the direction of* The Heiress, *adapted by Ruth and Augustus Goetz from Henry James's novel* Washington Square, *with Peggy Ashcroft and Ralph Richardson.*

1949

To Christopher Fry   *19 January, London*

I have just seen O. B. Clarence, who is really so beguiling and on the spot, and so enchanted with the play and the part, that I really think we should have a shot at it. He started by saying that he had the reputation of being a bad study, and if he couldn't learn it when the time came he would of course understand if we threw him out. After that I was lost, and I only hope we are not being rash.

Oliver's set becomes more delightful every time you see it, and I have persuaded him to narrow the proportions a little so that the two vistas are visible from different parts of the auditorium. I am trying to think hard about Thomas but my plans and concentration are disturbed at the moment as I have been called in to entirely re-direct *The Heiress* which opens this very next Monday in Brighton! An appalling botch has been made of the mechanics, and they are floundering in a morass of despair, so I can only try to do my

---

* Alizon was eventually played by Claire Bloom.

best. It's a sheer exercise in improvisation, and I only thank God I saw the play in NY and have read it a couple of times since, but I fear it can be but a patched result at best. You will have to forgive me if we begin rehearsals on 7th February without quite such a prepared production as I had hoped for. It is in my mind continually and I hope it won't take me long to learn when I really get down to it.

To Richard Myers   22 January, London

How very sweet of you to send the most amusing interview with Martita [Hunt] and to give me all the news. I couldn't have been more pleased with Marty's success [as the Madwoman of Chaillot in Giraudoux's play]. It is obviously the start of a new career for her, and if she cares to take Hollywood in she could be a sort of Ethel Barrymore and May Whitty in one, though I doubt if she would thank me for the compliment! I am amused to see her compared with Judith, and wish I could see those two gals in the same play, looking each other up and down! I wonder if you are seeing anything of her? She is the most wonderful company and brilliantly intelligent, especially about literature, clothes and cooking which she really knows a lot about. I am so glad Adrianne [Allen] has had a big success with *Edward* [*My Son* by Robert Morley], and imagine you are seeing a good deal of her. No, the *Importance* record with Edith is out of print, and though I believe it can be got for 20 dollars on the Black Market in America, one can't get a copy over here. It is a pity as it was a really good [*sic*], but I don't think they will repeat it now, and I suppose it will become a collector's piece.

The Return of the Prodigal ends tonight. It had a comfortable little run, but hardly anyone has cared for the play which they find bitter and inconclusive though an interesting period sketch. I have been preparing a production of *Much Ado* for Stratford with a Piero della Francesca décor by a Franco-Spanish painter, Mariano Andreu, of which I have great hopes. Diana Wynyard is playing Beatrice and Tony Quayle Benedick. This opens in April, but I have to rehearse in odd weeks beforehand as my own venture, *The Lady's Not for Burning* by Christopher Fry, has to be ready on March 7th for a road tour before we come to London. I have enormous belief in the play, I forget if I told you about it, a splendid cast headed by Pamela Brown, and Oliver Messel is doing a beautiful set in the Breughel manner.

Now this week on top of everything else, I have been hauled in to re-direct *The Heiress* which opens on Monday at Brighton with Peggy Ashcroft and Ralph Richardson. They didn't decide to get rid of the director, after the usual heartbreak and hysteria, until four days ago, and I've had exactly four nights and three days to do a completely new production as regards moves, furniture and business. I must say the cast behaved magnificently, and I even dare be confident that the play now has a good chance which is rather exciting, and I think it might even be another *Barretts* [*of Wimpole Street*]. Peggy gives a most touching and moving performance and the only weakness is the young man, James Donald, who is a dour Scottish character, very unskilled and stubborn as a mule, and if I get a good result from him in the end shall really think I am something of a wizard.

I saw the *Invitation au Voyage** [by Jean Anouilh] in Paris and was very taken with the play and particularly with the dual part which I had read in a rough translation beforehand. I was somewhat discouraged, however, when the curtain rose on a boy of seventeen who played so charmingly that I didn't feel it could ever go with someone as old as I am. He and the girl were quite enchanting among a lot of mediocre caricatures. Since then I have read two different versions in English, one by Clifford Bax, quite a distinguished literary man, and they were quite hopeless. As I have also read at least three versions of the *Voyageur sans Bagages*, which are also no good, I am beginning to think that Anouilh is a pretty impossible fellow to translate. However the Oliviers are now going to do his *Antigone*, I don't know if it is the same version as Kit [Cornell] did, and we'll see how that turns out.

To Dadie Rylands   *9 February, London*

Wasn't it exciting, my bringing off *The Heiress*, even though it meant trampling on the unfortunate Burrell's prostrate corpse, for which I'm sorry. But it was a remarkable test as I had to do the entire thing over again in four nights and three days, and it was fortunate knowing Ralph and Peggy so well, it made so much difference. She is absolutely radiant now, a rose in full bloom, and it's thrilling to have had a part in her enormous personal success.

We've a good cast for *The Lady* but O. B. Clarence is completely gaga and the moment is not far distant when I shall have to tell him so, not a very attractive prospect.

To his father   *12 March, Brighton*

Just a line to tell you the play [*The Lady's Not for Burning*] has really gone wonderfully well here and we are improving it every day, I think. The audiences have been most appreciative and do not seem to find the verse a difficulty.

We go on to Stratford tomorrow so I fear I shall not be able to get a chance to come and see you, but you know you are much in my thoughts.

Oliver's scenery and dresses are quite beautiful and have won great praise – the stage looks like a Dutch primitive or one of the early Millais pictures – Christ in the Carpenter's shop.

---

* Actually *L'Invitation au Château* which was produced in London as *Ring Round the Moon* in 1950.

To his mother   *14 March, Stratford-upon-Avon*

The play went wonderfully here tonight, far better than in Brighton – and Quartermaine, Diana Wynyard and the [Anthony] Quayles all enthusiastic about it, which is encouraging. The hotel beautifully quiet, and an excellent rehearsal of *Much Ado* – everyone knowing their lines and a splendid all-round spirit. I got through the whole first part in detail from 10 a.m. to 4 p.m. and then back here for two hours break before my own performance, so it all works out admirably.

To Ruth and Augustus Goetz   *20 March, Stratford-upon-Avon*

I saw *The Heiress* twice before leaving London. It was very well played – [James] Donald very much surer and with much charm and attack. I bullied Ralph [Richardson] a bit about his opening scene and tried to persuade him not to pick Peggy's handkerchief at the party as if he was Fagin teaching the Artful Dodger.

It was during the tour that Frank Gielgud, John's father, died after his long illness.

To Gabrielle Enthoven   *20 April, Leeds*

Thank you for your sweet and understanding letter. Yes indeed, it is a blessed relief for all, and it is wonderful to find Mother so calm under the blow. She suffered most in the sending him to the home last year, and now accepts the inevitable with her usual wonderful philosophy and sweetness. She even talked to me of wanting to go and work with you again to keep herself interested. Wonderful woman.

To Cecil Beaton   *27 April, Liverpool*

So very good of you to trouble to write on my father's death. It was a long drawn out and miserable business both for him and my Mother and sister who wore themselves out nursing him for two years and more, so one cannot but be thankful the end has come at last.

I would like you to see the Stratford *Much Ado*, for I think the scenic devices and brilliant colour might amuse you. It has really good flow and balance, and I enjoyed doing it very much. The company has a few good young people and none are really bad, which is unusual and refreshing in a repertory company. I'm planning to go there to act myself next year, as I want to work away from London and not play huge tragic parts eight times a week. *Lear* is only possible occasionally, to give a decent performance, and I'm sure *Measure for Measure* would only be successful in a repertoire. I want to do those two and perhaps direct one that I am not in without the responsibility of a huge sum to get back and the dangers of opening cold in London. At Stratford one has far more time and an assured audience. I mean to take a house nearby and settle down for a six months season – one could always do the most successful production later in London or New York. We shall see.

We have worked hard on *The Lady*, and it has gone wonderfully everywhere, so I have good hopes of it. It is, I think, very well acted and I love my part.

The Lady's Not for Burning *opened at the Globe Theatre on 11 May 1949 with great success.*

To Dadie Rylands   *May 1949, London*

Of course I was sorry you hadn't liked the play, but I was very anxious to know why. The people who dislike it are very violently off with its head – you, my elder brother, Christopher Sykes, Cecil Beaton – and the writers – Rattigan, Emlyn. Yet everyone else adores it, and I cannot believe it is in any way bogus! Weak in construction, yes, over-decorated, occasionally self-conscious, flowery but in its own kind, first rate. It has theatre magic, Alice in Wonderland character and fun, a mood atmosphere of weather and time of day and year that is wonderfully evoked, lyric tenderness and a real understanding of the inexpressible, tongue-tied, cliché-dreading, desperate vitality of the generations of the two wars – I mean in the love scene. It breaks all the rules and still delights and holds the audience, and it is full of fascination and difficult passages for the actors' tongues. Well, well, one day we will talk of it in peace at greater length.

To Christopher Fry   *14 July, London*

Isn't it wonderful that business is so good in spite of the terrific heat? This week we have had some of the best audiences of the whole run. The American managers came cavorting round, longing to present it in New York.

Pam [Brown] and I have overhauled the love scene a little, and I think it is better. Come and have a look at us again soon, so that we don't get too ragged with no one to see us from the front.

With **The Lady's Not for Burning** *running successfully, JG began rehearsals for* **Treasure Hunt,** *another comedy from the joint pens of M. J. Farrell (Mollie Keane) and John Perry.*

To his mother   *15 August, London*

I am so happy to think you are out of London – the heat terrific again the last two days – fortunately yesterday I had a car and went for the day to Midhurst and Arundel Park, which I'd not seen since Selsey days. Exquisite light and expanse of trees and green – and I lay by the Cowdray Castle ruins in the evening and watched a cricket match in the lengthening shadows – most restful.

Rehearsals of the new play shape pretty well, I'm glad to say, though Sybil [Thorndike] had to be away two days filming. On Saturday she filmed in the morning, took her daughter-in-law to the hospital to have a baby after the first act of the matinée of [*Daphne*] *Laureola* [by James Bridie] and was back in her seat to see the third act!

Donald Wolfit and Rosalind Iden came round tonight full of politeness and congratulations, so there is a hatchet buried indeed! I suppose he is only childishly petty like many actors and has decided the time has come to make amends. Anyway, he seemed quite sincere.

Dearest love to you – take care of yourself and relax all you can. I'm sure it must be doing you good to look at the country and not have to shop or order meals after so very long.

Treasure Hunt *opened at the Apollo Theatre on 14 September.*

To Christopher Fry   *16 October, London*

I read *The Boy with a Cart*, and loved it so. Asked John Perry if I couldn't direct it at the Lyric for Christmas with [Richard] Burton (I thought we might release him from the end of the run of *The Lady* to do it). It is enchanting.

*Love's Labour's Lost** – saw for the first time, never read it. What divine flashes of beauty and shape of things to come. A very worried, over-conscious production – one or two lovely bits from the comics. Otherwise most ill played. A great lesson in how not to carry on when speaking the verse. I learnt a lot, and Nora [Nicholson] and I haven't waved our hands on the stage since! I had a good afternoon a week ago rehearsing the first act, simplifying and freshening. I play all the beginning far more slowly and detachedly and try to get your bomb-happy tipsiness. It seems to me to be much clearer at last (to the audience, I mean) and I think there is much more reality and variety of pace and fun. Pam and I have also slowed up the opening of the love scene to get a truer feeling of awkwardness and gradual awakening of interest and familiarity.

I believe now we should sign the whole cast for America, even Esmé. The teamwork is so honest and well-disposed that I believe any newcomer, even if more perfect in detail, might break the quality of togetherness – and if we rest from the play for six months and then rehearse hard for ten days with the same cast, I have hopes we might achieve a really creditable result.

P.S. I don't really think it's much good trying to get anyone to replace me if

---

* Hugh Hunt's production at the Old Vic with Michael Redgrave and Diana Churchill.

it's to be only a second-grade actor – if I may be excused for appearing conceited in saying so. [Robert] Donat, Olivier and [Paul] Scofield seem to be the only real attractive possibilities and you'd not get any of them. [Eric] Portman, [Alec] Clunes, [John] Clements – none of these seem very exciting to me – but perhaps you disagree? I very much doubt if Pam would agree to any of them.

To Lynn Fontanne and Alfred Lunt   *25 October, London*

The Lady's Not for Burning is going strong after 200 performances, and I shall have to come out of it in January as I am going to Stratford for their summer season next year and we begin rehearsing in February and open in March. I am going to do Cassius, Angelo, Lear and Benedick, the latter in the production which I directed this year for Tony Quayle and Diana Wynyard and which they are now playing in Australia. Peggy Ashcroft is going to play Cordelia and Beatrice, and Gwen Ffrangcon-Davies is also going to be with us, and Quartermaine, so you can imagine how excited I am at the prospect. I have taken a funny little house eleven miles away in a beautiful village called Chipping Campden.

Streetcar* is an enormous success, but the newspapers have written it up almost exclusively on its sex sensationalism, and Vivien says it is rather wretched, for the audiences who come and pack in are rather like expectant apes. A pity, but I think it's something to do with the misunderstanding here of the Old South, which is Tennessee's strongest poetical card, that makes his beautiful talent less appreciated than it should be. The same thing happened over *The [Glass] Menagerie*.

JG directed Fry's **The Boy with a Cart** *at the Lyric, Hammersmith, and after coming out of* **The Lady's Not for Burning**, *he took a holiday before starting rehearsals for his season at Stratford.*

---

* *A Streetcar Named Desire* directed by Laurence Olivier, with Vivien Leigh as Blanche Dubois.

THE FIFTIES

1950

Our trip has turned out wonderfully. Exquisite weather after the first day in Seville. We stayed three nights there and saw a lot of superb building – only too many Murillos! The old quarter is fascinatingly romantic – tiny alleys and balconies almost touching one another, everywhere Roman and Moorish jostle the sixteenth century and the light continuously beautifies the prospect, even though not the fierce sunlight for which it is all designed. We went out to Itallicus [?] five miles away and saw an excavated Roman amphitheatre with fine marble pavements and bits of streets and houses still in preservation. The Alcazar is curious rather than beautiful but the Cathedral immensely impressive and you go up a huge tower like the campanile in Venice to survey the city – no steps up but a series of ramps – 35 of them – to get you to the top. Yesterday we drove here, a really superb drive through varying views of terrific variety and splendour, and got here in time for dinner. Lunched at Cordova where the Mezquita is incredible, an enormous Catholic church built *inside* a complete mosque which still remains intact, so that you look through hundreds of Moorish arches which run in arcades and vistas in all directions to the central choir, altar and nave which are almost on St Paul's scale. How it was all built is fantasy to me. This city is surrounded by high mountains covered with thick snow, and the sunset on them as we drove in was magically beautiful. Bright sunshine again today and we are off to the Alhambra and various other places. Our driver speaks perfect English and is excellent in every way and we had a good guide at Seville, though he got slightly muddled between Van Eyck and Van Dyck. The pictures everywhere are the most boring part – endless religious subjects, so very heavy and sombre. But the villages and countryside enchant one endlessly and even the best hotels are considerably cheaper than England.

To Ruth Goetz   *4 February, Cannes*

The Lady ended in a blaze of glory with three weeks of capacity business and a queue at the box office waiting half way through the first act in the hope of returned seats. I directed a one act play of Fry's at the Lyric Hammersmith which I like enormously and thought I did good work for – a Biblical story called *The Boy with a Cart* – written ten years ago, but after *The Lady* and

Olivier's play [*Venus Observed*] it was voted rather small Fry by the critics, I'm afraid.

The first play in Anthony Quayle's third Stratford season, Measure for Measure, *in which JG played Angelo, opened on 9 March 1950.*

To his mother   *3 April, Stratford-upon-Avon*

Edith Evans has been staying here and spent a nice evening with me dining at the house. [*Julius*] *Caesar* is going better, now that the young man from Birmingham [Michael Langham] has been nudged into an assistant position and Tony Quayle assumed authority. We began the other way round and wasted a good deal of time, as he is much too inexperienced to direct the actors. A pity.

JG spent many weekends at the Oliviers' country home, Notley Abbey in Buckinghamshire, and was always meticulous with his 'thank you' letters.

To Vivien Leigh and Laurence Olivier   *12 April, London*

Darling Viv and Larry
   What bliss at Notley – the daffodils and the green sticky buds and the company and good cheer and one thing and another. The decisions are harder and the telephone knells continual complications, but let us march philosophically into the dark tunnel of the farting fifties and be grateful for so many things – Ethel and the chequered maelstrom of playhouse, Sybil's cosiness, Edith's evangelical perversity and the sweetness of you both as my dear friends.

To his mother   *24 April, Stratford-upon-Avon*

We did the play last night up to the Forum with clothes, lights, scenery etc. for the first time, and the usual disaster ensued. Thank heaven my dress and wig seem to be one of the few that is satisfactory! The huge crowd and the fact that we have had the stage so little has held back the progress badly, and Harry Andrews terribly low and lacking in vitality which does not help rehearsals. Poor Tony (Quayle) in great despair at present, but no doubt all will sort itself. My fear is that he has attempted a rather old fashioned kind of production which is a bit cluttered and over detailed, à la Tree, and the speaking, as usual, has been neglected. Well, there is still another week, and miracles can happen in that time.
   All the festivities went off wonderfully well. Both the American Ambassador at the lunch and the preacher at yesterday's sermon boasted of their ignorance of Shakespeare, which seemed to me somewhat impertinent in every sense of

the word! But the flag unfurling, processions and the King's visit were all simple, well behaved and well organised, and the weather wonderful, which helped enormously. Two young boys drowned in the river yesterday almost under the windows of the theatre, which was rather a dreadful contrast to all the jollifications. It all happened in a few minutes with a boat only a few yards away. Horrible.

Yes, I always hoped to play Ivanov.* Komis' production in 1924 was wonderful, but the part is rather dismally repetitive, I thought, when I read the play again a year ago.

To Lillian Gish   *25 April, Stratford-upon-Avon*

It was lovely to hear from you, but I am most distressed to hear that Dorothy† has been ill, and do hope by now she is very much better and that you are able to leave her and get to Paris for the film of *Crime and Punishment*. If you do, is there any chance of your coming to England for a few days? I should dearly love to see you, and have a little house eleven miles from Stratford and could put you up for a few nights. It is something lacking in modern conveniences but Bernie [Dodge], my American manservant, is here with me, and continues to produce good meals.

My family are well, Mother quite recovered from the strain of Father's long illness and his death a year ago. She comes down for every first night and plans to spend several weeks here in the summer.

I am loving the work here, and of course am specially looking forward to *Much Ado* and *Lear* and working with Peggy again. She also has taken a house in Chipping Campden, across the street from me so we shall be able to drive in and out together which will also be very pleasant.

Julius Caesar, *in which J G played Cassius, opened on 2 May.*

To his mother   *May [?] 1950, Stratford-upon-Avon*

Still very dissatisfied with *Caesar* which is most exhausting and unsatisfactory. Am trying to persuade Tony to change certain things that are uncomfortable. I can't bear going on acting scenes in bad positions and feeling they fail of their effect. Masses of schoolchildren do not improve our tempers at the matinées either.

Much Ado about Nothing, *in which he played Benedick, opened on 6 June and* **King Lear** *on 18 July.*

---

* He would do so in 1965.
† Lillian Gish's sister.

To his mother   *14 August, Chipping Campden*

We had two *Lears* yesterday so I am taking it easy today and going in to Birmingham tonight to see the repertory company perform some new play* which I hope may not be unrewarding.

I have a suggestion of making a film of *The Tempest* next year, which I am looking into details of. It might have possibilities if they would postpone it till the autumn and give me a hand in the acting and treatment of it. The shortness of the play would enable one to play a pretty full version and all the magic etc. might be good on the screen. But we shall see.

Philip Carr wrote after *Lear* 'he didn't realise before that Lear's queen was a Jewess!'† Also that my make-up reminded him exactly of George Meredith!

To Dadie Rylands   *4 October, Stratford-upon-Avon*

I am tempted to send Arthur [Marshall] the *Lear* parody which I wrote for the Stratford party beginning –

> Our hearts belong to Daddy – BUT –
> Don't let's ask Daddy to stay,
> His knights are the Devil to pay.
> His boat hath a leak,
> And he dare not speak,
> And he's started to butter his hay!

Following the Stratford season JG took his production of The Lady's Not for Burning to the United States. Penelope Munday took over from Claire Bloom and George Howe from Harcourt Williams.

To his mother   *24 October, Boston*

As you see from the enclosed, the press is encouraging without being unstintedly enthusiastic. One of our crates was missing and we had last minute crises with replacing props and dressing, and only one rather hectic dress rehearsal yesterday before opening in the evening. The advance booking was so large that they were persuaded to book us into the Shubert, which is far too big. I played Hamlet there, but it is not really suitable for the pace and crackle of this play. We were all rather inaudible at first, but they seemed to hear me all right and Pamela [Brown] has never acted better. The cheap parts of the house were the first to warm up and then by degrees the whole theatre began to seem more at ease with us and the second and third acts went finely.

---

* *The Smooth-Faced Gentleman* by Peter Powell at the Alexandra Theatre.
† Gwen Ffrangcon-Davies, Maxine Audley and Peggy Ashcroft played Lear's daughters.

Of course we had not rehearsed for a fortnight and the two new players had never had clothes or the set before, so that all things considered I felt the performance and reception were most promising.

To his mother   *28 October, Boston*

Things going very well here – glorious, crisp autumn weather and the play settling down to all the same reactions as in London now that we have got used to the huge theatre. I have made one or two excisions and clarifications of words and phrases and changed a little here and there. All for the better. Enormous audiences and very good reception every time.

Saw a new play by Clifford Odets, *The Country Girl*, trying out here before N.Y. A very good performance by the woman – Uta Hagen – and a good level of acting and direction, but rather a tedious backstage story of a drunken actor being salvaged by his wife, with endless scenes in dressing rooms. Played slowly and with portentous seriousness, I didn't feel it convincing or moving, though it is a worthy effort.

I am much impressed by the lack of hoardings and signs on the roads in New England – everything much more countrified than the places near New York, and with the sunshine and autumn colouring everywhere, it all looks very elegant and picturesque.

Bernie is cleaning the flat, I gather, as thoroughly as Chipping Campden all over again. The Lunts have been very sweet and enthusiastic – raved about the play which they saw at the dress rehearsal, and we have had supper with them a couple of times.

The Lady's Not for Burning *opened in New York on 8 November.*

To his mother   *10 November, New York*

You will have heard from Binkie about the wonderful success we had. The press was practically unanimous and yesterday we had two capacity houses and people standing at both performances – plus a line at the box office all day booking seats, so I think we may now take a little time to relax and get into the general routine of a run.

I've settled down very happily in the flat and with Bernie, my new secretary and Toby Rowland who have all been on hand to obey my slightest whim, I've been indeed pampered and provided for in every way since we arrived.

I do wish you could have been here on Wednesday, not only for the success but for the wonderful welcome I had personally, both on my first entrance and at the end of the play. My little dressing room was literally awash with telegrams, champagne, flowers and presents of every kind – and the flat looked like the conservatory from *Ring Round the Moon*. I found it difficult to keep my emotion under control at so much kindness and love – that is both here and from home.

The company played splendidly and nearly all have individual notices as well as praise for their teamwork, so everyone is immensely happy and plans to send money home to appease their overdrafts!

Peter Brook is coming out to see New York and will stay with me for three weeks in December and we hope to plan then some definite production for my return. We are going to Edith Evans' tonight – she leaves tomorrow for London and one feels a little embarrassed to have come through where she didn't.* However, she is always good over her disappointments. Her own personal success was very great and I think she is full of offers as soon as she gets back to England and has turned down several attractive offers here.

New York was absolutely terrifying on Sunday, getting back from the comparative primness of Boston – it seemed like a gigantic monster waiting to swallow one up and I suppose my nervousness exaggerated the feeling. It seemed as though the traffic down below drove right through my bedroom the first night and I wouldn't be able to sleep – and the taxis drive with terrific exhilaration when you first begin to drive in them. But all that has settled now and I sleep perfectly and find everything curiously familiar. The comfort of the trains and their cleanliness is unbelievable after England, and it is hard to resist so much rich food.

I'm going to have some meat parcels posted to Eleanor because Bernie and I think a little red blood is what she needs.

To Christopher Fry   *November 1950, New York*

Wednesday was a thrilling night, and I shall be able to tell my stepchildren that I played for a whole year to not an empty seat. There's comfort for the fireside in the dog days to come. All the reporters clamour for details of your life and personal behaviour, till I tell them I am getting bored describing you as a dear and modest and ideal to work with.

I made one or two little cuts in Boston, and I do hope you wouldn't mind too badly. The first cut was tricky the first night. Richard [Burton] *will* drop the last three words of his sentences and gets too flat in his opening speech – Penny [Munday] and E[smé Percy] have come up splendidly, and Nora [Nicholson] has had a personal success, she is miles better than she was in London. I'm so delighted for her.

New York is a terrifying city but hectically beautiful in many ways. The kindness and welcome are overwhelming, but there is too much money, food and drink and too much respect for success, while endeavour and failure are just ignored, or swept away as if there wasn't any time or place for them.

Dear Christopher, thank you for the play and all it has given me in pleasure

---

* Edith Evans had appeared in an unsuccessful production of James Bridie's *Daphne Laureola*.

and worth. Your success will always be among my favourite theories – that good things will always achieve recognition in the theatre – and the people here are hungrier even than ours for new beauties, only sometimes the trash theatre, sold and fed them in such relentless streams, cloy up their spirits with vulgarity.

To Hugh Wheeler   *10 November, New York*

Isn't it marvellous that we have such a big hit here? The town is agog and I'm snowed under with presents, good notices and general jubilation. I've not had much time to do the town yet and felt that 42nd Street would bring me bad luck if I were seen there before the opening. Shall I be strong-minded enough to cold-shoulder it altogether? I wonder. Most of the bars seem to have changed hands and addresses but I suppose I shall smell them out before long.

Lennie and Arnold Weissberger both came for the first night but were *not* crammed together in the door of my dressing room as I feared they would be – and we had the pleasure of refusing Judith Anderson four seats as she applied too late – a touch of poetic justice which I could not truthfully pass without a touch of satisfaction.

Bernie and Jim Merrick are looking after me at the flat, which is spacious and comfortable. Do come and stay later on and see it. Peter Brook will be here for three weeks in December, but otherwise I have no bookings so far. However, you'd better fix the date fairly soon for fear I lose my head in the midst of all the excitement and become moved to install a permanent plaything!

To his mother   *16 November, New York*

Looking forward to hearing your account of the [Old] Vic opening. Edith felt happy she would be in it* to make up for the disappointment of her time here. I am glad she was back in time. I'm sure they must all have been proud to have you there and I've no doubt you held court between the acts.

All well here, beautiful weather, spring-like sunshine and the town agog with excitement about us and the play. There are plans for a big radio performance of *Hamlet* in January, but of course they want a film star for Ophelia! Jean Simmons, who was in the film with Larry, or possibly Jane Wyman. Pamela would do the Queen and the rest of our company in the other parts, but there won't be much left of them, I fear, as the whole thing has to be cut to 1¼ hours!

Do let me know if there's anything I can send. Sugar? White flour? Cooking fat?

---

* Edith Evans spoke a Prologue by Christopher Hassall at the reopening of the Old Vic Theatre.

To his mother   *23 November, New York*

I seem to go out every night, which means two o'clock before one goes to bed, with the 8.40 rise of the curtain that takes some getting used to after London. However, I wake at 9 without feeling overtired and am usually home by four in the afternoon to rest for two hours and have an early meal. Thus one catches up on the late nights.

The Shaw celebration* was rather nice, though too long and sagging at moments. Esmé Percy did a speech from *Far Fetched Fables* – the very last thing Shaw wrote – with great virtuosity and opened the proceedings well. I did Dubedat's death speech and [Katherine] Cornell the end of *Saint Joan*. Then an inadequate loudspeaker played a transcript of the singing of the Verdi Requiem aria and the Enigma Variations from the funeral service in London which was barely audible, and the house talked all through them!

I saw an excellent play yesterday, *Member of the Wedding* [by Carson McCullers], with negress Ethel Waters and two children in the main parts. Rather unpleasant, but brilliantly acted and directed with real atmosphere and sensitivity. A sort of modern version of *The Constant Nymph* and the Barrie plays – a girl of 14 [Julie Harris] suffering violent pangs of adolescence over the marriage of her young soldier brother, neglected by her father, and the old mammy cook trying to deal with the situation in her incoherent way of mingled ignorance and worldly wisdom. The little boy from next door [Brandon de Wilde], a child of eight, gives a wonderful performance and serves as an almost silent chorus, representing the youngest generation. He is on the stage playing all through the hysterical scenes of the young girl, sometimes vaguely aware of what it all means, sometimes just bored and longing for notice, and sometimes just thinking to himself – all done with extraordinary subtlety and emphasis. The old woman is a miracle of relaxation, passion, earthiness and resignation. A very original and touching piece of theatre, even though the story itself is loose and rather badly contrived. It is interesting how action has been stolen almost completely by the screen nowadays, and the theatre is more and more given over to psychological exposition, with almost embarrassingly realistic dialogue and atmosphere and character taking the place of story situations – not the long-winded perorations of Shaw and Ibsen, but the nostalgia mixed with violence which is also so characteristic of Tennessee Williams and other American dramatists.

To his mother   *27 November, New York*

I hope you got my wire of Saturday, as I not only wanted you to know I was thinking of you and greatly anxious to hear you were better, but also that all

---

* George Bernard Shaw had died on 2 November.

was well with me. I dare say there are reports in London of the terrific gale and havoc here on Saturday. It was quite a dramatic 24 hours, beginning on Friday night when the wind was fantastic on the East River here, and nothing would keep out the rain, which got through every crack in the very old window fastenings. The embankment flooded and boats floating down stream that had broken their moorings. On Saturday I got a cab down to the theatre all right, but there were windows out everywhere, awnings ripped and hanging signs torn from their hinges and littering the streets. The big sign on the Lincoln Hotel almost next door to the theatre broke in half and took half the afternoon to fall! Fire engines standing by and bits of the street roped off. We went up ten minutes late and had about 30 empty seats at each performance, though they were all paid for, fortunately! I was to have dined with Lillian Gish, but we were told not to leave the theatre, so Mary Martin again took pity on me and I dined with her next door in her luxurious dressing room in my make-up. By seven o'clock the storm had subsided, and yesterday was brilliant and calm again as if nothing had happened. Nothing happens in this country that isn't exaggerated and violent, it seems.

Peter Brook writes me a scheme that we should bring *The Lady* back immediately we close here and open it in London for a few weeks in June so that I could be playing quite early in the Festival,* and while it was running rehearse *The Winter's Tale*. He suggests I *double* Leontes and Autolycus – rather an intriguing idea, I must say. Or we might conceivably do *Caesar* with Ralph and Larry. Time will show.

To his mother   *9 December, New York*

Peter Brook has arrived from London and I have been showing him the city a little, but he is beset with hospitality and going to every play in town. Last night we were at a large supper given at the Stork Club by the international party giver Elsa Maxwell. The Duchess of Windsor was at the table, very well arranged (the Duchess, not the table) and excessively animated. I did not talk to her but she has an ugly voice and rather artificial vivacity it seemed to me. The Duke had retired early. Cecil Beaton and Mrs Astor, who was very nice and intelligent, sat next to me.

We have finally done with the Guild Subscription members and theatre parties – when the house is bought and re-sold at higher prices for a charity. These devices are a kind of insurance for the management but result in deadly audiences – late and sleepy and with no particular keenness to see the play, except that it is a hit. The last few nights when the ordinary public is at last in front are infinitely better and have given us all a new lease of life.

---

* The Festival of Britain, planned for 1951, was a celebration of Britain and the British people intended to raise the country's spirits after the Second World War.

To Laurence Olivier   *12 December, New York*

I was so delighted and touched to get your letter, and I feel I must seem very ungrateful not to fall in immediately with your plan of doing *The School* [*for Scandal*] next year. The difficulty is that I have been working since our *Measure* [*for Measure*] at Stratford with Peter Brook on a project for *Winter's Tale* for the Festival and he is very much in demand, as you know, and has kept himself free for June in order to do this production with me as soon as I am free.

I feel I want to do a *new* part when I next appear in London rather than one I have played before, and the reputation of my performances as Joseph [Surface] (a legend largely created by you!) is one I should hate to risk spoiling by trying to do it again and perhaps make a mess of it. Much as I should adore to work again with you – and Viv – I can't help feeling that a revival of something already done is somehow a confession of weakness – that is why I turned down the idea of *The Importance* which everybody thought at first to be the obvious and easy choice.*

If you and I and Ralph could have done *Julius Caesar*, I would have been keen on that, because the play also has not been done in London for a long time, but Ralph seems to be committed elsewhere and I did Cassius too recently. Although originally I thought it would be a good play to have us all work together for the fun it would be, it is also true that too many stars in one play will not be a good plan, for nobody would be able to get in, and there would be one great attraction and a lot of second rate ones at the other theatres. Whereas if each of us who can command an audience (one hopes!) put on a new show at three or four theatres, it will make the Festival more varied and divide the amount of work for the supporting actors to greater advantage. Does this make sense to you or do you think me very selfish?

I would so love to have seen you and had a real talk about the whole thing – it was very tiresome being at Stratford when the meetings were held at the beginning of the year, and I only got second hand accounts of what plans were afoot.

I hope Viv's play [*A Streetcar Named Desire*] turned into as splendid a picture as she hoped. How did she get on with Brando, I wonder?

My love to you and please don't think too badly of me for saying no to your offer. I do appreciate your suggesting it and wanting to work with me again.

To Lynn Fontanne and Alfred Lunt   *15 December, New York*

How I wish you were going to be in New York for Christmas. I miss you both on and off the stage. Sam Behrman came to the play and loved it and we went

---

* Gielgud had last played Joseph Surface in 1938; Olivier's production of *The School for Scandal*, with himself as Sir Peter and Vivien Leigh as Lady Teazle, had played at the New Theatre in early 1949.

out together and thought of you. It is really thrilling that it goes so well. And how I adored *Guys and Dolls*. I would love to go again with Alfred when he comes back, and watch his reactions. Peter Brook is staying here for a few weeks and the New York ladies are fighting over the pleasure of entertaining him – the telephone never stops ringing for a moment – and the Christmas festivities are a raging hysteria in the shops while the newspapers fill us with deeper gloom.

To his mother   *16 December, New York*

Very glad to see from your handwriting that you do really seem to be a little stronger. I do hope the enforced rest hasn't depressed you and made you miserable, for I know how you hate not being able to shop and find presents for everybody. I am glad to think Eleanor and the Vals will be with you on Christmas Day and I shall think of you all and perhaps try and telephone either on Sunday or Monday. We give performances on the 25th which always seem a bit odd to me – and on Christmas Eve Adrianne Allen gives a party at which the children are going to act!

Peter Brook is full of plans for *The Winter's Tale*, and has, I think, an exciting idea for a way to handle the scene changes throughout. We talked to Flora Robson the other day about Paulina. I think she would be excellent in it.

Business has slipped slightly this week, as Christmas shopping is in full swing. I supped one night with a delightful old lady here who goes at night to the theatre and gave a party for a dozen people after. She was still up and doing at 1.45 a.m. and goes by air to Paris to spend Christmas with her son. She is 89. So you are not the only marvel! I met her years ago in *Hamlet* days and feared she would be no longer alive, but there she is as intelligent and lively as ever, full of enthusiasm for Fry, all of whose plays she has read!

To his mother   *21 December, New York*

Lovely clear weather here with a nip in the air, and the city looks very beautiful in the main streets with the chains of lights, Christmas trees and the magnificent shop window displays, but everybody is of course nervous and apprehensive over the [Korean] War News, and the goodwill air of festivity heavily tinged with fatalistic dismay. Our play has suffered very little compared with most of the theatres, which shows what a really solid success we have – the audiences are really excellent. I have been to one or two musicals at matinées, but they are extremely indifferent on the whole, though excessively lavish in mounting, but too much money thrown away on heavy unimaginative material both in songs and dialogue. Peter Brook is very disappointed with the theatre here on the whole, but it is the most indifferent season I have known here – only about three first class shows altogether.

We spoke to Binkie the other day and settled *The Winter's Tale* for June. Diana Wynyard as Hermione, Flora is keen to play Paulina and we think of [Robert] Helpmann for Autolycus – he is a really inventive comedian and his star personality would be valuable to sustain the long middle act when we are off the stage. Also he could clown to his heart's content without upsetting any scenes for us! The difficulty will be to find attractive youngsters for Florizel and Perdita.

Larry [Olivier] has asked Peter [Brook] to direct *Caesar and Cleopatra* (Shaw) for him and Vivien, and he may do that in April before I come back. He (Peter) is certainly in demand for a boy of 26!

To Theodore Komisarjevsky   *23 December, New York*

George Hayes is a man who can never resist repeating an unkind thing. He is a clever actor but really not quite right in the head!

1951

To his mother   *New Year's Day, New York*

I was so happy to get your sweet cable for New Year and to hear from your letters and Eleanor's that you were really on the mend. Except for a fall of snow on Boxing Day it has been mild and beautiful here, and today I can sit and write by the open window with a welcome lessening of traffic streaming by and the ships hooting and puffing along the sunny river.

The party I had here for the company on Boxing Day was very successful and I think everyone enjoyed it. We had a tree and presents and Bernie did a very good supper and coped generally. He was much touched at your remembrance of him and the present I gave him from you, and is stocking up on his wardrobe with many gifts he had from the company and others of my friends. He also battled valiantly with Brook's endless telephone calls and got him off to his various appointments for which he is pathologically unpunctual.

We had a capacity week at the theatre, including a performance last night at increased prices which was sold out. Gladys Cooper came looking very beautiful though her face is covered with tiny lines and her hair quite grey! Cornell closed *Captain Carvallo* [by Dennis Cannan] after three disastrous weeks on the road and it never opened in New York at all. The Jeffers play with Judith Anderson* was not much liked despite Brooks Atkinson's rave notice, and failed to transfer after its two weeks at the ANTA Theatre. Helen

---

* *The Tower Beyond Tragedy* by Robinson Jeffers.

Hayes cannot find a play, so none of the big stars are on view this season. Jessica Tandy's new play* closed last night after a short run, and *Black Chiffon* [by Lesley Storm] comes to an end on Jan. 13th. [Louis] Calhern's *King Lear* opened on Dec. 26th and the *Enemy of the People* [by Henrik Ibsen] in a new version with Fredric March and his wife [Florence Eldridge] the following evening – rather heavy fare for Christmas week, and the notices rather mixed. People who have seen them both not overly enthusiastic. So you see we are very lucky to have a success in a play nearly everybody likes, though here, as in England, there are a few intelligent people who can't do with Fry at all, fortunately in the minority. The play list in London looks pretty dull to me.

I saw Orson Welles' film of *Macbeth*. Not uninteresting and some fine effects of battle and Birnam Wood, but slow and dragged out despite huge cuts and transpositions and the acting unmoving and conventional. Splendid costumes but the fine language is defeated by the limitations of the screen!

To his mother   *8 January, New York*

Pamela [Brown] and I do a television this week – my first. We are interviewed and then play the proposal scene from *Earnest* and a bit of Alice and the Caterpillar with 'You are Old, Father William'. They film it all and then put it out some days later. About ten minutes in all. It might be quite fun to do, though we begin at 9.30 in the morning – without make-up! What with that and the Sunday Benefits and the *Hamlet* radio, we shall be kept very busy the next few weeks. The play is still going strong and we have paid off the cost of the production.

To his mother   *14 January, New York*

It has been fine and mild here and I wish I did not have to picture you in the grip of a cold, dull winter with austerity restrictions making life perpetually difficult. It is still an incredible convenience to find every shop open here on Sundays, and cake shops, bars and tobacconists within a stone's throw ready to supply one's slightest need. We had a dull lot of audiences after New Year but they perked up again at the end of the week, and we were full again. McClintic is ill with three nurses, Kit didn't say what it is but evidently pretty serious. Pamela and I did our television interview on Friday – long and tedious business – 4 hours for a short session of ten minutes. They photographed it but I cannot help feeling it is abominably undignified to act to interruptions of advertising Pepsi-Cola!

Next week I am to do the 'Rogue and Peasant Slave' speech in costume with a live audience on a television programme. That may be a little less

_____

* *Hilda Crane* by Samson Raphaelson.

boring and they pay one large sums and one does touch a completely different and huge audience. We record the whole of the play for Decca on Friday, 9.30–6, which will be a long and trying day, I'm sure. Tomorrow is the ANTA Ball at the Hotel Astor and we have a benefit tonight, so I am kept extremely busy and have little time for outside engagements. [Richard] Burton leaves at the end of the month to rehearse for Stratford, which will mean fresh rehearsals too.

To his mother   *28 January, New York*

I am very sorry indeed to hear that you have not been so well again, and that Eleanor has had 'flu. The accounts here of the epidemic are alarming and I hope somewhat exaggerated – and I loathe the idea of your having less meat again. Shall I send more meat parcels – they are easy to arrange here and it would be nice to feel one is helping to feed you up a little! But I know how minutely you eat so perhaps it is not much use to you?

We have a great jump up in business this week, and many of the film people came round greatly impressed, apparently. Marlene Dietrich, who was really enchanting, and Danny Kaye! I am trying to think a little about Leontes. I think it is pleasantly untrammelled by tradition, like Angelo, and if one can carry off the difficult opening which, like *Macbeth* and *Lear* is the initial stumbling block for a modern audience, I think it could be a most wonderful part. They are talking about His Majesty's for it [*The Winter's Tale*]. Ellen [Terry] played Hermione there in 1905, with Charles Warner, Viola and Maud Tree. I expect you saw it, but E.T. must have been too old by then I fear. It will be hard to find a good Mamillius, Perdita and Florizel, but Peter is clever at casting. Sophie Fedorovitch is to do the décor, she has done lovely things for the ballet.

It does seem mad to me to be holding this festival in the present conditions – fuel and electricity shortages beside the food and general world depression – one dreads to think what London will be like with hosts of tourists grumbling and inadequately catered for. The newspapers here are terrifying – articles describing the rich in the Bahamas buying atolls and island hideouts against the wrath to come, and descriptions of how badly the American troops fight in Korea because they are spoiled by being so over mechanised and used to being taken everywhere by jeep!

The Oliviers are surely biting off more than they can chew with the *two* Cleopatra plays.* I fear Vivien has really too much control – she will never be able to touch the Shakespeare part, and he is not well cast for either play – the work alone of the two big productions is terrifying and I can't imagine how they can contemplate it, though I admit it makes a splashy announcement!

---

* For the Festival of Britain, Olivier and Vivien Leigh would present Shakespeare's *Antony and Cleopatra* and Shaw's *Caesar and Cleopatra* at the St James's Theatre.

To his mother　　　　　　　　　　　　　　　　*7 February, New York*

I have not yet heard the playback of the recordings we did of *The Lady* but they say they are pleased with them. We miss Burton in the play but the boy who has taken over [Trader Faulkner] does pretty well, for anyone who did not see Burton. We had to rehearse a bit, which was tedious, but on the whole improved our playing I think a little.

To his mother　　　　　　　　　　　　　　　　*14 February, New York*

The recording of the play came out very well, though I drove my own part rather too hard, and it is more declamatory and hurried than I would have wished. However, I think the general effect is good. With the new long-playing records you can hear nearly 45 minutes of music or speech without a break which is quite extraordinary, though I can't think anyone but students or invalids would want to hear a play that way. But it makes quite an interesting record for the future.

I took my Keats ring to Cartier's to have it polished. They tell me it is not an amethyst at all, but simply GLASS! Rather comic. So it is merely a valueless stage prop. However, it looks pretty and that is something, and I only hope it did belong to Keats!

Tennessee Williams' play *The Rose Tattoo* is very moving and beautifully acted and produced. Today I go to *Bell, Book and Candle*, John Van Druten's witch play with Rex Harrison and Lilli Palmer. I believe it is only good for two acts, but it is a great success, with the added appeal of two popular married film stars, which is always attractive to the public these days.

I know what you feel about the gloom of Leontes, but the play is so rarely seen and has none of the boring, hackneyed familiarity of the more famous plays. I think it may arouse the same interest as *Measure* and the part, like Angelo, is fresh ground for me, which I like. I wonder if Shakespeare was thinking of Henry VIII again – the unpredictable moods of jealousy, tenderness and violence over the Ann Bullen marriage must have seemed to onlookers something very similar, and Hermione in her righteous nobility very like Katharine. Claude Rains, with whom I had supper the other night – now past middle age and very happily married to a youngish wife – said he prompted at His Majesty's and described Ellen standing in the court scene with 'divine tears pouring down her cheeks'.

Take all care of yourself, my darling, and get really well again to enjoy the spring. It will soon be here now and it won't be long before I am home again. Fondest love as ever.

To Alfred Lunt　　　　　　　　　　　　　　　　*19 February, New York*

I am so distressed to think all your goodwill and fine trouping and generous giving of yourselves with such pleasure for your big audiences has tired you out, and that Lynn's trouble with her arm is still an anxiety for you both. Also, I know how deeply disappointed all your friends and admirers will be to hear that you cannot come to us this year in England. You and Toscanini both out of the Festival – that is a double tragedy for us. How I would adore to visit you at Genesee.* I have asked Jack [Wilson] to take the play off at the end of April and he has very sweetly agreed. Our business has dropped a good deal, as *Variety* will have informed you. (Did you notice the very nice heading two weeks ago – 'Pacific 25G, Tree 5, Coq flops out!') I am planning to go to Italy for three weeks, Rome and Florence, where I have never been, and perhaps Venice too.

New York has not been the same without you both in and out of the theatre. I did two television scraps which appalled me by their vulgarity of set-up and technical inferiority and the awful presentation with advertisements and frightful buttering up of the performers by the interviewers and presenters, and one comes out looking like a drowned, grey corpse, grimacing and prattling.

To Stark Young   *3 March, New York*

I was very delighted indeed to have your very kind letter and to know first hand what you felt about *The Lady*, which I had already heard from Billy [Harcourt Williams].

I find acting a far greater responsibility of work than I did once, and long runs are really difficult to bear. But directing, which I call my hobby, is really a joy and I think I am lucky indeed to have learnt something about it in the last few years. I hope soon to be able to direct plays that I am not in once or twice a year and take longer rests between acting in plays. Time the inexorable, however, presses one on to try and get in all the parts one really wants to play before 50 looms up on the horizon! And one fears to pass by any new script with a decent role in it, as they are so few and far between.

To his mother   *5 March, New York*

As you will see from the other notice, the *Hamlet* was done last night and I was very disappointed with it. I cut it to quite a tolerable 1½ hour version, but by the time the producer had done with it another ten minutes had to go – and what with 'commercials' from the sponsors and narrations from Horatio to make the action clear, the veriest skeleton was left – just the three big soliloquies and a smattering of the other scenes – the nunnery scene reduced to three or four *lines* and so on. Impossible to put over the character in such a truncated form – no humour left, no Rosencrantz and Guildenstern

---

* The Lunts' home near Milwaukee, Wisconsin.

or Osric, all the sentimental moments overemphasised and so on. I really hated the whole thing and wished I had never agreed to it. Masses of treacly music was played almost throughout by a large orchestra and the whole thing vulgarised for popular appeal. The passion for interviews and snippety bits of so-called straight acting to fill out programmes is nauseating and cheap and I cannot bring myself to do it again.

To his mother   *8 March, New York*

I was greatly saddened by Ivor [Novello]'s sudden death. He will leave a mass of sorrowing friends and was so greatly loved in the profession. I fear it will have cast a dreadful gloom over the West End, and I feel so sorry for all the casts in his two big shows who have to go on playing. But for himself it was a good way to go out in a blaze of glory and he had had a big new success and three months holiday with all his friends in Jamaica.

To his mother   *20 March, Washington D.C.*

It is pouring with rain today and I have only been down to look at the theatre – an old burlesque house in a narrow little back street next to a skittle alley and a 'striptease' house – but inside clean and agreeably shaped, about as big as the Globe, and tiny cabin-like dressing rooms up a steep iron staircase along the side of the stage.

I dined with the Lunts who have still two more weeks to tour and are rather at the end of their tether. She broke her wrist some weeks ago and though she is out of the plaster she has had bad reactions of rheumatism and looks old and tired. He is fairly well but worried to death about her as she will not complain and plays doggedly on. They have had blizzards and bad weather and uncomfortable theatres and feel they can troup no longer. They have cancelled coming to England very reluctantly and retire to their farm in Wisconsin for a year's rest, but one feels they dread giving up work which is their whole passion, yet fear to risk one or other of them collapsing in health. It is sad to see them but they were, as ever, enchanting to me and bitterly sad about Ivor's death. They are such lovers of England and all of us actors there.

I was fascinated by your account of the Vic, but Peggy seems to have had a great success personally despite the chorus and general production.* I fear the Greek tragedies are defeated by a picture stage still more than Shakespeare, and we have not the kind of stylised acting that can compass them sat-isfactorily. Still, I should like to have a crack at Oedipus one day when Olivier's performance is not quite so fresh in people's minds. I think I might do something with it.†

---

* *Electra* directed by Michel Saint-Denis and designed by the sculptor, Barbara Hepworth.
† He would play Seneca's Oedipus in the Peter Brook production for the National Theatre at the Old Vic in 1968.

To Robert Flemyng   *28 March, Washington*

We have had a very successful season with the play and could do a long tour of it if the Guild had their way. Me, I am tired and somewhat dispirited – reading dozens of queer novels with Koestler's latest [*The Age of Longing*] thrown in to really depress me. I hear you liked *The Night Air*, but wait till you get a load of *Double Door* by a young lady called Theodora Keogh – it is quite something.

Pam seems well and an occasional visit from her friend the chinless wonder* does her a world of good from time to time. Wish I had a good steady (or two) but either I am too old, too fastidious, or too lazy these days. Emotionally I starve and even physically too tired to roam unless something drops right into my jaded lap.

I met a friend of yours, Jack Thompson, whom I liked well, though to me is not attractive for the bed. Paul Morrison and Ben Edwards were my best cronies in N.Y. But most of the parties – except for three that Bernie and I gave! – were ghastly. Everybody lives à deux and one cannot muscle in on marriages, at least I try not to. Kit and Guthrie have gone off to Spain – she looks very elderly and cannot find a play – and he has been ill and looked, I thought, much better for it. Peter Bull is a dear and I go round with him a lot. Esmé [Percy] is keeping rather a horrid young boy and never stops romping, so there is hope for all of us yet. America has rejuvenated him and he appears in brocaded waistcoats and ties studded with rhinestones!

Rex and Lilli are the toast of the town and both enchanting in their play – I thought them very sweet, went to one of their parties where I met Sarah Churchill who seemed a dear too. Bernie does not enjoy America (too much of his past keeps cropping up, I fancy) and he is getting rather fat! He longs to get back to Cowley Street which I am very upset about being wrecked by those vile Coopers. But we shall soon get it back to rights again.

I wonder how the Stratford opening went off. Rather unfortunately Michael [Redgrave]'s photo in the S[*unday*] *Times* caught him practically doing a court curtsey! I would think Tony Q. has his hands full with that company – including the Welsh firebrands Messrs Burton and [Hugh] Griffith.

To Hugh Wheeler   *28 March, Washington*

They recommend the Eden Hotel in Rome, so I suggest you try it out and if you approve get me a double room. Bobbie [Flemyng] will come on the Saturday and I shall hope to be there by the preceding Wednesday. I suggest we take a three day drive to Florence, stopping at Perugia, Siena and San Gimignano where Adrianne has given me the names of hotels. We ought also to go to see the Piero della Francesca at Borgo San Sepolcro, and go through

---

* Pamela Brown's agent (and later J G's), Laurence Evans.

Assisi. In Florence there is Rosamond's Marquesa, Harold Acton and Mr [Bernard] Berenson if we wish to re-enter intellectual society for a day or two, and I hear that Baron Paulo Langheim in Rome is liable to lay on Fabulous Footmen and the Papal Guard at the dinner table at the drop of a hat! We have only to ring him up, it appears.

Washington is horribly relaxing and liverish and I feel like death and have lost all my appetites. A few kindred spirits have appeared and we are doing capacity business so I suppose one should not complain, but I am longing to dine at a Christian hour and be unbound by the routine of the theatre, and to see you and roam at will in new and beautiful places.

To Stark Young   *11 April, Philadelphia*

I am interested in what you say about the Pirandello *Henry IV.* I have toyed many times with the idea of doing it. It failed in London years ago. Did you see the Italian film of it? I saw it in N.Y. in '48 and thought it wonderfully good. The women, mother and daughter, doubled admirably by the same actress who wore hideous 1920 costume – scraped back hair, long earrings and a panelled skirt short to the knees in front with two long floating fishtails at the back. You gasped at the ugliness when she entered, and in five minutes she had made you realise why it was considered a glamorous fashion.

It is a pity that Pirandello is so bloody mathematical in his intricacy of construction, and the translations are all very flat-footed. But it is a fine part, certainly.

After the tour of The Lady's Not for Burning *and his Italian holiday, JG returned to England to rehearse* The Winter's Tale, *directed by Peter Brook for the Festival of Britain. It opened at the Phoenix Theatre on 27 June 1951. Eighteen years later JG recalled the production.*

To Professor Yoshio Arai   *4 November 1969, London*

Peter Brook, in the 1951 production, arranged the opening of the play as a sort of triptych. I was on the left in a doorway up a few steps, Polixenes on the opposite side, similarly placed, Hermione and the child in the centre archway. This arrangement, arrived at after many experiments, seemed to establish the triangle very effectively, as Hermione descended and met Polixenes, while I continued to observe them and comment from a short distance away.

It is long ago, so I don't remember when I came down the steps and spoke some of my speeches very close to the footlights. It seems to me that Leontes *is* slightly mad – increasingly so through the arrest of the Queen and up to the Oracle's dictum and the death of Mamillius. In the last act, I made up to look much older, grey hair and a long grey robe, very simple, whereas in the first part I wore red, breeches and doublet. I think my hair was reddish too, and in the trial scene I wore a close-fitting black skull cap with a severe gold crown encircling it.

I think the man had a kind of Shakespearean boyhood passion for Polixenes, which he has felt again in their reunion, perhaps with some kind of disgust or disappointment, and he almost wishes the jealousy with Hermione, as Shakespeare seems to do in many of the Sonnets as a kind of love-hate revenge both on himself and them.

To Edith Sitwell   *5 August, London*

I thought you might like to hear a comment made by an odd fellow, Martin Holmes, who was at school with me. He came round the other night at the end of the play and said 'Imagine the effect of the end of the play on the Jacobean audience, when Perdita's part was doubled by the boy who played Mamillius also.' I was greatly struck by this, as it continues the theory I suggested to you about the Fool and Cordelia.

Swinburne says the only cruel thing in the dénouement is that Mamillius, the one innocent victim, is forgotten by Shakespeare in the general rejoicing. But if the audience saw the miracle for themselves – the boy *and* the girl as one, restored to Leontes, the fable is complete without a word.

So I am sure did the exigencies of a small company (with probably only one really brilliant boy actor) serve as a means of turning the shortage to good account in the ingenuity and genius of the poet. Don't you think it is a good theory? Your luncheon party was such a pleasure the other day.

To Hugh Wheeler   *5 August, London*

The play is going wonderfully despite hot weather and holidays. I have had far the best press personally I have had for years – the only problem now is what to follow with, but I think we need not worry about that till next year. I am doing a radio *Lear* in September and probably will direct *Midsummer Night's Dream* for the Vic in December. Rather fun. I have asked Ben Edwards if he wants to come over and do the décor, subject to Guthrie liking his designs. But I fear there won't be much money in it – however, if they pay his fares and expenses and he stays with me, I should think it might be worth it for him from a prestige point of view if nothing else, and I know I would enjoy working with him.

Bobbie [Flemyng] is well. We go to Stratford for the day tomorrow. London is quiet and I am calm – Binkie and John return from the South of France on Wednesday. Toby will no doubt tell you he has a big hole in his heart. I told him to stuff it with bran, sawdust or Kleenex, and swallow the key! Unfeeling of me, of course, but I am a bit bored with that quadrangle.* Alan [Webb] goes to Edinburgh to play Higgins to Margaret Lockwood's Eliza – not very exciting, I'm afraid, but he must put money in his purse.

Had a mad offer from one Tom Hammond by telephone – would I redirect Miss [Olivia] de Havilland as Juliet beginning at St Louis in October and to open again in N.Y. in the spring. Lunatic.

All the French plays are to be done here this fall. *Colombe* [by Jean Anouilh] by Peter Brook, translated by Denis Cannan who wrote [*Captain*] *Carvallo*, [Yvonne] Arnaud, [Joyce] Redman and James Donald. *Bobosse* [André Roussin] with John Mills, *Nina* [Roussin] and *Ardele* [Anouilh]. I am sick of reading Anouilh plays – all too long – with the same plot and cast of characters switched round. They cannot all succeed. Have a good script for Margaret Rutherford if she would play it. It needs working on but a very amusing guignol true story about Rachel Leverson, the first beautician in London 1864, who gives her clients bran and water in oriental feasts and baths at ten guineas a time, tricks and blackmails them and is finally brought to book. Judith might be rather fine in it too if she could play with a German Jewish accent!

To Dadie Rylands   *11 August, London*

I am very glad you were pleased with us. It is wonderful that everybody seems to like me so well in it. Sexual jealousy not being one of my most besetting sins, I had to do it out of my head, but perhaps that is the best way in the theatre. I don't like the cuts of [the] opening scene and the oracle, but with dull actors it is better to cut than bore.

To Stark Young   *17 August, London*

Henry IV [by Pirandello] is so difficult for audiences because the title suggests Falstaff and Gadshill – English never imagine any country but their own has any historical characters except Napoleon, Marie Antoinette and Hitler!

Johnnie Butler and Woodie were here and we talked of you. They came to *Winter's Tale* and saw *Waters of the Moon* [N. C. Hunter] – Sybil Thorndike is indeed fine in it. She is remarkable in damped down emotion, and surprisingly commonplace and even sometimes absurd in high tragedy, in which she revels too evidently. Her Saint Joan was fine, though years ago, and her Jane Clegg in St John Ervine's play. She has a better part than Edith in this play – a near-Chekhov, not very distinguished piece, cast up to the hilt. Edith has a showy but unconvincing character which she does marvels with, but her clothes are hideous and it is not a patch on her acting in *Daphne Laureola* which was, to my mind, a masterly performance even though the play tailed

---

* Binkie Beaumont, John Perry, Toby Rowland and Alan Webb.

off unsatisfactorily. If you see Johnnie, he could tell you better than I can about *Winter's Tale*. I wish you could see it for yourself. Most people are very enthusiastic and, like Angelo, the part is wonderfully rewarding in its concentrated emotions of tyranny succeeded by repentance, so that the audience seems to be with you all the way. Whereas in *The Lady* one felt one was liked as expositor and protagonist, yet not really a very interesting character. Fry can't make his principal personages very real. They 'carry' the play yet one is not greatly concerned with their ultimate fate, something like Shaw's leading men. Would you like to read his new play [*A Sleep of Prisoners*]? Anyway, I will send it to you as I think you may. It plays *most* fascinatingly, though I don't like sitting on hard pews in an ugly church to see acting.*

I hope to do *Much Ado* in London at Christmas – the production I did for Stratford two years running. It was a huge success and great fun for us – a lovely semi-permanent setting and costumes à la Piero della Francesca by the Spaniard Mariano Andreu – and I have a succession of outrageous hats to wear – cartwheel, blancmange, charlotte russe and finally (my own addition) a little red flowerpot at the end to show I can see the joke!

To Frith Banbury   *12 September, London*

I have read the witch play [*Darkling Child* by W. S. Merwin and Dido Milroy] twice through and am very struck with it, though I must say I fear with John, that it might not find a public. However, this is often a very silly thing to say if one likes anything good – you can imagine how often the remark was applied to *The Lady* before it came on.

I do think it would need a rather stylised production, and personally I found the scene very revolting when they talked about the food and the smell of the corpse! He could, perhaps, modify this episode, or do you think he imagines it is comic relief?

I feel Mary Merrall and Catherine Lacey would be gnashing their teeth to be at those beldams. The witch scene is somewhat reminiscent of *Dark of the Moon* [by Howard Richardson and William Berney], but in costume would not look the same. I should think it could be done in a permanent set of white walls with dark cloths and props against it to give grouping and exciting silhouettes. I would have thought Eileen Herlie would be very good for the girl, she would certainly be far better employed doing it than the ghastly Dodie Smith play she is anxious to essay.

Thank you so much for letting me read it, and I do hope you get it put on soon. I am sure it's worth the trouble, and such an author should surely be encouraged. It is nonsense for John to say it is like Fry, because there is practically no comedy, and the poetry is entirely different in style. Though I

---

* *A Sleep of Prisoners* was first performed at St Thomas's Church, Tennison Court off Regent Street, on 15 June 1951.

am no great judge of poetry it seems to me to be full of atmosphere and would, I think, be much easier to follow than Fry, and ought to be effective when spoken by actors.

Sybil and Lewis both read it and you should talk to them about it.

To Christopher Fry   *? October 1951, London*

Went to Hammersmith today – loved *Thor* [*with Angels*]. [Jack] Hawkins splendid, Jessie Evans too. But oh dear, Miss [Diana] Churchill – and Martina [Dorothy Tutin] was a disappointment too. [George] Cole is good in both plays and Michael [MacOwan] has done them very well. What a rare pleasure and sweetness to see your work and hear it after that noisome *Ardele* which I suffered on Thursday for my sins.

To Stark Young   *11 November, London*

Winter's Tale goes on finely. We break the record for the play in London next week – 166 performances – held by Forbes-Robertson and Mary Anderson in 1887. She doubled the parts of Hermione and Perdita (using a double in the last act when the girl has but a couple of speeches), an attractive idea with an actress of suitable appearance and one that was evidently popular with the public. I am also planning two other Shakespeare plays which I am to direct – *Richard the Second* with Paul Scofield, and *Macbeth* with [Ralph] Richardson and Margaret Leighton for Stratford in June, and meanwhile I am rehearsing Bobby Flemyng and a good small company in a modern comedy [*Indian Summer* by Peter Watling] which opens in two weeks time in Brighton and comes in to London before Christmas. So you see I am not idle.

Orson Welles has had a certain amount of success with his *Othello* – I have not been able to see it myself. I gather he promises better than he can perform and the thunder grumbles but never breaks, and he is ill disciplined, they say, in the theatre and something of a terror to his company and management. Still the enfant terrible of Hollywood. He amused me when I met him, but he was rather stupidly touchy and lacked humility, must have the floor all the time or he fears he is not noticed. A pity, for he is obviously extremely intelligent and full of (rather disorderly) talent in many directions.

1952

JG's revival of Much Ado about Nothing *opened at the Phoenix Theatre on 11 January 1952 with Diana Wynyard as Beatrice.*

To Peggy Ashcroft   *13 January, London*

Thank you so much for your sweet good wishes. I am very happy it has all turned out so wonderfully, though I regret I could not have shared it with you with whom I worked on it so happily. But I know you will in your generous heart rejoice at Diana's wonderful notices and her great happiness. She gives a lovely performance and has been, as always, a wonderful friend to work with.

But soon we will work together again, you and I, and you know how greatly I look forward to that. Meantime, a thousand wishes for your new play [*The Deep Blue Sea* by Terence Rattigan] and may it turn out very wonderfully for you.

To Richard Myers   *17 January, London*

I gather the season is poor in New York, though I would like to see Julie Harris.* I can't imagine what Madge [Elliott] and Cyril [Ritchard] are living on all this time, but hope they are gay and well.

I wonder if you will like Irene [Browne]. She is a very good hearted woman and a stylish actress, but what is laughingly called her own worst enemy, liable to grumble and pout and lose her sense of humour over small things, not as intelligent as Martita, but nicer natured at heart. She was a great beauty in her youth and played parts like Belladonna in Australia and I think the finger of time has been somewhat hard on her. She may amuse you and I should think New York would do her good.

We opened with *Much Ado* last Friday and have the most wonderful success with it. Almost the finest reception I ever remember, and there are queues into the street booking at the rate of £600 a day, so no doubt we have a hit on our hands and I am very thrilled and grateful. It has to come off at the end of April as I am due to direct *Macbeth* at Stratford for Richardson and Margaret Leighton, but I don't really mind that, as four months is a perfect run with a success, we shan't have time to get stale or bored. I think quite possibly we might bring it over to New York in the fall, though it is a long way to think ahead as yet.

Alas, my sister-in-law who you like so much is parting from my brother,† but we hope we shan't altogether lose sight of her as we are all so fond of her here. Marriages in this family are not markedly lasting or successful, I'm afraid.

To Stark Young   *10 May, London*

Thank you so much for two letters and the books which safely arrived and I look forward to reading them, though this will not be for a few weeks yet as

---

* Julie Harris was playing Sally Bowles in *I Am a Camera*.
† Val Gielgud was separating from his wife Rita Vale.

I am in the throes of double work. *Much Ado* seven times a week and *Macbeth*, which I am directing at Stratford. I commute two or three times a week, and we don't play Monday nights here, but it is still something of a job flashing between two completely different atmospheres, and one has to observe a rather tight schedule.

Nothing is settled yet about the autumn. In some ways I would like to come over with *Much Ado*, but at the same time I would be much more excited if a new play should come along. I am terrified of being relegated to the ranks of an inveterate classicist.

Macbeth *opened at Stratford-upon-Avon on 10 June 1952 to poor notices.*

To Christopher Fry   *16 June, London*

How nice of you to trouble to write and pour in oil and wine. I must say I did think the critics a bit too much, especially for poor Ralph, who is so much more worth watching, even when he lacks the last jump, than some conceited and showy actors we could think of. I do hope he will recover from the blows and steadfastly build up the fine things in his performance, which are many. I am desolated not to be able to see it with an audience, and give notes on pace – that is, I think, where much of the weakness lies.

The Guild are pestering for your consent for the radio adaptation of *The Lady* – to which they say you will agree if I am responsible for cuts and transpositions etc. But surely you are the one to veto this. I suggest they submit a script to you, and that you must promise to provide any narrative links or new little bits to join up where cuts don't make sense. If you leave it to them there will be a disastrous clash of styles – they even wrote in a complete new scene in the version we did of *Earnest*, which was hell! The work you would have to do would be only a matter of a few hours and you really should not give them a contract to allow them a free hand with their terrible scriptwriters.

I think it would be possible for me to do it on my way back from Hollywood in late September. But where will they get the other players? I dread a New York cast.

To Sam Wanamaker   *25 June, London*

I was most delighted to have your charming letter about the play. We dread the matinées, when we feel that people may be in front whom we would like to play our best for, and the rest of the house is sparse and apathetic. I wish you could have seen it with a really responsive audience, but fortunately we are more conscious of them than you are, seeing it for the first time.

Congratulations on your success.* I saw the play in Boston when it was first tried out there, and even dallied with the idea of trying to get it for myself for England, but feared the atmosphere would be too strange unless the locale was changed, which would have entailed considerable alterations. It must have been beautifully handled by you to avoid that difficulty, and I shall hope very much to see it later on and to have the pleasure of meeting you.

After the run of **Much Ado,** *JG was to travel to Hollywood to play Cassius in Joseph Mankiewicz's film of* **Julius Caesar.**

To Hugh Wheeler   *30 June, London*

Laurie Evans, my agent (Pam's chinless wonder) thinks he may come with me for a week and start me off as I have now become one of his important clients. Ha!! Ha! He has been trying to wangle some sort of deferred payment scheme, but it seems unless you commit yourself to an option they won't play, and I don't fancy putting my head quite so far into the jaws of the Metro Goldwyn Mayer lion, so I shall treat it as pocket money and to hell with it.

Had a wonderful day in Sussex yesterday, *Idomeneo* at Glyndebourne to finish up with. Heavy going but exquisite music and the delphiniums fantastically beautiful against yew hedges and the downs in the entr'actes, with sheep and cows nibbling at the skirts of hideous musical ladies and their still plainer escorts.

To Stark Young   *31 July, London*

The Cecil question is a vexed one. It is certainly the custom among the old aristocracy in England (what's left of it) to pronounce the name 'Sissel', but I think it would probably bewilder an American audience and would sound odd spoken with an American accent. We always say Cecil Beaton here, but his lady secretary, who is one of the old school, always refers to him as 'Sissel', so I think you pays your money and you takes your choice.

After **Much Ado about Nothing** *closed on 2 August, JG left immediately for California.*

To his mother   *6 August, Los Angeles*

I have very luxurious quarters here – two huge ground floor rooms on a patio, and thick woods and a lovely garden all round – a most imposing swimming pool, and very quiet. I had hardly unpacked before Danny Kaye rang up and

---

* *Winter Journey* by Clifford Odets also with Googie Withers and Michael Redgrave.

sent his car to take me to his house for dinner – very rich crowd and very nasty food – but everyone frightfully agreeable and welcoming, the men in sports clothes and women in deep evening dress! It is rather too hot for comfort, and the town is a horror of ugliness, flat as your hand and crawling with cars. Nobody dreams of walking anywhere and shops and houses are miles apart.

The sudden change is a bit bewildering, and I shall be glad to get over the first few days. One feels a little like a new boy at school but it is all amusingly new, though exactly like one had expected really. I think I have already persuaded them that a beard for Cassius is not a good plan.

To his mother   *9 August, Los Angeles*

The climate is really wonderful here, almost cold after 7 o'clock and cool and misty in the mornings. The sun bursts out about 10 and the middle of the day is like a perfect June in England – windless and glorious. The studios are air cooled, and I have a grand dressing room in a separate building as well as one for titivating and visiting on the set. One can have meals sent from the restaurant and, with no theatre to worry about at night, the work is leisurely and relaxed.

[James] Mason is rather nasal as Brutus, like a somewhat conscious army officer. I fear his performance as Rommel in a recent picture is still with him, but he has a fine face and will not be priggish, at least. Certainly his reading of the part is more intelligent than Harry Andrews!

[Marlon] Brando is a funny, intense, egocentric boy of 27, with a flat nose and bullet head, huge arms and shoulders, and yet giving the effect of a lean Greenwich Village college boy. He is very nervous indeed and mutters his lines and rehearses by himself all day long. Very deferential to me, and dragged me off to record two speeches of Antony on his machine, where he listens to his own voice and studies records of Larry, Barrymore, Maurice Evans etc. to improve his diction. I think his sincerity may bring him to an interesting performance – his English is not at all bad, and he is obviously very clever and ambitious. He tells me he owns a cattle ranch, and after two more years filming, will be secure financially altogether!! He belongs to a students' theatre in New York and is desperately serious about acting, but I think he has very little humour and seems quite unaware of anything except the development of his own evident talents. It will be rather fun to watch him.

[Joseph] Mankiewicz, the director, is admirable – humorous, sensitive and sensible. I like him tremendously.

Burton is a huge success here. He is making Daphne du Maurier's *My Cousin Rachel* with Ronnie Squire and Olivia de Havilland. Last night he and his wife drove me to Malibu Beach to dine with the Selznicks. She is Jennifer Jones. Chaplin was there, and I had a long and fascinating talk with him. He is prissy, weary and neat, with completely white hair and wonderful little expressive hands, and alternates between rather pretentious philosophical generalities and sudden bursts of very natural sweetness and warmth. Funny, shy, little young wife* who obviously worships him. He talked with great nostalgia of London and his young days there – seeing Tree's productions from the Gallery – and of the Irving book, which he has read. He suddenly gave a fantastic imitation of an Italian actor. How he went to see Duse, and this actor – he (Chaplin) mimed the whole thing – gave the most skilled and voluble speech which fascinated the house – twirling a chair, sitting down astride it, hands on the back, the gestures and a marvellous imitation Italian dialogue, made up to sound like the language – and suddenly there was a stirring behind the piano, some huge chrysanthemums on it moved, and the old lady suddenly appeared from a concealed entrance, and by her utter simplicity, as she first arranged the flowers, slowly sat down and held her wonderful hands towards the fire, the man was completely blotted out and forgotten by the audience in a moment. It was all so expressively described that it was quite extraordinarily vivid. I hope I shall get a chance to see his new film [*Limelight*] one day soon – he has just finished it and is, of course, mad to have opinions of it before he opens it in the audience.

The parties are grand, but clumsy – awful food, too much drink, rather noisy and the weirdest mixture of clothes, women in beach clothes or full evening dress and the men in every crazy variety of sports clothes. But it is not difficult to pick out the people one wants to talk to, and the rest of the guests don't seem to trouble one or expect one to trouble about them.

To Laurence Olivier and Vivien Leigh   *13 August, Los Angeles*

James Mason still talks through his nose and Marlon looks as if he is searching for a baseball bat to beat out his brains with.

Richard Burton is a great success in [*My Cousin*] *Rachel* and invited me to call on him and Ronnie Squire on the set. I believe Miss O[livia] de H[avilland] threw a temperament after I had gone – the first so far in this picture – but whether I was the unwitting cause is not apparently confirmed.

To Robert Flemyng   *15 August, Los Angeles*

I am beginning to enjoy myself here, and I only wish you were along to giggle with. Your friend Hugh has twice had me down to his charming house. He has a son (rather fat) and a very handsome boyfriend who flirts outrageously with me. How nice he is, and how he loves you. Allan Davis, if you please, has directed a picture at MGM† (but I don't think it is a success) and has a sweet little house up in the hills, where I was bidden to a small boys' party

---

* Chaplin had married Eugene O'Neill's daughter Oona in 1943.
† Probably *Rogue's March*.

(the party, not the boys) the other night. Peter Watling is staying with him, and Rex Evans and Richard Cromwell (no longer so pretty or prosperous, alas!) were also there.

Johnnie Fever has come to be my bonne à toute faire, and drives me around in the car I have hired, which is very agreeable for me, and everyone rings up and invites me out. Spent last evening with the Grangers* and Deborah and her husband† in a strange restaurant where we had Cantonese food and Jamaica Rum cocktails – a somewhat dangerous mixture.

To his mother   *16 August, Los Angeles*

I have been to half a dozen parties, with all the Hollywood knobs [*sic*], and everyone is very agreeable, though the conversation is pretty local and one begins to scent the jealousies and disappointments and ambitions much as in the theatre, only rather more concentrated out here, like actors crossed with Anglo-Indian civil servants who have a perpetual chip on their shoulders!

I dined with the [William] Goetzes who have fabulous pictures – Matisse, van Gogh, Daumier, Picasso etc. and afterwards we sat in a vast room heavy with these masterpieces – and one wall slowly rose into the air with half a dozen masterpieces securely screwed into it, like the flap of a dining table, so that a film projector could emerge from behind! Soft music played, the lights dimmed and a screen descended through the ceiling. The film they showed us was, unfortunately, the musical version of *Charley's Aunt*, which is vulgar without being in the least funny, and let down the tone of the proceedings in magnificent anti-climax. It was quite an experience, and with all the showing-off and bad taste they suddenly endear themselves by getting up and making embarrassingly cordial speeches at the end of dinner, welcoming the principal guests and so on.

Tonight I go to the ballet in the Hollywood Bowl which is, I believe, a most beautiful open-air setting. The houses and gardens in this part of the town are really lovely – beautifully designed either in modern style or in imitation Spanish, American Colonial, Tudor, Regency etc., and though the final result is rather artificial, they have great charm in their cleanliness, bright colours and elaborately kept gardens and lawns. And everything seems to grow, from roses and carnations to palm trees, hibiscus and jasmine. Everyone is brightly dressed in rather outlandish beach clothes of brilliant colours, everyone is sunburnt and looks healthy, there is abundance of everything – the fruit and flowers and vegetables laid out open in the markets, and there is endless variety of design in the shop fronts and windows, like an exhibition at Earls Court that has only been put up for a month or two and will be torn down and rebuilt next year.

---

* Stewart Granger and Jean Simmons.
† Deborah Kerr and Anthony Bartley.

My costumes are very fine, also my wig. We have done tests both with and without beard. I think I look like the 13th apostle in the beard, and much too noble and Biblical, and hope when they see the tests next week on the screen that they will agree to discard it. Perhaps a bit of stubble in the scenes where I wear the armour may be a successful compromise. Anyway, I do not think they will insist on my playing in a make-up I do not feel happy in, and, as Brando and Mason wear so little, I am sure it will mar the general effect if I am obviously reeking of the make-up room.

To his mother   *26 August, Los Angeles*

I have taken a little house, really two bungalows, and am moving there on Wednesday. It is extremely cheap, quite simple and comfortable, and it seems silly now that I have had the fun of two weeks in this hotel, to go on spending so much money on bed and breakfast, which is all it comes to really now that I am beginning to work every day. My secretary will have his own quarters and we are a hiring a cook – valeting, cleaning, laundry etc. are all available and much cheaper too, of course, than in an hotel, so I think it is a very good plan and I might stay on there for a week or two after the picture is finished instead of trailing all the way to Europe, where one can never trust the weather! Here it is sunshine the entire time and there are endless places to drive to – country, beaches and so on, and I want to go to San Francisco for a weekend some time.

Today they began to shoot the film and I watched the opening scene with real sheep, pigeons, goats and dirty water running in the gutters. Herbert Tree's ghost must have breathed approval. Of course nobody speaks very well and the accents sound a bit peculiar – 'May the GUDS so stead me' – and so on, but the acting generally is no worse than the American company I acted with in *Hamlet*, and Mason, with whom I have all my scenes, will be quite good. He has pace and style and phrases intelligently. [Louis] Calhern very ham as Caesar and the ladies English but rather simpering and affected, I'm afraid.

Lavish entertaining still continues, and I have dined out every single night. The quality varies, naturally, but quite a few people are intelligent and nice, and they love to display their elaborate homes, which are all like sets in a play, and everyone drinks for an hour before dinner, nibbling at elaborate canapés and appetisers and *then* they sit down to an enormous meal.

To his mother   *30 August, Los Angeles*

I have seen some 'rushes' but only feel dismayed, as I always do, by the telltale eye of the camera which registers fatally the slightest slip, hesitation or lack of concentration and I catch myself pursing my lips and making what J.P. calls my Shylock face. Technically the work is extremely difficult, and I am only glad that Mason is very skilled at it and keeps me in balance by a very steady, relaxed performance which I think should make a much better foil to mine than Harry Andrews' sonorous showiness which I always hated. Everyone is, of course, madly impressed because I can rip off the long speeches with such speed and accuracy without losing the meaning, but I think I overact and don't quite know how to avoid doing so without losing urgency.

Why not let me give you a nice little holiday at the Hyde Park Hotel? It would give me so much pleasure, and I could claim it off my Income Tax!

To his mother   *11 September, Los Angeles*

We are now at the killing of Caesar, a very messy proceeding – the daggers spout mock blood which splashes over clothes and faces, and then they want to photograph the scene again from another angle and everyone has to wash and change and make up all over again, making endless delays on to the already tedious procedure.

The nicest Hollywood gag I have heard so far happened the other day, when the live pigeons were sitting patiently all day on the plinths and columns of the Forum. They are apparently clipped so that they can't fly about, but one daring bird was bold enough to flutter to the pavement, where he was strutting about. The cowboy character who looks after the animals noticed him and went over and was heard to remark severely 'Now get back up there. Go on, didn't you hear me? Don't you want to work tomorrow?'

So sad, Gertie Lawrence's sudden death [6 September], like Novello's at the height of her career.

To Hugh Wheeler   *September 1952, Hollywood*

I have one more day, then nearly a week off, then the tent and battle stuff which will be hell, as the armour weighs a ton, ditto the helmet (Tweedledum's coalscuttle) and there is a HORSE somewhere in the middle distance to be coped with, principally, I trust, by my dear double.

We thought to go to Yosemite and back by the Redwoods, Carmel and Monterey. I am told it is quite needlessly extravagant to book at the Mark Hopkins. One should just dump one's baggage at the Y. and move in to Jack's Baths for the nights. We should also visit the Opera, I understand, but if so, does one sit primly in a good seat or is there delicious wandering behind the partition which I have always been led to understand is the great attraction at the Met!

To Edith Sitwell   *23 September, Los Angeles*

There was a rumour going about that you might be coming here to give historical advice on a film of *Fanfare for Elizabeth*. Can this be true? I fear you would find it terrifyingly unreal though, as always, there are one or two kindred spirits to be found amidst the milling hordes of vulgarians. The climate is divine, and the working people (crew in the studio and the simpler folk) are kind and very efficient. But the rich and fashionable higher group are, on the whole, appalling, though hospitable in a wild way.

The film is, on the whole, dignified and the director civilised, which makes a great difference, though I fear it will be overlaid with the over-smooth veneer which is the symbol of all the big companies of Hollywood. They fear anything rough or 'arty' and will probably achieve both qualities in the wrong way. But I hope at least the text, though cut severely, will all be Shakespeare's, and the Brutus, with whom I share all my scenes, is human and not priggish and has an English voice.

To his mother   *23 September, Los Angeles*

All thanks for your most amusing and descriptive letters about the Lunts' play.* I am sorry for Noël that the press has been so bad for him, but it seems as if his early brilliance cannot find a stronger phase as he gets older, and I fear he suffers from his own inability to judge his work dispassionately. His friends too, do not criticise him with any discrimination and he is very obstinate, though I think he is less arrogant than people think.

Mankiewicz is very nice indeed and talks of wanting to film *Much Ado* in England. It might perhaps be interesting if one could also plan it with him on the lines of the production I did which he admired very much. The attacks in the Press upon Chaplin, now that he has left, are very violent and hysterical. I am glad to see a kinder attitude in a note in the *Observer*, and hope his reputation in London will console him. I should think it would be just as well if he did remain in Europe, though it would be a big wrench for him after 40 years in America.† He told me he does not see Aldous [Huxley] any more – evidently they have had a row of some sort, but Chaplin is appallingly touchy and it is very difficult to say the right thing to him on any subject, even himself! So he is probably largely to blame for all the trouble.

I am to meet Stravinsky at lunch today, which may be interesting.

To his mother   *4 October, Los Angeles*

We are now on our last three days of shooting, and I am growing my beard for the end and look like a burglar or the thirteenth Apostle. The tent scene came off pretty well, though I blink and fidget still in close-ups and my eyes

---

* *Quadrille* by Noël Coward opened at the Phoenix Theatre on 12 September 1952. The press were complimentary about the Lunts but critical of the play.
† Chaplin was barred re-entry to the United States after being accused of having Communist sympathies by the Committee on Un-American Activities.

wander as if I was looking to see if a policeman was coming to arrest me. Mason is so steady and clear in his facial acting that I get very jealous. He gives such a good performance of Brutus and will, I think, make a great success in that difficult part. If they cut me cleverly, I think I may pass muster but I hope they won't think I give a theatrical and over vehement performance. I have seen nothing of Brando's scenes, but they say his Forum scene is fine.

I am looking forward to finishing here, though I have enjoyed all the people's company with whom I have worked – much nicer on the whole than the society high-ups – a little of them goes a very long way – and the English who are voluntary exiles have become extremely complicated and unsatisfactory, even the nicest of them.

To his mother   *10 October, Los Angeles*

Yesterday I did my last day's work on the picture – location shots for the battle. Behold me on horseback, biting the dust under a shower of arrows, and fighting hand to hand with shield and broadsword in a very dusty quarry under the blazing noonday sun. I stood it with remarkable sang-froid, and it is an amazing sight to see such big scale tactics in progress – cranes, horses, lighting equipment, food, tents etc. all sent down and manoeuvred (with endless delays and appalling noise and chaos) throughout the day. But they got everything they needed and I am completely free at last. So we are off to spend the night at Yosemite and on to San Francisco for the weekend.

To his mother   *19 October,* The Chief

Riding across America in this very de luxe train – technicolour sunsets over [illegible] vast and deserts idle. We stop at Chicago tomorrow for six hours before moving on to New York. I love the cleanliness and good food and service – one of the best and most modern luxuries of the U.S.

I seem to have acquired a great deal more stuff, but fortunately MGM is paying excess baggage.

I went to the *Don Juan in Hell* [by Bernard Shaw] reading, with [Charles] Laughton, [Charles] Boyer, [Cedric] Hardwicke and Agnes Moorehead in Los Angeles before I left, but I found it a most affected exhibition of faked spontaneity and a terrific bore, as I am no Shaw addict anyway. However, it was packed to the roof and the audience adored every minute of it. I also saw the rough cut of *Caesar* – up to the Forum scene, and on the whole was not displeased with it. It seems to me to be quite lively, dignified and vivid, and though personally I think Calhern is dreadful as Caesar, the plot comes over very clearly and the poetry not at all badly. I could not judge Brando's Antony in such a short bit as I saw, but Mason and I do seem to be all right, and the Casca [Edmond O'Brien] is excellent. I have great hopes of it on the whole.

Returning to England, JG embarked on his season of classical plays at the Lyric Theatre, Hammersmith, with Paul Scofield. Richard II, directed by Gielgud and with Scofield in the title role, opened on 24 December 1952.

To Robert Flemyng   26 December, London

I was so touched at your thinking of me and sending me the fine cheese all the way from U.S. I hope you are enjoying things better now that Carmen and your daughter have come to cheer you – and I am sure Kit and Guthrie will have exerted themselves to the full to give you a festive Christmas. I only got a glance at Chicago en route back from California and was enormously impressed with the pictures in the big gallery – also the camp of the Pump Room with Mrs Siddons on the dinner plates and the footmen with crew cuts and silk knee breeches! To say nothing of the D.A.R.* champing over their salads and sirloin.

Last night there was a great tamasha at Lord North St. Johnnie [Perry] is fairly perky despite his tragic time in Ireland, where he found his poor old Mum quite non compos, and had a horrid fall (J.P. did) and nearly broke his bloody neck, which gives him a good deal of pain. Mrs Lunt was looking terrific last night, with one tit provokingly popping in and out. Noël, Joyce [Carey] and Adrianne [Allen] disciplining strictly in 'The Game' and me slyly flirting with Graham [Payn] and P[eter] Glenville whenever their husbands' backs were turned!

Richard opened well on Christmas Eve and Paul had a great ovation. Now for *Way of the World* [by William Congreve] which we begin to rehearse on the 5th or so. We have a very fine cast for it, and Mrs [James] Bailey† has run up some entrancing frock designs and delicious sets, so it should look well at any rate.

1953

To Vivien Leigh   6 January, London

You do remember everything, kind friend. Your pin is in my tie, your berries on the piano, the butter in the frig. and at any moment now, the ointment will be dripping from my horny hand – so you can see on every side I am beholden to you, and I had such a divine weekend – cut and thrust, hot and cold, sweet and sour, comfort, causerie and complication. Thank you.

---

* Daughters of the American Revolution.
† Male homosexual slang often refers to individuals in this way – cf Mrs [Arthur] Marshall.

To Stark Young   *17 February, London*

I'm so glad you like the Denton Welch Journals. There is now a collected edition of his work – three or four novels – which I will have sent to you. He had a frightful accident, it appears, was run over and only existed in appalling pain and recurrent illness for a few years. I never knew him, but he had, of course, a great succès de scandale in the great world with his outspoken homosexual atmosphere and tastes. Edith Sitwell was his just cicerone, but I have never asked her about him. I believe he was rather odious because of his neuroses, but I have always been fascinated by his talent.

I am to fly to Bulawayo in Rhodesia in July to play Richard the Second for a week at the Rhodes Centenary celebrations, which may be fun, except that they are building a theatre to seat 3000! We open tomorrow with *The Way of the World* which we played last week at Brighton with much success and I got some good rehearsals and improved it all greatly with familiarity and general tidying up. I think it is a much simpler and lighter production than *Love for Love* – all summery – light costumes, delicate drop scenes, very little furniture and stage business – much spoken straight on to the audience, which is essential with such a wordy and involved text. Mirabell is not much of a part, but I am beginning to enjoy it for the sake of the style and balance with the other parts.

On 25 February JG's eldest brother Lewis died in Paris following an operation.

To Stark Young   *1 March, London*

The beautiful scarf arrived yesterday in its elegant envelope of Tiepolo. I like it so much, both the pattern and the lovely material and shall love to wear it and especially in reminder of you – not English, is it?

Our Congreve has gone off well, though with very controversial notices. I was appallingly nervous on the opening night and made slips and hesitations in my short part, which did not help the confidence either of myself or the other players. But we are packed out at every performance and I do think the balance and ensemble very successful and we have an enchanting décor. We start work on *Venice Preserv'd* [by Thomas Otway] in April and play it for May, June and July. It is rather a fearsome melodrama, but I hope may prove effective and curious under Peter Brook's direction.

To Noël Coward   *5 May, Brighton*

Your azalea was a dream of beauty, but as soon as it saw me undressed – and I really cannot blame it – withered and shrank like a parable in the Bible! I am happy to report, however, that a night immersion – and possibly my pretty transformation into a tragic juvenile – revived its drooping spirits to a surprising degree and today it blooms again in pristine splendour. I think it must have missed *you* at first.

I hear nothing but superlatives of *The Apple Cart* [by Bernard Shaw] and Magnus* – and we had a very nice opening waltz ourselves, I'm happy to say, so perhaps May is not to be an unhappy month as the cherry stones prophesied. Couldn't you dash off a little repartee of some comic import for me to do with Larry at the Midnight Matinée?† Otherwise I would do the Bag scene with Edith from *Importance* if Gingold, who is supposed to be appearing with her in a sketch, should remain indisposed. Or what?

Venice Preserv'd *opened at the Lyric, Hammersmith, on 15 May 1953.*

To Edith Sitwell   *30 May, London*

I am more flattered than I can say that you should have thought of me for Henry, and I always loved your seeing so much of Lear in him, but, alas, for the screen [*Fanfare for Elizabeth*] it would be a physical impossibility. My tallness, beaky nose and general air of diffident arrogance (!) would betray me at once. You *must* have a man of something near the right build and cast of features – small eyes and mouth, stocky, athletic, these things even make-up wizards cannot accomplish, and a lot of maquillage and padding on the screen destroys all authenticity and turns actors into unconvincing dummies.

I should say Richard Burton is your man – stocky, Welsh, tough, yet beautiful in repose – only he is a bit phlegmatic and may lack power and aristocratic authority. But on the screen all that could easily be emphasised with close-ups and clever photography and direction. Besides this, he is the new rage, and *really* a good actor, intelligent, sensitive and full of potentialities. I am sure you ought to try and get him. He will soon be back in England – he is playing Hamlet at Edinburgh and later at the Old Vic. Do make a point of seeing him play and meeting him – I believe it would be both an artistic *and* commercial triumph to have him for the part even if it means waiting for a year.

Meanwhile, remember me if you want a Philip of Spain or Charles the Second – which I could play in bed – with tears and fainting fits to satisfaction! But alas, alas, no Tudors.

After Laughton – who is Henry to the World (!!!) it would be so much better to have a very handsome *young* man in complete contrast – don't you think?

JG received a knighthood in the Coronation Honours List in 1953.

---

* Coward had just opened as King Magnus at the Theatre Royal, Haymarket.
† *Stars at Midnight*, a gala night in aid of the Actors' Orphanage and the Jewish National Fund Charitable Trust. JG appeared with John Mills and Laurence Olivier in a number called 'Three Juvenile Delinquents' from Coward's musical comedy, *Ace of Clubs*.

To Edith Evans   *3 June, London*

I am very proud to be in such a noble company, and will do my best to be a credit to you all. Your fine example and brilliant achievements are something to wonder at, and it is a very great day for me to join you, and to have you for a friend. Thank you for being so pleased for me.

To the Lunts   *3 June, London*

Your congratulations mean so very much to me. I am overwhelmed by the kindness of all my dear friends – so many that I knew I had and many more that I am so glad to know are pleased. But above all you two brilliant and heavenly artists who are such an example and inspiration to us all.

To Edith Evans   *9 July, London*

Peter Brook was recently in Vence and brought me messages of greeting from Edward Gordon Craig, who, at the age of 82 is living in one room in the South of France on a very tiny income.

Peter and I discussed the possibility of some kind of Charity Performance for his benefit, but felt he was only a name to the majority of theatrical people today, and that we could hardly ask them to give their services. But it seemed to me that if we could send him a cheque in honour of his 80th birthday, with the signatures of a dozen leading theatrical personalities, it would be a gesture of admiration which would mean much to him, apart from the material advantage.

Sidney Bernstein, an old friend of Craig's, has given me a most generous cheque to start the ball rolling. I wonder if I might ask you to let me have £5 so that this small sum from each of you would, with Sidney's cheque, easily make the £100, which is the total I am hoping to be able to send.

Please for give my trespassing on your generosity and time.

The season at the Lyric, Hammersmith, finished on 11 July, after which JG flew to Bulawayo to play Richard II.

To his mother   *21 July, Bulawayo*

Madness. Madness. Icy cold. But the audience huddled in rugs and overcoats and I really thought the last act would never end. However, they sat through it like Trojans and couldn't have been more enthusiastic or attentive. Great rounds on every exit and scene change, but of course the long distances on the stage slowed it all up – the speaking too – so that we played till 11.30 (beginning at 8.15).

Idiotic conditions everywhere – Tottenham Court Road hotel – hot water on and off, more generally off – the simplest order wrong – called at 6.30 instead of 9 – no spoons – an hour to get a cup of tea sent up – everything shut at 9 so that there are no supper facilities of any kind – now today [Herbert] Lomas is ill with blood pressure and I fear won't be able to play tonight.

J.P. is very good in this kind of emergency do – his Irish philosophy laughs off the difficulties and with Alison [Colvil], who is always a wonder of Scotch imperturbability and warmheartedness, we manage very well. It is quite good for one to be shaken out of one's luxury-loving orderliness and be forced to improvise and put up with a little inconvenience.

I dread going out and have refused several invitations. Boring strangers would be more than I can bear, even with the lure of a decent meal! I think I shall diet strictly till we leave – it will be good for my figure. David Webster arrived yesterday – he is really an epicure and what *he* will do for food, I can't imagine.

To his mother   *24 July, Bulawayo*

Poor David has 200 people to cope with – opera singers, orchestra and chorus and *four* operas to present, including *Gloriana* [by Benjamin Britten], which I should think they will hate. Also he has to stay two or three *weeks* – and he is far more of a sybarite than I am!

The people are kindly, but with the usual small town defensive attitude. They like to pretend they are very critical and unimpressed – at the same time they are pathetically anxious to acquire a reputation for hospitality and to be thought welcoming and appreciative. Their first question is always 'Are you pleased with your reception?' rather than 'We did enjoy the performance'.

To his mother   *26 July, Bulawayo*

We visited a Mission where a strange man trains the 100 young natives in his care to draw and paint, without models or books or any derivative influence. They have drawn murals all over the walls of the chapel, inside and out, illustrating Bible stories in their own childlike idiom – some quite beautiful like Matisse and Rousseau – all curious and touching. Saints and Virgins and Christs – all black types – and some in modern dress extremely original and striking. The man, Patterson, trained in London, was a friend of Middleton Murry and knows Sybil Thorndike, with whose enthusiasm and altruism he has much in common.

Returning from Bulawayo, JG had a holiday in Rex Harrison's house in Italy.

To Stark Young   *15 August, Portofino*

The knighthood was a great experience not only in itself, but in the wonderful affection of so many friends, and I had the real pleasure of reading all sorts of nice things about myself that I only expected *might* possibly be said if I were to drop down dead! At the same time they gave me a D. Litt. Degree at Oxford, the first ever bestowed on an actor, and in some ways a more rare and distinguished compliment. So I have been greatly spoilt one way and another. Only it was all at the end of the long and arduous Hammersmith season and I was rather tired and in need of a rest. Now I am having it in this lovely place, and go on next month to Grasse, where I have a villa for September. After that I rehearse a new play [*A Day by the Sea*] by the man who wrote *Waters of the Moon* [N. C. Hunter], my first modern dress piece for 15 years – a pseudo-Chekhovian conversational study with a fine cast. Ralph Richardson, Sybil Thorndike, Irene Worth (who was in *The Cocktail Party* in N.Y.) and Lewis Casson. My part, a rather embittered diplomat who ought to have married long ago, but preferred his career which, it turns out, is not as successful as he thought it would be! It is well written, though no masterpiece, and will I think be interesting to direct if the parts come out as well as they read. I only agreed to play it for six months.

Meanwhile I took the liberty of giving your address to Alan Dent, an erudite and charming Scotsman who is the 'Jock' of Jimmie Agate's 'Ego' books. He was J.'s secretary for many years, then became critic of the *News Chronicle*. He goes to N.Y. for four months this September to report on the American Theatre, and I am sure you will like each other.

On Monday I go over to Rapallo to call on Max Beerbohm. I hear he remains perky and delightful even since his wife's death two years ago – and in France I shall meet Gordon Craig, whom I have not seen since 1931. He writes gaily, but I fear has rather a struggle for existence in his old age.

I wish you could have seen *Venice Preserv'd* – it came out quite astonishingly effectively thanks to Peter Brook's brilliant direction, and I achieved some brutal but necessary cutting which enabled it to avoid ridicule in the sentimental passages. The lewd scenes between the harlot and the old Senator went enormously well, and Scofield was splendid as Pierre. We played it in a simple Guardi–Piranesi setting with low arches which sank and rose to give different height, and one painted drop of the great hall of the Doge's Palace (with figures *painted* on it) was beautiful and strikingly original. I had a powdered wig and a black and gold suit, and Belvidera 'stark mad in white satin' – we quite looked like the Zoffany pictures of Garrick and Mrs Cibber.

To Hugh Wheeler   *28 August, Venice*

Fancy me after the African jungle, two Comets, Rome and Portofino, ensconced here with Cecil Beaton and – Truman [Capote], who has become a great chum! I have dined with the Windsors – the horror of it – revelled with the Rex Harrisons (who I think are *dears*), spent a fortnight with Binkie and John, and thought of you very often, particularly yesterday when it poured with rain as we know it only can here! On Monday, after a party at the Volpi Palace, I go to Grasse by train to meet Eleanor, Bernie and Esmé [Percy] at the Castello Opio, which we have for a month – it should be restful and relaxing, if Miss Dodge doesn't learn too much French temperament to add to her Scandinavian and American relish, and will only lack your sweetness to complete the house party. Well, I can't concentrate, and I must go to the Lorenzo Lotto Exhibition and find the Carpaccio Chapel again, and cruise a little too and admire the Italian Packets. Such a lot to tell you, and I *can't* write letters.

Did you know that Cecil Rhodes – yes Sarah Gertrude Millin says so – didn't after all say 'So much to do, so little done.' No, his final words were far more poignant, more human. He turned to one of his secretaries and murmured 'Turn me over, Jack!!' So you see how Africa speaks.

To Cecil Beaton   *2 September, Grasse*

All thanks for your farewell note. You were whirling so vivaciously in the arms of Anne Marie that I had not the heart to disturb you with farewells and banal expressions of thanks for all your good company and sympathetic discourse throughout our meetings and journeying. I am sure you know how much your presence and friendship added in pleasure to my holiday, especially with such a one as Truman to complete our so fashionable threesome.

You left some bathing things and your coffee-coloured gabardine suit at the hotel, and I prevailed on Chips [Channon] to bring them back for you rather than risk the uncertainties of parcel post. So ask him for them when you (and he) get back.

Fulco [di Verdura] referred to the Volpi Ball as a Rat's Fuck. Of course, Chips thought the Bastagni dinner divinely chic, but what with the smells from the canal and the odour of mortality emanating from all those elderly aristocrats, I confess I found it almost terrifyingly moribund and should not have been surprised if the whole palace had slowly sunk in to the mud and vanished amid a gutter of candles and the cries of the veteran élite. You and I of course (and perhaps the pretty Baron Rudy [?]) would have been saved by the two handsomest gondoliers on the premises and supported to safety in dripping triumph.

I had a filthy day-long train journey here, but it is rather a fascinating villa – once monastic – rather sad and a bit ghost-ridden but full of character. We go to see Gordon Craig tomorrow. See you soon I hope, and we will have a nice game of Lorenzo Lotto (like the last act of *The Seagull*) and talk everything over in retrospect. Perhaps you will let me come and see your garden one fine October Sunday and we can draw some conclusions on our summer solstice. Hope your trip to Paris is a pleasant interlude before you trek back to the English scene.

To Cecil Beaton   *8 September, Grasse*

Many thanks for your letter and for sending the cheque so promptly. I do hope you have found all well at Pelham St and in the country, and are relaxing in your garden after all the excitement. The house and party seem so far to be a great success and it is not as expensive here as I had feared.

Paul Anstee* sends you the enclosed for your album.

Gordon Craig was very picturesque – in a huge straw hat, a sort of surgeon's white overall with a turned up collar à la William Nicholson, and a white burnous thrown over one shoulder and tucked across his lap so that he could adjust his truss at meal times with discretion – toothless and deaf, but with exquisite long white silky hair and prodigious vitality and appetite. Living in a sad little room of a clean but arid pension surrounded by exquisite carving tools and little book covers and collections of theatrical archives of every sort. Talked wonderfully well and *far* more vitality than Max. I wish you could have been with us to meet him. We saw the Picasso ceramics and drawings in the Antibes museum, very exciting and beautifully shown in white walled rooms with thick loopholes looking out on the sea. Otherwise I have eschewed the coast, but we are going to take a motorboat one evening and go to St Tropez.

My love to you – I miss you very much.

After his holiday, JG began rehearsals for A Day by the Sea *by N. C. Hunter which he directed and in which he also played. In October he was arrested in Chelsea for soliciting and fined £10. Many of his friends wrote letters of sympathy and support. After his conviction, the production went on a four-week pre-London tour.*

To Noël Coward   *22 October, London*

Ever thoughtful and kind friend – you shame me by your wonderful sympathy and understanding. I suppose it might have been worse, and I must try now to justify the superb faith of my dear friends by going on with the play as if nothing had happened. I know you would do the same.

Thank you.

* A young designer and decorator who had worked with Beaton. His relationship with JG began in the early 1950s and continued for a number of years. Although their physical relationship came to an end, Paul Anstee remained a close friend and confidant and is one of JG's executors.

To Cecil Beaton   *28 October, Liverpool*

Thank you very much for writing. It's so hard to say what I feel – to have let down the whole side – the theatre, my friends, myself and my family – and all for the most idiotic and momentary impulse. Of course I've been tortured by the thought that I acted stupidly *afterwards*, insisting on tackling it without advice of any kind – but I expect it would all have come out anyway – and I just couldn't bear the idea of a case and weeks of obscene publicity – even if I had got off with a clean sheet the slur would still have been there, and everyone would have gossiped and chattered. As it is – well, I can only feel that I've been spoilt and protected all my life and now it's something basic and far-reaching that I've got to face for many years to come. The miracle is that my friends have stood by me so superbly, and even the public looks like letting me go on with my work. Both things would not have been so twenty years ago (though I don't think either the press would have been so cruelly open).

There are many other things to be thankful for. For one, I don't think my Mother has realised the full significance of it, or else she's the most wonderful actress in the Terry Family! For another, I wasn't actually playing in London at the time, and these four weeks of the tour are a sort of test both as regards the public and my own nerves. There are some tricky lines in the play, but many are also compassionate and charming, and the character I play has sympathy without seeming to ask for it too much. That is all to the good.

To Laurence Olivier   *21 November, London*

Your constant thought of me in my travail with all you have of your own to worry about has touched me so deeply – I cannot tell you how I have been helped and encouraged and above all by you and Viv and Ralph and Mu* – all of you have shown such heavenly tact and sympathy, the kind one can never forget or thank for adequately.

A Day by the Sea *opened at the Theatre Royal, Haymarket, on 26 November 1953.*

To Meriel Forbes, Lady Richardson   *27 November, London*

Your friendship has been so very dear to me these last weeks – your exquisite tact and sweetness – and of course Ralph has been the most superb friend. I can never tell you what it has meant to me to know you did not want to stop knowing me, and that you could still find it in your heart to spend time encouraging and cheering me when I needed it so badly. I do hope the notices

---

* Ralph Richardson's second wife, Meriel Forbes.

have not disappointed you – the only *real* comfort has been Ralph's success, which is as undisputed as it is brilliant. I never stop thanking the Gods for such friendship and loyalty as you both have given me so freely.

To Edith Evans   *27 November, London*

Thank you for your wire which was very precious to me last night. You know I love you as a woman, and esteem you greater than any living player, and I could not have borne to feel that you no longer wanted to know me or look on me as a friend.

Strange are the ways of experience – but you know that better than anyone – and I hope you will believe that I have learned some truth, however bitterly, along with a wonder at the intrinsic fairness of human beings even in bad times. So much has happened, vile things and glorious kindnesses all mixed together in a few short weeks. I hope to sort it all out and learn from it in days to come.

To Stark Young   *1 December, London*

We opened last week in the new N. C. Hunter play, which has had a superb reception, and will, I think, be a big hit, though the critics find it lacking in power and inconclusive – as indeed it is. However, it gives fine parts to all the players, and the teamwork is beautiful. I know it wouldn't do for America, but it is the kind of thing they like here very much, and I think it has been a good idea for me to play in modern dress again after so long in costume. [*Julius*] *Caesar* is playing just across the road, so I can hardly fail to be in the public eye one way and another.

Unfortunately I have been in it a great deal too much lately, a disagreeable incident of which no doubt rumours may have reached you. I can't write about it, for it has been very loathsome, and might have had even worse repercussions than it has, but I did as I thought best in the circumstances to get it all over quickly. Unfortunately the press got hold of it, and blew it up to terrifying proportions and the world repercussion has not been pleasant. It may affect my coming to the States next year with Stratford, but they have been very charming to me about it, and are waiting to decide for a few weeks until everything is more settled and further in the distance.

To Stark Young   *31 December, London*

The play goes enormously well here, and the picture is still running across the road. The Stratford people have decided that I shall not go there after all for the end of their summer season, and then on to America for the tour. This is something of a disappointment, of course, but at the same time I feel rather relieved at not having to bear the responsibility, or come up against any possible check through the press or the Immigration people. Everyone has been awfully nice about it, and the inquiries in high places were all very favourably received. I was to have left this play in June in order to get a holiday, and then go to Stratford, but now I may stay on a few months longer.

Mankiewicz started his own independent company in Italy, and spoke to me a few weeks ago of being anxious to make another classic with me and (conceivably) Audrey Hepburn. He suggested *Twelfth Night* but I tried very hard to woo him to the idea of *The School for Scandal*, which I have long thought might be an excellent vehicle for the screen, especially with an all-English star cast. For on the stage one can never afford to cast it up to the hilt, whereas even the smallest parts could be played by stars in a picture. Sheridan's style is so much more leisurely than Shakespeare's as regards construction, and would allow of cuts and transpositions without harming the quality of the text. The order of scenes – so important in Shakespeare – matters far less in Sheridan, and the humour seems to me universally comprehensible today for audiences everywhere, whereas in Shakespeare – particularly the comedies – there are so many archaic jokes that you have to keep cutting or leaving dead wood, especially with the low comedy parts and passages. I hope he may see the force of this, and possibly let me work with him on the adaptation, for I would dearly like to have a say in the scenery of such a picture and not only play a part in it. Joseph Surface would be a most effective contrast to Cassius, and I think it more suited to me than Malvolio, but we shall see.

1954

*To Zita Gielgud**   *9 January, London*

It was very sweet of you to leave me those things of Lewis' – I am so pleased to have them in memory of him. I feel very sad to think he was in an unhappy state those last two years, and that we never got to know each other really well. But as a family we are, as you know, crippled by self-consciousness and find it incredibly difficult to break through our shyness, especially with one another.

It was good to see Maina so confident and happy in her enthusiasm and promise, and I did so enjoy taking her out and getting to know her a little, and I think Mother had a very happy day too.

---

* Zita Gielgud is the widow of JG's brother Lewis who had died in February 1953. Maina is their daughter.

To Richard Myers   *4 March, London*

Caesar has been, and still is, so enormously successful everywhere. Did I tell you The Players Club refused to let me resign – they made me an honorary member there in 1936, and have never let me even pay dues – and that touched me so very much – to feel the American actors could still respect me.

During the run of A Day by the Sea, *JG directed* The Cherry Orchard *at the Lyric, Hammersmith.*

To Hugh Wheeler   *6 August, London*

The play settled down again after the loss of Sybil and Lewis,* but now Ralph [Richardson] has had a domestic tragedy culminating in attempted suicide (what a play this is for apt quotations!) and a discovered love affair† – all most melodramatic and of course it has to be covered up, not discussed and kept out of the press at all costs, so that has not made any of us very cheerful.

I am supposed to do Clarence‡ but it seems the money is not yet guaranteed, though they are scheduled to begin Bosworth Field (in Spain) next month. If it *is* done, Ralph may play Buckingham and we might close the play in October and I might get a holiday by the end of that month.

Bernie has had a typically disastrous week in Cornwall, culminating in being thrown out of the hotel for asking for a different menu to the English boiled chicken and cauliflower! You can imagine the scene. He is still implacably hostile to poor Paul [Anstee], so my life continues in a somewhat disjointed fashion between Mrs Keppel and Queen Alexandra. Trevor Howard leaves *The Cherry Orchard* this week to do a film, so I've had to rehearse a new Lopakhin (Brewster Mason). He is not bad, but business has already dropped, and I fear they will only run on for another week or two at most. Peggy follows in as Hedda early in September. She is said to be superb, despite a muddled and inefficient director (Peter Ashmore, who made such a hash of *Three Sisters* two years ago). The new Rattigan one act plays§ (two episodes of one story) are brilliant, I believe – Eric Portman, Kay Walsh and Phyllis Neilson-Terry, P. Glenville directing – they are in rehearsal now. No plans for next year at all. Peter Brook is over engaged, so can't do *Othello* for me as I hoped he might – he is to do *Titus Andronicus* at Stratford with the Oliviers. Made great friends with Marlene [Dietrich] while she was here – do you know

---

* Sybil Thorndike and Lewis Casson left the production in June for a British Council tour of Australia.
† Richardson's wife, Meriel Forbes, had a brief affair with the director Garson Kanin. Sir Ralph bought a gun and Mr Kanin left for America. I am indebted to Bryan Forbes for this background.
‡ In Olivier's film of *Richard III*.
§ *Separate Tables.*

her? Unfortunately she always had Ken Tynan in tow, which cramped my style. Didn't think much of her act but she seemed a pet to meet.

To Robert Speaight   *8 August, London*

Thank you so very much for sending me the Poel book.* I am quite enthralled by it and have ordered several copies for friends who I know will be interested. Frankly I imagined it an almost impossible task when you told me of the project. You have, to my mind, achieved a remarkable picture and a thrilling record which will appeal to all modern Shakespeare enthusiasts and make Poel a great deal more to people than the vaguely pedantic figure which I, for one, had imagined him to be. And to think one might have worked with him and known him – how one regrets lost opportunities of one's youthful unawareness.

To Hugh Wheeler   *10 August, London*

I shall be free for certain by the second week of December and as I'm going to direct *Twelfth Night* for the Oliviers at Stratford for their opening there in April, I shall be able not to work between December and March 15th when we begin rehearsing.

My first thought was to try to get Noël Coward's house, and I have made a tentative bid for it. On second thoughts, however, I don't believe it would be a very good plan. One couldn't take it without asking several women to stay. I should be terrified (a) of snubs (b) of social demands, calls etc. and it would be bound to get into the papers. All far too spectacular, I think.

But I should enormously like to take a house for eight weeks – mid-December to mid-February – somewhere in the West Indies and above all with you if you would feel inclined to come. But if so, I think it should be smallish, and taken in *your name*, so that I come as a guest. Then one would only risk a photo at the airport, and of course I would come alone. I thought of getting Paul Anstee to come later for a week or two, if he isn't working, and perhaps Ben Edwards or Paul Morrison if they had free time.

You do see, I'm sure, that the less publicity I get the better, and to have to import Lady Olivier, Miss Gish and Virginia Whitehead [wife of Robert] to colour the proceedings would hardly be my idea of a perfect hol.

To John Masefield   *16 August, London*

May I thank you for the penetrating beauty and wisdom of your republished essays on Shakespeare [*William Shakespeare*]. I always loved the original little

---

* *William Poel and the Elizabethan Revival* by Robert Speaight.

book and have given it and lent it a dozen times. It is wonderful to read it again with the new additions. Especially I admire your words about the Queen Mab scene in *Romeo*, and to know that the present generations have such a joy before them in reading the book. I also read the other day *The Faithful* for the first time, and found it enormously impressive, though I should tremble for an English company trying to bring it to the stage.

You may not remember – but I always shall – my coming to your house with Miss [Mary] Jerrold in 1941 and you talked to me with such graciousness and illumination about *Macbeth*.

Now that [Granville-]Barker is gone, alas, one is more than ever grateful for such leadership as yours in studying Shakespeare. Thank you for the inspiration, and please forgive me intruding on your privacy with so inadequate a letter. It is none the less sincere – and I had to write. No answer, *please*.

Most admiringly ever, John Gielgud.

A Day by the Sea *closed on 30 October, after which JG started filming for Olivier's* **Richard III**, *in which he played Clarence, as well as directing a revival of* **Charley's Aunt** *with John Mills.*

To Cecil Beaton   *6 November, London*

I really was so delighted with your décor for *Love's Labour*,* and I do think the press and general attitude towards it has been monstrously stupid and unfair. The simplicity and ingenuity of the whole design serves the play most admirably, and the clothes are most beautiful, striking and poetic. The dress of Mercade with its use of contrasting materials and the black and white used so sparingly and to such sharp effect particularly entranced me. The only costume I didn't like was the King's – but he is to my mind a beastly actor ([Eric] Porter) and I thought he wore it badly and was ill made up. But Armado and the little Moth wore theirs splendidly. The women looked heavenly, only they don't move well enough to do them justice.

The play is extraordinary – so like what Fry is trying to do in the early scenes, don't you think? – and the end is pure bliss – the scene of the messenger and the final song sent me out transported to walk across the bridge in great ravishment. I felt something of the same kind when I saw the Vic production,† ugly and common as it was, but I hardly expected, seeing it only for the second time, to gain the same sense of wonder at the genius of the young Shakespeare emerging from his chrysalis in such peacock splendour.

That other production was so busy and cheap, I thought, and this one, with all its inadequacy of verbal virtuosity (which is, of course, a bad fault) still seemed to me sincere and beautiful in conception and completely trying to

---

* Beaton designed the Old Vic production directed by Frith Banbury.
† A reference to the 1949 production.

serve the play, which must always be a very difficult one for a modern audience. I hope you won't let yourself be depressed by the ignorance of the people who have no eyes and fail to bring their imaginations into line with yours. I was quite alone and felt I subjected the whole thing to my most critical scrutiny and examination, and I found your part of it well-nigh perfect.

I am filming sporadically with Larry, but am beginning to relax after the long run. Saw the first night of *The Matchmaker* [by Thornton Wilder], which seemed to me very well done, though it doesn't interest me a bit as a play, and I don't know why Wilder should have ever bothered adapting and elaborating such a crusty old farce. Ruth [Gordon] and Eileen [Herlie] are both admirable, however, and Guthrie has done it as well as it could possibly be done.

Mankiewicz' new film, *Barefoot Contessa* a grievous disappointment, contentious, melodramatic, and as slow and silly as a melodrama by Arnold Bennett in the twenties – odd, because I read the script and it seemed on paper amusing and vivid, but Joe has fallen in love with his own dialogue and everybody talks interminably in what he thinks a pungent and witty way about Hollywood and the smart European set and none of it rings true – the colour is hideous and it is all a cracking bore.

I go to spend Christmas with Noël in Jamaica, and I've taken a house with Hugh Wheeler about nine miles from Noël's for January and February. Paul A. is coming out via N.Y. and hopes to see you en passant. I'm not going to risk that, much as I should like to, but if you would have time or leisure to come yourself to Jamaica, while I am there, do suggest yourself.

To Hugh Wheeler   *16 November, London*

I have done five days of Clarence and shall be through with it in ten days' time – then I go to Paris with Esmé for a long weekend. I do hope you won't be bored with Paul. I have to be so surreptitious in seeing him in London it will really be something of a joy to me to have him for a real holiday – and he adores you and is, of course, thrilled at the prospect.

I do hope all goes well with you, and that you aren't regretting your decision to come. I can't wait, and it is wonderful already not to go and act every night after so long.

1955

To Harry McHugh   *22 January, Jamaica*

Having such a happy and wonderful holiday here. I do hope you are keeping well, despite snow and cold, and that business remains good at the Haymarket.

Thank you for looking after the house at Christmas time and nursing Bernie when his leg was bad. He is certainly an unlucky fellow. Wish you could see the beauty of this island, and the natives in all their gay colours with flashing white teeth, and the adorable black children with their Sunday school frocks and little plastic parasols trooping along in the sunshine.

To Stark Young   *27 January, Jamaica*

I can't resist showing you the two enclosed letters from Nevill Coghill, a delightful Irish don at Oxford who directed *A Midsummer Night's Dream* for me in '44. It wasn't a success, alas, he couldn't manage professionals, but the *ideas* were all pure and splendid. He has done many excellent productions with the undergraduates, especially a *Tempest* in Worcester Gardens in which the masque came across the lake on a barge, and Ariel literally *ran* across the water on a plank cunningly placed along the edge of the shore just under water level.

I am having a most wonderful holiday here. Noël is 8 miles away and we call and swim at each other's houses. I stayed with him for Christmas. Sam Behrman was down and lunched here two days ago, as sweet as ever. I gave him an amusing cutting from London about Edith – 'How great acting can ruin plays!' She must have loved it.

Claudette Colbert was here and keen for me to do *The Guardsman* [Ferenc Molnar] with her in N.Y. on T.V. I have been making a few inquiries and I wouldn't do it unless Alfred [Lunt] would consent to help me direct the whole thing, if possible. I imagine C.B.S. is pretty powerful with the press and columnists and wouldn't risk engaging me unless they were sure there would be no adverse publicity, but we shall see.

I wonder if you'll like the Fry play [*The Dark Is Light Enough*] that Guthrie is doing. I hated it, even with Edith. What with Christopher's Quakerism and Edith's C.S. [Christian Science] it was a perfect triumph of non-dramatic uplift.

To Stark Young   *12 February, Jamaica*

I am going over to Haiti for the weekend of Mardi Gras, and as I can't see *House of Flowers* [by Truman Capote and Harold Arlen], that is no doubt the best way to get an idea of the Voodoo and native life there. I have to go back on the 23rd to meet [Isamu] Noguchi who is in London discussing his décor with the director [George Devine] of my new *King Lear*. Did I tell you we had engaged him to do it? I have never met him, but everyone tells me he is the very man, and I have had a sort of 'hunch' about him for that play since I first saw Martha Graham's Ballets in 1947. I hear the designs are most original and exciting, and hope devoutly we shall get on. It will be an interesting collaboration, I am sure.

To Hugh Wheeler   *9 March, London*

How sad, yes, that it is all behind us, and what fun it was! It was dreadful coming away, but the journey soon over and not as bad as I feared. My mother seems much better, thank God, though not able to go out yet which is just as well, as the cold is horrendous. The main attraction here is Antonio who is dancing superbly. Miss [Siobhan] McKenna's *Saint Joan* can be passed very lightly over and there are no new plays to see.

We had a party last night which was a great success. 58 people and hot food for most of them – Bernie surpassed himself and it was all very agreeable. The *Lear* plans seem to be going well and Sunday I begin at Stratford.

I have got a party for Paul to do for Adrianne Allen in July and also have suggested Toby [Rowland] might give him a room while Alan [Webb] is away. He says the house is very expensive to run alone and I think it might be pleasant for both of them – but we shall see.

To Stark Young   *3 April, London*

I'm in the throes of *Twelfth Night* at Stratford, which opens April 12th. Then I go to Venice for ten days respite before we rehearse *Much Ado* and *Lear*. Noguchi has done such exciting décor for the latter, and I only hope the director (George Devine) can devise the production to be worthy of it.

Olivier is brilliant as Malvolio, though he is very ultra-realistic in his approach, and his gift of mimicry (as opposed to creative acting) sticks in my gizzard at times. His execution is so certain and skilled that it is difficult to convince him that he *can* be wrong in his own exuberance and should occasionally curb and check it in the interests of the general line and pattern of the play. The truth is he is a born autocrat, and must always be right. He has little respect for the critical sensitivity of others; on the other hand he is quite brilliant in his criticism of my directing methods and impatient with my hesitance and (I believe) necessary flexibility. He wants everything cut and dried at once, so that he may perfect with utter certainty of endless rehearsal and repetition – but he is good for me all the same, and perhaps I may still make a good thing of that divine play, especially if he will let me pull her little ladyship [Vivien Leigh] (who is brainier than he is but *not* a born actress) out of her timidity and safeness. He dares too confidently (and will always carry an undiscriminating audience with him) while she hardly dares at all and is terrified of overreaching her technique and doing anything that she has not killed the spontaneity of by over practice. It is an interesting problem, the pair of them – Lynn and Alfred, I suppose, in parvo.

It is fun not to have acted for three months, and I am much refreshed in spirit by the rest and hope when I get back to playing, I shall find myself a bit new again – there's no consolation in middle age except to find one has better selective taste and a bit more power technically, especially in roles one has tried before.

After the opening of Twelfth Night *JG began rehearsals for* Much Ado about Nothing, *directing and playing Benedick, and* King Lear *in which he played the title role.*

To Hugh Wheeler   *4 June, Brighton*

We are safely ensconced for the two weeks in a very agreeable flat. Weather really divine at last, and our final run-through of *Much Ado* very encouraging on the whole. The *Lear* costumes seem very exciting and I can't wait to see them in the sets and lighting – the Edgar/Claudio [Richard Easton] is really excellent, and we only lurch somewhat dangerously now where Edmund [Harold Lang] and Goneril [Helen Cherry] are concerned. Bernie is positively beaming as the flat was all his idea and I think the sea always affects him favourably anyway!

Paul and I caught Denholm Elliott cruising the King's Road Chelsea coffee bars, which gave us furiously to think!

I have had quite enough rehearsing and shan't be sorry to poke my painted nose round the scenery at last, though I rather dread the first few nights' experience.

After the Brighton opening, the two productions went on a short European tour.

To his mother   *June 1955, Vienna*

Wonderful reception for *Much Ado* despite a rather crumby old music hall with poor acoustics where we play. The music died on us for the procession to the church, otherwise the staff did wonders, though the lighting is very sketchy. About fifteen curtains at the end, and a crowd of a hundred or more at the stage door (with soldiers to restrain them) who yelled and applauded us as we drove away in great state.

Enormous party at the British Embassy – about 500, but not very amusing. Dancing and no food till midnight! A lovely house and some pretty women. Six embassies attending the opening, including the Russians who were heavily serious at the party looking like caricatures of their kind – fat, dowdy women and close-cropped, stocky men. They know all the cuts and thought the Claudio rather inexperienced!

Peggy's cold is better and so are my feet and voice. I went to a charming skin man who wouldn't accept a fee but asked for two seats for *Lear* instead.

To Cecil Beaton   *2 July, Zurich*

I too was very sorry not to see you at Brighton. The consensus there seemed to be impressed, though distracted at the beginning by the strangeness of the designs. That seems to go here too, and in Vienna, and it makes the first act difficult work for me – also my clothes are hideously heavy and uncomfortable. I'm hoping to have them remade in lighter form for London. The receptions are sensational, audiences rapt, critics very divided and controversial in both cities. Also, of course, lighting and timing – on which so much depends – have perforce to be sketchy and incomplete with only 24 hours to set up and light the play with foreign technicians. However, I think there is no doubt the production comes off in quite a new way, particularly the storm scene which is a big achievement. Irene [Selznick?] saw *Lear* at Brighton and muttered a few eyebrow-wagging compliments – if only she didn't look so *sallow.* Couldn't you invent a make-up for her and persuade her to use a microphone! Isn't it sad about poor Edith?* I do hope it's only a temporary setback – was the play right for her, I wonder? I was crazy about Vienna and staying at Sacher's – unfortunately the weather was Singapore – murderous, thick, damp, muggy heat, and I got a rash of athlete's foot which ruined all my sightseeing and made the performance torture. However, it's better now and we have had a few days off here and only four performances in a nice smallish theatre with good lighting. The picture-postcard smugness is undeniable but it is rather pleasant to see everyone grazing contentedly in such clean and prosperous surroundings. Paul said he was seeing you – I hope he is behaving nicely while I am away.

King Lear *and* **Much Ado** *then played a short season at the Palace Theatre.*

To Edith Evans   *22 July, London*

It was lovely to get your message of good wishes the other night, and to hear from Gwen that you are feeling your old self again. It is lovely being with Peg again and George has been most helpful and constructive over *Lear,* who is now fixed in my mind as a kind of wicked Churchill! The production is very original and powerful. It will cause a lot of controversy but I'm sure it breaks new ground which is what we hoped.

During the run, JG had a number of offers of future work, including Oscar Wilde's **Salomé** *in New York.*

---

* Edith Evans had been rehearsing *Nina* by André Roussin which was due to open in Liverpool before moving to London. After various casting vicissitudes, Dame Edith was taken ill and had to withdraw.

THE FIFTIES • 1955

To Hugh Wheeler   *28 July, London*

Salomé is not the thing itself. It's a decadent old piece (pace dear Oscar) and reeks of the nineties and Morris wallpapers, and who can say what Eartha Kitt would do – Herodias too would have to be played by a coloured lady – Mae Barnes?? – and I think the whole thing is far too much of a stunt. The money would be nice, so would the chance to be back in N.Y. but I'm quite sure the right occasion will eventually occur and then one will not hesitate – but it must definitely be 'class' and there is obviously no hurry. Dick Myers spent lunchtime trying to persuade me to do *Much Ado* with Kate Hepburn – then Oliver Smith rang from N.Y., would I like to do Higgins in the musical of *Pygmalion* as Rex is now problematical. I remain flattered but refuse to be rushed. Sam Spiegel also suggests I should do the part they wanted Noël to do in *The Bridge of Kwong Hai** but I have the script and it is anybody's part – à la *African Queen* – and even the lure of Bogart, Monty Clift and Guinness does not shake my indifference to the part.

Bernie and Paul tell me they have sent you the notices. Raves for *Much Ado*, an onslaught for *Lear*, but we are packed to standing room notwithstanding. I have had rather a bitter struggle with athlete's foot, George Devine's criticisms and far too many opinions all round, but am feeling better now and am greatly restored from the dismay of the notices by the feeling that I am playing better and there is enormous interest and enthusiasm on all sides for the production. I wasn't well abroad, but still managed to adore Holland – where Paul came and we had a divine week – and saw a few lovely things in Vienna, including Mozart's Coronation Mass in the Hofburg Chapel.

To Laurence Olivier   *9 August, London*

I can't begin to tell you how deeply I was touched by your sweet letter. Such generosity and thoughtfulness, above all, when you have so much to occupy and absorb you. What a lucky man I am to possess such a friend – and I always seem to be making unwarrantable demands of friendship and receiving them back a hundred fold. I am ashamed of my own weakness in being so downed by bad notices and I confess to having been very low over the weekend when the last hope of the weeklies failed to console my wounded vanity – but to have your sympathy and understanding has healed me as nothing else could, and I faced the audience tonight with defiant and glaring imperturbability and really felt I played better and found myself again. George [Devine] thought so too, and sends you his love and thanks with mine. I shall always remember, with so much else that I have to be grateful to you and Viv for, this sweet and infinitely thoughtful gesture of yours.

---

* Pierre Boulle's novel was eventually filmed as *The Bridge on the River Kwai* with Alec Guinness, William Holden and Jack Hawkins.

To Edith Sitwell   *26 August, London*

I hope I have not let you in for an exhausting time tomorrow at *Lear*. It is so dreadfully hot and I fear I am something of a husk after this especially tiring week, but I will hope to interest you a little, and I think you may find Noguchi's décor imaginative and original. People are so divided that I never know whether to expect blank disapproval or enthusiasm on people's faces after they have seen it. So I try to keep my own belief in the production unassailed, which is sometimes rather difficult.

To Hugh Wheeler   *26 August, London*

Here I sit in rather melancholy state saving myself for *Lear*, which is no joke to plod through these rather boiling days, even though we have wonderful audiences which, after the awful press and the long unprecedented heat wave is something of a miracle. In three weeks' time we paddle off on our tour again, and those beastly English provincial towns to dread through November. The company is not interesting (in any way, least of all to act with) and Peggy in a high state of emotional tension owing to domestic disharmonies, poor girl.

Paul is in a frenzy of preparation to open his shop* in the King's Road which he takes over next week – his Dad has put up half the money and Adrianne [Allen] the rest. We end mid-December and my plans are not made after that. There are a mess of half offers and suggestions – a revival of [*The*] *Gay Lord Quex* [by A. W. Pinero] with Peggy, but she won't do it till September of next year – the Leonard Sillman *Serena Blandish* which I rather like the script of, but it is not yet cut and finished (the book) and I've not heard the music or the names of the possible stars.

I'm doing the proposal and bag scenes† with Edith and Margaret Leighton next week for the opening of Commercial Television, and if that is a success I imagine I could spend the spring reviving some old successes for that medium – *The Lady, Importance, Circle* etc. if no new script should materialise. I certainly intend to take a bit of a holiday in January.

I highly recommend for your perusal – *Snake Wine, a Singapore Diary* by Patrick Anderson, an ex-professor from McGill, *The Unsuitable Englishman* by Desmond Stuart and *The Capri Letters* translated from the Italian of Soldati – if you can't get them in N.Y. I will send them over. They would all amuse you, I believe.

Dodie Smith has removed her piano after lending it me for 16 years. She has come back odder and more escapist than ever, and will, I'm sure, write no more successful plays. The drawing room is now rearranged and looks much

---

* Interior decoration and antiques.
† From *The Importance of Being Earnest*.

bigger. Gwen [Ffrangcon-Davies] is going to stay here when she begins rehearsing her new play* for Toby [Rowland], with Dirk Bogarde. I do hope it will be a success for them all. Joe Reed, en passant, trying to suggest I should do Stratford, Conn. next year but I think no more Shakespeare for the time being.

My mother is finding the heat dreadfully trying, and worrying herself silly over her poor mad old sisters. Oh, what W.S. didn't know about the terrors and distresses of old age. Eleanor manfully bearing the burden as usual. They are pulling down and building up houses all round us in Cowley Street which makes the mornings noisy and the dust lies thick on all the furniture – otherwise life goes on much as usual. The town is packed with tourists and visitors of every clime, costume and varying degrees of attractiveness. The National Gallery is so packed with shorts, lederhosen, corduroy and other distracting gentlemanly attributes that one is tempted to spend long hours there – almost the only place in London with air-conditioning too, and there are always the pictures! A lovely Tiepolo of the Banquet of Cleopatra lent by the Melbourne Art Gallery – how on earth did it ever get there?

To Vivien Leigh and Laurence Olivier   *14 September, London*

I can't begin to tell you how happy you both made me with your praises on Saturday night. The production has been a great responsibility and worry to me as I was the person who first suggested Noguchi and in all loyalty both to him and George it has been necessary to remain patient and to continue to try and dominate some of the very great difficulties under which I labour. It's too mighty a part to have to worry ceaselessly against a general consensus of disapproval – so many people liked me better before and accuse me of deliberately spoiling what was good for the sake of restlessness and change. This is not true, of course – I mean the intention, the result maybe, I can't tell that – but it was obvious that the different style of this production [*King Lear*] had to be matched if possible by a performance that goes with the make-up and general pictorial effect. But the clothes and furniture are both very hard and exhausting to manage, and with the emotion and vocal strain as well, I find it a very wearing business that only a masochist could find much enjoyment in! But if you were really both convinced and moved, then the labour is infinitely repaid and I am happy to think you troubled to come and see it.

After the season at the Palace Theatre, the two productions resumed their European tour, followed by a tour of British regional theatres.

---

* *Summertime* by Ugo Betti.

To his mother   *21 September, Berlin*

Berlin is extremely depressing – endless miles of ruins, with a sort of half-hearted ghost town rebuilding and scarred in the middle in uneven patches. We went by underground on Monday night to the Brecht Theatre in the Eastern sector, where they played Farquhar's *The Recruiting Officer* in a strange propaganda version with rather an indifferent company, but with an attractive décor and production. I gather it is not one of their best shows, but I found the presentation very interesting, though I resented the twisting of a light comedy into a savage satire on English Army methods and the grinding of the poor.

Our own first night went extremely well but, as we began at 6.30 and finished at 10.15 with endless intervals (*Lear*), Peggy and I staggered from a frightful foyer party which went on till after midnight – champagne but nothing to eat, of course – and sought a meal before falling into the hotel. A wonderful reception and I had even to go through the Iron Curtain (literally!) to take a final call. The theatre is very small and hideously ugly, standing like a Baptist Chapel amid a half-mile of rubble, but it seemed to me rather a good performance and received with rapt attention.

To his mother   *4 October, Copenhagen*

Very short flight here from Hamburg and we do not open till tomorrow night. I enjoyed Hamburg very much – marvellously comfortable hotel and [Gustav] Grundgens, who is star and director of the theatre, gave me his dressing room with private bath, sent flowers and champagne, altogether very grand and welcoming. Two magnificent audiences for both plays, and wild scenes of enthusiasm – the safety curtain lowered twice and raised again for more calls. In all the German towns the curtains were extraordinary – applause lasting ten minutes and more, and we had to go back after we had gone to our dressing rooms. The town itself is very fine with the lake covered with yachts and sailing boats, and there is great space and air and luxury. Only it all seems very peculiar after the great wars! And the meetings with Germans not very rewarding – one simply can't trust them, however they bow and gush, and the women are all so ugly and dowdy.

Moira Lister [playing Margaret and Regan] took me for lunch to Fredericksruhe Castle to the Prince and Princess von Bismarck. He is grandson of the old chancellor and was at the London German Embassy from 1928–36 (with Ribbentrop, I suppose). They have a beautiful house, though half of it was bombed down. Six children and horses and servants in the best English country style, and couldn't have been more charming. She is Swedish and has been a great beauty, but I gather she was an ardent Nazi, so one doesn't know how to feel about them. It was certainly an agreeable day, the weather beautiful as it has been all along. Peggy has had a tummy upset and didn't go out much.

She really hated Germany and her spirits rose at once as soon as we landed here.

To Hugh Wheeler   *12 October, Oslo*

Germany was extraordinary and I must say I enjoyed the wicked quarter of Hamburg. Tony Ireland picked up our taxi driver, a cream-faced loon dressed entirely in leather. I trembled and shook, but he turned out to be quite a dear, intensely sentimental, and never left our sides for three mad evenings. Their young men are certainly attractive, and of course they are mad costume and uniform fetishists, so my eye was continually titillated with corduroy, breeches, jackboots et cetera! Marvellous audiences everywhere and quite pleasant times in between the labours of *Lear* and the tedious official parties with their eternal speechmaking and insincere polite conversations with complete strangers whom one never wants to see again.

Paul's shop has opened the day after I came away and seems to be doing extremely well. I think he's very happy and madly busy. We get back to England next Wednesday and I am off to Stratford to see *Macbeth* and *Titus*. Then we have a weary eight weeks grind round the provinces, ending at Stratford in mid-December.

No plans as yet for next year. I want to do a Season – Marlowe's *Faustus* and Buckingham's *The Rehearsal* (in one bill), perhaps *Measure for Measure* or *Ivanov, The Gay Lord Quex* of Pinero, and maybe a Viennese play by Hofmannsthal, *Der Schwierige* – everyone on the Continent says it would be good for me, but I gather it needs a rather skilful version.

Richard the Third comes out on Dec. 13th in London – I am longing to see it. I wonder when it opens in America. I saw the new Clouzot film *Les Diaboliques* in Copenhagen (*Wages of Fear* director). A marvellous piece of Grand Guignol, but I should think the Western scissors will be busy before it is shown in London or New York.

To Noël Coward   *15 October, Oslo (of all places)*

This is the last week of our tournée. Oslo appears to have been built by the L.N.E.R. and there is a very disagreeable smell in the theatre which I thought was probably Ibsen's unpublished plays, but turns out to be a particularly nauseating kind of carbolic soap which they use for cleaning – otherwise it is just another touring date, like Aberdeen. Moira Lister is quite a dear and talks affectionately of you. I make perpetual speeches trembling (as does the company) on the most slippery edge of disaster possible, but a tear at the right moment in the voix d'or generally manages to save the day. I have reluctantly to confess that the Germans couldn't possibly be a better audience, but of course they think Shakespeare was a German, and who but Winifred [Ashton], Dover Wilson and Alan Webb shall prove he wasn't?

To Hugh Wheeler   *26 October, Newcastle-on-Tyne*

The English provinces are typically grim, but we have only eight more weeks to tour, and I had a very good half week in London. Went to Stratford with Paul and Dick and saw *Macbeth* (very disappointing except for Larry) and *Titus [Andronicus]* which was simply wonderful – Peter's masterpiece in every department, except for poor Vivien [Leigh] who seems in a very bad way. She is utterly ineffective on the stage – like paper, only not so thick, no substance or power – and off stage she is haunted, avid, malicious and insatiable, a bad look-out for the future and for poor Larry who is saint-like with her and play-acting most beautifully as well. We also saw [*Waiting for*] *Godot*, which we loathed, and *House of Bamboo** (with Noguchi's wife [Shirley Yamaguchi] in it) which is rather fun.

I am deep in the Bloomsbury twenties with two biographies, John Lehmann and David Garnett. It's funny to be old enough to read biographies covering quite mature periods of one's own life (though perhaps mature is hardly the word). The Hofmannsthal play I heard of in Vienna has arrived in a literal translation. I rather like it and it's obviously a wonderful part for me, but it remains to be seen whether J.P. and Binkie like it enough to have someone really good get to work on adapting it. It dates a bit, but I think has a lot of charm and humour. Sort of Molnar cum *Reunion in Vienna* – Maugham. Noël has rewritten the Jamaican play about Lady Edwina [Mountbatten] and the coloured gentleman, and it is terribly funny, though not in the best of taste!† Vivien proposes to do it after Christmas with Peter Finch, and wanted me to play in it – a very good part (obviously Nell [Noël Coward] herself) but (a) I don't think she will be fit to do it, or (b) be very good in it, and (c) I don't think it's quite good enough for me, and there are rather too many jokes about Public Conveniences to suit my taste and reputation. A pity.

To his mother   *8 November, Glasgow*

Very disappointing house here last night, though I've no doubt the good notices will drive them in. Odd how the public in the big shipping places, this and Liverpool, is so much less good since the war for anything of any class. *Can-Can* [by Abe Burrows and Cole Porter] which follows us here, and was a failure in London, is already booked out for several weeks! Not very flattering, and *Florodora* [by Owen Hall and Leslie Stuart], which is a thousand years old, followed us at Edinburgh! I fear the fact that so many good London

---

* Film directed by Samuel Fuller.
† Barry Day says, 'The play started life as *Home and Colonial* intended for Gertie [Lawrence], then turned into *Island Fling* which was played by Claudette Colbert briefly at the Westport Playhouse in 1951, then became *South Sea Bubble*, starring Vivien Leigh in London in 1956 and was quite successful.' Edwina Mountbatten was reputed to have had affairs with both Paul Robeson and Jawaharlal Nehru.

plays don't tour at all these days has spoiled the provincial market, and they sit at home and watch TV, unless they can hear a great row and lots of music.

Coward's comedy [*Nude with Violin*] is very funny, I think, though Peggy read it yesterday and didn't think so. But I am very inclined to do it if he liked the idea. It is wildly farcical, but the part – a dago valet of extremely doubtful background and perfect English manners – might, I think, come out amusingly if I could get a good wig and make-up – and it's the last sort of character anyone would expect me to play. I long to do something frivolous, if not for too long. We shall see what Noël himself thinks of the idea. He obviously wrote it for himself, and my only fear would be giving an imitation of him. It is very broad and a bit vulgar, but full of sure fire situations and brilliant curtains, and I think it couldn't fail to be a success – but I should have to be rather clever at creating a character out of a 'type' which doesn't really exist in life.

To Vivien Leigh   *25 November, Liverpool*

I imagine you are relieved to think you are free after tomorrow* and the long exhausting spell achieved at last, and I do hope you are going to have a real rest, both of you, and emerge as lions refreshed next year with new and wonderful successes. I shall miss seeing you both very much and am myself longing for my holiday after Christmas. I shall long to see notices of *Richard* and know it will be another triumph for Larry and a reward for his many months of labour. Take great care of yourself, my darling, and relax all you can and look back on this season as a great achievement.

I see you married off the many-splendoured Thring† and now he is going to terrify the children as Hook!

To George Pitcher‡   *1 December, Stratford-upon-Avon*

Dear George Pitcher

Your charming and enthusiastic letter gave me the greatest pleasure. My performance has not been much liked generally in this production, and it is very gratifying when I feel it has got across to someone like yourself so fully.

---

* The Oliviers had been appearing in *Titus Andronicus* at Stratford-upon-Avon.

† The Australian actor Frank Thring who played Saturninus in *Titus Andronicus* married the fashion model Joan Cunliffe, much to many people's surprise. Laurence Olivier gave away the bride and Vivien Leigh was her matron of honour.

‡ This is the first letter JG wrote to George Pitcher, a young American academic working in Oxford on a Harvard scholarship. On a visit to Stratford to see *King Lear*, he had been taken backstage to meet JG. The attraction was mutual and instantaneous. Although George Pitcher returned to the USA after his year in England, the relationship continued for the next eight years; with the understanding of his lifelong partner, Ed Cone, Pitcher returned whenever possible to Europe to resume the affair, and JG would meet him during his New York seasons. Their friendship continued to the end of Gielgud's life and George Pitcher's photograph was found by his bedside at his death.

The main lines were taught me in 1940 with the most brilliant lucidity by Granville-Barker and I have tried to develop the character since on the lines he showed me. The intention of the production is, I think, more successful than its execution, generally speaking, but I think it was a worthwhile experiment despite its weaknesses and limitations.

I hope you will come and see me again and sometime – if you should be here for *Much Ado* perhaps you would like to join me for a meal or a drink. If not, look me up in London when I am playing there next year.

With my best wishes – sincerely yours

John Gielgud

To Edith Evans   *13 December, Stratford-upon-Avon*

I cannot tell you how delighted and happy it has made me that you will work with me again on this very original and exciting play [*The Chalk Garden* by Edith Bagnold]. I only hope I can bring some constructive ideas to it and not hinder or confuse you in your creation.

I am spending Sunday night and Monday with Enid Bagnold, and will hope you can lunch with me at Cowley St on Tuesday round one o'clock, and we can talk everything over. I shall be most fascinated to hear your views about the play and also your ideas for casting the other parts.

I do feel sure that if the right balance and atmosphere can be achieved, the play could be sensationally good. But it draws a very fine line, does it not, between farce and melodrama, and needs superb all round style, it seems to me, to bring it to real achievement on the stage.

To Stark Young   *13 December, Stratford-upon-Avon*

How are you and did you have a wonderful summer in Italy? I often thought of you in Venice where I had a heavenly ten days in April. Since then I have had an exhausting but interesting tour with the Noguchi *Lear* – very controversial, not well directed and abominably cast, but interesting all the same, and *Much Ado*, my own old production of five years ago which, with Peggy Ashcroft's help, I have managed to bring out with fairly satisfactory results despite the weakness of the rest of the company. I stupidly allowed the Stratford people to engage the cast while I was in Jamaica last Christmas, and the result was disastrous.

After Christmas I go to Paris for a week, and then I am to direct *The Chalk Garden* with Edith Evans, which is a most exciting assignment. I loathed it at first reading, but now have fallen quite in love with it, and it should be a marvellous role for Edith, though she somewhat complicated matters by wanting to play the governess, in which case, Enid Bagnold said, we should have had to get Ellen Terry back from Heaven to do the old lady. However, she has now agreed to play the veteran, and I hope either Pamela Brown or

Irene Worth will do the other part. Neither the author nor Irene Selznick
want to use Beaton's set here, and I am still not sure what will be decided. He
is a great friend of mine, and will, of course, be deeply hurt if his prestige is
insulted by using another designer in England.* But I should not have
thought he was the right man for this play. It seems to need a kind of
stylised realism with shadowy overtones, more like the Mielziner settings for
Tennessee's plays only, of course, English. I am getting the photographs to see
before deciding, but I should value your opinions on setting, direction and
acting, and your views as to how the play ought to be treated, very highly
indeed, if it would not be too much trouble for you.

There is talk of my playing a valet in a new comedy of Noël's in the spring
[*Nude with Violin*]. It is almost farce and very well constructed and funny –
but I rather fear I shall seem too aristocratic and aloof for it. He is supposed
to have a perfect veneer of sophistication, speaks beautiful English as well as
three other languages, but must at the same time look like a dago, and
convincingly suggest that he is an adventurer, a criminal, and of very common
background, but I confess I am intrigued by the idea of trying to play it,
though Olivier or Alfred would take it in their stride better than I can. We
shall see.

1956

To Stark Young   *19 January, London*

All thanks for your kindness in sending me your impressions of the Bagnold
play. We are now held up for a month. I agreed suddenly to make a film for
MGM in April. The father in *The Barretts* [*of Wimpole Street*] with Jennifer
Jones, which immediately fired Irene Selznick with the plan of engaging Peggy
Ashcroft for Madrigal.† She accepted, but has now to have an operation which
forces us to postpone, so I am twiddling my thumbs till the end of February.

The part in *The Barretts* is somewhat of a cliché. Hardwicke and Laughton
both played it as a sort of ogreish Pecksniff. I don't see why it must be like
that and would hope to reduce it to a more comprehensible narrowness of
nature, more like Angelo, if I can. Anyway, I needed the money, and think it
may lead to advantageous publicity for the future for America, so I hope I
won't regret it.

I have no great opinion of Siobhan McKenna, though she was charming
enough as Lady Macduff when I directed her at Stratford a year or two ago.

---

* *The Chalk Garden* had opened in New York in October 1955, where Cecil Beaton had designed
the sets and costumes.
† A character in *The Chalk Garden*.

But her much-vaunted Saint Joan was to me like an angry Irish housemaid and devoid of all variety of voice and development of character – not a patch on the original performance of Sybil Thorndike which I was lucky enough to see. I am sure she would miss the implications of a Madrigal.

The photographs of Cecil's set look to me like a villa for a farce, and I particularly disliked the look of the pebble well you mention. Cecil is a really good friend of mine (and also of the authoress) but I gather he has risen above the situation and is not to declare lifelong war, because, conveniently, he is already in New York, so there is the obvious point that he can't be supervising a production in London. The designer we have chosen [Reece Pemberton] is not as distinguished or original in quality, but I think he has conceived a far more interesting looking scene with a step up to an archway leading to a square hall and a view of the staircase – the room half grand, half shabby, and with a feeling of garden and sea which should create a good feeling. The play seems to need (as did *The Lady*) a stillness to absorb the rather stylish and highbrow dialogue with a flexible and elegant arrangement of movement and pauses in counterpoint, so that the audience receives a digestible impression of satirical comedy (*not* farce) with some subtle undertones of dramatic wisdom and suspense. Edith is, of course, ten times the actress Gladys Cooper is – the latter only excels in broad melodrama and a certain effective comedy broad style which she learnt from Charles Hawtrey and which serves her well enough to amuse an audience.

Edith has a new house in the country (Kent) with a rich girlfriend [Judith Wilson], which seems to be giving her much pleasure to arrange, and is in tearing form. I hope the mood may last during our rehearsals. It sounds as if it were quite an interesting season in New York this year. Very disappointing here, and the Scofield–Brook *Hamlet* is really disgracefully bad – not even a correct text spoken, and not *one* decent performance. Such a pity it should have been seen in Moscow. They must have thought us sillier than ever.

To Edith Evans   *March 1956, Brighton*

Much distressed not to have seen you after the play tonight [*The Chalk Garden*]. We were arguing over improvements over dressing the set. The performance was splendid – growing all the time – and I was so delighted to feel you were all so much happier in the smaller house. My love and thanks as ever.

The Chalk Garden *opened at the Theatre Royal, Haymarket, on 11 April.*

To Edith Evans   *12 April, London*

I know you don't mind or read the critics, but I think you would be pleased by the universal approval. I thought last night when you all played with such admirable balance and drive that they could hardly fail to appreciate our work and the beautifully mannered yet spellbound enthusiasm of that perfect audience. You will be tired and yet relieved, I know, that the strain is done with. I do hope you will have a long and enjoyable run, and I hear Pamela Brown has agreed to follow Peg, which pleases me greatly, not only because it shows her generous intelligence and lack of resentment but also because I think she will give an admirable performance and you will be happy working with her.

After the opening JG took a holiday in Spain.

To Paul Anstee   *2 May, Camp de Mar*

This is a mad ramshackle house with a magnificent view of umbrella pines, mountains and the blue, blue sea. Very like Jamaica in a way, only with the brown Spanish earth and olive trees, which are more like Provence or Estoril. Off to the beach, which is just down the road. Daphne* has a strange collection of house guests, a Jewish M.P. with his daughter aged 8 and a gipsy looking companion for her who appears to be the girl-friend of the father, long black hair and a wall eye – said to be wonderful at fortune-telling and served with the French forces during the war – also spent much time among the Bedouin Arabs!! Also a young American couple out of every play who fill in as small parts. As the newest arrival I kept the table in a roar with all the stories you are sick of hearing. But I would rather you had been here, as it would be much nicer and would probably not have prevented me telling them just the same! Much rich food and vino. I shall have to be very strong-minded or return as Robert Morley.

To Stark Young   *1 June, London*

I am having a very boring time trying to keep patience with the *Barretts [of Wimpole Street]* film which will not be finished till the beginning of July. We are about half way through and the director – an elderly man called Sidney Franklin – is very uninspired though thorough, courteous and efficient. I fear it will be a very routine job when it *is* finished, but it sets me up for two years so I can't complain. The part is very stagey and on one note. I find it very difficult to convince myself in it, let alone an audience.

Peggy Ashcroft was made a Dame during the run of The Chalk Garden.

---

* Probably Daphne Rye, formerly casting director for H. M. Tennent.

To Paul Anstee   *1 June, London*

Great celebration at the Haymarket for Dame Peg last night. She was very sweet and Edith very gracious, curtseying to P. all over the place.

Effusive and gracious note from Patrick Burkhart saying goodbye on coroneted notepaper from Gavin Faringdon's in Berkshire! Reminds me of the story of [Alice] Delysia leaving Juliet Duff's. She held out her hand to say goodbye and all the Wilton notepaper flew out and scattered at Juliet's feet!

To Paul Anstee   *June 1956, London*

I do feel such a treacherous bitch, and I do hate to make you unhappy. I don't defend myself – you know me far too well, and all my weaknesses – and you do, I think, know that I am utterly devoted to you, admire you both for your personal sweetness, your pride, your cleverness and your physical beauty. I adore being with you and I value beyond words all you have given me of friendship, love and loyalty. Now it is for you to decide if you are made too unhappy by my behaviour and want it all to end? Of course it seems as if I am trying to get the best of two affairs, and dropping you when it suits me and picking you up again when I feel inclined. Truly I don't mean to do that. I suppose it seems impossible to you that one can have strong continued feelings for another person while remaining equally devoted to you – the worst kind of Rex Harrison bad compromise. Well, I just can't stop writing to George [Pitcher] and hearing from him and hoping to spend a bit of time with him once a year, because I am devoted to him too. It's all a question of different people with completely different personalities, and all hopelessly involved, I imagine, with basic sex appeal which will not be denied. It was ridiculous of me ever to imagine that you and he could ever like each other and believe me, I regret infinitely that you ever knew about him at all – no good has come of it – and in some ways, if I had been a better liar, I wish I had kept the whole thing quiet.

But you must please feel free to do exactly as you want, and if it hurts you to be with me and you would rather make a complete break, you must say so, even if it makes us both very unhappy. I don't want to pretend with you and feel wretched all the time and make you wretched too. But I couldn't bear to lose your friendship and your company. I won't go on because I don't feel it is any good churning up everything in such an impossible situation. You are in the strongest position as the injured party! And you have your life and career before you. I can't really share my life completely with anybody, as you know, and wouldn't know how to if I could, I don't suppose. However, I'm not going to appeal to your heart on the grounds of advancing years, loneliness, need of companionship and all the rest of it. If I've been seeing you less lately it is because you are so busy in the shop where I always feel slightly embarrassed hanging about, and you are tired in the evenings and you don't like coming here because of Bernie, and I don't like to come to you because of John P. and so it has come about. But heartless and selfish as I am, I don't live without deep feelings about someone I love as much as I love you, and nothing can change that in my case. If you should fall in love with someone else, you will want to review the whole situation again I've no doubt, but meanwhile cannot we still be the same? Or is that too much to ask? I don't believe I've written you a letter since the one that hurt you so dreadfully last year when I went to Paris and said everything wrong.* I do hope you won't find this one equally tactless and hurtful. I sometimes think it is better not to put one's feelings into words – but that seems cowardly too. So forgive me if you can, and thank you, darling, for all your patience and the things you *haven't* ever said when you had every right to say them. I am quite unworthy of your devotion and I truly do not want to humiliate or hurt you in any way at all. You have been infinitely sweet and forbearing and at my age I ought to know better than give you cause –

My love always, John

To Richard Myers   *10 July, London*

Today I finished *The Barretts* film with Jennifer Jones. It has been a long and rather gloomy affair – since April 11th – but I only hope it will not prove a damp old squib when it comes out. I have found it terribly difficult trying to breathe some humanity and conviction into the Simon Legree of an old father. Rather a comedown as a character after King Lear! And the dialogue stilted and old-fashioned. I am glad I never saw Laughton in the part, but many did and admired him greatly, so I have much to rival.

I am busy also with a long playing recording of *Hamlet* with the Old Vic Company – 3½ hours if you please. I am glad I am not at school to be forced to listen to that! But it will be a voice for posterity of a sort! Then I rehearse Pamela Brown who takes Peggy Ashcroft's place in *The Chalk Garden* – then three weeks holiday at Portofino, and then the Coward comedy [*Nude with Violin*] which we open in Dublin so that the Master may have a glance at it before we come to London. The *Measure* reviews† fill me with dismay – I'm sure I should *hate* it. The Guthrie *Troilus and Cressida* (at the Old Vic now) is much the same shimble-shambles of a production – and I cannot bear Shakespeare messed about with in a modern analogy – whatever Noguchi's *Lear* may have been like, we did not try to belittle the *stature* of the play. And *Measure* can be so wonderful. Peter Brook did it beautifully at Stratford when I played Angelo, and one day I hope we may bring it over.

Martita [Hunt] is filming here *Anastasia* with Helen Hayes, Yul Brynner

---

* This letter has not survived.

† Possibly for the American Shakespeare Festival in Stratford, Connecticut, which was done in 'modern' dress, as was the Old Vic production of *Troilus and Cressida*.

and Ingrid Bergman. They say Helen's presence will restore Bergman to favour with the matrons of the Middle West!

To Stark Young   *22 September, London*

I received your letter yesterday, dear Stark, and hasten to reply to it. *The Quare Fellow*, which I chanced to see only a few nights ago – and found greatly impressive too – is certainly presented on the billboards as being presented by Theatre Workshop, a rather left wing but most interesting group, who have been operating in a shabby old theatre at Stratford East down beyond St Paul's, and had a great success in Paris last year with *Arden of Faversham*. It is a prison play by an Irish writer named Brendan Behan, written with great power and humour à la O'Casey and I must say, in spite of the gruesome details of a hanging which is the central core of the play, I was enthralled by the writing and presentation, though it could never be more than an 'art' success with the general public.

Something of a feat, though, to achieve an all male play without dirty language or any homosexual cracks or innuendo, and they play it admirably (the director is a Miss Joan Littlewood) with the simplest possible décor (but what there is, is *most* imaginatively selective) and a tiny company of ten or eleven men, all of whom double, if you please, some playing warders as well as prisoners.

They did a *most* interesting *Edward the Second* [by Bertolt Brecht and Leon Feuchtwanger] some months ago, also presented on a shoestring, with the scenery and their own trousers and sneakers showing under sad little string-mail coats and hoods, and the direction was so intelligent and the teamwork so unpretentiously sincere that one quite forgave their utter lack of sophistication, the doubling and the drabness of the affair from conventionally glamorous standards. They also did *The Good Soldier Schweik* [by Jaroslav Hašek], but I hated the play so much that it bored me, though I saw the intention and ensemble was interesting. There is a strong influence of Brecht, whose company we have just had here – fascinating production of *The Chalk Circle*, *The Recruiting Officer* of Farquhar and the famous *Mother Courage* in which Helene Weigel (Mrs Brecht) gave a superb performance. Alas, I have no word of German, so I couldn't criticise fairly, and got dreadfully bored and irritated in the long dialogue scenes, but the whole thing was so stimulating and exquisitely rehearsed and executed that it was a great inspiration, all done since 1949 when the Brechts returned to Germany and founded a theatre in East Berlin, largely financed, I fear, by the Russians! I only wish [Eric] Bentley had not written so much boring and highfalutin stuff about Brecht, and that the plays did not seem so pulpitty and propagandist. But I suppose that kind of man is fanatical to present his own views and make disciples, as Shaw did too.

I leave for Dublin tomorrow and we open a six-week tryout of Noël's comedy. It seems to be fairly funny. He is arriving on Wednesday and I hope he will be pleased with the way I have done it. The company is excellent, but I have only had three weeks rehearsal and feel my own performance leaves a lot to be desired. I'm hoping the audiences will help me on the way a lot, but I am rather alarmed after not acting for nearly a year.

If a young man called George Pitcher should write to you, will you find half an hour to be nice to him? I met him this year in England where he was doing a Philosophy course with a scholarship from Harvard, and is now teaching same for the first time at Princeton. He is such an equable and delightful fellow, and I ventured to give him your address in case he was able to meet you one day when he is in New York. I think he would not bore you, and he would love meeting you.

To his mother   *September 1956, Dublin*

Noël has done wonders with cutting the play and simplifying the production. The improvements are really striking with all the dull patches gone.

Nude with Violin *opened in Dublin on 24 September.*

To his mother   *25 September, Dublin*

The play had an uproarious reception and we were all very relieved. The gallery rained paper darts on to the footlights during the intervals, but this was only a display of native exuberance, it seems.

It is dreadfully muggy and stormy and the city very much as I had imagined it, even down to the chatty waiters and dreadfully shabby streets with Georgian fanlights – a few less bare feet than I had expected!

To his mother   *7 October, Dublin*

Noël has gone back to Paris and sails for America on Tuesday. He is very satisfied with the play in its final shape. We have worked very hard, changed one actor, and he has written up my part in two scenes to some advantage. The trouble is that, after an effective first act with the reading of the letters, my character only hangs about all the middle of the play and the final scene is not really good enough to redeem it, as it lacks any punch surprise dénouement.

Still, there has been a lot to do trying to get right what I *have* got in the play, and though I think everyone will say it gives me poor opportunities, it may get by on its gags and amusing collection of types. I am very interested to see how the critics and public like it in the North, and no doubt now we have all the changes set, it will be smoother and gayer as the nights go by.

Dublin is damp and rather disappointing. I never think any provincial town is bearable for more than one week, and I shan't be sorry to see Liverpool.

To Paul Anstee   *October 1956, Newcastle-on-Tyne*

Standing room only last night and very appreciative till the last scene which went down the pan as usual. Damn it! *Quite* agree with you about [A] *View from the Bridge* [by Arthur Miller]. Very hardworking rep. performance – everyone trying too hard to get an effect one has seen, alas, too often on the screen acted by the real types. Mary Ure's wig join really a disgrace – a sort of mobcap effect. Tony [Quayle] and Megs [Jenkins] were increasingly good, I thought, as it went on, but the awful chorus and Michael Gwynn putting on the holy voice every time made one shudder – ruined the final curtain. I loved the production and Brian Bedford's green manch.* When I went round he had got into some terrible check ones with a large rent in the knee, the manch lying on the floor in a tousled heap. I was tempted to pick them up, smell them gingerly in the crotch and tell him to put them on again. However, the room was full of people so it would have been rather odd behaviour.

Our Bishop was on the train, shuffling round the King's Cross bookstall and just restraining himself from buying *The Story of a Nun*! I gave him a beady look but he pretended not to notice and got into the other Northern Express so I couldn't pursue the matter further.

Nude with Violin *opened in London at the Globe Theatre on 7 November.*

To Noël Coward   *20 November, London*

I think you would be pleased now, both with the pace of the whole performance and the way it goes. Except for two appalling benefit audiences last week it really seems to amuse them vastly, and to be just the right length. Between the two benefits the Queen came (last Tuesday) with a private party of Peter Carter's. She sat in the front of the dress circle, and they tell me she seemed very amused. Fortunately her presence did not seem to inhibit the audience at all and the play has never gone better. The company did not know until the end which was a good thing too as they didn't underplay – and I hope I didn't overplay. Of course I am much more fluent and certain of myself with practice and I think you would hear no more Terry tones.

To Dadie Rylands   *3 December, London*

I am giving your symposium – I mean the Shakespearean excerpts from your anthology – next Sunday for the Apollo [Society], as you no doubt know. It was a great success in The Hague last summer, and I enjoy doing it. I hope you would approve of the selections.

---

* As far as I can tell, this is an invented word and seems to mean corduroy, frequently corduroy trousers.

To Richard Myers   *12 December, London*

It is fairly quiet here – my Mamma, at 86, still managed to venture out to grace a small family party here, and we have two performances today. The Coward play goes to very fine audiences. I am a bit disappointed in it myself, though I ought to emulate the Lunts and refuse to hear a word against it until the run is over. I am not usually so disloyal to authors, but this is such a good part and idea that it is rather irritating to play it with success knowing how much better it ought to have been. Noël's being away made it impossible to get the last two scenes rewritten. If only that had been successfully coped with, it would have been a very much more amusing piece of work all round – however – I have a lot of other irons in the fire for the New Year – Warwick in the [Otto] Preminger film of *Saint Joan* – a very clever adaptation (and condensation) by Graham Greene of Shaw's play. Then in May I am to direct Berlioz' *Les Troyens* with [Rafael] Kubelik at Covent Garden, a somewhat alarming and mammoth undertaking. Finally I go to Stratford in August for the last play *The Tempest* under Peter Brook to play Prospero. 'A life crowded with incident' as Lady Bracknell would say.

To Stark Young   *14 December, London*

Your welcome gift of the Chekhov translations arrived just as I was approached to play Astrov in a television of *Uncle Vanya* – in a translation, I regret to say, by David Magarshack. I have not read it because I wasn't free to accept it, but I'll stake my oath it is not a patch on yours, which I *am* reading with the greatest enjoyment. Thank you so much for sending me the plays. I shall enjoy them all at leisure, and when next some Chekhov is done here, we must certainly use one. I always wanted to do *Ivanov*, although it is in some ways less satisfactory as a play, and the character an irritating and doomed study of irresolution (but something of Hamlet too, and of Fedya in *The Living Corpse* of Tolstoy, which always fascinated me somewhat). Perhaps one day I will try and tackle it. Have you a version of that play tucked away in your files, perhaps? If so, I would love to read it, please.

Coward's play is a great success with the public, despite a maddeningly weak last act which drives me to despair every night. I try to cover its paucity of invention with nods and becks and wreathed smiles – which I suppose is what the old actors prided themselves on being able to do. But they had strong fustian melodrama and emotional situations to clothe with their magnetism and striking tricks of stagecraft. This is a pseudo-Molière comedy (of bad manners) with cheap cracks and phoney witticisms which make one blush to utter them, and you know I am not a theatrical snob! Never mind, it is good for my diction, and I like to pretend I have Noël's own technical skill but, I hope, not his curiously thick-skinned lack of self-criticism and poor opinion of his audience's sensitivity. Anyway, I am condemned to play it for a few months and it was my own choice, so what the hell!

To Hugh Wheeler   *14 December, London*

We are to do the Troy opera as well as Carthage, but I can't get any records of
the former. I don't think there are any, but I love the Carthage French [?]
ones. I'm having long discussions with Kubelik, who seems to know both
works very well – did them in Prague in 1938. Amy Shuard is to be the
Cassandra, and Blanche Thebom the Dido. She looks very handsome in her
pictures and is said to be a fine singer. Mariano [Andreu] is to do the décor,
so I write endless letters in pidgin French to him and only pray he will be
inspired to new ingenuities and brilliance – a chorus of 120 and eight scenes
in a four hour evening – and all for only eight performances – seems a
terrifying stint to look forward to, and one must try and foresee all the
difficulties beforehand.

Pamela Brown has succumbed with a slipped disc and is not going back to
The Chalk Garden – what a piece for changes and illness. Gwen Ffrangcon-
Davies is going in and I have to rehearse her next week. Enid Bagnold has
gone into a nursing home to have her face lifted, if you please.

My mother seems to be better again, Eleanor fairly well and Bernie is in
good form. I am determined henceforth to send him abroad for at least a
fortnight every year – the sun certainly restores his equanimity in a quite
astonishing way.

I loved *Christophe Colomb* [by Paul Claudel] greatly against my expectation
(but *Occupe-toi* [*d'Amelie* by Georges Feydeau] bored me) and made great
friends with the Barraults* who are sweet. He gave me a lovely poster – the
last thing Dufy did for them.

To Lillian Gish   *19 December, London*

I had a nice Christmas card from Judith [Anderson] saying she forgave me
and was still friends – so the Christian spirit is still abroad at a suitable
moment! I am glad – I am really fond of her, and do hate estrangements with
old friends.

1957

To Robert Flemyng   *22 January, London*

Bless you for sending the *Barrett* notices. I am rather thrilled about it, as I
never saw the rushes, and felt sure I should be badly compared with Laughton.
I hope it may lead to that famous visa being granted again one of these days.

---

* Jean-Louis Barrault's company was playing a season at the Palace Theatre.

I start on *Saint Joan* tomorrow, which is only a few bits and pieces and shouldn't be too unbearably strenuous, I hope. It must have been fun having J.P. with you. He wrote very amusingly about it, and George of course was bound to meet him, though J.P. didn't mention that encounter!

To Hugh Wheeler   *11 February, London*

Did I ever thank you for the Judy Garland record? Anyway, you were sweet to send it. George P. has passed his thesis and will take his degree this month, at which he is delighted and so am I. He says he only talks to you on the telephone, but perhaps you have met again by now. I hope so – he writes me long sweet letters which touch me very much, and I trust he will spend a month with me at Stratford in August and September.

I am almost finished with *Saint Joan* and hard at work with the technicians and Mariano on *The Trojans*. John P. and Binkie are back today from their Caribbean cruise – they enjoyed staying with The Master, but found the nightly finger-wagging rather a trial. In addition, transport was seldom available and Nellie has taken to cooking in a big way, with the result that Worcester Sauce flavours every course exclusively, even the mousse. Also the new house at Firefly – which Terry Rattigan christened Cape Wrath – has glass windows all round the living room, and no verandah, so that the guests fry by slow degrees under the Master's lash.

I saw *The Barretts* last week – it is very poor indeed, except for colour photography and décor and Virginia McKenna and Jean Anderson give the only two decent performances in it. Bill Travers' tight pants do not, alas, make up for the amateurishness of his acting, and Jennifer [Jones] is a nice, technically skilled Dutch doll. I fear I spout like Donald Wolfit and am tedious and repetitive in my effects, though they are moderately professional in comparison, but I was on the whole greatly disappointed with the whole affair, and not at all surprised to read we had grossed a new low (only surpassed by Alan Webb's *Lassie* film) at Radio City.

Toby [Rowland] is in a terrible plight with *The Crystal Heart* [book and lyrics by William Archibald] directed (apparently disastrously) by Bill Butler! It opened with every possible jinx at Edinburgh two weeks ago – lights fell, Gladys Cooper took a call and fell flat on her arse, and could neither sing or dance, apparently. Then she bruised and fractured her breast bone, being flung about by the boys, who were apparently tough and inexperienced dancers. She was off for ten days and nobody came to see it. Terrible notices and rockets in the London press too. Now they have the Saville Theatre for a month, dark for one week, and about £30,000 in the red. All very unfortunate. It seems a pity they have not the courage to cut their losses and can the whole thing. One dreads another disaster here.

I have bought a lovely little post-Canaletto picture of a Venetian square and a beautiful Queen Anne mirror. Paul now says the drawingroom is too like a museum and the one uncomfortable room in the house! There is no pleasing some people. Adrianne says she is not going to act any more. The shop is a great success, and Paul's flat is very attractive. He has a lodger, an American student at the RADA called John Perry, believe it or not, a pretty but rather boring Texas beauty like a young Jean Marais. No love and little cash, but of course I pretend to be excessively jealous.

To Felix Aylmer   *14 March, London*

Flora Robson has sent me the enclosed facts in a letter. I wonder if I might ask you to send me £5, so that we could send a cheque to Harry Kendall. I am asking eighteen people to do this, and if we could thus collect £100 altogether, I thought Flora should send it from 'some friends in the theatre' without any name except hers. I hope this idea may seem good to you and that you may feel inclined to give help to a man who has had a long and worthy career in the theatre. It seems very sad that he is in such low water with illness to make things more difficult for him.

To Hugh Wheeler   *25 March, London*

We are having terrible Aunt trouble – poor Eleanor as usual stooging to the detriment of her health and nerves – a most Strindbergian situation with my Mum and her old sister which would inspire a horrific short story – Bernie and I weep but are not much good. Paul is very busy and successful – his new flat, his lodger (John Perry the Second). I languish for the unattainable (G. P. Princeton) in my idiotic way, and Noël's silly play is driving me to madness but I have to do it for another 100 performances before my blessed release in late June.

The Brooks are gravid with plans, Peter more beguiling, Natasha more idiotic, late and passive than ever, and he as sweet.

Vivien [Leigh] and I saw the rehearsal of *Petrouchka* today at the Garden – great nostalgia for me after all these years. I think it will be quite good, though the young men are all too slim and sly for that broad Russian peasant stuff. Madame [Edwige] Feuillère is delighting (though not greatly me) in *Dame aux Camélias*, *La Parisienne* and *Phèdre*, and [Harold] Hobson and [Kenneth] Tynan vie with each other in damning and overlauding her, and I have to go to innumerable parties to kiss her hand and murmur inadequacies.

The Trojans *opened on 6 June at the Royal Opera House, Covent Garden.*

To Hugh Wheeler   *13 June, London*

I believe Paul has sent you [Ernest] Newman and [Philip] Hope-Wallace, both of whom crushed me rather unmercifully over *The Trojans* – a dose of heavy powder after the jam, and I had rather a bitter letter from Mariano [Andreu] complaining of my inadequacy over the lighting – which, of course, I admit damaged his work considerably. However, I hope to get that part of it reorganised if we do it again next year.

I met Gloria Swanson at Arnold [Weissberger]'s party – she seems quite a little old monster and killed me by saying (not knowing I had done the production) 'Dear Blanche [Thebom] begged me to go to Covent Garden on Friday, but she told me not to dream of arriving before 7.45 as the first 1½ hours would bore me stiff!' Noël announced last night that he is going to delight N.Y. with Sebastian [in *Nude with Violin*] in October!! (He also rather likes my idea of a new last scene, and I shall be amused to see if he writes it – and how!) The company is rather cowed (sorry) under his rehearsal whip. Patience [Collier] in mild hysterics and M[ichael] Wilding* at the sleeping pills. Thank God I haven't got to rehearse myself. The Lunts came last night and were very gracious.

To Dirk Bogarde   *22 June, London*

Having suffered considerable slaughter in the making of *The Barretts* and *Saint Joan* recently, it occurred to me again what a much better film could be made from the stage play of *Richard of Bordeaux*. It seems to me it would be a wonderful part for you. If you were interested, and felt inclined to interest in your turn, a director and producing company, I would be only too delighted to try and help in any way I could, both in working on the script, and possibly even working with you on the part if you would like me to. The great advantage of the dialogue is that it is completely modern and colloquial. The love story, though slight, is charming (the Queen might well be played by a little French girl) and the other parts are all showy and some rather amusing. There was a lot of comedy in the play as well as its excellent dramatic thread. And of course there is a wonderful opportunity for you to get gradually older, beginning as the flighty hysterical youth, then the embittered tyrant, and, in the final scenes, the saintly gentle victim.

Somebody once told me you disliked wearing tights, but I can't think that would be an insoluble obstacle. Or would it?

After Nude with Violin, *JG returned to Stratford to play Prospero in* The Tempest.

---

* Michael Wilding was to take over from JG as Sebastian.

To Ralph Richardson   *1 August, Stratford-upon-Avon*

Peter [Brook] is doing most imaginative work and the company has some clever people in it. [Alec] Clunes is a very doughy Caliban and I miss a certain fine actor in the part.*

The Tempest *opened on 13 August.*

To Robert Flemyng   *12 September, London*

Now it must out – after all your sweetness and the good time I had with you and Carmen. I was nearly telling you a dozen times, but dreaded to spoil your holiday and create an embarrassment for us all. Binkie now has *The Potting Shed* [by Graham Greene] again and is mad about it and has asked me if I will do it between the two Shakespeares. I have read it again and confess I like it enormously. I don't know what was done to the script after I first read it, when Donald Albery sent it to me two years ago. I suppose it was rewritten a lot before New York, and now there is a new third act too since then.

I feel simply terrible to do you out of a part you love for London.† It seems revoltingly unfriendly as well as greedy, when I have two other parts to play, and I despise myself for being such a turncoat. I seem to have no judgement left nowadays, for I did exactly the same thing with *The Chalk Garden* – don't seem to know my own mind any more – and I am not yet sure if dates would fit or a cast and director would be available, but I suppose, as I was originally thought of for the part, they will be keen to have me do it, even for a limited season.

Can you forgive me? I would not have dreamt of coming to Majorca with all this so fresh in my mind if I had known you and Carmen would be there – but the accursed chance of coincidence brought it about (I only decided to come on a mad impulse). But I feel I must write and tell you myself before you hear it is in the wind from other sources.

We had not been together for such a long time, and I was so happy being with you again and feeling we were still such good friends after all these years, if this wretched scent had not been gnawing at my vitals all the while. Even now it seems rather selfish to blurt it out when you are still in the happy sunshine and the sea is between us.

I would most gladly withdraw from the scene if I were certain they would offer it to you but I once did that (*Laughing Woman* [by Gordon Daviot]) because I thought Emlyn should have the part, and Bronnie promptly gave it to Stephen Haggard! When I see Graham Greene I will put the situation clearly before him, and I do hope you will believe me when I say that if he

* Richardson had played Caliban to JG's Prospero in the 1930 Old Vic production.
† Robert Flemyng had recently created the part of James Callifer in *The Potting Shed* in New York.

would rather have you for the part, of course there is no question that you must have it. It is an impossibly embarrassing situation to me and I feel I must tell you of it in all frankness before it goes any further. Do forgive me if you can, and again thank you for a perfect week of friendship, which I can only pray this sword of Damocles may not sever by its cruel blade.

Love to you and Carmen and forgive my causing you this pain – believe me, I really feel it is all most unfair and wretched.

To Stark Young   *25 September, London*

I am commuting up and down to Stratford for two performances a week as Prospero – a very uneven but in some ways imaginative piece of direction by Peter Brook – the musical effects and the comic scenes are extremely successful, the Lords and spirits less so, the Masque a disaster, the Miranda [Doreen Aris] and Ariel [Brian Bedford] inadequate, the Caliban so-so. We come to Drury Lane with it for eight weeks at Christmas time, but I hope Brook will yield to my pleas and do some work on it meanwhile, as so much of it is admirable, but it is not as good as it ought to be – yet.

Afterwards I am to do Graham Greene's *The Potting Shed* for twelve weeks, then Wolsey with Edith Evans as Katharine in *Henry the Eighth*, for May and June at the Old Vic. So it looks as if America must again be postponed, at least until the fall of next year, which is sad. But my Maman, who is now 88 and an invalid, rejoices that I do not go so far away, and I am glad for her sake. I hear the Lunts are in Paris, Alfred and his coloured man, Jules, going daily to the Cordon Bleu for cooking lessons, Lynnie with her satchel to the Berlitz for French, which must be an amusing sight!

In the midst of all his other activity, JG was rehearsing Robert Helpmann who was to take over from Michael Wilding as Sebastian in Nude with Violin.

To Noël Coward   *11 November, London*

Today I had an excellent first rehearsal and was simply delighted not only with Bobby [Helpmann]'s industry and quickness, but also of course with all the new touches and material which, with the addition of Bobby's vivacity, should revive the spirits and attack of the company, who are not unnaturally somewhat drooping with holding the scattered shreds of the play as it sags under Michael's terrifying pathological deficiencies. What you must have suffered rehearsing him I can well imagine. Even in the ten days I worked with Zena and Geoffrey Dunn* he reduced me to a helpless welter of shame and impotence, especially when he sat down on the footlights, in imitation

---

* Zena Dare took over from Joyce Carey and Geoffrey Dunn from David Horne.

of Danny Kaye, with a cup of tea and gave a spirited résumé of his own inability to perform, with all the attendant reasons for it. Yet one cannot really dislike or blame him, though I came to the resentful conclusion that he is fundamentally lazy and incapable of dealing with it in any way.

To Stark Young   *2 December, London*

I do thank you for your generous letter, and I am delighted to think the record [*Hamlet*] gave you some pleasure. It was quite difficult, after so many years of playing the part with different actors and directors, to decide on a consistent rendering of the character as far as possible, and to adapt it and control it to the medium of recording, which requires, I find, as individual a technique as filming does. The acting training is of basic value, of course, but one has to work again from scratch, and listen (agonisingly) to playback and try and criticise oneself objectively and decide what sounds the truest. Coral Browne (Gertrude) is an Australian, hence the common diction which, of course, you picked on. I had to use all Old Vic actors (except the Polonius and Ghost and Laertes) and considering I had never worked with them before, I think they did well with only ten days to record that whole mighty play.

I gave two lectures recently, one at Cambridge University to the Marlowe Society, and one to an amateur group at Leicester, on Actor and Producer. I used your last book of essays for both talks extensively, reading extracts from your admirable surveys on the subject, to great enthusiasm, and I have ordered another copy of the book from America to be sent to George Rylands, the Bursar of King's College, Cambridge, himself a considerable expert on Shakespeare and English Literature (he directed *Hamlet* and *The Duchess of Malfi* for me during the War, in London) as he didn't know your work and was very anxious to read the whole book for himself. So you see you are much in my thoughts and a continual inspiration to me in my work.

I meant to speak to you of Billee [Harcourt] Williams too. His death was so tragic and his illness horribly painful and, it seems, mismanaged. And Jean* has lost her mind and is a pathetic half creature now. Oh, dear.

The Tempest *opened at the Theatre Royal, Drury Lane, on 4 December.*

1958

To Richard Myers   *1 January, London*

Things are good here, except that my darling Mother has been lying bedridden for several months, rallying at intervals but no longer able to take much

---

* Jean Sterling Mackinlay, Williams' wife.

interest in life, and far too many people have been ill and dying. But *The Tempest* is a real success at Drury Lane, and my dressing room is full of children and parents who really seem to love it. I have the Mary Martin–Ivor Novello suite, and feel a real star at last! Brook did quite a bit of work on the production after you saw it, and I think it is much improved, especially the Masque of Goddesses, though the cast will never, alas, be more than adequate.

I went to Paris and did my Recital there twice early in November. I have been given the Légion d'Honneur, which pleases me very much, and the success of the Recitals was very great, considering it was the worst weekend possible, with the French enraged against England over the Tunis business. I did one for about 900 students on the Sunday at the Université de la Cité and another on the Monday at Bernstein's Théâtre des Ambassadeurs – and all the nobs and a lot of leading actors and actresses came – a lot invited, of course, but none the less gratifying.

We play another four weeks at Drury Lane, and then open immediately with *The Potting Shed* – a week at Brighton then London, probably the Globe. Gwen Ffrangcon-Davies in Sybil's part, and Irene Worth as the wife. There is a new third act – apparently [Carmen] Capalbo persuaded Greene to alter it completely for N.Y. without even hearing the original read – and as he and Greene were both mad about Leueen MacGrath at the time, the act was altered to build up her part at all costs, which made hay of the original scheme! I hope ours may be an improvement. Did you see the play? It is morbid and gloomy but very sparely and concisely written and the first two acts are really fine in an Ibsenesque way.

In February 1958 JG appeared at the Globe Theatre in Graham Greene's The Potting Shed. *His next appearance as an actor was to be as Cardinal Wolsey in* King Henry VIII *at the Old Vic, and he also began to make preparations for his productions of Terence Rattigan's* Variation on a Theme *and Peter Shaffer's first stage play* Five Finger Exercise.

To Meriel Forbes, Lady Richardson   *27 February, London*

I am very distressed to hear that you know about the Shaffer play which I am to direct in the summer, because it was only a wild idea of mine to cast you in the part, which is an affected, insincere woman with a son of 18! I did tell Ralph about the play and said that *if* we really wanted you to do it, I would ask *him* to read it and give me his opinion before speaking to you. But I expect he must have mentioned it, and I am so sorry, because now we have all decided that you would be *much* too young and sympathetic. Brenda de Banzie was the first choice, and now Adrianne Allen, which I am sure will convince you that it would not have been good casting, however clever a character actress you are, to choose you.

I am very sorry it has happened this way, but you know how I always talk too much and too soon. Do forgive me. I do truly hope to work in a play with you one day. I wanted you to know how matters stood over this.

To Hugh Wheeler   *14 March, London*

We have had freezing weather here with all the usual attendant inconveniences and ill effects on business and general perambulation. It seems to suit my Mamma, however – she has returned from the very perimeter of the exit door for about the third time in the last six months, and seems as indomitable as ever, though still with two nurses and bedridden.

I am in the throes of Terry's new play which I am directing while I rehearse Wolsey and open with that at the Vic May 14th, so you see I'm not exactly idle – with *The Potting Shed* (mercifully short and no great strain) thrown in for good measure. The Rattigan play is admirably constructed and should, I think, be a sort of *Heiress* tearjerker, *strong* scenes, love interest, a dash of queerness – in fact all the most vendible ingredients. I think it is very happily cast, and Miss Leighton is a dream to work with. Paul [Anstee] has done a clever set – huge Riviera villa circa 1880 – on the terraces of which it all takes place – the boy is Tim Seeley who was a success in *Tea and Sympathy* [by Robert Anderson] here, though I didn't see him in it. He is only 22, rather mean and Teddy looking, but with enormous talent – poignant, funny and butch – a rather unusual mixture – a *great* friend of Brian Bedford's. But that won't mean much to you. I am enjoying rehearsals immensely. Terry is so good to work with too, and the Censor has passed almost everything we were a bit afraid of, so I have great hopes of it. I have also another new play to direct in June while *Henry VIII* is on – only five people, three of whom are to be Adrianne Allen, Roland Culver and Brian, and that should be quite interesting too. Then we go with *Henry* to Paris, Brussels and Antwerp for two weeks in July, and I plan to meet George at Cherbourg and motor with him around France.

I have told Paul A. about the George trip – naturally it was not very well received, but I cannot be bothered this year with intrigues, lies and subsequent recriminations. Anyway, I'm going to try to pass it all off with a gay shrug, and it seems Ed Cone* is in the picture and does not object. Life is short, and I am inclined to make a bit of a fight for one week's independence in the year, so I hope all will be well though, as usual, I feel a bit of a heel for doing it. George is nothing if not overwhelmingly persuasive, and of course that flatters me no end. Also I am rather excited at the prospect of seeing something of him again in America if I really go. I'm afraid he has really rather wound himself round my cockles in a rather special way, but I know you would understand all that.

Did I tell you I had got the Légion d'Honneur – permission from Mrs Battenberg to wear it, the citation and all – but I have not yet been kissed

---

* George Pitcher's partner.

and given the rosette, which I intend to wear on all occasions in France to guarantee good hotel rooms, I hope, wherever we go.

To Richard Myers   *12 April, London*

We begin rehearsing *Henry the Eighth* on Monday, but I am still playing for three more weeks in *The Potting Shed*, so there isn't much time to play at anything else. I have also directed the new Rattigan play *Variation on a Theme*, a modern version of *Camille* in which Margaret Leighton gives a heavenly performance. They are on the road now, and follow us at the Globe on May 8th. The provincial press has not been good, and there is trouble over the leading young man, who may have to be changed before London. If so, Margaret will have to rehearse him, as I have no time, alas, now.

There is a good chance I may bring my Shakespeare Recital to Canada and the States in the fall, leaving New York till round Christmas, if the other cities seem to like it – a 10 week tour including the West Coast. But it is not yet signed and sealed and there is a lot of scheduling and general planning to be done before it is sorted. I hope it may be.

The winter has been going on for ever here – icy winds and dark, cold days – very depressing. My poor Mamma is declining fast and has little memory or activity left her, but she sits in her bed and smiles and seems to be unaware of pain or suffering of any kind, which is a blessing.

To Hugh Wheeler   *13 April, London*

Hope it is warmer with you than it is here, for icy winds betray us and I ache in every limb despite the blue skies and waving daffodils.

I am rather low and exhausted. Terry's play opened at Manchester to fair notices and business, and was panned to hell in Glasgow – the boy will probably have to go and I have no time to rehearse Laurence Harvey who, rumour has it, may be put in after Brighton where they play this week. J.P., Binkie and Terry are going down tomorrow to make the final decision. I think the play is great fun but the boy is hopelessly inexperienced and has broken my heart with his lack of discipline and stupidity. I really shan't care if he is thrown out, and I am pretty sure it is essential he should be. I'm only glad I haven't got the final decision to make.

Poor Bernie got beaten up last night by two burglars who bashed in his little bedroom door in the yard. I heard shrieks at 2 a.m. and the police removed the two intruders before they had stolen anything, but poor B. is badly shaken and bruised with a black eye and a cut in his head. The police (helpful as usual) said 'We advise you not to press the charge' and removed the thugs, so I suppose it is better *not* to do anything about it, as I imagine (though I remained myself incognito, leaning, like Jezebel, from my bedroom window but reluctant to make an appearance until I knew what the form really was!) B.'s occasional evening sessions with gentlemen have probably not gone unobserved in this inquisitive quarter and the thugs probably made 'other suggestions' to the policemen and, quite conceivably, pressed a pour-boire into their incorruptible palms. It seems rather disgraceful, but as I have no means of checking anything more decisively, there it will have to rest. I'm only grateful they didn't ransack the house and all my bibelots, or kill B. with the broken glass they were brandishing. All highly melodramatic.

To Hugh Wheeler   *19 April, London*

The New York lecture trip is temporarily off. John P. rashly signed an option with some presenting agents who have turned out to be highly suspect. Fortunately the contract they have now offered is quite different to the one we first agreed, and Roger Stevens is being called in to set matters right without lawsuits and recriminations, or so we hope. The idea will be to drop the whole scheme for a few months, and *possibly* start again from scratch. J.P. really was rather rash and impetuous in liking the personality of the young man so much (I didn't remember he had almost as fatal a weakness as I have for young Americans) and Binkie has been very quiet over the whole matter, but I think is working decisively behind the arras.

I'm still doing *The Potting Shed and* rehearsing Wolsey *and* redirecting Terry's play on Sunday because we've had to throw out the boy after three weeks' tryout and put in another one [Jeremy Brett] before the London opening, so all is bustle and confusion, and I am a bit on edge juggling with three balls at once, so to speak.

To Hugh Wheeler   *6 May, London*

This is a frightful week for me, as Terry's play opens on Thursday and next Tuesday Wolsey at the Vic. Thank God *The Potting Shed* is at last behind me. I haven't yet fixed the autumn plan – whether I do the lecture tour or not – or what – or when – so please bear with me for the next few weeks when it should all begin to sort itself out.

Managed to see [*My*] *Fair Lady* last night, but was a bit too tired to really enjoy it, and on Friday I am going to the opening of Verdi's *Don Carlos* at Covent Garden, having dinner with the Margrave* tonight to meet Visconti who is directing it. I had an offer to do *The Trojans* at the Scala but did not dare to accept it!

Variation on a Theme *opened at the Globe Theatre on 8 May and* **Henry VIII** *at the Old Vic on 13 May. In July the latter production travelled to France and Belgium.*

---

* David Webster, General Administrator of the Royal Opera House, Covent Garden.

To Paul Anstee   *16 July, Antwerp*

Antwerp is very dull – damp, raining, livery and provincial. Yvonne Arnaud certainly comes from here, judging by the local standards of feminine beauty – *very* few pretty gentlemen, and jeans and manch only so-so. Bernie apparently took a room in Montmartre for the weekend and had a succession of mad affairs with legionnaires – he is subdued (comparatively) and triumphant in consequence, but of course finds Belgium very dull!

Five Finger Exercise *opened at the Comedy Theatre on 16 July 1958 while J G was in Antwerp.*
   His beloved mother, Kate Terry Gielgud, died in August 1958.

To Irene Worth   *11 August, London*

My darling mother died this morning. There will never be anyone like her, but I cannot help being glad, both for her sake and especially for Eleanor's, that the long struggle has ended peacefully at last.

To Gwen Ffrangcon-Davies   *13 August, London*

Bless you for your sweet wire in the midst of all your work – it was like you to think of it at once – and to Marda [Vanne] too for hers. It is dreadfully sad to think she is really gone at last, but I think she was 'half in Heaven' for many months gone by, and I am very thankful for her incredible example of love and care, and glad to think that Eleanor can pick up her own life again, though of course she feels utterly exhausted and bereft after all she has had to bear ever since Father was taken ill nearly ten years ago.

To Lillian Gish   *13 September, London*

How sweet you were to write so warmly about my darling Mother. It has been a very sad time as you can guess – the only good things are the relief for my sweet sister, who has battled with everything so long and patiently, and the fact that I can now go to America without feeling I ought to be here in case I was needed. She did not suffer greatly, but it was a long, sad road of gradual diminishing in mind and body that was distressing to watch, unable to be of any help.

To Stark Young   *15 September, London*

I thought the enclosed might amuse you. [Kenneth] Tynan is a brilliant but rather odious young fellow, who is good when he is enthusiastic, but cheap and personal when he dislikes anyone's work (he hates mine). I said once

'Tynan is very good to read as long as it isn't you' but he is shrewd and readable all the same, only lacking in any respect for the tradition and of course he has seen nothing earlier than 1946! *And* he thinks theatre must be propaganda of some sort, and if it is merely entertainment (even if it includes it being art) it is not worth anything at all, which seems very boring to me.

My mother died at 91, after a long sad decline, and I went to try and enjoy a rather unsatisfactory holiday in Italy and other places, but the Mediterranean is pretty hopeless in August with screaming families and children everywhere, roads jammed with traffic and Vespas screeching like demons everywhere. However, I did see Karajan's *Fidelio* production at Salzburg, the mosaics at Ravenna, Nancy with its lovely square and palace, and the Etruscan tombs at Tarquilia [?] – not to mention Lucca, S. Gimignano and Pisa, so it was worth while though rather hurried and exhausting.

In September, JG set off on a long North American tour of his one-man show, Ages of Man. *The tour was produced by Jerry Leider and Tennent Productions; Patsy Ainley was the stage manager and factotum. John Perry (J.P.) came out for the early part of the tour.*

To Hugh Wheeler   *21 September, Toronto*

We're off. Seemed to go pretty well last night, though I was very nervous, and we had a rather gruelling day with two drives of 100 miles each besides the recital and a reception! Splendid hotel, and Patsy and J.P. twin towers of strength. Don't fancy the Canadian Sunday much, but slept till 12.30 so not much of it left. I am beginning to recover from the upheaval. What horrid tasteless food in this country. Otherwise I love it. Great prettiness everywhere of *all* kinds.

To Paul Anstee   *21 September, Toronto*

The Crest Theatre *Salad Days* [by Dorothy Reynolds and Julian Slade] was rather fun – much better than London – and Dick Easton was excellent. He and Donald Davis are giving a boys' party tonight for me and J.P. which should be a relief after all the official efforts, Patsy discreetly retiring to friends of her own. I did a twenty-minute TV interview on Friday which they say was a great success. None of the interviewers could get a word in edgeways, and I babbled of green fields and told practically the whole story of my life as far as it is repeatable.

To Paul Anstee   *28 September, Toronto*

Our long first week is over at last, and I move on to Kingston today, then Ottawa and Montreal. I have had piles, a heavy cold, and no trade, so you can imagine I am not especially gay, also I can't taste a cigarette. However, we did 17,000 dollars here and over 7,000 in one night at Stratford and there has been nothing but praise and bravas, so I really mustn't complain.

Will send you back *Lolita* [by Vladimir Nabokov] by J.P. when he leaves on the 8th. Really! What a book. You may think you have not the slightest interest in 12 year old girls, but I assure you, you will change your mind. The first three-quarters are really something. Almost as good as Genet.

Such a pretty boy came round yesterday – about 23, at the University, fair hair, blue eyes, perfect skin and teeth, a red blazer and brand new short blue manch which creaked along beside me as I hurried him into my dressing room to give him advice about the future! I restrained myself with the utmost difficulty from trying to make a date. The town is awash with such entrancing creatures, all in the best kind of campus deshabille which is so attractive. The girls, on the other hand, wear ankle white socks and sneakers and look simply hideous.

To Paul Anstee   *1 October, Ottawa*

Enormous cinema last night to play in – 2,700 people if you please – and it went awfully well. Reception afterwards at the High Commissioner's, usual sort of stand-up boredom. The night before we were in Kingston, and I played in a dreadful gothic hall – awful coffee and sandwiches party afterwards with a lot of boring faculty and *hideous* students who presented me with a tam o' shanter with no bobble on top of it and a tartan lining – apparently an undergraduate compliment – they all wear them in the first year! Strong Scottish influence everywhere, hence the anti-alcoholism, dreadful Sundays, hundreds of dreadful gothic churches and a lot of pseudo-Highland castellated architecture, but the roads are marvellous.

A lot of manch about in Kingston, and a boy came to photograph me in three different kinds – a thick manch box coat in one colour brown, and needle cord trousers in another – unfortunately he had a *wig* – bright yellow – and Stanley [Hall] would not have owned it even at the Judgement Day!

To Paul Anstee   *3 October, Montreal*

Well you're a nice one, Julie Jordan. John Perry Jun. indeed! And what is he living on, pray, besides you? And is there honey still for tea? Perhaps he will do for Tony Forwood and you can start a Country Quartet, with Philippe as matron and the girls' school beating the bounds with saucepans. Or perhaps they will set on Dirk [Bogarde] in a lonely lane and eat him in gobbets and send back the empty riding breeches in a sealed packet done up with bloodstained sealing wax.

Gregory Peck is here giving a personal appearance for his new picture [*The Big Country* or *The Bravados*] and I believe he's coming on to see me and

wants me to sup with him. Jean Vilar and Gérard Philippe also in Montreal
and I hope to meet them tomorrow. Appalling dinner party arranged by Patsy
on our one free night this week with Lord and Lady Hardinge of Penshurst –
awful bores and snobs, hideous house but very good eats and we got a good
giggle out of it as J.P. will tell you when you see him.

To Paul Anstee   *4 October, Montreal*

Rather disappointed in *Gigi*, though [Leslie] Caron and Iso [Isabel Jeans] are
really delightful in it and the décor is all it is said to be. But [Hermione]
Gingold is very bad indeed, like an old Jewish wolf in drag, [Maurice]
Chevalier *very* old, though admirable of course (but I knew him so well as a
young man that it depresses me a bit – shape of things to come – or not to
come?) and [Louis] Jourdan, though he acts well (and *appears* to have a big
one) wears his clothes very badly and has an awful figure.

   Called on Gregory Peck – very affable and wants me to come and act and
direct in a theatre he is building in La Jolla in two years time! But very shy
and correct – he really does need jeans to glam him up – and a pretty little
French wife.

   Tried on a smashing pair of Italian manch – cream-coloured, very forward
pockets, but they were 35 dollars and thick as thieves so I should boil to death
in them in this central heated continent *and* they were very bulky to pack –
but I could hardly bear to pass them up. They had them in divine black and
very dark green too. Still, it was ten minutes Lillian Browse and no questions
asked!

   Life is painfully proper and J.P. nods and pats me on the back for my
impeccable behaviour with boring hearties at boring parties. Today I lunch
with the Kenneth Clarks. They are doing a lecture tour too. My catarrh still
hangs around. Gérard Philippe is supposed to come to the matinée today, so
I shall probably meet him. A quartet of *fairly* attractive French queens never
stopped ogling at supper last night, I think probably from the Vilar company
playing here (he asked me to direct for him at Avignon too) but I merely
gazed adoringly at Patsy and played with some rich jewel.

   From Brian: *Child*   Mummy, mummy, can I lick the basin?
                     Mother No, dear, just flush it.

To Paul Anstee   *8 October, Rochester, N.Y.*

It hardly seems possible that I have only been three weeks away. Such a lot of
reciting and motoring and chattering seems to have gone on – but it goes
very fast really, with all the moving, packing, checking in and out and so on.
The hotels are wonderfully comfortable, despite a tendency to foam rubber
pillows and mattresses which spring about under you and almost throw you
out of bed. Perhaps they are good for romping – I haven't had an opportunity

of trying! The food is good if you stick to American things like oysters and frankfurters – the toast is soggy and the coffee weak and the meat cut in doorsteps so that you rather dread it. Wonderful fast, roomy and low-slung cars which are very comfortable indeed. The most marvellous drives the last two days, past still lakes with woods turning to gold and orange reflected in the water, white wooden houses and fine roads with very little traffic or people.

To Paul Anstee   *13 October, Boston*

I do a show at Lancaster Pa. tonight and have tomorrow OFF, the first for 15 nights! But I have done 24 performances out of 76 so I feel that I have bitten off the first third in a chunk. There is more free time after the next 30 days which are the worst. But I am well and I do enjoy being in a high room with a view over the skyscrapers and the Common (tempting!). Hugh [Wheeler] has been here which was a lovely break, and the three shows went wonderfully. A very nice lunch at Harvard with professors and a lot of most unattractive but agreeable eggheads in hideous Ivy League suits.

To Paul Anstee   *16 October, Delaware*

I've heard nothing for ten days either of you or Eleanor – and you are the most important, and I feel very lost without news of you.

Patsy and I gave our big suitcases to the publicity man to take by car over the weekend (as we were going by plane) and both were stolen at 4 a.m. from the back seat in N.Y. Imagine my rage and bafflement – about 16 shirts, new shoes, two suits (fortunately old ones), three pairs of lovely slacks – my check, whipcord and silk ones – and my lovely blue coat without lapels. *And* it is now ragingly hot and I am simply stifling without any thin clothes to wear. Also laundry problems – had to buy evening shirts ready made in Philadelphia which I hate. I hope the London insurance is O.K. Patsy lost a lot of good things too – shawls, two evening dresses etc. Anyhow I shall *have* to buy some new clothes now, and have a field day when I get back. And there is always Jerry Rothschild's in Hollywood.

We stay in these motels a good deal for the one-night stands – far more comfortable and less chi-chi than hotels (we were in a horrid one in Philadelphia). Everything going pretty well otherwise, but one never stops packing, unpacking, resting, meeting a lot of vague people, doing the show and eating rather drearily in coffee shops and university restaurants which are like ladies' teashops in England. Still, it is all comfortable, intensely clean (new strip of paper over the loo seat to assure you it has been disinfected after the last tenant!) and the wonderful weather. Some of the halls are hell – movie houses and basketball courts with audiences spread deep and horizontally –

but now and again there is a stunning audience and a nice place to speak in and one really enjoys it and gives a decent performance.

To Paul Anstee   *19 October, Pennsylvania*

Glorious weather still, really almost too hot. We had terrific drives yesterday and the day before – 285 miles yesterday and then the show. The motoring I've done this year, one way and another! And Jerry Leider hums a good deal and Patsy in her clipped little sergeant major voice is discreetly bossy. I get rather sick of them both as you can imagine, but it might be far worse. The students at the schools and universities are a wonderful audience, and a good deal of needle cord manch is worn (very badly cut, and usually only partly zipped!) so my eyes occasionally wander. The R.C. college at Cleveland was rather fun, and I *thought* the skirted Father who managed the show (who had been at Oxford) squeezed my arm with a rather familiar warmth after a few heavy scotches, and threatened to come to Detroit to hear the Recital tomorrow as he was too busy behind the scenes in his own college! About 42 and not unattractive, so I may yet achieve a Catholic pass – but Patsy orders me off to bed every night at about 12.30, which is very handy, *unless* I happen to be enjoying myself, which does not happen often. Perhaps I can elude her just for once.

To Paul Anstee   *22 October, Detroit*

Detroit is the most deadly city – we drove to Mount Pleasant on Monday, 126 miles each way – and going out of the city (and coming back) there is an absolutely straight and unbelievably hideous street at least fifteen miles long with two storey shops and garages and lamps and traffic lights every 200 yards, and not a variation of any sort or kind. Like driving to Hell, and exhausting and BORING.

I have two queer books to send you, but of course Patsy wants to read them first!! If I tell her they are not in her line, it will make her even more curious, so you probably won't get them till about Christmas. The Japanese one is quite exciting, and the *cover* of the other is very you – not a bad story but the queer part rather dragged in for sensationalism, I should say.

To Paul Anstee   *25 October, Chicago*

At last, at last, four lovely letters from you, and your sad little picture with the appealing calf like eyes? Oh dear, what nostalgia. I simply couldn't give Patsy a civil word over lunch, I was so excited, and I am manching every bit of you as I write, from top to toe. What a heap of news – darling I miss you so *very* much and long for you too.

I was offered *Valmouth* [by Sandy Wilson] to direct and thought it vulgar and horrid and wouldn't touch it with the end of a bargepole – wrong again, well, well.

I've had a frightful week. We flew to Atlanta yesterday – no, the day before – back yesterday, 60 mile drive to Lafayette, and 100 mile drive here this morning, with 'fast time' and Eastern Time and Summer Time making us ruin our watches and shatter our schedules, hours losing and hours gaining, and the clocks go back again here tonight! It is quite mad. The planes and cars are roomy and comfortable, and the roads wide and straight but oh! so deadly boring and flat. And the motels are passable, but food utterly filthy and monotonous and Patsy and the Leiders 24 hours a day is pretty trying, I can tell you. This hotel is just luxe and a welcome change, just for 48 hours. I must say the halls are wonderful on the whole, but they vary a lot. The faculties and parties are ghastly and everybody thinks Patsy is my wife which is rather embarrassing for us both! No prettiness, absolutely! But I go for two nights to Bobby Lewis next Thursday and he has promised me a party with Lena Horne and some pretty boys, so that will really be an excitement for 48 short hours, then on we go again.

You don't say if you have seen J.P. since he came back from Canada. I've only had one note from him saying will I do an AUSTRALIAN tour in '59. Thank you *very* much. What a horrible idea.

To Paul Anstee   *3 November, Chicago*

Well, dig those gorgeous deep front pockets with the split linings, what a lovely joy it was to chat with you over the great big, beastly ocean. And today a sweet and happyish letter as well. Bless you, darling boy.

Just returned from seeing *Cat* [*on a Hot Tin Roof*], in which Paul Newman looks absolutely divine in cigar brown manch (but only when the film was getting very longwinded – a great relief to brighten the last half hour). He acts well too, and so does Miss [Elizabeth] Taylor, who looks as beautiful as Vivien used to, and not unlike her either. But there is a deal too much talk and noise and hideous colour.

New York was so divine, and I even got a couple of bites at an old cherry, which relieved the long strain on my starving basketwork after so many weeks of frustration. I seem to live in Chicago airport. Thursday I have off and have (rather madly) decided to rush in to N.Y. again for the night to see *Pleasure of Your* [*His*] *Company* [by Samuel Taylor] – Cyril Ritchard's smash hit which he has directed and plays the lead in and thinks I may like to do in London. Hugh saw the play in Boston and rather liked it, so I feel I should go while the iron is hot, for there are sure to be other offers for it for London and I want to see for myself. Shall try and take Marlene on my arm! *That* would please the boys. It sounds rather fun, and a nice one set grand room overlooking San Francisco Bay for you to design.

Do you know what a circumcised cock reminds one of? Yul Brynner in a turtle-necked sweater. Bobby Lewis joke.

To Paul Anstee   *8 November, St Louis*

Lovely day in New York – glorious summer weather, no overcoats – met Miss Garbo on Park Avenue looking like a displaced charwoman. I'm sure she cuts her own hair with nail scissors. Distantly gracious, and that beautiful smile. 'Don't touch me,' (as I made to shake hands) 'I am ill – on my way to the specialist!' Wild greetings from my barber and manicurist at the Plaza, and a lovely cruise round all my favourite streets, window-shopping. In the evening to Cyril's play with Marlene on my arm. Dreadfully disappointing – two jokes, one about semen and the other about stool (a word I have *not* yet heard before for a stage laugh) were the only times I smiled. Phoney, badly constructed idiotic play – old-fashioned and badly acted too – shocking in a thoroughly dreary, bad taste way, like a poor man's *Roar Like a Dove* [by Lesley Storm]. I'm sure it would die the death in London, unless Rex Harrison or the Lunts gave it the benefit of their particular brilliance. I'd rather die than play it. So that's that.

On to '21', which was pandemonium and rather boring, and Miss D. went off to the village with Daniel Gélin and J.-P. Aumont, sighing very sweetly. She told an endless story about meeting [Michael] Wilding, whom she evidently had had a big thing with before, on his honeymoon with Mrs Nell in Las Vegas, and how he insisted on begging her to join them, and how Mrs N. held her hand *far* too long. I gather she always tells stories about ladies making passes at her. She also said she was mad about Visconti, 'but of course no one had told me it was hopeless!' Very sweet and intelligent on Noël, too.

Bobby Lewis as sweet as ever – an extraordinary boy keeps house for him, and a beautiful, spotless house it is (but they NEVER open a window, and the air conditioning is stifling). It seems he did the whole decorating for Bobby and it is really very pretty in a Hollywood kind of way. And the boy's wardrobe! Like an advertisement in *Esquire* – about 20 pairs of slacks, belts, ties all on racks exquisitely arranged. He cooks too, in a spotless kitchen (but not very well – oh, American food is *awful*) and discreetly slides about the house in the discreetest possible way. Jolly clever of Bobby and the boy seems utterly content. Not very pretty, however – just as well perhaps, though I gather there are many admirers.

Impossible halls the last two nights, each holding 5,000! I drew about 1,100, which looked like a bunch of Brussels sprouts huddled together in an empty desert, but they seemed to like it very well all the same. Van Cliburn and Peter Ustinov in opposition so I was hardly surprised not to have a very big house, but so silly to put one anywhere so vast.

I see the Lord Chamberlain has lifted the ban on homo in the theatre.

Well, well. And Madame Callas has got the sack from the Met. so she will be closer in David [Webster]'s arms than ever.

To Paul Anstee   *14 November, Denver*

Arrived here for four whole days, and completely unpacked for the first time since Boston – you can't imagine the relief. A very plain Jewish professor with dyed black hair drove us to Central City to look at the relics which were rather fun. So was the driver – a really attractive boy of 21 with exquisite Californian grey flannel trousers and a Tony Curtis cut – just breaking in to Hollywood – enormous dark glasses, of course, and a lot of charm. With Patsy in the car I was hardly able to try my Lolita act, but it was fun to think I might have if she wasn't.

To Paul Anstee   *16 November, Denver*

My few remaining hairs are going very grey. I think I shall be an old gentleman by the time this tour is over – but I am a bit rested with this four-day break. A German in Chicago sent me a new translation he has done of Pirandello's *Henry IV* which is the best I have read of many over the years. It might be a possibility for London. [George] Devine begged me months ago to do it at the Court, but I don't see why I shouldn't do it on my own in the West End. Will send it to the boys and see what they think.

To Paul Anstee   *19 November, Idaho*

The ad in the (New York) *Sunday Times* is the one thing they take a month beforehand. They buy an enormous space and hope to get huge advance sales from it immediately – parties etc. This is always done, in some cases they sell out for weeks on it, and hope to do so with me. Alas, I originally promised another two weeks option (if it is a real success) and can't get out of it now. Of course, Kolmar (William Morris [Agency]) and Arnold [Weissberger] both tell me that Jerry [Leider] is making too much money – they say *he* will make 30,000 dollars out of the tour! Why didn't I go to them direct? W. Morris put up *all* the money originally and only take their 10 or 15 per cent, which annoys them. Well, never mind, and don't tell J.P.! I think H.M.T. [H. M. Tennent] get 1000 or so, which is really more than they deserve! But still I think I've saved a lot of money. No sitting rooms, except in Boston, and I spend very little with so much travelling. Mean to have a shopping spree in Los Angeles, though. I had a very sweet wire from Don [Bachardy] and Christopher [Isherwood] and a note from Rex Evans, so it ought to be fun there. Not a word, however, from G. Cukor, so I fear he is not inviting me to stay with him.

Bernie's sister has left her husband and become an alcoholic! so I expect to enjoy a Tennessee Williams scene with her if I can find her in the dives of Costa Mesa!

On with the plans and take all care of yourself. Maurice's cords sound a dream of beauty. Why don't you borrow them to dazzle me – or even have them copied for yourself in oyster grey or merde d'oie? Lots of lovely frontier pants around here. Did you see *Cat*, with Paul Newman in the divine brown manch! (I hope I shan't go completely dotty in the next five years and get put away in a Corduroy Concentration Camp for my last remaining time on earth.)

To Hugh Wheeler   *24 November, Portland, Oregon*

Very sick of travelling, and poor Patsy, who is metallic and patient, but oh!, not so close for so long! – and the endless moving and meeting new people is agony. However, they have cancelled one recital at San Francisco, as all the students at Berkeley are away from it for Thanksgiving (they might have thought of that before) so I have four clear days which should be wonderful. I tried to get George to meet me there, but he is maddeningly promised to his old Grannie and cannot get out of it now. Paul is coming to N.Y. and we propose going to Havana for Christmas.

To Paul Anstee   *27 November, San Francisco*

Sweet letter from you this morning to cheer up Thanksgiving, which is a complete holiday here like Christmas in England. Not a shop open or a car in the streets, but glorious weather after a filthy fog last night, and a horrid drive to and from Sacramento (88 miles) and a dreary, po-faced party for Callas at Whitney Warren's which Patsy and I arrived at very late. The fat parlour maid was the nicest person there and the food wonderful, though I was too tired to enjoy it much – the crab kept Patsy awake but not, thank Heaven, your old friend.

To Paul Anstee   *3 December, Beverly Hills*

San Francisco was a bit of a disappointment, except for the Saturday night when I went on the town with my friend from the reception desk and the bars were simply fabulous – people squashed together in milling hordes of jeans and manch, packages galore, and I finished up at 4 a.m. with a rather bashful teacher from Santa Barbara with a very handy property and a beige corduroy SUIT. So that was quite an evening, though I was a little the worse for wear next day, especially as I had two shows!

This hotel is simply divine – the first real luxe – Mediterranean heat, blue skies and palm trees, and wonderful service. My dear little garden to have breakfast in and absolute quiet – no radios or TV bawling. Had an exhausting lunch with Don and Christopher who sent you much love, and a mad shopping spree in the morning, of which more anon! Saw *The Defiant Ones* and loved it. Today we go to Disneyland which I hear is great fun, and tonight I dine with Cukor and Clifton Webb. Tomorrow Rex Evans is having a party for me – chaps only, so I am beginning to cheer up at last.

New York theatre is still not decided. Long letter from Binkie offering me to direct Sir Ralph in a new Graham Greene comedy in the spring – also, will I do *The Potting Shed* on TV? Mmm? Not altogether smitten.

To Paul Anstee   *4 December, Beverly Hills*

Patsy and I and friends of hers went to Disneyland yesterday. It was simply divine and I *longed* for you to have been there. You get in to a little launch on Jungle River and glide away past crocodiles, gorillas, giant butterflies etc., and the divine young man at the helm (in very tight white ducks and jersey and a peaked cap) does a commentary of wonderful camp – now steady here, folks, it's dangerous here – over the rapids, shooting off a pistol at intervals as a huge hippo rears its head into the boat, and rubber arrows go flying past, mad life-size clockwork (I suppose) animals and natives. I can't tell you what fun. Then we went on two *mad* rides – the Snow White one with shrieking witches and sound effects, pitch dark passages, sailing through walls that open and close behind you, figures leaping out as you pass – and another Peter Pan, in which you go up a slope in a small boat through opening windows and appear to fly over London, model Big Ben and all, and descend at a hair-raising angle passing Hook and Smee and the Pirate Ship all posed and shaking their fists from the decks below – and a ridiculous mining train with the driver and guards in ten gallon hats (and jeans) puffing through caves and deserts and descending to a brilliant cavern of jewels and waterfalls. It really was a hilarious afternoon. *And* it is 85 degrees here in the daytime!, hotter than the South of France. So it is all rather fun but a bit exhausting too. The *pace*, and the cars and the mad ladies and sexy looking boys on every corner. If ever I do a picture here again you *must* come out. You would simply adore it.

To Paul Anstee   *12 December, Tallahassee*

We have had a most vile week – travelled all night on Thursday. At 1.45 the plane left after a show and awful party – arrived at Dallas 8 a.m., waited three hours, on to Beaumont – back to Dallas, with a filthy snobbish audience and impossible hall to seat 2,700 and vile acoustics – up at 5.45 this morning and changed at New Orleans – have just arrived here, but a lovely place and lots of nice letters including one from you. So I feel better already – tomorrow back to New Orleans, four hours wait, lunch there and I will investigate the hotel someone recommended, which I *think* is run by the same Queen for whom Bernie worked at the Lafitte when I met him. If so, it is sure to be a madhouse but perhaps amusing! I have some other divas for you there, but no *people*, I'm afraid. On Sunday we have a night off at Washington, then two more dates before I see you – and the travelling outfit! I bet it's stylish too. Only five more days – imagine.

Paul Anstee met JG in Washington and they enjoyed a holiday in Havana before Ages of Man *opened at the 46th Street Theatre on 28 December.*

1959

To Paul Anstee   *14 January, New York*

Well, my little one, so you are back again at the loom and I do so wonder if you had a terrible time getting away and arriving and how you managed with the parcels and the customs and all. It did seem terrible to go back into Goddard [Lieberson]'s house where you had been sitting just a minute before and realise you had all that coping to do by yourself and I shouldn't see you again for another two months. You must have thought me a shit not to come and force you to let me go with you to Idlewild,* but I was a bit afraid of being voiceless after that very late night and I went back to bed and wept a little for my sins and hoped so deeply that you had at least enjoyed *some* of our time together here. Havana, at any rate.

I'm not going to dig up the old problem again. It distresses me nearly as much as it does you, but I suppose not quite as much or I would be strong-minded enough to do something about it. But I think you do know I am very deeply devoted to you and adore being with you and *hate* to give you cause for pain or unhappiness of any kind. I know I am not worthy of your great affection for me and have made you suffer for it and I am very sorry.

Darling boy, do try and forgive me, and understand if you can. It was lovely sharing this success with you, even at second hand, and I like to think it gave you some pleasure too. Everyone here was so delighted with you and I know you made many contacts which should prove both pleasant and perhaps advantageous in the future.

It is very empty in the house without you – the girls are in semi-deshabille cooking a grand dinner and discussing how many maids and coloured boys they must engage for a *respectable* cocktail party they insist on giving me before I leave. I shall try and rustle up an imposing guest list and Patsy can do the honours for once.

* Idlewild Airport became John F. Kennedy Airport in December 1963.

To Paul Anstee *16 January, New York*

The house is very dull and empty without you. Mad parties and lunches every day and I spend the morning trying to squeeze out crocodile tears for the photographers. *Life* Magazine and [Richard] Avedon both insisting I should weep for them! Really!

To Paul Anstee *20 January, New York*

Turned down 25,000 dollars to do *Potting Shed* on TV *here* with Alec [Guinness]. Also 15,000 to do the Recital on TV. Get me!

We played to 36,650 last week, and Sunday night was 5,300!! They queue up all day for seats, and asked me if I would come back and do four weeks more of it in the autumn. Certainly not.

To Lillian Gish *24 January, New York*

I have been extremely worried during my stay here to learn that dear Flo Reed has fallen on hard times and often finds it difficult to pay her Hotel Bill.

Knowing her pride and how she would hate to accept anything from us, I was wondering if you would join me in paying her Hotel Bill for six months or more? I had thought if six of her good friends gave 200 dollars each, we could give it to the Manager of the Hotel Windsor as an anonymous gift.

Of course she must never know where or from whom it came. I leave here February 5th, but if you would like to send me a cheque before I leave, I will gladly take it to the Manager of the Hotel and he can tell her some friends have placed the money to her credit.

To Paul Anstee *26 January, New York*

Went to the Actors' Studio and had a terrific welcome – lots of pretty characters and some toothsome manch – a boy and girl did a very sexy scene from *Anatol* [by Arthur Schnitzler] – in bed – he in tight black trousers (no pockets) and a vest only, and she a sort of Shelley Winters type in a negligée – rather fun at such very close quarters.

You will enjoy this. Irene [Worth] invited George [Pitcher] to take her to the first night of *Rashomon* tomorrow and offered to put him up. 'Only one bed, of course, dear, but you could sleep on the sofa!' How little she knows her future might be in deadly peril! I'm not sure he won't accept too!! He was very evasive when I asked him what he intended to do about it.

Very tricky dinner with Diana [Wynyard], as she is going to California to do a T.V. with Maggie Leighton and I am in the throes of trying to fix the latter for Beatrice. I shall probably make lifelong enemies both of Peggy and Diana, but it is a ticklish problem all round.

To Paul Anstee   *28 January, New York*

Rather sharp letter from you this morning, but I do love the sight of your pretty hand on the breakfast table just the same.

Bob Gable gave a very crowded party which was fairly fun and I popped home to a flat in the village with a very well-equipped young fellow (rather like *you* to look at – very gentle and sweet for a drink) who is a designer at Bob's TV. Decided to leave at 4 a.m. and left my keys behind, so the poor Darby and Joan here were rudely awakened by their wandering guest. I must say they were very sweet about it. Called on Jacques the other day to find him in bed with a young chap in chinos with a basket like a bunch of ripe bananas which I stroked appreciatively before discreetly leaving!

To Paul Anstee   *30 January, New York*

It is strange to be packing up, both here and at the theatre. Patsy fetching and carrying and bossing about as usual. Wonderful moment at Irene Selznick's the other night, when Mrs Lee Strasberg, a large Germanic cow, was talking to me with her batty daughter [Susan]. Irene leaned over us with a drink and Mrs S. cooed 'My dear, what beautiful garnets!' Irene had on a blood ruby that had cost David S. 110,000 dollars, so you can imagine her face. It was rather a nice party, and Tennessee and [Elia] Kazan have asked me to go to a run-through of the new play on Tuesday which might be exciting. I am also going to *Rashomon* on Monday.

Mad business again. I hear the standing room only allows 38, and by the time the intermission was over they counted 52 the other night. I suppose the gentlemen retire from their seats to indulge in a little groping during my second act, as other dear friends of mine have been known to do in their time. I go to the Plaza today and lunch with [Roger] Stevens and [Robert] Whitehead to look at their theatres and discuss *Much Ado*.

Tomorrow we close and there will be present giving and tears and a party at Sardi's for the troupe. Sunday the boys have a cocktail party here for me, highly respectable, and in the evening a rather more al fresco gathering arranged by Ben and Louis for my gentlemen friends.

To Paul Anstee   *4 February, New York*

Hugh came on Saturday and we went together to see Tennessee's new play [*Sweet Bird of Youth*] run-through yesterday – very striking, unnecessarily violent, but Geraldine Page and Paul Newman (in pyjamas, and then putting on some *very* dishy beige jeans with huge patch pockets *underneath* the front ones, in full view of audience) were both simply wonderful. The first and last acts much the best. Our last night was very hysterical. I did 'Fear no more' as a sort of encore at the end, with a good many chokes en route, and a large bunch of red carnations tied with orange ribbons was flung on to the stage as the curtain finally fell. All very moving.

Apparently Irene's invitation was quite without arrière pensées after all. George thinks she is in love with Claire Bloom! Irene is going to Stratford Ontario to play Rosalind, so perhaps she is already practising in tights and boots!

After Ages of Man *closed in New York, JG went on holiday to Morocco.*

To Paul Anstee   *8 February, Marrakesh*

We lunched in Paris with Ginette [Spanier] and Paul-Emile [Seidmann], at La Perouse where I have never been before – very nice, but I was in rather a jumble from the journey from New York, though I had slept a bit on the plane. Then five hours to Casablanca, where we stayed the night. On by car through very green plains, with camels and donkeys and minarets and Arabic inscriptions on walls and gates, and a delicious lunch – oh, to be back to European food and drink again – and so to this hotel, where Adrianne [Allen] was celebrating her birthday. Flowers for us in our rooms, and champagne etc. She and Bill, Tommy [Elliott] and Billy [Chappell], John, Binkie and I. Churchill is here but I haven't seen him yet.

It was wet and cold yesterday, but today was glorious – we sat out on our three adjoining balconies with nothing on, while the palm trees swayed and birds twittered and the pink walls of the garden and the green pepper trees and laburnums twinkled against a background of snow mountains. And this evening we spent hours in the huge square of the Arab town watching every kind of goings on, and plunged into the alleys to see herbs and fruit and meat and materials piled high in every corner – like a glorified version of the Flea Market – and the children are divine, and the snake-charmers and funny old carriages packed with veiled ladies and bundly gentlemen in turbans and slippers. And you go up on the café roof and watch them all pack into the mosques at sundown, and it gets quite cold and all the little lights go on in the shops and everyone is intensely busy and talks in low voices – also a nice change after America – and nobody bothers you or stares or touts – unlike Havana! Tonight we go out to dinner (Adrianne to poker with the Churchills) and I expect Binkie and I will try a little luck at the casino. How you would love it all. I miss you very sadly – a holiday is not the same without you, not at all.

Gladys Cooper is to play Sybil's part in *Day by the Sea*, and possibly Maggie Leighton for Irene's. I suggested it because I want to do something I really know for my first go at TV. Anything new would make me far too nervous, and I didn't want to appear in a costume part.

Some talk of doing the Recital in London in July, perhaps to open the Queen's, if I fix *Much Ado* for September in N.Y. I am hoping to approach

Peggy first but they say not to upset her at the moment as she is in heavy trouble with her new play [*The Coast of Coromandel* by J. M. Sadler] which is on the road. I agree with you that she ought to be the first choice, and Maggie if she fails. M. was really very good as Rosalind, and she is a big draw in N.Y. after *Separate Tables*. We shall see.

To Hugh Wheeler   *11 February, Marrakesh*

Your glasses are a triumph of chic. I love to wear them and fold them and show them off – what pretty presents you gave me so sweetly, and I fear I only thanked you so very casually.

I am dreadfully homesick already for New York and miss you (and George) most terribly. The last two days at the Plaza were almost more than I could bear. That awful feeling of rooting oneself up from a time that could hardly be possibly so good again. Here I cannot sleep till 3 a.m. and, as there is nothing whatever to do after dinner, about 10, I find it a bit trying, though of course it is fun to be with the boys again and discuss endless casting possibilities and future plans. Also the place itself is marvellous, and the weather divine – but there are distinct drawbacks. Only two restaurants at which we eat alternately, and a maddening French air-training field. The planes buzz like angry wasps the whole day long, disturbing the divine beauty of the pink walls and distant mountains and the twittering of birds which would otherwise constitute a veritable khayyam of privacy.

Old Churchill and his entourage hobble around rather touchingly. Adrianne and Bill, Billy Chappell and Tommy Elliott were all here but are already gone, alas, so we are left to our own devices, and I have a sneaking suspicion that I am going to be very bored and depressed with another whole week to go. However, I suppose the enforced rest and let-down of activity are good for me.

To Hugh Wheeler   *27 February, London*

We drove to Fez for three days and saw Rabat, Meknes and Casablanca on the way back. The blondes [Binkie Beaumont and John Perry] were very sweet, but I was heartsick for George and spent hours writing him ridiculous love letters and mooning about. I just can't get him out of my system, and the snatched times in America are madly nostalgic. I think I have frightened him to death for fear I shall make a belated effort to drag him away from Ed altogether. I would too! But of course I won't. Do reassure him of this if you write to him. He does still love me rather, but I just mustn't bouleverser him again – his life is suitable and comfortable from every point of view and I must be content to be just sweet for a drink – lucky to get *that* at my time of life, and one must not be greedy for too much. Look what the Oliviers have got from that! And those five weeks after Christmas were really something to treasure always.

Saw *La Grande Illusion* which I missed before – how divine – and a wonderful *Lucia* [*di Lammermoor*] at the Garden with Joan Sutherland sensational – Serafin in the orchestra – a dear little 80 year ball of fire – and lovely sets and costumes (and lighting) by Zeffirelli, a pupil of Visconti, who also directs. Thrilling evening. Tonight I go to *Five Fingers*, in which I hear Adrianne is over-acting her drawers off, and tomorrow to *A Taste of Honey* with Peter Brook. Went to Stratford to see Peggy's new play – no good, though we argued about it till four in the morning. Fear it won't come in, though she gives a lovely performance as usual, and I'm afraid Eric Porter, my bête noir, is excellent in it too, but the play falls between several unsatisfactory stools – written by some inexperienced little lady.

I envy you at Rio Chico – give them all my love and greetings. Nuns at luncheon and Nell to cocktails, what a time you will have.

My Spoleto dates are June 28th to July 5th inclusive – three recitals, so I shall stay there all that week. Do you think you would like to come? If so, I might try and get a flat, as I want to persuade G. to come for a week before and then on with me. He and I might go to Rome, I thought, about June 18th, if Ralph's play* is launched by then. I may do the Recital in London after Spoleto in July and August, then, please God, America again some time in September, but Stevens and Whitehead are terribly vague and Binkie says it will cost 150,000 dollars.

Very embarrassing ditching Peggy, Diana *and* Irene (who they say is too old to do *Day by the Sea* on TV). I fear none of my ladies will be speaking to me. I hear Noël is not speaking to Roger Stevens either – in fact the pots are all at boiling point in the Avenue one way and another, and Binkie's secretary has given notice!

My record was full of buzzing voices too, and I wrote Goddard – hope to God they deal with the fault before it is generally released. I have had one or two splendid notices for it already, so perhaps it will sell well and swell the coffers, which really are quite full for once – and nobody around to spend them on!!

Paul is well and busy and gave a splendid party for me at his flat. Brian [Bedford] gave another which was rather a shambles. Bobby Lewis and Toby [Rowland] dining here next week. Paul seems to have acquired a lot of miscellaneous admirers all of a sudden – this is not just braggadocio I believe – and says that now he is 30 he begins to be able to get some trade, ever since his success at 72nd Street, I think. So that is rather a relief to me, and I think he has settled at last for G. being No. 1.

Send me a letter and I will forward it to Keith [Baxter] – his address takes

---

* JG was to direct Ralph Richardson in *The Complaisant Lover* by Graham Greene.

too long to write! He was at the Margrave's the other night. The Fearfuls* are triumphant and the house packed with new expensive treasures, but Jimmy [Bell] looks like Kit Cornell, sagging and squat, and David's teeth appeared to be rather here and there – they are beginning to droop a little, I fear, despite all their riches. Aren't we all? All but you and me.

To Noël Coward   *11 March, London*

I am very much hoping to do *Much Ado* in September with Maggie Leighton in New York. Binkie is busy now trying to arrange it all, but Roger Stevens seems to be a bit complicated to deal with. Kit Cornell says it is always so hard to pin him down as he is secretly deciding about Park Avenue – whether to buy it or pull it down!

I have seen a lot of plays since I got back. *Taste of Honey* [by Shelagh Delaney] and *Long and the Short and the Tall* [Willis Hall] both hideously ugly and squalid but both very well played and impressive, I thought. And I loathed *Valmouth* [Sandy Wilson]. Low camp, if ever I saw it. I think C[hristopher] St John's book on Ethel Smyth might amuse you – I will send it to you. The photos alone are worth the money – and Vita S[ackville]-West's poem at the beginning. Why are Lesbians always so humourless, even the cleverest of them?

In April JG returned to New York to make a television adaptation of Terence Rattigan's The Browning Version. *It also starred Margaret Leighton and Robert Stephens and was directed by John Frankenheimer. He began to make plans for the North American tour of* Much Ado about Nothing *later in the year.*

To Paul Anstee   *8 April, New York*

New York is a summer festival, but I don't see much of it buried in my rehearsal room miles down in the Bowery. But we are progressing well, and he is giving us Friday off to learn our lines! We are trying to get P. Ustinov for Dogberry – a good idea I think, but of course he may not be interested. Graham Greene and Ralph have apparently had a row and he nearly threw up the part because he disagreed with an essential point – that he hadn't done it for years with the wife! Binkie suspects Lady Mu of being at the back of this, but he will enjoy patching it up I have no doubt.

To Paul Anstee   *11 April, New York*

We rehearse interminably in our enormous black ballroom, but I have got my way about the script and am beginning to know my lines. I think the

---

* JG refers to 'The Fearfuls' twice in letters to Hugh Wheeler and once to Paul Anstee. It appears to refer to 'Binkie' Beaumont, John Perry and David Webster.

director is excellent, though he is full of infuriating adenoids and mannerisms, and yells within two inches of one's face. Bob Stephens, who was in [*Epitaph for George*] *Dillon* [by John Osborne] is quite a dear and turns up in skin-tight manch, which is something to cheer one up. Trousers seem tighter than ever this season, though I don't have much chance of taking them in.

Jacques turns out be a terrific drag queen, and sews all day when he isn't in bed, either buffing his nails or being fucked by strange gentlemen – some people have a very easy life, do they not? He lives for the big balls – in every sense, I imagine.

To Paul Anstee   *13 April, New York*

Wonderful ovation for me at the Waldorf Astoria [for the Tony Awards] last night – about 1000 people present and great scads of people from the theatre, of course. I got the biggest applause of the lot, except perhaps Ingrid Bergman and people tell me it was very impressive on TV. I made a demure speech with a few discreet tears and it went down extremely well.

Frankenheimer, the director, and I have become great buddies and between us have fashioned a really striking new beginning *and* the original end. I think it is going to be quite good altogether. Maggie is wonderful too, and I simply love the part – a riot of props, though, spectacles, books, gowns, medicine taking etc. etc.

I miss you very much, though I'm sure you don't believe a word of it.

To Paul Anstee   *18 April, New York*

Oh, what sharp letters I get from you, fairly bristling with innuendo and mischievous retaliations. You needn't imagine I am having a very amusing time, and it is a bit tantalising to slave away all day long and be so tired by the evening that one doesn't really enjoy the few social moments I have managed to squeeze in – the Bolshoi first night should have been fun, Margaret and I went with Arnold [Weissberger] (and the *ghastly* Milton [Goldman]) in the front row of the stalls if you please! (But of course I offered to pay for my ticket and Arnold graciously allowed me to!) Garbo and Valentina [Schlee] sat just behind us, and Nellie [Noël Coward] and Marlene quaffed champagne with us during the interval, and I saw masses of people I knew, but we had had nothing to *eat* before, and after three and a half hours of *Romeo and Juliet* and an endlessly slow service in the Oak Room as guests of that awful Ethel Rainer, we were starving and speechless with exhaustion. Ulanova was divine, but she is cold, you know – nothing in the least Italian about her – still, I'm glad to have seen her and she had a fantastic ovation. But oh, the white paper roses and those awful silk bloomers the men wear over their tights – the fights and general efficiency very striking, but all hideous to look at and incredibly old fashioned in invention.

Last night a cocktail party at Neal's. The usual 30 piss-elegant queens standing up for hours nibbling canapés. Again no food, and I staggered at 9 to a frankfurter joint in Times Square before an exhausting conference with Maggie and Whitehead about *Much Ado* which lasted till 1 a.m.

On his return to England, JG directed Ralph Richardson and Paul Scofield in Graham Greene's The Complaisant Lover.

To Irene Worth   *28 April, London*

Got on like a house on fire with Frankenheimer, who is rude, brash and brilliant, but showed Maggie and me great politeness and co-operation. Bob Stephens was excellent too as the lover, and a dear boy to boot. Cecil Parker something of a sad wreck – knew even less of his lines than Gladys [Cooper] in *A Day by the Sea*! – and wasted much time and energy thereby. We taped all his scenes the day before the live recording in the end, which made him seem all right, thank God.

I managed to see *Raisin in the Sun* [by Lorraine Hansberry] – divine – and *A Majority of One* [by Leonard Spigelgass] – dreadful soap opera sentimental with Gertrude Berg (a sort of Jewish Yvonne Arnaud) – Cedric [Hardwicke] quite absurd as a Japanese. Coming home the jet ran out of emergency oxygen and we went all the way back to Idlewild and started again, which was really hell! 20 hours on the journey instead of 6½ – and I missed the reading of Graham's play and had to start rehearsing next day more dead than alive. Now I am beginning to recover and I think the play is wonderfully good and Ralph and Scofield both will be splendid in it – or I hope so anyway.

T[yrone] Guthrie has had fine notices for his *All's Well* at Stratford (Eng.), the same production, I gather, he did for you and Alec.* I shall hope perhaps to see it while Ralph's play is on the road.

To Hugh Wheeler   *13 May, London*

Pause in our rehearsals before final run-through. Everything promises amazingly well. The play is quite brilliant, and the two men splendid – only Phyllis Calvert† un peu constipé and overlaid. I trust an audience will prise open her rather shuttered technique. Binkie comes tonight to see it, and we go to Manchester on Sunday for the opening. Now as to your piece [Wheeler's play *Big Fish, Little Fish*].

---

* In 1953 Tyrone Guthrie directed *All's Well that Ends Well* in Stratford, Ontario, with Irene Worth as Helena and Alec Guinness as the King of France.

† Angus Mackay tells of being in JG's crowded dressing room during the run of *Forty Years On* when Phyllis Calvert was among the visitors. As she was about to slip away, JG noticed her and called, 'Oh goodbye, Phyllis! So glad the hysterectomy went well!'

J.P. has read it twice and promises me to write a criticism to you direct, Binkie also. Peter Brook is away seeking locations in the Canaries but of course I will give it him when he returns. Meanwhile I want to read it again myself.

J.P. thinks it too short, and lacking in motive generally. Both he and Binkie agree the dialogue is brilliant but they think the implicit queerness should be tempered, as it is apt to shock, because all the characters are so middle aged. There is some truth in this but I feel, as it has never been done in the theatre, New York at any rate might be fascinated by the middle aged professorial problem. *Provided* of course that they are also continuously amused. I think the play would certainly not do for London anyway. I picture someone like Henry Fonda as William, but Binkie says why should he want to play such an unpleasant half-queer man? Of course he doesn't know as many American gentlemen as you and I, and he thinks *Pleasure of His Company* brilliant (I saw it here the other night and it is, I must say, about 100 per cent better than in N.Y., direction, acting, set, everything, and is a big success). Binkie also adores *Majority of One*, which I thought quite contemptible, and he is very prissy – naturally, I suppose – about anything queer in the theatre.

If you have a spare copy, why not send it to Irene Selznick at the Pierre Hotel? I believe her views might be intelligent and pungent, and a woman's reactions would be very interesting. She was here two weeks ago on her way back from Israel, her hair undyed and looking rather fine like a white Cassandra, and she was very intelligent about the Greene play which she saw an act of in rehearsal.

Bernie has a lover he is mad about who hopes to get a job at Stratford with Charles Laughton as chauffeur-companion, whatever that may mean! B. happier than I remember him almost ever and Eleanor has put on weight and says she never remembers feeling so good. Only Paul's a bit piney and peaky and temperamental about not coming to Italy. I am taking him to Copenhagen for four days at the end of this month to try and make up to him. He is frightfully busy and I think rather over-worked. His mum back from Rhodesia for the eighteenth time, tiresome, unhappy lady that she is.

G. very agitated because Ed is being blackmailed by some Florentine ex-bit, demanding 1000 dollars or he will send photos and details to the Princeton authorities! Rather midget-like* and alarming for the poor men, but I suspect it is only a try-on and they should be firm and undismayed!

The Complaisant Lover *opened at the Globe Theatre on 18 June 1959. This was followed by a short visit to Italy to do* **Ages of Man** *at the Venice and Spoleto Festivals. George Pitcher joined him in Italy.*

---

* Terence Rattigan's lover, Michael Franklin, was referred to (by Rattigan) as 'The Midget'. The word seems to have been adopted by the homosexual coterie, with variable meanings, whether or not they bore any relation to Michael Franklin.

To Paul Anstee   *June 1959, Hotel Cipriani, Venice*

Needless to say, Patrick loomed up in the Piazza last night, chewing an ice-cream cone, and accompanied by about the best looking young American I have ever laid eyes on, green manch and extensive property by the outward seeming, and tanned to a divine shade of olive brown. So of course I asked them both to lunch today, and also one of the terrible Beatnik poets from Tennessee's table at Nicolson's. Well, well. Small world.

George missed two trains to Milan, so I did a good deal of hanging about. He arrived by 9 p.m. however, and all was well. The hotel is charming. No sun today, but very hot. Strange to be actually here. It is beautifully quiet away from the Canal, and the memories are thick but sweet.

To Paul Anstee   *24 June, Hotel Cipriani, Venice*

It is at last blazingly hot – yesterday Patrick escorted us to 'the beach that likes to be visited' – extraordinary cruising ground with 'nests' in long grass and occasional gun emplacements (now empty and forlorn) which give excellent vantage points for voyeurism. People walk up and down in their bathing slips (mostly with *enormous* bulging erections) smiling and beckoning and disappearing at intervals into the undergrowth in pairs. I had one or two vagrant fancies, and G. went swimming with an 18-year-old Australian (freckles and a *hideous* accent) and was not seen for about two hours. I must say it was rather fun, though a bit barefaced in the full glare of the afternoon sun.

Athene [Seyler] and Beau [Nicholas Hannen] are here – coming to lunch today with us – also the inevitable Bob Nesbitt and his wife, the Bernard Delfonts, David Lean – very dishy I always think – and those iridescent twin charmers – hold your breath – Kitty Black and Vivienne Byerley. I didn't stay long enough with them to notice if the famous Hope diamond was still on Kitty's finger, but she looked comparatively human for once in a plain linen frock, and *no hat.*

To Paul Anstee   *24 June, Hotel Cipriani, Venice*

Wonderful weather today. Another visit to the likely beach made me witness to a quite interesting gangbang in which the principal performers were Patrick (and equipage, rather to my surprise) and a German of remarkable handsomeness and royal physique. I merely held the gloves, as it were, but it was quite interesting en plain air. G. and I have decided that Patrick is *death* and boring, but he never leaves us and threatens to follow us to Spoleto. I shall soon begin a little gentle wrist slapping but he is obviously *very* thick-skinned and determined to introduce us to *all* his friends, some of whom are undeniably attractive! A strange character. Scuola di Rocco, the Frati and the

Accademia this morning, and tomorrow I have to get busy about the Recital which is to be at the Fenice after all – but nobody seems to know anything about the arrangements, nobody speaks English, nobody ordered wolves! I hear the employees have not been paid for months. People are told that (a) it is completely sold out and (b) that no tickets are available till the day itself. All very mystifying.

Darling, I *do* miss you – very much – and many pangs of nostalgia (and muddling of Christian names, which is not popular here either, I can tell you) assail me from time to time.

Take care and stay fond of me a little. I will never cease to be devotedly yours.

To Paul Anstee   *June 1959, Spoleto*

The Venice Recital was very successful at the Fenice. A very good house, and great reception, though I was nervous to begin with, having not done it for so long. Afterwards Briggs gave a v. grand party in the great salone at the David, candlelight, musicians, bath tubs of champagne and an elaborate supper served by gondoliers on silver plate.

Today is gorgeous, and this place mad – Festival of Fifty Queens, it ought to be called. Marvellous characters and camp little restaurants and art shops. Americans, gorgeous Italian boys, gents and trade alternately, sweep round eyeing one another. The little theatre is divine, but tiny. They could have sold it out many times they say. Lots of people I know and a good many more that will swim in and out during the week. We stay in [Gian-Carlo] Menotti's house, a simple flat with an enchanting and smiling houseboy, who G. thinks very dishy. As I foretold, he is sitting across the room (G. I mean) writing to Ed! He thinks you may not care to be sent his love but still he sends it to you. Tomorrow there is the Verdi Requiem in the Duomo here, then we go in the car to Assisi, Perugia, the Palio (horse race) at Siena on Thursday for which we have been invited to sit on a balcony overlooking the square, which should be wonderful. George saw it once *standing* and said he was groped silly, but perhaps it's just as well I am too old for such frivolities. Back here on Friday for the Robbins Ballet, the *Duc d'Alba** of Visconti, and my two other Recitals. It's all a bit mad and over-social, but a *wonderful* little town. Television cameras and lights all over the place at 2 a.m. while Nora Kaye dances bits of Juliet in the open air with a pretty young Romeo wearing a black velvet doublet and skin-tight grey manch! What more can one desire? What a lucky boy I am. This was only a rehearsal, of course, and went on till 2 a.m. Food is filthy and hard to get, but it is all kind of al fresco and fascinating, and it is nice not to be all the time in an hotel, though Cipriani's was simply superb – food and service the best I think I have ever known anywhere.

---

* *Il Duca d'Alba* by Donizetti.

G. adores Edward and talks about him nearly all the time, which is sort of funny. (I talk a lot about you too.) He bought me a very nice new queer book which I will bring you – two sensational scenes in it. Take care, my darling, and miss me a little. I shall soon be back.

On his return to London, JG opened the rebuilt Queen's Theatre in Shaftesbury Avenue with a short season of Ages of Man. *At the beginning of August, he left for the USA to begin a tour of* Much Ado about Nothing. *Margaret Leighton played Beatrice, Micheál mac Liammóir, Don Pedro, and Malcolm Keen, Leonato.*

To Paul Anstee   *1[?] August, London*

Silly one – cruel one – you devastated me last night, and I couldn't sleep and you never rang even when you got home, dreading, I suppose, our usual fruitless arguments with the long empty pauses in between. Yes, of course, you know me only too well (but just not all that well as you think you do).

I shall always love you, but your sudden turns from sweetness to venom rather terrify me, though in a way I understand, being somewhat (and lamentably) senior.

To Paul Anstee   *4 August, Boston*

Lovely weather here and a very nice suite looking on to the Park. Slept till 12 yesterday and tottered out to see *The Scapegoat* which was simply dreadful. Alec [Guinness] just the same (BAD) in both his dual roles and everyone else acting their heads off. You will have to see it for Irene W[orth] as the wicked wife and P[amela] Brown and B[ette] Davis giving their all.

We went over to the theatre, which is just as it looked in the photographs. *Macbeth* is a flop, I gather. We go tonight to see it. But everyone is agreeable and anxious to please and I have decided to ask mac Liammóir and M. Keen to dress with me and treat it all as a big lark.

Off now to meet the company – hope there will be some prettiness *and* talent. Rarely combined, but both, fortunately, in you.

To Paul Anstee   *5 August, Boston*

How quickly the oceans part us, and one takes up another hectic and strange life. We saw *Macbeth* – the theatre is as dreadful as I feared – a great tent with canvas walls, not closed at the top, so that air comes in (and plenty of light too) and a sort of sloped saucer concrete dome on top with microphones hanging on long strings like cocoons over the actors' heads. You hear the voices well enough but oh!, the sound effects – bagpipes, crickets, wind mingled with endless noises of cars, riverboats and aeroplanes from the outside world, so that one is worn out with trying to concentrate. It is impossible, however, to judge by this production as ours is to have a built-in proscenium, a curtain and the side seats moved to the centre and forward – and I *hope* the mikes will be relegated to the footlights and side walls.

Actually, the *Macbeth* was not wholly unimpressive, though [Jason] Robards was rather over parted and got very tired halfway through and Siobhan McKenna yelled as if she was in Marble Arch in the sleepwalking scene, which she chose to play in a flowing white Hollywood negligée which floated round the stage like a Christmas angel. 'Callas Athene', I christened her rather wickedly. Dreadful acting in all the other parts, but some of the lighting and staging *very* fine, especially in the early scenes. A huge and indiscriminate audience appeared to love every moment of it, and we shivered with cold by the time it ended (11.45). Endless dangerous-looking but unnecessary fights in the last act, and a *ridiculous* invention by which Macbeth left the stage when his wife was announced to be dead and reappeared (after an absurd pause of nothingness) carrying her body in his arms (à la Lear) and did 'Tomorrow and tomorrow' holding her corpse on the ground and rocking it in his arms. Oh, these absurdly impertinent improvements by clever directors!

Our rehearsals go very well, but it is simply maddening to be in a town with five theatres empty and closed (including several more in universities – we are rehearsing in an excellent one) and then going out to appear in the ridiculous echoing tent, with Hell breaking loose on every side. If there should be wind and/or rain, it will be a swamp too and *quite* impossible for us to be heard. I suggest we should record the whole play on tape, and mouth it like an Ice Show or the Bernard Brothers!

The hotel here is lovely, and quiet! Myles [Eason] and Bob Schear are my Charmian and Iras, and the S.M. has a shaved head like Yul Brynner and wears skin tight Sun Tans with an *enormous* packet! So you see I have really little to complain of.

To Paul Anstee   *11 August, Boston*

New York was awful – pouring rain all weekend. *Gypsy* [by Arthur Laurents, Stephen Sondheim and Jule Styne] was quite fun, [Ethel] Merman really superb, a sort of musical comedy Edith [Evans], relentlessly powerful, tragic, funny and certain, with incredible selectivity and confidence in every word she speaks or sings. The show only so-so. I hate heavy sentimentality about Show Biz, awful child prodigies etc., but there is one wonderful comedy scene of three girl strippers doing grinds and bumps. But no dancing to speak of, and no male beauty or interest at all, which doesn't suit me, needless to say. I doubt if we could cast it in London.

I saw a wonderful small house on 62nd Street [New York] with four lovely rooms, well furnished, a piano and a small garden, and I think I shall take it, though it is dreadfully expensive. It belongs to a character actress who is going to Europe for several months, and she seemed nice and to like me. I think it is pretty certain I shall get it, for two months anyway, and it is really delightful.

The play coming along quite well, but all the troubles of the dance and church scenes to negotiate and get under control. Margaret simply sweet and most helpful and all the English company excellent. [Micheál] mac Liammóir in his Frankie Howerd toupée, a great joy. I am so afraid he and Barrie Ingham [playing Claudio] may get their wigs mixed in the dressing room and appear parti-coloured blonde and brunette.

Story. Written up in a loo. 'I like girls. Do you think there is something wrong with me?' Underneath. 'No. Unless you're a girl.'

To Paul Anstee   *21 August, Boston*

Don't talk to me about heat. We have had 95° here, and today there is a mad sirocco blowing too, so one sweats the whole time even sitting or lying still – and the clothes in the play – and the make-up! The tent is something of a shambles. I dress with Keen and mac Liammóir in a sort of box divided with curtains, and Niobe* dives about behind me tearing clothes on and off. But Ray Diffen has made everything beautifully – the clothes as a whole better than Stratford and London, and only the scenery very tattily and poorly painted, like Anthony Holland doing a panto for Hull, as Myles wittily remarked. Tonight we have the horror of 1st full dress rehearsal. mac Liammóir looks a bit like Widow Twankey and camps dreadfully. Otherwise I think the play not too badly acted – BUT we still have the lighting to contend with and, above all, the amplification. One can do no work in the daytime, as bulldozers and electric drills hurtle about everywhere levelling ground and building art galleries and concert halls (for *next* year) and light streams into the tent, everything blows about and the noise and heat are quite unbearable. So we have to wait till dark falls, then the work begins – and there are photos to do before we open. Very hard to know what to eat, but one pours juice – tomato, grapefruit and an odd whisky remorselessly down one's throat and yells through a microphone, which terrifies the actors. The girls and boys who walk on are, at least six of them, moronic, and will undoubtedly fall flat on their faces the moment they try to dance in their costumes. The boots and shoes have not yet arrived etc. etc.

I don't think I shall ever have a success with anyone again. I have my usual skin rash, prickly heat, uric acid, and too much shellfish, I suspect, and feel rather hysterical and low alternately – but no doubt I shall be better when the curtain has finally gone up on our revels.

---

* This appears to be a reference to his manservant and dresser, Bernie Dodge, and his predilection for tearful fits.

To Vivien Leigh   *24 August, Boston*

mac Liammóir plays Don Pedro a little like Dorothy Ward,* but we rely on
the sentimental passion of the Americans for the Irish to drag him through.

To Paul Anstee   *27 August, Boston*

Teeny-weeny bit previous in sending you that triumphant cable as the *C.
Science Monitor* suddenly spoilt the score a bit with that last review. However,
it went wonderfully last night following an appalling daylight matinée at 5.30
with a small inattentive audience moving about all the time to dodge the sun
which streams in above the canvas and below the dome. Oh, the filth and
discomfort of it all – Elsinore, Rhodesia and now this. The clothes will be
filthy by the time we get to N.Y. and they are so beautiful. We have made
some discreet cuts in scenes where the actors can't sustain. I really think it is
a pretty good show. Maggie looks like Lucille Ball as Lysistrata, but I am
trying to tactfully persuade her to wear headdresses – at present she is entirely
out of period, though the dresses themselves are lovely.

To Paul Anstee   *3 September, Boston*

Yesterday we arrived at the tent for the 5.30 matinée to be told that a steam
shovel had broken through the main drainpipe, and there was no water of
any kind. Margaret almost refused to go on and we rang up a quarter of an
hour late, leaving only twenty minutes between the two shows. The Fire
Brigade arrived to pump in emergency water from the river, but only succeeded
in making a hideous row – buckets and urns of water were brought in and
slopped about. The toilets did not work, of course, and then came the rain,
drowning out the church scene completely. M. Keen exhausted and drying
up all over the place, and backstage a misery of exhaustion and discomfort. It
really is rather hard to bear, and all so amateurish and unnecessary. Only 12
more performances, thank God. They are to repaint all the scenery next week,
which is essential, as it looks at present like a third rate Italian coffee bar.

To Paul Anstee   *9 September, Boston*

The Margrave rang me today – would I direct *Macbeth* of Verdi at the Garden
in March with Callas and [Tito] Gobbi. John P. says don't touch it, but I
confess it is rather tempting. I shall try to stall for time.

Bought myself a raw silk grey suit in Filene's Basement yesterday to try and
cheer me up, as I have been deeply depressed. Nobody much to show it off
to still.

---

* English actress best known for playing principal boy in pantomime.

To Paul Anstee   *11 September, Boston*

I have been hideously depressed, piles, rash, liver all combining to make me feel a thousand and the play such impossibly hard work to put over in that vile tent, where the mikes and planes and boats combine in a cacophony of accompaniment and one can time and place nothing with any certainty. However, we have changed one of the girls, I have stood over the scene painters who have improved the sets considerably, and the audiences are much better with cooler weather and also more numerous and responsive these last few nights. Still, I can't wait to shake the dust from my shoes and be in New York.

My two scrambles were not very interesting. The Italian boy is too young and dewy eyed to get involved with, though he is really very handsomely proportioned and walks around the theatre naked to the waist in bright yellow tights with such a basket of kisses that it is impossible not to look rather interested. The other with the stage manager, who is an absolute dear – 35ish and glasses and a crew cut, was rather hairy and unsatisfactory and hardly likely to be repeated, I think, though no bones were broken on either side.

To Paul Anstee   *15 September, New York*

At last. We are installed. The house is very agreeable, and I have moved from the mistress bedroom into the back in order to avoid the noise from the street. Niobe has the front one. The maid is very nice and there are four huge rooms to wander around in. Decorations fairly harmless and trees in the street and a little garden below.

Went to Kay Kendall's Memorial Service* yesterday to support Maggie, who spoke very charmingly. Moss Hart read an eulogy – congregation largely Jewish! Irene Selznick looking like a mad prophetess in an unsuitable white girlie straw hat.

Lovely weather. I have a fine dressing room, the theatre is very handsome and they hope to have a quarter of a million dollars advance before we open.

Much Ado about Nothing *opened at the Lunt-Fontanne Theatre on 17 September.*

To Paul Anstee   *20 September, New York*

It has been a terrific week – we were awfully disappointed that *The Times* and the *Tribune* didn't like the production much – but they were the only flies in the ointment. We did nearly 40,000 dollars in six performances and the

---

* Kay Kendall died of leukaemia on 6 September 1959.

matinée, the first, yesterday was sold out – bravos and screams at the end of every performance, so I really think it will be a big hit. The theatre is just too big, which is a pity, and three or four of the small parts very vilely played – Margaret, Antonio, Friar, Don John all most indifferent, despite my endless cajolements, cuts and hard work on them. But the rest are pretty good, and Margaret, George [Rose] and I have received unstinted praise.

Dietrich, the Lunts, Helen Hayes, Hugh [Wheeler], [Hermione] Gingold, Harry and Mrs Truman (*not* Capote), Martha Graham, [Simone] Signoret and [Anna] Magnani made the first and second nights very glamorous. Bob gave a big party (sit down) at an hotel for the whole company which was much more agreeable than those things usually are, and all my old fans are rallying in force. The theatre is vulgar but beautifully clean and smart – air conditioning in my dressing room, carpets on the stairs etc. etc. What a joy after Boston.

I have strictly forbidden myself the queer bars while I am playing. So many people seem to know me now, and talk to me in the street and in restaurants, it really seems important to behave very circumspectly indeed, alas. I go to Dick Easton this afternoon, who is having a housewarming for a new flat, and tonight Ben Edwards is taking me to a preview of Yves Montand's one-man show.

Toying (as usual) with the temptation to buy myself a green manch suit – they are all the rage this fall, and so pretty.

Very pleased with the house. Niobe very gay and faithful to her London love, and sings about the house. Goddard [Lieberson] has lent me an enormous gramophone and sent a huge bunch of records – not my choice, of course, but very kind of him, and the resident maid is a dear. The weather is divine – sunny but not too hot. New York looking its very best. So I am feeling relaxed and happy for the first time in many weeks. Myles went to *Sweet Bird* [*of Youth*] and said Geraldine Page has ruined her wonderful performance in six months. What a pity.

To Paul Anstee   *24 September, New York*

All well here. Fine notices in *Time*, *Newsweek* and *Variety*, but Tynan has destroyed me more spitefully than usual, and I smart a bit under his lash. I am going to see a run-through of the new Mary Martin, Rodgers and Hammerstein musical [*The Sound of Music* by Howard Lindsay, Russel Crouse, Richard Rodgers and Oscar Hammerstein] on Sunday, which might be fun. Found myself in a very odd studio in Amsterdam Avenue at 3 a.m. this morning, having a tiny romp with an extraordinary Negro who was leading dancer in *House of Flowers* [by Truman Capote and Harold Arlen] – do you remember? Most weird character – paints rather well, and does a cabaret act in the Village – rather sweet for a drink!

To Paul Anstee   *28 September, New York*

The Mary Martin/Rogers and Hammerstein run-through was ghastly. I thought Ivor's ghost would come down on a wire to bless it. Cute and appallingly sentimental by turns – *seven* children, singing nuns, and M. looked as old as God and was frisking around as if she was 17. Hideous men, no dancing or chorus and an endless boring plot.

To Paul Anstee   *1 October, New York*

I went on the Jack Paar Show last night very late – he is away (fortunately) and I was sandwiched between Paul Newman, dental plates, and deodorants, and some frightful girls in velveteen slacks with enormous bottoms showing fashions – rather depressing, but they say 30 *million* people see it and it is good for the play. I am said to have comported myself with comparative dignity, and Arlene Francis, who did the interview, was amiable and tried to put me at my ease.

To Paul Anstee   *5 October, New York*

Yesterday I had about 20 chaps to brunch for Binkie – rather fun, though of course Niobe was distracted, with a heavy cold and a cough like a volcano erupting. However, needless to say, there was a mass of rich food, and several people got rather pissed. Ed and George took me to the Stravinsky opera and *Carmina Burana* – a 1930 Nazi collection of folk songs sung by a choir with a lot of *very* rude ballet by John Butler, which was quite boring except for the gentlemen, who were mostly stark naked and half of them with (real) beards! I imagine they think they look more hearty but actually they just appear as rather poetic looking beatniks.

Went to the Bru Soir one night where the groping was marvellous and apparently almost unanimous! But I am frightened of going anywhere at all. I am recognised everywhere in the most extraordinary way. TV and *Ages* I suppose, and I simply dare not do bars or anything except private parties – and not too many of those, I fear. It is such a bore, and yet I know it is a sign of success and one simply must not risk anything going wrong. People point and nudge and talk to me in the street and everyone knows me in the shops. Supper at the Barrister, an all gents bar as it turned out, which made me very uncomfortable, as I was highly conspicuous in a white dinner jacket before going on to a party for Yves Montand! I left as soon as I politely could.

Irene gave a boring cocktail party for B., Lauren Bacall, Ingrid Bergman, Moss Hart etc., and today I lunch with Lillian Gish, so you see I do behave rather correctly in my spare time. Have not seen my Jamaican enchantress again.

Squib today saying the lower cloakroom in Noël's new Swiss villa will be wallpapered with his SHEET music – oh shit! The opera programme has an announcement of all the new attractions coming. I *dread The Miracle Worker* [by William Gibson], and *Sound of Music* is revolting.

Keep those crabs right out of your hair! Of course you will buy that suede jacket and I think you will want a black leather waist length jacket, or mac, much worn here. The Negroes, whose legs seem to begin at their shoulder blades, look wonderful in them, and I think one would suit you too. Oh, the young men in the streets here – my eyes are on 6" stalks all the time.

To Paul Anstee   *9 October, New York*

This pestilential weather *will* not stop. The humidity is appalling again, and one is fit for nothing. I am very low indeed, owing to a horrid anonymous phone call which upset me very much last night, and we had to bring in Binkie, Whitehead and [Aaron] Frosch to deal with it. B. will tell you all. I really can't bear to write it down, but it has been a vile 24 hours of suspense. I think only a cheap little blackmail attempt but it makes one feel the ground is crawling.

Trying to keep the play up to scratch, but the company too is affected by the heat, and I have continually to be giving notes. mac Liammóir waltzes on (and called Leonato Benedick the other night, right at the first entrance too, confusing the audience hopelessly), camps, blows kisses in the air, fidgets and reacts, killing laughs in all directions and driving us all to fury. He is a dear man too, and I don't believe he really knows he does it. Starring so long with bad companies in the bogs, he imagines he is bound to steal all the thunder for himself and is hopelessly bad in a team.

Well, the Tories are in, so you will be happy. And *what* a notice in *The Times* for Beverley Cross's play [*One More River*] at the Duke of York's. Did you meet him at Judith's – with a funny little Eurasian wife – he is very pretty too, or was when he played Balthasar with us on the Continental tour.

This recognition is really too much of a good thing. Two friends of Hugh's took me to the Waldorf Astoria to supper the other night and to my horror and dismay, the chanteuse, a very untalented young lady, suddenly announced that 'the greatest actor in the world' was in the audience and would I please take a bow. At the Downstairs lunching with Lillian Gish, photographers rush up and insist on taking me and apparently the news that Maggie L. and I left after the first half of the Mary Martin run-through struck horror into the entire audience and is the talk of the town – very unfortunate, as I hate hurting theatre people's feelings – but no doubt we can live it down in time. Larry Harvey is here for the weekend, which is nice for M. I am going to get very depressed creeping around the town behind an enormous bee-veil, not daring to be seen *anywhere*.

I do miss you very badly, and now I feel I don't even dare to phone and have a little love pat over the wires. Oh dear, life can really be very difficult.

Success, money and where does it get you in the end? Masses of offers for the Recital, TV, directing plays, but I think I shall take Binkie's advice (as usual) and do nothing for two months at least in the New Year.

To Paul Anstee   *14 October, New York*

This doesn't seem to be my lucky month. I don't know how to write to you, dear Paul. J.P. has written me a terribly violent letter, and no doubt he and Binkie will have seen you by now and told you all the horrors. It has been a hard and horrible week, as you can imagine, having to discuss things with Frosch and Whitehead and feeling that nameless people are trying to destroy me. All the miseries of 1953 come surging back and I have to go round smiling and frisking about on the stage as if everything was fine.

I don't quite know what to do now. All parties must be out except the boring, respectable ones with ladies. Frosch even talked of getting someone to fetch me every night at the theatre so that I am never alone in the streets or restaurants. If one is to go about with a perpetual bodyguard, life is not worth living at all. B and J.P. will obviously never trust me again and everybody is going to worry and suspect the worst whatever I do and wherever I go.

The blackmail business is so abominable and cannot be called my fault, but obviously the man told Frosch I had been seen in places and my habits were known, all of course exaggerated and made to seem worse, and I can't account for every person and place over the months, and almost begin to think I *have* behaved very badly, which I haven't. The lunch here for Binkie was a mistake, of course, and Bob only comes in for three hours a day and does my accounts and letters and I never go anywhere near him. Oh, it is all so wretched and unnecessary, and Heaven knows if I can now *ever* be sure that some unforeseen disaster may break over my head. They have examined the wires here and say they are practically certain the phone could not have been tampered with. But *any* conversations could be a proof though I don't think the blackmailer could possibly use them except to try and get money out of me. They have found out that he has a criminal record in Boston, but one can't arrest him for *this* for fear something might come out if the police were brought in – one is helpless with the fear of publicity of *any* kind being unthinkable in my case. And so the days go by with no real assurance of the possibility being lifted for certain. And now you won't be able to come, and I know this will be a dreadful disappointment to you as well as to me. I only hope you will understand and try and forgive me. Perhaps we could go to Paris for Christmas – I feel now that I only want to get out of New York as soon as I can and try to forget it all. I seem to bring nothing but worry and disappointment to those I love best and very little pride or satisfaction to myself after all these years of experience and work, and it makes me very wretched and rather despairing of the years ahead.

Write soon and tell me you understand. I can't bear to write more fully.

One is dry of feeling after a big shock, and it is very hard to get through the days and work without giving away one's wretchedness. Try not to worry about me unduly. I will be all right, and I suppose I have only myself to blame. It is a hard and wicked world.

To Paul Anstee   *16 October, New York*

Your letter was very kind and comforting and soothed me a bit after all the dreadfulness. The man rang the theatre again on Wednesday just before the matinee and Frosch sent for Bernie, who was consequently half an hour late for the evening show, with me sweating with fear at what might be going on. Apparently they brought the man *here* and grilled him until they found he had *no* proofs or tapes, didn't know where the wires were, tried to escape etc. etc. Pure melodrama, with seven people to assist. But Frosch swears that now it is all over and there will be absolutely no risk of further trouble.

Bob is leaving, you will be glad to hear. I don't believe he deliberately did anything wrong, but went to the bars and talked about working for me, what a dear I was, so easy to meet and natural to talk to, and some character or other pieced everything together.

I'm hoping to get Ben Morse to take over my correspondence and money and be on hand to see me home or vet strangers. I am only going to accept invitations in future from people I actually know, and find out before leaving where they propose to take me – one cannot be too careful now. People pretend to be friends of Hugh's or say they have met me before, and of course I can't remember for certain. It is all quite hideous and has exhausted me dreadfully, as well as having to go about apparently unconcerned and get through the play. Bernie has been very good and loyal, makes no friends (as usual) and is *most* proper and respectful in the theatre. He really is very faithful in a crisis, though so often maddening at other times. Don't say anything to B. and J.P. about Ben Morse. I want Frosch to approve before taking him on, as B. insisted I should refer *every* detail to him first. He has really been wonderful and I can't be grateful enough for his help. He is sending me to a doctor tomorrow, as I need something to restore my nerves, and don't want a recurrence of double vision or suchlike aftermath as I had in '53 when it was all over. The reaction is always bad after strain and shock.

You will, I suppose, understand by now that your coming here simply cannot be, though it makes me most unhappy to agree to it. You know I would always give you a trip to come *alone* some time for a week or so if you wanted to. You could stay with some of your other friends and have a gay time, but I fear the boys are right in feeling that to come as my guest and stay at this address would be dangerous and cramp any chance you would have of a good time. I told B. I was so afraid you would think it all a trick of mine to prevent you coming in order that I could be with George. He met George and Ed and will assure you that they are devotedly together. I do see them when they come to N.Y. and I am to give one Recital at Princeton next month. I shall always be devoted to G. but there is absolutely no chance that he would alter his life for me, though he is very fond of me as a friend. The sex side is entirely on *my* side, and so very unsatisfactory as you can imagine, and I do all I can to repress it altogether. Does this make sense to you and do *you* still feel as fond of me as ever?

With **Much Ado About Nothing** *established, JG began rehearsals for the New York production of* **Five Finger Exercise.** *Jessica Tandy was to take over from Adrianne Allen.*

To Paul Anstee   *20 October, New York*

Your letters have been such a comfort. I am much better and the weather is divine now – a cool breeze and blue skies. New York looks so wonderfully beautiful, and we both love it so. It does seem so unfair that we are not allowed to share it. The doctor – a very simpatico young thirty-ish (but married) – tells me I am perfectly sound in wind and limb, and gave me a tonic and tranquillisers for my poor old nerves. Peter Shaffer and I have started work on the play with Jessica. P. has some excellent ideas for rewrites and little cuts and additions, so I think it should be interesting to do it again, and we only have 23 more performances of *Much Ado.*

Victor Saville has approached me with an idea of directing a film in the spring. He has a script of a novel by Rumer Godden called *The Greengage Summer,* about five children in a sort of hotel in the north of France – the film would be done there. The book is very charming and I am rather taken with the idea if he supervised all the technical side – it would be something completely different and, I should think, absorbing.

I fear you will have rather a wretched time when you do see Binkie and John – they are sure to be in finger-wagging mood. Went with Maggie to *Heartbreak House* [by Bernard Shaw] opening on Sunday. The play bores me a good deal and was very patchily acted. Maurice Evans, Diana Wynyard and Alan Webb the best. Pam [Brown] overdid it rather, and [Diane] Cilento was appalling. Last night with Arnold and that awful Milton to the Persian Room – Celeste Holm and Ronnie Graham in not a very good revue. I am gritting my teeth and going everywhere with ladies for a bit – don't suppose I shall be able to keep it up for long. Rehearsals will keep me very occupied for the next three weeks anyway.

Take care of your dear self. I see your [Margaret] Lockwood play* is turning *One More River* out of the Duke of York's, but I suppose they will easily make

---

* Paul Anstee was the designer for *And Suddenly It's Spring* by Jack Popplewell.

a transfer somewhere else. *The Edwardians** sounds disaster – poor Jeremy [Brett] doesn't have much luck, does he?

Fondest love, dearest boy. Write whenever you can and don't be sad for me.

To Paul Anstee   *25 October, New York*

Micheál mac Liammóir's dresser bought him some green manch trousers and Bernie caught him *sewing* the creases in! I murmured in the wings to him (unable to resist it) 'I hear you sew in your creases', and he replied unblushingly 'Yes, I find it gets me more success!!'

Terribly overworked with the other play – rewrites and new moves all through – the set is so wide (and the theatres too) that I have to put the dining table straight on to the audience. They don't like it much, nor do I, but it is necessary if they are to be seen and heard. Jessica fits in splendidly and is a dear to work with. Brian [Bedford] a bit pouty over changes. [Fred] Brisson [the producer] insists he should wear his hair shorter and brush it back to show his forehead – I agree, but oh, the black looks from Miss B. She has brought an entire wardrobe from London – a *very* common green suit and some *very* sexy brown manch – to entice me, I opine!

Natasha [Parry] is playing in Rex's play [*The Fighting Cock* by Jean Anouilh] which Peter B[rook] is directing. Miss [Odile] Versois was thrown out! Hope she can make the grade, though I have little confidence in her acting prowess. Edith [Jackson] is trying to run a huge flat for Rex in Sutton Place and can't get any servants. Rex's sister also here and a great thorn in her flesh. She and Bernie great cahoots together. E. seems to think Lilli [Palmer] will return to Rex eventually, so perhaps Carlos [Thompson] will be thrown back upon the boys again. Brian went to see *Cheri* [by Anita Loos, based on the novels of Colette] and of course fell madly in love with Horst Buchholz and had dinner with him afterwards. I see him in the street occasionally, and he looks very midgety to me! The production is said to be very common, but I think it may run for a bit on matinée ladies and queens who flock to see the love scenes, H. in pyjama trousers and a lot of rucking, I gather.

To Paul Anstee   *31 October, New York*

It is very hard work doing the play again – they hate altering *anything* and are inclined to pout, especially lazy Brian, and [Roland] Culver holds forth for hours and wastes time on unnecessary details. However, I think it is going pretty well and I am delighted with Jessica, who makes all the difference. Peter S. keeps on putting bits in and taking them out again.

Apparently our business with *Much Ado* has been phenomenal. Over 49,000

---

* Adaptation by Ronald Gow of Vita Sackville-West's novel.

again this week, and they have paid off the production. No Shakespeare play has *ever* done so well on Broadway, so that is some consolation for the feeling of disappointment I have had to fight with the bad performances, ill painted sets and the hugeness of the house, which makes it very hard to put over satisfactorily.

I miss you greatly, as always, and my life is painfully celibate. I just look longingly out of taxi windows and Ben Morse sees me home every night. I feel rather like Princess Margaret with a hangover. Did I tell you Charlton Heston came round to see me, with the most extraordinary chatelaine of gold coins and chains hanging from his trouser pocket. A gold buckled belt, a divinely cut blue suit, priceless vicuna overcoat in blue with a high collar slung about his vast shoulders. Quelle assiette – but he went on to Maggie and bored her for hours talking about himself and his career, so I got the best of him!

Saratoga [by Morton da Costa, Johnny Mercer and Harold Arlen] has opened out of town – they say it is very dull, but gorgeous. One of Cecil [Beaton]'s dresses is covered with hundreds of bubbles, and the leading lady screamed out 'I just can't manage this. My balls keep getting tied up.'

To Paul Anstee　　　　　　　　　　　　　*4 November, New York*

It is very late and I am dead tired and I don't want to seem hateful and unreasonable. But is not your attitude a bit selfish. You don't say 'I long to be with you' or 'I want to do what is best for you' as I would say if I was very fond of someone. You go on about 'what people will think' if you don't come to New York, and you fuss about whether my friends take trouble about you except when I am there. Yet you don't really like Binkie or David Webster very much, and so often at Knots Fosse* you are bored with the people there. So why bother if you don't go there?

I cannot *bear* this tearing of devotion between my best friends and lovers, and I seem to do nothing right these days. Once we have opened next week at Wilmington, I will be able to pull myself together and think more clearly about the future. Meanwhile, don't be sad and furious with me. I love you very dearly, and only wish my long time with you could have brought you more steady satisfaction and security of position, but you have made a great success of your work and can stand in your own right and live your own life – and if you still want me to share it as far as I can, you know it gives me joy to be with you and have you as my dearest friend.

After Much Ado *closed, the pre-Broadway tour of* Five Finger Exercise *began in Wilmington, Delaware.*

---

* Binkie Beaumont's country house in Essex.

To Paul Anstee   *9 November, Wilmington*

On the road once more! A vast hotel with endless terrifying snake pit corridors. Peter Shaffer, Ben Morse and I in an enormous suite, with 4 T.V. sets! Marvellous view of autumn woods in the distance, ruined by millions of cars parked like shining tin beetles in huge lots. The theatre is actually in the hotel and rather nice, though a bit big. The new set is rather picturesque, but all the details are very peculiar and un-English. Mock Tudor mixed up with a *Victorian* door to the kitchen, with engraved glass in the panels like digs at Clapham! But I have to walk warily in my criticisms and remember that the Americans are touchy about their idea of England.

We had a great closing of *Much Ado* and I made a little speech. But I am very tired and delighted to be done with acting for a bit. I was only sad to say goodbye to dear Maggie who goes on to Texas to play cowboys with Larry Harvey who is making a Wild West film there [*The Alamo*].

To Paul Anstee   *November 1959, Wilmington*

Awful post-mortem drinks in Brisson's room last night – all the actors grousing about their moves and positions killing the points and P. Shaffer waving his arms hysterically. They were all inaudible – including Jessie – and the audience couldn't catch on at all till the middle of the second scene. There were virtually no laughs at all, which of course enraged and baffled the actors. But once they project and time better and *phrase* better and cut out all the 'wells' and 'ohs' which they have sprinkled so lavishly all over the text, I think it will be a very good performance. They have simply got to find the way to put the dialogue over in a more selective and broader way. But God, what a crashing bore Culver is. [Michael] Bryant is rather smug and Brian as obstinate as a mule. Fred Brisson is rude and bossy, and has ordered down a voice coach from N.Y., at great expense, as he informed the cast at 2.30 a.m. with a shark-like coldness. You should have seen their faces! I think we are all exhausted and bad critics after the last mad ten days and I am determined to go back to N.Y. on Saturday and try and see it with a fresh eye next week – Peter also. The company *must* find their own confidence and get used to the new production in their own way for a few performances and not rehearse till everything has been really tested a few times. I am convinced the play itself holds as well as ever, even if they don't think it funny in the parts they did in England.

You need not feel *you* are treated like a naughty schoolboy. What about *me*? Ordered about at 55 and told I am like a child of sixteen with too much money in my pocket! Well, they mean it all for the best, but I do find it as maddening as you do. All my own fault, of course, but that doesn't make it any easier to put up with for either of us.

To Paul Anstee   *17 November, Washington*

Not a moment's peace have I had yet. Endless rows and rehearsals, Brisson
rude, indefatigably interfering and insulting the company, who are increasingly tiresome and gave a dreadfully bad performance last night here. Rave
notices, however, to my amazement. Today we rehearsed all day, and Peter
has rewritten the first ten minutes to great advantage and more clarity than
ever before. After endless argument and rebellion we got it rehearsed and they
played the new version tonight, and it was a different thing altogether. Clear,
audible, lots of laughs and no coughing and I really do think it is a big
improvement and should increase the chances of the whole play. He has
invented a new curtain to the first scene too – much more final and effective.
But oh, God, I am so sick of them all, and can't wait to get through these
next two weeks and be done with work for a bit. These re-hash jobs are far
more exhausting than any new assignment, and one has to bully and coax
and everyone is so disagreeable. Jessica is a pet and has been very sweet, but
she is rather tentative still in her performance and a bit high-pitched in voice
and too fluttery. I think she will be all right in the end – her strong scenes are
infinitely better than Adrianne's but she does not dominate the first act and
set the character properly.

To Paul Anstee   *21 November, Philadelphia*

I think my labours are almost done now. I hope so, anyway, as I am terribly
sick of the play and rehearsing it every day and watching them every night.
Brian and Rowley [Roland Culver] have two of the ugliest voices I ever heard
when you have to listen to them continuously for weeks on end.

    J.P. comes tomorrow, and on Tuesday I go back to N.Y. to do a twenty
minute bit of the Recital at the Waldorf for a lot of terrible Jewish ladies –
some charity do of Mrs Richard Rodgers.

To Paul Anstee   *25 November, New York*

We went to Philadelphia and saw *The Fighting Cock* – very muddled and
disappointing. Rex [Harrison] was good and Natasha [Parry] quite enchanting – her scenes the only really good ones in a very dull play indeed. I tremble
for it when it comes in. Back to Washington on Sunday, where we heard a
lovely concert conducted by that dish, Mr Karajan whom I only saw before
through the mist at Salzburg when we heard *Fidelio*. He played a Strauss waltz
for an encore on Sunday and I really was smoothing my elbow white gloves
and twirling you round the ballroom in my imagination.

    J.P. arrived safely and was delighted with *F.F.E.*, which has settled down
out of all knowledge and is playing to capacity all the week. Yesterday the
weather changed and we sat for four hours in Washington airport – flew at

last to Newark where we arrived at 3 p.m. (instead of N.Y. at 12.15 as we had planned). Met by a car, I was driven headlong to the Waldorf Astoria where the audience (what was left of it) was impatiently awaiting me – Claudette Colbert wildly filling in as commère. I flung myself on to the platform – no time to comb my hair or change out of my sports coat – and obliged with quarter of an hour of *Lear, Henry V, Sonnets* etc. Rather exhausting and nerve-racking. However, it is all over now and Brisson says I need not return to Washington, so I am free at last.

Very cold today and I bought myself a thick, black overcoat at Whitehouse and Hardy. Took J.P. to lunch at Toque Blanche, and we went to a matinée of *The Miracle Worker.* Anne Bancroft and the little girl [Patty Duke] – aged 12 – quite wonderfully good, though the play is a bit sentimental and unnecessarily elaborate. Tonight we dined with Hugh at Sardi's and saw *Cheri* which was quite fun, though very over-produced by Bobby Lewis. But Mr [Horst] Buchholz is very dishy in a succession of lovely Edwardian numbers – stripped to the waist a good deal, several scenes in bed, and takes off his trousers at least three times during the course of the action. Silly, bad adaptation, and Kim Stanley rather brilliant in spite of being utterly miscast.

J.P. brought the new script* from Enid – first two acts greatly improved and an amusing idea of an EGYPTIAN in the impersonation scene – fez and a Welsh accent! But the last act is a muddle and I won't agree to do the play unless it can be radically strengthened and my part in it rationalised and made a convincing climax. At present it is all theatrical tricks and effects, and a death scene with no proper motive or development from the early part of the play. J.P. agrees with me, and I shan't decide about it till I get another version.

To Mrs Richard Rodgers   *25 November, New York*

So many thanks for so kindly sending me that fine brandy. I did not feel I had deserved such a handsome present. It was so kind of you. I am glad I managed to put in an appearance and at least fulfil my promise, but I feel it was very careless of me not to have come earlier by train, as of course I would have done if I could have foreseen the change in the weather. Air travel is very fine and convenient until it goes wrong! I am so very sorry to have had to disappoint many of the audience. I was sent today a most handsome gift of champagne from Mrs Fishman and Mrs Fischer. There is no address to write to, so might I ask you to convey to them my sincerest thanks for their courtesy and kindness and apologise for my shortcomings.

---

* Enid Bagnold's *The Last Joke* was to be JG's next London appearance.

To Paul Anstee   *1 December, New York*

Ben-Hur was simply *divine*, not really even too long and Charlie (Heston) is definitely my darling, though he has a *little* too much hair on his stomach for my money. Stephen Boyd is a bore, but Hugh Griffith – my unfavourite actor as a rule – is really delightful for once. And the galley slaves and charioteers – ma foi! I am being given a lunch by the Lambs Club today – rather nice of them. It is very odd not having to work at last, and John [Perry] is in excellent form and quite enjoying himself, I think. Silly old Niobe – I am so sick of her neuroses and persecution mania – perhaps she will settle down again now that she is back with Ray. I do hope so.

Wish I could see your lovely window. The shops here are already wild with decorations. Macy's has about ten tableaux of 18th century scenes on the façade – Rome, Naples, Paris, Vienna, Venice all with doll figures that bow, curtsey, play the violin, climb poles, dance etc. Very pretty and ingenious, but you can't get by for the crowds on the sidewalk. Organs playing carols peal forth from Saks and frightful Santa Clauses and Salvation Army ladies play harmoniums and rattle tambourines and moneyboxes as you pass.

To Noël Coward   *2 December, New York*

Tonight *Five Finger Exercise* opens, so I am nervous and apprehensive. A lady was violently sick at the preview, right in the middle of the stalls, and about fifteen people round her stampeded from their seats during the most important moment in the first act, which hardly served to delight the actors or the rest of the audience. However, it went wonderfully last week in Washington, and I have some good hopes.

To Paul Anstee   *6 December, New York*

Well, it is exciting that *Five Fingers* is a success. Today Johnnie leaves, which is sad. I have much enjoyed my first leisure and going to the plays with him, and I think he has quite enjoyed it too, though we liked very little. *Take Me Along* [musical by Joseph Stein, Robert Russell and Bob Merrill] and *Ben Hur* were the most enjoyable – *Silent Night, Lonely Night* [by Robert Anderson] is very well acted by dishy Hank Fonda and Barbara Bel Geddes, but the play itself is very sentimental and early John Van Druten, and it has had rotten notices. J.P. went to *The Tenth Man* [by Paddy Chayefsky] and *The Fighting Cock* yesterday and hated them both, and I was taken to a very boring Beatnik dope play in the Village, called *The Connection* [by Jack Gelber] – all junkies with a jazz combo and a lot of people being given heroin jabs in the loo – just offstage – and having their boils squeezed (onstage). 'Gosh, look at all this green pus on my hands' and 'shit' every other word.

B[inkie] has evidently caught J.P. out in a little escapade he had in Paris a few weeks back, judging by a ¾ hour conversation conducted in hushed tones across the Atlantic one afternoon last week, so even in the properest dovecotes there is yet an occasional flutter, is there not?

I sent you some records, but not [*The Boys from*] *Syracuse* [by George Abbott, Lorenz Hart and Richard Rodgers] which seems to be out of print. There may be one at Cowley Street which you could filch with pleasure. Ask Niobe or Mrs Marshall.* *Sound of Music* is so unspeakable that I sent mine to Arthur M. as a joke present. If you want to hear the full horror of it you can pop round to No. 16 and play it, but I am sure you wouldn't want it to keep.

To Paul Anstee   *9 December, New York*

Saratoga was pretty awful, and even Cecil [Beaton]'s work rather tired, I thought. You will see that Natasha has a marvellous notice and the play too, though Hugh went with Peter and says the audience hated it. *Les Amants* is a divine film – manch, polo breeches and a quarter of an hour love scene – they do it in a boat, in a bath, on the bed and finally he puts on her woolly bathrobe, opens it and wraps it round the two of them together. Very exciting indeed. And I saw it entirely alone, and in an almost empty cinema, so no nudging was even possible!

To Paul Anstee   *12 December, New York*

Life does not cease to be hectic here. I gave talks at the Stella Adler School and the Neighbourhood Playhouse School, and a two-hour recorded interview to a man at the *N.Y. Times* who is writing a book on acting. Consequently, I dozed through most of the first act of *Figaro* in [Rudolph] Bing's box on Thursday, and last night at *The Tenth Man* I fell completely asleep in the first act and came home and went to bed. Brilliantly directed by Tyrone Guthrie and lovely lighting, but I couldn't understand what it was all about – a lot of dreary old Jews in a deserted synagogue and a girl who was possessed by a Dybbuk – too boring. And the most appalling late audience of the most horrible Jews imaginable did not make the theatre any less oppressive in front.

We have a whole seven days rehearsals for the T.V., which is pretty stupid work, though Carol Channing is rather a camp [*sic*] and quite a dear. Eva Gabor idiotic and sweet for a drink, like an overblown Viennese bath bun. I don't seem to be able to discover whether Nell [Noël Coward] herself will be presiding at Blue Harbour when I go – I rather hope so, as I have not seen her for so long.

I was not greatly impressed by *Seven Deadly Sins* [by Bertolt Brecht and

* Arthur Marshall.

Kurt Weill]. I had perhaps heard too much about it. Lotte Lenya is nice but Kurt Weill's music means nothing to me, and the *Figaro* performance was very routine. Oliver [Messel]'s décor nice, but much the same as it was at Glyndebourne, and the Met is really rather too big a house for Mozart. I enjoyed meeting Stravinsky at the Liebersons.

To Paul Anstee   *December 1959, New York*

I have been thinking about you since your last letter – so full of suspicions and veiled reproaches. I know you have had a frustrating time and a disappointment over New York, but it is unworthy of you, as you *can* be, to let it make you resentful and martyred. Of course I scrupulously avoid mentioning George and Princeton – what is the point of mentioning it when you hate him so much, to risk upsetting you? Of course I do see him at intervals, when his professor spares him, once or twice a month, and they are both very sweet to me and assure me that my presence is not unwelcome to their own happiness together. But as I have one guilt complex about disturbing their relationship and another to feel *you* think I have behaved disgracefully to you, it is not a particularly comforting situation either way for me, as you ought to understand, I think.

You seem unable to be fond of me as I am of you. You want the doglike devotion of a lifetime and, after knowing me so well for so long, you know perfectly well that I cannot give you that completely. I do everything I can to show how fond I am but, although you must be fond of me to take such trouble writing and take such an interest in everything I do, you do seem to spoil it rather by being over-possessive and feeling so critical about my friends and doings when you are not involved with them. As I have already got Bernie and the hard blondes* to cope with, I get terribly trapped and depressed by all this refusal to allow me *any* independence of my own. I do so look forward to your letters, and when they come at last, there always seems to be a sting in the tail and a hint of the pleasant impression that you think me a silly old thing who is only to be tolerated and put in his place. If our long friendship has any value, it is surely some sort of mutual trust and sweetness, regardless of what we may either of us think of the other's weaknesses, friends and pursuits.

You can be so very sweet and tender and thoughtful when you like. I know the situation is difficult, but being away doesn't make me any less devoted to you. Only sometimes I feel you only want me to come back so that you can make snide remarks about my time here and how boring I will think your company by contrast. This is just plain silly. We have had wonderful fun and happiness together, despite all kinds of hazards and distractions which are, I fear, inevitable, especially in two people of distinctly feminine natures (and

---

* Presumably Binkie Beaumont and John Perry.

iron determination in strange ways, too). Our sex relations have never been amiss, at least as far as I am concerned – you know it gives me always enormous pleasure being with you and sleeping with you – but there are far too many years between us to make it possible to have a completely shared life together. I have so few people that I really care for, Patrick [Woodcock], Hugh [Wheeler], Bobby Flemyng, Dick. You mustn't make impossible demands, though I know your jealousy is a great compliment. It only distresses me and I'm sure it makes you unhappy too. Life is not all that amusing and there is little to look forward to, I find, except struggling to find jobs that absorb one, and mutual sweetness and confidence in the people one loves and who forgive one's trespasses. I don't mean to preach, but it is Sunday, and I am sad.

To Paul Anstee   *19 December, New York*

Dearest boy, thank you for your very sweet wire. I always think I have gone too far when I write snappily to you, and I regret it the moment I have popped it into the letterbox.

I must fly out and buy a few baubles for *very* few people. Xmas is much cheaper at least away from home. Neal [Berry?] and Charles are back – of course the first request was for seats for *F.F.E.* (and peril take me if they are not in the third row. Why can't they buy them in the ordinary way, silly cunts!), and I am bidden for a drink this afternoon. 6 o'clock, I said. No, 5.30 would be better, was the reply. I do find all that prissiness very odd in two people who are fundamentally very sweet. But I must try not to be intolerant and bitchy.

To Paul Anstee   *23 December, New York*

Your *very* sweet letter came today. I do thank you far it, darling boy, and forgive me so much past thoughtlessness and distress I have given you at various times. I love you very much and I always will.

Saw *Orphée le Negre* [*Black Orpheus*] film with the Gish girls last night. It was divine – marvellous colour and a voodoo Black Mass – all so like Haiti it gave me great nostalgia. Also heard Stravinsky conduct his *Les Noces* and *Enfance du Christ* of Berlioz – very lovely. *Tiger Bay* I enjoyed too – pretty Horst [Buchholz] and clever Hayley Mills. Huge party for Cathleen Nesbitt – Tallulah [Bankhead], Shirley Booth, B[arbara] Bel Geddes etc. etc. but rather boring – all parties are these days, it seems, and the boys' ones are full of elderly cover girls. I met Chita Rivera at Jerry Robbins', who seemed rather a dear. Shall not be sorry to pack up here and get off to Blue Harbour and the heat.

THE SIXTIES

1960

It is so very strange to be here again – and without you. The house is just the same, the sea as blue, the palms waving in the wind, three cats, May [Simpson] and Alton,* the natives in the roads with bright shirts and bundles on their heads, the corrugated iron shacks and funny, warm smell of cooking. *After the Ball* on the gramophone, bamboo furniture and drum tables – all as if they had stood quite still from all those years ago. Funny feeling, rather sad making, but beautiful in its own way. The peace is certainly comforting after New York – only the wind and sea and twittering of birds and whirring of insects.

I went rather mad while we were waiting for the plane at Idlewild and had all my hair cut off. I have been longing to try it for ever so long. Now I am terrified at my appearance, though Hugh and Ben both assure me it is a success. Anyway, as I am not working, there is plenty of time to grow it again if it strikes dismay into everybody when they see me. Don't mistake me for Bobby Lewis when we meet again, that is all I beg of you. Like Nellie [Noël Coward] herself, those long strands draped over the bald patch have depressed me these many months, so I thought I might as well go the whole hog and sacrifice the sides as well – maybe it will grow a bit stronger after the sun has shone on it for a couple of weeks, and I can always wear a skullcap or a beret in public if the worst comes to worst.

Rouben Ter-Arutunian suddenly decided to come with us at the last minute – the *very* hairy Armenian designer I'm sure I told you about.† He is rather sweet for a drink – very like Costa, with the same kind of accent and very camp clothes, excellent company, talks endless music shop with Hugh and is generally rather fun. I have to go to Kingston tomorrow week for the Recital and have to stay with the Governor which I hope won't be too much of a bore.

To Paul Anstee   *11 January, King's House, Jamaica*

Feel like Delysia at Juliet Duff's! Must use the notepaper. Very beautiful here but I am intensely depressed by Jamaica. I look very peculiar with my

---

* Noël Coward's Jamaican staff at Blue Harbour.
† Known sometimes as The Forest of Arden.

shaved head and a light sunburn and my skin agog with prickly heat. Usual Government House set-up. Dinner party for 18, including Mr Gaitskell.* But I managed to sidestep politics and discuss the Moscow Art Theatre with him! Read Rupert Croft-Cooke's book about his case,† which was extremely upsetting. I suddenly tremble for Knots Fosse but I suppose it is silly of me.

We lunched at Goldeneye, where Annie [Fleming] was wizened gossipy, and I felt they were on the verge of a frightful row. Also met Blanche (Crosse and) Blackwell, Noël's new cicerone and apparently Ian [Fleming]'s mistress, a very rich widow with a toothy smile and Joyce Grenfell voice. Received two charming offers from different gentlemen just as I was leaving N.Y. Tempting but too intense and not a grain of humour in either, so I gracefully bowed out, flattered but firm. What am I coming to?

To Noël Coward   *13 January, Blue Harbour, Jamaica*

Enid Bagnold has a new script [*The Last Joke*], rather exciting for two acts, and she is busy with Glen [Byam Shaw] working on the third. I hope it may be good for me – mad Roumanian Prince with a paralysed face, drawn, I gather, from Etienne Bibesco, whom you probably knew?

Let's hope we shall meet again soon – it seems such an age since Dublin and all our trials and tribulations. By the way, *never* act with Micheál mac Liammóir, delicious creature though he is in every other way. His Don Pedro in New York was simply awful – as undisciplined as Esmé Percy and bigger laugh-killer than Lewis Casson!! But what an angel Maggie is – I had such real joy working with her.

Hugh [Wheeler]'s play [*Big Fish, Little Fish*] is so brilliant – everyone likes it, Binkie, Irene, Moss Hart, but nobody seems ready to put it on! The director is the difficulty, and so important. I would love to do it, but the boys think it not a good plan and I fear I must agree with them. I'm going to show it to Tony Guthrie who I think might be taken with its originality. It is very funny and rather sad too. I think the time is just ripe for it – middle-aged unmarried gentlemen have not yet been used much on the stage!

To Hugh Wheeler   *21 January, London*

All is bustle and confusion – had my usual bad luck at Idlewild on Monday night. We left at 1 a.m. being scheduled to leave at 9 – awful hanging about but O.K. in the end. George came for three days and was divine and we went to the Frick, the Met., a fascinating day at Stamford with Rouben, Philip Johnson and Lincoln Kirstein, and a beastly day saying goodbye and packing.

---

* Hugh Gaitskell was Leader of the Labour Party and having an affair with Ian Fleming's wife, Ann.
† In 1953 Rupert Croft-Cooke was found guilty of an act of gross indecency with another man and sentenced to nine months' imprisonment. His book was called *The Verdict of You All*.

Paul and the boys very sweet here, and Bernie cheerful – the drawing room painted Adam green – now I have to find new curtains for it.

Enid's new last act is amazingly improved, and I have agreed to do the play, rehearsing in May–June to Christmas here and then in New York, if it should be successful, so I have a wonderful time off first. I have offered to do six Recitals in Italy at the end of March. Could you, would you care to come with me? It would be divine, and I would adore it if you felt like it. They would pay your return from London to Italy and back, and expenses too, so it would cost you nothing but your passage from America. If it is agreed, I have suggested to George that he comes to Rome April 8 and we go to Greece for a week, which he has free at that time. We could all go together – wouldn't that be rather a lark? You will surely be done with Jamaica by then. Do pray Ed will not object!

Taking advantage of his time off, JG went on holiday to Morocco with Paul Anstee, Binkie Beaumont and John Perry.

To Hugh Wheeler   *16 February, London*

It is icy cold here, but vast crowds throng the Mall waiting for news of Mrs Mountbatten's imminent accouchement.*

The Morocco holiday was fun, and Paul was sweet and seems to have settled at last for a more mild relationship. Binkie and John didn't have a cross word, and the Arab boys at Agadir never left us for a moment. One rather pretty sardine-fisherman, part Spanish, enticed Paul into the dunes two days running with apparently satisfactory results. I did not look on, oddly enough, nor misconduct myself in any way. My juices must be running low at last. As Mrs Maugham remarked in an interview last week, 'The dinner table finds me out. I can no longer eat what I like, only nibble what I must.'

Nelly [Noël Coward] is on crutches after phlebitis and Graham [Payn] is nursing a sick mum in London.

To Hugh Wheeler   *25 February, London*

Ed [Cone] is not coming to London after all, *but* I am planning to go to New York for a fortnight – hoping to do two recitals to excuse it (Yale and Stratford Conn. I hope). Ed will be in Spain and has sweetly said O.K. so I can have a divine time with George. He has found a new hotel called Hotel 14 on 60th Street where he says we can live (in a suite) like anonymous princes for 15 dollars a day!! Anyway, I am thrilled about this, and he may come to London on his way back from his holiday in June with Ed – I suggested Ed should

---

* They had quite a long wait; Prince Andrew was born on 19 February 1960.

stay with *me* and G. with Binkie – and Elvira* and Bernie could be umpires and stuff us all so full of goodies and wine that no-one would know who was sleeping in which street when!

Do you think Moss and Goddard [Lieberson] have something in common (besides racial characteristics and extensive properties in the Midlands?). I always feel they are a little bit alike – their black hair and gold props and beautiful but rather frigid wives! [Kitty Carlisle Hart and Brigitta Lieberson]

Enid's play is postponed till July, as Ralph [Richardson] is to play the tycoon, but he has to do *Exodus* (the British general I turned down!) in Cyprus all through June after he leaves the Greene play.

Going to see *Giselle* with Fonteyn tonight, taking Vivien. I am rather dreading discussing the Larry situation. I gather his N.Y. play is N.G.† and he wrote, Brian [Bedford] says, a very carping article on American acting in the Sunday *N.Y. Times* the other week. I had one in the following Sunday, which I gather was *better* received! Ha ha. Brian says he is taking lessons in technique from Bobby Lewis to balance the ones of *feeling* at the Theatre Studio. I should have supposed the other way round to be more likely, but it seems not!

Saw Margaret Leighton's Mortimer play [*The Wrong Side of the Park* by John Mortimer] last night, and was mad about it. It is a big hit, but no one seems to like it except me. Joycie [Carey] excellent in a poor part, the writing and acting very good. But Binkie, J.P. and Paul all loathed it, and I hear the Royal Court boys as well.

Splendid new ballet of Freddie Ashton, *La Fille Mal Gardée*, marvellous production of *Cav and Pag* by Zeffirelli (whose *Lucia* was so good last year). I am supposed to help polish up *The Trojans* in April. New Cassandra and Dido (don't know who yet) – and I am hoping Peggy Ashcroft will do Andromache – isn't that exciting? Her Rebecca West in *Rosmersholm* [by Henrik Ibsen] is superb – but finishes, alas, before you come. Nothing much else to see. We caught *Hiroshima Mon Amour* in Meknes (of all places) but found it a bit slow – beautifully acted, though, and not too painful as I feared. The Japanese young man in it is a very hot assiette with the most lovely back. Bought a lot of dirty books in Morocco and managed to get them all back safely. Two you will like – don't forget to make Paul lend them – I think he will make a fortune as a lending library!

To Irene Worth   *9 March, London*

I am more than delighted by your success and that of the play [*Toys in the Attic* by Lillian Hellman]. How good, too, that you like the others, and

---

* Binkie Beaumont's housekeeper. Beaumont lived in Lord North Street adjacent to Cowley Street
† Olivier had directed Charlton Heston in *The Tumbler.*

everything happy behind the scenes also. I always thought Lillian H. a bit of a battleaxe and I imagine she might be difficult to work with, but she has always been charming to me, and I believe she had a vile time in the Red Purge, which saddened and almost destroyed her, which probably accounts for her rather formidable manner.

Vivien leaves on Friday and is staying at the Navarro. Do ring her and be sweet. She's in pretty brave shape, but terribly sad and Notley is sold, which has been hard for her. I've not seen Larry since his return.*

A lot of poor stuff here in the theatre. [The] Aspern Papers [by Michael Redgrave, based on a story by Henry James] disappointing, though the women are all excellent, but it is slow and old-fashioned and I liked neither direction, setting, nor Michael [Redgrave] himself. Marie Bell rather transpontine as Phèdre in a very elaborate hair-do which makes her look like Edith Sitwell playing Queen Elizabeth and the men rather embarrassingly over-undressed! Maggie [Leighton]'s play very fascinating and she is splendid in it.

Everyone agog, of course, over the Wedding,† which is to be May 6th. We shan't be able to move in the neighbourhood. Let's hope it will be good for the theatres.

To Dadie Rylands   *22 April, London*

Bernard Levin, who is something of a know-all, has taken me to task for saying 'the imperial votaress passed on' as he says it should be 'vot'ress passèd'.

I am always ready to be corrected, but would like to know your opinion. I have tried both and think mine sounds the best.

In May JG returned to the USA for performances of Ages of Man in Connecticut and Massachusetts.

To Paul Anstee   *17 May, New York*

The Westport Recital was not fun – huge, beastly new school auditorium and a lot of boring ladies and inefficient students, bad lighting etc., but the one at Boston on Sunday was a real joy. A superb new hall in the shape of a shell – audience close and rising in tiers in a semi-arch – perfect acoustics and a friendly audience. I never did it so well and probably never shall again.

Bye Bye Birdie [by Michael Stewart, Lee Adams and Charles Crouse] is simply *divine* and I am taking Hugh to see it on Thursday. You would go mad. Music, décor, acting, dancing all utterly charming and light, and young attractive people for a change. I hear the man who put it on has gone over to

---

* The Vivien Leigh–Laurence Olivier marriage had been troubled for some time. Olivier had now asked her for a divorce in order to marry Joan Plowright.

† Princess Margaret was about to marry Antony Armstrong-Jones.

London to arrange to do it there himself. Apparently up to now he was only a stage director! [Gower Champion] Extraordinary the way these things happen here. But it is infinitely the best thing I have seen since *Guys and Dolls*.

I was delighted with *Five Fingers* – saw a packed matinée with ladies gasping at each dramatic moment and kicking their shoes off under the seats and then finding them very difficult to retrieve.

To Paul Anstee   *21 May, New York*

Walked out of *The Fugitive Kind* – Brando enormously fat and quite incoherent – pauses for hours between every unintelligible word – and the whole thing a crushing bore.

Did you know Tammy Grimes is going to marry Rex [Harrison] at any moment?

Vivien [Leigh]'s play [*Duel of Angels* by Jean Giraudoux] coming off in three weeks time. I dread getting involved with her – she is so exhausting and dotty again, poor lady.

To Paul Anstee   *24 May, New York*

Camino Real [by Tennessee Williams] was interesting, but far too long. I hear Tennessee went last night and cheered and shrieked with laughter all through à la Brendan Behan, which must have been jolly for the cast in a theatre the size of a small room – even I found it a bit embarrassing having them act in one's lap.

To Hugh Wheeler   *14 June, London*

I feel very cut off from you since I got back. George has arrived from New York and is asleep upstairs after his flight. He stays till next Monday before joining Ed in Spain – returns to Princeton July 3rd. Ed comes here the last week in July.

Glen [Byam Shaw] has had a heart attack and is recuperating with Dick as Nurse! Hope to God he will recover in time for our play [*The Last Joke*]. Enid [Bagnold] bombards me with notes and rewrites and I dread having to take on the direction as well as act. Felix Kelly has done lovely sets, and the readings were quite encouraging. Anna Massey brilliant, Bobby Flemyng is to play my brother. A good idea, I think. He read it admirably.

Saw *Rhinoceros* [by Eugene Ionesco] – boring piece but Larry [Olivier] brilliant. Lady Viv back in London with a good many straws in her hair. Terry very triumphant over *Ross*.* I loved it (saw it last week with Paul) except for

---

* Terence Rattigan's play about Lawrence of Arabia.

one or two mistakes – angel voices and Alec [Guinness], who is brilliant otherwise, a bit overdoes one or two of his important reactions.

My poetry recital went very well, though I cried far too much and misted my spectacles, making several howling textual errors in consequence ('fresh *fields*' instead of 'woods' in *Lycidas*). Paul very well and sweetly forgiving over G.'s arrival, though there were storms at first. I am taking him to Antibes for four days to make up, which seems to have cheered him up considerably. Trust there will be no delicate meetings this week.

To Hugh Wheeler   *21 July, London*

I used to like Burgess [Meredith] in 1936 (!) when Peggy Ashcroft came over to act with him in *High Tor* (an awful Max Anderson play). He was married to Margaret Perry in those days – the wedding was said to have been a mad romp (as all her ushers were well-known queens) and it didn't last long. I must have told you about us going to the country to stay the weekend with them, and how the Great Danes had been locked in, and after we had put the car away we found Burgess's wife and Peggy with dustpans trying vainly to remove at least eight steaming piles distributed round the dining room floor! When I met him briefly again (at the time of the Recital), he seemed very much aged and hung over, but perhaps that was only my impression.

George came here for a blissful week, except that he had violent hay fever *and* strong reaction from anti-typhoid shots which he insisted on Patrick [Woodcock] giving him for Spain (he really is a bit of a hypochondriac, I must admit). We went to Glyndebourne – *Falstaff* – what a marvellous work – and I got drunk on Bernie's lethal martinis, fell head first in the salmon, and didn't even remember I had done so five minutes later! G. was rather perturbed, of course, but I recovered miraculously. Drink only seems to hit me violently for a few moments and then leaves me perfectly readjusted! Also we saw *Ross* together, *The Caretaker* [by Harold Pinter] and *The Merchant* at Stratford, and spent a day at Oxford for him to visit old chums. The weather was divine all the time – the driving rather too much, but pleasant, and we went to Knots Fosse for the Saturday night, where tennis was played violently with J.P. (G. won after the first set, of course), and off he went again to join Ed in Spain. Ed is now in Paris and arrives here next Monday for a week. I hope he will not be bored. Concerts and operas are mostly over for the summer unfortunately, and I am in rather a dither, but I hope I can keep my head and not bore him too badly.

Paul and I went to Cap d'Antibes just before rehearsals began for five days and had a lovely time, I must say. He was very sweet, and we dined with Edward Molyneux and Willie Maugham, and P. won £40 at roulette, and altogether it was a great success – lovely weather again, though *here* it has been *vile* – thunder storms, cloudbursts etc. all these last three weeks. (The *New Yorker* had a very virulent anti-English article, complaining we talk of nothing but the weather.) Our rehearsals very hectic – terrific rewriting and bits cut and put in. The first act seems pretty good, but the second and third hang badly at present. On the other hand, we had a whole week on Act I (without Ralph) and we've only had two on the rest with endless arguments and readjustments. So we are barely right on moves, texts and business at present. Binkie and John come tomorrow to see a run-through and decide if the final version will at least hold up for the opening as it is at present. After that we have four or five weeks – how I dread them – to redirect, so we shall see. I plan to take Paul to Paris on Saturday for 24 hours before the last lap (and Ed) in order to see the Poussin show, which I hear is sensational, at the Louvre. I gather you can't get near the Picasso Show at the Tate, but will probably try to take Ed there next week. He sent me quite a funny crossword puzzle this week, composed in Brittany by himself – one of the clues 'evidently found in the Forest of Arden' in five letters – the answer, of course, CRABS which was wittier than I thought him capable of – or is that only my childish appreciation?

Two good stories for you. Youthful American (worn out after exploring all the churches of Rome, Florence and Venice): 'If she doesn't put that child down soon, it will *never* learn to walk.'

The other, Harold Hobson, fancying himself no end in the French, insisting on being the only London journalist to interview Jean Genet when he comes over for *The Balcony*. On arriving at Genet's hotel, silence ensued for some minutes, and Hobson's completely gravelled for an opening.

Genet (breaking silence, suddenly): 'Donc! Vous êtes pédéraste?'
Hobson (leaping for cover): 'Non, monsieur, je suis critique!'

The Last Joke *had a long tour prior to its London opening.*

To Hugh Wheeler   *11 August, Liverpool*

The play is very odd. The *Guardian* loathed it and tore it to shreds – the *Liverpool Post* liked it very much. Business is incredibly good. I alternate with thinking it will get by and that we should not bring it in to London at all. Ralph feels rather the same. J.P. and Binkie appear optimistic, we have stipulated we do not finally decide until Oxford (the week after next).

August is loathsome – vile stormy weather and a kind of hiatus everywhere. Glen [Byam Shaw] is sweet and helpful and the company is nice – Bobby Flemyng dreadfully bad and drives me mad in the play, but he is a dear off, and fortunately his part is short – he doesn't now come back in the third act at all. Enid and Irene [Selznick] potter about, rewriting and arguing endlessly. E. seems unable to see the real weaknesses and cavils with phrases and little clevernesses of no real value. It is all rather dreary to me.

Ed's visit was an unqualified success, I think, and I really like him immensely, though I found it somehow agonising, discussing George with him – not surprising really, I suppose. He staggered me by telling me that after he had met G. first (and found out about me), he held his hand for some time, invited G. to a concert where he was playing which G. evaded to his (Ed's) disappointment. Then one day G. came into his house and said quite calmly 'I feel we could have a life together, if you wanted it!' All this before they had been to bed! Isn't that an extraordinary sidelight. What a risk and how curiously certain G. must have felt to embark on such a thing so deliberately. He grows more interesting hourly! Ed did *not* sleep with me. I indicated as tactfully as possible that I would be willing, and he countered with the charming excuse that I should be disappointed with him after G! What a dialogue for a short story. I was really upset when he left, but probably largely because I couldn't bear to think of him back with G. G. writes that he is seeing something of Jean[?] (but this is *not* for Ed's ears) and is very upset by his loneliness and sad background – no doubt he will manage an odd rendezvous with him from time to time. He is unlucky, isn't he (or is he?) in having so many admirers in lonely agonies at his absence. Ed says, however, that he enjoys having me to hover over his head and would be *very* upset if he thought I was no longer carrying the torch, but I feel it is all mighty frustrating and unsatisfactory, really. Paul met him (Ed) and was polite, though frigid.

The Paris trip with Paul was quite a success, though there was a tricky moment when we ran bang into Ed at the Carousel! We found a little Poussin went a long way, but loved the exhibition of Louis XIV objets and furniture. Dreadful dinner at the Méditerranée with Ginette [Spanier] and Nancy [Spain] (in trousers), Ginette dimpling up a good deal. Dined at Maxim's, where the Americans all wanted autographs and two who were at the next table finally said 'We *must* know who you are!'

Enid was interviewed at Manchester at the first interval by a *deaf* reporter.

'How did you think the first act went, Miss Bagnold?'

Enid (ecstatic): 'Oh, Sir John, Sir John!'

Reporter: 'I quite agree with you. Too long!'

The first night here I made a short speech ending 'Thank you for your enthusiasm and *sympathy*.' Fortunately Enid did not notice, nor did the papers take it up.

To Hugh Wheeler   *24 August, Oxford*

Fred Hebert wrote offering me to direct the musical of *The Quiet Man* – Rouben and Jack Cole for décor and dances respectively. I hated the film, but it might possibly be worth considering if only for the trip. As you know, I always longed to direct a musical but Rouben wrote me that Bobby Lewis is directing. Irene is closeted at Rottingdean with Enid but I don't believe anyone can patch or mend now – we've all had our cuts at it for so long already. I went to Knots Fosse and Cowley Street at the weekend. Bernie very cheerful and brown from his Barcelona hol. which seems to have been quite a success, though I gather he bossed his companions a good deal, aired his atrocious Spanish with former acquaintances and [illegible] at Ray for disliking the local dainties (food, not gentlemen – the latter were, I gather, *most* accommodating to all parties).

To Hugh Wheeler   *7 September, Birmingham*

We totter on, in pouring rain, doing a handsome £5000 a week, at raised prices everywhere. No one is bored, though no one thinks it a good play. We open Sept. 28th at the Phoenix – Brighton and Edinburgh after this – and B. says we have already £15,000 advance, so I suppose we can't fail to get our money back. A nice three months – but not another *Nude* nine, I do devoutly hope, and it might be all through by Christmas with any luck. Enid is quite incapable of patching or reconstruction – of course she ought to *collaborate* from the beginning with someone amusing and reasonable like J.P. but it's too late now. If only she would give us another ten good jokes (besides the last one). All we get is highly charged fantasies about sputniks and fatal lines like 'You had a joke. Yes, Mr Portal, and it fell flat!' 'But I don't understand you at all', and suchlike sure-fire gallery booers, none of which, naturally, we accept. Glen is white with exhaustion, Roderick (Enid's husband, aged 80-odd) very seedy, and might, I gather, be gathered to his forefathers at any moment now.

Ralph enormously improved, but not very flexible, Bobby self-conscious in his wretched part, dealing packs of cards with his hands on every line – the weather unspeakable – ye Gods!

No other news. I shower poor George with articles on music and the theatre, and impassioned wavings of my spluttering torch – oh dear, five years is too long for such remote controlled devotion.

P. is well. Took me to Judy Garland last Sunday (awash with queens and sentimental vociferations) and has a pretty but common new admirer to whom he introduced me. He may go to N.Y. for a week at Christmas. My own sex life is at a complete standstill, except for passionate love notes from Enid, which are faintly embarrassing considering how I am maddened by the play. Bernie and Ray continue to bill and coo. I sent the record of *Oliver* [by Lionel Bart] to Goddard [Lieberson], but hardly think you would like it enough to send it to you. The stagecraft is the thing, the music very amateur, though catchy and appropriate, but I thought it might amuse him.

To Vivien Leigh   *15 September, Brighton*

We have had rather a wretched tour. The play is not right and never will be, I'm afraid, though there are attractive and brilliant things in it. But the story line is impossibly weak, and Enid is quite incapable of mending it – only produces more flowery fancies, paradoxes, aphorisms and what all, which confuse and over decorate an already overblown text.

Ralph has a magnificent new Bentley and has given Mu a superb new mink coat as a birthday present, but I think he is longing to get a nice juicy film contract to pay for them!

To Irene Worth   *21 September, Edinburgh*

Val has married again (5th!) and gone off to Venice! Eleanor went to the wedding, but it was all a great secret, and I've not met the girl who is 25 and nothing to do with the theatre. I don't know where he met her.

What a wonderful run your play [*Toys in the Attic* by Lillian Hellman] has had. I'm sure it won't do for London, though. Gwen is not working, I fear, and Edith Evans lost her friend, who shared her country house – she suddenly died of cancer and I fear the shock will have shattered her. No-one seems to have seen or heard of her since. I hope she will find a play and be able to work again soon.

Binkie and John have been in Spain on holiday, returning tomorrow. Edinburgh looks superb in the autumn sunshine, the first after weeks of appalling rain and storms. Fountains Abbey, where I took Ralph for the first time, was more divine than ever, otherwise it has been a grisly eight weeks.

The Last Joke *opened at the Phoenix Theatre on 28 September.*

To Noël Coward   *1 October, London*

So very good of you to think of me – the play is something of a disaster but, as usual, everyone in the theatre behaves their best in adversity.

Loved you in the film [*Surprise Package*], though I fear Yul [Brynner], in spite of being (to me) an undoubted dish, is no comedian and I think he kills the film as a whole by his poor acting – though you shine brilliantly in every scene you have.

To Hugh Wheeler   *10 October, London*

Bless you for your consolations – it is a miserable business playing the wretched thing – we did nearly £3500 last week, and now with the Motor Show the town is full of visiting firemen, so I fear we may go on doing well for another few weeks – not much hope of being through before the end of November or beginning of December. We all loathe it and so do the customers, but they come in all the same. Enid sent Ralph a p[ersonal] and confidential note begging him to influence me to abandon the shooting and poison myself instead in the last act!! More time then, she said, to let me *explain* myself.

Christ on a bicycle! She is a dear gallant old amateur dairy-bags [?] and I fear she is written out, over and on.

I have signed with the Margrave to direct the Britten *Dream* at the Garden, rehearse Jan. 4th, open Feb 2nd. So I am desperately hoping to get to America in December, and perhaps spend Christmas with G. The only awkward thing is that I promised Paul *he* should go to N.Y. and it would be a bit complicated all round if we were there together, though he is now quite resigned to our affair being over, and talks quite freely about G. Probably the London Fearfuls will make their usual difficulties about him coming also. I'm having a terribly tricky time with J.P. and Binkie anyway, as they are a bit ashamed about our play, and consequently defiant, and they are mad with me because I began tentative negotiations to do *Cherry Orchard* (Peggy and Michel St-Denis) and *Othello* for next fall for Stratford, London and New York.

Zeffirelli (who is charming and obviously very clever) has done a most controversial *Romeo and Juliet* at the Vic – Hobson loathed it, Tynan three columns of rave. I go to see for myself next week. He might be the man to direct *Othello* if I could get the right Iago too. Albert Finney would be wonderful. I saw him last week in a funny play called *Billy Liar* [by Keith Waterhouse and Willis Hall] in which he is superb – he understudied and played for Larry last year in *Coriolanus* and is going to be Martin Luther in John Osborne's new play [*Luther*] at the Court later this year, but now, of course, he's greatly in demand – turned down a £60,000 film contract, for which I much admire him.

Ray socked Bernie (blood all over my sofa, which has gone to be re-covered) while I was on tour, and was dismissed, bag and baggage. I gather he is living elsewhere and think they are slowly making it up!

To J. R. Ackerley   *6 November, London*

I do want to congratulate you on the novel [*We Think the World of You*], which I read last week with great pleasure and [illegible]. The relationships are so marvellously exact and compassionate, as well as the all over perfection of style and understatement. Everything implied, nothing over-emphasised – it is poignant, funny, absorbing – I could not leave it till I had read it all.

I hope its praises and success are giving you pleasure, and that you will also have it published in America, and that it will bring you financial as well as artistic rewards, as you deserve. I have always loved your talent, and regretted not seeing you more often, as in the old days of Hammersmith and the Café Royal.

I had to write and thank you and tell you what pleasure you have given me. I hope you are well and happy – or something like it!

The Last Joke *did not last long, and JG took a holiday in America. He played* **Ages of Man** *in Florida before returning to New York to continue preparations for his production of Hugh Wheeler's play* **Big Fish, Little Fish.**

To Paul Anstee   *11 December, Florida*

I must say it is divine here – tropical sunshine, rich, purring limousines, swimming pools etc., a dear little theatre in an art gallery where I play tonight. Unfortunately I must return tomorrow to N.Y. to get the casting etc. under way and talk to Hugh about the rewriting and so on.

Boring big party on Wednesday – met [Ethel] Merman, who was very unattractive, and Cary Grant, as dishy as ever. Went down to Princeton to see the drag show of the students – very bad and boring – but we had a lovely day driving in the country and a wonderful lunch in a riverside hostelry run by an ex-radio star. G. very pale and wan with a bad stomach – no doubt alarm at my approach! Ed very sweet and cooked a grand dinner for me, after which I returned to N.Y. and popped into the Bon Soir, where N. discovered me – the bar was extremely busy, as it was Saturday night, and I found I had my hands quite full in a very short space of time, only don't mention such a vulgar thing to the Fearfuls, will you.

1961

After Christmas JG returned to England to rehearse Britten's A Midsummer Night's Dream, *conducted by Georg Solti.*

To Hugh Wheeler   *9 January, London*

It seems very odd to be back, and plunged into *The Dream*, though I am glad to report that I am quite delighted with [John] Piper's sets and the enthusiasm of a cast that seems to be really remarkably well chosen. I had a punctual and satisfactory flight home, only marred by developing a heavy sinus cold next day, and then having to do two night journeys by train in order to give two recitals in Cumberland (heavy snowstorm!) for David Webster's Hungarian silkworm friends* (who own a very charming private theatre in Rosehill, Barrow-in-Furness) to which an audience of 200 flocked – in deep evening dress – to hear me! I returned, a little the worse for wear and tear, to a Sunday rehearsal at Covent Garden, which was unexpectedly hopeful. So I live in hopes, though I cannot yet smoke a cigarette, which maddens me.

His production of A Midsummer Night's Dream *opened at Covent Garden on 2 February. He then returned to New York, where he stayed in José Quintero's*

---

* Sir Nicholas 'Miki' Sekers, a Hungarian immigrant, whose company had silk mills in Cumbria.

apartment, to rehearse **Big Fish, Little Fish.** *The cast included Hume Cronyn, Jason Robards Jr. and George Voskovec.*

To Paul Anstee   *12 February, New York*

Sweet of you to Valentine me – très amusing card. The journey was hideous last weekend, but I recovered quickly with my usual sang-froid and recuperative potentiality. We are working like demons and I have hardly had a moment to ring anyone up or see or do anything – or anybody! P. Brook appears completely in purdah. Even Arnold [Weissberger] refuses to divulge his telephone number, nor does Hugh know it. Most peculiar. The play is *very* promising – wonderfully good actors in all the parts.

We rehearse on the roof of the New Amsterdam (now a movie house on 42nd Street). It is a tiny derelict old theatre and one can really camp down for the day, undisturbed except for the water pipes which emit ghostly explosive crackles about once every two hours. The snow has almost gone, and days are crisp and blue, though it is still pretty cold. The apartment has been repainted and looks spick and span – have a new morning negress who is very unpunctual and hysterical. Ben left 100 dollars in my dressing table drawer for me the day before I arrived and it promptly disappeared – also a bundle of mail for José – great mystery – nothing else seemed to be missing but we had to have all the locks changed. Perhaps one of José's admirers had an old key! They say he was always leaving the front door wide open when he was here! I *don't*.

To Paul Anstee   *18 February, New York*

We slog away at the piece, and I am really hopeful about it. The rewriting and cutting has been endless, but Hugh is patient, sweet and infinitely resourceful – his professional mind so quick to see where bits drag or are harmful. The cast quite excellent, though Robards is rather behindhand owing to nightly potations which make him slow to learn. But he is a dear and indeed I like them all immensely.

To Paul Anstee   *1 March, New York*

It is suddenly marvellous spring weather and we are all set to leave tomorrow to the Philadelphia tryout. Monday was very hectic. Jason didn't come in the morning, and arrived late in the afternoon saying the whole last scene was wrong and he couldn't play it, it wasn't the same play we had begun rehearsing etc. etc. All worked up out of his own guilty conscience, as he goes out every night and gets drunk apparently, so does not study his lines and is consequently behindhand with the ensemble. Also, the others are so good and have such effective parts that he thinks he will come off second best, which may be true.

But Hugh worked like a black and changed two speeches very cunningly, and I think in the end it has worked out even better than before – the end is now strong and touching and a bit ironic. I like it immensely.

I have been terribly tired and gone out very little. Dined with Nelly [Noël Coward], who was perfectly sweet, but both he and Coley [Cole Lesley] (whose hair is now black *velvet*) are much aged, I thought, though as delightful as ever. No doubt they thought the same of me – the age, I mean.

Peter Glenville rang from the Coast to suggest I should go into *Becket* [by Jean Anouilh]!! Play Larry [Olivier]'s part and Larry would take over from [Anthony] Quinn, who is leaving to do a film. Thank you very much. Still, I suppose it is nice to be thought of.

Peter Brook told us a divine story. He met a tart in London and was talking to her. She said, 'You know that torture room in Curzon Street?' (Peter didn't, of course.) 'Well, I had a client the other day with rather special tastes and I thought I would book us there for an hour or two, and we went, and imagine, when we got to the room, there was Alec Guinness on the rack!'

To Paul Anstee   *9 March, Philadelphia*

The play is now in good shape, with a new and more optimistic final curtain, but the actors are a bit low and uncertain. We cut five minutes or more out on Monday and rehearsed all day. I think they will recover by the end of the week when they regain confidence and are more sure of their effects. It needs endless watching and coaxing to get them all up to scratch, and they conceal their weaknesses under all kinds of pretexts and a desire to be sympathetic at the expense of character. I don't think Jason likes the new end, but I think Miss [Lauren] Bacall* does, so I hope to persuade him eventually to play it up. When he doesn't believe in a speech he recites it blankly and of course it doesn't go. He is so awfully good and very sweet in many ways – a big, spoilt baby, like most good actors!

Rather a fraught visit to Princeton. George got a bit tight and started groping a young S. American under the table at dinner, which threw both of his elderly admirers into a pet! Hugh took a dislike to Dick Easton and another actor who were at the party, and it all ended in profuse apologies and sympathetic protestations in every possible direction. Ed naturally felt *he* was the prima donna, having played very well in his concert, and Hugh and I are both extremely nervous with all this stress and strain, so it wasn't altogether a very happy visit, despite heavenly spring weather. Well, well.

---

* Miss Bacall would shortly become the third Mrs Jason Robards.

To Paul Anstee   *12 March, Philadelphia*

Leaving Philadelphia at last and on to the great event. It has been a trying time. Hugh is in a lather of nerves and detests everyone we meet, the actors, me etc. but he also hangs on one's heels almost pathetically – has no matches, typing paper, finds everybody inefficient! I think once Wednesday is over he will recover his equilibrium.

Goddard [Lieberson] came to the matinée yesterday and produced some last minute suggestions for alterations which had, I think, better be ignored or the actors will lose their confidence so near the opening. Of course he saw a very poor matinée performance – Jason with a hangover, fluffing right and left and infecting the rest with jitters – the evening show as good as possible and 4,000 dollars up on the first week, which is encouraging. They really seemed to like it here, and Noël is staying in New York to grace Wednesday with his august presence.

Wonderful Cecil [Beaton] story. The first night of his *Turandot* the curtain rose on his carefully graded colour scheme. To his horror, he suddenly espied a chorus girl dressed in bright orange, the costume he had designed for a scene in the *last* act. He rushed through the pass door and had the stage manager haul her off, where he ripped of the offending dress from her back in the wings. Returning to his seat somewhat breathless, he asked [Rudolph] Bing at intermission how he thought it was all going. 'Splendidly,' said Bing, 'except that the entire chorus has gone on strike and the curtain won't go up again unless you go round to their dressing rooms and apologise personally.' Which he had to do forthwith!

Big Fish, Little Fish *opened at the ANTA Theatre on 15 March.*

To Dorothy and Lillian Gish   *20 March, London*

Hugh's play hangs in the balance – it was rather agony to leave it. If the publicity and interest is sufficiently arousing I believe it may still be a hit. The press was just under-enthusiastic, alas, though its tone was really distinguished and encouraging on the whole, but I fear that may not be quite enough to drum up the customers in sufficient numbers.

After the opening of **Big** Fish, **Little** Fish, *JG returned to England to direct Margaret Rutherford in* **Dazzling** Prospect *by M. J. Farrell (Molly Keane) and John Perry.*

To Hugh Wheeler   *27 March, London*

I do hope you are better by this. I'm not surprised to hear you collapsed when you got home after all the strain and stress. Beastly of me not to ring you –

but there was the usual rush and parting with George etc. The Saturday night I saw them all at the theatre and had a farewell drink with Ben E. The audience seemed to love the last act, which I saw, but I gather business is not very encouraging and do not feel very hopeful for our chances unless some unforeseen miracle occurs.

We start rehearsing the Rutherford play today. I am not much looking forward to the next two months, unless the play turns out more fun than I anticipate. They have already *built* the set, and it is rather ugly and inflexible and too late to change it. I look back with some nostalgia to our work together – at least the result is something we can all be proud of, I believe, and it was an exciting if wearing time.

Knots Fosse looks a dream of beauty – daffodils, lions and hyacinths jostling for position, only a bitter March wind, despite which the boys dig and delve indefatigably. I saw *The Devils* [by John Whiting] which is wonderfully directed by Peter Wood, and well acted too – but rather too horrific for my stomach – disembowelling, rackings and bloodstained aprons practically in one's lap.

I met Edward Albee, who seemed very solemn and intense – hear he *hated* our play – said it was bound to succeed on Broadway as it was so commercial!! – but also that Bill Inge and Gore Vidal liked it.

To Hugh Wheeler   *20 April, London*

The Irish play is neat and funny, and I think they are all good in it. Brook [Williams] is so like father Emlyn, and Joyce [Carey] so like mother Lilian [Braithwaite] that I seem to be back twenty years. Margaret [Rutherford] is immense, in every way, and such a duck. I think it bodes admirably if the critics don't slash it as being snobbish and old-fashioned. We have had very agreeable and unhurried rehearsals. I hope we are not over-optimistic.

Dazzling Prospect *opened, without great success, as the Globe Theatre on 1 June, after which JG took a holiday in France with George Pitcher.*

To Paul Anstee   *13 June, Saint Jean Cap Ferrat*

It is divine weather here, and a very attractive unpretentious hotel run by Mrs Michael Powell, who is deadpan and mysterious and, I believe, a martyr to the bottle. Dear little harbour and beach. Went to Cannes yesterday which was a bedlam of road mending, traffic and a film festival – did not linger long, but up into the hills for dinner, all very restful and pleasant.

To Paul Anstee   *19 June, Saint Jean Cap Ferrat*

Today, lunch with Willie [W. Somerset Maugham], and Tuesday to see old [Edward Gordon] Craig. Also went to Menton and sought out Mimi de

Gielgud,* an extraordinary little old lady now living in a large ground floor flat in a derelict hotel – very sweet and absurd and unchanged.

I alternate between great enjoyment and usual divine discontent when on holiday. My various guilt complexes come and go spasmodically. There was a travelling circus here last night with all the local children screaming with joy at it. Very pretty in the open air. There is to be a fête on the 24th too – all the harbour being decked out with little flags and coloured lights.

To Paul Anstee   *21 June, Saint Jean Cap Ferrat*

We have marvellous weather still here and the visits to the aged locals went off agreeably enough. Old Craig very deaf indeed, but ate a good lunch and seemed pleased to see me, and Willie *most* affable. Sunday we go off towards Avignon and plan to eat at TWO three star restaurants en route if our digestions permit and we don't lose the way!

After George Pitcher returned to America, Paul Anstee joined JG in France and the two of them moved on to Italy, where JG was to talk to Franco Zeffirelli about their forthcoming Othello.

To Hugh Wheeler   *18 July, London*

The three weeks with George in France were heavenly, if sometimes fraught for me with certain emotional disappointments which I ought by now to have expected. But he was very sweet, though Ed has turned him into a perfect demon Michelin sightseer.

Then I met Paul, and on to Livorno where the goings on were quite unbelievable. How we longed for you to put it all into a book – or play – 14–18 people staying and visiting, a divine fat Auntie and her companion-housekeeper, who produced two meals a day – hot and at least four courses – horrid hard beds, empty rooms, little hot water, jagged rocks to bathe from, storms, mad trips in Franco's car, Joan Sutherland and an entourage of *six*, people sleeping two and three in all the rooms, a good deal of this and that, a mad trip to Spoleto to see the Robbins Ballet, and Franco started so late that we arrived just as it was over! Paul adored it all and was the pet of the party. I slept a lot and with so much Italian clamouring around me, found considerable periods of enforced silence rather relaxing. *Othello* and several operas being designed by various minions on the top floor, TV blaring in the sitting-room, one patient maid sweeping and making beds and washing (and losing) everyone's clothes from morning to night – the whole thing was fantastic and really great fun.

---

* Lewis Gielgud's first wife, JG's former sister-in-law.

Judith [Stott?] has left her husband and retired to her Mum in Oxfordshire –
rumours that she is in love with Albert Finney quite unconfirmed so far! Dick
Easton still living at Binkie's!! Brian [Bedford] staying next door with J.P.!

To Hugh Wheeler   *4 August, London*

Took Irene W[orth] to the Robbins Ballets – quite fun, most of the old stuff,
but very young, pretty and lively. Going to *Luther* next week, and Franco is
arriving with the designs and we shall drive to Stratford and cast the other
parts. Iris Murdoch wants me to talk to her about adapting *A Severed Head.* I
think it *might* make a play – but difficult. John P., Dick Clowes and Paul all
loathe the book, but Patrick [Woodcock] and Irene W. agree with me that it
is brilliant – have now given it to Binkie to read – shall be amused to hear his
reactions. I do think it is very much in the feeling of the moment, somehow,
and so *not* for the Establishment. I may go abroad again if I could get Franco
to come – feel desperately in need of a bit of a fling before settling down to
work and it is dull here.

Lovely art shows – Italian bronzes at the V and A, Daumier at the Tate,
Dufy at Wildenstein's. Don [Bachardy] and Chris [Isherwood] came to lunch.
Don did some drawings of me – fair – also of Paul, Pamela B[rown], Irene
and is now to do Margaret Leighton – he is to have a show at the Redfern in
the autumn. Irene may do *Oh Dad* [*Poor Dad, Momma's Hung You in the
Closet and I'm Feeling So Sad* by Arthur Kopit] (which was a terrific flop here
with Stella Adler) with Jerry Robbins directing. Might be a good idea – I've
not read or seen it, but John P. says it needs a brilliant comedienne – so who
knows?

To Hugh Wheeler   *28 September, Stratford-upon-Avon*

Ralph Richardson is leaving for N.Y. to make *Long Day's Journey* [*into Night*
by Eugene O'Neill] with Sidney Lumet, K. Hepburn and Jason [Robards]!
Wonder how he will get on with the latter. Delighted for R's sake, but why
didn't they have Freddie March who was supposed to be so wonderful in the
part?

Zeffirelli is extraordinary – maddeningly undisciplined and more unpunctual than Peter Brook and Binkie put together. Hours wasted every day
through starting late, and endless distractions – offers by cable and telephone
from Paris, Rome, Dallas, New York and Chicago, and he dallies with them
all and reads (and writes) endless letters, and pores over his damned press
cuttings and photos of the *Romeo and Juliet* in Venice with the Vic, which
was apparently a furore, and Elsa Maxwell, the Strasbergs and God knows
who from Italian café society had a ball and filled every newspaper for weeks
with glorious publicity for him, which he loves.

His work is quite brilliant, but he dallies and dickers, and everything's behindhand, scenery, dresses, as well as the play itself. All the cast, save Peggy and me, playing in two or three other plays in the repertory, with three matinées a week – consequently, actors are continually unavailable or have to stop rehearsing owing to having to act at night, and Peggy and I wander round Stratford in a dither of frustrated impatience. Ian Bannen, the Iago, plays also Hamlet, Orlando and Mercutio, is overtired, neurotic, a converted Catholic, tricky, a bad study, interfering, inefficient and impertinent, and makes rehearsals a misery when they could be really very stimulating. I've had one or two real rows with him already, and fear there may be more in the offing. If the production fails it will be largely his fault. The rest of the cast is weak but willing, and Peggy and Tutin both quite splendid. Franco is excellent for me, won't let me sing or declaim – but without a balancing Iago my big scenes are agonisingly one-sided, and the great duets fail completely at present. If the young man can be somehow forced into giving some sort of a concrete reading (and be made comparatively *audible*) he *may* yet weigh in with something of a performance – but I have the direst forebodings, alas.

Paul has opened his second shop in Cale St only a few yards from King's Road – the decorating now done from there and only antiques from the old shop. He seems to have opened excellently, with a big page in the *Sunday Telegraph* with a drawing of the new premises, showing how cleverly he has adapted the building, and I think the publicity should be splendid for him. He seems in very good form – is coming down here at the weekend.

Toby [Rowland] and Alan [Webb] came down last week – very sweet. Alan off to N.Y. to be in Tennessee's play [*Night of the Iguana*] with Maggie Leighton. They saw *Richard III*, *Romeo and Juliet* and *Much Ado* and said they had never seen such bad acting in their lives!!

Have you read *Rabbit Run* by John Updike, who appears to be an American. Very clever and really – the detail! Can such things be said so openly in print, and somehow manage not to be really pornographic? Apparently they can.

Have found a marvellous flat for George next year in a superb country house,* built by Calamity [*sic*] Brown and restored by Sir John Soane. Some rich people called Brunner, whom I know only slightly, (I.C.I.) have restored it with the aid of £35,000 contributed by the Govt. (or some Trust or other) when it was on the verge of being demolished. In the middle of a huge park, with lakes, gates, railings – a sort of Petit Trianon – only 20 minutes away from Oxford. He will be mad if he doesn't jump at it. They want to make four flats on the top floor (and give concerts and Son et Lumière à la Glyndebourne) and he is *just* the kind of tenant, apparently, that they would most like to encourage!

I live here in a suburban cosy cot like the set for *Hay Fever*. Franco also, which is something of a strain, but only for two more weeks. Bernie and he get on wonderfully, thank God, though his inconsideration and lack of order

---

* Wotton Underwood, whose South Pavilion J G would buy some years later.

are so often infuriating. Eleanor has taken over some of his correspondence and, as usual, Marthas us all remarkably.

To Leon Quartermaine   *30 September, Stratford-upon-Avon*

Don't talk to me about Iago – he is a neurotic, tiresome boy – like a budding George Hayes – shouts or mumbles and capers about in jackanapes fashion, impossible to help, and well nigh impossible to act with – no sense of timing or rhythm and madly in love with tricks and business. Peggy and Dorothy both wonderful, and the director clever and fascinating though, alas, no good on the SPEECH. I fear it will be uneven and ill-balanced, though less ignoble, I *hope*, than the four current productions, which are a disgrace. TV, films and the division of the two companies for the Aldwych venture have resulted in a more rabbity crowd even than usual, and [Peter] Hall is young and has none of the discipline and control of Tony Q[uayle] and Glen [Byam Shaw]. It's a great hazard for me.

As You Like It is the best thing here. The Redgrave girl* is very charming and talented, though dreadfully tall. She will have the same difficulties as Phyllis Neilson-Terry had – no leading man capable of topping her. No Shakespearean joke intended!

Othello *opened on 10 October.*

To Irene Worth   *4 November, Stratford-upon-Avon*

We have had a terrible time with *Othello* thanks to a ghastly number of mishaps on the first night, which lasted four hours. The impossibility of working with Ian Bannen, and Franco's irresponsible and irrepressible charm, mixed with his dreadful lack of discipline and punctuality, wasted important time in every department. He and his designer both left for America the next day, and we are trying hard to patch up some of the mistakes without him. Except for [Harold] Hobson and [Victor] Cookman, who gave me very good notices indeed, the entire press was disastrous, Zeffirelli attacked violently, and Dorothy and Peggy almost ignored. The settings are beautiful but cumbrous, the dresses ditto, and the pace is snail-like. Far too many blackouts, realistic business and pauses as if playing Chekhov, and no earthly good in Shakespeare. If Franco will let Peter Hall re-direct the play with a new Iago, which is the present idea, we might get better notices the second time, but it is rather a horrid responsibility.

Poor Hugh [Wheeler] has had a disaster with his second play [*Look, We've Come Through*], though all my friends say it was beautifully played and

---

* Vanessa Redgrave played Rosalind and Ian Bannen, Orlando.

directed, and the top press very encouraging, but not good enough Box Office notices, and it has closed after five nights – so disheartening for him. Glen [Byam Shaw] seems to have a success with *The Complaisant Lover*,* in spite of great shenanigans on the road with [Richard] Johnson and [Michael] Redgrave, and no doubt Mrs Selznick stirred the pot with her usual witch-like inanimation!

When will you be back I wonder, and have you found a flat? Paul is doing my dining room at Cowley Street against my return, and I have bought a most beautiful Harpignies at the Marlborough Galleries, two rather shameless extravagances after not a very good year – but one must cheer oneself up somehow!

Quite a lot [of people] have come round after *Othello* with tears in their eyes, but whether from boredom, horror or pity for my temerity in attempting, is rather difficult to judge.

To Robert Flemyng   *7 November, Stratford-upon-Avon*

We have had rather a disastrous time down here. I have finally decided not to bring *Othello* to London – sad, but also something of a relief. I cannot cope with rows and recriminations, and without both the production could not be made practical technically or patched for the better as far as the company is concerned. Ian Bannen is not right in the head. James Donald is a dishclout to him and yet he has had a lot of excellent notices, though he wrecks the play. Zeffirelli, a dear, mad, brilliant creature with not a grain of responsibility and absolutely no idea of time or discipline. So we play it seven times more and then put it to bed. *Cherry Orchard* on the other hand goes wonderfully and Michel [Saint-Denis] is a miracle of thoroughness and inspiration, so I hope it may make up for the other disappointment.

To Leon Quartermaine   *7 November, Stratford-upon-Avon*

Since you came, I have decided not to bring it in to London – too many difficulties involved. I *cannot* work with this Iago – and he had, in a lot of the notices, more success than I, which makes it most difficult to get rid of him without appearing to be jealous or malevolent.

Zeffirelli's Othello *was not a success, and it was followed by JG's own adaptation of* The Cherry Orchard, *directed by Michel Saint-Denis. When the production, in which JG played Gaev, transferred to the Aldwych Theatre in December, he began rehearsals for* The School for Scandal.

---

* Graham Greene's play had opened in New York.

1962

To Kitty Black   *30 January, London*

I am enjoying *The Cherry Orchard* very much, though many people don't
much like the production and some of the performances, but it is very relaxing
to be in. We tape it for BBC at the weekend, and I don't know when it is to
be shown. *The Dream* was fun too, and I thought it came out well, though
they are apt to change the cast about without rehearsal. But I wouldn't tackle
an opera in a foreign lingo. I asked [Benjamin] Britten if he wouldn't do a
Tempest, leaving me to speak my text as Prospero. He seemed rather intrigued
with the idea, but don't know if anything may ever come of it.

To Hugh Wheeler   *12 February, London*

George arrived for a blissful 48 hours, then his usual stomach collapse and 24
hours groaning and starving – my usual unfortunate effect on him! However
he recovered on Saturday and seems to be wild with joy at the flat, as I hoped
he would be. I shall probably go to see it at the weekend. Great meeting with
him and Paul at Covent Garden – I feared the worst, but no such thing.
Paul – 'I had no idea he was so gentle!!' George – 'I had no idea he was so
attractive. What does he like doing in bed??' So there we are. Rather a relief,
I must say, to my battered old carcase.

The [J. B.] Priestley *Severed Head* arrived and I have been agonising over
it – however Peggy and John P. and Binkie all say firmly No! No! No! so of
course I have given in and sent it back. I do think I'm too old to play the
part, and anyway am not so sure that it's very LONG rather than very good,
like that? I have a translation of *Le Dindon* [by Georges Feydeau] to read –
wonder if it might be fun to play a real farce again.

The School for Scandal *opened on 5 April at the Theatre Royal, Haymarket.
Most of the rest of the year was taken up with performances of* Ages of Man, *both
in the UK and abroad.*

To Hugh Wheeler   *27 May, London*

I hope you got the card G. and I sent from Italy. The ten days holiday was
really pretty successful except for G.'s bronchitis, which disabled him for two
of them, and a trip to Capri, after which we missed the boat back to Sorrento,
and almost froze on an open small boat. Black looks and crossness, as it was
my fault entirely for not listening to the Head Porter at the Hotel! However,
we were mad about Paestum, Herculaneum and Ravello (Pompeii less so) and
the two Breughels and the Bellini in the Capodimonte Museum at Naples

make that endless trail through acres of boring pictures worthwhile. The weather was pretty marvellous, and we stayed two nights in Positano with a friend of Franco's, Robert Ullman – enormously rich but sad (of course) à la Edward Molyneux – the most beautiful villa, food and servants. How sad that those people never radiate real warmth or fun. Terrible journey home via Frankfurt owing to BEA strike, with a horde of muslin-bedight Indians being sick into cardboard boxes, and back to icy cold and wintry weather here. Not a hint of summer yet, except for two fine days last month. We go to *Pelléas* at Glyndebourne today – no picnic – it is far too cold and wet – with Judith Stott and Paul. On the way back we are to call on Vivien and see her house, which P. has finished. She says it is a dream of beauty and I am longing to see it. He is also doing the set for the new Pinter play [*The Collection*] at the Aldwych, which is lovely for him so he is awash with success. Wimbledon Common claims him too often, I fear, though.

I went to the Consecration at Coventry Cathedral with Peggy A. and on to Stratford, where we saw a really *beautiful* production of *The Dream* by Peter Hall – I never saw a better – such a welcome improvement there after last year. Also a heavenly Chekhov film of the short story *The Lady with the Little Dog*, made by the Moscow Arts for the Centenary – enchanting, Boudin-like scene at Yalta, and Moscow in the snow, beautifully acted and directed. Buñuel's *Viridiana* is also fine in its rather sickening, wicked way.

Richard Easton takes over from John Neville in *S for S* tomorrow. It is a great success, despite the Press, I'm glad to say. I miss you always and long to see you. Noël is on the verge of opening but seems too busy to be seen in private, which I well understand.

To Hugh Wheeler   *26 June, London*

Nothing new comes in, except a musical of *The Relapse* by Paul Dehn and Jimmy Bernard which I *might* perhaps direct.* I think the lyrics are brilliant but the music a bit ambitious and lacking in melody.

Paul has done an enchanting small house for Lady Viv who has returned pretty far gone, I fear, with Jack Merivale in rather doleful attendance.† Fine Francis Bacon show – also Graham Sutherland. They say old Willie M. is rather round the bend – all those injections have gone below the waist and the brain seems to have suffered. He sold the pictures he had left to his daughter and she is now suing Sotheby's – and he *now* proposes publishing the autobiography (which was not to come out till 50 years after his death) which discloses that she isn't his daughter at all!!

---

* *Virtue in Danger* was directed at the Mermaid Theatre in 1963 by Wendy Toye.
† Vivien Leigh's relationship with Jack Merivale had begun in 1960 after her divorce from Laurence Olivier.

JG with his siblings and mother (left to right: Val, mother, Lewis, Eleanor, John).

JG at the wheel of a car (August 1927) 'I had her decarbonized and new exhaust valves and she is now "as new" once more.'

John Perry and Paul Anstee.

JG with Edward Gordon Craig –
probably in 1953.

JG and Hugh Wheeler – holidaying in
Jamaica, 1955.

Paul Anstee – after he and
JG met in 1953.

JG and Bernie Dodge, his American manservant.

Paul Anstee, JG, Truman Capote on holiday.

JG and George Pitcher.

George Pitcher in the 1950s.

Binkie Beaumont at Knot's Fosse.

Noël Coward and Cole Lesley – finger wagging in Jamaica.

JG, Paul Anstee, Somerset Maugham – Cap d'Antibes or Cap Ferrat, 1960.

Martin Hensler, the companion of JG's last forty years.

With Ralph Richardson in *The School for Scandal* – Theatre Royal Haymarket, 1962.

John Merivale, JG, Vivien Leigh, shortly after she saved him from drowning – St Vincent, June 1966.

JG and Harold Pinter – probably New York 1967.

With Lauren Bacall – possibly 1961.

JG and Irene Worth
at Wotton.

John Perry in the Great
Room at Wotton.

JG in the garden at Wotton.

To Jerome Kilty   *16 July, London*

I have only had time to read the revised script* once since it arrived, but it certainly seems to be remarkably strengthened and improved. I imagine from the urgency of your letter you were now hoping to do *Ides* this fall in New York. This will not be possible as far as I am concerned, and really I think it would be much better to work further on the script and plan it for the fall of next year. But of course if you feel you want to do it at once I would have to give it up, although reluctantly, as I do believe there are great possibilities in the project.

Hugh Beaumont tells me he has had a copy of the play, and he thinks it *extremely* interesting. Perhaps you would consider a project to do it here first with H. M. Tennent next summer. I believe we might be able to cast it more perfectly here than in America. Might we not collaborate on the direction?

To Paul Anstee   *3 August, London*

Took Hugh, George and Ed to the Aldwych – first night of *Penny for a Song* [by John Whiting]. Lovely set by Lixie [Alix] Stone, but oh! the boredom. Torture – as little humour as Osborne and little good acting either. Marius Goring as comedian – disaster. Last night to *Don Quixote* in which a little dancer from down under, Lucette Aldous, was simply ravishing. Our rehearsals [for the television version of Anouilh's *The Rehearsal*] drag on – enjoyable save for stinky (literally – his hair has not been washed since dung-spreading) Alan Badel, who is bad, obstinate and non-co-operative. He nearly got flung out today, but we all kept our tempers admirably and crisis finally averted.

To Paul Anstee   *30 August, Venice*

Glorious here all the time, but very proper, comparatively speaking, though I confess there is a small group of elderly American queens (one of whom offered to lend me his flat in N.Y. but he is so *awful* – like Humpty Dumpty and always pissed, that I don't think I shall take him up on it). Also a rather squat (German?) with a large gold earring – Peter Shaffer says his friend wears another in the other ear but I haven't seen that myself. But the Piazza closes down at midnight, lights are put out, shutters slammed. Most of the cottages have gone or been redesigned with open entrances and thick glass partitions, so evidently the purge has been thorough and considerable. Well, well, it helps to remove temptation, though a little boring for us senior girls.

Exquisite concert in San Giorgio the other night, and a wonderful dinner party at Countess Brandolini – a colossal flat on the Grand Canal – the most

---

* Jerome Kilty had made a stage adaptation of Thornton Wilder's novel *The Ides of March*.

beautiful decorations I've ever seen – wooden parquetry floors, a library, bathroom decorated by Lila de Nobili, divine food. Tonight to the Ciogna house which is also beautiful, but on a smaller scale, grey, pale green and silver, pictures mounted in panelled walls with wonderful grisailles (are they called) over doors and on ceilings. John P. refuses defiantly to be involved in any social engagements, but I must say I do enjoy the beautiful houses and ladies – wish there were a few dishy men to add to the gaiety. Peter Glenville queening it at the Ciogna house.

To Paul Anstee   *4 September, Ischia**

Do wish you were here – you would love it. [Beatrice] Bumble Dawson the only lady guest, taking mud baths for her rheumatics. Wonderful sandy beach – three sweet little Italian maids – delicious food – great beauty in all directions.

Endless talk of Terry [Rattigan]'s new TV play [*Heart to Heart*], new film script [either *The VIPs* or *The Yellow Rolls-Royce*] and screaming quarrels (by letter only, thank God) with the Midget.† Eight page letters of vilest Bosie recriminations read out for our entertainment – a titsy bit boring, if you ask me. £25,00 has been squandered on Brighton but not even a desk or a pen provided for the landlady! The drawing [room] carpet was dyed – at £9–10 a yard (you should have seen J.P.'s face when this was discussed) – to match the *pebbles*, if you please, in a second rate Victorian picture unsuitably hung in the place of honour etc. etc. etc.

We had a horrid journey getting here. Alitalia buggered up the reservations from Rome to Naples, and J.P. and Binkie spent ten minutes shrieking at the hostess, shaking her by the lapels, while I sat on the luggage looking like Peg O' My Heart.

To Leon Quartermaine   *13 September, London*

I have just come home after a wonderful five weeks of perfect weather, S. of France, Israel where I did four shows of *Ages of Man* to enormous audiences, only unhappily the halls were also enormous and I had to use microphones – then Venice and Ischia. Now into the corsets and try to pretend I am still young enough to get away with Joseph [Surface]. I am somewhat cheered to think how divinely you acted Scandal [in *Love for Love*] – and Mercutio too – with hardly a touch of make-up, too.

In October, J G took over his old part of Joseph Surface in The School for Scandal and rehearsed other cast changes preparatory to a tour of the United States.

---

* Terence Rattigan rented a house on Ischia from William and Susana Walton.
† Rattigan's lover, Michael Franklin.

To Hugh Wheeler   *September 1962, London*

I struggle with the somewhat recalcitrant chums at the Haymarket – the Richardsons really are rather tough nuts to crack, the one the best Brazil, the other an anthracite brick (Madame, needless to say). Dined with Irene W. tonight – she spoke warmly of the gay pub crawl you had with her at Stratford.

To Hugh Wheeler   *20 October, London*

Are you now being capped and shredded in the molar regions? How horrid – I believe Ed spent a thousand dollars on his teeth, when he first contemplated permanent matrimony, and the result I must admit is striking, though I hardly remember how he looked before! I hope George fully appreciates the agonies he must have endured on his behalf!

I opened at the Haymarket on Monday, after *Five Finger* like struggles with the cast. Talk about drawing teeth – Brian [Bedford] and [Roland] Culver were nothing to the arguments and obstinacies of Ralph [Richardson] and [Laurence] Naismith. However, all was finally sorted out and the critics came again on Thursday and did us proud all round. I saw *Curtmantle* [by Christopher Fry] which is a crashing bore, and not well done either. Gwen's bracelets started to jangle early in the first act, and I began winding up my watch, so no doubt the actors found it hard to make themselves heard.

I have a strange Hungarian [Martin Hensler] now, whom I picked up rather shamelessly at the Kokoschka exhibition, who is mysterious, intensely shy, and highly demonstrative – an agreeable once a week diversion.

To Hume Cronyn and Jessica Tandy   *6 November, London*

It is fun working again every night, and I do find it much easier to go on working in detail with the actors at every performance. It has improved very much, I think, even since Jessie saw it. We are packed to the roof, and I only pray the size of the American theatres will not destroy our confidence completely.

I was not absolutely mad about the *Man for All Seasons* [by Robert Bolt] myself, but I rather wanted to play it and direct it, so I was probably rather prejudiced. Scofield was wonderful in the second act, but I thought he lacked bonhomie and humour, and I should think Emlyn would be (between ourselves) too sly and prissy. It is a wonderful story and a fine character.

The beautiful attaché case you gave me is so elegant I hardly dare use it. I am sure I shall get it stolen in an airport by someone who thinks I must be a cabinet minister!

To Paul Anstee   *11 November, Philadelphia*

Very good flight, then a press reception at Idlewild and three hours coach ride
here, so we are all pretty exhausted. The theatre is huge, but quite pretty, and
the scenery looks very pretty in it. We rehearse with changes and orchestra
this afternoon and tonight a preview with an invited audience. [Alexander]
Cohen [the producer] is amiability itself and thinks he has found me a flat. I
have an enormous sitting room with purple, coral pink and striped upholstery
that would make your hair curl, in the hotel here. Gogie* comes on Saturday
and Hugh on Sunday – for a day or two. Brian [Bedford] was here to meet
us, very gay and living with Roddy McDowall in N.Y. with little hopes of his
play [*Lord Pengo* by S. N. Behrman] lasting long I fear. The Richardsons
have arrived safely and Mu [Meriel Forbes, Lady Richardson, playing Lady
Sneerwell] has to dress with Pinkie [Johnstone, playing Maria] and Gwen
[Ffrangcon-Davies, playing Mrs Candour] with Geraldine [McEwan, playing
Lady Teazle]. Only 8 dressing rooms in the theatre – the ones on the top floor
unfurnished and disused because American actors don't like to go upstairs!

To Irene Worth   *27 November, Philadelphia*

What a stunning Clytemnestra-Goneril you play.† I was so *very* much impressed – your whole manner and look – the sunken cheeks and prim,
repressed fury, and the development of the performance, as if you had a
terrible inner cancer eating you away – wonderful – all congratulations.

I loved it without reservation up to the end of the Dover Cliff scene – then
I thought the Albany [Peter Jeffrey] and Edmund [James Booth] could not
lift the fourth act and that Peter B. has failed strangely in the awakening
scene – the NOT looking at Cordelia does not come off at all, in my opinion,
and the lack of contact between them – gazing, gazing, can it really be her? –
destroys any chance of pathos. Also his sitting upright, both in the chair and
at the death, ruined those scenes for me, I'm afraid (going to prison scene
lovely, though – couldn't Kent be persuaded *not* to shout and spit at 'Vex not
his ghost. O let him pass' etc.) – and I thought the battle poor and slowly
drawn out. But then – one cannot hope in such a mighty work to achieve
more than ⅔ perfection – and that I think this production really does – and
you, Paul and Alan are all three magnificent in your different ways. I confess
to being disappointed in McCowen, whom I admire greatly, but not in
Shakespeare. For me, his Mercutio was far too lightweight – now in this he
seems stolid and a bit heavy-handed – don't think his costume is a great help,

---

* I believe this may be a nickname for George Pitcher, although Mr Pitcher himself has no recollection
of JG ever using it.
† Peter Brook's production of *King Lear* with Paul Scofield as Lear; Irene Worth as Goneril; Patience
Collier, Regan; Diana Rigg, Cordelia; Alan Webb, Gloucester; Tom Fleming, Kent; and Alec
McCowen as the Fool.

it is baggy and clumsy. All the rest of the clothes and scenery are wonderfully successful, I thought, and some of the grouping and pictorial effects – dinner-party, storm, Edgar [Brian Murray] and Gloucester at the opening of Part Two – really inspired. Lighting and effects splendid, all but that disastrous tea-trays battle bangs which he will surely cut or change before London – they just sound funny and are *most* damaging.

Do show this to Alan if you will, otherwise I will have to write it all again to him – oh, how wonderfully good he is – amusing, authentic, moving, tragic – and you too, all sides of the character, so difficult with those wicked ladies.

To Paul Anstee   *12 December, Philadelphia*

The play [*The School for Scandal*] goes splendidly now. I have brought Lady Mu practically into the front row at the opening and altered the beginning of the party scene so that they are all heard better. Everyone seems to enjoy it very much. Saw *The Manchurian Candidate* but couldn't sit through it – appallingly silly, I thought. I start today on my records of the Sonnets, and work a bit on my book. Otherwise, lots of sleep and rather boring meals and walks around the streets.

To Paul Anstee   *19 December, Detroit*

Appalling city this, as I knew. The theatre huge and vulgar (but lovely big dressing rooms) and very hard to get the play going in the first act, as will always be the case in America, I'm afraid. Too much of the women, and too much talk which confuses the audience, and of course I have so little to do that I'm not much help. A pity. The weekend was great fun – huge party on the St Regis roof, masses of people I knew.* I never stopped being kissed by gentlemen! Peter O'Toole, Jason Robards, Tennessee, Quintero etc. – and a few ladies too! Maggie [Leighton] was hysterical all the evening – late, no taxis, trouble with her dress, tired, sitting so long at the picture – 4 hours etc. etc., but she was, as usual, very sweet. Alec Guinness is not very good, rather like a benevolent old lady. It is a great pity I didn't play it – it would have been a marvellous part for me. Never mind. O'Toole is wonderful – and dishy too – and the whole picture is superb, except that it is really two films – one the story and the other the spectacle. But it is dignified, breathtakingly beautiful to look at, moving, exciting and everything. Only some common pseudo Rachmaninoff music which is vulgar and the only blot, I thought. All the other men wonderfully good, even Wolfit! Mad audience – wigs, rocks, stars, the lot. I did enjoy the evening.

---

* The opening of the film *Lawrence of Arabia*.

I have got the flat I wanted. It has nice things and quite a lot of character. Several beds which can be adjusted to taste, and two bathrooms. So now you can stay with *me*, and you *must*. Have just promised to do a poetry reading at Hunter College on Jan. 6th in place of T. S. Eliot who is very ill in England. They had a sell-out to hear him, and I thought it churlish to refuse under the circumstances. I shall do the Milton Nativity Poem, some sonnets and a kind of Christmas programme which they are composing for me to choose from.

I'm trying to persuade Martin [Hensler] to come to Toronto, but of course he havers and shrinks at accepting the ticket. I rang him up last week and talked to him for a minute or two. Glad J.P. seems to like him and thank you for being so sweet as to have him out with you. I do hope he doesn't bore you. Oh, I do wish some decent work would come his way.

To Paul Anstee   *25 December, Detroit*

What a good boy you are to find time to write me such good and amusing letters. They are welcome in this awful city, I can tell you. I sleep for ever, as there is no noise at all in this hotel – a great blessing. The play is dreadfully hard work and Ralph's performance becoming daily more indescribable – a mad, slow marionette jerking and distorting and completely false. God knows what he will be like in another four weeks. Well, well.

Did I tell you poor Ben Edwards' flat was burnt down in N.Y. Everything soaked and frozen that wasn't burnt. He opened a drawer and found a sheet of ice water with one shirt refrigerated at the bottom of it. Books, clothes, designs, everything gone – he has been there 15 years and only has 15,000 dollars insurance. Someone saw the fire on the telly, if you please, and rushed off to find him four hours later. He has been amazingly good about it, poor fellow.

1963

To Paul Anstee   *2 January, Detroit*

New Year's Eve I had supper with the Richardsons (the boy* has arrived too, poor brute) and Gwen, whom they suddenly decided to be nice to at last, and her performance immediately improved under Ralph's rather excessive flattery. He is the most extraordinary character. Still hates Geraldine [McEwan] and I'm sure that is why their scenes have been so forced. I shall

---

* Ralph and Meriel Richardson's son, Charles.

obviously have to have a few sharp words in N.Y. before the opening. I only trust Binkie will come to back me up. Bernie alternates between utter gloom and embarrassing high spirits. I think everyone else dreads him, which does not altogether surprise me. I had a terrible row with him after the party the Cohens gave for us last week, when he arrived after supper was *over* with a complete and *very* unattractive stranger, and made a mad prima donna entrance in front of the whole company – very shaming – but of course there were tears and apologies afterwards as he said he thought it was a *buffet* supper and nobody would notice.

Business disappointing – the theatre is much too big and they just don't understand us, either our accents or the dialogue. It is odd that in spite of all the efforts of the rich here – wonderful museum with huge, superb Van Gogh show, always packed – they can't really force culture out of big business, and it makes the work tedious and unfruitful.

I am on tenterhooks to hear if Martin will come next week. I did have a few words with him on the blower a few days ago, but he didn't seem to be very hopeful. Can't make out if J.P. really approves of him or not. Martin, of course, says John hated him on sight. He really is a terror for self-depreciation. Can't make out if it is pathological or something of a pose. He writes me adorable little notes in dreadfully fractured English with no news in them at all, especially as regards *work*, which makes me very anxious. Do you think he was educated to be idle rich and now despises it, but has no talent for anything?

To Paul Anstee   *9 January, Toronto*

We are all in despair after shouting and mugging our way through three weeks in that ghastly Detroit, where there was hardly a single reaction or laugh the whole way through. This theatre is enormous – Festival Hall – but the amplification is marvellous and every line got heard last night – bravos at the end and a terrific reception, but *now* we have to work again to try and balance things a bit, bring up Lady Mu and Gwen and get Ralph to play quickly and drop those dreadful affectations and tricks, which I have been trying for weeks to tactfully explain to him. I had a long talk to Mu just now, and she is really very sensible about it all, and will do all she can to help.

Of course I am very excited Martin is to come tomorrow. Johnnie has, I think, been a bit fascinated with him and doing what he can to help. If only he could help him to a job of work! He had, he told me, a terrible time getting him to accept ticket and hotel, but seems to have contrived it in the end, thank God. I have been chaste too long.

Spent a hectic weekend in N.Y. Took George to see the flat, which he was mad about, lunched with Brian and Jack and did the poetry Recital in the evening – huge success, especially a mad chorus from *Sweeney Agonistes* (of Eliot) which brought down the house, though I was simply terrified doing it off the cuff for the first time. Finished with 5 sonnets and the waking scene from *Lear* – lots of blubbing, of course.

G. is very excited because they have approached him about a Fellowship at Corpus Christi, Oxford, which is his dream, though Ed is very upset at the idea! I do hope the dear boy gets it. It would be wonderful for him, and nice for me too.

Had three letters from Craig (91), Ernest Thesiger (85 and blind) and a long one from Edith Sitwell. These Victorians – wonderful.

To Paul Anstee   *12 January, Toronto*

Very exciting week here – marvellous houses – and they are divine audiences and take every point. If only Gwen could get it, but she is sadly under proof I fear, and always will be. The bad notices did Ralph a lot of good, and in fact the whole performance is much better again with the encouragement of the good response.

Martin is here, very strange and well-bred, like Millamant. Tomorrow I take him to New York for 24 hours and Gogie (who is agog to meet him) is coming up to lunch with us. It will be fun to show him Rockefeller Center and Central Park. Oh, he is difficult to manage and to pry open that Slav oyster of a temperament, but his sweetness and diffidence are very touching.

What a notice for *The Physicists* [by Friedrich Dürrenmatt] and dear Irene. I must be madly out of date. I read it and only liked the first act – after that it seemed so involved and cold-blooded, and I didn't think her part was really so wonderful – but Peggy [Ashcroft] was mad to play it, so I expect it is. Ralph read *The Physicists* and agreed with me it was very clinical and aseptic, but I wonder if it will really be a success with the public. *The Visit* never was – horrible old Swiss Dürrenmatt.

Went to a very piss-elegant queer party the other night with Richard Easton. I did not stay long, but he was there till 6 a.m.! Martin was rather seedy with his vaccination and cried off. But he seems all right again now and dear Aaron [Frosch] fixed his New York permit quite easily for me – invaluable, he is.

To Paul Anstee   *16 January, Toronto*

Fun weekend in New York. Martin is suitably impressed. Pouring with rain on Sunday, but we lunched with Gogie at the Oak Room. Went back to shave at the hotel leaving Martin and George together for an hour – do not think any misbehaviour ensued, though it was a rash act on my part. They seemed to like each other very much, however. Dined at Cavanagh's with them and J. who took us on to an odd party at the flat of a polio queen over Carnegie Hall. Found Rouben, J. and a young Negro doing it together in the kitchen with a lot of writhing and reeling between the stove and frig(idaire), and watched a married couple doing it (between breaks of dressing, undressing and watching TV) in the flat opposite with the lights and no blinds down. Martin got very drunk and I walked him uncertainly home about 3 a.m. culminating in Slav suicidal protestations and a lot of you know what.

Monday night two odious queens whom I met at a party last week invited me to supper. Martin was tired and would not go. I arrived at 12 at a vilely over-decorated flat, they plied me with drinks for nearly an hour and then remarked 'I'm afraid dinner won't be ready for 45 minutes', on which they both rolled me on the floor and tried to have me – together!! Really, at my time of life. A very nasty collation of rock hen stuffed with wild rice was served at 2 a.m.! My face was purple, and it was so icy cold that I couldn't walk out for fear of not being able to find a cab. Did *not* tell Martin and don't you tell *anyone*. But quel adventure – they were pretentious and horrid, though one had a very remarkable property.

To Richard Sterne   *17 January, Toronto*

I do hope all will go well with your plans and ambitions (and that you will fall happily in love soon) and achieve your heart's desire in the career you want. You were very comforting in that awful Detroit. This city is very much nicer – fantastic business and most appreciative, responsive audiences. Also a lot of nice people to entertain and flatter us. And now New York is near.

To Paul Anstee   *January 1963, Philadelphia*

Had lunch with the Tiffany window man, Gene Moore, who is a *dear*, in spite of a rather unconvincing toupée. He is mad to do the Caesar play [*The Ides of March*], and seemed to love my ideas, but of course the script hasn't arrived yet so I haven't even seen the last post-Berlin version myself. Am longing to show it to Moore.

Ben Gurion cabled to the Pope – 'Cancel Easter, we've found the body.'

The School for Scandal *opened at the Majestic Theatre, New York, on 24 January.*

To Paul Anstee   *28 January, New York*

I never thanked you for the sweet roses I had on the first night. I was so touched at your thinking of it, and my eyes glistened with a little tear. My room was a bower of beauty, and presents and telegrams rolled madly in – and poor old Ralph only had one little sad bunch of pussy willow!

Howard Goorney [playing Moses] is very unhappy – they never mention him in the notices, and are shocked everywhere by Moses – extraordinary people. He said 'If I wasn't Jewish, this place would make me anti-semitic.'

To Paul Anstee   *2 February, New York*

Charming lunch yesterday chez Florence [Reed] – Lincoln Kirstein and a
man called Van Truex – about my own age – with whom I believe I scored a
big hit, as he took the trouble to ring up to say how much he had enjoyed
meeting me, so I asked him to lunch next week. A little wholesome flattery
does one so good at my age, and my sex life appears to be at a complete
standstill since Toronto, alas. Still no word from that wretched Martin – I
think I shall have to abandon the quest. I really can't hold these torches
endlessly without a little encouragement.

Will you go to see Peter O'Toole [in Brecht's *Baal*] – sounds an awful piece,
but he does a lot of romping in it and his performance sounds worthwhile. And
he is so very dishy. Do go and tell me details – what he *wears* etc.

To Paul Anstee   *8 February, New York*

Of course I will meet you. Am sending Bernie to a hotel so that you can have
the whole basement to yourself – there is no proper spare room – and you
will then have your own bathroom too. With Eleanor around, it would not
be tactful to put you in my bed! How lovely it will be to see you again.

Today Eleanor and I lunch with Lillian Gish who is mad to do Irene's part
in *The Physicists* in Oct. here with Peter Brook. No word if Irene likes Claudia
Pulcher [in *The Ides of March*] – everyone refuses the parts in the Caesar play.
[Geraldine] McEwan and [Dorothy] Tutin, Bryant, Dan Massey – all N.G.
So we must look for some blinding new talent from somewhere, I suppose.

I believe M. is sort of bowing out, with all his neuroses and humiliations –
perhaps, as he says, our world is not for him after all – makes me rather sad.
We shall see.

Saw Tutin and Paul Hardwick at the Rink yesterday – such a lovely warm
day, the first, and it was divine in Central Park – and took them to lunch at
the Four Seasons. They have a great success with [*The*] *Hollow Crown*,* but I
don't think they are doing very well as they have no NAMES and people
hardly know it's on. Bad luck for them.

To Paul Anstee   *15 February, New York*

Don't worry about Bernie. He will enjoy being on his own for a fortnight and
it will be much more convenient to have this flat to ourselves. He rather
touched me by saying the other day (with tears in eyes) 'Would you like me
to leave, and offer my job to Martin!! Perhaps he would make you happy, and
it would be the only way to persuade him to live with you to offer him work.'

---

* Anthology on the Kings and Queens of England devised by John Barton.

Not a good idea, but rather a sweet thought, don't you think? Not a word from her, strange Hungarian woman of mystery that she is.

Irene Selznick was burgled the other night at the Pierre – 300,000 dollars worth of bijoux, including the Tiffany diamond valued at 130,000!! Get her. Fancy leaving it in drawers in her bedroom instead of the hotel safe. Do you think she puts it all on Binkie after lights out? I imagine she is heavily insured and can hardly raise a sympathetic tear, can you?

To Paul Anstee   *22 February, New York*

I am wondering whether we should have a party on March 17th – Sunday – beginning about 2 p.m. and working up! Bobby Lewis gave one for me last Sunday at 9 and everybody went home at midnight (including Tony Perkins – I was promised Johnny Mathis too but he didn't turn up) because of work on Monday.

I have a new elderly admirer whom I met at Florence's – his name is Van Truex and he is about my own age – not handsome but *very* nice – gave him your address and telephone – I think you would like him. He goes to London next week. Works at Tiffany's (not the one who is doing the *Ides*) and moves in the café society circle, but charming and sympathique. Gave me a beautiful gold brazil nut to keep saccharine and cocaine in! Useless but enchanting.

Irene W. was very depressing about the *Ides* and I don't think she will do it. However, I will show her the rewrites when they are done. I think they should strengthen it very much, and we are to see a set model next week.

Have not seen Franco Z. but they are rehearsing [*The Lady of the Camellias* by Giles Cooper and Terrence McNally], and rumour is rife around the town. Coral Browne leaving in tears for England – had to pay her own fare back, as well as 300 dollars excess baggage! Apparently she found a different script to the one she read in London. I hear 'whore' is said every few minutes and 'piss' several times. Who's afraid of Susan Strasberg?* Almost everyone, it seems.

To Paul Anstee   *21 March, Boston*

My North Western boy fan (21, if you please) arrived last night to stay, but beyond a goodnight kiss he did not appear to welcome further investigations or intimate contacts, so I fear I am just the old father figure and likely to remain so. As he appeared for breakfast in some brand new brown manch, I must say I was somewhat disappointed. He thinks of nothing but his career and the theatre and evades all questions about his sex life – odd!

It's like a Xmas Carol here again this morning, pretty but a bore. Today we have a matinée. The dressing rooms are unspeakable – my taps tied up with string – nothing has been done to them since I played here in 1937!

---

* Susan Strasberg was playing the lead in *The Lady of the Camellias*.

To Isabel Wilder   *21 March, Boston*

So many thanks for your sweet letter. I was *so* sorry not to come with you to Tiffany's – Heaven knows what we might have bought each other! But the doctor gave me the most violent penicillin injection and pretty well knocked me out. I broke a shoehorn, smashed my glasses and lost *two* pairs of gloves – (one I could have left in a taxi – but *two*) so by the time I went to bed I looked at the calendar and there suddenly it was – The Ides of March. So heaven knows what we are to think of such peculiar and variegated omens. Love to Thornton – all fingers crossed – even my poisoned one which is almost well again, though it is the colour of brawn, and strange little envelopes of dried skin begin to detach themselves, with a nice healthy finger underneath, thank Heaven.

To Paul Anstee   *27 March, Boston*

A poorish weekend at Bobby Lewis', except that I was taken to 'The Ramblers', a section of Central Park (West) with paths, bridges, walks etc., which is the Rotten Row on Sunday afternoons. Never have you imagined – or seen – the *parade* of gentlemen – with or without canine adjuncts – such baskets, such chinos, gazing and giggling, circulating and camping. A ghastly evening at *Hot Spot*, which has nothing whatever to recommend it save Rouben's pretty décor. I slept through most of the first act, and wished I had not woken up for the second. It cannot possibly do. Notices horrendous in *Time* and *Newsweek* both for *Tovarich* [by David Shaw, Lee Pockriss and Ann Croswell] and *Camellias*, and Ruth Gordon's play [*My Mother, My Father and Me* by Lillian Hellman], Bobby Lewis says, is also a disaster. Quel saison!

Today I lunch – at *3.30 p.m.*, if you please, with the Richardsons. Then Ralph and I go to receive an award from the City of Boston – another of those plaques, I suppose!!

Bernie got beaten up by a white man and a Negro outside his hotel the night before last – bruises on his face, his glasses smashed and his room key stolen, but lost neither his money nor his wristwatch, fortunately. Bloody but unbowed. What dramas he always manages to involve himself in.

George has just missed his Corpus Fellowship by a whisker, apparently. He is rather disappointed, and so am I, but Ed is, of course, delighted. Now, perhaps, they will find a decent house in Princeton!

To Paul Anstee   *6 April, Washington*

The Kennedys came to our opening, and Jackie used my loo between the acts (I tactfully retired into Ralph's room) and left me a pencilled note of thanks which will look well in my scrapbook.

Bernie has had one of his most outrageous crises – rang me this morning and wished to leave as soon as we finish next Saturday. Perhaps I shall really let him go – I am so sick of his idleness and tantrums but dread the emotional scenes of parting and the worry of wondering whatever sort of job he can possibly get. It really would be a major decision in my rather circumscribed existence and I dread facing it, though it would be nice, I must say, to have a really good cook for a change, and not to have to listen so much.

I shall be glad to be done with this play. I am sick of the company and feel I have acted the part long enough.

To Paul Anstee   *12 April, Washington*

The performance has got very tired – the women worse than ever, and Ralph and [Laurence] Naismith [playing Sir Oliver Surface] bored and tetchy if they lose a single laugh – I shall be very glad to end it tomorrow night.

Just spoken to the Margrave, who promises I shall meet Nureyev before I leave. Jealous?

To Paul Anstee   *17 April, New York*

Rachel [Roberts] and Rex [Harrison] everywhere, accompanied by Lindsay Anderson – he seems to dislike me as much as I do him. But the Harrisons are always sweet and went on like mad about the Recital. [Alexander] Cohen gave a very good party for me at Sardi's East. Florence [Reed] came, flanked by a table full of queens, including the Margrave.

The School for Scandal *closed on 13 April and J G went off to Italy before starting rehearsals for* **The Ides of March.** *Martin Hensler accompanied him.*

To Paul Anstee   *9 May, Venice*

Wonderful here – weather perfect the last few days – we went to the Villa Maser – wonderful Veronese paintings all over the place – velvet slippers to wear so as not to spoil the polished marble floors – dispensed by a *very* dishy N. African servant (who, I suspected, was having a romance with the painter who was cleaning the mosaics!). Martin is absolutely charming, but goes off at intervals into extraordinary silences and disappearances and begs me to find alternative delights – not a bit necessary, as I vainly assure him!

To Jerome Kilty   *9 May, Venice*

Had a look at the play for the first time today. Hope you have had some good thoughts, and perhaps Wilder has sent his notes by now! I gather we have all the cast, with the possible exception of John Stride, who I believe is playing hard to get.

Returning to London, rehearsals began for **The Ides of March.**

To Richard Sterne   *22 June, London*

All thanks for your two letters. I am delighted to hear Ashland [Oregon Shakespeare Festival] is so much to your liking, and that you are to try a fall with Romeo. You will find the part a great challenge and often unsatisfactory, for Juliet has all the best *positions* in the text – the Banishment must not seem an anti-climax after her great cords scene – similarly the Mantua scene is hard to put over after the Potion – and the mourning. You only manage to beat her to it in the Tomb – and you will surely get a crick in the neck, while *she* queens it up on that damned balcony! *Don't* let the director convince you that the love scenes are *realistic*. The ball scene meeting is a SONNET, the Balcony the epitome of longing and romantic imagination and 'getting to know you'. The Wedding is the only scene when he really declares his most complete surrender to her (and she to him). The farewell is *not* a rough and tumble on the bed. It ought to be played on the same balcony as the other one – only they are worn out with the *past* night and the agony of parting – morning light, bleak despair = EPITHAL[AM]IUM – foreboding on both their parts which they try vainly to hide from each other. The evanescence of youth and passion – the hectic hopelessness of the moment they are both strangely aware of – then in the Mantua scene, *he grows up* in a single moment 'Then I defy you, stars!', he is suddenly a man and not a boy, no longer affected (Rosaline scene), not rash (encounter with Tybalt at the Ball and the Mercutio death). He has *no sense of humour* – he is a doomed young madman (but must not be too conscious of it himself!). In the tomb he is tired again suddenly – (the effort of control when he heard the news of her death, the long ride from Mantua to Venice, the blind rage as he kills Paris) and, marvellously, he shivers in the cold silence and dimness (just as SHE described it in the Potion scene) and he promises to stay there and look after her in that icy stillness. SIMPLE. (I only found this extraordinary truth in doing the death speech *by itself* out of context in the Recital.) It is a wonderful part. I know how to play it well now, but I could never convey it on the stage. Olivier *was* Romeo (though he couldn't speak it in those days) because he was absolutely the lover of all time in the way he *looked* at Juliet and leaned against the balcony, and flung himself on Tybalt, but he was VULGAR in the farewell because he insisted on lying on top of Juliet and giving a *physical* violence in the love scenes which Shakespeare could not have imagined (or risked) with his boy Juliet! The *words* must do it. But they must give you a beautiful SIMPLE costume, and every help with wig and make-up. The first entrance – from a distance – is very important for the first impression, and grace of manner and deportment must be blended to a feline sensuality and sudden violence at a few important moments. You need to relax with a Latin indolence, but always with an underlying athleticism and a power that is ready to strike – like a flame – in the moments of fury and expressed emotion. So full of feeling at one moment – and an emptiness at others for contrast –

the utter spontaneity which Latin people have when they are very attractive – and very young!

I am sure Iago must have been informative and good experience, despite the difficulties – it is a fascinating part and no one could play it without learning a lot from the experiments, and even from the mistakes!

The Ides is fascinating. I go to Oxford tomorrow – we open on Monday there, and then tour, probably for a month before coming to London. I am delighted with the cast, the rewrites and the general feeling of the play – but we shall learn much the moment we have an audience. I worry too much about the production as a whole and the other performances, and shall be glad to be forced to play my part – however inadequately – for several weeks, and finally to be forced to concentrate on my own performance. At present I barely indicate what I hope to do in time, and I stumble over the many words, trying to simplify them every day and find the right shape for scenes and speeches.

Good luck with your struggles – it may give you heart to know that my own are equally tortuous and unsatisfactory – one does not find anything easier, even with old and long experience! Take care, be happy.

To Isabel Wilder   *27 June, Oxford*

Well, it all looks quite promising, I believe. Excellent cast, beautiful simple décor in perfect taste – the first act very successful, only needs a bit of cutting and tightening here and there.

The Cleopatra party scene is a bit banal at present, and Marie Löhr (otherwise admirable as Aunt Julia) is very slow and ponderous – but she is an old lady and has to conquer her nerves and acquire sureness and confidence. The Cleopatra [Valerie Sarruf] excellent but inexperienced. We will work on that scene of course.

The men are all good and Irene [Worth] excellent, though inclined to be inaudible and too slow (Brecht and Ibsen influence) but she is better at every performance – looks wonderful and is strikingly intelligent and effective, of course. I think we have to curb her tendency to be too subtle and intellectual (she has Shakespeare's Cleopatra up her sleeve a bit, one feels!). But they are such a good co-operative enthusiastic company that I feel sure we can do great things in the four weeks tour. The theatre here is dreadful – big and echoing, and a huge spread auditorium with noisy, banging seats, and rather a common provincial audience. Brighton should be much easier to play in and to judge reactions.

Kilty has been very helpful and amenable, and gives in to my rather stringent criticisms and rearrangements. The lighting was not very good, but we get it better each performance – it is, of course, especially important for this kind of play. It comes out as a comedy – plenty of laughter and in the right places. But the Clodia party scene is moving and fascinating to listen to, as is the death of the Poet. I wonder if or when you will be able to see it. I shall long to hear your reactions.

The Ides of March *opened at the Theatre Royal, Haymarket, on 8 August.*

To Isabel Wilder   *18 August, London*

The press has smashed our hopes grievously. The company has behaved beautifully and many people have encouraged and consoled us with praise, but I fear we cannot hope to survive more than a few weeks. Irene and the rest are splendid. I should have loved you and Thornton to have seen it. I fear I could never have the courage to play it in New York, though I do think it would stand a much better chance there. It is the Americans who have seen it who are the most enthusiastic. Do give Thornton my love and tell him how sorry I am – and all regrets for us all.

Following the brief run of The Ides of March, *JG made a short visit to New York before setting out for Australia with* Ages of Man. *Whilst there he began preliminary planning and casting for his production of* Hamlet *with Richard Burton.*

To Paul Anstee   *25 October, New York*

Went to Martha Graham in the evening with Hugh who is in excellent form and dying for news of you and everyone. *Circe, Embattled Garden, Judith* – nice sexy selection. Not such a camp audience as in London, but a good many duos of gentlemen and loads of ladies. The Lunt-Fontanne Theatre is unbelievably hideous from in front – no wonder we hated it so in *Much Ado* – ice blue and gold – ugh!

To Meriel and Ralph Richardson   *25 October, New York*

New York is a sweltering Turkish bath and I had sixteen Ophelias before lunch yesterday – something of a marathon, even for Hotspur! It is very alarming having to make snap decisions on characters one has only seen for a few minutes, mostly murdering the text. One needs limitless patience and perspicacity.

To Paul Anstee   *5 November, Perth*

Hellish journey – nineteen hours flying and TV, press interviews and radio whenever we came down – Sydney, Adelaide – the day seemed to last forever and we missed a whole night somehow, arriving here more dead than alive.

Incredible place – spotless hotel, landlady with pince-nez – Dorothy Wilding portrait of H.M. on the stairs with the dress (in material) appliquéd on to it in relief, enormous oak furniture in the rooms, pitch dark, awful food! The town a cross between old Brighton, (pre-war) Singapore and Bombay – sort of Victorian Colonial with an occasional skyscraper, hideous war memorials, bowling greens and ladies in unsuitable white hats. The theatre manager's son (an ex boy actor) appeared in a swept-up hair-do with grey becomingly streaked through it, a green moiré dinner jacket, a sort of diamond in his bow tie, very fancy waistcoat with silver buttons, trouser pockets practically wedging his crotch, and winkle picker shoes. Quite sur-prising – Italian shoes are definitely in for the young man – also chinos – but not a packet or a hint of corduroy anywhere! Mad accents. The opening seemed to go very well and splendid write-ups despite hot competition from a jazz combo in the club next door to the theatre which almost drowned my best speeches and ruined my concentration. The people are really very sweet once you get over the strangeness of their awful voices.

To Paul Anstee   *10 November, Adelaide*

Endless stupid interviews with moronic ugly young men, uneatable deep fridge food, but otherwise things are not too bad. We played to £3,700 in only six performances, which is a good deal better than the English provinces, and people are very *polite* which is a nice change, and warm and agreeable too. The flowers are beautiful and trees in blossom everywhere – but most of the houses are hideously ugly, and most of the people too.

To Paul Anstee   *20 November, Brisbane*

Heard the Peter Sellers–[Anthony] Newley record about [Christine] Keeler and the Queen and Philip – *Fool Britannia* it is called. It is very funny. I bought a copy to send to George and Ed – just their cup for one of their Prissy Princeton Professor Parties, and wanted to send one to you too, but as it is banned in England I thought they would probably confiscate it at the Customs. I believe it is to be had in the Soho gramophone shops under the counter – I think it would amuse you considerably.

To Paul Anstee   *26 November, Sydney*

Had a mad weekend at a seaside bungalow. Visited various rich queens in the neighbourhood (Whale Beach). Rather exhausting altogether, but quite fun too. They all have wonderful views out of huge glass pseudo-modern houses, but no space round. Everyone seems to build on top of everyone else. Pretty hideous furnishings – bars the central feature of every sitting room. Most of them have good pictures – the locals are very expensive (I mean the artists' *pictures*) and everyone vies to have a good collection before they go to England and become top price best sellers like Sidney Nolan.

Most of the gentlemen in Sydney wear shorts with white stockings – only successful on the young and slim, of course. John [Perry] is thrifty as a bead bag and won't let me fritter money, so I dare say I shall return quite a wealthy old lady.

To Paul Anstee   *3 December, Sydney*

Eleanor writes that Bernie is in a Nursing Home in Fitzroy Square, poor fellow. [John] Janvrine diagnoses a hernia in the diaphragm. X-rays have been taken, but treatment for a fortnight, diets, no drinking or smoking, seem so far to have been ineffective. I do hope it isn't anything more serious. I am quite worried about him. If you had a minute to pop in or send him some mags and papers, I'm sure he would appreciate it very much.

Martin hasn't written for about ten days, wretched creature. Eleanor wrote he *hoped* to do some modelling at Simpsons. Perhaps that is occupying him, or can he be sitting on Miki Sekers' knee? I do hope not.

To Paul Anstee   *6 December, Sydney*

All thanks for your two letters today. Entirely agree with your criticisms of the book [*Stage Directions*] – it doesn't really add up to much, only a series of reprints and articles written without much raison d'être, but I tried to keep it fairly light and not lay down laws or put down too many local anecdotes. I'm sure it will annoy the avant-garde boys, if they ever bother to read it, but I am not prepared to enter the lists too forcibly in defence of my rather old-fashioned views about the theatre. I feel my pioneering days are done, yet I don't want to shut myself away from possible new developments. The last few years have been disappointing. Since the Recital, no one seems to have any good ideas for me, nor do I find them in myself. I wrote to [Albert] Finney and Scofield suggesting a *Caesar* revival with them (me as Brutus) for the Lane or Her Majesty's next summer, but neither has so far even bothered to reply! I'm sure they won't do it. Might try O'Toole, but it seems the *Hamlet** has been a great disappointment and he is off to make *Lord Jim* – he would be a good Mark Antony. Alan Webb *might* play Cassius, but it really needs *three* equal stars. [Christopher] Plummer, perhaps? Who knows? *Measure* is no good without an equal star Duke *and* Peter Brook. What about his mad Artaud season at LAMDA?† Way out, of course, elusive creature that he is.

So sweet of you to go and see Bernie. Do hope he will respond to the

---

* The opening production of the National Theatre at the Old Vic, directed by Laurence Olivier.
† London Academy of Music and Dramatic Art.

treatment and that they will really find out what the trouble is.

Martin RANG up the other morning. J.P. came into the room just as he got on, and was so outraged at the extravagance that I couldn't talk properly to Martin, who kept saying 'What is the matter? Do I disturb you? What time is it?' and other wasteful remarks, and refused to discuss his transport to Jamaica. 'Oh, I think I will not come, you do not want me' etc. etc. What a fellow! I suppose I shall get him there after a lot of the usual palaver.

To Paul Anstee   *12 December, Melbourne*

Melbourne is not half so much fun as Sydney. Sort of Cheltenham-Edinburgh atmosphere – nothing open after the show – rather square people so far. We have a mad Margaret Rutherford flat – three huge rooms (from which we shout madly at one another), bathroom and kitchen in a huge private hotel – stained glass windows in the hall and passages, vast creaking lift with a letter box in it – old ladies and gents tottering about. Fine view over the park. We had a fine press and wonderful reception on Monday and I played my best, but I suppose the publicity has been less good and everyone is Christmas shopping. All the decorations look very silly with the warm, damp weather and it is odd to be eating strawberries and raspberries in mid-December.

Weather poor since we arrived – humid and dull. We drove out to an animal sanctuary – great fun though squashy underfoot. Koala bears (divine), emus, masses of wonderful screeching birds with Hieronymus Bosch beaks and plumage, parrots, snakes etc. Saw two kangaroos fucking – it took *hours*, and they looked dreadfully bored. The lady chewed grass and looked furtively about, like me when I am bored at a party! – and the gent clasped her round the stomach with those two sad little forepaws and banged away remorselessly.

To Paul Anstee   *15 December, Melbourne*

What a *dear* you have been to Bernie. Of course I am dreadfully distressed about him – only pray that they find the trouble and that it is something twisted that they can put right and not what one always dreaded. Poor fellow, it is miserable for him, and with his gentle and lonely naiveté, he must feel dreadfully apprehensive and every kind of horrid possibility must be racing through him. I feel wretched at being so far away and unable to do anything, but we shall soon know, I suppose, what is the verdict, and Eleanor will cable or telephone as soon as the operation is over. We've been together fifteen years and I am deeply fond of him in spite of the drawbacks. He has been through so many crises with me one way and another, and he is like an animal when he is down. I know you understand how I feel about him.

To Noël Coward   *19 December, Melbourne*

Poor old Bernie is very ill in London – had a serious operation last week. I don't think he knows how serious it is and I hope he won't. My dear sister is, as usual, coping valiantly but of course it has made me terribly sad after 15 years of such close companionship and I feel very badly being so far away. Food and clothes and rooms are so horribly personal and everything I touch and remember seems to be a painful reminder. Do be very sweet and send him a Merry Christmas card or a tiny note to Cowley St and Eleanor will take it to him in the Nursing Home. I know he would be thrilled to hear from you, and it's all I can do to hope he will feel sustained by thoughts from my friends – he has so few of his own. I wanted to come back to London instead of going to Jamaica, but Eleanor says it would only alarm him and perhaps make him realise the worst, so with a heavy heart I think I will not change my plans.

To Paul Anstee   *21 December, Melbourne*

No need to tell you this has been a most unhappy week. Memories crowd in at the most unexpected moments, and though I find I can go for several hours perfectly all right, I suddenly find myself overcome by some overwhelming sadness and don't know how to fight it down. If only they had let him die under the operation when they found it was fatal. What is the good of dragging on for a short while with all the work and worry for everyone concerned and nothing for him to look forward to, and all the pretence to keep up that he is going to get better. Of course everything in Cowley St is so bound up with him that I dread imagining going back there – rooms, clothes, food, all my possessions – but I suppose I shall get used to the idea after a few weeks. But what I feel in a way the *worst* about is leaving everything to Eleanor – and you, who have no real reason for being bothered with it all. Of course I should dread and loathe being in London to watch it all, but it is really shaming to feel one *always* escapes the really serious crises of life and leaves someone else to take over while one idles in comparative ease, imagining all the weary, miserable time that everyone else is having to bear, which is difficult for me too, because I can't *do* anything.

I was away when my Father died, and my eldest brother died in Paris. There always seems to be an escape, and so many people are fond of me that I know they think I am too sensitive to stand up to a crisis and must be spared all possible experience. '53 was the only time I've ever had to face something really serious on my own, and even then, the way you all rallied round me was a marvel to me.

Of course I told Eleanor I would scrap the Jamaica holiday and come home instead with J.P. but she begged me not to. You will tell me perhaps more truly whether you think it would give Bernie some happiness and what sort of condition he is in. I've no idea how long it is likely to drag on, but perhaps it is kinder not to stir him up emotionally by seeing me again. It would be difficult for me to disguise my feelings but I am not a bad actor and I do feel so desolate at the thought of never seeing him again.

To Paul Anstee   *24 December, Melbourne*

John says José Ferrer is awful in *The Girl Who Came to Supper** and why don't I play it in London. Of course it was a good part in the play, and Larry and Ralph (in this country) had successes in it, but Tessie O'Shea (who has nothing to do with the plot) has had all the success in New York, and I fancy the plot is the dullest part.

To Paul Anstee   *25 December, Melbourne*

If Ophelia had groped the men and thrown her skirts over her head (showing her codpiece, of course – or was she coccinelle), Shakespeare's audience would have shrieked with laughter. They thought that kind of lunacy a fair scream right up to Hogarth and Dickens, so obviously he wrote the silly charming scene he did, and it drives me mad myself when they try and stage it for sensationalism. Such an easy solution.

Saw *Charade* yesterday and regret to have to admit that Cary Grant really *does* look 59 at last.

To Irene Worth   *25 December, Melbourne*

I suppose you are now rehearsing *Lear* again, and without Madam Patience [Collier],† I trust, tiresome old maddy that she is.

Eileen Herlie is to play Gertrude for me – a relief after all the stupid ideas put forward by the management – Ingrid Bergman, Greer Garson and Lilli Palmer if you please!! I have also Hume Cronyn (Polonius), George Rose (Gravedigger), George Voskovec (Player King), David [Dillon] Evans (Osric). It remains to be seen what Burton will turn up with – besides his Serpent!

To Paul Anstee   *28 December, Melbourne*

Very glad to hear Bernie seems more cheerful – I simply can't bear to think of all the pretended gaiety that must be demanded of you and Eleanor and the imagined improvement that I suppose he will feel for a little while. Of course, I have no idea of the course of the malady and whether there is a

---

* A musical adaptation by Noël Coward of Rattigan's *The Sleeping Prince.* José Ferrer played the Grand Duke and Tessie O'Shea, Ada Cockle.
† Pauline Jameson took over the part of Regan.

chance he may have a real period of apparent hopefulness and be allowed to go out again. I have myself such a dread of being shut up and not to be able to see people and places that I love – but I shall hear from you how everything goes and how Eleanor bears up under all the strain.

We had a nice Christmas with Googie [Withers] and her very sweet children, swimming in the pool etc. and a day at the races, which was very grand indeed and much more comfortable than Ascot, only the women (dressed to kill) all have to eat and sit in a separate stand! Very Old World. John and I both won a few pounds. Saw *Casse Noisette* dress rehearsal yesterday and a party at night given by Peggy Van Praagh and Roy Powell. The snow fell in the ballet in lumps of clotted rice, drowning and blinding all the children, some very funny décor out of Williamson's stores, and wigs not to be believed. You would have loved it. A pretty girl called Kathleen Gorham was very accomplished and a rather dreadful boy called Garth Welch who looked a cross between Lord Harewood and Peter Glenville! Stanley Lloyd takes us to a queer party tonight, but I think I shall be too tired to enjoy it much. Happy Birthday, happy New Year, happier than this last one for us all, let's hope. Take care. I do miss you.

To Lillian Gish   *31 December, Wellington, New Zealand*

We rehearse *Hamlet* in Toronto for a month, not my favourite city, but perhaps it is a good omen? I've found a girl called Lisa [Linda] Marsh for Ophelia whom I think very hopeful, though I don't expect she can live up to a certain beautiful rendering I seem to remember.

1964

To Paul Anstee   *1 January, Wellington, New Zealand*

Happy New Year, dearest Pauly. Letter from you arrived yesterday – very welcome, with your cheerful news of Bernie. Do hope his improvement may continue, at least for a while. I'm so glad to hear he is behaving so well, though I've no doubt his grandeur must amuse (and I hope not dismay) the people who have him to look after.

The Strindberg translation is in hand, but I fear the man who has to do it is not a first class writer, and I fear another Kilty fiasco. We shall see when I read it. After all, I am tied up – like Michael Redgrave – till April which is plenty of time to formulate some ideas and, I hope, receive some offers and suggestions.

To Richard Sterne   *4 January, New Zealand*

I'm very glad to hear you are all set for *Hamlet*. I was a bit afraid they might have double-crossed you, as they seem to have delayed so long in getting the contracts, and the Toronto rehearsals have obviously complicated matters. I have been 'down under' all this time and only get the picture by odd cables and the occasional telephone call.

Last two performances here today, thank God. There is a charming night-club next door to the theatre with a steel guitar band which plays non-stop throughout the whole two hours of my recital and nearly drives me up the wall. Don't try it ever – though it is a great exercise for the concentration! Not a tear can I squeeze out of myself (except of baffled rage) even in *Lear* and *Richard*. Such a pity after coming all these thousands of miles, and a nice theatre and splendid audiences.

After his Antipodean tour, J G took a holiday in Jamaica before starting rehearsals for Hamlet.

To Noël Coward   *17 January, Blue Harbour, Jamaica*

We had such a wonderful afternoon today at Firefly. The pool is stunning and the view fantastic. What a lovely place you have made up there. Everyone is so kind and sweet to us, and we miss you more than we can say. It is wonderful to be here again, though I am always a bit nostalgic over days gone by. Work is, I'm afraid, the only panacea as ever, but I know the rest and beauty will be good for me.

Had a long sweet letter from Bernie – dictated – saying how touched he was to receive your letter – it was so sweet of you to bother. I fear it will not be long but all my friends are being wonderfully kind, visiting and encouraging him and he thinks, thank God, that he is getting better and talks of plans to go for a holiday to recuperate, which rather breaks my heart. John Janvrine promises he will not suffer but go gradually into a coma and then slip away. I find it very hard to accept, but we all of us have these things to face, I suppose, with the wicked finger pointing onwards.

Had a good time at the Broadway, but I must agree that Tessie O'Shea does steal the show – how *lightly* and skilfully she handles herself and her material – and I *did* find José F[errer] a bit reminiscent of Arnold Weissberger, although he puts over his numbers surprisingly well with, obviously, a good many hints from a master hand! How I wish you had played the part yourself. The girl* is charming, but no G[ertrude] Lawrence! As John P. is so fond of saying, 'We have seen some Majesty, and should know.' I thought Irene

---

* Florence Henderson.

B[rowne] very elegant and effective, but was saddened to see her so thin and aged – but it is wonderful for her to be in a success and have such effective scenes and clothes – her last get-up a masterpiece – and the house was packed and enthusiastic.

To Paul Anstee   *19 January, Jamaica*

The weather is very changeable here – some appalling days of storm and rain – but in between it is as beautiful as ever. Tommy Steele and his wife are coming over this morning and we are all going up to Firefly for a picnic lunch and to spend the afternoon. Martin roams about and of course adores getting browner than ever – chummed up at once with Tommy Steele's wife!

Peter wrote me a long letter from Bernie – so touching and sweet – it upset me, of course, but he does really seem to imagine he is getting better. Thank God for that, though it is heartbreaking to think he plans that holiday that can never be.

Clinton Wilder, Dick Barr and Albee, who are doing [*Who's Afraid of*] *Virginia Woolf?* [by Edward Albee] in London, have asked me to play a wonderful part in a play by Ugo Betti, who wrote *The Queen and the Rebels* and *Summertime*, called *Corruption in the Palace of Justice* – a grim but powerful piece. The part is a guilty judge – the others old men and one young girl. They did it with success in an off-Broadway production last year, and now propose doing it in London with Donald Albery! Don't know how the boys will react to this – of course I should like them to be in on it, for their own offerings seem very low to me. I think it is a marvellously new kind of part for me and a really fine dramatic play, with some kind of spiritual implications that are not too dogmatic or churchy. It is exciting, moving and tragic, so I do hope it may materialise.

To Paul Anstee   *24 January, Jamaica*

The afternoons up at Firefly are really memorable with the new pool – fresh water and the fantastic view. Otherwise it is all a bit the same. Still, the rest and sleep have done me good and we have worked out the whole production which I really believe should be very exciting – a whole lot of new effects and ideas I have never used before, but still classical and basically simple. I'm rather longing to get down to the work with the actors now.

To Paul Anstee   *4 February, Toronto*

Rehearsals have begun unbelievably well – the first two acts already placed in less than a week, and we have the rostrums and steps and most of the sound effects all the time. Hope to get on the stage on Sunday and Monday. Extremely satisfied with the cast – everyone seems excited and obedient. It seems the booking is fantastic and we shall be sold out for the whole engagement. Richard [Burton] looks pretty gross and red, but he is so beguiling and gifted that one succumbs the moment he begins to act, and he is utterly amenable to every suggestion and extremely skilled in adapting any idea one gives him. I really think he will be wonderfully moving and effective.

Saw *Dr Strangelove* which I thought over-rated – bitter and only occasionally funny. [Peter] Sellers is very unlovable for all his brilliance and I thought the whole thing in rather odious taste.

Ghastly crowds of morons besiege the hotel where Burton and Taylor are staying – every drink and conversation they have is paragraphed and reported. It really must be hell for them, and now some Ohio congressman has demanded that his American visa be rescinded for moral turpitude, comparing him, if you please, to [Christine] Keeler and [Mandy] Rice-Davies! Quel vie de dog!

To Harry McHugh   *6 February, Toronto*

So many thanks for your letter. I fear Bernie is far more seriously ill than he knows, and I am very sad indeed to be so far away from him and to have to leave poor Mrs Ducker to bear the burden of his long illness – but it seems he has become a patient and model invalid – and Mr Anstee, Miss Ffrangcon-Davies and Miss [Nora] Nicholson have all been untiring in their kindness and thoughtful helpfulness. But it is very sad to think that perhaps I shall never see him at Cowley Street again. You of all people know how close he and I have been over the years, and what changes and crises we have been through together. And of course he has now no family or intimate friends except mine who are fond of him. Well, well, there it is. These sadnesses accumulate inevitably as one grows older.

Bernie Dodge died shortly afterwards.

To Paul Anstee   *13 February, Toronto*

I know this week must have been sad for you, and dreadful for both you and Eleanor. I feel ashamed to have been able to be absorbed at work and only occasionally overwhelmed with the thought of what you must have had to see and experience over all these weeks. I had a most remarkable and touching letter from Peter K. telling me of Bernie's 'farewell' to you all at the Nursing Home – extraordinarily vivid and well described, and though it upset me terribly when I read it, I was greatly impressed by the simplicity and friendly loyalty implicit in it. I will keep it to show you one of these days, for I am sure it would amaze you. Somehow I felt glad to get the news from *him* first – a kind of first-hand commission from Bernie himself and of course I knew from your and Eleanor's silences that it must be pretty near the end.

I telephoned twice to London last week (once at 5 a.m.) in the hope of getting a word to him before the morning injection, but each time it was too late, and now, of course, I feel so sad that I didn't call a week or so earlier when he might perhaps have been able to hear and talk to me for the last time. Eleanor seemed marvellously calm when I spoke to her yesterday but I feel sure she is concealing a terrible weariness and grief which will no doubt break out at last, in spite of her wonderful control, as soon as the funeral is over. She hinted that she had had a bad time with the American authorities over the arrangements for the burial and the distribution of his possessions. It does seem very hard that she should have been put to that extra strain and distress, but I suppose it is a question of government red tape. Well, I am deeply glad that it is all over now. I only hope to God he did not miss me too badly at the end, and above all that he did not feel I had failed him in his hour of need. How unimportant everything else seems when the basic facts of life and death are really before one's eyes, and I can't help wondering whether I shouldn't have disregarded all your advice and come back to give my best acting performance by his bed for a day or two instead of going to Jamaica. No more of that. I suppose it is the natural reaction and nothing can change it now – alas.

An extraordinary rumour that Peter O'Toole and *Nureyev* are shacking up in Hong Kong or somewhere during *Lord Jim*! This is *too* much!

Martin is rapidly becoming a cordon bleu. The bell rings for supper. I have had too many scotches – so no more.

Friday morning
Martin says I was really drunk when I came in from writing this last night.

To Emlyn Williams   *23 February, Toronto*

Richard is at his most agreeable – full of charm and quick to take criticism and advice – but he does put away the drink, and looks terribly coarse and heavy – gets muddled and fluffy and then loses all his nimbleness and attack. But he has given one or two really beautiful rehearsals, and I have a wonderfully good and enthusiastic company, so I live in hope.

Hamlet *opened at the O'Keefe Centre, Toronto, on 26 February.*

To Paul Anstee   *28 February, Toronto*

I hear Alfred Drake [Claudius] may throw up his part (no bad thing either!) but it would mean rehearsing someone else (some talk of Harry Andrews).

Cohen hates the Ophelia – Richard and I stand up for her and feel she only lacks experience and is baffled by the vast theatre, as many of them are, of course. So there are many problems besides getting the lighting right and gradually rehearsing and tightening all next week. Then I have to go to New York for a week as Edith Evans arrives and we must rehearse our Shakespeare programme [*Homage to Shakespeare*] for a week for Lincoln Center and Princeton, Maggie Leighton also appearing. Have worked out quite a good selection, I think, but we have to plan links and more or less learn it all – quite a business.

Am staying away from *Hamlet* till Monday night to get a fresh eye on it before rehearsing again. They are all tired and need to gain confidence and play it in. The set is *wonderful* – Gordon Craig would own it. The dresses are a problem and don't really work properly yet – most tricky to get them to seem casual yet to help the effect of character properly. Richard dreadfully uneven, but brilliant enough in the best bits to be well worth working on, and so patient and agreeable. He looks suddenly years younger and his costume (though not yet quite right) makes him quite boyish and attractive – the company adore him. Hume Cronyn [Polonius] is brilliant – the rest very adequate – but Drake and [Eileen] Herlie [Gertrude] at present seem like an ex-croupier from Monte Carlo who has eloped with a fat landlady who keeps a discreet brothel on the Côte d'Azur. A really nice and hardworking team. Not one cross word all through rehearsals. Jean Rosenthal has lit it brilliantly too, but did not have enough time, of course. But the theatre is hell – holds 3,200 people, and at least 100 seats where you can neither see nor hear properly, which of course makes them restless and cough. We play a very full version – only one interval – and it lasts exactly three hours and two minutes, which I think is excellent.

J.P. wrote me such a stupid idea of a season – (they are obsessed with this one) – *The Apple Cart*. Oh God! Even Noël, who was brilliant in it, couldn't interest me in the play in the slightest degree – and *Twelfth Night*. No, no. I suggested *Faustus* and *The Rehearsal* of Buckingham – the first perhaps directed by Joan Littlewood. I have always thought this a possible double bill. But really, I am in no hurry. I saw a private showing of *Becket* this week and *loved* it, though Martin thought it awful! Quite marvellous colour and spectacle and I infinitely preferred it to either of the stage productions. Richard and O'Toole both extremely good, I thought. I think my little scenes do come out rather well, though I wish I didn't squint so much under the lights. D. Wolfit hams it up and is pretty bad, I think – all his most typically common faults come out – but apart from him, I thought it beautifully acted, and quite a credit to the British studio. Martin is very good and sweet and really a marvellous cook! Bernie would have found this hard to bear! Dear Paul, I never thanked you for writing about the funeral and everything. You know how touched and grateful I was for all you did.

Trying to persuade M. to come and live at Cowley St. I think he longs to come, but is frightened Eleanor will resent him. Well, bridges to be crossed in due course!

To Paul Anstee　　　　　　　　　　　　　　　*10 March, New York*

Recital here on Sunday and at Princeton March 22nd, so all is bustle and confusion. Edith in fine fettle, Maggie madder than ever – glasses askew, dropping everything, laryngitis etc. but her usual professional self whenever the work begins.

I have offered to play *Claudius* if they can get rid of Alfred Drake – mad idea but I am rather excited at the possibility. So is Richard, but it all has to be settled in the next 24 hours. J.P. and Binkie *not* pleased as they heard the news this morning. But I do believe it might be wonderfully helpful to the play and quite fun to do. Stanley [Hall] will have to make me a gorgeous, modern wig and perhaps I can take to it for private life.

To Paul Anstee　　　　　　　　　　　　　　　*17 March, Toronto*

Everything still in the melting pot here. More mad auditions for Ophelia in New York – Sarah Miles etc. – but I have no faith in any of them. Linda Marsh has improved tremendously – everybody has, in fact. Drake is better in the second half and I may be able to help him in the first scenes. If he gets a terrible press in Boston he may ask to be released, but I am not all that keen to play the King, though I have some sly ideas that I believe might be very effective in a new way. The part is always acted as a sort of ogre, but I think I could be Borgiaesque and charming!

The Recital went very well, great ovation for the *Richard II* Prison Scene and Edith for the *Merry Wives* and Queen Katharine. Maggie is a bit under par – but huge and rapturous audience. We shall change a few things before the other two Recitals if the girls don't become too hysterical. M. is subject to hysterical fits of coughing and general malaise, and Edith is terribly timid and nervous, and has to be told everything a dozen times. However, they both looked stunning and I think it was very good to have them both instead of doing it alone.

We went to *The Deputy* [by Rolf Hochhuth] – Emlyn [Williams] *awful* – beautiful décor by Rouben. The play impressive and moving – Jeremy [Brett] *very* good, and one or two others, but it is a bit cheap as a whole – an enormous success. Peter Brook has offered me [Cyril] Cusack's part in *The Physicists* with Alan Webb and Irene W. for the autumn tour, but I've just read the play again and really, I can't abide it.

Can't bear *Timon [of Athens]*. An indifferent version of *Lear*. I've seen it twice and it just doesn't play.

To Paul Anstee   *27 March, Boston*

Crises now more or less over – rave notices here and everybody staying on in the cast, thank God. Threats to Burton's life (!) so police and fans make it impossible to get in or out of the theatre, front or back – I have to stand or have a chair in the aisle! Applause (for me!) when I returned to my seat after the interval last night – well, well! Burton improving by leaps and bounds – the others too.

Could you get the sofa and armchair in the drawing room at Cowley Street reupholstered before I get back? I always hated that stamped white. Will leave you to choose colour and material – all one colour, I think, no pattern – velvet, silk?? Maroon, green, grey? I leave it to you. But I would like that room to look *different* when I return. The mahogany chair seats want doing too – cleaned or re-covered or something. If you choose the materials and put it in hand *at once*, could it all be finished by the time I return?

Hamlet has paid off before opening in N.Y. according to *Variety,* a profit of 140,000 dollars on the tour covering a 133,000-dollar production. Not bad eh! Longing to see you – will have tickets for you to take Florence and will try and get seats for [*Hello*] *Dolly* [by Michael Stewart and Jerry Herman] and [Barbra] Streisand's musical [*Funny Girl* by Isobel Lennart, Bob Merrill and Jule Styne]. I loved *Dylan* [by Sidney Michaels] – Alec [Guinness] and Kate Reid are both wonderful, though the play is a bit diffuse and weak.

Hamlet *opened at the Lunt-Fontanne Theatre, New York, on 9 April 1964; JG returned to London.*

To Lillian Gish   *11 May, London*

I am just off for a month's Recitals – Scandinavia, Helsinki, Warsaw and a fortnight in Moscow and Leningrad! Martin goes with me but a woman from the British Council will look after me in Russia. Then at the end of July I go to Los Angeles for a few weeks to do *The Loved One* with Tony Richardson – a short but, I think, effective part. Isherwood is writing the dialogue which should be distinguished. Larry's Othello is a sensation here, also Maggie Smith as Desdemona – unfortunately a wretchedly dull Iago [Frank Finlay] which is a major blot on an otherwise fine production, the others flat and poor in consequence. But the two are superb. Peggy lovely as Arkadina in a good but uneven *Seagull.* Peter Finch rather disappointing, Vanessa Redgrave splendid as Nina especially in the last act. No autumn plans as yet. But Ralph Richardson returns soon and I hope to do a season with him, perhaps *Volpone* [by Ben Jonson] and *Ivanov.*

To Paul Anstee   *May 1964, Hotel Kamp, Helsinki – Fancy!*

Helsinki is rather nice, Warsaw rather grim. Copenhagen quite the same. The Recital seems to go as well as ever everywhere, thank goodness. Tomorrow early we go to Stockholm and play at the Drottningholm theatre, which should be delightful, then off to Moscow on Saturday, and Martin goes home. Only just obtained my Russian visa – what a ridiculous fuss they do make. Shan't be sorry to get back to England.

To Irene Worth   *21 May, Helsinki*

So sweet of you to wire about Diana [Wynyard].* It does seem terribly sad and I know Peggy will be heartbroken. Hope you are enjoying N.Y. though I went to the opening of the Ballet at your theatre just before I left and feared it would be unmanageably big for your two productions, though of course I couldn't judge the acoustics. The lines of sight not very good either.

Ralph's *Dream*† got a terrible panning in Paris, it seems, and he wasn't even mentioned by name in the *Times* notice, which will, I fear, upset him terribly. I want to plan a three play season with him in the autumn.

To Paul Anstee   *28 May – I think – have lost sense of days! Moscow*

Very hectic here but it has been an extraordinary success – pin-drop audiences, slow claps, and flowers and endless curtain calls. Very gratifying, though the interviews, speeches and impromptu recitations at clubs and dinners embarrass and exhaust one somewhat. Tonight to the Bolshoi – *Don Quixote* – and tomorrow to Leningrad. The interpreting is terribly difficult – if one looks at the person who is speaking to one, one misses the translation and if you watch the interpreter it seems so rude to the other person. Don't think I have dropped any bricks so far.

To Paul Anstee   *June 1964, Leningrad*

Most beautiful city – fantastic treasures at the Hermitage. Matinée at the Kirov, the Mariinsky theatre lovely,‡ the river and canals, green 18th century palaces etc. – most elegant and romantic, rather like Paris with a dash of Venice. Went into a church this morning with mass baptisms going on one end, babies carried around squealing, their prams holding candles – and

---

* She died suddenly aged fifty-eight on 13 May of kidney failure after a short illness.
† Ralph Richardson was on a British Council tour with *A Midsummer Night's Dream* and *The Merchant of Venice*.
‡ In 1935 the Mariinsky was renamed the Kirov; in 1991 it would again become the Mariinsky.

funerals the other end, a lot of singing and lamenting round an open coffin. All very striking and picturesque.

To Laurence Olivier   *29 June, London*

Bravo for Brazen.* I loved your performance, as usual, and much of the play, though it is a bit cumbersome here and there. Liked Colin Blakely so much, also Lynn Redgrave, [John] Stride and of course Maggie [Smith], who is brilliant. [Robert] Stephens plays well but somehow seems to lack charm, needed for so long a part. Lovely décor. I didn't come round, thinking you would want to get away to Brighton.

After a brief return to London, JG travelled to Hollywood for his appearance in the film version of Evelyn Waugh's The Loved One, *directed by Tony Richardson.*

To Hume Cronyn   *20 July, London*

I am sorry to read that Richard [Burton] has been ill again and hope he has recovered by this. Alex [Cohen] asked me to fly in for the August 5th celebration, but much as I should like to be with you all, I would not dream of it unless I had at least three days off from the studio. Please give everyone my love and congratulations on breaking the record.†

Alex made some frightful suggestion of a tour of *Hamlet* with [Robert?] Burr,‡ and gathered the understudies to support him. A sixteen week guarantee, and I suppose he wanted to use my name for prestige value. Jean Varrere is to direct, copying everything. I told him I thought it a horrid idea and I will certainly not be a party to it. It really would be cheating the public though I suppose it would give some needed employment. But I don't approve of the idea at all.

I was trying to do *Julius Caesar* here in September, but Chris Plummer, whom I approached for Antony, has refused it, so I am scrapping the whole scheme, and we are now toying with the idea of two plays, with mostly the same company, if I can get Vivien Leigh and Alan Webb to appear with me. *The* [sic] *Ideal Husband* [by Oscar Wilde] and *Ivanov* would, I think, make an effective contrast.

I hope you aren't too sick of Polonius by this time. I shall always be grateful and proud of your performance in it.

---

* Olivier played Captain Brazen in *The Recruiting Officer* at the Old Vic.
† The production of *Hamlet* with Richard Burton broke Gielgud's own record for the longest-running Broadway production of the play.
‡ Robert Burr was an extra in the production and may have understudied as Hamlet.

To Paul Anstee   *22 July, Beverly Hills*

Vivien [Leigh] has invited me to stay with her, so I hope to move in over the weekend. Dining with her tomorrow and with Maggie [Leighton] and Michael [Wilding] tonight. Make-up test as the strangled corpse this morning – very macabre. T. Richardson is great fun and very sweet and easy. Bobby Morse a great bore and all my scenes are with him.

To Paul Anstee   *1 August, Hollywood*

Vivien and Jack [Merivale] are simply angelic to me – the house is a welter of luxury – so many gadgets and air conditioning, electric washing machines etc. etc. that there is a continual undercurrent of buzzing which makes one wonder if the whole place may suddenly blow up. Gold fittings everywhere (swans on the taps!) and a dreamy view over all the valley below – glorious in the morning (if there is no smog!) and better still at sunset with all the lights twinkling on.

The film is the greatest fun – everybody is good in it, and they are mad about my performance so far. Saw a long scene yesterday in the rushes, and we all roared with laughter – I even thought I was rather funny myself – and Tony lets me improvise lines and chatter so that I seem natural in a way I have never been before on the screen. I get up at 6.45 and we work till nearly seven each day, and usually a party afterwards every evening so I get pretty tired and it is good to have Saturday and Sunday off. Tony R. is delightful to work with and all the other actors too – excellently contrasted types.

Great party for me last night at the Brissons – Yul Brynner, [Simone] Signoret, with whom I have made great friends, Maggie L. and Michael (but I never hear a word he says!), old Binnie Barnes. I *danced* my shoes to pieces and got home at 2.30. The night before, another party with Gladys Cooper, Cathleen Nesbitt, and Rock Hudson, who seemed to be quite a dear. Vivien has about 12 people coming here tonight. She is looking wonderful and seems to be enjoying her film [*Ship of Fools*] too. Have had two offers of films I don't want to do – one a colonel in a Japanese prison camp story [*King Rat*] for Bryan Forbes – the other a Druid priest with Charlton Heston. One of my lines 'My son, are you ever a prey to improper thoughts?'

Jonathan Winters, who plays two parts in our film, is a duck and a brilliant comedian. Does improvisations all the time between takes, one hysterically funny one of a queen tying to grope a cowboy in a movie house, getting his wrist slapped and then, when he has apologised, nearly got turned out, and given up all hope, the cowboy suddenly puts his hand on *his* knee! Was my face red!

To Paul Anstee　　　　　　　　　　　　　　　　　*7 August, Beverly Hills*

We are finishing my scenes in a mad old estate – derelict house and grounds – an empty, macabre swimming pool – terraces, glades, statuary, all overgrown and disused – a weird little children's cottage which has become my house, with a studio littered with incredible props by Rouben – Nouveau Art telephones, mother of pearl lampshades, oriental bric-à-brac etc. Terribly hot and exhausting working under the lights in small rooms on boiling days, but I am really delighted with T. Richardson and everyone is very pleased with me. I do think the part has come out effectively and I have seen quite a lot of rushes which are amusing and quite touching too. I am having a splendid time, though it is a bit distressing when Vivien gets her fits of depression and wilfulness. Jack tries very tactfully to manage her, but of course she is really labouring under the depressing fact that she is playing a supporting character part for the first time, and that makes her feel she is slipping and getting old, and if she has one drink too many she gets resentful and difficult. I think Jack is quite glad to have me in the house to share a bit of his responsibility for her. She really is such a sweet and touching character – so generous and thoughtful and mad about her work. Wish she would agree to do the plays with me. We shall see.

　　We go to a party at Joan Cohn's tonight (Larry Harvey's lady), and tomorrow I dine with Christopher [Isherwood] and Don [Bachardy]. What about Bob Boothby?* O, I do hope he hasn't perjured himself to no purpose. I suppose London is ringing with rumours. It would be wonderful if he could sue those vile Sunday papers and get enormous damages – but frightful if they really have evidence against him and it went the other way.

To Paul Anstee　　　　　　　　　　　　　　　　*14 August, Beverly Hills*

I have finished all my scenes, but still have two more appearances as a corpse. It has been great fun. We have had a nasty crisis with Vivien, but it seems to be averted now, thank God. Her mother arrived too, so it was all a bit of a business, and I felt very sorry for Jack. But Kate Hepburn and Cukor rallied round, and she has till next Tuesday before filming again. But of course, she refuses to stay quiet and to put off our day in Disneyland tomorrow, and shops and dines out regardless. Her vitality and recuperative powers are really extraordinary – a bit frightening too, at the bad times.

　　Saw the film of our *Hamlet* and was appalled. Richard assing about and giving the most mannered and vulgar performance, shouting, grimacing, all sorts of tricks, everything I did for him destroyed. Hume [Cronyn] overacts

---

* The Conservative politician Lord Boothby (1900–86) was accurately accused by the *Daily Mirror* of having a homosexual relationship with the psychopathic gangster, Ronnie Kray. Boothby refuted the allegations and won damages from the newspaper.

his head off. Only Eileen [Herlie] and one or two of the others – including [Alfred] Drake, to my great surprise – are human. But it lasts three hours and I almost died of boredom watching it. It is to be shown in several hundred movie houses for 4 perfs. only, at a dollar and a half entrance fee all over the country on Sept. 23 and they say it will take 12 million dollars!!! I have one per cent, and a big percentage too on the record album, which has apparently broken all records, too – isn't it mad? My artistic soul revolts, but what would you?

I have an offer to play Henry the Fourth (Shakespeare) in Spain in October with Orson Welles – might be fun – but will Keith [Baxter] be Prince Hal again, that is the question? I hardly think our accents would sound very good together.

Laurence Olivier wrote to JG inviting him to appear with the National Theatre Company at the Old Vic and asking for any ideas he might have for parts he would like to play.

To Laurence Olivier   *3 September, Venice*

I was greatly touched by your first letter but at a bit of a loss how to reply to it. There have been a few tentative schemes afoot, but so far nothing definite, and, as Edward Albee has told me he is writing a new play [*Tiny Alice*] with me in mind, I have postponed deciding anything until his script arrives. If it should prove all that I hope, I should be in America again early in the New Year. I am sad to be away from London so much, but a really new play would be so exciting. I am rather dubious whether I could do anything startling with *Love for Love*. I fear I may know it too well, but I do think you will be wonderful as Foresight, and of course Joan [Plowright] ought to play Miss Prue. Ben is sure-fire and Tattle and Valentine both extremely effective. Sir Sampson and Scandal are the two most difficult parts to cast and make amusing, and of course we cut enormously when I was in it originally at Oxford and again at the Phoenix. Angelica can be dull but Pam Brown played it brilliantly in New York.*

I stayed with Vivien and Jack while I was making *The Loved One* last month. Got on marvellously with Tony Richardson whom I didn't know at all before. Vivien was as generous and sweet as ever, and Cukor and Kate Hepburn – also Signoret who is in the film [*Ship of Fools*] and seemed awfully sweet and affectionate – are looking after her pretty well, though as you know it is terribly difficult – especially for Jack – to moderate her restlessness and

---

* Olivier and Peter Wood, the director, had their own ideas about casting when the play was produced by the National Theatre a year later. Olivier himself played Tattle; Miles Malleson, Foresight; Lynn Redgrave, Miss Prue; Colin Blakely, Ben; John Stride, Valentine; Anthony Nicholls, Sir Sampson; Robert Lang, Scandal, and Geraldine McEwan, Angelica.

seemingly inexhaustible vitality. I do hope she will come home next week and rest for at least a month or two at Tickerage* before she starts any more work. [Stanley] Kramer and everyone seemed to be delighted with her performance, which is the great thing, but one can't help feeling helpless and sad sometimes to see her getting out of control.

Maggie Leighton and Michael appear to be Romeo and Juliet, though M's father, aged 92, had fallen downstairs and later moved in on them with a broken arm. Maggie immured and cooking him three meals a day. What love can do?

Did you know Bernie died while I was in Australia and now I have Diana [Wynyard]'s cook – seems rather indecent somehow, to benefit so basically after losing two lifelong friends!

To Laurence Olivier   *23 September, London*

I saw John Dexter in Venice the other day and enjoyed talking to him about things. He murmured something about Shylock but I felt that I did not bring that off in 1938 and doubt if I would now either. In spite of my nose, I have never managed to have much success in Jewish parts.

After filming The Loved One, *JG took a holiday in Italy and Switzerland before moving to Spain to film* Chimes at Midnight *(Orson Welles' version of the life of Falstaff). This was to be followed by his appearance as Julian in Edward Albee's* Tiny Alice *in New York.*

To Paul Anstee   *12 October, Madrid*

Keith [Baxter] met us – no hotel – hung about for two hours hoping to get into the Hilton. Finally driven here arriving round 8 o'clock. Nothing ready, armour, clothes etc. Shooting supposed to begin today, but 10.30 and no one has turned up yet. Court scenes to be shot in mountain village near Barcelona beginning Wednesday. Obviously impossible to write from there, so don't expect to hear. Icy wind and stormy day – jolly prospect for location work! The whole thing quite mad. Have not seen Orson yet, only a bunch of amiable, shrugging and obviously inefficient executives. Perhaps we shall pack up and come home again?

To Paul Anstee   *October 1964, Berga, Spain*

Really very fascinating working here, about 20 of us in a summer hotel specially opened for us – and drive each day 25 miles to this fantastic castle at

---

* Tickerage Mill, Vivien Leigh's home in Sussex.

Carbona where we film in a colossal disused church – gothic kind of Torcello – which is magnificent but gets very cold at night with the stone pavements and no windows – open embrasures! However, everyone is agreeable and Orson immensely funny and talented. Keith very sweet and enthusiastic – mad about Welles and works very hard.

To Paul Anstee   *14 October, Barcelona*

Mad two days filming battle scenes on a plain – icy wind. Orson works very fast and despite improvised costumes and mad inefficiency over calls etc., it is all rather fun. Strange polyglot cast, Italian, Spanish, French and English. O. like a benign Santa Claus striding about in a huge cloak with hair and beard flying, like Laughton as Lear.

To Lillian Gish   *30 October, London*

I am very excited about the Albee play [*Tiny Alice*], and expect to come to New York on November 16th to start rehearsals, although I have not even read the third act yet. Irene Worth is to play opposite me, which I am delighted about as I love working with her. As you know, I have always wanted to create a part in New York, and to work with American colleagues. I have waited so long for an original play, and *Ides of March* and *The Last Joke* (to say nothing of *Othello*), were great disappointments, and I began to think I would never choose cleverly again – touch wood!

To Laurence Olivier   *7 November, London*

How splendid *Hay Fever** is and what a success. I had a grand evening and Edith seems really to be getting into her stride, I was glad to see, after, I gather, a sticky start.

I have a rather charming picture by Roger Furse of a dress rehearsal of *The Merchant* at the Old Vic in 1931 – the first professional production I ever directed, just after I did *Romeo* for the OUDS. In the picture, besides me and Billee [Harcourt] Williams (who played Aragon) are Malcolm Keen as Shylock, Peggy Ashcroft as Portia, Roger Livesey (I think) as Gratiano, Charles Hickman as Bassanio. Motley did the décor. I thought it might perhaps hang at the Vic in a corridor, bar or lobby if you have room for it, as it is quite an amusing and characteristic sketch and I think it ought to go where it has the right associations. Anyway, have a look at it and see if you would care to have it.

---

* Coward directed his own play which opened at the Old Vic in October with Edith Evans as Judith Bliss.

To Paul Anstee   *22 November, New York*

Fair Lady film is half an hour too long but Rex is really superb, and I thought
Audrey [Hepburn] much better than Julie Andrews. Mona Washbourne's nice
too, but Stanley Holloway a bore, also [Wilfrid] Hyde-White, and poor
Gladys Cooper quite eclipsed by Cecil's over elaborate wigs, hats and dresses.
The Ascot scene is really splendid but the Ball – as on the stage – an anti-
climax and all the Queen of Transylvania business unnecessary and tedious.
You will like all the Nouveau Art décor, but it is, as usual, too much and
showing off at the expense of the play. Audrey's last pink frock and hat quite
staggeringly successful, but the colour (especially the green foliage and the
day street scenes) is not really good – not a patch, for instance, on *Topkapi*,
the new Dassin jewel robbery picture in Constantinople, which is divine, I
thought. Jeremy Brett typically colour*less* in *Fair Lady*. We saw *The Knack*
[by Ann Jellicoe] with Brian Bedford and Brian Murray – and a very funny
girl* – beautifully directed by Mike Nichols and a very amusing evening
altogether.

Rehearsals are interesting and I find the director [Alan Schneider] patient
and helpful. Have managed to learn the first act so far. Thank Heaven we
have four more weeks to rehearse. Albee is said to be altering and cutting the
other two – he has not been to see me since the reading.

Not going out at all till I get really to know my part, except for a day in
Washington on Dec. 2nd when I have to recite a Shakespearean speech for
the Breaking of the Ground at the Kennedy Memorial – rather an honour to
be asked, though I rather dread those kind of things. I have also been offered
an honorary degree at Brandeis College near Boston, which George and Ed
tell me is a good thing.

To Paul Anstee   *14 December, New York*

Little news. Working like mad. Albee has telescoped two scenes – much
better, and I almost know the hellish words of my last speech at last. I shall
get some very kinky letters if the play goes at all! Riding boots and a clerical
collar and a cassock and a riding crop (not breeches, alas!) and with my toupée
(tell Stanley) I look as good as gold. Hm!

The scenery is O.K. but all the accessories – carpets, furniture etc. – are
horribly common. A pity. The designer [William Ritman] has no taste or
colour sense unfortunately, and not much authority. Albee, Wilder and the
others all bring patterns and samples and the result is a muddle. Irene's
Mainbocher dresses are simple and very effective – if they aren't ruined by the
dye on the hideous *painted* carpet.

---

* Either Alexandra Berlin or Lee Lawson who took over the part.

To Paul Anstee   *27 December, New York*

The rain has poured down all day today. We trudged out by bus to see the Pet Show at Columbus Circle, which was rather enchanting, except for the SMELL and the screaming children. Martin entranced with the monkeys, puppies and parrots. We are supposed to go to a party tonight given for Dirk Bogarde by Roddy McDowall and Sybil Burton in the Village, but I don't think I can face struggling into a D.J. at 10 p.m. and facing a crowd.

Spent Christmas Day in bed! turning down a lunch at the Kanins.* We have been working so terribly hard – new bits and transpositions and cuts every day, and then putting them in at night with an audience in front. Tomorrow we have a run-through in the afternoon and a final D.R. at night. Of course, in the end they have cut my final speech to 2½ pages from 8, and at least another ten minutes or more have been finally cut, but Albee was obstinate and I learned the whole lot with sweat before he would agree to get it to sensible length. He never speaks about the play to us, which is clever in a way, but also a bit damping. Everything is done through Schneider, who has been most patient and tactful, but is no Peter Brook. The other three men are only so-so, but no doubt they will pass in New York – the lawyer especially indifferent – a poor man's Vincent Price. Irene is splendid, though.

Terrific interest and controversy – outbursts of booing at the end drowned in bravos, so Heaven knows what Tuesday will bring in the way of reception and criticism. Have tried not to listen to too many people – everyone gets out of it by telling me how wonderfully *young* I look. Hm! Always makes me suspicious. Martin has seen it three times at various stages, and has been extremely intelligent and helpful to me about my mannerisms and tricks. I think I have got it more simple now, and as good as I can get it for the moment. Of course, I am very nervous and apprehensive.

I was very sorry to read about old Moura Budberg – those elderly patrician ladies go a bit round the bend, it seems. Less humiliating though, I suppose, than cottage-crawling!! Poor old Clemence Dane has had a big operation – fear she may not recover.

Alfie [by Bill Naughton] doesn't seem to be a success, with Terence Stamp, nor is *Hughie* (O'Neill's one-acter with Jason Robards), nor *Bajour* [by Walter Marks and Ernest Kinoy] with Chita Rivera, nor the Jean Kerr *Poor Richard* with Alan Bates – a sorry season so far!

Tiny Alice opened at the Billy Rose Theatre on 29 December 1964. JG began working on his adaptation of Chekhov's Ivanov.

---

* The director Garson Kanin and his wife, Ruth Gordon.

1965

To Paul Anstee   *8 January, New York*

You probably saw the London *Times* notice yesterday, and the one by Alan Brien in last Sunday's *Telegraph* – both bad. The reviews continue very poor, except for two raves from Boston critics – odd! – but the management here seem to be delighted and prophesy a six month run – I should be inclined to give it three – but we shall see.

Rather smug to read Paul Scofield is to do *Timon* at Stratford, for once accepting something I turned down first!!

To Paul Anstee   *12 January, New York*

The play going wonderfully well. They say it will last till June. I would think April nearer the mark, but the audiences seem raptly attentive and the advance is excellent. A lady screamed out 'Oh, it's all a lot of SHIT!' the other night and was escorted with her husband from the theatre without more ado. I thought she was drunk, but I hear that friends of Albee were sitting near them and *they* said she was so excited by my hallucination scene that she had a tiny frisson and screamed out at the climax! Who shall say?

Irene wears the most alarming underclothes when she strips for me in the play – a sort of armoured, flesh coloured corset and thigh length pink combinations. I shut my eyes and lunge to death every night, but I must say we giggle a lot about it. So difficult not to knock her down when I bury my face in her stomach, and not to trip over my riding boots while I am doing it. Her clothes, incidentally, are I think most disappointing – only Molyneux and Valentine as professional couturiers ever seem to bring it off on the stage. The negligee makes her look like Lady Dracula, and in the get-up for the last act, with a short skirt and hooded cloak, she looks like a Blue Cross nurse who has mislaid her collecting box. The sets are horrid too, only so high and vast that everyone thinks them beautiful and impressive. A ghastly carpet and awful poor French furniture. The walls are pickled oak, the whole effect like a particularly gloomy reading room at the Athenaeum, and the Cardinal's garden has enough creeper to smother Walt Disney. Well, well.

I'm sure I shan't do it in London. Both J.P. and Hugh [Wheeler] thought the seduction scene very nearly funny and feared it might get the bird in England, though I must say they love it here – and I never stop having to say 'I don't understand', 'What is this about?', 'What is going on here?' etc. etc., all good cues for nice cries of assent from an unruly gallery, which I thought all playwrights had discarded in the melodramatic twenties. But I shall keep them guessing for four or five weeks before definitely refusing. It will be interesting to see what management will offer to take it and who they get to play my part.

Albee has cut his hair again. He always wears tan corduroys, but so short and wrinkled that they are poor things. Very skinny legs and huge feet. A lovely flat, though, decorated in chocolate coloured cork (à la Proust, I suppose), very good modern pictures, a horrid yak-like rug and three cats. He is very like one in character, I think. Absolutely refuses to discuss the play or acting at all, though he is always charming.

To Paul Anstee   *18 January, New York*

We were very bored with *Aida* last night – an incredibly vulgar new (!!) production, with Katherine Dunham dancers doing appalling jungle bunny ballets at intervals – most unsuitable – prehistoric picture scenery and Radames in a tea-cosy gold helmet on top of a fat Jewish face. He is a cantor at one of the synagogues and looks like it. 35 dollars a ticket and a hideous audience for some Israelite Benefit. [Leontyne] Price sang beautifully, but acts like a barmaid serving drinks to the cowboys!

To Paul Anstee   *26 January, New York*

I am half way through *Ivanov*, which seems much longer and more difficult than *Cherry Orchard*. Of course I don't know the play nearly so well. Martin types it for me, which is very good for his spelling.

Can hardly believe it is only a month since we opened, it seems so much longer. Margot Fonteyn came last week and seemed to love it (but no Rudi [Nureyev], unfortunately) and Lynn Fontanne and G. Cukor. The matinées are always excellent here, so much better than in London, full and attentive and it makes the week so much less tiring. I have my usual colds and catarrh, and snort and sniff a lot, but that is nothing very unusual.

Heard the Churchill programme on TV last night at Irene's. Didn't much care for my contribution, but thought Larry O. was splendid. I found it very hard to distinguish my own bits, but they seemed a bit 'recity' and over-romantic to me.

Binkie wants me to direct *Barefoot in the Park* [by Neil Simon] in August in London. Just got the script to read. Hm.

To Val Gielgud   *11 February, New York*

New York is as impossibly noisy and hard to get about in, especially in bad weather, as London, and not many amusing people or parties. Took Irene [Worth] to Trude Hellers, the new dance hall in the Village – unbelievably jungle dancing and steel guitar (amplified) band in a tiny place, the floor shaking up and down – [Marcello] Mastroianni looking rather pensive at the next table! Am trying to get hold of the rights of *Death in Venice* which José Ferrer appears to have bought. Think it would be a wonderful film for me if someone like Orson [Welles] would direct it.

To Paul Anstee   *23 February, New York*

I had never noticed that Albee has such big ears! Tiresome party last night at Irene's for the Moscow Art – about six of them – all that shouting insincerities through interpreters and not to bed till 3.30 a.m. Wonderful Rubinstein all Chopin concert last Sunday – with Florence [Reed] who gave a lunch party first, Irene W., herself, and eight queens! Rouben, Martin, me, Billy Baldwin and several other more or less elderly chaps! She really is the Den Mother of all time.

Stanley [Hall] wrote me a sweet letter enclosing all the *Much Ado** articles. I must say the Sunday ones made me a bit furious. Maggie Smith seems to have brought it off again, though, and I gather it is brilliantly done in typical Franco fashion, and very gay and pretty to look at. But I do resent Shakespeare being made a scaffold for deliberate distortions of producers. They seem to say the Claudio-Hero-Leonato story is more *convincing* this way.

Going to see *Barefoot* again next Sunday, and must decide whether or not I direct it London in August – rather despondent about the idea – I could only copy the production – it is so good – and unless Mildred Natwick would come, I feel rather disposed to say no. Oh, plans, plans!

The Loved One is due next month, but I was rather depressed when Rouben told me it only began to be funny after I was dead! Did you see I was nominated for a best supporting role Oscar for *Becket*? What next! Hope it may at least put up my film price! I gather Orson's film is almost done, with Keith [Baxter] doubling all the parts and voices of members of the cast who were unavailable – mine included.

To Paul Anstee   *18 March, New York*

The play drags on, dropping a bit more each week. Not much fun, really, but I suppose we must grin and bear it. [David] Susskind has again offered a *huge* sum for *Ages* on TV and, as I am doing it for the President and Congress in Washington on the 29th, it does seem a good publicity moment to accept. So I hope to tape it during April or May and come home rich.

Grim week of local horrors. The Women's Prison on 10th Street condemned as a sink of horror – rats, bugs, cockroaches and a *hotbed* of homosexuality. Ghastly murder in the subway of a 17 year old white boy by a Negro delinquent

---

* Franco Zeffirelli's production for the National Theatre opened at the Old Vic on 16 February 1965, with Maggie Smith as Beatrice and Robert Stephens as Benedick.

aged 17, and no one who saw it would dare to come forward to give evidence – and, of course, Selma.* A big benefit to be given to aid the blacks organised by Sammy Davis for April 4th. Irene and I are thinking of doing the proposal and bag scene from *Importance* with Mildred Natwick as Lady B. Feel we might get away with it in a big theatre with the aid of wigs and chokers to disguise our seniority!

To Paul Anstee   *4 April, New York*

Heavenly Spring beginning and the view from our terrace is divine, only it gets cold at intervals too, flurries of snow and icy wind. Even so The Ramblers seems to be agog with mackintoshed gents cruising, even in a midweek afternoon! I really don't dare to walk through the Park even in the daytime any more.

To Paul Anstee   *14 April, New York*

The TV script I think I told you about is very exciting – a new Anouilh on – whom do you think – Sir Thomas More! A wonderful part and they want to film it at MGM in July in England with a star cast to be directed by George Schaefer, who does all the big straight plays for Hallmark here – (the Lunts, Maurice Evans, Julie Harris etc.) so that would mean a lot of money and also it would be shown in England and America. In colour too. I am seeing them today about it and feel it is a very good omen for the year. They talk of Plummer for the King, Sarah Miles, Anne Boleyn, and Flora Robson as Lady More. It's a bit too talky and needs cutting – the dear French are so mad about dialectic – but I do think it is a noble play and just as good – and a bit more vivid – than *Man for All Seasons*. Odd that everyone seems to be taken by the same subject.

We drove down to Stratford, Conn., on Monday and saw – thank God only half – of their *Romeo and Juliet* with a children's audience. Sort of OUDS† standard – most undistinguished – a little boy, Terence Scammell about as much like Romeo as a messenger boy and Juliet, who is only 22 but managed to look like Edith Sitwell. Lillian Gish impossible, alas, as the Nurse – Rebecca of Sunnybrook Farm with a dash of Mary Poppins.

A huge party on Staten Island for Margot Fonteyn on May 7th. Airports kept open all night, parking facilities, two pages of notes and directions for getting there! I shan't go, of course.

---

* On the orders of Governor George Wallace, civil rights protesters had been attacked by state troopers when they tried to march from Selma to Montgomery, Alabama.
† Oxford University Dramatic Society.

To Paul Anstee   *9 May, New York*

A lot of news suddenly. The play comes off in a fortnight – May 23rd! Trying
to fix the More play for TV, but fear there is no dough! But I am trying to
get A. Cohen interested, also to arrange definite dates for TV of *Ages*. Various
places are asking for Irene and me to do the Sitwell–Eliot programme, so am
hoping to do one or two dates with that – might do *Ages* at Philadelphia
where I've never given it, too, and they want me to record the narration for
The Play of Daniel.

Terribly excited about *Chimes at Midnight*. I saw a lot of snippets when I
dubbed for two days last week – the photography and angles are terrific. I
look a million, but very *real* and, I think, quite impressive. It is supposed to
be finished in June and released in October – same time as *Loved One*. Hope
I shall live long enough to see them both!

The record of the Ravel I made with Gina Bachauer with the [Christopher]
Fry poems is just out,* and I think it is the best I have ever made – even
Martin thinks it is really good! Goddard just rang to offer me a seat in his box
for Horowitz Recital this afternoon – very exciting as he has not played in
public for years, and seats impossible to get – people queuing for several
nights past. Martin saw Margot and Rudi in *Swan Lake* last night, lucky
thing.

To Paul Anstee   *18 May, New York*

Everything still in the melting pot about future plans. They sent me *The
Cavern*, the Anouilh play that has been done at Nottingham, suggesting I
might play the author in it, but I really don't care for the part and there is
nothing to it that I could do better than lots of other character actors, so I
refused it. So we are back to *Ivanov* and an undecided second play. I want
Vivien for both, with *Ideal Husband* or [*The Gay Lord*] *Quex* (but not a word
to her yet, please), but am not yet sure whether they will agree.

We close on Saturday and next week I do the TV of *Ages*. The director
seems nice and intelligent and I do hope we make a decent job of it, as it
should be a property for me for some years to come, as well as a fat sum of
money down. Still hoping Rouben will do *Ivanov* for me. The RADA notices†
were rather encouraging, I thought. *Mother Courage, Saint's Day* [by John
Whiting] and *Oedipus* won't do much to cheer London up. The [Anthony]
Newley musical [*The Roar of the Greasepaint, The Smell of the Crowd*] opened
here to dreadful notices, but the music is already a great success and they have
700,000 advance so I don't suppose they care. Liza Minnelli had a personal
success in another musical [*Flora the Red Menace* by John Kander, Fred Ebb,

---

* *Gaspard de la Nuit* with poems by Aloysius Bertrand translated by Christopher Fry.
† JG's (uncredited) version of *Ivanov* was done at RADA on 8 May, directed by John Fernald.

George Abbott and Robert Russell], which appears to be dreadful except for her.

To Paul Anstee   *29 May, New York*

I have been immersed in the studio making *Ages* all week long, and there are still two days work to do. You can imagine what agony it is judging the rushes, with enormous close-ups of one's face going on forever, but I hope we can make a fairly successful thing in the end.

J.P. is quite busy casting *Ivanov* – Claire Bloom wants to play Sasha and should be good, I think. We go tomorrow to see the new Balanchine *Don Quixote* – a great spectacle apparently, though probably a bit of a bore too.

After a holiday, J G returned to England to rehearse Ivanov. *In addition to himself and Claire Bloom, the cast included Angela Baddeley, Roland Culver and Yvonne Mitchell.*

To Noël Coward   *8 August, London*

I am in the throes of rehearsal and I think the company is a good one and the play itself coming out better than I had feared – the marvellous humour and compassion are most evident, even though not quite so subtly blended than [*sic*] in the four more famous plays of his – and my own part, though something of a [illegible] self-confessed weakling, is nothing like as tedious, I hope, as that boring creature in the Osborne play [*Inadmissible Evidence*], whom everyone but me seems to find so touching and interesting. Wasn't the Pinter piece [*The Homecoming*] extraordinary? And how beautifully done too.

Ivanov *opened at the Yvonne Arnaud Theatre, Guildford, on 30 August.*

To Nancy Hamilton and Katherine Cornell   *4 September, London*

I have been meaning all this time to write and thank you for your two sweet letters. Are you still up in the Vineyard? And is there honey still for tea and a puzzle for restless guests? Martin and I think so often of you and our happy days at the Haven. Do the plans for the new house go well, and is there any water in New York – we could send you a few casks with pleasure – it has poured unceasingly for weeks and the papers are full of floods, avalanches, as well as the usual plethora of politics, wars and crimes – to say nothing of friends dying and being ill in all directions. Ah, youth, youth!

Ivanov opened last Monday at Guildford and today is my first breather, though we have performances at 5 and 8 today which I greatly dislike – twice nightly was only for music hall performers in *my* time – but plus ça change.

The cast is really splendid and I had a fascinating job working with them –

everyone extremely pleased with the whole production, though of course there are details still to improve, and my own performance especially, which has got a bit behindhand in my general supervision of everything. Rouben Ter-Arutunian's décor is very beautiful, despite some wardrobe and executive crises – mostly over money – which made me rather sad, as I had to suffer as referee between him and Binkie and J.P. but I think it has all come out wonderfully, though I hope it has not put Rouben against English managements for ever. Well, there always has to be difficulties in one department or another, and at least this time there was no trouble with the actors or the play itself, which has emerged as fresh and funny as well as dramatic, rather to everyone's surprise – not nearly as old fashioned as I had feared when I adapted it.

Did you read that Bill Ball did *Tiny Alice* at Pittsburgh with Brother Julian stripped to the waist and swathed in white tulle as the Bride of Christ, if you please, in the last act.

Martin has his beloved white Peke back after an operation on his eyelashes to stop them growing in and making him blind, so that is a relief. The parakeet I brought back chirps away despite the rain and cold, and M. is decorating a little room at the back of my house in burlap for a studio, which will be very pretty when it is finished.

Ivanov opened at the Phoenix Theatre on 30 September.

W. Somerset Maugham died on 16 December 1965. JG wrote to his secretary-companion, Alan Searle.

To Alan Searle   *16 December, London*

It seemed very sad and final to see the news boards here this morning. After the alarm earlier this year I imagine you must have been quite prepared for the end, but obviously Willie's strength must have been extraordinary, like the stalwarts of his generation so often seem to show.

It will be extraordinary for you to be freed from the cares of the last few years, and I hope when you become used to being without him you will find a new interest for the time to come.

I always remember the wonderfully affectionate way you spoke of him to me the last time I visited you both at the Villa. He was always very kind and generous to me, and I shall remember the privilege of knowing him even in so slight a way – his going must be an incalculable wrench for you after so many devoted years of companionship.

Don't bother to answer – you will have hundreds of letters, all better expressed, I'm sure than this one.

1966

After its run at the Phoenix Theatre, JG's production of Ivanov *went to the United States. Vivien Leigh took over from Yvonne Mitchell as Anna Petrovna and her companion John (Jack) Merivale took over from Richard Pasco as Lvov. The American actress, Paula Laurence, took over Angela Baddeley's role as Madame Lebedev.*

To Paul Anstee   *6 February, New York*

Rather disappointing week. We walked out of the Henry Fonda play [*Generation* by William Malcolm Goodhart] and [*Man of*] *La Mancha* [by Dale Wasserman, Mitch Leigh and Joe Darion], a dreadful Don Quixote musical. *Condemned of Altona* [by Jean-Paul Sartre] interesting but inadequately staged and acted, though the theatre (in Lincoln Center) is quite beautiful in itself. But there is really a dreadful feeling of apathy and failure about the theatre here, as per.

Rehearsals rather bleak and boring and very hard work – you know – a great bare empty theatre – the Broadway – eight hard chairs, no props. Jack and the American lady in Angela's part are not good – otherwise we seem to have adequate players for the party scene, though it is very slow and hard work getting it into shape and, of course, no fun to do compared to creating it in London. Never mind.

To Paul Anstee   *13 February, New York*

The play is ready really, though we go through it every day. Jack still very awkward and rather gloomy – Vivien seems all right but fusses about her dresses and feels a bit neglected, of course, having so little to do. I hope to God she will get good notices and enjoy things a bit when we get started. We go to New Haven on Wednesday morning – dress rehearsals there and three previews Friday and Saturday before the opening tomorrow week.

Loved *Cactus Flower* [by Abe Burrows] with Betty Bacall and Barry Nelson – the only unqualified good evening we have had. *Sweet Charity* [by Cy Coleman, Dorothy Fields and Neil Simon] beautifully staged and some very dishy dancers and numbers for the boys and girls, but Gwen Verdon is never off the stage – an excellent dancer but not young, and with protruding teeth and a hideous little skimpy black dress throughout. She has neither glamour nor appeal for me. Lovely scenery and lighting, but a very boring evening in the end. I read the much-praised Truman Capote [*In Cold Blood*] with great disappointment – could not be really interested, though I suppose it is very clever and well done in its way, but so sordid and depressing and rather sentimental too, I think. Lunched with [Peter] Shaffer who goes home tomorrow but threatens to return to some love affair he has embarked on here. Hm!

To Noël Coward   *23 February, New Haven*

Do so hope you are really better by now, and full of esprit and energy again. Also that Cowley Street will give you a friendly welcome – am having a bit of decorating done so I hope you'll find it clean and neat. And do try and use the two cooks (one Jill Esmond's girlfriend! 'tis, really). They are both excellent and so convenient – shop, make the menu, cook, wash up and away with them before you can say knife.

To Paul Anstee   *24 February, New Haven*

I *hated The Loved One* – cheap and revolting – only Liberace, Maggie Leighton and Milton Berle were good – and I am O.K., I think, in the short bit I have, but the whole thing misses fire badly and is endlessly long and vulgar.

I think the play is in good shape. We have cut about seven minutes and tightened it up. Business good but not a sell-out. However, they do seem to like it very much and there are bravos (for me) at the end. Vivien is restive, but I think she is beginning to be happier. The other new people have fitted in all right, except for Madame Lebedev, who is a pronounced Jewess with a Bronx accent you could cut with a knife.

To Irene Worth   *4 March, Boston*

The enclosed* will, I think, amuse you. I must say I was rather shocked when I saw it – 'false face doth hide' etc., but I suppose he is sore over the failure of *Malcolm.*† Anyway, it is not attractive behaviour, is it?

Tennessee's plays‡ were a disaster – no wonder it was so hard to raise the money for them. Margaret [Leighton], Kate Reid and Zoë Caldwell all brilliant and utterly wasted – the most painful evening to watch and I didn't

---

* Newspaper cutting with a quote from Edward Albee during an interview with Leonard Probst for the NBC radio show, *Monitor*. 'I've only had, in the nine plays that I've produced, one unhappy experience with an actor and that was with John Gielgud, who refused to learn the lines that I had written, and I had to cut the third act of *Tiny Alice* in shreds because he was petulant and refused to learn it ... Most [actors] are thorough-going professionals and I haven't had any problems with them. Curiously enough the only one I had was with the man who was supposed to be the most thorough-going professional on the English-speaking stage and he's not, he's a child.'
† Albee's new play had nineteen previews and seven performances before it closed.
‡ Tennessee Williams' two plays, *The Mutilated* and *The Gnädiges Fräulein*, directed by Alan Schneider, had sixteen previews and seven performances before closing.

think Alan Schneider had helped. He came to our seats and beamed in on us through the glasses but fortunately did not ask our views – probably our faces told him.

To Paul Anstee   *6 March, Boston*

Took Vivien and Jack to a beautiful house to lunch yesterday, about 30 miles away – mad old couple, both half pickled, but the claret was as good as the lunch! He is Ava Anderson's brother and knew my eldest brother in Paris. Hates Malcolm Bullock – good show. Described how hideous the poor wife was – the one who knocked off her poor head riding under the bridge – and how Molyneux made his first success by flinging yards of scarlet satin round her and sending her to a party! This old man is pretty dotty – they are mad about the ballet and had a party of 80 for a champagne picnic lunch when they were in Boston – Margot, Freddie, Bobby etc., but they are only half compos and said they dreaded Chekhov, so I do not think they will favour the play with a visit. But you would have been mad about the house – looks like a country cottage – clapboard – on two floors only. Exquisite Aubusson rugs and some good pictures, sprinkled with awful Edwardian ones, and curved Adam ceilings put in, I suppose, in the elegant big drawing room.

Great trouble with sound effects – some radio station close by interferes with our tapes, and strange orchestras mingle with owls and carriage wheels. Jean Rosenthal comes tonight, thank God, to look at the lighting and get it corrected I hope, once and for all. I have a sweet coloured man to dress me who was with [Charles] Boyer and Joseph Cotten. Wonderful old Ethel Griffies (88) fell against a chair in her hotel bedroom and cracked a rib but insists on playing – did not miss even one performance once and professes to be perfectly all right – wonderful. You would adore her both on and off the stage.

To Paul Anstee   *11 March, Boston*

How wonderful for you about the cottage. I thought nostalgically of the day when J.P. and I drove down to Essex on a gloomy winter's day in 1932 (or 3) and saw Foulslough looming through the mist and we said 'Yes, of course we must have it!' and rushed back to London like maniacs to be in time to act in *Richard of Bordeaux*!

Not much news here – business still very good – think we shall do over 50,000 this week, though I am slightly peaked [piqued] to discover (as I suspected) that Vivien is getting *much* more salary than I am! Well, she has Laurie Evans to fight her battles and I am a silly cunt not to use him too. I shall in future. No doubt she is a very big draw and I am devoted to her, but I do all the hard work! Have won over the lighting, and I am told 8,000 dollars worth of extra equipment is going in for Philadelphia and dear Jean Rosenthal is to start again from scratch, but not till the end of next week. All the bills have to be changed, of course, and the booklet has been rushed through with a dreadful picture of Vivien and me on the cover without showing it to me first. All these silly decisions are made and accompli – then they have to spend a huge sum changing them and meanwhile hundreds have been already printed. So absurd and wasteful and unnecessary. However, I suppose it would be dull if there was nothing to grumble about!

To Paul Anstee   *23 March, Philadelphia*

Wonderful Japanese exhibition at the Museum here – scrolls and screens and sculpture etc. We went to the Zoo also, which is very well arranged and clean. A colossal hippo climbed out of the water, put its hooves on the rails and reared up with its great pink stomach within a few feet of us to hold the pose for a few photographs. Anteaters – which I never saw before – and some marvellous orang-utans with long red hair and pale green, wise old men's faces. Only I can't bear seeing the lions and leopards trudging backwards and forwards in narrow cages.

To Paul Anstee   *9 April, Toronto*

Do hope you have had a wonderful time – lots of glorious photographs to show for it, and congenial company. But I must say as a race I don't find those Egyptians very winsome, do you? Were they always scratching their balls and whisking their dressing gowns above the knees while they were showing you Pyramids and things?

Vivien very low indeed with a heavy cold and a rash on her face, brought on, she thinks, by taking some raw quinine that old Ethel Griffies persuaded her to take. Business has been simply phenomenal – 85,000 last week and almost the same this. Of course it is impossible to play it in such a huge theatre – 3,000 people and we had 13 standees last Saturday matinée – but they cough a lot and, of course, the atmosphere is completely non-existent. Anyway, now we've played it in every size and medium except on ice or through glass, which I think would surprise the dear author if he could only see it. Binkie came over and was hand in glove with David Merrick. I think those two and Irene Selznick would make a very unholy trio and might combine in management at any time.

To Paul Anstee   *20 April, Washington*

Noël's notices* are good, aren't they, and Irene has had wonderful praise. Toby [Rowland] wrote Vivien that there had been terrible rows – N. calling

---

* Coward's *Suite in Three Keys* with himself, Irene Worth and Lilli Palmer had recently opened in London.

Lilli a fucking Nazi* and Irene slapped somebody's face – Lily Taylor's, no doubt.

Have you seen the Feydeau [*A Flea in Her Ear*] at the Vic? I hated *Morgan*,† rather like the film of *The Knack* – very 'in' and fashionable but it just didn't amuse me, though Vanessa [Redgrave] is rather enchanting and Bob Stephens hardly doing justice to his corduroy suit! [David] Warner is only a freak and not a top star farceur, but Irene Handl is very good.

To Paul Anstee   *28 April, New York*

Rather irritating previews with 'party' audiences – trouble with the sound effects and the dear Shuberts don't turn on the air conditioning in 44th and 45th Streets till tomorrow, so we have been pouring with sweat from the lights and the audience falling asleep and fanning themselves with their programmes.

John [Perry]'s full of London news, but rather deaf and forgetful I find these days, which saddens me. Keith [Baxter] seems to be quite an obsession – he says Noël is mad about him as giving a superb comedy performance in the Shaw play [Valentine in *You Never Can Tell*], and he has turned down a Josh Logan film and is to play Bob Acres – good heavens!

Reading a divine book by Barbara Tuchman called *The Proud Tower* – study of England and Europe before 1914 war. Divine story in it of Wilde meeting a terrible bore who said, 'You know, Wilde, I feel there is a conspiracy of silence against me these days. What do you think I ought to do about it?' 'Join it,' said Oscar.

Chimes at Midnight is now to be shown definitely at Cannes in May and is supposed to be up for The Golden Palm – whatever that is – so if it is a success we might be able to get backing for *The Tempest*, I hope.

To Irene Worth   *1 May, New York*

I have not seen E[dward] A[lbee] but Hugh says he is back in New York – some scheme for him, Zeffirelli and Nureyev to make a film about Nijinsky, only it is not to be officially about him! Rather an eclectic trio, I should say. Don't quite know what I shall say – or not say – if I meet Edward. I fear the icy stare and 'How do you do, Mr Worthing' is indicated but I so hate all that kind of [illegible] cutting and bitchiness.

Have not seen many people here except for one of Arnold's usual mad celebrity parties – Cathleen Nesbitt, Tallulah etc. etc. Can't do with those fiestas any more, I find.

Ivanov *opened at the Shubert Theatre, New York, on 3 May 1966.*

---

* Lilli Palmer was an Austrian who fled Nazism, but she was married at this time to Carlos Thompson who was a Nazi sympathiser.
† Adapted from David Mercer's play, *Morgan – a Suitable Case for Treatment*, directed by Karel Reisz.

To Paul Anstee   *13 May, New York*

Rather gloomy here, I fear. I sent the early reviews for J.P. to see and pass on to you. They are depressing reading and very stupid and disappointingly unanimous. I don't think I ever had such bad personal notices in my life, and it seems so odd since it is the same performance which was so praised in England, both in the theatre and TV. Well, well, it can't be helped. We are doing fairly well at present thanks to advance booking and parties, but rather dread what will happen in the next four weeks, especially as there is now a taxi strike (as well as three big newspapers out of action), and the weather is at last brilliantly fine. Vivien is not very well – can't get rid of a skin rash which she can't find a cure for. But she behaves well in spite of the disappointment.

I talked to Sol Levine (another of those Spiegel–Todd–Preminger film tycoons) about the possibility of getting backing for my *Tempest* film idea with Orson Welles. He was gracious and seemed interested, but unless *Chimes at Midnight* gets better notices elsewhere than the one in the *N.Y. Times*, which is very damning, I fear no one will risk him for another Shakespearean picture.

They have offered me a huge part in a MUSICAL – don't laugh – with Geraldine Page. The music and lyrics are quite delightful, I think, but there is no proper book yet and the big directors – [Jerome] Robbins, [Gower] Champion – are both unavailable, so I think it would be a terrible risk for me. I can hardly believe a very middle aged couple as the leads in a musical would draw the town. Still, it was amusing to hear it and to be asked to do it. I'm pretty sure I shall turn it down, but will chew on it for a week or so. I am tired and depressed and not in a good mood to make decisions – anyway, I always think I jump into things too quickly and they always want to involve you so that they can hold you to promises. Rex's success is a kind of temptation but also a very dangerous precedent. Mr Jule Styne (*Bells are Ringing, Gypsy* etc.) is a very potent salesman and played the songs very well and the lyrics are brilliant – sort of cosy, melodious, witty family stuff – no dancing or modern sprightliness (it takes place in 1906) and is an adaptation of Arnold Bennett's novel *Buried Alive*, afterwards made into a play, *The Great Adventure*, and two films have been made of the same story – one with Monty Woolley and Gracie Fields. Sam Behrman has done a book, but they are apparently throwing most of that out! It does need a good actor aged 58! Well, there it is – probably no good at all.

To Paul Anstee   *24 May, New York*

Rather gloomy week. We dropped 7,000 dollars and Vivien and I go on cuts for the next three weeks – matinée audiences good, crowds at the stage door etc. – but thin at nights, a few wild enthusiasts as usually happens with a failure! To console me a little, I won an award on TV for *Ages*.

Heard the musical score again yesterday at Florence's, whose aid I sought for advice. She was very enthusiastic, but of course nothing can be decided until the book is finished and a director I agree to, fixed. I've no doubt it will all fall through but it is quite fun to dally with the idea.

To Paul Anstee   *1 June, New York*

We totter along to rather thin houses except at matinées. They are still pressing me to say I will do the musical. I tried out two or three songs with Jule Styne and thought I could probably manage them. But not a word of dialogue has yet been produced – they promise *part* of the script at the end of this week. Can't somehow believe it will materialise. Much enjoyed a tiny revue called *The Mad Show* which I went to because the man who directed it, Steven Vinaver, has been mentioned as possible director for the musical. This was brilliant, but a very fast little cheap revue, mostly TV and *Mad* Magazine jokes which were completely incomprehensible to me but I greatly enjoyed it all the same.

Vinaver did *Divorce Me Darling* [by Sandy Wilson] and Binkie says he is frightfully clever, but Sandy Wilson wouldn't listen to him. Also greatly liked *Philadelphia Here I Come* [by Brian Friel], which Binkie is doing eventually in London. Sentimental Irish whimsy, but awfully charming and touching. But it is a huge success here and will run for months.

Ivanov *closed on 11 June 1966 and JG went on holiday to St Vincent in the Caribbean with Martin Hensler, Vivien Leigh and Jack Merivale.*

To Paul Anstee   *15 June, New York*

Just off for our island fastness. Vivien is very excited about it and should be nice to have along and Hugh [Wheeler] *may* come for the second week. It is good to be free again. Saw the revival of *Annie Get Your Gun* [by Irving Berlin, Herbert Fields and Dorothy Fields] – marvellously well done, better than the original production and [Ethel] Merman, looking like the back of a cab, sang and played simply splendidly. The designer had obviously taken more trouble with the *gentlemen's* costumes. The hero – a sort of Harry Andrews 40ish glamour boy, was breeched and fringed to kill and was really very attractive, at least to my old eyes, and a splendid chorus of dancers with very little on.

The maddest offers keep coming in, and Vivien has half a dozen to choose from too. So we don't feel we did ourselves any harm by doing *Ivanov*, thank Heaven.

I have to decide about the musical as soon as we return. Arnold [Weissberger] is away until the 25th. I'm hoping he can make a stunning contract for me this time! *If* I decide to do it.* The present book is untidy but has great possibilities, I think and I like the proposed director, but no one will commit themselves without the other, so we are all chasing each others' tails like cats. Do you know Millicent Martin whom they now propose for the girl? She was in the *Crichton* musical† and one of the Newley films. Dora Bryan would be ideal, but she is tied up with [*Hello*] *Dolly*, I fear.

To Paul Anstee   *19 June, St Vincent*

It is rather divine here. The island is only a short boat's throw from the mainland, but more remote and Robinson Crusoe-ish than Jamaica. Very sweet native boys and fat ladies look after us and we practically have the place to ourselves. Vivien and Jack have a hut and Martin and I one each, with hot water, loo and outside shower. The boys wear striped shirts and tight white cotton trousers to the knee – very becoming – one is like Yul Brynner and another rather like Fred Webb when his hair was fuzzy. Very stormy bad weather at first – gales and rain – which was a bit forbidding, but it is better every day. The food rather good in a spicy sort of way and a little local band comes in to play after dinner. No telephones or newspapers. A pool with turtles and blowfish, a donkey, parrot and a cage of pretty coloured birds, so Martin coos at them and gets coal black with the sun. We go on a schooner trip tomorrow. Vivien is very sweet. We all read and sleep a lot. I nearly drowned in the sea the first day – an unexpected dip in the ocean floor – but Vivien rescued me.

To Leon Quartermaine   *9 September, London*

I was disappointed with the Feydeau farce [*A Flea in Her Ear*] which has been so greatly praised. I think they have changed the cast since it opened (Finney has left‡) and the French director [Jacques Charon] has evidently not been back. Consequently they all shout and take each other's tone, and the admirable achievement of great pace has deteriorated into a gabble, and misses the dogged sedateness which would make it far funnier. Also they are mostly too *young*. I think Feydeau needs solid middle-aged actors who are *almost* past the time for sexual frolics! Then the bourgeois respectability caught in outrageous situations makes a hilarious effect. Only young Edward Hardwicke (Cedric's son) is quite excellent, I thought, in a difficult part.

---

* He didn't. *Darling of the Day* eventually opened in New York in January 1968, starring the unusual pairing of Vincent Price and Patricia Routledge. It lasted for only thirty-one performances.
† *Our Man Crichton* by Herbert Kretzmer and David Lee, based on J. M. Barrie's play *The Admirable Crichton*.
‡ Robert Lang had taken over the dual role of Chandebise/Poche from Albert Finney.

Olivier and Gielgud had resumed discussions about the latter's possible appearance with the National Theatre company.

To Laurence Olivier   *9 September, London*

What do you think about doing Pirandello's *Henry IV* if we could get Visconti to direct it? I would suggest Zeffirelli but after the *Othello* fiasco I am a bit wary. If I do *The Misanthrope* [by Molière] I would love [Jean-Louis] Barrault to direct it, as I know he has made a great success in the part himself, and I admire and like him so much personally as I know you do too.

To Laurence Olivier   *8 October, London*

In detail, I feel as follows. *Tartuffe* [by Molière] – I like [Richard] Wilbur's translation enormously, it has great buoyancy and lightness, and to my mind makes Miles [Malleson]'s version seem very stuffy by comparison. As we agreed on the telephone, Orgon is vitally important and very difficult, and if you would play it I would be much more interested in doing Tartuffe – or would you prefer to cast it the other way round?

When We Dead Awaken [by Ibsen] is very powerful and haunting but The Huntsman seems to me to verge on the ridiculous and the wife's part is hideously difficult too. I cannot think how one would stage the play either, what with forest streams and mountain fastnesses. Ibsen obviously visualised great realistic sets. I gather *Little Eyolf* which was done at Edinburgh last year got laughs in all the wrong places and would be rather afraid the same thing would happen with this play, and yet there is a grandeur and terror about it that is rather wonderful.

The Pretenders [by Ibsen] seems to me a much more suitable play for your theatre and might, I should think, have the same sort of success as *Royal Hunt* [*of the Sun* by Peter Shaffer] if well done. The Bishop is a wonderful part and of course I would love to play it, but Skule really carries the play and if it is done I do hope you will play it.

I imagine you would not do *The Bacchae* [by Euripides] in the Gilbert Murray version? It is a terrifying piece, but no doubt [Jerome] Robbins could do wonderful things with it. I have never been in a Greek play and it would be interesting to see how it came out. As you say, the old gentlemen dancing together would be something of a problem.

Nice letter today from Peter Shaffer, not wanting to work on the Pirandello, but agreeing that the published translations are hopelessly dull. Have you any ideas for another adapter? Who speaks Italian and can write good colloquial dialogue?

Just read the Seneca.* Very vivid and terrifying – and *Tartuffe* again, with

---

* A version of Seneca's *Oedipus* by Ted Hughes.

Orgon in mind, which does seem a good idea for me – much better than T. himself.

To Laurence Olivier   *20 November, Hollywood*

I am delighted to hear you have got [Tyrone] Guthrie and I loved [René] Allio's décor in *Recruiting Officer*.* I shall hope to see John Dexter when I am back in New York. Have you had any more ideas for a translator of Pirandello's *Henry IV*? I mentioned it to Moura Budberg but do not know if she would do it well? Everyone tells me that Giorgio Strehler is *the* Italian director – might he perhaps be interested?

Towards the end of the year, JG and Irene Worth took their Recital, Men, Women and Shakespeare, *on a British Council-sponsored visit to South America and thence for a few more performances in the United States.*

To Paul Anstee   *1 December, Rio de Janeiro*

It seems rather improbable being here in tropical heat – humid like Israel, Bombay or Melbourne. Sweltering away, packing, unpacking, flying, lunches, press conferences, parties, all the usual British Council camp in between rehearsals and Recitals – hugely unsuitable opera houses to perform in, and a general kind of Graham Greene hotchpotch of opulence and squalor. Pretty nasty food and drink, but everyone is helpful and agreeable, and some of the views – beaches, mountains etc. – are pretty stunning. We opened last night in São Paolo – an hour's flight only – a ghastly city with huge potholes in its roads, unbelievable noise and traffic – rather marvellous from the air but hideous when you see it all close – huge half finished skyscrapers and an Art Gallery with about a dozen masterpieces in a very gloomy building, and the paintings cracking and badly hung and cared for. Apparently the Brazilians are very uninterested in the cultural arts though everyone, including ourselves, are endeavouring to make them so.

The Recital is far too long and we have to cut at least ten minutes. Irene looks very fine in her two dresses provided by the Wool Board and made by Belinda Belleville, one white, the other yellow, in caftan style. She did well as Rosalind, Lady Macbeth and Cleopatra, but Volumnia will have to go! Everyone very agreeable, but all the politeness and small talk a bit of a strain and I have done it all so often. We have to live down the disappointment of Vivien [Leigh]'s and Ralph [Richardson]'s two somewhat disastrous visits, but I have hopes we shall succeed in doing so.

---

* Guthrie and Allio would be director and designer for *Tartuffe*.

To Paul Anstee   *16 December, New York*

Arrived back here after a 10 hour flight from Santiago, very exhausted with
heat and British Council entertainment. Irene chose the last performance to
insult the poor impresario for not having the floor of the stage cleaned
properly and her dress was ruined etc. Very tiresome and I had much ado to
prevent giving her a good slap!

I wrote to you at least twice on the tour – hope they will arrive sometime,
but you know what posts are like in Latin countries. I'm terribly tired and
don't make much sense, but I am so very devoted to you and always will be,
and don't you dare to think otherwise for a single moment.

To Paul Anstee   *29 December, New York*

Saw [*The Killing of*] *Sister George* yesterday for the first time – well played by
Beryl Reid and Eileen Atkins, but the last act is cheap and false, I think, and
Lally Bowers a caricature, so that it all falls to bits in the second half.

Silly Ralph [Richardson] doesn't like the Ustinov comedy I am so keen on.
I long to buy and direct it but can't think of anyone else to play the part –
John Clements – Tony Quayle – not interesting enough.* Wonder if Vivien
will finally do the Chekhov TV [*From Chekhov with Love*] for Susskind with
me. They talk of getting Peggy A. and Dorothy Tutin for the other two
women, and as they *both* had affairs with Sir L. [Olivier] at various times, I
hardly think her little ladyship will be too keen to co-star with them.† We
shall see. Jonathan Miller is to direct in March in London.

We have a rest till Jan 5th. After that twelve Recitals – Yale, Chicago,
Washington etc., one in New York on the 22nd. A lot of money but a bit of
a chore. However, Irene needs to make some dough to help her poor girlfriend
whose flat she is staying in in the Village. The wretched woman slipped and
fell into a boiling bath and is appallingly burned – in a public ward until
April and no job to come back to. A sad story and I must say I do admire
Irene for coping – she goes every day for two or three hours.

Oh – *The Chelsea Girls* – an *outrageous* film by Andy Warhol – voyeurism
in the Chelsea Hotel. It lasts 3½ hours, and is mostly out of focus – a double
screen – *everything* going on – mostly queers and lesbians, but you can't see
anything clearly and the sound track is deliberately distorted. One can't tear
oneself away, but it is a crashing bore – yet the audience sits spellbound and
packed. Really decadent and incredible that it is allowed. Two small *children*
came in with their Dad, and I almost had a stroke – but I'm glad to say he
removed them after about ten minutes. Yet the Catholic Church have banned

* *Halfway Up the Tree* opened on 23 November 1976 at the Queen's Theatre with Robert Morley in
the leading role.
† She wasn't, even though her marriage to Olivier had been over for some years.

Blow-Up, which doesn't seem to me indecent at all. The birth scene in *Night Games* – and the little boy in bed with his Mum is pretty strong too, but done with great artistry and beautifully shot and acted. Do see it. It is really quite exciting fantasy.

1967

To Paul Anstee   *7 January, New York*

We did two Recitals at Yale – very successful and wonderful audiences – the boys all very sweet and enthusiastic. Big party at the Liebersons – Bernsteins, Irene [Selznick], Kitty Carlisle etc. – the two boys, almost grown up, arrived from the theatre as we were leaving, in extraordinary *Guys and Dolls* suits - black and white stripes and bell bottoms, spotted ties and handkerchiefs, long hair, and two beatnik girls, one in a minimus skirt. Extraordinary to see the American version of the Chelsea Set. Goddard looking old and tired, but Brigitta rather wonderful for the mother of two grown-ups. Anyway, they are evidently *normal*, which must be a relief to Mum and Dad.

The Homecoming had a miserable, grudging notice from Walter Kerr – no praise for anyone – acting, production or set, the actors barely mentioned, and he says the first act is a cracking bore and the whole thing would be better as a one act piece. I am furious – with such a ghastly season it should have been hailed, and I hear there is little advance so it may have to close at once. Bad luck for Cohen too. I think we forget the essential difference in *dialects*. Probably that kind of Cockney idiom is quite foreign and annoys them, just as Tennessee's plays have never really seemed convincing to London audiences.

To Paul Anstee   *20 January, Indianapolis*

Here I am holed up in the most preposterous suite with fantastic fake Louis XV furniture, to appear at a college called Butler tonight. Had to give a two-hour press conference yesterday, if you please, to drum up business. We turned hundreds away at Boston but evidently in outlying bailiwicks I am *not* a name to conjure with.

Have agreed to do [*The Charge of*] *the Light Brigade* April, May and June and Shaffer says he is writing a TV play for me (an English professor in Greenwich Village who takes LSD) that he would like me to do here in August, so the year seems pretty full of interest one way and another. Jonathan Miller is back in N.Y. and I hope to see him tomorrow about the Chekhov.

Also Tony Guthrie, directing for the Met, so I may be able to discuss *Tartuffe**
with him a bit.

Arnold [Weissberger] had a 60th birthday on Monday – huge party at his
mamma's – all the old trouts, Radie Harris, Anita Loos etc. – and Rouben
went to a 50 strong boys' party for him last Sunday, but we were *not* invited.
Met Harold Pinter at last and liked him enormously, *Homecoming* fighting
for its life – much advertising – they think they will save it. Shaffer's *Black
Comedy* and his new one-acter [*White Liars*] a huge success in Boston. He
looks very shagged out, however. Have you seen *Blow-Up*? I imagine David
Hemmings is very you – met him in Hollywood with Vanessa [Redgrave] –
he was nice but hearty, I would think.

This is a ghastly little town. Had to see *The Bible*† last night as there was
nothing else to do, and fortunately the news shop opposite is packed with
dirty books. I read *two* last night. Well, well.

To Paul Anstee   *15 February, New York*

How I loved Patrick [Woodcock]'s joke about the Signoret *Macbeth*‡ – 'Aimez-
vous Glamis?' I feel sure Emlyn must have coined it.

To Laurence Olivier   *11 April, London*

I was talking to Michael Powell today who gave me affectionate messages
from Pamela Brown, whom I've not seen for more than a year. He says she is
much better in health and more confident after two blackout scares some
time ago, and seemed to think she might dare to work again in the theatre,
but not eight times a week.

If Irene [Worth] doesn't want to do Jocasta – I gathered she was rather
tricky and demanding other roles as well – would it not be a good idea to
approach Pam? I admire her so much as an actress, and her strange no-age
beauty would surely be rather splendid – and the deep voice – if she were not
to have to appear too often – that kind of special engagement might appeal
to her.

To Lillian Gish   *11 May, Italy*

Here for a week before going to Ankara to film *Light Brigade* with Tony
Richardson for six weeks. We did a few scenes in London and it seems a very
fine, pungent script. I play old Lord Raglan – one arm and a bit dotty, but

---

* JG had agreed to play Orgon in *Tartuffe* at the Old Vic in November and *Oedipus* the following
year.
† *The Bible – In the Beginning* directed by John Huston.
‡ Alec Guinness and Simone Signoret appeared in *Macbeth* at the Royal Court Theatre.

rather a dear! Trevor Howard and Harry Andrews are the rival Lords of the Brigades. Rang Alec [Guinness] before leaving London hoping to hear news of you, but Matthew answered and it turned out it was his wedding day! I gather Alec is very pleased about it, but Merula has been ill so he had to cope with everything without her. We think of you often and send much love.

To Paul Anstee   *21 May, Ankara*

We are bien installé ici – a very new, swank hotel and a large suite on the 12th floor – two bathrooms, loos and a sitting room. Fine view but over-sunny when it is hot, and there is a nightclub and pool which is apt to be a bit rowdy till 4 a.m. on a Saturday night!

However, we get up at 5, drive to the location (about 20 miles), make-up, breakfast, work till 3 p.m. then lunch in the canteen and drive home. Early to bed, of course – a long day, but beautiful in the early mornings. Enormous unit – about 100 people and all kinds of Turks, Persians, peasants, Turkish children, horses etc. etc. Yesterday a downpour for about half an hour which turns everything to mud, but I was safely ensconced in my caravan and after it cleared up we were able to go on working.

Martin has been put into the uniform of a French officer with moustache and imperial, and done quite a bit of background work! He chums up with all kinds of characters and brings tales of their grievances and private lives when we get home.

I had two days on horseback – well, half an hour each day. The first time the horse lay down to roll in some sand and coyly heaved me off, but I managed to stay on the rest of the time while it was *walking*, only holding the reins with one hand – quite clever of me, I thought. There are lots of people to choose from and one can avoid the bores. Don't fancy the food much but the yoghurt is delicious and said to be very health giving. Fish, lamb and endless oily hors d'oeuvres. There is a pleasant feeling of lack of personal responsibility quite unlike the theatre and it is interesting trying to play comedy with so much grim reality alongside it.

To Paul Anstee   *30 May, Ankara*

Battle of the Alma today – 1500 troops, horses, flags, drums etc. Turks very squat and ugly and not a bit like the Highlanders and English troops they are dressed up to represent, but very effective en masse. Big advance in a valley, over a stream and up a great hillside – explosions, cantering horses, drums, bagpipes etc. etc. Quite exciting. I've done a lot of work – only five or six more scenes, I think – so imagine I will easily be through in two weeks or so. Doing *Ages* at the theatre on Sunday week. It's all rather fun, really, and everyone so nice to work with – excellent canteen, caravan to rest in between shots etc. The young men all very polite to me. There are compensations for being elderly after all.

To Paul Anstee   *16 June, Ankara*

We watched the Charge from a hill above the valley sitting under sunshades – very much in character! And also some gory battle scenes. Great trouble with the army who are difficult to manage and costing a fortune. I do an odd shot or two on horseback in between the big scenes. Now Tony says he won't want me for ten days, so we are trying to plan a trip to the South to see Izmir, Ephesus and several other places where there are temples, amphitheatres, beaches etc.

Too many deaths in the London papers. [Claude] Rains, [Spencer] Tracy, Pamela Frankau, Richard Ainley – now poor old Quartermaine is having a prostate op. at 91. I hardly feel he is likely to survive it, but you never know with the Victorians.

Binkie is off to Venice with some strange new chum of Cecil's – do you know him? Could it be an affaire du coeur?

Leon Quartermaine died on 25 June 1967.

To Barbara Quartermaine   *29 June, Ankara*

Dear Barbara

Only heard today – the Monday newspapers did not reach me. I am so sad for you, but if he went painlessly and did not know, what better end can one wish for? It's only sad for *us*.

My memories of him must go back quite a way further even than yours. That cheering house for his Mercutio, with Ellen [Terry], in 1919, was I think the first time I saw him act, and then, greatly daring, I asked him to play it again in 1935 on the tour following the London run when Larry did not go. And of course I fell for him at once – his marvellous youthfulness and brilliant sensitivity with the verse. His affection for me over the years was one of the greatest pride and happiness to me, both in and out of the theatre, and I shall not forget his artistry, his high standards and his personal sweetness. He was a really *poetic* man, one of the few I ever met. (Barker was another and, I suppose, Harry Ainley too, but he was a kind of beautiful lost soul.)

To Paul Anstee   *8 July, Ankara*

J.P.'s sister, Sive, died suddenly in Ireland. I am sorry not to have been in London when it happened and Binkie has gone off on a holiday, so I fear he has had a lonely and wretched time flying off to Ireland for the funeral. I'm afraid it will make him gloomy and sad. But she had been crippled with arthritis for a long time and was such an outdoor person, like him, that I think she no longer had much use for living. But he was awfully fond of her and she is the last family link, which he always felt very strongly.

No news really – wonder how *Three Sisters* went.* Larry wrote me such a sweet and cheerful letter. I do admire him, but tremble a bit for everything.

To Colin MacInnes   *28 July, London*

I only got back from Turkey, where I have been filming, a few days ago, and was so pleased to receive your Music Hall Book [*Sweet Saturday Night*], which I have thoroughly enjoyed reading.

Though not really a music hall buff (I too thought the mystique of Chaplin and [George] Robey rather overdone by some of the highbrow critics), I have some very good memories of evenings at 'Variety', though being very squarely brought up, the Coliseum was usually where I saw the great comedians, alternating with serious sketches (Bernhardt, Irene Vanbrugh, Arthur Bourchier etc.). I love to remember a fearfully grand turn called Olga, Elgar and Eli Hudson – three posh vocalists performing amid a welter of shaded standard lamps and bearskin rugs. I even once played there myself, in the Balcony Scene from *R. and J.* with Gwen Ffrangcon-Davies (in 1924). We were top of the bill, and a great flop, sandwiched between Teddy Brown and his xylophone (an enormously fat man) and the Houston Sisters (who gave slight imitations of us and vastly amused the customers). There was also a silent clown called Robbins, who did a marvellous act changing his costume twenty times in front of the audience. From the wings one could see all the paraphernalia he discarded tangled up behind him, and I used to wonder who unravelled and replaced it all for the next performance. I think he was German.

I saw Grock a couple of times, but he didn't amuse me. I can't bear comedians who make to play instruments and never do – Jack Benny, Vic Oliver and the Danish man who is so popular but whose name I forget [Victor Borge].

I was only about 12 at the time, so my memory is probably at fault, but I *think* I saw Sarah Bernhardt in a patriotic playlet *and* Vesta Tilley *and* Albert Chevalier all in one evening! I remember 'My Old Dutch' and Vesta Tilley's elegant figure in tails.

But I did see Marie Lloyd just before she died, at the Kilburn Empire. She sang 'If you show the boys just a little bit, it's the little bit the boys admire' – in a grand dress with the diamond headed stick, and 'The Old Cock Linnet' – and she sat down on a park bench with very narrow slats and said 'Oh, I'm nipped in the bud!'

---

* Laurence Olivier's production of *Three Sisters* opened on 4 July 1967 at the Old Vic. Olivier was being treated for prostate cancer at the time.

I loved Harry Tate, but only saw him in revue or at the Coliseum – *Motoring* and *Fishing*.

You don't mention Nora Bayes or Sophie Tucker. I was a terrific fan of them both in the late twenties, and used to follow them from one hall to another when they played in several different theatres on the same night – Palladium, Alhambra and sometimes the outlying halls. By the way, I'm *sure* *The Bing Boys* was at the *Alhambra*, not the Coliseum.

Thank you again for sending me the book. I've been an admirer of your novels for a long time. Perhaps we shall meet one day – I hope so.

On his return, JG began rehearsals for Peter Ustinov's play Halfway Up the Tree *with Robert Morley.*

To Ariadne Nikolaeff   *6 October, London*

The Ustinov play goes wonderfully in Manchester, after a black dress rehearsal. The old omen* seemed to come true – a great relief though it still needs some work and playing in.

I've been recording a tribute programme to Leon Quartermaine, a reading of E. Nesbit, and go to Aylesbury tomorrow to read in memory of another friend – the reaper is so busy lately.

Following the opening of Halfway Up the Tree *on 23 November, JG appeared for the first time with the National Theatre company, playing Orgon in* Tartuffe *and, early in 1968, Oedipus in Peter Brook's production of Seneca's play.*

1968

To Richard Sterne   *10 January, London*

Many thanks for your letter and the copy of the book,† which arrived safely. I think it has come out very well, and you have obviously taken endless trouble in vetting all the details and small points. I find the text with the stage directions etc. especially well done, and I also feel that the rather slangy reportage of the rehearsals has (after all this time) a rather attractively spontaneous ring and accuracy of atmosphere. Congratulations. Redfield's book‡ amused me – he is so *very* complimentary about me at first and then the worm turns! He was so disappointed that I evaded his continual hopes of

---

* Theatrical tradition has it that a poor dress rehearsal presages a good first night.
† *John Gielgud Directs Richard Burton in Hamlet.*
‡ *Letters from an Actor* by William Redfield dealt with the same subject.

buttonholing me in corners to discuss motivation and character in Guilden-stern who is, after all such a very minor person – and he played him perfectly adequately. But I think, after my persuasive attitude in engaging him, that he felt I would find a way for him to make his performance spectacularly outstanding, which was of course impossible. Not a bad book, though, all in all, though it is rather annoying that he should have got in first.

Tartuffe is miscast in my opinion. I have not had a success in it and only enjoy it as a sort of exercise. Now we are rehearsing *Oedipus* (Seneca) with Peter Brook – 10½ weeks' rehearsals, which ought to produce something interesting, I hope. I also go to Rome next week to do a short part – a dying Pope – in the film of *Shoes of the Fisherman*.

Light Brigade comes out in April. I have seen a rough cut and like it enormously. I also saw the Chekhov T.V. when I was in N.Y. The women are very good in it and the colour extremely pretty, but the script is rather haphazard and hard to follow, and I spend too much time sitting at desks! A few connoisseurs may like it but not the general public.

To Barbara Quartermaine   *29 April, London*

[Raymond] Mander and [Joe] Mitchenson are a strange, freakish pair – no taste but enormous diligence and they have a remarkable collection of materials of various kinds and are really dedicated collectors – middle aged, one rather dandified, the other with a broken nose, looking like a Shaw burglar.

Yes, I hate memorial services. Vivien Leigh's* was an agony – all the fans and reporters and the solemn faces of the actors and actresses. Lewis Casson and I rang Paris when [Harley Granville-] Barker died to try and arrange some sort of tribute, and were told firmly that his wife wanted no kind of comment from the English theatre! She was certainly a Tartar, and they say he turned against her when he was dying and died herself only a year later, rather mad. How his genius was wasted, except for the Prefaces, of course.

Oedipus *opened at the Old Vic on 19 March. It was a great success but, according to Olivier, casting problems made it impossible to keep it in the repertoire.*

To Laurence Olivier   *9 May, London*

Of course I understand. I am only sorry if I have seemed intractable over the suggestions you have made and of course it is sad that *Oedipus* cannot be revived after all.

I only hope you may like to ask me back another time if something should come up that you feel I can do justice to. It has been so very happy for me,

---

* Vivien Leigh died in the July of the previous year. Her memorial service took place at St Martin-in-the-Fields, and Olivier asked JG to write and deliver the address.

working for you and getting to know Joan a little – and everyone has been so kind and welcoming. I am devoted to Colin [Blakely] and Ronnie Pickup* and even old *Tartuffe* has settled down a bit with playing and makes a pleasant task in contrast to the balancing feats (all on the end of my nose) of *Oedipus*.

To E. Martin Browne   *6 August, London*

Of course you may use the letters. Perhaps you never heard the full story. I agreed with T. S. Eliot to co-direct the play [*The Family Reunion*] with you. We lunched – twice, I think – at the Reform Club – surely you were there on one of the occasions. We had a fine cast lined up – May Whitty (Dowager), Sybil [Thorndike] (Agatha), Martita Hunt, Freddie Lloyd for two of the chorus. All seemed to be going very amicably. Suddenly one day I met Sybil who said gaily 'You know Eliot won't let you do his play. He says you have no Faith, and therefore are not right to play it.' I was amazed. I don't know how he told Binkie Beaumont but the upshot was that we did *The Importance* instead! Later I met Eliot and he was nice but vague. I sent him a record I had made of 'The Journey of the Magi' and he said he had wanted to hear me do *Family Reunion* on the air but he had missed it. He was quite ill already, so I never really found out what tactless thing I may have said or done, and of course I was sorry never to have played Harry. I think he got alarmed at the idea of Shaftesbury Avenue and feared I should put a vulgar commercial smear on his writing and force him to accept it.

To Cecil Beaton   *31 October, London*

I have missed the pleasure of your friendship very much over these last years. I always valued it and regret our long estrangement. Now that it is all such ancient history I may as well tell you that the first thing I asked about when they asked me to direct *Chalk Garden* here was whether your décor would be used. I wanted to fly to New York to see it, but Binkie said he didn't wish me to see it, that neither Enid [Bagnold] nor he wished it to be used here, that Edith [Evans] had not been happy over *Heartbreak House* and must not be upset – she was in a bad state of health at that time, as you probably remember – and anyway you were fully occupied in Hollywood with the film [*My Fair Lady*]. I dislike having to blame other people, even at this late date, but as you obviously thought it was all my doing I feel I must give you the facts. It was no use my going into them at the time, but anyway that is how it was.

On 31 October JG opened as the Headmaster in Alan Bennett's Forty Years On at the Apollo Theatre.

---

* Colin Blakely played Creon and Ronald Pickup the Messenger in *Oedipus*.

To Lillian Gish   *3 November, London*

Wonderful notices for us all and huge houses immediately. I had had great misgivings at Manchester where it was quite a failure and a real baptism of fire, but by the time we got to Brighton I had begun to be much more hopeful, though I hardly dared hope for such an unanimously favourable reception.

To Alec Guinness   *30 November, London*

Thank you so much for your warm and generous letter, too generous as usual. How nice that we can both be in real successes once again – and your directing part of the Eliot play [*The Cocktail Party*] has, I think, been considerably underrated, as it usually is when the director is also successful in the leading part. (Bronnie, silly old thing, said, 'Oh, but it's such a small part. We see so little of him.') None of the actors with you have been as good before, in my opinion, and I was so pleased at that.

Yes do let us have supper on the 10th, but won't you be my guest this time? I am always eating at your expense – you, like Ralph, always seem to beguile everyone into letting you pick up the check! It's so maddening one can't have supper at home any more, but we all have the staff problem to contend with. Such a pity.

1969

To Hugh Wheeler   *25 March, London*

I do envy you St Kitts and Tobago. Still icy cold here and beastly grey, windy weather. I got 'flu and was off for three performances – felt like death, but better again now, thank Heaven. Great troubles over income tax. My accountant died suddenly, and we now find he had paid nothing since 1966!! A colossal sum has to be found, as I have made really big money these last three years for the first time in my life! They now say I oughtn't to have brought back the *Light Brigade* money, but stashed it somewhere abroad. All very boring and complicated – now they take 60% of all I earn and put it into a separate account, so we cut down all we can.

The play is still packed out, and I expect to stay in it till August – some talk of Wolsey with Burton in *Anne of 1000 Days* – also Caesar with Orson as Brutus in a new Shakespeare version. Don't know if I can do either as well as 8 times a week – we play 6 and 8.45 matinées twice a week, really twice nightly, which is very hard work, though better for the box office.

Hated *Lion in Winter*, [*The Prime of Miss Jean*] *Brodie* and *Madwoman of*

Chaillot. Dear Miss Hepburn just doesn't act any more – only cries in every close-up, and they are all over-coloured play transcriptions, false and theatrical – and long! *Isadora* better. Vanessa [Redgrave] really splendid, but also 40 minutes too long, and a preposterous Gordon Craig [James Fox]. A few lovely scenes, though. I loved *Pretty Poison* – [Anthony] Perkins and Tuesday Weld – did you see it? Doing a Dürrenmatt half hour play with Alec Guinness – very effective sort of psychological thriller – *Conversation at Night.* I think it was written for radio but should be effective on TV, if we can iron out a very stiff translation.

To Hugh Wheeler   *2 April, London*

A man called [Ronald] Hayman is doing a book on *me* – going through all my scrapbooks and old letters – a somewhat Herculean task – and interviewing various friends and colleagues. I've seen nothing written yet, only long talks about myself, rather boring and time-taking.

Fabia [Drake] is, of course, a veritable pain in the neck, except in very small doses. She and I were both protégés of Leslie Faber in the twenties and she used to drag me round Quaglino's dance floor and nudge me going home in taxis. Fortunately her parents (her Dad was a floorwalker in Maples and I think she was a bit ashamed of him!) were very strict, so I never got inveigled anywhere near her bedroom. (She was in love with Bobby Harris, too – much good that did her!) She was an intelligent young actress, but Stratford (where she played Rosalind and toured in America playing that and Portia, under Komisarjevsky) rather went to her head. She retired on her marriage to a distinguished legal man, who then died hideously of some ghastly elephantiasis which made him a monster to look at. She and Joyce have been on holiday together before. I imagine the Carey deafness must have been a great advantage on the Greek Islands. She is a good sort but a great bore and so bossy!

To Robert Speaight   *1 June, London*

Baroness von Hulton (Richard Ainley's mother) once told me that I reminded her of [Josef] Kainz – I would love to hear the record. Years ago Faber gave me some 78 records of [Alexander] Moissi, a rather dull 'To be or not to be' and a very fine *Faust* with bell effects which I loved – both, alas, long disappeared. Fascinating.

The actor Richard Bebb was preparing a series of talks on JG's work, illustrated with recordings from his unique collection. He sent the script to JG for his approval.

To Richard Bebb   *11 August, London*

I think it is admirably chosen and argued with great perceptiveness and skill. I'm glad you left out Hamlet and put in the Ghost, which I was rather pleased with myself. Of course, *that* was done for the microphone and not live. You are very right about the audience domination – so very difficult to recreate on the microphone, with the necessary control of projection in the loud passages and danger of sibilance and exaggeration. One is always impossibly self-critical in listening to playbacks.

Brook always made me feel convinced I was in the best isolated or strong position on the stage for making the best effect – in Angelo, Leontes and Prospero, for instance. Zeffirelli cluttered the stage and was utterly useless at giving me confidence – so disappointing after his enormous success with Callas and Sutherland. The great difficulty, once one is a skilful technician and established star, is to find a director who understands one's problems and is highly critical as well as positively creative. One *has* to trust a director, and then develop as one finds out how to manage the audience! *Oedipus* never *really* satisfied me, though I trust Brook so much. The physical limitations he insisted on were extraordinarily difficult to accomplish, and I couldn't help secretly suspecting I could have done it better my own way, but that would not have fitted the enormously complicated plan of ensemble which he had conceived. Irene Worth was much more sure than I ever was, and consequently achieved it far better.

Saint-Denis, in *Noah* and *Three Sisters* and even to some extent in *The Cherry Orchard*, also imposed too much of his own over-all conception to make me feel really free to expand, but with those performances and even with the rather untilled *Tartuffe* with Guthrie, I began to find myself a great deal better as the performances progressed, and I began to find what the audience seemed to want of me. Of course one shouldn't toady to them – they prefer one's mannerisms and well-known effects – but one does learn inevitably from playing to a *live* audience as one never can in TV or movies or recordings – or even at rehearsals.

Following his earlier appearances with the National Theatre company, there were further discussions to tempt JG back.

To Laurence Olivier   *24 September, London*

I'm afraid I hated *Danton's Death* [by Georg Buchner], though I see it could be a great director's vehicle. [Leslie] Faber once described the Reinhardt production which he saw in New York – and I saw it myself once when the OUDS did it with Komis. But Robespierre doesn't seem very exciting to me, nor the translation, which is surely leaden.

Of course I am sorry to think *The Pretenders* is out, because I loved the part in it, but if you don't play Skule, I do see the balance would not be good.

Did Ken [Tynan] speak to you of my idea of [*Julius*] *Caesar* – you as Julius – such a short part, but I am told when Ralph did it on a record, the importance of a great personality helped the whole play immeasurably – and [Robert] Stephens (?) as Cassius. I always thought I might do something with Brutus – he is usually so dull and priggish – and could not one think of an Antony (*not* Laurence Harvey, but that kind of arriviste personality). Lots of other good parts and an *Elizabethan* décor – permanent stage and Renaissance clothes with bits of Roman additions à la Veronese and with an upper stage, pillars and a few benches one could have a swift and vivid production without waits and a new look, after all the years of togas and heaviness. Good to do a play in fine *English* after two translations, don't you think? The Forum scene would be so much better with a *small* crowd, and not the cripples and old ladies with infants in their arms. Some sort of stylised reactions, except for three or four real personalities who have the lines. Would you direct it or who? You and [Frank] Dunlop together, perhaps?

Binkie has the rights of *The Cocktail Party* and would let you have it, I think. But although in the same way I'd like to do something in modern clothes (though it *should* be '20s, I think), I am not madly keen, or sure it would be the right moment to revive it.

It would be best of all if Charles Wood came up with his new play* – or Osborne? – but I gather you are not very friendly (and no wonder) since the Spanish epic.†

To Hugh Wheeler   *4 December, London*

The holiday was somewhat fraught – if you did hear from Beirut, that was our final port of call. The revolution broke out – fortunately after we had made some fine excursions, Byblos, Saidon, Baalbek, and we were put under curfew the last few days. Irene W. came for the last week and was very agreeable as usual. She now goes into rehearsal with *Tiny Alice*, which the Royal Shakespeare are doing in January at the Aldwych – David Warner to play my part. A young man called Robin Phillips directs, said to be very clever – an actor also, he has just played Copperfield in a great star TV with Sir Ralph and Edith Evans which I'm told is a great success.

No, I didn't go to Japan, but Attenborough still says Paramount are mad to do *The Tempest*. Finney is toying with the idea of playing Caliban, and Britten is O.K. and says he thinks Bali would make a better location than Japan. His brother (who is a big noise in TV production) is soon to show me

---

* *Veterans* was eventually produced at the Royal Court in 1972.
† John Osborne's *A Bond Honoured*, an adaptation of Lope de Vega's *La Fianza Satisfecha*, had not been a success for the National Theatre.

some documentaries he made there (in Bali). Might be more exciting. Pray God it all works out sooner or later.

Meanwhile I start rehearsing Shaffer's play [*The Battle of Shrivings*] on Monday. Peter Hall, who is to direct, says the cuts and alterations are very good, though I've not yet seen a new script. Patrick Magee is to play the other big part. Larry, I'm told, is somewhat miffed at it being taken away from the National, but he havered too long and no-one seemed to trust him to promise to go through with *playing* in it himself which was, of course, the whole point. Wendy Hiller is to be the wife. There is a young boy [Martin Shaw] whose work I don't know and a girl of 22 [Dorothy Lyman] whom they have found in America and are bringing over.

Noël was here for pre-celebrations,* but was laid low in the Savoy with a carbuncle in the groin, if you please, and had to cancel his engagements – one of them a great Foyles lunch (for the book) which Chaplin had flown from Venice to be present at. I sat by Margaret Lockwood, whom I found a bit surly and very hard work, and had to make an impromptu speech. Patrick [Woodcock] apparently pulled N. together and sent him back to Les Avants. He returns next week for what he calls Holy Week! A midnight matinée, which I have to open with a poem he wrote as a boy about child actors, and a great dinner the next night at the Savoy at which he, Mountbatten and Larry are speaking – all for the Theatrical Charities, so the general shenanigans will cost me about 50 guineas, which one cannot grudge, but I don't see why the people who *should* be at the dinner should have to pay, especially if they can't afford it. However, it's a good cause, I suppose.

The animals are flourishing, thank Heaven, though a couple of the little songbirds died while we were away. Workmen still far too obsessive – central heating, rewiring, the cellar cleaned and turned into a storeroom. Now the kitchen (riddled with mice) has to be decorated again, and so it goes on. I have bought a superb Bentley (2nd hand, of course) and enjoy it very much, except that the Greek boy (whom Martin chose out of the hire firm we used to use) is needless to say, another problem child – how I do seem to attract them – rather nice fundamentally, but rather spoilt and I fear, somewhat sly. Not sure whether he will stay the course.

Joyce [Carey] has had rave notices (and stolen the play from Flora Robson) in a revival of *The Old Ladies* – moving to the Duchess next week from the Westminster – apart from her they say it is no good – old-fashioned – but I feel I must go – so nice for her.

Do you see Rouben? Or George and Ed? Are they happy in their new house? They don't write either. I mean, you do, they don't.

Great Elizabethan portrait show at the Tate, Claude at the Hayward, Berlioz at the V & A. Saw *The White Devil* [by John Webster] at the National – very

---

* Of his seventieth birthday.

striking décor by an Italian [Piero Gherardi*] who worked with Fellini – but a bit too with-it – see-through lace shirts for all the gentlemen! – interesting evening but too long and not really quite well enough acted or directed. Rex Harrison has a terrible turkey† and leaves it (and bequeaths us the theatre) to do a film of *Scrooge*!

---

* When asked for his design for the set, Gherardi sent the National Theatre production manager a close-up picture of a stone wall with a note on the back: 'The bricks move.'
† *The Lionel Touch* by George Hulme at the Lyric Theatre.

THE SEVENTIES

1970

The Battle of Shrivings *opened at the Lyric Theatre on 5 February but had only a brief run.*

To Hugh Wheeler   *21 March, London*

We had a wicked Sunday and weekly press and wretched business for three weeks, now much fuller all of a sudden – but they have already let the theatre, and unless they can get a transfer, we shall probably close on April 11th, which would not be unpleasing to me, as I am not very happy in it, and would like to take a holiday.

My biography is a disaster and I have spent weeks rewriting and cutting it for the stupid man (but nice) whom Heinemann have commissioned to do it. I am insisting on a completely new start, but it wastes a lot of time.

I was approached by the Royal Court to do a very fascinating new play [*Home*] by David Storey to be directed by Lindsay Anderson but do not think it is really right for me or for the dates proposed. A pity, for I think it brilliant and original.

My new (second-hand) Bentley was stolen from the garage yard where it was being tested and abandoned next day near Newmarket. Fortunately it is one of the grandest London firms and they were responsible for all the police and insurance complications, which was a blessing. We sacked our young chauffeur. Can't help suspecting he may have had something to do with the stealing.* Anyway, he has gone and we have a very nice chic middle-aged LADY now – like the WAAF ladies who used to drive generals about in the War. She seems extremely efficient and reliable, thank God.

I've seen no plays save *The Revenger's Tragedy* [by Cyril Tourneur] which was awfully good. I loved *Z* and *Zabriskie Point* which all the critics hated. It is simply beautiful to look at and I thought it most exciting and poetic.

Claudette [Colbert] is announced here to be doing *Coco* [by Alan Jay Lerner and André Previn] in London, which sounds a highly dangerous project to me. Can it be true? She hasn't graced a stage for years – some play in N.Y. with Boyer, I seem to remember, and Noël's stories of her in the TV *Blithe Spirit* sounded distinctly discouraging. The theatre season has been awful here too. Poor Maggie Leighton opened in some awful unisex comedy†

---

* There is no evidence that he was involved.
† *Girlfriend* by David Percival at the Apollo Theatre.

and closed again after only a week. I hear she is now to play Gertrude in Richard Chamberlain's TV *Hamlet* for Hallmark. They offered me Polonius but I just couldn't face the idea of that.

Meanwhile I am rehearsing the Caliph in *Hassan* (with Ralph R. as Hassan), which we do in colour at the beginning of April. It is hard work with the play at night, but I love the part and think I should be good in it. King Charles TV (Shaw's *In Good King Charles's Golden Days*) with a most successful scene between me and [Elisabeth] Bergner (as Catherine of Braganza) was really good. I hoped they might perhaps buy it for America, but I fear it is too tacky for the other side.

Goddard [Lieberson] and Brigitta were here for two nights and I loved seeing them. [Robert] Whitehead also, with Zoë Caldwell, who is to play Emma Hamilton in Terry's Nelson play* in August, who told me about their country house designed by Ben Edwards, apparently with great success. I am delighted for him. Paul Morrison turned up with them – he is still a dear, but I find I haven't really much to say to him.

Martin has bought a little S. American owl to add to the menagerie, who is very sweet. All the basement, kitchen, cellar etc. have been completely done over and it all looks very clean and sweet. Enormous bills, of course, and I am still in confusion paying vast back arrears of Income Tax. Paul has an impossible truck driver friend at the moment too, but do not think he will last!

To Irene Worth   *8 April, London*

[*The Gay Lord*] *Quex* has fallen through owing to the demands of the American ladies who have bought the rights to turn it into a musical and now want to co-produce and interfere here if we do it, which Toby [Rowland] is not prepared to settle for. Very disappointing.

I may do the new David Storey play at the Court which is funny and fascinating, though very unusual and peculiar. Can't make up my mind if I would be mad to take it on, but I loved the author and it would be interesting, I suppose, to work with Lindsay Anderson whom I have always disliked personally but admire the work both on screen and stage.

We go on one more week at the Lyric – they still talk of transferring, but I think that is only to assuage the Peters [Shaffer and Hall] as there is no empty theatre and several new plays waiting to come in.

To Irene Worth   *19 April, London*

The Shaffer play came off last night and I must say I feel that a load has been lifted from my elderly shoulders.

---

* *A Bequest to the Nation* by Terence Rattigan.

I hoped to get away for a short break but it does not seem likely now as I am doing the Ghost (heavily truncated, of course, in a version by John Barton) for the Richard Chamberlain Hallmark TV *Hamlet*. They offered me Polonius (which [Michael] Redgrave is now playing) and came back with the other, which I thought was not too undignified and helpful for the pocket money. Only a few days, of course, with Peter Wood directing. Then I have a Recital with Dadie [Rylands] and P[runella] Scales next Sunday at Wigmore Hall and on May 4th I begin rehearsing the new David Storey play with Lindsay Anderson for the Court. I think I told you something of it. Ralph has agreed to play the other man, though he is dubious if the play will hold, with absolutely no action. We shall see. Mona Washbourne and Dandy Nichols and one younger man [Warren Clarke] complete the cast. I think it can't fail to be interesting, if somewhat hazardous and experimental. I only hope experience and good orchestration will bring it to life. It is very funny and a bit poetic, too, and something quite new for us. I think of growing a moustache to change my image somewhat!

Did you hear that poor Marda [Vanne] has cancer? She has been in U.C. Hospital having treatment for the last two weeks, and is now being allowed home, but according to Mavis and Binkie they only give her a year to live. They say she is behaving as gallantly as Irene Browne and Barker did. These death sentences seem to have the most extraordinary effect of purging character, which is touching and I suppose a sort of blessing. Her only grief is that she cannot speak of anything to Gwen [Ffrangcon-Davies], who resolutely refuses to accept the situation. One cannot help admiring such courage, but it will be a sad time for them both. It appears that Marda is older than one thought, about 75. There seems to be little one can do except keep in touch with Gwen and hope she will be busy with work and her house and garden. Oh dear.

The animals are flourishing and there is a new one, a small owl (called Gideon*) who is very sweet but has to be fed on live locusts (without honey!) – very hard to obtain, even in London.

Home *opened at the Royal Court on 17 June.*

To Irene Worth   *20 June, London*

They [the notices for *Home*] are really splendid and almost unanimous and so we are packing the Court with cheering every night at the end. I am mad about Lindsay Anderson and David Storey – everyone has been so kind and helpful and the cast is impeccable. Jocelyn Herbert's set perfect. And everyone loves and is moved by the play except for odd people (like Val and one or two

---

* Named after the character JG played in *The Battle of Shrivings*.

others) who find it, stupidly, painful or tenuous – or both! I get so enraged by my old fans who think that Ralph and I are wasting our time, but that always happens when one tackles anything new. They are never satisfied with what one is actually doing and only thirst for new plans of star vehicles or revivals – so annoying.

Went to Jonathan Miller's *Tempest* at the Mermaid yesterday (greatly praised by the critics) with Fabia Drake. Couldn't bear Jonathan M.'s production – ponderous, ugly, slow and flat-footed, no sense of grouping or movement though a packed and enthusiastically attentive young audience – hundreds of pretty girls with crackling shopping bags and sunglasses pushed up into their hair. Only Angela Pleasence (Donald's daughter) most interesting as a real child Miranda, very plain indeed, but hushed and eagerly intense – one could really believe she'd never seen a man except her Dad! – and a very good red-haired, toothless, Negro Caliban [Rudolph Walker]. But the rest – my God – awful pseudo Velasquez costumes, everyone in *black* including Ariel [Norman Beaton], a *grave* 30-year-old Negro also, and three awful coloured goddesses who never looked at the lovers and sang the whole Masque to pseudo Monteverdi. At Cambridge the whole thing would deserve praise as an interesting and promising experiment but not in London. I won't go and see *The Merchant** – couldn't bear to sit through the gimmicks. Portia and Bassanio in red hunting kit, comic Victorian ballad singers for 'Tell me where is fancy bred', Larry with false teeth and a fur coat à la Rothschild, and the garden scene sent up with Lorenzo smoking a pipe (before ladies in the '80s) and putting a handkerchief on the steps for Jessica (who has the curtain at the end) to sit on. I don't think anyone really likes it much, though of course the new look intrigued the critics.

Much enjoyed the [Robert] Bolt play [*Vivat! Vivat! Regina!*] at Chichester. Not at all a deep or great play, but a very effective production admirably staged (Carl Toms and Peter Dews) for the Chichester stage. A lot of second rate acting, but of course it is a huge cast to pay – Richard Pearson and [Edgar] Wreford both good. Sarah [Miles] surprisingly attractive and really well bred in the early scenes but neither she nor Eileen [Atkins] are really up to the ageing business. Eileen quite admirable in the beginning and also handsome and dignified. Makes the old Queen a bit Widow Twankey at the end – her face and *hands* can't live up to it, and she shouldn't put on rouge which is particularly unbecoming to her rather housemaid-y face, but she does at least make an effective change, whereas Sarah only puts on a plain brown dress and less make-up and doesn't pad her body or wear an obvious wig which would so greatly add to a fine theatrical effect when she opens her black cloak in her last scene to reveal a brilliant scarlet dress. But it is good romantic theatre, better, I thought, than the More play [*A Man for All Seasons*],

---

* Jonathan Miller's production of *The Merchant of Venice* with Laurence Olivier as Shylock had opened at the Old Vic in April.

which I always found a bit overrated, and will certainly come to London afterwards. Nice for Binkie, who owns it, and handed it to [John] Clements when Peter Hall reneged and they couldn't get a cheap enough company for London. Now he says it has cost £35,000 but he will be able to present it in town for £10,000 which is, I suppose, a very big consideration.

Marie Löhr writes very feebly. I hope to go and see her in a week or two, and Sybil [Thorndike] still moves with terrible pain but, of course, goes out to the theatre and down the stairs and *all* the dressing rooms afterwards. Marvellous creature.

Ralph is, I think, very happy indeed and splendid in the play. It is really beautifully cast and directed. I think we shall move in after our six weeks, perhaps to the Apollo which I only hope would not be too big. The Criterion would be better, but I don't think it is available. The play is blessedly short and compact – and so exciting to play a part with *no* long speeches (Albee and Shaffer!) with a life to live all through and only a few short sentences full of implication and sensitivity. But, as you can imagine, it was hell to learn – hundreds of little cues and non-sequiturs. Thank God we had five weeks' rehearsals and the week at Brighton.

Binkie tells me he has sent you a play? He sent *Cher Antoine* (Anouilh) to me and I thought it dreadfully old-fashioned and filled with the cliché characters and situations of all his former plays. I was also asked to direct the Mart Crowley play [*The Boys in the Band*] for Los Angeles and New York – how common and awful it is. I well understand how it disgusted you.

To Hugh Wheeler   *23 June, London*

Here are the reviews of the new play, which is a huge success after all doubts and fears. Even Martin lyrical about it and when we read *The Times* review we both sat holding hands and weeping – very surprising spectacle, I must say. I do wish you could see it, I think you would love it. Whether we shall be able to hold the shape and concentration over the months is another question, but certainly at present it is as good as we can make it. It looks as if we shall transfer after the six weeks at the Court but I'm hoping the Court management will present it and not sub-let to Binkie, [Michael] Codron, Albery and others who are begging to take it over. It seems to us silly to let in middlemen when we did it as a gesture to the Court, and the director, author, actors and theatre should make the money to further the admirable record of the Court in getting interesting new work written and produced under the best conditions.

I've been somewhat low, as usual, with an eczema rash in my crutch and athlete's foot – my cross in nervous emergencies always – but am gradually recovering and beginning to enjoy the scene a bit more. Mac [his dresser] is able to go on with me, as it is such a simple play with no changes, which is nice. Also it is blessedly *short*, after the over-indulgence of Albee and Shaffer and I am rather proud of bringing off a part which, for once, hasn't a single long speech or opport[unity] of declamation or sustained rhetoric – quite different from anything I've ever done.

[Fred] Zinnemann is supposed to be making a film of *The Dybbuk* here in September, in which he wants me to play the old Rabbi who exorcises the spirit from the young girl – an effective part – but a gloomy (though powerful) script by David Rudkin but neither the money nor the leading lady yet decided, and I think it may fall through. Also there is a location stint (in Scotland!) which I couldn't agree to do if I was still acting in London. We shall see.

Meanwhile *Eagle in a Cage* is still to be released from last year. [*Julius*] *Caesar** is now on view and awfully bad, though I manage to be fairly effective in it. Jason [Robards] and Heston dreadful, awful colour and amateurish décor and costumes. A pity. I also gave a (highly truncated) Ghost in Richard Chamberlain's *Hamlet* TV for Hallmark – done à la Monk Lewis in 1820 costume – I look like Napoleon at Ascot, hardly have a word left and only manage to look fairly convincingly transparent! Would you kindly send on the cuttings to Irene W. I gather her Hedda is splendid, though she quarrelled with Peter Gill, the director, whom she had chosen herself. The review in *Newsweek* – a rave – was somewhat marred by a very ugly landladyish photograph, and the preface that she was 54 and 20 years older than Ibsen intended!

To Hugh Wheeler   *5 August, London*

We moved to the Apollo last week from the Royal Court where we never had an empty seat and are doing smashing business. I couldn't be more surprised and delighted. Everyone is mad about it – we do eight or twelve weeks there and Alex Cohen wants us to do it in N.Y. for Nov. and Dec. if we can get the Morosco or the Golden. It would be nice to go again and perhaps have Christmas in N.Y. – you know how I always hate it here.

Very hot here, but lovely walking the dogs on Hampstead Heath. I'm putting a seat near Kenwood House with a lovely view over the lake in Bernie's memory, much nicer than a dreary gravestone, don't you think? London packed with visitors and tourists, but that is good for business fortunately. They are taking up the road outside this house, which is rather hell with the drills, but we shall soon have a smart new street. M. is converting the cellar into a study for his books etc. so as to make room for more cages in the studio! Two owls now and a new white cockatoo. Madness, madness, but it keeps him busy, which is good.

---

* A new version in which JG played Caesar, Charlton Heston, Brutus, and Jason Robards Jr., Cassius.

Much enjoyed *Patton* – greatly to my surprise – and even *Woodstock*, though the noise drove me out after an hour. The Zinnemann film of *The Dybbuk* is postponed till next year. I think it may never be done. *Nijinsky* seems to be off too. Tony R. quarrelled with Saltzman and withdrew. I only hope he gets his money. Zeffirelli was supposed to be taking over, but now is announced to be casting again for *Francis of Assisi* (surely a part for M. somewhere!), so he can't be doing *Nijinsky*. I wonder how Scofield and Nureyev are placed, who were both supposed to do it.

Binkie has a dull programme of four plays announced, including Terry's Nelson piece with Zoë Caldwell. *Blithe Spirit* revival has opened next door to us and is said to be a success – Beryl Reid as Arcati. Noël, Coley [Cole Lesley] and Graham [Payn] came to the play last week. N. has been in bed at the Savoy for three weeks with pneumonia, but now recovered and they all went back to Switzerland yesterday. They look rather a sad and senior group, I'm afraid.

Irene ecstatically successful in Canada. Some talk of her doing *Hedda* [*Gabler*] in N.Y. with Claire [Bloom] alternating in *Doll's House*. I should think that a v. doubtful proposition and might be the end of a devoted friendship, as Claire would undoubtedly come off second best. Went to [*Oh*] *Calcutta** – seats presented me by Tynan! – very boring and unwitty.

In November, Home *transferred to the Morosco Theatre, New York.*

To Meriel Forbes   *November 1970, London*

I feel sure you know what happiness it has been for me to be with Ralph again in such an equal and firm success, especially when I think how we were both troubled in the initial stages. I only hope our dizzy dames [Mona Washbourne and Dandy Nichols] will stand the strain of the transplant without further mishaps, and that the New York theatre parties, whom I am sure are being vigorously proselytised for action at this very moment, won't make us regret that we ever left this none too salubrious metropolis!

To Paul Anstee   *12 November, New York*

I retired to bed as soon as I got here and have been miserable all week, crawling about the flat with aches and pains all over – just beginning to feel a bit better today. I suppose the bug I had in London was still lying in wait to pounce again. However, we had our first preview last night – marvellous audience and it couldn't have gone better. More laughs than in London and pin-drop silence in the sad bits. Everyone very excited and various people thronged

---

* Erotic revue devised by Kenneth Tynan.

round in waves of enthusiasm, so I hope all may be well. The old girls played up like anything and all their scenes went splendidly.

To Paul Anstee   *21 November, New York*

Big success, thank God, only competing with Keith [Baxter] and Tony Quayle next door [in *Sleuth* by Anthony Shaffer]. We have to go on three TV shows now to advertise ourselves, and engagements seem to come thick and fast. I may do a part in a film next month in N.Y. as well as the play, which would be nice dough and a change of clientèle – have not seen the script yet.

To Dorothy Reynolds and Angus Mackay   *27 November, New York*

The success is wonderful, press even better than in London. A few passages seem to confuse the public. Vale of Evesham and Gloster [*sic*] are curiously puzzling to them, it seems! But after a very exhausting first week, we are beginning to settle down. However, Ralph hates New York, and Dandy has to go back to England for her TV serial [*Till Death Us Do Part*], so I think we shan't be able to go on after Jan. 9th.

Martin has made the flat very handsome and comfortable, but misses his animals. Everyone all over us, of course, as we have a success! New York very beautiful in autumn sunshine but unbelievably expensive and thronged. However, it's all quite fun if one insists on resting between times. *Sleuth* [by Anthony Shaffer] next door has already paid off after only 23 performances. *Hay Fever* (with Shirley Booth) and Danny Kaye's 'Noah' musical [*Two by Two* by Peter Stone, Richard Rodgers and Martin Charnin] have been dreadfully slated. *Conduct Unbecoming* [by Barry England] is not the big success they hoped when it opened. The new Warhol *Trash* has to be seen to be believed.

To Irene Worth   *4 December, New York*

Glorious sunny weather here and we are to break the house record this week, which is rather smashing. But both Ralph and I dread the TV shows – now over thank God – David Frost yesterday, a whole hour of rather boring questions and answers.

Went to the Juilliard Drama School with [John] Houseman and Suria St Denis – wonderful classrooms, two theatres, superbly equipped – about 70 students who seemed to be a nice lot, but what it must have cost and where will they all find work after a 4 year course!

We are probably to go on after Jan. 9th when Dandy Nichols has to go back for a TV serial. L[indsay] Anderson back today to recast. We hope for

Mildred Natwick, a brilliant actress and Ralph is devoted to her – they were together in *Toreadors*.*

To Paul Anstee   *10 December, New York*

Our houses are still wonderful – broke the house record last week. They are trying to get Jessica Tandy to replace Dandy and we expect to go on four weeks after Jan. 9th and possibly 8! Also – believe it or not – I have been asked by Dick Barr to direct Albee's new play [*All Over*]! They want Peggy Ashcroft and Irene [Worth] to star in it. A powerful melodrama on the same lines as *Delicate Balance* – wonderful parts for everyone – all the characters in their sixties – all about deathbeds – extremely depressing but should be most effective and not obscure like *Tiny Alice*, thank God. So I expect I will do it – here – probably for March, which would mean being away a long time. Martin terribly worried about his animals – two of the iguanas have died – and I must say no light and heat, with fog and Christmas thrown in, sounds absolutely wretched for everyone. How lucky I am. Wonderful sunshine here in the flat and lots of parties and goings-on. Keith [Baxter] and the other English actors greatly fêted everywhere. We are going to put Bumble [Beatrice Dawson] in a hotel – can't face her falling flat on her face from this very abominable bathtub.

Now off to a lunch party at Florence [Reed]'s and to hear Leontyne [Price] sing some songs.

To Irene Worth   *18 December, New York*

Well, so you are to be in [the film of] *Nicholas and Alexandra*. I do hope it is a good part and a *lot* of money. Of course I am extremely disappointed you can't be in Edward's play, especially as I am certain the burying of the hatchet (as with Cecil [Beaton]) is greatly due to your influence and sweetness. I am very glad when feuds are made up – life is really too short for them (poor Molly Williams so suddenly gone). I am only hoping I may be able to work well with Albee and do a good job on the play, which is grim but powerful and has very fine acting parts for everyone. Have you read it? It would have been so fascinating to work again with you and Peggy, but perhaps we can all do *Borkman* together instead one day not too far distant.

The off-Broadway strike is over here but no taxis still. Fortunately for us, Ralph and I have both been provided with cars by Cohen for which I am extremely grateful. The play is still doing huge business and we have agreed to go on till Feb. 20th. Jessie Tandy is replacing Dandy Nichols on Jan. 11th – do hope (for her sake and Ralph's temper) she will be good. It is rather unlikely casting, but she wants to do it and is an old friend of mine.

---

* Ralph Richardson and Mildred Natwick appeared in *Waltz of the Toreadors* in New York in 1957.

1971

To Paul Anstee   *3 January, New York*

You can't believe how beautiful it is here – the snow on the Park and really hot sunshine on one's neck at breakfast. We read the Albee play today with a substitute cast for his and our benefit – possible cuts etc., quite a good idea, I think. Real cast not yet settled. Did I tell you I'm for Chichester in May to play Shaw's Caesar? Seems to haunt me, that one. Hope Anna Calder-Marshall will be good – saw her in a TV but not in *Vanya*, in which most people liked her but Martin didn't! Don't know if she is a comedienne. Will have to find a home for the four months – no money, of course, but I feel I ought to do it. Took Bumble to see *Trash* and a *filthy* film called *Hollywood Blue* in which a lady was fucked by a large dog! Also nipped in for half an hour to the boy cinema (used to be Henry Miller Theatre) and saw a bit of *Boys in Chains* – rather fun though utter tosh, of course. Had to leave for my theatre but plan another surreptitious visit – somewhat afraid of being recognised and Martin finding out. You would love it. Stills of naked boys to while away the interval! Jessica Tandy begins rehearsing tomorrow and takes over from Dandy next week.

To Alan Schneider   *9 January, New York*

I feel somewhat embarrassed about being asked to direct the Albee play [*All Over*], knowing that you have done so many of his previous plays and remembering your kindness and help during [*Tiny*] *Alice* – and the subsequent quarrel between him and me. I do suspect that our dear Irene had a lot to do with the reconciliation which she effected between us during Edward's visit to London last year. Even so, the last thing I ever expected was to imagine he would ever want to work with me again – and of course I was flattered to be asked! But I do feel it strange that you should be passed over and it seems a bit disloyal to you to accept the assignment as I have done.

I hope you are not badly hurt over the matter. I know you are busy with [*Waiting for*] *Godot* and only hope we may soon meet again. I just wanted you to know I am not so insensitive as to be unaware of the situation. Please accept my apologies if you can.

To Dorothy Reynolds and Angus Mackay   *14 January, New York*

I shall be staying until about the end of March or so, doing the Albee play, not altogether happy about it. Peggy [Ashcroft] and Irene [Worth] both unavailable, alas, now it is to be Jessica Tandy and probably Colleen Dewhurst and Madeleine Sherwood – three fine women's parts.

Now I have promised to play the Shaw Caesar at Chichester, May to Sept. with Anna Calder-Marshall and Robin Phillips to direct. I wrote asking who is to play Ftatateeta – couldn't they ask you? I think it is the best of the other parts, but perhaps you wouldn't fancy it? But we could have some fun, if only counting the house right, left and centre!

Jessica Tandy took over from Dandy who left, alas, last week – not a patch on her, of course, but it affects me less than Ralph and Mona, who are a bit depressed by the change. Alan Bennett's new play seems a long time in the womb, as no doubt he was himself!

To Paul Anstee   *17 January, New York*

Huge party last night given by Tony Shaffer and Keith [Baxter]. I had a long talk with an extraordinary transvestite who is a complete woman and pressed a fascinating photo of herself on me!

Thank you for sending the Calder-Marshall article – she had a very bad notice for *Wuthering Heights* but maybe they are wrong, as everyone in England seems to think so highly of her. Carl Toms is to do the *C. and C* décor, which will be nice, as I have never worked with him.

We go to see [*No, No*] *Nanette* [by Vincent Youmans, Irving Caesar, Otto Harbach, Frank Mandel and Burt Shevelove] next week, which everyone is saying is divine. Peter [Brook]'s [*A Midsummer Night's*] *Dream* opens on Wednesday. A big Jewish musical *Ari* [by Leon Uris and Walt Smith] opened to disastrous press. They are *not* wild about *Ari*! Our business dropped badly for a week but I hope is picking up again and will see us through. We are presented with *Evening Standard* Awards on Tuesday (TV and photos to be shown in London) and I gather we shall get a 'Tony' here, too. Ralph and I are a sort of twin team like the Denisons* now!

Emlyn Williams' wife, Molly, died in December 1970.

To Emlyn Williams   *24 January, New York*

I didn't write before because you were so short a time in England. I have thought about you very often, and remember the wonderful way you and Molly used to ring up almost every night to see how I was getting on when I had my 'trouble'. I am glad of course that you are working again so soon, but the eternal packing, and making polite nothings to strange people, and never knowing quite what city one is in, must be infinitely trying to your nerves and patience. Still, the old cliché of 'work the great healer' has, I imagine, something to be said for it. You must be glad to have the biography to occupy

---

* Michael Denison and Dulcie Gray.

you in between times. But then you have always been so industrious and interested in so many things. How long ago it is since *Spring 1600** – and Molly fresh from *Battling Butler* [by Stanley Brightman, Austin Melford, Douglas Furber and Philip Braham], and Rodney [Ackland] with his first play, and old Pa [Richard] Clowes and Frank Vosper – and then the success of your marriage and your own enormous success – and Daphne Rye and Richard [Burton] coming into our lives, and now it's all like a dream – very strange isn't it, getting old – somehow one never thought it quite possible – for oneself, I mean. What I hate so much is my own intensely selfish attitude when other people's tragedies occur. One immediately thinks 'What horror will *I* have to face – illness, operations, losing the few really important people – accidents? Plane crashes? Losing one's memory, unable to work? What next?' But I'm sure it all happens for each person in the most expectedly hellish way, and some curious instinct of resilience creeps in from somewhere and nudges you to go on in spite of all the misery.

Dear Emlyn, my love and admiration for your courage and devotion and be sure Molly would not have wanted you to grieve too desperately, though I can well imagine what a ghastly time this is for you to bear.

To Irene Worth   *28 February, New York*

I struggle with the Albee play. Jessica T., Colleen Dewhurst, Madeleine Sherwood, Betty Field, [George] Voskovec – a good cast and they all work very willingly and well – very difficult text, of course. I feel it is in such danger of becoming a gloomy and monotonous litany of woe, though the individual parts and speeches are all most interesting – integrating them terribly difficult, however.

Rehearsals for Chichester begin May 19th – I rather dread open stage, which is a new experience for me. Sure Edith will jib at it. I can't believe she will really go through with the Anouilh play [*Dear Antoine*] which is announced for the second attraction. I read it and thought it a great bore anyhow.

Alan Schneider has had fine notices for his new production of *Godot* in the Village. I gather he is very hurt at having been ditched by Dick [Barr] and Edward [Albee] without a word of explanation. I wrote him a little note which he acknowledged very sweetly. I do wish you had been able to be in the play – perhaps later on if it is done in London?

My niece Maina had quite a success here with the Béjart Ballet, which is common and crude, but a great success, especially with the young, despite a great panning in the press. She is a very dedicated and striking young woman (26!), independent and steely (with some of my hauteur!) on the stage, and everyone seems to think very well of her.

---

* JG directed Emlyn Williams' play in January 1934.

To Ralph and Meriel Richardson   *2 March, New York*

The Albee play is going more hopefully now, I think, in the third week of pregnancy. We had to sack our two deafies – the Nurse and the Doctor – and we have much more satisfactory replacements. Colleen Dewhurst is interesting if only she didn't slur all her most elaborate speeches.

I saw *Eagle in a Cage* yesterday. What a pity it is such a mess, because our scenes, and the boy Michael Williams, are really lively and good. But the rest – the two women mean nothing, the Negro and Ferdy Mayne lend no help, and [Kenneth] Haigh is efficient but awfully dull. The cutting and tempo only come to life in our bits. I fear it will never see the light of day (or Odeon?) and does not really deserve to.

I much enjoyed *Doll's House* and Claire Bloom was excellent, also [Patrick] Garland's direction and quite a good company. A great relief to be able to go round with honest enthusiasm. I had two awful evenings at *Applause* [by Charles Strouse, Lee Adams, Betty Comden and Adolph Green] and *School for Wives* [by Molière] – the latter had rave reviews and I thought it simply dreadful. Brian Bedford – of whom I am very fond – completely absurd and utterly miscast, like a promising RADA student trying to play Richard III! I don't think I shall risk *Hedda* or much else in the theatre – rehearsals are a good excuse.

Will you really come back for the awful Tony ceremony? I wish I had the courage of George Scott and could just say 'Don't suggest us, please.' It appears we closed to a delicious profit of 1,000 dollars – well, well!

To Paul Anstee   *13 March, New York*

It was so lovely seeing you, and you were so sweet and understanding, as always. Your letter to Martin gave him *enormous* pleasure – in his strange way. He told me he burst into tears reading it in a taxi! He does so long for personal approach – apart from me – and many people who really like him for himself are ready to give it him, if only he would make himself more approachable. Oh dear.

Dined with Robin Phillips – very nice and intelligent – excellent ideas for Carl [Toms], but my God – *six weeks* rehearsals in Chichester – no money all that time, so I must be clever about living. Hear the Wildings may have bought a house there, so possibly I can P.G. with them, which would be a wonderful solution. What a rave for P. Scofield in *The Times*. Don't fancy that play, though [*The Captain of Köpenick* by Carl Zuckmayer at the Old Vic].

To Paul Anstee   *24 March, New York*

Our previews go very well – critics begin to come these last five days – official opening on Saturday – everything depends on notices. A few rows over clothes and cuts, but on the whole fairly calm. The set and lighting are both splendid and it is very well acted. I think I have done a good job on the production. Albee has to be handled very carefully. The company splendid to work with and I have really enjoyed the work, and find the play far more fascinating now. But I don't know a bit if it will find a public in that huge house – there were great complaints of inaudibility at first, but I think it has been conquered now.

The awful Tony Awards on Sunday. Ralph flies back to sit with me, but it is all very embarrassing, as I gather only *one* award is given. Brian [Bedford] and Alec McCowen also nominated, so maybe one of them will get the 'best actor'! I gather they can't divide it for R. and me! Two hour programme at the Palace – excerpts from 20 years of musicals, speeches etc. etc., full TV coverage. Prudential pays Cohen a huge sum, and it is supposed to be great publicity for the theatre all over America. I dread the whole thing but will have to endure it.

All Over *opened at the Martin Beck Theatre on 27 March 1971.*

To Dorothy Reynolds   *28 March, New York*

The Albee opened last night and we wait for the critics with some trepidation. We had scenery and costumes and lights for a whole week in the theatre (Martin Beck, much too big unfortunately) before we began previews (ten days of them), so it was comparative luxury, and none of the agonies of a touring tryout. Not a 'likeable' play, none of his are, but fine acting parts and very fine speeches. The whole sad and a bit grim and needs concentration from the audience. Good notices would be the making of it. We shall see tomorrow.

[David] Hockney is supposed to want to paint me and Martin in one of his conversation portraits – might be fun.*

To Paul Anstee   *30 March, New York*

Great agony over the Albee play – a near rave from Clive Barnes, lethal attacks from the cheaper papers – *Time, Newsweek* etc. They have put up a preliminary notice to close this Saturday, but have taken a big ad in *N.Y. Times* tomorrow and say they will keep it on if weekend business warrants. Albee himself has had a collapse, and put to sleep for 24 hours. So I shall leave on Friday without knowing the play's fate – have offered to forgo my royalties if they keep it on, much to Martin's indignation.

Brian Bedford got the best actor Tony Award over me and Ralph!! The

---

* As far as I can tell, this picture was never painted, although Hockney did draw Gielgud solus in 1974.

Richardsons and Mona Washbourne both came back – paying their own fares. The ceremony was fairly jolly, all hands to the pump, but I thought it agonising, embarrassing and invidious, not that I care about winning. Brian was very sweet and suitably demure about the decision. The show rather good, because everyone mucked in and showed professionalism and goodwill, but I do hate the whole affair.

Saw the *Follies* [by James Goldman and Stephen Sondheim] – awful – *Company* [by Stephen Sondheim and George Furth], which bored me terribly. Shall learn Caesar and hope for the best.

All Over *ran for only forty performances. From New York, JG went to stay with Tony Richardson in the South of France before moving on to Tunisia.*

To Paul Anstee   *16 April, Saint Tropez*

Very sweet of you to remember my old birthday. Great time here – masses of odd visitors – Hugh [Wheeler] and Peter Bull both staying. Mad opera performance in the garden of *Cavalleria Rusticana* last night by two crazy Italian boys. David Hicks lunched (with the head waiter from the Casserole), said to Tony on leaving 'You live very casually here, don't you?'

To Paul Anstee   *21 April, Hammamet*

Martin met me and Hugh safely (of course, there were two different airports) and we are well ensconced here – big, cosy rooms with high ceilings, chilly at night and morning but hot sunshine all day. Lovely garden with sea at the bottom of it – expeditions and picnics – fine Roman ruins – towns and amphitheatres – general effect much cleaner than Morocco. Everyone very kind and gentle – sweet Arab cook who has no English and can't even write!

After his holiday he returned to England to begin rehearsals for **Caesar and Cleopatra.**

To Irene Worth   *31 May, Chichester*

You heard, of course, that the Albee play was an utter failure – no interest from the public at all, despite a fine notice from Clive Barnes, and they went on cuts after a week and staggered on for another three. I gather Peggy A. is still keen to do it at the Aldwych in the autumn, and Peter Hall is to direct. I greatly enjoyed working with the cast. Colleen Dewhurst and Madeleine Sherwood were particularly good – also Jessica and Betty Field – but Albee, though over complimentary to me caused great distress to the cast. I didn't feel I really wanted to be involved with the play a second time, though it may be far better in repertory.

Everyone very sad because Edith E., having opened triumphantly in the
Anouilh play, completely lost her nerve after the second performance and
ordered a car and drove home. I did not see her myself, but evidently her
nerve has gone for good and she will never act again – most tragic for her,
and of course an agony for poor Clements and Robin and the company, who
had worked so hard to make her happy and help her through. It's bad luck
on the public too, though the advance was huge and won't, I think, suffer.
The understudy adequate but quite undistinguished and now, with most of
the cast rehearsing the later plays, there is no possibility of another actress
coming in. Binkie, of course, wants to transfer it and talks of Lynn Fontanne,
but Robin says he won't direct it again for London, though his work on it is
brilliant.

Ralph is filming, doing a TV of *She Stoops to Conquer*, and is to be in the
new Osborne play in August. I am tying to get the Hammamet villa for him
to go there next month with Mu for two weeks' holiday. I know they would
love it. We made a TV of *Home* as soon as I got back with Lindsay and the
original cast. Rather a misery, as L. had never worked in the medium before
and was in violent disagreement with the technicians, so it took an extra day
of waiting about and exhausting adaptation, though what I saw myself seemed
pretty good.

Gwen is in S. Africa playing Edith's part in the same Anouilh play. I am so
glad for her, but wish she could have been in England as I think she is the
only person who might have staved off the disaster. I hear Sybil is still lively
despite her crippling arthritis. Amazing woman. Alec [Guinness] is filming
with Zeffirelli and does the [John] Mortimer play [*A Voyage Round My Father*]
(which was done at Greenwich earlier with Mark Dignam) at the Haymarket
in the late summer. Very bad luck on Mark, but he is now in the newly cast
Vivat! [Vivat! Regina] which I hope is a consolation. I've seen nothing except
Death in Venice, which I think is very disappointing though heavenly, of
course, to look at. Marvellous costumes and compositions, but the film itself
melodramatic and a bit vulgar, I thought, but maybe I was just jealous. It has
been hugely praised.

To Lillian Gish   *4 June, Chichester*

I've been living down here for six weeks rehearsing *Caesar and Cleopatra*.
The Cleopatra is a delightful and talented little girl [Anna Calder-Marshall]
(the film of *Wuthering Heights* did not do her any justice). She is tiny, only
22, and though she has a slight limp (from early polio) and big ears, she
is enchantingly pretty and acts most beautifully. I am mad about her and
feel she will make a big success. The production is most original and
daring, a sort of child's nursery with rocking horses, dolls, hoops etc. and
two chutes which we slide down on our behinds when we come down
from the Sphinx and dive into the sea in the lighthouse scene! I think the

serious passages are not at all diminished by the 'larks' of the comedy scenes, and the play emerges very well, with most of the gimmicks to cover the changes on the open stage.

It is a bit nerve-racking having no prompter within easy reach, and I have not yet experimented with an audience. However, we have a house full of schoolchildren tomorrow, and a charity preview on Tuesday before the critics come on Wednesday, so we hope to solve at least a few of the problems in the next few days, though naturally one is full of doubts and fears. The young director, Robin Phillips (who did *Tiny Alice* in London, and *Heloise and Abelard**) is extremely talented and we all love working with him, so the rehearsals have been very stimulating. This hotel only holds about 20 people and is run by two nice ladies, with excellent food, and the little village is almost on the creek, with a squat old church, the churchyard smothered with rose bushes, and a cluster of Dickensian timber cottages looking on to the flats, with many yachts and sailing boats.

How I wish you were to be in England this year. Do take care of your dear self, and I long as always for the sight of you.

Caesar and Cleopatra *opened on 6 July.*

To Irene Worth   *23 July, Chichester*

Well, Martin and I saw *Lear*† and were stunned with the beauty and power of it. Sat just behind Paul and Joy [Scofield]. (Patience [Collier] was there, of course, but I didn't see her afterwards to look if her nose was out of joint!‡) The notices today are maddeningly lukewarm – the first film critics seem to be away on holiday and the others give all their space to horrific notices of Ken Russell's obviously dreadful *Devils*. You were magnificent – absolutely convincing in every way, and the rest of the acting is without one mistake. How clever to use all those Irish actors so well, and [Tom] Fleming, Alan [Webb] and Susan Engel all as good as they could be. The story comes out so clearly, and Paul infinitely more satisfying (to me) than he was on the stage. His grating quality of voice and rather limited range vocally all works so much better with the close-ups – you see every thought and emotion as it comes to him – and he looks like Tolstoy. All the melodrama tempered with underplaying and strength – the cutting admirable. The only things I didn't much like were the titles (which seem suddenly old-fashioned) and a certain scanting of Cordelia's part. She is so good, but he gives her very little. The awakening scene (as in his production in the theatre) seems unlocalised and rather rushed over. I suppose Peter

---

* *Abelard and Heloise* by Ronald Millar.
† Peter Brook's film of his stage production, with Paul Scofield as Lear.
‡ Susan Engel played Regan, the part originally played by Patience Collier.

dreads being sentimental, but Shakespeare's *tent* with the silent doctor (we don't see him in the film) and Kent, and Lear carried in 'asleep in the chair' are so wonderful after all the storm scenes – though I love the two being hurried off and *separated* in going to prison (but we never see her as Queen of France, or the general of the relief army).

But everything else was *perfect* and by far the best filmed Shakespeare I have ever seen. If you don't get a wonderful contract offered you, I'm a Dutchman. I only hope the Sunday critics will be more perceptive. I was just enraptured by the whole conception and its superb achievement.

Our *Caesar* has also had a very mixed reception, though one or two of the critics (*Times* and *Financial Times*) loved it. I wasn't at all good on the first night. Too many hazards on the strange stage and pitch dark at the back – all those passages, no prompt corner – but now I am getting much happier and it goes wonderfully, though I have said I won't come to London in it as the whole production would have to be altered. Loved working with Robin who, of course, adores you, and the little girl is enchanting to work with. If only there had been a Bérard or Whistler to do the décor. Carl Toms is clever and efficient, but the scenery and costumes are all white – a great pity after *The Dream* and *Winter's Tale* and it is all a bit Peter Jones with a dash of Casa Pupo! He can't bear to be told (Robin) that he is influenced by Peter [Brook], but after *The Dream* it is a bit the same *kind* of production, only a bit camp, with all the young men in flimsy scanties, and I think that annoys some people. Martin, of course, detested it, and said 'Of course, it is a very good part for Rex Harrison' which I must say made me laugh. There are several excellent performances (Peter Egan, Pat Nye, [Michael] Aldridge). It's rather fun here, I must say – marvellous audiences and a delightful company though, of course, disastrous for the exchequer.

Peter Wood rang me to say the Shah [of Iran] wants me to make a Golden Disc welcoming the potentates to his Festival in October and to invite me to come out as a guest! Rather flattering, I must say, but I would rather have a new play. Ralph is rehearsing the new Osborne [*West of Suez*] with Anthony Page at the Court. I gather it is a fine part.

To Hugh Wheeler   *14 August, Chichester*

Martin thinks me stupid to have refused the Lear play [*Lear*] by Edward Bond, but though I have read it several times, I couldn't bring myself to do it. Harry Andrews is now doing it. They are mad I should do the Light Brigade-making comedy [*Veterans*] by Charles Wood (who wrote the dialogue for the film). It is certainly very funny, but I fear it is too much of an 'in joke' and there is argument about the director. [William] Gaskill wants to, but I would prefer Lindsay – have promised to consider it again if considerably cut and pulled together. After the New Year some possibility of a few days in a horror film, playing Robin Phillips' father!* Shall I end by competing with Vincent Price? Pirandello's *Henry IV* at Oxford? No!

Everyone seems to be getting terribly old. John P. so lame and deaf, Alan Webb living in his cottage at Haslemere – a sweet little house and a very nice small garden – but he typically left for America (having liked it) without discovering that they could build all around him. New houses are going up within a stone's throw. His sad brother lives with him, working and taking the blows, which I gather are manifold. I think he (Dennis) tipples on the side, and Alan in the open. He says he wants to act again, but looks very thin and frail. Enid Bagnold also tottering about (everyone I know seems to be wearing plastic hips!) and very miffed at not being wanted in the theatre. Quarrelling with Gladys Cooper, though she did manage a month or two at the Haymarket with *The Chalk Garden* revival, and is now taking it to the O'Keefe in Toronto (heavens!) and a Californian tour, so Enid really shouldn't be too cross.

I was mad about *Diary of a Mad Housewife* – and also Peter [Brook]'s *Lear* film, which had rotten notices, greatly undeserved in my opinion. I think you should see it if it is still around, but I feel the critics have killed it – it only ran three weeks in London. Peter and Irene W. should be back in London next month from Persia, I imagine. Scofield was much better, I thought, than on the stage – and also brilliant in [*The Captain of*] *Köpenick* which I saw at the National.

It is said that Larry is to remain officially head of the N.T. but Peter Hall – who was announced for Covent Garden but slipped out of it after an apparently disastrous *Tristan* and big row with Birgit Nilsson (who refused to do the arranged business in the production when she appeared in it) – is to take over at the National, though this has not yet been officially announced.

Paul Rogers has taken the N.Y. flat for a year – going over to replace T. Quayle in *Sleuth*. Tony Shaffer is now a millionaire. So you see you simply *must* dramatise a Patrick Quentin,† as we have all begged you to for so long. Now that the flat is let I am sure to get a New York offer, I suppose.

Wasn't *The Devils* awful? I couldn't sit it out. Now [Ken] Russell is making a film of *The Boyfriend* with Twiggy, if you please. Must go to lunch with Christopher Fry, who lives near by.

To Hugh Wheeler   *23 October, London*

I had a marvellous two weeks at Nid du Duc. Tony [Richardson] only stayed a day or two as he is trying desperately to get backing for one or other of his still abortive films. Have been working quite hard on a little book of theatre reminiscences to be called *Distinguished Company*. I started it at Chichester

* For whatever reason, he did not play the part.
† The nom-de-plume under which Hugh Wheeler wrote a number of detective stories.

and I think it is almost finished. Heinemann seem to fancy taking it. I hope so. It may amuse you as it is nostalgic for our generation, though I don't suppose it will mean anything to anyone under 40.

I have a big TV interview coming out on Nov. 7th – my Jubilee if you please, with Patrick Garland. I did it in a garden by the cathedral at Chichester and I hear they have a lot of good photographs and film clips. I am to see it next week. Also I did the narration for Charles Castle's programme on Noël, in which everyone takes part. It is not bad, though Noël himself looks sadly bewildered and talks very slowly. I was just in time, however, to prevent them closing it with a shot of him sitting lonely in a very unsuitable sky blue jacket in the sitting room at Les Avants, accompanied (imagine!) by Cleo Laine singing 'Mad about the Boy' at the top of her voice!! There was a nice Chelsea party for the [Norman] Parkinsons, where Michael York was more velvety divine than ever, his wife too, of course.

Joyce C[arey] seems very sprightly, but they chose a day when she had a bad cold to photograph her for Noël's programme and she seems sad and old in it which is a shame. The Lunts have been here more indefatigable than ever, though he's very blind and walks with difficulty. They had been to Paris, and to see Noël in Switzerland where they reported he was very much better and in good form. As Chaplin and Mountbatten were also there, no doubt he made a special effort. Sybil Thorndike (89 tomorrow) was expected to die but I rang this morning to hear she had gone out for a drive! [Margaret] Rutherford and Edith Evans both seem to be waning fast. Oh dear, the fell hand.

Went to the Round House with Irene. The French *1789* was a bit like *Orlando Furioso* – 2½ hours standing on one's feet turning like a teetotum to see what one was missing on the various stages. I think they make a big mistake to have so much dialogue when they play out of their own countries. One narrator (or two) speaking in English and plenty of music would set the whole thing off far more satisfactorily.

The Gorky play *Enemies* and Etherege's *Man of Mode* both rather so-so, though each had two good performances from the same actors, Helen Mirren and John Wood, both new to me. Alan Bates good in *Butley* [by Simon Gray], a rather unequal play but fairly amusing, and I thanked God it wasn't Nicol Williamson. The new Alan Bennett play [*Getting On*] with Kenneth More bored me considerably, but has had excellent notices and is a smash hit. Lucky Toby [Rowland]. Of course he is delighted as there were hideous rows at rehearsals and during the tryout, and Alan won't come near the theatre. Mona Washbourne divine as usual and much the best thing in it.

Ronald Eyre, who directed *Three Months Gone* [by Donald Howarth] and *Voyage Round My Father* [by John Mortimer] is to direct the Charles Wood play. I wish you could read it but I have only one copy and that is subject to a lot of alterations.

Paul [Anstee] has sold his cottage. His dad died, the stepmother is a confirmed alcoholic so I think it will not be long before he is quite well off. Good.

1972

At the beginning of 1972, JG started rehearsals for Veterans, *a new play by Charles Wood.*

To George Pitcher   *13 January, London*

Thank you so much for sending the *Eagle* [*in a Cage*] cutting. I am only in the last half hour of the picture, so if you go to it to see *me*, you need not rush your dinner! – Irene has a new play [*Notes on a Love Affair* by Frank Marcus] – three characters only – goes into rehearsal next week. I've not read it but she is excited about it. We work terribly hard. I have an enormously long and difficult part but very fine material if I can hammer the words into my head, and I think the play is very distinguished and should be extremely amusing. A sort of skit on Christopher Fry dialogue and comic situations, most original. Like the director very much and all the cast save one young man who may have to go!

I like *French Connection* but could not attempt to understand the plot. Did you?

Veterans *opened at the Royal Court on 9 March 1972.*

To Hugh Wheeler   *13 March, London*

Surprise, surprise. After an appalling four weeks of ghastly disapproval at Edinburgh, Nottingham and Brighton, people walking out in rows and writing insulting letters (I had one enclosing a postal order for 40 pence, as I must be hard up to appear in such a play), we opened at the Court last week to a hysterically amused audience and rave notices. Harold Hobson the sole disapprover – common, vulgar rubbish, how could I soil my talent etc. However I am not going to bring it in to the West End as I think it far too special and shoppy. All the pros adore it, but it bewildered and irritated the hoi polloi.

Luckily enough we finish April 8th and I have to fly to Hollywood to play that silly old H. B. Warner part in *Lost Horizon* with Peter Finch – 10 or 12 weeks and a *huge* salary, so I could not turn it down, and it all fits splendidly.

M. and I were invited to Budapest for the Burton do, but I couldn't face all those celebrities. Emlyn's son (my godson) made a scene at the party and was thrown out. Poor Emlyn – and his great friend Ann Plugh is the mother of the girl who was murdered by Malcolm X in Trinidad. What a year he has had, poor Emlyn.

To Peter Hall   *21 March, London*

So good of you to write. An extraordinary division of opinion – so many people detest the play, think it cheap and smutty and resent my being in it – and then such praise and appreciation from the other side. Anyway, I think it's something of a charade, and not very well cast (or, between you and me, directed) and I know I am right not to transfer in it or do it in America. Charles Wood is clever, but very obstinate and eccentric – could not find ways to tidy it up on tour. Now, of course, he is very disappointed.

To Edith Evans   *9 April, London*

I am off to California to do a remake of *Lost Horizon* with Peter Finch. Your *Chalk Garden* man, Ross Hunter, is the producer. I have Gladys Cooper's house in Santa Monica – now belonging to Marti Stevens – which should be infinitely pleasanter than an hotel as well as less expensive. The part is an idiotic walkabout, not a moment that gives one the slightest opportunity to act and I feel a bit ashamed of the bribery that makes me accept it. But I had a bad income tax disaster three years ago and this should help to put me straight again (and leave another vacancy at Denville Hall* with any luck!).

To Paul Anstee   *15 April, Hollywood*

The film is going to cost 6 million dollars, so let's hope the music will be the making of it – nothing else will! I have christened it 'Hello, Dalai'!

To Dorothy Reynolds and Angus Mackay   *May 1972, Hollywood*

Strange, improbable life here. I am Portia in the Trial scene with a hint of Von Stroheim's grandson by Yul Brynner. The last of summer (my remaining locks) shaven and shorn and bits of glove-stretcher stuck in the corners of my eyes next my nose to make me look Chinky. Yards of fox fur for the blizzard scene to be shot in Bronson (Albery?) Canyon in blazing heat. I shall strip beneath the coat in order to survive, as Graham Robertson told me he did when he sat for Sargent in that long black overcoat with the jade walking stick and the poodle (only to achieve the thinness, he hastily added), the one in the Tate.

---

* A home for retired or less fortunate actors.

We have an enchanting bungalow house with roses blooming, a heated pool, a sweet Italian maid like [Anna] Magnani who also cooks, and a view of the golf course, on which all the players trundle in little white go-cars – not like my own exhausted reminiscences of trudging round Crowborough carrying my brother's heavy clubs and drinking my first gin and ginger beer on the terrace at the end of it.

An extremely tame blue jay swoops in and out of the windows, nipping food out of the kitchen and eyeing us as we sit at table. Martin will no doubt carry him round on his shoulder before long. We are getting brown. Saw a hilarious cartoon *Fritz the Cat*, very rude and violent but brilliant and refreshingly un-Disney (though I much enjoyed a day in Disneyland as usual – marvellous new ride, Pirates of the Caribbean).

Hedda on the box, indeed! And Jill [Bennett] doing it in the new Osborne version at the Court. Those pistols do trigger off a lot these days. Ingmar Bergman is doing *his* version of *The Wild Duck*, I see, in Oslo (or Stockholm?). The Greeks seem to have had far too many words for it at the Aldwych and *Yerma** sounds a bit tricksy, to say nothing of the heaving billows in *Coriolanus* at the New Stratford (The Nunn Story).

They say the Bacharach score is splendid but I have not heard it, and thank God I don't have to pretend to sing as [Peter] Finch and the others do. Liv Ullmann (also from the Bergman stable) is a beautiful girl and a lovely contrast to the other two girls, Sally Kellerman and Olivia Hussey. Fantastic monastery set going up on the back lot – rebuilt it from the castle in *Camelot*! Well, well.

Ross Hunter, the producer, looks and behaves like Stanley Hall, beaming and enthusiastic with large Olivier tortoiseshells and a very indifferent toupée!

To Paul Anstee   *22 May, Hollywood*

I did five days gruelling work on the canyon set, swathed in my furs, wind machines hurling plastic snow in our faces and appallingly uncomfortable and hot. Now we have moved to the Fox Ranch where there are pastoral scenes and a big number with the children to be shot. I have a fine caravan to retire into when I work – colour TV, air conditioning, a folding bed and heating and, of course, a loo! So I don't think I can complain of un-star treatment!

Martin is more copper colour than ever and planting furiously as he tends the garden. Rena screams à la Magnani a good deal and plunges about like a giraffe. Hugh [Wheeler] threatens to come in June – his new musical [*A Little Night Music*], Hal Prince-Sondheim, is announced – adapted from *Smiles of a Summer Night* (the Bergman film you probably remember).

---

* The Nuria Espert Company from Spain appeared in Lorca's play in the World Theatre Season at the Aldwych Theatre; the set, designed by Victor Garcia, was a raked trampoline.

To Nancy Hamilton   *24 May, Hollywood*

I see that your revue is opening or has just opened and I wanted to send you my good wishes. I hope you are pleased with it and working with a company and director that you like and that it will be a great success again for you.

The film progresses very slowly and I have a difficult walkabout part. They have shaved my head and put pieces in the corners of my eyes to make them Chinky, and the sets are colossal Hollywood erections, if you know what I mean.

To Maina Gielgud   *7 June, Hollywood*

Very sweet of you to take time to write and tell me all your news. I am so glad you are pleased with your new contract and decisions. You evidently believe, as I do, that a success in classical work is the best thing to lay the foundations of a career. I imagine it is in some ways the same in dancing as in the theatre.

My love to your mother and please thank her for her last card from Newcastle. I have always detested touring, but I suppose it is inevitable in your world, and you don't seem to hate hotels and a lack of your possessions around you as I have always done.

Weather very changeable – 100 degrees one day and 65 the next, thunder and rain and we have lost several days because of the weather. We are still working on location exteriors for which sun is essential. Crowds of Asiatic extras, water buffaloes, goats etc., marvellous sets, half fake, half natural, but the dialogue is boring and sentimental. Peter Finch and Michael York are nice, also the Norwegian actress Liv Ullmann, beautiful and sweet. The music is clever but mostly the voices are doubled as the actors can't sing! I am not supposed to, I'm glad to say.

To Paul Anstee   *13 June, Hollywood*

Ghastly do for the Lunts last Sunday.* I sat at the grand table with them, Ronald Reagan and wife, Jack Benny and wife, George Burns and others – a stupefyingly bad band, wretchedly badly placed mikes and a show of sorts – film clips and endless 'turns' with tributes. 8 to 12.30. Couldn't hear a word, either at the table or elsewhere. I did a couple of sonnets at midnight. Uneatable food and scores of photographers and fans thronging the hotel lobby and sidewalks. They looked dreadfully old, she had had a fall and hurt her back, and he is almost blind, but they were manoeuvred into a little box at the side of the stage and suffered nobly through the endless entertainment, ending by making a charming double speech – the only bearable event in the evening.

---

* *An Evening with the Lunts*, Beverly Hilton Hotel.

Of course, I had to get up at 5.45 next morning and had a long speech in close-up to do at 7 p.m. Then my eyes were cracking as usual and they will have to retake it! I believe we are about a week late on schedule. Read a really *filthy* book called *Lord of the Dark Places* by Hal Bennett [published in 1970], in paperback. If you should see it on a bookstall, it is worth a glance – far dirtier (as advertised) than *Last Exit to Brooklyn*!

Nobody drinks round here except me and Peter Finch!

Tony Newley asked me to play God in a dreadful new musical concocted by him and Leslie Bricusse. Very dull music, I thought, and an extremely vulgar book. For Broadway in the fall. No, no.

To Alan Schneider   *24 June, Hollywood*

I am playing a very stupid part in the remake of *Lost Horizon* in Tibetan Portia robes and a shaved head. The make-up man will be the only one to take any credit, as the role is practically non-existent, a sort of Fitzgerald travelogue character. But I am glad to earn some over-payment after two seasons of 'art' at Chichester and the Royal Court, which do not help to swell the exchequer and I must have a nest egg against senility, loss of memory and the other impending onslaughts of the enemy!

To Michael York   *June 1972, Hollywood*

The earth was so dry yesterday that all the yellow flowers died on the hill and they had to *paint* them in again. Well, well. See you soon.

To Paul Anstee   *25 June, Hollywood*

I gather Martin told you about the offer to direct the musical – revival of *Irene* [by Hugh Wheeler, Harry Tierney and Joseph McCarthy] – in October. I am rather keen to do it. They will pay me a good percentage, and I believe it might be very successful. Met Debbie Reynolds, who sang five or six songs to me with great energy and charm. They do have indefatigable application those ladies, [Carol] Channing, [Mary] Martin, [Lauren] Bacall etc. and she seems similarly dedicated and enthusiastic. The numbers are old but very pretty and melodious – lots of songs and dancing, 1919 period. Billy de Wolfe, who is to play opposite her – a male dressmaker but not very camp – is said to be very amusing and nice too. The only drawback – they want to rehearse *here* all through October, then four weeks each in Philadelphia and Boston – a new theatre, the Astor in Times Square to be opened with it beginning of January, so I would have to give 12 weeks to do it.

We stagger on – hours and hours of waiting about. I saw one sequence on the screen – a number with the children, sung by Liv Ullmann (dubbed) and Finch and I wandering by. I looked all right and fairly *thin* and imposing, though the lines are such awful clichés. Otherwise it was really rather beautiful to hear and look at.

Cukor is back from Spain, v. pleased with his film* and working with Maggie Smith and Alec McCowen. We are to go to Las Vegas and on to the Grand Canyon with the [Michael] Yorks next weekend. Mrs Y. is very like Adrianne [Allen] – great bossiness and pressing telephonage, but Martin has taken a great fancy to them both – I prefer *him*, natch. They are mad health cranks – no spirits and endless health foods, so I feel more gluttonous than ever, and M. won't even cook fish or eggs any more – however!

I loathed *The Godfather* and have seen nothing else. Oh, yes, *Cabaret* which I enjoyed. M. [Michael York] is charming and [Liza] Minnelli extremely clever, though quite miscast. Joel Grey wonderful – loved all the numbers.

To Lynn Fontanne and Alfred Lunt   *24 July, London*

Oh that evening . . . so maddening to be with you and not able to talk for the bloody band, and the way you both stuck out that endless entertainment so well meant but so protracted. Noël's festival at the Phoenix last year was so splendidly timed and efficient. Nobody ought to be allowed more than ten minutes each, at most, on those auspicious occasions, and Mr [Raymond] Burr was not the most cheerful master of ceremonies. It was all well worth while for the glimpse of you both and your enchanting speech of thanks, but you must both of you have been exhausted. How I should adore to come and see you at Genesee. Alas, I had to spend four gruelling days in New York – impossibly humid and tiring. Saw a school musical called *Grease* [by Jim Jacobs and Warren Casey] which might have been in Choctaw – only a few rude words could I hear or recognise – and the Bernstein Mass was appallingly vulgar.

Noël was here last week, very bright and on the spot, but receiving in red pyjamas and not much good at the walking, I'm afraid.

Back in England, JG directed Maggie Smith and Robert Stephens in Noël Coward's Private Lives after which he returned to New York to rehearse Irene.

To Paul Anstee   *29 October, New York*

I am amused at your going to Byam Shaw's school (Glen's dad, as I'm sure you knew). I once took a few life classes there myself in my extreme youth – fascinated, of course, by the model's jockstrap – a term that always embarrassed me so much that I didn't dare to pronounce it. I once (aged 19) entered a rubber shop in the Charing X Rd to try and buy one (for the theatre, of course) and was presented with a medical version!!

---

* *Travels with My Aunt.*

I sat in a rash draught and have acute rheumatic jabs in my lumbar region in consequence. We rehearse in fourth floor studios on 56th St and Broadway – quite convenient but hellish noise of traffic, and the cast two inches from one's nose. Looking glasses all round the walls, telephones ringing interminably and endless deprivation of company to go to singing or dance rehearsals in adjoining rooms. So I have had two days and a half already when I could do no work myself at all – very frustrating. Designs beautiful but dreadfully late, costumes only half designed, estimates far too wary and demands that things should be cut down. Hugh very helpful but somewhat hysterical, sitting beside me and *hating* Billy de Wolfe, who is a silly old closet queen in a wig (about my age) and no actor at all. I refuse to sack him, as we have had so little time to work so far, and Patsy Kelly and la [Debbie] Reynolds obviously love him and want to help him on. He still dances quite well, but with Hugh's speeches, which are rather good – oh la la! Maybe he will give up gracefully of his own accord, or we shall have to replace him on the tryout, but I feel I must give him a chance to learn the words and relax a bit. He is obviously terrified, after some years of TV short appearances, but I must admit he is something of a liability so far.

The juvenile is a heavy bore, square as Trafalgar and heavily 'method' – wants a psychological reason for everything, but I think I can knock some sense into him in time – à la Bob Stephens.

Kitty Carlisle (Mrs Moss Hart) turned down the part of the boy's Mother, in which she would have been perfect, on the grounds of salary, billing, No. 4 dressing room etc., so we have to make do with a very untalented Winifred Evans-ish lady of very little acting talent, who sings quite well but is devoid of style and can't time an acting speech to save her life.

So there are three heavily weighted disadvantages in the cast. Debbie and the others – Patsy Kelly especially – will be excellent however, and it is early days to make final decisions, I suppose. But as Hugh has written so well, it is a shame not to have better performers to speak his lines.

The choreographer is a dear little (non-queer!) Italian called Peter Gennaro, very efficient indeed, and most inventive and helpful. He is also stone deaf, and even with a hearing aid has to stand practically touching me in order to hear anything I say, and then I talk too fast and he doesn't get half of it. The boys and girls and stage management etc. very sweet and work their guts out all day long, but a lot of the music – entries into numbers, accompaniments etc., and even a couple of actual songs are not yet decided on or composed, so it's all a bit fraught as you can imagine.

Rouben was mugged the other night on 1st Avenue – only 20 dollars but all his credit cards etc. and I gather he has a large black eye. All the elderly ladies, Gish, Cornell, Florence, sound on the telephone to be breaking up apace, though Margalo [Gillmore] is still indefatigably gay. Emlyn (who gives three Dylan Thomas Recitals next week) is staying with her, and they come to dinner on Friday.

Silly old Harry Rigby (the producer), anxious to get in with Martin, dropped some hint to him on the telephone about Hugh and the going to the queer movies, so that was a mild crisis which I endeavoured to lie my way out of. Actually, I always go alone, and maybe not any more as *everyone* seems to know me in the filthy streets, and television seems to make one impossibly familiar.

Saw a preview of *Pippin* [by Roger O. Hirson, Bob Fosse and Stephen Schwartz] – terribly boring book – with a message – but brilliantly directed (Bob Fosse) and designed (Tony Walton). It will certainly be a big success but, with no interval, a somewhat exhausting evening.

To Paul Anstee   *12 November, New York*

Having a perfectly dreadful time – Billy de Wolfe resigned on the plea of illness, returned, lost his voice, we spent (and wasted) two days trying to get James Coco and he got a film and turned us down. Endless discussions and suggestions, wasting hours, so that I get no rehearsal. Now de Wolfe is back *again*, making great effect with generous offer to open after all in spite of strain. I try to insist he should only play Toronto and that we have a good replacement *now* for matinées in Toronto and opening in Philadelphia. All the scenery and costumes are late, half of them not even designed, but scrabbled together out of contemporary magazines, immense costs of over-time, and no dress parade till we get to Toronto, where I am hoping we shall be announced as previews and the critics staved off for the first three nights at least. New lyrics and musical arrangements coming in all the time, which they have to go off and learn, so Hugh and I sit on hard chairs wringing our hands and drowning our sorrows in the bottle. Debbie is, thank God, extremely helpful and does all she can to force them to organise properly, but she can't, of course, do everything and doesn't know her words yet. Still, I think she at least will turn up trumps.

Maddeningly, de Wolfe's part needs a funny man – at all costs, able to be married to Patsy Kelly in the last scene, with a lot of fairly elaborate dialogue which needs skill, and two numbers, one of them with a dance. Not important enough for a star like Danny Kaye or Zero Mostel, but a broad comedian – and they all seem to be on the Coast earning vast fortunes in TV. I keep auditioning N.Y. actors without success. Cyril Ritchard would be perfect, but tied up in *Sugar* [by Jule Styne, Bob Merrill and Peter Stone]. It's all madly flustrating* and just what everyone said it would be, only more infuriating because I can do nothing much to get it fixed. Get very tired and come home every night, have dinner and stagger off to bed.

It appears that poor old Florence [Reed] has artiosclerosis. I spoke to her one day but she was hopelessly gaga and repeated the telephone no. wrong

---

* A Bernie Dodge neologism.

about six times. Very sad. Lillian Gish is laid up too, and Cornell also has hurt her back, so everyone is breaking up apace.

To Irene Worth   *8 December, Toronto*

The temperature goes up and down with the work just as the weather does. Cold and gusty one minute and comparatively mild the next. All sorts of rows and emergencies which blow up and last for 24 hours and then simmer down again as the next crisis comes heaving into sight. Most of it is unnecessary and highly exhausting. I am not used to inefficiency in so many different departments, *three* producers to consult or appease or accept suggestions from, and fury from each individual boss (choreographer, conductor, designer, to say nothing of the cast – 50 strong) if things are interpolated, cut or changed without them being informed first and given a chance to air their separate views.

New songs are needed, costumes still unfinished (Debbie R. has a completely new set by Irene Sharaff to go in at Philadelphia – she has been wearing a whole set of her own up till now, as the ones designed for her were quite hopeless and she rightly threw them out).

Hugh very temperamental about his book, resenting changes and cuts which he does not approve and the actors all gagging and disputing lines they don't like (with some of which I am bound to say I agree). He has now left us to start his other musical for Hal Prince (a version of the Ingmar Bergman film *Smiles of a Summer Night* with Glynis Johns and Hermione Gingold), but he telephones me furiously all the time with new lines and suggestions for the show, and two young writers are being brought in to add some funny bits and pieces which are very necessary. So I see myself umpiring desperately with the three of them for the next six weeks.

To add to all this, Debbie lost her voice and has had a chill, cutting her two ballads at night and making a speech of apology to the audience at the end. Luckily I get on extremely well with her, though she is a bit bossy and interfering, and hates the leading man [Monte Markham] – and he her. He is very good in the part, but a crashing bore who argues interminably and tries to bring Method motivation into his scenes as well as directing and criticising Debbie quite impertinently. We have an impossible dowager [Ruth Warrick], who looks splendid in the clothes and sings quite well but can't act *at all*, and Patsy Kelly is a splendid old vaudevillian low comedy film girl, whom the audiences adore, but outrageously overacting as long as they encourage her, which unfailingly they do. George Irving, who replaced Billy de Wolfe (thank God!) is brilliant, easy to work with and a tower of strength. I am only afraid he shows up Debbie, who dances and clowns most resourcefully and delightfully, but finds it impossibly difficult to project effectively without the hand mike which she is used to in nightclubs, and though there are hidden mikes all over the stage, she sounds thin both in the ballads and long spoken speeches.

All this must sound very boring to hear about, I'm afraid. One becomes obsessed by the irritations of having to stand through it every night (we do packed business and they seem to love it, despite all the bad patches) and trying in an hour or two (we only can rehearse from 1 till 6, and the dancing and singing coaches insist on most of that time) to put in the cuts and tightening up that is required. Everything seems so slow. But I try and be patient and believe that, if too many people don't split up everything so far achieved, we *may* be ready for New York after the five Philadelphia weeks.

To Ralph and Meriel Richardson   *19 December, Philadelphia*

We have our ups and downs. Endless conferences, arguments and tantrums. Frustrating days of twiddling my thumbs while dances and songs are endlessly rehearsed, and new book material discussed but as yet unwritten. The word scenes are only links between the numbers, and the naive plot has to be nipped in somehow to the continual dismay of the actors (who can't really act) and their lines are cut, improvised, wrongly remembered or transposed in the most desultory fashion. Pages are retyped and lost, stage management tearing their hair at changes in setting and striking necessitated by altered dialogue, choreographer and conductor screaming for their rights, an inefficient lighting expert (?) and *three* producers to appease, each with individual urges for alterations. So you can see I live in an amazing world of intrigue, internecine feuds and bafflement of every kind. We open here on Thursday with five more weeks of this kind of chaos to try and ride. Then a fortnight of New York previews in a brand new theatre yet untried for sound.

The press here says that Celia [Johnson] and Maurice Evans are wanted for *Lloyd George [Knew My Father* by William Douglas Home] in New York! They did approach *me* too, but not on your Nellie! American managements are so extraordinary – they want to do *Days in the Trees*, that rather boring [Marguerite] Duras play which Peggy [Ashcroft] played at the Aldwych. So far Irene [Worth] and [Elisabeth] Bergner have been approached – now they talk of Ingrid Bergman!

We live in barren dance studios and ghastly hotel ballrooms with everyone knitting or doing petit point (the chorus boys, of course), munching sandwiches and spreading endless gossip. The outside world seems quite remote.

Martin has had the New York flat painted and redecorated the big bedroom very cleverly with blue material walls, doors and curtains – looks extremely pretty. I saw the *Travels with My Aunt* film – very heavy and uneven. Maggie Smith brilliant though, a caricature which the others can't match. Alec McCowen very good. Maggie is far more like Queen Elizabeth than Glenda Jackson.

To Paul Anstee   *29 December, Philadelphia*

I am slogging away rather miserably – everything is so appallingly slow – learning new dances and numbers, re-shaping dialogue, putting in cuts etc. etc. The business is frightfully good, but I stand through every performance, more and more aware of the weaknesses and able to rehearse about an hour and a half a day, so I hang about biting my nails and trying to keep calm. It looks as if we shall stay here an extra week and not open till the second week in February in New York. It is a seemingly endless stint, and I shall really be glad to get through with it, for better or worse.

Dismayed to hear *Lost Horizon* is terribly bad – hideous colour, Peter Finch far too old – and that it has been chosen for the Royal Performance in London in March – hope I may be otherwise engaged that evening. Poor Mrs Windsor – the things she does for England.

The new writer, a Jew called Jo Stein, who wrote *Fiddler* and *Zorba* has put in some good new material, jokes etc. for Patsy Kelly, but the cast are so slow and obstinate about learning and substituting lines and business, and of course it's a dreadful bore rehearsing one version and playing another, with orchestra, scene changes and stage management all involved in any different bits, and a lighting or scene rehearsal costing the earth in crew wages.

Arnold and Milton [Goldman] were here yesterday – quite encouraging, but Milton got very drunk at a terrible dinner they took us to – two middle-aged queens as hosts with a hideous house – well-meaning, and I was promised a superb meal, which was a hideous exaggeration. Well, well.

1973

JG was sacked during the Philadelphia try-out and replaced by the American director Gower Champion.

To Irene Worth   *6 January, Philadelphia*

I am so very sorry to have felt I couldn't do *The Seagull.* You know how I would have loved to work with you again, but I just feel I can't cope so soon after the rather horrific three months I have had here, much as I love the Chekhov play – and you.

I am getting out of *Irene* – they have decided to remain on the road for another month, so will not open in New York till March. Everything is still a chaos of disagreements and suggestions for improvement, and I have given so many weeks to go along with it, but Gower Champion has suddenly become available to take over the whole thing and I am very relieved to be done with it all – though it does seem to have been rather a wretched waste of time, especially with no-one around to trust or make friends with, though Debbie Reynolds has behaved very well indeed and I do like her very much.

To Paul Anstee   *20 January, New York*

The whole *Irene* business was most unpleasant and rather humiliating. I will tell you all about it when I come back. They are now having the impertinence to ask me to cut my royalties by 50 per cent, and leave my *name* on the production for the 4 weeks in Washington! Audrey Wood, Arnold, Milton and Laurie [Evans] all say I have a cast iron contract, and they play in Philadelphia to only 100,000 dollars a week, so I am determined not to give in as it was all done in the most backhanded and insulting way.

Terrific do last Sunday for Noël's visit to *Oh! Coward* Invitation Performance. Everyone in the theatre was there and I really enjoyed it a hundred times better than *Cowardy Custard* – only three people, all good, and admirably slick and selective – not a minute too long. Noël shuffled in, poor old pet, and held court in the interval. Marlene in dark glasses, velvet bandeau and pink and gold Chinese pyjamas, played nursemaid, and Iras and Charmian* sat discreetly in the row behind. A big party afterwards in a tatty restaurant, and Noël was almost carried in and out by two hefty gents whom I didn't know. Marlene's TV a great disappointment, and now she's suing Rex Reed, to whom she gave a rashly frank interview panning everyone and everything, and Alex Cohen is said to be suing *her* for what she said to Rex Reed about him and has cancelled the tour she was expecting to do.

Binkie urging me to return at once (as usual!) to discuss directing Maugham's *The Constant Wife* with Ingrid Bergman. But Laurie [Evans] says she doesn't want to do it much. Eight weeks on tour and television to follow for Granada, but not London. I can't imagine why not – it reads very well and would be fun to do, but sophisticated and tacky in the old 1926 French windows style. I should think it would not get over in the big provincial theatres, but is ideal for a moderate sized house in London. We shall see what happens. It would have been a great bore to go on tour with it and it needs a slap-up cast in all the parts, especially with the statuesque Miss B. who is a dear but obviously no great shakes as a light comedienne, although she draws enormous audiences.

To Hugh Wheeler   *17 March, London*

I am doing a TV play with only two characters – sort of thriller, set in deepest Cornwall where we did four very mushy days in deep mud and sporadic

---

* Probably Cole Lesley and Graham Payn.

downpours on location before we started rehearsing – the cart before the horse, it seemed to me, but apparently the studio has to see the weather first and match up to it. It's a very good part, eccentric old clergyman who imprisons the organist (don't laugh) he has advertised for in his terrible old house. He conducts services in an empty church and paints the bedroom doors with Biblical names. Apparently the episode really took place in the tiny church we filmed at – very spooky.

The Constant Wife is fixed for the end of July, and I have to rehearse John Standing to replace [Robert] Stephens in *Private Lives* – he is leaving to play Trigorin with Irene at Chichester, directed by Jonathan Miller. Maggie [Smith] is hysterical, voiceless and distraught – the marriage on the rocks etc. so I don't look forward to the work. She is giving a dreadful caricature of a performance – mad clowning and exaggeration and permanent laryngitis. Not easy to remonstrate, especially as the houses continue packed.

Very delighted with your [*A Little*] *Night Music* success.

Have seen nothing but *The Misanthrope* – quite brilliant – at the National.* Diana Rigg wonderful and Alec McCowen very good, though not quite enough variety and range – the whole thing transposed to Paris 1966, beautifully directed and decorated.

On 23 March 1973, Hugh 'Binkie' Beaumont died in London. Five days later, Noël Coward died in Jamaica.

To Irene Mayer Selznick   *26 March, London*

I don't know how much you have heard about Binkie's death, but I know you will have been dreadfully shocked and saddened, as we all are here. The last time I saw him was about three weeks ago, when Ingrid Bergman and I sat and talked about the Maugham play. He was in bed, and in considerable pain, just leaving for the Nursing Home where he stayed for nearly a week having X-rays etc. Then they let him come home and he went to the country for the weekend. I didn't see him again, alas, but we spoke several times on the telephone and all who did see him in those last days – Jane Edgeworth, Mary Evans and others – said how much he seemed to have improved in spirits. He was hardly drinking at all, and full of fun and plans.

The post-mortem certified a massive heart attack, and it seems he knew absolutely nothing, had no pain at all, and was smiling peacefully when Anna found him in the morning. John P. says that the verdict about his spine was not good – a slow, crumbling arthritis, which might well have crippled him in time, so one feels that there is some mercy in escaping such a fate.

But of course the shock has been terrible for everyone who loved him, and

* Molière's play in a version by Tony Harrison.

all the readjustments and business commitments will have to be solved and coped with somehow. I gather that last holiday at Barbados was one of his very happiest times, and I am so glad of that. Also, his fortunes did seem to have turned after that long period of ill luck, and he must have been proud of the way he ignored the implication that his empire had foundered, and went on, as he always did, with dignity and humour. Of course I am dreadfully sorry to have seen so little of him during the last few years, but you know how things changed, and he didn't like discussing intimate problems with me, so I never intruded on personal matters more than I could help. I know we were always deeply fond of one another, and I shall miss him most dreadfully.

He was so devoted to you, as I know you were to him. I hope you will take courage and believe that this sudden farewell seems to have been blessedly contrived to spare him anticipation and a long illness. He was so dedicated to his work – and the need to get on with it and concentrate – that he may have missed, quite willingly and deliberately, a more contented private life. But you probably know more of that than I do. I always felt his woman friends were more valued than the men. I only wish I could feel I was half as good an influence on him as he was on me.

Much love and sadness – as ever, John.

To Hugh Wheeler   *13 April, London*

All thanks for your sweet letter. So very glad for you – hope you are making a lot of dough. Still not a dollar from the Minskoff [Theater] and they say it will take another couple of months before the arbitration is held. I imagine they will offer a settlement – all very annoying and pigheaded of them, it seems to me, if they really have a big success. I suppose they will probably tour it later on – and perhaps London too – well, well.

London is rather dull and these two impending Memorial Services are not very cheerful to look forward to. Graham and Coley are back, but I've not seen them yet. John P. back at his – or rather Binkie's – desk at the Globe, rather pale and wan and lame with his arthritis, but working hard – and his beastly little boy friend as horrid as ever.

Working hard on John Standing who takes over in *Private Lives* on Monday. The others very obedient and willing, and Maggie has quite returned to her old form, after several months of hysteria and appallingly grotesque embroideries, which she abandoned most agreeably when I pointed them out. Audiences still packing in, and it will run as long as they will play it. Noël's Charles Castle documentary has been sold everywhere – great luck for him, of course, but I resent him being quoted as one of Noël's oldest friends. It didn't come out badly on the box once they had cut and edited it to great advantage after the time I saw it last year.

To Lillian Gish   *1 May, London*

We have had such a sad two months. Binkie's sudden death – and then Noël – as well as several other friends gone. I had a bit of a fall and cut my head quite badly but am quite recovered now, and my head almost invisible, the scar I mean.

Martin is well and tends his animals devotedly. John Perry has gone back to the office to continue the five or six projects which Binkie had already undertaken. He died in his sleep – a massive heart attack – very good as far as he was concerned, but a great shock to us all. I had known him since 1924 and of course worked with him from 1939 to now, a long and valued friendship in work and play. Irene Selznick wrote me a dreadfully sad letter – she was so devoted to him.

I am to direct Ingrid Bergman in a revival of *The Constant Wife* in August. Done here twice – and a failure each time – with Fay Compton and then Ruth Chatterton. Hope we may be 3rd time lucky!

To Emlyn Williams   *25 May, London*

We miss you here – tremendous turnout for Noël's service yesterday – Joan Olivier in sky blue beach trousers and Margaret Whigham Argyll making a stink because she hadn't better seats! About 800 people or more – I think Noël would have approved, but I am mighty glad it's over.

The Constant Wife *opened at the Albery Theatre on 19 September.*
   In 1974, JG would join the National Theatre Company at the Old Vic to play Prospero *again.*
   By this time, Peter Hall had succeeded Laurence Olivier as director and other possibilities were also under consideration.

To Peter Hall   *3 October, London*

I still think Rattigan's *The Browning Version* with Buckingham's *The Rehearsal* might make a good double bill. Bayes is a very funny part, it seems to me, and someone should cut it from five acts to one, and I picture it as developing from a first to a dress rehearsal with possible changes of scene – stage door, bare stage and finally perhaps the stage at the D.R. seen from the back, as Peter Brook did in *Colombe*, if you remember?

I'm rather alarmed at the idea of Marianne Faithfull* – if a girl what

---

* Marianne Faithfull made her acting debut as Irina in Chekhov's *Three Sisters* at the Royal Court in 1967.

about Nicola Pagett. But a boy might surely be found at one of the choir schools?*

No chance of Alan Bates, I suppose, for Caliban? And there is an Anglo French actor, Michel Lonsdale, wonderful in the [*Day of the*] *Jackal* film – a very good face and obviously splendid actor.

Late in 1973, JG bought the South Pavilion, Wotton Underwood, Buckinghamshire, although it would be three years before he and Martin Hensler were able to move there.

1974

To Hugh Wheeler   *7 January, London*

The house begins to get going and we are very lucky to have achieved a set of local workmen who fortunately know my accountant, a very nice chap indeed who lives in Aylesbury himself and is of inestimable help. M. has very attractive plans and we are buying furniture and decorating like mad. They begin on the exterior next week and I think if we are lucky, we might manage to get in by May or June at earliest. Meanwhile, I have to try and get rid of this house – 16 years lease to go – and try and find a small flat in town for working from.

Irene W. is doing the 'Oedipal' plays at Greenwich with Jonathan Miller, in a unit set and costumes – *Ghosts, Seagull* and *Hamlet* opening one after the other and then in repertory till March. Sounds a bit grim to me, but she seems happy to be working again and is full of her usual enthusiasm that always comes over her when she feels she is pioneering – not much good, though, to her bank balance, I'm afraid.

Joyce Carey had a tiny bit in the TV episodes in which I played Disraeli and it was fun to be working together again – was glad to see the director and other actors treated her with deference and sweetness. It means so much to her to keep working, even in the smallest capacity.

We began rehearsals for *The Tempest* last week, the set-up already in skeleton in a permanent West End rehearsal room, which is a great relief after those awful huts in the Waterloo Road where we rehearsed last time – and I like P. Hall's ideas and the cast seems promising. We don't open till March 5th so there should be plenty of time to get a really slick production. Nice to be speaking Shakespeare again.

---

* Perhaps casting Ariel?

I meant to write to Christopher [Isherwood] at [W. H.] Auden's death but felt it rather an uneasy chore. Oddly, I met him [Auden] on two TV shows last year. He was very amiable but I found him a bit affected and disappointing, though of course there was no opportunity of talking to him properly. He looked quite terrifying.

Everybody around seems to be ill or dying or both, which adds to the general gloom. Alan Webb is now a frail little old man, but manages to work still. (He found his brother, who kept house for him, dead on the floor a month or two ago.) John P. is very lame, but working hard with [Arthur] Cantor to keep HMT on its feet – still no word of Binkie's will, and I hear no one wants Lord North Street, which stands empty with all the furniture still in it. Elvira went back to her family in Italy – very resentfully – but Anna is back and now working next door to Binkie's house.

Parks [Norman Parkinson] and Wenda had a splendid wedding for her son at St James, Piccadilly and a huge party at the Ritz afterwards. Very grand, and they brought over all their Tobago staff and dressed them up in black coats and striped trousers from Moss Bros. They made a fascinating group sprinkled among the white guests, all in Ascot finery and the two blacks – page and bridesmaid – were enchanting – a beautiful bride too, so it was all most gala, and I was most flattered to be invited.

To George Pitcher and Ed Cone   *2 March, London*

We rehearsed eight weeks for *The Tempest* which opens next Tuesday. I think it will be a beautiful production, but very elaborate – designed for the new theatre (next year),* so is a bit cramped on the small stage at the Old Vic. Flying goddesses and Ariel too – a brilliant young boy [Michael Feast] who sings counter-tenor and manages to be convincing also as Ceres in the Masque and the sea-nymph who brings on Ferdinand in the first act.

I nearly killed myself (and Ferdinand) when they rashly opened a trap door I was standing on at the dress rehearsal. I fell about 4 ft. on top of the young lovers who were on either side of the chess board waiting to come up, and neither one of us was hurt at all – miracle really – but a slightly alarming experience, to say the least. We have had two previews – the first a bit shaky, but last night went splendidly and I had a real ovation at the end, which, of course, delighted and encouraged me very much. I go to the Court for August and September to play Shakespeare (!) in a most fascinating new piece [*Bingo*] by Edward Bond which was tried out at Exeter last year – it reads wonderfully, though of course I did not see it. The same woman director [Jane Howell] is to do it in London. I know nothing of her but she seems interesting and nice. It is a bitter study of W. S. in the last week of his life at Stratford – fine prose writing, and a most interesting follow-on to Prospero.

---

* The new National Theatre on the South Bank did not open, in fact, until 1976.

Have not yet sold Cowley St or found a new pied-à-terre for London. The Pavilion [Wotton Underwood] won't be ready till May or June so there is time yet, but everything is bad money-wise and I fear I shan't get as much as I hoped for this house. I'm selling my Boudin at Sotheby's in April to pay for some of the work in the country. We have started massive repairs and decorations and it should be glorious – but of course dreadfully costly – and we haven't yet done anything about staff. Will probably have to make do with dailies, if we can be lucky enough to get them. Martin goes down almost every day and works like a Trojan both in the house and garden. Fortunately it has been a mild winter and the snowdrops, crocuses and daffodils are all bursting, as well as the fruit trees.

Terrible alarms as well about 'the Enemy' (the farmer who lives in the Lodge at the gates) who has gone off with an appeal to build a house 40ft high just over the wall of our garden. He was refused planning permission by the District Council in 1972 but is evidently bent on getting round that. Please God nothing will come of it, for it would simply ruin the view and all the privacy, besides being an eyesore and a ruin to the value of the property.

Binkie's will still not proved – another three months before probate – all very mysterious. John [Perry] is *not* an executor, and the last boyfriend [Roger Stock] is the chief beneficiary, but everything left in a muddle, which one would have thought most unlikely. Paul has an enchanting new chum – a young Canadian designer with a beard. Paul has grown a moustache to balance, but I don't think it suits him! They are to move in to a studio penthouse in Chelsea, and are blissfully happy. I do hope it continues for him, as he has always needed someone permanent.

*To Martin Hensler**   *12 June, Bristol*

On such a beautiful day I think I must write you a tiny love letter and tell you that I am never really happy when I am not with you and I do thank you for all these years and for managing to get over the difficult times which are bound to happen now and again.

I know the house is going to be a dream of beauty and I so appreciate all the thought and effort and imagination that you are putting in to it. Take care of your sweet self – I'm so proud of you and grateful for everything you have given me and stand for. Take care of everything.

Dearest love to you and the animals from old Grandad

After **The Tempest,** *JG returned to the Royal Court to play Shakespeare in Edward Bond's play* **Bingo.**

---

* I have it on good authority that Martin Hensler destroyed virtually all the correspondence between him and JG almost certainly without JG's knowledge; this and the later (undated) letter in this book appear to be all that have survived.

To Ralph and Meriel Richardson   *22 July, London*

I am rehearsing *Bingo* hard and last week did two days with [Joseph] Losey in *Galileo* (as a dotty old Cardinal – yards of scarlet satin and a faint!) and a reading of Walpole's letters at Strawberry Hill, which was rather fun and seemed to go well.

We have a good cast for the new play. A wonderful old lady called Hilda Barry, who says she is 90 and was word perfect for the first rehearsal! Arthur Lowe is fine too – my own part very difficult. An extremely stripped (not literally!) and sensitive production by a handsome lady who rehearses in caftans and bare feet!

To Gwen Ffrangcon-Davies   *16 August, London*

The play is very black and the part quite devoid of humour, which makes it difficult. People don't care to think of W.S. like that, but Prospero has no humour either, and Bond is rather terrifying in his analogy – much of Lear in it as well.

To Georg Solti   *20 October, London*

I was most touched and delighted to read the charming message in my book. Dear Irene took so much trouble to get my friends to contribute, both in England and America, and I was particularly pleased that so many musicians were included, especially after the very timid way I approached my work at Covent Garden, where both you and Kubelik (egged on my [by?] poor departed David Webster, of whom I was very fond too) were of such invaluable help in encouraging my tentative approach to the magically complicated world of opera.

I follow your increasingly brilliant career with the utmost pleasure, and hope you are well and happy and that one day we may work or/and meet again.

Martin Jarvis played the title role in a radio production of Richard of Bordeaux.

To Martin Jarvis   *1974, London*

Congratulations on your splendid performance in *Bordeaux*, which I listened to last night with the keenest pleasure. The whole play came over faultlessly and the version and all of the performances seemed just right, and knowing the whole thing by heart and having spent two years of my life playing it, you can imagine I was hard to please.

I wish you might have the opportunity of giving it in the theatre for it seemed to hold up wonderfully well, and I believe the authoress would have been as satisfied as I, especially with your own performance.

After **Bingo** *JG* **re-directed** **Private Lives** *and* **The Constant Wife** *for visits to the USA before returning to the National Theatre to play Spooner in Harold Pinter's* **No Man's Land.**

To Alan Schneider   *4 December, London*

I saw Edward Albee for a minute as he was passing through London. I gather he has given up the grape. He looked like a surly pirate with drooping moustache, but was very amiable and I felt much more easy with him – though he also seems less attractive and rather removed.

1975

To Christopher Isherwood   *9 February, London*

I know you will like to read this* and I send it, as I don't imagine it will be published in America. I found it enormously interesting and deeply sad, bringing back vivid memories to me of early days before the War, when I often lunched at the Café Royal with Heard and Christopher Wood and Joe [Ackerley] and we had great fun together. I remember Joe acting in *Troilus* at Cambridge and it was brought to the Everyman in Hampstead for a week after (this was in the early 20s). Don't remember which part he played, but fell rather for his good looks and charm. Later we went occasionally for walks in Richmond Park, and I visited him once or twice when he had a flat in Chiswick Mall (years later) overlooking the river. The main decorations a plaster figure of Narcissus – or was it Apollo? – and a plate of bananas. Highly symbolical! Was rather snobbishly shocked to meet a stalwart young tough, a trouser-presser by profession (more symbolism) with whom he was enamoured at the time and quickly understood why *I* had had no success with Joe in that department!

The letters make very gloomy reading. And I don't think they are particularly well chosen, cut or assembled. Far too many repetitions, for instance, giving almost word for word versions of small occurrences which one does not want to read again in a letter to someone else a page or two later on. And of course the animal thing becomes an absolute obsession, and that, with the drinking and death wish adds up to a very sad and dreary dégringolade.

But what a dear talented fellow he was, and how he loved his few friends. He was obviously devoted to you and Don, but lashed himself into such loneliness and disillusion that nobody and nothing could come to his help.

---

* J. R. Ackerley's book, *My Father and Myself.*

To Irene Worth   *14 February, London*

Wotton is looking really splendid and the carpets are due to go down next week – also a sort of offer from someone to take this house, but I feel I can't possibly move out till June, as I have the Pinter play and *Quex* to deal with. We read the former on Monday, blocked the whole action on Tuesday, if you please, and walked through it on Wednesday with our books in our hands! It all seemed to fall into place with almost terrifying felicity and Pinter was simply delighted. I only hope we are not being too optimistic. We have three weeks off now to study and learn, and begin rehearsing properly on March 3rd for five weeks. Very exciting, I must say, and there is also talk already of a transfer to the West End after the Vic, and Roger Stevens offering Washington and New York for a limited season just before and after Christmas, which is all rather overwhelming so far ahead.

Alan Webb has been ill with some wretched bladder infection, but returns to *Borkman** tonight. They don't play next week as *Heartbreak House* is opening, so I shall wait to see it until the week after. Wonderful press, though some of them say Peggy is too sympathetic. Ralph (who will be wonderful in the Pinter) begs me not to come till he has settled down, but I think he is touchingly and secretly delighted at the success and seems in wonderful form.

I dined with Maina, who is in great worry about her future – all the usual backstage intrigues and complications, worse even, it seems, than in the theatre, if possible! I got Ninette de Valois to see her, and I hope she will be able to make constructive suggestions. M[aina] says she is almost 30 (Heavens!) and must make it properly or be forever lost.

To Irene Worth   *5 March, London*

Borkman was very impressive – very good teamwork, I thought. Excellent décor and lighting and all of them good except Frank Grimes who plays Erhart and is not, I think – after seeing him in three or four different roles – the budding genius that Lindsay Anderson appears to think him.

Heartbreak House† is a great success and I hope to see it soon. One of the Sundays had the grace to compare *your* Hesione very favourably as opposed to that of Eileen Atkins, which was good to read.

We are rehearsing the Pinter at last. His wife [Vivien Merchant] was taken ill in Hong Kong when she was acting at the Festival there and he has had to go over to fetch her home. She has to travel by ship so I fear he won't be back for a week or two. But Peter Hall is in excellent form and we have, I think, begun well.

---

* The National Theatre production of *John Gabriel Borkman* by Henrik Ibsen opened in January. Ralph Richardson played Borkman; Wendy Hiller, Gunhild Borkman; Peggy Ashcroft, Ella Rentheim; Frank Grimes, Erhart Borkman; and Alan Webb, William Foldal.
† John Schlesinger's National Theatre production opened in February.

To Irene Worth   *28 March, London*

Ralph has a bit of a chill but fortunately we have Easter off from rehearsals
and there are no *Borkmans* till next week. The play going very well, but it is
not much fun rehearsing in that dismal Aquinas Street* with water dripping
in to pails through the ceiling, and the canteen smelling and aeroplanes
drowning one's efforts to remember the lines. Fortunately after next week we
move in to the Royalty Theatre and have the set for a whole week before the
previews.

No Man's Land *opened at the Old Vic on 23 April. During its run, JG directed
Judi Dench and Daniel Massey in* The Gay Lord Quex.

To Irene Worth   *29 April, London*

Do hope things are moving to better prospects for you and that you are not
too depressed. Spring is wonderfully bursting out all over here, the lilac and
roses almost ready to flower, and daffodils just ending and giving place to
hyacinths and bluebells.

The Pinter play went wonderfully on the opening night and everyone
seems very pleased with both Ralph and me. I dried up stone dead in my long
speech at the end of the last preview – tried to replace a line I had left out,
and fumbled the whole thing badly, so I was in terror of doing it the next
night, but God – or proper concentration – was with me, fortunately. Very
good press all round – all a bit baffled by the obscure passages and whatever
moral one takes away – or leaves behind? But it is funny, menacing, poetic
and powerful, though possibly the blending of the components is a bit
startling and confusing to the audience. But this is true to some extent with
all the Pinter plays.

We are in a maddening money pickle – still undecided whether to get rid
of this house, or put Wotton up for sale without even living in it! My American
royalties are eight weeks overdue – they have to 'clear' dollar cheques, whatever
that may mean, and Laurie [Evans] has done a merger with another big agency
so that their books and efficiency seem to be all at sixes and sevens. I'm still
trying to sell the Boudin, so far without success. Wotton is very nearly ready
but we need steady cash to complete it and prices rise like mad in every
direction. Everyone says 'Hold on' but that doesn't mean the Bank enjoy
overdrafts and tradespeople have to be paid. Well, it's all a great muddle and
worry – worse for Martin who has to cope with it all personally. You know
how blinkered I sail through life, like Micawber always fairly sure something
will turn up at the eleventh hour.

---

* During its tenure of the Old Vic, the National Theatre's administrative offices and rehearsal room
were in temporary buildings some 400 yards from the theatre.

Two nice anecdotes of Ingrid [Bergman in *The Constant Wife*].

She said to Barbara Ferris one night in the last act 'I like you. I think you are a cheat, a liar and a hamburger – but I like you.'

And once she asked Dorothy Reynolds why she had lost a good laugh she was used to getting, and Dorothy said 'Well, I think if you turned your face to the audience, you would get the laugh' and Ingrid cast her eyes to Heaven and remarked 'All these rules!'

To Irene Worth   *18 May, London*

So very sweet of you to offer to help the money crisis, but I am sure I shall find a way out.

Am working very hard on *Quex*, driving them all mad by changing their moves every five minutes! The big cast is, I think, well chosen, but the minor members have to be taught by numbers. I think Judi, Dan and Siân Phillips will all be excellent and the sets are very pretty indeed – Alan Tagg.

We start previews June 5th. Bumble [Dawson] is, of course, fractious at her inability to get about,* but I hope she may be well enough to supervise final dress parade etc. I spent my day off yesterday visiting invalids. Edith Jackson back in the Clinic and threatened by a gastric operation which I hope may be proved unnecessary though I fear for her. Sybil [Thorndike] in bed having traipsed up to Golders Green in pouring rain on Friday in memory of Lewis's death – but intrepid and gallant as ever, though the companion told me she had a bad heart attack a week ago, but she insists she will be coming to the Vic next Friday night. Astonishing.

We are to move to Wyndham's at the end of June for a hopeful three month run and Cohen is bargaining to get the American production from [Robert] Whitehead and [Roger] Stevens, making a much more advantageous offer. But I believe Pinter is morally bound to Roger, who helped him at his first beginnings. Whatever happens, I am determined to stick out for a fat salary and, if possible, not too big a theatre and no mikes! I heard they use them for *Private Lives* in the 46th Street Theatre where I *never* had them for *Ages of Man*. But audiences seem not to mind, though I do, desperately.

The Gay Lord Quex *opened at the Albery Theatre on 16 June.*

To Dorothy Reynolds and Angus Mackay   *18 June, London*

Thank you so much for your telegram. As you will have seen, the press was pretty grudging, but I hope they survive with a little luck and perseverance. I

---

* Beatrice (Bumble) Dawson had been involved in a serious car accident.

am cutting quite a bit – stupid not to have done it before, but didn't want to upset the cast.

Thought *Edward VII* splendid this week, didn't you? Martin kept handing me Kleenex to stifle the sobs!

To Irene Worth   *12 July, London*

I believe I never said a huge thank you for the offer of the Aubusson carpet – what a very sweet thought and I long to see it. But we are still in a turmoil of indecision over our future, and though Wotton is really *almost* finished, the floor in the big room has still to be stained and painted and we shall only take our good things down if Cowley Street is really sold – which *may* go through in the next two months, I hope. We go down almost every day, but the animals and birds complicate matters and we have to come back to London each afternoon.

Arnold [Weissberger] and Milton [Goldman] are here, people giving parties for them all over the place, and I have a business conference with them and Laurie [Evans] and the accountant next week. Everything is madly difficult financially, and I really don't think I can possibly afford to come to America in October in the Pinter play, as Roger Stevens is begging us to do. Well, maybe it will all sort itself out. I do odd days filming and recording for quite large sums, and the taxes reduce them to ten per cent left for me! Was offered £20,000 to do a commercial and almost agreed – a sherry ad! – till I worked out that £17,000 would go to the Government, £2,000 to Laurie and £1,500 left for me! Too humiliating! Well, we shall see what happens. Mr Micawber is nothing to me!

Martin is worried to death, eats nothing, drinks less, toils away at recalcitrant workmen. Caesar still lives but is very delicate, the other animals flourish, thank God, the birds too.

Jonathan Miller smarting after leaving the National in disagreement with P. Hall. Very spiteful interviews announcing (for the nth time) that he is renouncing the theatre and returning to medicine.

No Man's Land *transferred to Wyndham's Theatre on 15 July.*

To Cecil Beaton   *19 July, London*

It was nice of you to mention *Quex*. Business has improved a bit, but it is losing too much money – £40,000 to put on and £9000 a week to run! The management has behaved very generously indeed, ploughing in more money and not cutting the salaries. But Dan Massey has been a disappointment, and it has to come off in a fortnight's time, alas.

The Pinter, on the other hand, is a huge success. If you do come up to see it, please let me know so that I can get you aisle seats. There are only a few steps to the stalls – almost on street level – so it would not be taxing for you. But wait till the weather is cooler – terribly oppressive at the moment. I think you would enjoy the play.

Did you hear that Diana [Cooper] went out in a yashmak to see *Shampoo* the day after her bad fall, and after covering the looking glasses for a day or two, finally decided to face the worst and remarked 'My God, I look just like a Francis Bacon!'

I am still trying to sell this house, but the landlords ask £30,000 for the freehold! There is only 12 years lease as it is. I hope I shall get a decent offer for it. The Aylesbury house is a dream of beauty, but I have spent all my savings decorating it and have not yet even slept a night there – go down most days and hope I may perhaps get in at the end of the summer.

To Irene Worth   *12 August, London*

Wyndham's is packed despite a terrific heat wave, thank God. I love the play and my part, though the wretched Pinter is in hiding after huge and unattractive publicity which no doubt has reached your ears even so far away.* Huge front page articles for a day or two, but I expect it will all die down quite soon – a godsend for the gutter press and columnists in the dog days. However, he has directed a new Simon Gray play [*Otherwise Engaged*] with Alan Bates, which opened last week to excellent notices, though, of course, he was not to be seen at the first night.

Michael Codron has stepped in to Binkie's shoes – four successes cheek by jowl in Shaftesbury Avenue. He certainly has flair.

What other news? Ralph is well, though he finds the hot weather a bit hard to take. He has to fall down three times in the first act of this play – six times on matinée days – but seems to manage it without mishap. His manservant of 20 years died on holiday the other day and I fancy will be hard to replace. He was very nice and quiet and efficient. Also Jim, our demon ex-chauffeur, suddenly died of a heart attack. I think he was older than he admitted and we were certainly lucky that he left. We have a nice man now, though a maddening lot of troubles with the big car, which is always being repaired at huge cost and still keeps going wrong.

Have hardly seen anyone as we go down to Wotton every day and water the garden, and I have been trying to help Martin gild and paint. Still waiting for news of selling this house. It is nice to be in a West End success again with such a splendid part that everyone seems to like me in, and I have already been able to pay a lot of outstanding bills – we eat here alone and don't go out at all, but I find that rather a pleasant change.

---

* News of Harold Pinter's relationship with Lady Antonia Fraser had been seized on by the press.

To Hugh Wheeler   *30 August, London*

The play continues to do very well indeed and we are booked to stay at Wyndham's till December. Then Ralph is wanted back at the National – *one* of its new theatres now said to be opening definitely in November for a revival of *John Gabriel Borkman* [by Ibsen], so America would not be possible till next year.

I have a lot of odd jobs to do this autumn – *Pilgrim's Progress* for radio with Vaughan Williams music, two days as a Headmaster in a film and a 20 minute monologue for TV taken from the Grand Inquisitor chapter in *Karamazov* – the latter rather a terrifying prospect, but I think one ought to force one's memory to learn at least one new part every so often, so that one's capabilities don't get rusty, vide wonderful old Sybil Thorndike, who can still spout yards of poetry and Gilbert Murray in her nineties, while Edith Evans can't remember a word any more!

Irene Selznick came last night – *didn't* think the play would do for the U.S. and I must say I have always been doubtful myself, though people would probably come for a few weeks to see two old hams (for the last time?), but I would only agree to a really small house, and you know how tricky the managements are about that.

Lots of casualties around here. Terry Rattigan has been in the Clinic for 6 weeks and they don't seem to agree what is really the matter with him. Bombs keep going off in unlikely places – they cleared our theatre for ten minutes last night, but it was a false alarm – rather scary and very bad for the theatres and cinemas. Tennessee was here, very quiet and well behaved – said he loved the play and did not moan about his own débâcle.

We have been working like mad at Wotton, staining the floor of the big room, lacquered with a hand painted pattern gold motif – it looks rather splendid now it is almost finished. Martin is so clever *and* painstaking, and I amble around trying inefficiently to help. We have done a lot of gilding too in the hall and on the stairs – all the workmen away and also the chauffeur on holiday, so we get up early and totter down by train to Aylesbury, returning in the afternoon – something of a chore but it all begins to look so splendid – the birdhouse cleaned and painted, but we had to cut down 12 trees in the woodland because of the elm disease which is ravaging the countryside everywhere.

Still nothing really settled about selling this house, but now the play is a success I've been able to pay off quite a lot of bills and have sold my pretty Tissot of the lady reading the letter for £3000. I paid £150 for it in 1945 so I feel I have a nice profit and many years pleasure, though I hated to part with it – and the Boudin is going to Johannesburg in the hope of selling well in a Sotheby's sale there.

Of course the Tissot was not signed, and the man who bought it says it isn't a Tissot at all, but by a man called Stevenos [?], a Belgian, who admired and copied him – rather sad, as it would have been worth much more if it had been by Tissot. Ah well! Goddard sent me the *Chorus Line* recording – wish I could see it.

The dogs are flourishing, but poor old Caesar really on his last legs, I fear. When he does go – which one really hopes as he looks such a wretched little morsel – it will simplify comings and goings quite a bit, but I fear Martin will take it very hard as it was the first dog I gave him when we met.

To Irene Worth   *31 August, London*

I give a reading on Sept. 14th at the big house [at Wotton] in aid of Friends of the Vale and renovating the Church Tower. Thought I had better keep in with the locals if I am going to live there. Horace Walpole's and Lord Hervey's Diaries – amusing 18th century gossips.

Alec [Guinness] is splendid in his play [*A Family and a Fortune* adapted by Julian Mitchell from Ivy Compton-Burnett's novel] and Rachel Kempson and Nicola Pagett also excellent, but it is rather chilly and discursive – and Maggie [Leighton], though she does wonders and is incredibly brave to tackle acting at all with her lameness, is to my mind not rightly cast – too imposing and obviously malignant when I would have thought an outwardly benevolent sweetness concealing the bite is more what was required, the sort of thing Lilian Braithwaite used to do so well. Alan Bates has made a big success in a new Simon Gray play, directed, brilliantly it seems, by Harold Pinter. But his divorce* with Lady Antonia Fraser has been a nightmare of publicity for all concerned. He (Pinter) asked Ralph and me to supper to meet her, and I must say she is very beautiful, sweetly spoken and, of course, excessively bright-brained. R. thought her quite a Cleopatra.

London is hideous with tourists and their litter, bombs go off daily, they keep clearing theatres and streets with false alarms, and there are quantities of Arabs about, buying flats and big houses for enormous sums and shoplifting in Oxford Street in their spare time.

To Barbara Morley Holder   *28 September, London*

Of course I remember *The High Constable's Wife* [by Cecil Lewis, after Balzac] – and Lewis Casson terrifying us with his vocal inflections. I knew him much better later on and grew very fond of him. Sybil (at 93) is still marvellously vital and gallant despite crippling arthritis – she goes about and reads voraciously still. So delighted you enjoyed the little book.† I enjoyed putting it together though some of it is a bit scrappy I'm afraid.

---

* The divorce from Vivien Merchant did not take place until 1980.
† A collection of his writings, *Distinguished Company*, was published in 1972.

I *think* Cecil Lewis is still about. He had a great success for a little while when GBS took him up and he filmed one of the one-act plays.

To George Pitcher   *1 December, London*

Am quite amazed that you liked *Travesties* [by Tom Stoppard] so much. I really detested it – chop logic and not so much as a wry smile for me in the endless 1.40 hour first act, after which I fled. I was so disappointed, as I went alone, having to bribe my way in, and expected I would enjoy it. But then I loathed *Jumpers* too, and a lot of *Rosencrantz* [*and Guildenstern Are Dead*], though that got better after the shove halfpenny was done with. I thought that opening scene would go on for ever. I just can't get on Stoppard's wavelength at all, and I must say it rather bewilders me. Christopher Fry – except for *The Lady's Not for Burning* – has the same irritating effect for me. But I gather *Travesties* is really a hit – here it played in repertory, and for about five weeks in the commercial transfer, rave reviews from the critics, very mixed reactions from people who saw it, but a lot agreed with me! Mr [John] Wood, whom I admired in a Gorky play and a Restoration comedy, but deplored as Brutus and only mildly admired in *Sherlock Holmes*, is enormously praised both sides of the Atlantic. It appears he has been around for years. I never met him myself. Well, he's the clever new boy.

Cowley St is sold at last. We move out, and into Wotton the last week of February 1976 – seems impossible. Martin has done marvels with the house, and the garden is bursting with bulbs and seeds, so I hope we shall have a wonderful spring there – and a new life! I've had an awful time with money this year. Sold two pictures – one at a profit, one at a loss – some books and silver – never *earned* so much money as I have in the last three years, and this ghastly tax – 83% and 10% to the agent – leaves me £10 in every £100.

No Man's Land goes on till Jan. 24th, then I do a TV of *Dorian Gray* with Peter Firth – who was so good in *Equus* [by Peter Shaffer] – and possibly a bit in the Zeffirelli *Christ* series – Joseph of Arimathea, I believe – (Lew Grade is supposed to have said 'Such an expensive budget – couldn't we manage with only *ten* disciples?') – and a very fascinating part in a new Alain Resnais film – two weeks in Providence, New England in May and one in Paris in July. Also we do the Pinter again in repertory for only ten performances in April and May. So I hope to get quite a bit of time to live in the country, and yet not be idle.

1976

To Richard Bebb   *30 January, London*

The effect of rapid movement does greatly fascinate me, both in the case of
ET [Ellen Terry] and HI [Henry Irving]. Have you noticed how Edith Evans
never moves if she can help it? I never remember her entrances, and in
Millamant's she was foiled by a stupid great gate, and had to enter through a
narrow side archway. But she scarcely ever moved in that part. She was like a
Venetian glass figure in a vitrine, turning slowly now and then with slow,
deliberate movements of her neck and arms, never using her fan except as a
kind of weapon! And whenever I have directed her – [Lady] Bracknell, *Chalk
Garden*, the Nurse – she always wanted to stay still and let the voice do
everything.

Even her Rosalind was not *physically* lively, I think. But how she played it!
Perhaps she hasn't good legs! But I doubt if Ellen had either – anyway one
never saw them, though she did magic things with her long skirts. They say
her hands were mannish and ugly but she used them superbly.

To Irene Worth   *1 February, London*

We really *move* on Feb. 23rd. Martin goes up and down every day, but of
course I'm not much use. The gramophone is installed in the big room and
sounds marvellous, and I am arranging books and records when I am able to
go down. Violent cold weather suddenly with ice and snow. Don't know how
M. proposes to transport the birds! I don't dare to inquire as it is a sore subject,
but the bird *house* is floored and heated – only the cages have to be built.
Otherwise everything is really ready, but a lot of tiles came off the roof in a
huge gale recently and the insurance co. wouldn't play because we are not
living there! The car has also had to be mended, but thank God we have a
very nice new driver – Burmese in origin, really sweet-natured and obliging,
which is a great help.

Have not dared to see the Finney *Hamlet* [at the Old Vic]. Everyone says
the performances are poor all round. Philip Locke, as an *elderly* (why?) Horatio
in spectacles and Robert Eddison as the Player King have come off best, it
seems, and all the critics say what a splendid *play* it is uncut. Well, I think
some of us had guessed that already.

Ralph seems well and still insists on driving that alarming motorbike. He
has taken a week in Brighton and now goes to Tunisia to play for two days in
the Zeffirelli *Christ* TV serial. They offered me a wretched part in it which I
had the temerity to refuse! Everyone seems to be in it, but the script of the
bits I saw didn't read very inspiringly, except for the quotes from you know
who.

To Irene Worth   *14 March, Wotton Underwood*

The holocaust of our move from Cowley St depressed and exhausted us considerably. A few boxes still unpacked, but on the whole we are amazingly well settled and I do think the house and garden are lovely. The Spring just on the verge of busting out all over but some cold days last week put it back again after an early start.

Great night at the Old Vic farewell. Ralph and I supported and Finney and Peggy did the hard work and turned out a wonderful show, though they read their parts from scripts. Sybil was wheeled down the aisle in her chair and had a fantastic ovation. Everyone very nervous about the new theatre, *partly* opening this week. *Borkman, Happy Days, Plunder, Hamlet* and the new Osborne play [*Watch It Come Down*] which no one seems to like much. I have seen none of them and am glad to be away from the Sturm und Drang. A great strain on everyone's nerves. But the critics are all trying to be encouraging about the building, though I found the theatre which *is* open [Lyttelton] very drab and rather dreary when I went there to be photographed a few weeks ago. Dreadfully wide, like all the American stages, and no central aisle, surely a mistake. I hear the dressing rooms are tiny and cabin-like, but Ralph and Peggy refuse to be daunted and Peter Hall is amazingly resilient. Larry cried off the Vic farewell – said he could not face an audience. He is said to be much better, however, voice back and he has made two films – went to one of the previews, I gather. I've not seen him myself.

Are you well and happy? We do so miss you and long to hear more good news, but the best would be if you decided to come back, if only for a bit. London is very horrid and I don't a bit mind being away from it and I know you would be thrilled at what Martin has done with the house. He works so damned hard I feel ashamed – cooking, gardening, sewing and the birds and dogs to tend. Eats and drinks nothing and smokes far too much.

To Hugh Wheeler   *4 April, Wotton Underwood*

Financial affairs still in a maddening muddle. The U.S. Government won't give up the big sum they hold there in Withholding Tax, nor do they seem to decide what is to be done with it. My agent here and accountant, Milton and Arnold, do little to help and pass the buck to one another all the time, with the result that we live tremblingly (and thriftily) under the sword of Damocles, which threatens to fall upon our heads at any moment.

However, it is lovely here – the dogs and birds were transported safely at the last moment, and the spring flowers are just coming out – a week or two later than in London, where the crocuses are already over.

I start again with *No Man's Land* in a week's time – twelve performances in the new National (which everybody seems to hate) over two months. I'm doing a tiny bit in Tony Richardson's new Fielding film to be shot near Bath –

18th century knockabout stuff à la *Tom Jones* – and then I go to Limoges and Paris for three or four weeks for Alain Resnais – a very fascinating part with Ellen Burstyn, Dirk Bogarde, David Warner and [Elaine] Stritch – a rather odd, abstract sort of film [*Providence*] by David Mercer. I also have to go to Dublin in July to play a terrifying preacher (nine page monologue sermon about Hell) in James Joyce's *A Portrait of the Artist as a Young Man* for Joseph Strick – so shall be sporadically busy all summer with, I hope, several weeks to stay quietly here and enjoy the country. In September we are supposed to go to Toronto, Washington, New York – four weeks each for Stevens and Whitehead, with *No Man's Land.* We (Ralph and I) have resisted so far, but are now on the verge of signing, only I do want a N.Y. theatre to be agreed and confirmed before we settle. I so dread a big theatre and the fears of amplification and I bet they will try to push us into somewhere too big with the promise of bigger profits.

I simply love it here, but Martin has a very tiring time doing everything – cooking as well as the house and garden. Our dear two dailies come down to clean three times a week and we have a very nice – and co-operative – new chauffeur – a Burmese with a Spanish wife! – which is a great help. But the accountant keeps worrying us and telling me I should sell the house – which seems impossibly silly after all the money and love that has gone into it.

No Man's Land *opened in the Lyttelton Theatre, part of the new National Theatre on the South Bank, on 12 April.*

To Douglas Fairbanks Jr.   *23 June, Wotton Underwood*

Of course I agree with you about Cathleen [Nesbitt]. Fay Compton, like Ellen Terry only got their awards when they were too old to appreciate them. I always feel Isabel Jeans, Gwen Ffrangcon-Davies, Athene Seyler and Emlyn Williams have been very unfairly passed over. I suppose one can't make too many recommendations. But there are not many of the old Brigade left and they would all be worthy and I'm sure very pleased to be remembered.

I will certainly write to Callaghan* about Cathleen if you think it would help. Very distressed to hear of her accident. She was here in such good form just before she left for America, after rather a struggle with Equity to get her permit. Hope she may still recover in time to work. She can't bear to be idle.

To Hugh Wheeler   *27 June, Wotton Underwood*

Unbelievably beautiful here, and unbelievably hot. How lucky I am not to be working, and to be able to be in the country. My back is broken picking up

---

* James Callaghan, Prime Minister at the time.

weeds and leaves and snipping dead heads, the only things I am to be trusted to do in a garden. Martin is black as black and toils unceasingly. Had 17 people to a party last week – food on the terrace and it seemed to be a great success – and Ralph and Mu are coming on Tuesday. The garden is agog with flowers and really looks divine – do wish you could see it. Had a strange three weeks at deepest Limoges, filming with Resnais – very interesting but foully cold. I lay out in a glorious park on a long chair in a Palm Beach suit pretending it was lovely, while the wind whistled and all the crew sheltered in windcheaters! Also two weekends with public holidays, so wasted about six days – wandered round trying to find a place to learn my Irish preacher part amidst French families with children and sinister Algerians lying about in groups – and of course the non-working days were the only fine ones. Fortunately the town has five restaurants and five cinemas – two porno-graphic! – with fairly constant changes of menu and programme, and I even managed to save quite a big sum to bring home out of my living allowance! [Elaine] Stritch and her husband [John Bay] and Dirk Bogarde and his friend Tony Forwood were OK but not wildly exciting, but I thought the rushes did seem to be.

I finally succumbed to play a small part for a lot of money in the *Caligula* of Gore Vidal. Martin is very cross with me for accepting it as I was originally offered Tiberius (now to be played by Peter O'Toole) and my first scene was to come out of a pool, with a plaster over my nose and eczema all over my face, to reveal two children, boy and girl, emerging from under my tunic where they were dallying with me. So I loftily refused and had a stinkingly rude letter from Gore saying he supposed I'd never read Suetonius, and how dared I go round saying good actors would be ashamed to appear in such pornography. Then a week or two ago came an offer of this other part – an old Senator who cuts his veins in a bath and disapproves of everything, and I thought well, why not? What Vidal and I will say to each other if and when we meet, I tremble to prophesy. I must say I never liked him. It is backed by the owner of *Penthouse* magazine! [Bob Guccione]

Dear old Mac [Harry McHugh] died suddenly yesterday in Folkestone, the heat did him in. I think he was 87 or 88, so another funeral and one does not really grieve for such a good life, but he was a sweet character to remember. Chris Isherwood and Don came down to my party, driven by David Hockney – in most peculiar clothes and a very wet cigar and that boring Peter [Schlesinger] boy friend (no doubt you saw the film).

Arnold and Milton due in a few weeks time. Joyce has had her hip operation and I believe it is successful – shall hear more from Patrick W[oodcock] with whom I lunch next week, preparatory to giving a talk to some American speech group for Paul Gregory. Can't think why I agreed to do it. I remember last seeing him at Blue Harbour with [Charles] Laughton. Rather shocking Elsa [Lanchester] prefacing the new life of him* and digging up the skeleton. Have you read it? Sounds horrid.

Hoped to hear from George and Ed giving me their address in France. I might have visited there from Limoges on an off day, but they haven't written.†

To Irene Worth   *5 July, Wotton Underwood*

Go to Paris tomorrow to do a last five days on the Alain Resnais film – very interesting. David Warner is an odd fish, but devoted to you – full of wretched complexes, dreads working on the stage but seems to be much in demand for films – a bit pampered by his entourage, but basically sweet and timid – drinks too much and wife (ex., rather nice) and Israeli mistress arriving at intervals – faithful and quite amusing Bernie-like dresser who does look after him very well. He is certainly most effective on the screen to judge by the rushes I saw, and Ellen Burstyn is a lovely actress and most charming woman.

Great service at the Abbey for Sybil,‡ whose ashes are interred there. First actor since Irving to be so honoured – very right and proper. Wonderful music and fanfare of trumpets. Paul Scofield and Ralph read, and I gave the address – a greatly difficult job as everything seemed to have been said already, but people seemed to think I said the right ones and got one or two laughs, which I feel Sybil would have liked – enormous congregation, of course.

To Cecil Beaton   *22 August, Wotton Underwood*

Good to see your diaries coming out and lately in Rome, Franco Rossellini showed me a charming new book of yours which he said you had illustrated with drawings from your left hand.§ To have achieved these must have given you much satisfaction, and I'm delighted you feel able to go on working with such indefatigable determination. I had hoped to propose myself for a visit but, alas, I have to go back to Paris for several days to do the post-synching of the Alain Resnais–David Mercer film I was in during the early part of the summer, and as soon as I get back, I begin rehearsing *No Man's Land* again for the U.S. The original boy [Michael Feast] cannot go, so we have to start again with a different actor [Michael Kitchen], and we fly to Canada on Sept. 8th, which is alarmingly soon.

I wonder if you saw the National Theatre programme last night – not very edifying, I thought, and Larry and Peter Hall ducking in and out with Tynan gnashing a prehensile tooth between. It's a pretty beastly house to work in, I can tell you – awful passages, dressing rooms, endless opening and shutting of passage doors, no centre aisle, dress circle so high that it has no kind of

---

* *Charles Laughton – An Intimate Biography* by Charles Higham.
† In fact George Pitcher wrote several times, but his letters were intercepted by Martin Hensler.
‡ Sybil Thorndike died on 9 June 1976.
§ Beaton had had a stroke in May 1974.

contact with the stalls, dreary buff upholstery, open light boxes – rather like the Everyman Theatre in the twenties.* One can only approve of the acoustics (though I'm told they are not universally perfect) and the lines of sight.

I've been playing a small part in *Caligula* in Rome. Backed by *Penthouse* Magazine to the tune, they boast, of 12 million dollars. Ideological pornography, says Gore Vidal, who wrote the script, and stars in letters of gold on the cover. He's certainly right about the second appellation. (He has now quarrelled with everyone concerned and retired to Venice and Ravello in high dudgeon.) Unbelievable non-costumes and sensational sets by Donati, who seems to be something of a genius. Stark naked youths and girls in hordes, nurses with huge exposed breasts suckling tiny babies wrapped in gold lamé, shrieking all day long, and being coaxed with comforters that look like clay doves but on closer inspection turn out to be modelled on cocks and balls! Peter O'Toole, Malcolm McDowell and Maria Schneider (the girl in [*Last*] *Tango* [*in Paris*]) all appear, but I can't believe the Empire or the Odeon will house it – the Curzon possibly! Well, well.

After his various film and television commitments, J G returned to North America for a tour of No Man's Land, *once again with Ralph Richardson.*

To Paul Anstee   *15 October, Washington*

The play goes intermittently well – as I anticipated a lot of people are bored and mystified but we have big houses and fine notices. Have to do a lot of radio and interviews, a little TV sketch about crosswords – only three minutes in the Pinter style which they cooked up for us in Toronto and paid us well for doing.

Fantastic, fine hot weather. I walk endlessly about the enormously long streets with mammoth buildings everywhere. The Kennedy Center, beautiful and impressive place, the theatre reasonable size and good acoustics. Lots of galleries and museums, but a dearth of decent films. Don't want to see *Marathon Man* or the new [Ingrid] Bergman–[Liza] Minnelli film [*A Matter of Time* directed by Vincente Minnelli]. A few porno parlours but they look very sordid and I seem to be recognised everywhere here so I try to keep to the straight and narrow.

Goddard [Lieberson] was here last night for a presentation dinner at the White House for Martha Graham. We were invited, Ralph, Mu and I, but having no dinner jackets with us decided to make our excuses. I'm sure it would have been a great bore and we didn't want to seem rudely conspicuous, arriving when it was half over.

His future plans included further appearances at the National Theatre.

---

* J G refers to the Lyttelton Theatre.

To Peter Hall   *1 December, New York*

I thought of Coral Browne for the much-married lady in the play.* Also of
George Rose for the servant, but I doubt if either of them would be inclined
to return to Albion?

Does [John] Schlesinger *really* want me to play Caesar? I should hate to
push in – don't think I've ever suggested myself before – and Ralph told me
he offered himself too. We laughed, I must say, over that.

No, I don't think Lindsay [Anderson] for *Lear.* I gather his *Caesar* and
Dream at the Court were both very unhappy. Did he not direct *Twelfth Night*
there too, with Patrick Procktor décor? Would much rather you did it yourself.
I so distrust the new directors of the Bard, and shuddered at [Donald] Sinden's
photo in *The Times* with Goering medals and cigar.†

Play going almost too well. The opening scene tends to emulate *Charley's
Aunt* reactions now, and we have to be very firm to keep the hysteria in check.
And people applaud in the street when we come out after the matinées,
something I've not seen since Bergner in *Escape Me Never* in the 30s. Well,
well, old age has its compensations after all.

To Cecil Beaton   *1 December, New York*

So many people here inquire for you and miss your presence in the New York
scene – Anita, Lillian, Arnold and Milton and so many others. *Fair Lady*
seems still to be going strong and I hope it still makes money for you. The
Pinter play is a huge success, thank God, and we have packed houses and a
throng of people coming round after every performance. So I feel we are very
lucky indeed, though the previous month in Washington was rather a bind,
too big a theatre and a sticky lot to play to. Toronto, on the other hand, has
become very fine and impressive – mirror tiled skyscrapers, space between the
buildings and trees and flowers sensibly planted – the best of New York and
California – very striking in contrast to the squalor of Rome and Paris, both
of which seemed dreadfully sad and run down to me when I spent some
weeks in each city this summer. New York, of course, does manage to keep
its unique combination of sordidness and splendour, and I am greatly enjoying
being here again, especially in a success, which people seem genuinely to *like*
in America, whereas at home there always seems to be a bit of resentment and
envy, don't you think?

Back to the National in the New Year with a very promising new comedy
by an author I didn't know of – Julian Mitchell – a sort of Dadie Rylands part
for me. Also Shotover in *Heartbreak House* for TV and various other hopeful

---

* *Half-Life* by Julian Mitchell.
† Donald Sinden was playing Benedick in John Barton's production of *Much Ado about Nothing* at
Stratford-upon-Avon.

projects, if only I can still learn the parts and keep going! Larry seems to have achieved a remarkable recovery and is working great guns in films and TV, though he can't face the live theatre. Michael Redgrave, too, is supposed to be much better and also able to work. I know you have managed to write again yourself – and draw too – someone is sending me your new book. I am looking forward to that – it has not arrived yet.

Eva Rubinstein, daughter of the pianist, photographed me the other day – a charming creature and the pictures she showed me were very striking. Do you know her? I've never quite forgiven [Richard] Avedon, who asked me to *cry* for him as I did it so well, and I did for about an hour, and he never showed me a print or put one into his book – I suppose the result was so horrific!

To Paul Anstee   *11 December, New York*

New York is so hectic – people crowd my dressing room, which is so small that it is like the cabin scene in *Night at the Opera*, with everyone squeezed in and out. It has really been a marvellous success, and the city, with its squalor and luxury all mixed up, more beautiful than ever.

A lot of the people here, Margalo [Gillmore], Paul Morrison and some others have aged most terribly since I saw them last. Florence [Reed] made an effort to let me come and see her, but funked it at the last moment. Still, it has been a great experience to have such success – if it is one's last New York visit, it will certainly be something to remember! George and Ed are a bit *boring*, I'm afraid! Talk about their mongrels the entire time – and Christopher and Don are here, and I find I haven't much to say to them – oh dear. Hugh looks very old and rather depressed. He had to escort Elizabeth Taylor back from Vienna – *alone* with a dog and a cat *and* a jewel case, of course! He says she can't *write* and was incapable of filling in a form or remembering her *name* – not surprising. They were re-routed to wait 4 hours in Frankfurt, and then to N.Y. instead of Washington, so he was terrified of being asked to fork out for her at Customs etc. Gather he was divided between delight at being her cavalier and terror at what might happen. You can imagine it, can't you?

1977

In the New Year JG was back at the National Theatre rehearsing the title role in John Schlesinger's production of Julius Caesar.

To Dirk Bogarde   *January 1977, Wotton Underwood*

Your very sweet and generous letter touched and pleased me so much. I think we shall all gain some prestige from the quality of the film [*Providence*] and the distinction of the direction, art direction, photography and performances. I only saw a rough cut when I went to do the dubbing in Paris at the end of the summer – without music – and even in that form I was greatly struck by its beauty and general integrity. I knew from the moment I read the script, that it had no chance of appealing to anything but a highbrow public, and the popular press in New York have been pretty damning, which must be a bad disappointment for Alain.

But what fun it was – even with the vileness of the weather, hot and cold in all the wrong taps, but I shall always feel proud to have worked with you so happily and to have got away with a character which I frankly feared was too butch for me to make convincing. I know I could never have done it on the stage, but somehow the location and strange speeches gave me a sort of courage to let myself go in a new way – for me – in trying to act for the screen.

To Meriel Richardson   *9 January, Wotton Underwood*

Dear Harrods! Sheaves of notepaper all wrongly stamped, hence the clumsy corrections!*

Our Arcadia has been somewhat chilled by a fault in the central heating furnace – out with the screwdriver and some shivering hours in consequence. It would happen at the weekend when nobody would think of assisting in any quarter – oh dear!

Miss you both very much, and rather bouleversé by the number of familiar faces in the Actors' Canteen [at the National Theatre], half of whom I can't put a name to. Struggling with David Storey's prizewinner,† which I find terribly gloomy and monotonous, and slightly yearn for Harold Robbins and Jacqueline Susann. Does America vitiate one's palate as badly as that! I fear so.

The *Julius Caesar* setting and general plan is very original, simple and exciting I thought, and Schlesinger extremely intelligent and sympathetic – but of course John Bury's costume designs are beastly and I can see myself making myself very disagreeable at the fittings. Fortunately Stephen,‡ the tailor at the National, is something of a genius and perhaps we can work out something possible between us. I trust so.

Did you see *Love Among the Ruins*?§ I thought it in very bad taste – like making fun of the old ladies, which I always hate, in Gilbert and Sullivan – and Miss Hepburn, whom I love, made to look so awkward and ridiculous. But the others acted very well, Larry in particular, of course.

---

* Harrods had put Wotton Underwood in Berkshire instead of Buckinghamshire.
† *Saville* was published in 1976 and won the Booker Prize.
‡ Stephen Skaptason, chief cutter in the National Theatre wardrobe. Canadian by birth, he was indeed regarded as a genius by actors and actresses for whom he cut clothes; he died sadly young.
§ Television film written by James Costigan, directed by George Cukor, with Laurence Olivier and Katharine Hepburn.

To Peter Hall   *26 January, Wotton Underwood*

Someone has sent me a play about the last days of Wilde – no good, but it reminded me of what I always thought should be staged – a one-act play by Laurence Housman about Wilde. It is called *Echo de Paris* and has three or four characters, Wilde and three friends sitting in a café. He tells stories and is finally cut by some old friend passing. Beautifully written and very vivid. I have no copy, alas, but I imagine you could find it at the London Library or somewhere. I can't think why it has never been put on. Would it make a double bill with *The Browning Version*, I wonder? I don't think I could possibly play Oscar with any conviction! (or without!) but possibly one of the other men? Anyway, you might think it worth getting your henchmen to dig it out. I am sure it has real distinction and would be a bit of a find.

To Irene Worth   *17 February, Wotton Underwood*

Had rather a boss shot at Shotover I fear – a very indifferent production [*Heartbreak House*] by Cedric Messina, who has no talent as a director, whatever qualities he may have as a producer. The young Ellie – a girl named Lesley-Anne Down was very willing and extremely pretty, but not experienced enough for that difficult part. Dan Massey awful (and tiresome too) as Hector, Siân Phillips not at all right for Hesione – no comedy – she played it as a Burne-Jones romantic, Barbara Murray rather good as Ariadne and David Waller and Richard Pearson excellent as Mangan and Mazzini, but it was all very uneven – enormous baroque sets! quite unnecessary and rather unsuitable, everyone rushing about to try and justify the amount of talk. I was very glad to be finished with it.

We have started on *Caesar* which will, I think, be very interesting. I like [John] Schlesinger immensely, and Brian Cox as Brutus and Ronnie Pickup as Cassius seem both to be promising. Hardly any crowd, nondescript period clothes – semi-uniforms, no togas – and I find my small part full of tiny indications which may, I hope, justify my trying to play it. Then I do a small part in *Volpone* (Paul Scofield) – Sir Politick Wouldbe. Peter assures me it can be very funny – I do hope so. I can't see it from reading but perhaps he will guide me to something. We finish *No Man's Land* next week for good. It will be sad to leave the part, and part with Ralph. He starts on his new [William] Douglas Home play *The Kingfisher* with Celia Johnson and Alan Webb for four weeks tryout and then the West End. I've not read it but everyone seems to think it is excellent – specially written for Ralph.

P. Hall tried to lure me into accepting Tony Page to direct *Lear* later on for me, but I don't feel confident enough to agree, and hope for Peter himself, Dexter or possibly Schlesinger. The idea is to do it very simply at the Cottesloe which opens next month. I think the theatre is horrid – like a black coffin, but it isn't quite finished yet. A good size (Royal Court) but thoroughly depressing in atmosphere. Oh dear, everything at the National is *awful* – dressing rooms, passages, decorations etc. Last week our curtain broke down – refused to budge and we had to send the audience home after the first act!

It seems Natasha Brook has made a big personal success in Paris with [*Night of the*] *Iguana* – how clever of her to act in French.

To Richard Findlater   4 *March, Wotton Underwood*

I was interested to talk to an old man called [R. W.] Hart, whom I sat next to at lunch at the Garrick one day recently. He was Ellen Terry's lawyer and managed her affairs in the last years. Knew her evidently pretty well and was full of chat on the subject. Unfortunately he is very deaf and most of my questions didn't get through to him at a noisy table. Edward Robey tells me he is considered the club bore and everyone dreads being buttonholed by him, but of course I found him interesting, being so full of information, and there are so very few left alive who actually knew her.

Bryan Forbes was completing his biography of Edith Evans which would be published later in the year under the title Ned's Girl.

To Bryan Forbes   5 *March, Wotton Underwood*

I am fascinated by the Shaw excerpts and find that ill opinions of my acting from so long ago do little harm to my vanity. I had no idea the old boy still took such an interest in the current theatre. Of course they must be published just as they are.

As to my own letters to Edith, I am amazed to hear I ever wrote her any! I never thought we were on corresponding terms and I'm sure she never wrote *me* any that were interesting or I should have kept them. We had a strange friendship over the years, but never an intimate one and I always regret that I didn't make better use of the many weeks we were on tour together in the thirties, though I have a few memories of good times together. But as you know, I'm sure, she wasn't at her best in a company, and I think she feared my gossipy side and that she might be quoted and misrepresented if she confided in me as a private person. In the theatre, of course, she was a model of behaviour and professionalism, but she was basically so shy of committing herself – a strange mixture of arrogance and humility. I annoyed her once at Brighton when I said 'Wasn't it wonderful to find you had this amazing talent for fascination and coquetry after those early years of spinsters and mothers?' And she answered grandly 'Well, I never had to tour, you know. Always played in London with the best players and directors.' I suppose her plainness had always irked her, and she was never recognised at stage doors – always a small coterie of passionately enthusiastic admirers, but no big general acknowledgement from public or managers, though the critics were so laudatory almost from the time of *I Serve*. I said to Bronnie Albery (at *The Seagull* time) when I was leaving to go to New York in *Hamlet*, 'Why don't you put Edith under contract and we could do more work together when I come back, and she could hold the fort here!' And he answered 'Edith Evans? I can always get her if I want her. Why a contract?' She needed a man behind her as [Katherine] Cornell had [Guthrie] McClintic and Sybil [Thorndike], Lewis [Casson], to give her the confidence managerially, but I don't think she ever trusted anyone very close to her to advise or manage her. What a pity you came into her life so late, and how lucky for her that you did.

To Howard Turner   *5 March, Wotton Underwood*

How nice to hear from you after all these years, and how pleased I am to receive such praise from you for the film [*Providence*]. I loved doing it and was enormously impressed with Resnais himself. What a pity the obliqueness of the script denies the chances of a commercial success. It has not yet even been bought, it seems, for England, though according to the ever-ubiquitous *Variety*, most of the other European countries have bought it and it has received a prize in France.

So glad your work is prospering over the long years. I am at the National all this year, and trying to find some time off to enjoy this beautiful house and garden – much too grand for me really, but my chum has done a marvellous job on the redecoration and slaves away for me, cooking and gardening and trying to manage my impossible finances. So absurd and maddening having to scrimp and save and worry and not be able to entertain or indulge in the smallest luxuries when one is still earning large sums and am [*sic*] lucky enough to be still in considerable demand.

To Bryan Forbes   *12 March, Wotton Underwood*

I was asked to recommend an 'intimate portrait' by Jean Batters* which is coming out. I didn't like it at all, though it is sincere. But I'm sure Edith herself would have detested and resented it so I said no. I gather there is one of the same kind on Vivien Leigh by Anne Edwards. The personal feelings and behaviour of well-known people whom the public admires should not be seized on the moment they are dead. There was a scheme to write about Binkie, which all his friends have stamped on firmly. But I know your book will be quite another matter and give a proper account of Edith's greatness as an artist, and her extraordinary dedication as a woman. I always thought of her as Florence Nightingale, amazed at her own genius and guarding it like a dragon for fear it would get out of hand, and she forwent so many of her

---

* Edith Evans: *A Personal Memoir*.

natural impulses to devote her whole being to preserve it and present it to the greatest possible advantage.

I would love to see you and Nanette [Newman, Bryan's wife] one day, but I am driving up and down for two sets of rehearsals and only spend weekends here. If you were ever in *this* neighbourhood, do ring up and come over. I think you would like this lovely house, though you won't get much of a meal!

Julius Caesar *opened on 22 March 1977.*

To Ralph and Meriel Richardson   *24 March, Wotton Underwood*

The notices were pretty brutal and naturally I found it a bit embarrassing to meet the company last night – and John Schlesinger is, I think, bitterly disappointed. I fancy he thought the Bard an easy wicket, and he says he wanted [Colin] Blakely, [Alan] Howard and Alec McCowen, but they all turned it down! I would have thought Albert Finney and Paul Scofield nearer the mark but one does realise the awful difficulties of juggling casting at the National. But *Caesar* ain't much good without big personalities and really powerful *speaking*. All that black, and meagre crowds don't help much either. Of course that stage needs a big Reinhardt crowd, which seems nowadays to be absolutely out of the question. Ah me!

To Dorothy Reynolds and Angus Mackay   *24 March, Wotton Underwood*

As you no doubt saw, the production is not much liked – a pity as it's a wonderful and enthusiastic company – but the *voices* are ugly and the principals lack stature. I suppose they are at the same stage we all were years ago when we started in Shakespeare at the Vic, but with all the ballyhoo of this mausoleum more is expected. I do think Peter Hall has had an impossibly difficult task to tackle at this particular moment when everything is so impractically expensive and complicated.

Fondest love to you both, and I do hope the medicos are succeeding with Dorothy's trouble. I can't bear to think of her not being able to work.

Dorothy Reynolds *died in early April 1977.*

To Irene Worth   *27 March, Wotton Underwood*

I'm having a much dreaded meeting next Wednesday with my bank manager at the present accountants. Of course Martin refuses to come with me, saying he has not been asked, so I shall be my usual vapid ignoramus and try and take in what they are talking about.

Caesar had a fearful slanging from the Press, and I was greatly over-praised myself, which was very embarrassing when I had to meet the company the following night. But I fear it is rather a conventional show – what the Vic might have got away with, years ago. The huge stage hung with black velvet and the drab (but quite adequate) semi-modern uniforms make the whole thing a bit dreary. There should have been some judicious cuts and some primary colours somewhere at some time. There are a few original ideas and touches, but the text does not ring and vary – both Brutus and Antony [Mark McManus] have strong accents (Scotch and Scotch-Australian!) and there is inadequate orchestration of climax, pause, and all the musician's expertise which, in this play especially, is of such vital importance.

I think he [Ralph Richardson] was upset over the Tynan interview – and so was I. He said Mu was hideously distressed but refused to mention it. Tynan is a devil – he did much the same years ago with me – you can't trust him an inch – and especially annoying as so much he writes is admirably well observed and written, I thought.

After Julius Caesar, *JG played Sir Politick Would-be in* Volpone.

To Pat and Michael York   *2 June, Wotton Underwood*

Did I tell you of the awful moment when Princess Grace came round in New York and for one ghastly second I *almost* greeted her as Deborah Kerr! Such is the fate of advancing years and confused dressing-room technique! I wonder if she guessed as she tactfully mentioned Monaco a few seconds later which caused the penny to drop with a fearsome clunk.

To Bryan Forbes   *2 September, Wotton Underwood*

Had such a splendid time reading the book – devoured it at two long sessions, one far into the night! I think you have drawn her [Edith Evans] most splendidly and truthfully and feel sure you would have pleased her with it as much as you will surely please countless readers.

Much amused how well Enid [Bagnold] comes out! I am devoted to her as you know but, like all female playwrights, she is a devil to work with in the theatre – really a thwarted actress herself and as autocratic and self-centred as Edith who, I always thought, was slightly resentful of her snobbishness and arrogance. I think Enid was deeply jealous of sharing her (undoubted) talents both with Gladys [Cooper] and with Edith and both of them realised and resented it and became understandably difficult as a result. I shall never forget the job I had in the Birmingham tryout of [*The*] *Chalk Garden* to keep them from each other's throats. But of course Enid's letters are fascinating (always with an eye to eventual publication!) and she will be delighted, poor old girl, to see them in print. But they don't give any idea of the trouble she can make!

Guy's letters* are remarkable – met him quite often at suppers at Malkin St. and he used to sit in a corner and never say a word. Michael [Redgrave]'s are extraordinary too. What an odd fish he is – so talented but now a wreck, yet determined to go on working – a real pro.† Rachel [Kempson, Michael Redgrave's wife] is a wonder.

JG came out of the production of Volpone *for a prostate operation but returned to the cast and began rehearsals for a new play,* Half-Life *by Julian Mitchell, directed by Waris Hussein.*

To Irene Worth   *15 September, Wotton Underwood*

Thank you for the wonderful roses – *two* lots – which came for me to the hospital. Angelic of you. They let me go in exactly a week, and of course it is wonderful to be back in glorious Indian summer weather, though I am very weak and tired. But I eat and sleep well and I know the next three weeks rest will enable me to get back my energy and enthusiasm again. I don't begin rehearsing my new play till Oct. 10th and go back on the 21st to my little part in *Volpone*. We play the new play, *Half-Life* by Julian Mitchell at the Cottesloe for 20 performances from Nov. to Jan. 16th with occasional *Volpones* and some off nights, so it will keep me busy. After that my contract is over at the National and we shall either hope to transfer *Half-Life* to the West End or, if it turns out to be no good, sweep it under the carpet and hope to find something else. There is a play about Diaghilev in which I am rather interested and so is Lindsay Anderson and managements both in London and New York, so that is a vague possibility up one's sleeve if the Mitchell play is no go. I suppose I ought really to come to America again to make some money. The bank and accountants are pressing me to go away for a year, but I dread that. If only I could make a couple of well-made films for a month or two, and come back between, that would calm the situation a bit. I'm selling more pictures meanwhile and am determined to hold on to this house somehow. Of course our transport expenses are dreadfully heavy but I do feel it is worth it. London is more hateful than ever and I don't seem to miss theatres and cinemas as there is so little to see, though Ian McKellen and Judi Dench have the most extraordinary praise for their *Macbeth*, which Trevor Nunn has brought to the Donmar, and I should really like to see it – a 'chamber' production without scenery or any kind of costume presentation, which is the way Peter Hall talks of doing *Lear* for me – perhaps!

Lynn [Fontanne] arrived a week or two ago – came to Ralph's play one night and to see us in *Volpone* the next. She is bowed and has let her hair go white, but looked infinitely distinguished and brave. Is staying at the

---

* George 'Guy' Booth, Edith Evans's husband.
† Michael Redgrave was suffering from Parkinson's disease which would take his life in 1985.

Dorchester for 3 weeks, where I hope to go and see her soon. I want Ralph to write a tribute, signed by a dozen of us here, to be read at the N.Y. Memorial Service [for Alfred Lunt who died on 3 August], perhaps by you? I will talk to Lynn about it, but don't know how soon it will be. We talked of a service in London (Ralph and I) but decided it might not be well enough attended as it is so long since they played here.

To Lillian Gish   *13 November, Wotton Underwood*

My operation seems to have been very successful. I was only just a week in hospital, in a lovely room looking over the river to Big Ben, though I was extremely depressed and easily tired for the rest of September. I was able to go back in to *Volpone* for the last five weeks, and have been in rehearsal for the last five in the new comedy which opens this Thursday in the small theatre, the Cottesloe, which is attached to the National. It's rather a horrid building, I think, no carpets and all painted black, no curtain or proper proscenium, but I suppose it is a good tryout place. We are already sold out for the 25 performances we give there over the next three months and I very much hope we may be transferred to the West End in March. Naturally I am very nervous as I have a hugely long and complicated part, but like the company and the director very much. I only pray it may turn out well. Also, Ralph and I are to make a TV version of *No Man's Land* in February, which I shall enjoy.

I do miss my American friends, especially Marti Stevens and Irene – and you! I wonder if Rosamond Gilder has recovered. I heard she had been very ill and she is much older than she looks. I would hate to think of her as an invalid. She is such an intrepid, enthusiastic creature.

Half-Life *opened at the Cottesloe Theatre on 17 November.*

To Richard Bebb   *26 November, Wotton Underwood*

Do you think one of the American universities would perhaps buy from me a bunch of my rehearsal scripts? I have about 20 fairly recent ones, covered with notes, directions, copyings out and doodles! I'm told they often like to collect such things. I have no real use for the scripts. I wouldn't offer the film ones, but the theatre ones are more interesting. Anyway, you might ask tentatively when you are next in the U.S. I'm afraid there are no Shakespearean ones, though. I should be embarrassed to ask for myself, but have been in bad money troubles since I left London and bought this beautiful house, just at the wrong moment. Everyone tells me I ought to sell it, but I am determined to manage somehow. My best pictures have gone already, alas.

To Irene Worth   *22 December, Wotton Underwood*

I'm glad to say the new play goes marvellously well, even at the Cottesloe
with no proscenium or curtain – very self-conscious making in an old-
fashioned kind of play as this one is – but apart from that the auditorium is
intimate and good to play to, and I begin to feel more at home in my long
part which was hard to learn with so few performances and ten day gaps
between.

We had a rather mixed press at the opening, justly I think, for many
reasons, but I think we can live in fairly good hopes of it going well in the
West End. It has masses of laughs and a few serious moments – witty and
well written on the whole – but a bit patchy here and there as the author is a
novelist and this is his first play. I'm very aware of the flaws where it has been
cut and filled in, but I don't think it shows much as far as the public is
concerned – rather the quality in general of *Day by the Sea* and *Chalk Garden*
if you can imagine that marriage!

Ralph had a 75th birthday and many tributes and I had my interview with
the Queen when I got my CH [Companion of Honour] and a degree at
London University, which darling Gwen attended and was mentioned, to my
great delight, in the speech they made about me, so all that was very nice.

I've been to Lord Goodman about my financial troubles and he has been
absolutely charming, taking over my lawyer work as well as finding me new
accountants and suing Coutts, so I'm hoping very much that I may be able
soon to get on to a more even keel again next year. Just wretched luck that
the massive inflation and crippling tax laws should have come over these last
three years when it is so expensive paying for the continual car expenses and
trying to keep this big house warm, to say nothing of the outrageous price of
food and drink. But everyone I know is in the same boat, and Martin slaves
away and spends literally nothing on himself. His animals are his only real
pleasure, but I can't help wishing they didn't tie him quite so much.

1978

*A dinner in honour of Dame Peggy Ashcroft's seventieth birthday was held at the
Garrick Club.*

To Peggy Ashcroft   *6 January, National Theatre*

I did feel so very badly not to come to your Garrick dinner last night. Really
I find it so difficult to believe you are joining me in the Seventh House! I just
can't stay up after the play any longer with the long drive back, and yesterday
we had a rehearsal as well as a performance, with two hours at the BBC – so

you see it was an impossible day for me. We hadn't done *Half-Life* for more than three weeks! So it was all the nerves of a first night all over again.

Would you care to have the enclosed trifle in memory of our long and dear friendship. I still cherish the little mourning brooch you gave me with H.P. (Hamlet – Prince) on it when we opened at the Haymarket in '44.

Fondest love and long life and happiness.

Half-Life transferred to the Duke of York's Theatre on 2 March.

To Cecil Beaton   *24 March, Wotton Underwood*

Your impeccable manners don't diminish. I was so happy to see you again, if only for those few moments, and of course delighted that you had enjoyed the play. The notices for your book could hardly have been better, and I enjoyed it so very much, despite the sadness which all of us in the age bracket are bound to feel. (Beverley Nichols came round last week on two sticks after I gather, some pretty horrendous operations, but still attended by Cyril Butcher!) But you have triumphed remarkably over all your miseries and you can still write and paint and occupy yourself with your lovely house and garden.

Larry and Michael Redgrave are both equally to be admired for their courage and determination. There must be something about the theatre and social life which manages to drive one against all reason, to continue to be lively and interested and to refuse to lie down. What price Enid and Diana Cooper? Shall we last as well as that? Well, perhaps we shall, you know.

To Irene Worth   *2 May, Wotton Underwood*

Very depressing start to the summer. May Day (new) Holiday complete washout – pouring rain and everything closed – Hampton Court, Kew, Museums and Picture Galleries, Garrick Club, restaurants! Everyone trudging about with macs and umbrellas, mass demonstrations soaked – only the pubs (and porn shops) still open. Oh dear.

An American called Robert Patrick, who wrote *Kennedy's Children* – great succès d'estime here (though it only had a season at the Arts after being first produced at the King's Head) has sent me a play about Pontius Pilate, Judas and Christ in modern dress. It was done at a University Theatre in California and the notices are very encouraging. Many things wrong with it, especially inordinate length, but I am greatly taken with it and hope to meet the author when he comes to Europe. It is very original and well written, though I don't know how it might offend Jews and Catholics, and don't quite understand the political credo, as I am so stupid about those things. Will show it to Lindsay Anderson who might be interesting about it.

Ralph very worried about his new play [*Alice's Boys* by Felicity Browne and

Jonathan Hales]. They are at Richmond this week and open next week at the Savoy. Trouble between director and authors.* I do hope all will solve itself. Was it after you left that Binkie's house in Essex caught fire – a terrific gale, sparks from a fire J.P. had lit in the sitting room fired the thatch in many places and the whole house, except the bungalow, burnt down in half an hour. Under-insured, of course, and the Will still not cleared up – after five years!† He had just moved all his London things there and got rid of his London flat.

To Irene Worth   *18 May, Wotton Underwood*

Tony Richardson has sent me a play by [David] Mamet called [*A*] *Life in the Theatre* for two actors, originally played by Ellis Rabb, now I believe by José Ferrer off Broadway. I don't see anything in it myself, but he thinks it would be fine for me – another *Home*. Would you be an angel and give me your opinion of it. I hate to seem stupid, but I do imagine it comes out quite a bit differently on the stage – in reading it seems nothing to me. So do see it if you can bear to and tell me what you think.

Spring is here at last, and we are doing very well at the theatre with the influx of tourists, but poor Ralph has come an awful cropper with his new thriller which closes next week after disastrous notices and a lot of trouble beforehand – director changes etc. I fear it will be a most dreadful blow to him, and Mu has not been well also which is such bad luck.

Providence has just opened here to rave reviews, but I felt very embarrassed to read them on the same morning of Ralph's débâcle.

To Ed Cone and George Pitcher   *15 September, Great Yarmouth*

Well, here I am holed up in an appallingly gimcrack hotel – sing-songs in the evening, plastic walls and unspeakable food and furniture making a ridiculous half hour television special (!) of a Roald Dahl short story [*Neck*] in which I do my Orient Express deadpan butler performance with Joan Collins as a randy chatelaine and one or two others. We move to Lowestoft to finish it next week and film at a dreadful 1926 stately home with Edwardian furnishings and rather pretty run-down gardens with a maze, flocked to by tourists twice a week at 70p a head while we lark amid a welter of cables and cameras in the bedrooms upstairs. All pretty boring, especially as the weather's endlessly squally and uncertain which drives everyone in and out and wastes the time of the crew. I sit about a lot and do my crosswords and work desultorily on another little book of reminiscences‡ which I've almost finished.

---

* The original director, Eric Thompson, was replaced by Lindsay Anderson before the play opened.
† Binkie Beaumont's sudden death in 1973 left his affairs in considerable disarray.
‡ *An Actor and His Time*, written in collaboration with John Miller and John Powell.

Meanwhile at Wotton the enemy flourishes as well as ever. We have got the road mended at long last, with a lot of chicanery from Elaine [Brunner] and the neighbours about sharing in the paying for it. We're struggling to get a flue directed from our big chimney down to the fireplace in our big room so that we can have an open fire in the winter, and trying to mend the clock tower which has split and leans ominously askew. Attempting to prevent the enemy from building a bungalow just over the end of our garden wall (for which it seems he succeeded in getting planning permission back in 1974, before we took the house). Elaine not at all concerned as she won't see it, if it is built, from *her* windows, and so on and so on.

Lord Goodman's solicitors and accountants have now taken me over and if only Arnold [Weissberger] can get me back the big sum that your tax people have withheld all this time, I may be able to get a bit tidier by next spring, but we have scrimped or saved all this year, forgoing having people to stay and going out to meals. I sold about four of my pictures which rather broke my heart, but they were the only things of any real value that would get me cash, and of course there is a capital gains tax even then. Fortunately the walls don't really need pictures, and I managed to save the Dufy and a few others that I couldn't bear to part with.

I've never stopped working. *Half-Life* ran 200 performances and finished a week or two ago. Much more successful than I dared to hope – a very uneven play by a novelist, his first, which needed a lot of tinkering and readjustment, but it amused people and I had a very long and fairly amusing part – sort of Maurice Bowra don with a lot of Noël Coward acidity, and an emotional breakdown about an ex-lover (killed in the Spanish War) in which I burst into tears with my back to the audience – thought that way might make a change – at the end of the second act.

Besides the play I did a TV of Shotover in *Heartbreak House*, Chorus in *Romeo and Juliet*, John of Gaunt in *Richard the Second*, and two short cameo (!) bits, one in *Les Misérables* (film and TV) and one in a very silly Sherlock Holmes–Jack the Ripper film [*Murder by Decree*] with Christopher Plummer and James Mason, in which I appear as Lord Salisbury behind a desk in a Masonic Hall in a huge beard, so one way and another you see I have not been idle.

Martin slaves away, cooking and minding the dogs and birds, smoking endless cigarettes and eating and drinking nothing. He has also started mending the garden wall and the pretty masks on the front of the orangery which Arthur Bryant [a former tenant] had allowed to crumble. We quarrel with Elaine when she gets too brassy and she racks [?] it up by sending Nanny with consolation prizes of vegetables and purring endearments on the telephone.

Various lodgers come and go at the big house – agreeable American dons, the Silversteins and Ellises (who asked me to dinner to meet John Bryson, an erstwhile lover of mine in the 20s, whom I was delighted to see again – and then he died a few weeks later – shock from seeing me, no doubt!) He left a large fortune and his pictures were given to the Ashmolean – he had very good ones.

To Irene Worth   *29 September, Wotton Underwood*

I just finished a record for Caedmon of *Ages of Man*, hoping the affectations and mannerisms I listened to with dismay on the playbacks will smooth themselves out. I do find recording finds one out, and Shakespeare is more difficult in that medium than narrative prose and poetry. You manage your breathing so well – one is never conscious of it, while I puff and blow like a grampus if I'm not very careful.

We are taking *Half-Life* to Toronto for 4 weeks in November – two weeks here first at Oxford and Richmond – but they left it so late that all that good company got other jobs and we have to rehearse a new one – three weeks at least, but I shall make my understudy do some of it. Hope to get a few cuts and tidying up and hope the fresh people will be equally good and help me to attack it a bit more satisfactorily. After that I have no idea.

I cannot be accurate about the date of this next letter, but the subject of the memoir had been dead for a number of years.

To Dr Haffenden   *10 October 1978?, London*

I was at preparatory school (Hillside, Farncombe, Godalming) between 1914–1915 and John Hayward became one of my best friends there. I even remember visiting him at his home in Wimbledon where his Mother greatly resembled him with the same large eyes with big doll-like eyelashes. He was an ugly boy with a big sloppy mouth, but very amusing and likeable. We would lie out on rugs watching cricket matches and eating cherries. When I moved on to Westminster I completely lost sight of him. Then, in Cambridge during the Second War, I was giving shows for the troops in nearby stations and Boris Ord, whom I knew slightly, invited me and the company to an organ recital which he gave for us in King's Chapel, including Delius' First Cuckoo in Spring – a strange effect it made adapted for the organ! As we sat waiting for the music to begin, a cripple in a wheelchair was rolled up the aisle and stopped opposite my pew, and I immediately recognised Hayward. I spoke a few embarrassed words to him as he left, and as I hurried across the Court, I looked back and saw to my dismay that his chair had slipped off the step of the chapel as it was guided towards his car and he was tipped out of it on to the ground. I could see his dreadfully misshapen back and shoulders and he was obviously cursing furiously at the man who propelled the chair.

Peggy Ashcroft was staying at Merton Hall with Lord Rothschild, then her brother-in-law,* awaiting the birth of her child and when I went to see her there a few days later, I found Hayward staying in the house too. He was cataloguing the library and avoiding the raids in London (this was 1941, I think), and so of course I had an opportunity to talk to him a little. He had become, naturally, rather bitter and acid, but I was told he was very popular, especially with women students who used to take him out in his chair and with whom he was said to flirt rather outrageously. I didn't see him again, however, till the 50s when he was brought to dine at Peter Brook's house off Church St, Kensington, where I met him again. (Mrs George Orwell was the other guest.) He was pretty alarming by this time, and everybody took pains to try and keep him amiable and amusing, which he could be when he liked. But we never met again, and I only knew afterwards of his long friendship with T. S. Eliot and the disappointment he suffered by the poet's second marriage. He was obviously a tragic and brilliant creature. I always wondered if his wretched physical martyrdom was in some ways hereditary, remembering the looks of his Mother, which were so curiously and alarmingly similar. He never wrote to me at all.

To Lynn Fontanne   *16 October, Wotton Underwood*

What a sumptuous occasion.† What a Lucullan feast. And such a gathering of dear and faithful friends, and all contrived and organised by your radiant and unchanging self.

How like you to have thought of it all, and to put yourself to all the enormous trouble. How we loved to be at your table and to look round it at all those devoted faces – so many wonderful memories to look back to, and your own unflinching courage to admire. The joy of thinking what happiness you gave us all in your unforgettable years with Alfred. I'm sure he – and Binkie and Noël – were all hovering about with loving wings and blessing you with the comradeship and *hard work* of all the years you laboured together to bring so much happiness and fun to so many different lives. Most fond love and admiration and thanks much more than I can possibly say.

Take care of your most dear self and continue to flourish. Come back again soon. You are a great lady, an unmatched actress, and a most dear friend.

To Irene Worth   *6 November, Wotton Underwood*

What plans for next year? Do you think I could tempt you to play Lady Bracknell? You are the only person who could satisfactorily follow Edith and I would dearly love to do the play once more, in correct 1895 fashion – bonnets and bustles (we made it Edwardian so that Edith could have the big hats) and

---

* Victor Rothschild was then married to Jeremy Hutchinson's sister, Barbara.
† A dinner party at the Dorchester Hotel.

of course we were all *too old* when we did it at the Globe, the Phoenix and New York in the 40s.

When I first played it for Playfair in 1930 with my aunt Mabel Terry-Lewis as Bracknell, we were all the right age and it was so much lighter and more attractive. The men and girls should be in their twenties. I ask you because the Triumph people* who now have the Haymarket are anxious to put something on there from March to September when I gather they propose to do *Othello* for Paul Scofield.

I know I could make a charming thing of it, and the revivals since I did it – one very bad at the Haymarket with Dan Massey and Isabel Jeans, and one on TV with Coral Browne, then one at Greenwich directed by Jonathan Miller with Irene Handl (with German accent, God knows why) – all these were disaster. And it is such a perfect play which I know so intimately.

Would it interest you to do it? If so, I will urge the idea, but have no interest in it with anyone else. Do think it over and let me know what your reactions are.

The other great difficulty for *Earnest* is the casting of the two young men. But if you were to agree to do it, I would begin looking carefully now for the four young people. I think Annette Crosbie would be a splendid Miss Prism.

1979

To Irene Worth   *5 February, Wotton Underwood*

We miss you so much as always. Yesterday a hideous Foyle's lunch for Betty Bacall to promote her biography [*By Myself*], which is awfully good, I think, and will surely make a fortune for her, but she is absolutely exhausted with promoting it, both in the U.S. and here, and still has Australia and Paris to cope with. Larry was at the lunch too – agony to see him so changed and withered, but he talked gallantly, made a speech – a bit rambling – and even said he might be tempted to try and act in the theatre again. He is really very brave.

We played *Half-Life* for two weeks at Brighton, but I was glad to see the end of it – awful weather and wretched houses, icy cold and I spent my spare time visiting invalids, Enid Bagnold and my sad brother Val, who has hardening of the arteries and is a shadow, tottery and slow of speech – nothing to be done – very sad for his young wife who looks after him devotedly.

Maina has done her show in Paris and had a fine notice in the *Telegraph* the other day – so clever of her to have conceived and executed it all by herself both in London and now abroad. I am so sorry to have missed it – and

---

* Managers Paul Elliott and Duncan C. Weldon.

apparently she rescued [Svetlana] Beriosova who had retired and become an alcoholic. Maina got her to do a scene in which she taught her a classic ballet role and it was the hit of the show. I think [Yvette] Chauviré and some other famous ballerina is doing the scene in Paris. Maina even directed and lit the show herself!

You are very lucky not to be in England just now. The cold weather lasts forever, and the news is abysmal. Strikes everywhere (the National had to close twice last week), hospitals, ambulances, lorries all picketing and only working with voluntary help and London is piled high with garbage. Rubbish heaps mountain high, almost up to the head of the statues in Leicester Square, Piccadilly almost impassable, and they say the rats are out scavenging all over Soho.

I'm quite glad of a bit of a rest after my year and more in the play. Off to see *The Double Dealer** tomorrow – the first time I've ever been in front at the Olivier – everyone says it is brilliantly done, and [Dorothy] Tutin, [Robert] Stephens and Michael Bryant all extremely good. I feel it is quite an outing as I've been so seldom to a play or film the last year.

My twelve radio talks (about myself, oddly enough!!) were a great success, I'm glad to say, and are to be put out again later on and also to be published as a book with a lot of photographs, which is nice, as the work is really done already.

Oh for the Spring and your return.

To George Pitcher   *17 June, Wotton Underwood*

I am in something of a frenzy of work. Just returned from five weeks in Warsaw where I made a film for Andrzej Wajda [*The Conductor*], my part in English (including a 4 day crash course in conducting a 50 piece Orchestra – Beethoven's Fifth – not easy, I can tell you) and acting with delightful but incomprehensible actors speaking in Polish. The other parts are to be dubbed into English for the Western version, and mine dubbed into Polish for the local one! Everyone marvellously kind and helpful, including an excellent interpreter. A terrific heat wave – no script, everything improvised and translated (by me, from impossible literal dialogue) and shot in one or two takes only, mostly with hand-held cameras, as they can't afford expensive American equipment, which has to be imported at great cost.

I play a kind of Toscanini character returning to his native Poland after success in the West, and finally die there. Very good part and brilliant director, but a bit taxing one way and another. The Poles have wonderful manners and are defiantly hard working and optimistic despite all sorts of dreary stringencies and lack of comfort and luxuries of all kinds. Then I made friends with the *N.Y. Times* correspondent who gave me his room in the big hotel

---

* The National Theatre production of Congreve's play by Peter Wood opened in September 1978.

just opposite Victory Square, from which I saw the whole Papal Mass. 250,000 people standing for 3½ hours in the blazing sun – marvellously staged and sustained – the Pope reminded me vividly of Harry Andrews! By and large it was a really thrilling experience. I only hope the film may come out in the not too distant future and that my performance may be adequate – the bits I saw were splendidly photographed and lit, anyway.

I got back to start a commentary on English Gardens, a programme for television. I am driven about to various beautiful houses and gardens – weather dreadfully disappointing, gales and rainstorms, which spoils it rather, and the speeches are very commonly written, sort of guidebook jaunty. I try and adapt these a bit to make them sound more human. After that I do two days in Otto Preminger's film of Graham Greene's new novel, *The Human Factor* – a very small part – and then off to *Libya* for a week to play a really tiny bit in an elaborate epic about Graziani and Mussolini called *Omar Mukhtar*, with Anthony Quinn, Rod Steiger and Irene Papas – huge money for absolutely no part – a week in Rome for another scene in it in August, and in between I do *two* TV films of three weeks each.

So all is bustle and confusion, and I hardly know if I am on my head or my heels. Piles of letters to answer of which this is about the only one I can find time for. So do forgive the slight note of hysteria!

The new government has mercifully reduced the top rate of income tax to 60% instead of 83%, which is certainly a relief. I really feared I should have to sell the house and go to live abroad. But of course everything is going to be hideously more expensive, and they say they won't give us any more oil till December. As this affects the hot water system as well as the central heating, the winter prospect looks decidedly grim.

To Irene Worth   *15 July, Wotton Underwood*

I've had such a mad time these last three months.

I went for a week to Libya!! Idiotic war epic about Graziani and the Bedouins with Anthony Quinn and Irene Papas, millions of pounds invested in it, and I had one short scene, covered in beard, blanket and Arab get-up, but it was kind of interesting. Wonderful ruins at Cyrene and Apollonia, stayed in a huge camp like Camberley, pine trees and lovely air – no flies – a hut with hot shower, loo and comfortable bed. 250 people installed there, all nationalities, film every evening, tennis court, swimming pool, games room, huge canteen, laundry – all laid on. They have built two of these camps for the unit and they go back to the Libyan army when the film is over. Dreadful waste of money it seems to me, and Gaddafi is supposed to be backing it along with various Americans and others. I have to go to Rome at the end of August to do another small scene – thought my travelling days were over, but it seems not!

Hume [Cronyn] and Jessie [Tandy] open in *The Gin Game* [D. L. Coburn] at the end of the month. I fear I have no new address for Larry but ICM would forward a letter. He is to play MacArthur in a big film* for a colossal salary, filming in Tokyo, Seoul and Hollywood. Amazing gallantry, and Michael Redgrave is acting again, an almost silent part† in a play at the National [*Close of Play* by Simon Gray] directed by Pinter. Peggy A. was to have been in it but is laid up for 3 months with a cartilage in her leg operation – such bad luck for her. Ralph is well and working in 2 plays at the National.

---

* *Inchon* was financed by the Revd Sun Myung Moon, directed by Terence Young, and was an unmitigated disaster. Olivier was reputedly paid one million dollars.
† Redgrave had only one line in the play although he was on stage almost throughout.

THE EIGHTIES

1980

In Michael Rudman's National Theatre production of Arthur Miller's All My Sons, *Stephen Greif played Biff.*

To Stephen Greif   *25 January, Wotton Underwood*

I would like to congratulate you on your very moving and powerful performance in the play, which I saw yesterday with so much pleasure. It was really a delight to see such perfect interplay and so many good performances in a beautifully integrated production. I thought your big scene immensely touching and real.

To George Pitcher and Ed Cone   *17 February, Wotton Underwood*

Delighted to have your two letters and to know the book [*An Actor and His Time*] arrived safely and that it amused you. It has done marvellously well over the Christmas sales, though I simply loathed the lunches and signing sessions and interviews which the publishers insisted on – so embarrassing having to publicise one's own work in a way that, thank God, is never necessary in the theatre. Now it has been sold for paperback (Penguin) for next year and bought for America in the fall. Realising my whole American career is not touched on in the book, I am going to do two more radio talks soon, which can be edited for an extra chapter in the American edition – seems a good idea. I was very embarrassed to realise I had completely ignored Irene. 'Not even her name in the index,' Martin cried, the moment he examined the book, but I will put that right in the new chapter. I wrote her a profound apology which she answered very sweetly. I am dreadfully distressed at the immediate failure of her play, but hardly surprised – remembering the fiasco of *All Over* – that there was difficulty in raising money for a play all about cancer and the Angel of Death! Albee was on television here a week or two ago, looking like Robert Louis Stevenson with his Mexican moustache – his dogs were beautiful, but he was very pretentious and boring, I'm afraid.

I can hardly believe that for the first time in my ancient life I haven't acted in the theatre for a whole year, but film and television offers have poured in (and one or two silly offers for plays in N.Y. which I turned down, too), and are, of course, much less responsibility, very well paid – including living allowances and travelling – and quite fun to do, especially as they are spread out over short periods with weeks between when I can relax quietly here, which is a great joy. Martin slaves away at the house and garden, and gets very tired – eats nothing (not even FISH!), does not drink at all, but smokes interminably. We have only three dogs left and five – no, six – parrots, two tortoises. One greyhound died suddenly and before that our third shitzu, but the others are a great comfort and get on splendidly together.

I'm in a mad frenzy of work at the moment. Stayed for a week at Castle Howard in Yorkshire, playing a very amusing part of the eccentric father of the hero in a TV serial of *Brideshead Revisited* [by Evelyn Waugh]. Olivier plays Lord Marchmain, though we don't have any scenes together.

The film I did in Warsaw last April with Andrzej Wajda is being shown this month at the Berlin Festival – can't imagine how they have put it together, as they wrote they couldn't find a Polish actor with a voice suitable to dub mine, so are leaving me in English with subtitles!

Last week a tentative offer for a film with – hold it – *Sinatra* – to be made on location in New York the first weeks in April. My agent says it is quite an amusing part. If they make a firm money offer I might say yes, but only if they will pay Martin's fare too. It would be fun to be there again and perhaps see you.

To Pat and Michael York   *17 February, Wotton Underwood*

The theatre is in a parlous condition and nothing to excite one, though I do want to see *Amadeus*, the Mozart Shaffer play with Scofield which has aroused much controversy. Oddly enough, the two big successes of the RSC and the National seem to be revivals of American plays, *Once in a Lifetime* [by George S. Kaufman and Moss Hart] and *Death of a Salesman* [by Arthur Miller]. I dragged myself up to see the latter because I had to present a prize to Warren Mitchell, and thought it amazingly well done, accents included.

I can't quite believe I have not been acting in a theatre for a whole year – never happened in my life before! But thanks to the new government, money problems have been considerably lightened, and I have been amazingly lucky doing a succession of quite effective (and not too much responsibility) parts in films and television.

To Hugh Wheeler   *23 April, Wotton Underwood*

My poor brother Val is in a very bad way. Hardening of the arteries and pretty dotty. They are trying to get him home to his fortunately devoted wife, but he has been in hospital several weeks now. Awfully sad – and, oh God, the World situation. The news seems to get worse and worse.

To Douglas Fairbanks Jr.   *10 May, Wotton Underwood*

How very kind of you to think of me and send me those happy snaps of Ellen [Terry] and James Carew.* Of course Edy Craig and her 'gang' disapproved of him very much, but I never really knew why they parted. Ellen is supposed to have said, 'He kicked my dog!' The pictures are taken at Smallhythe – have you ever seen the cottage? Now a museum, beautifully preserved with many of her stage dresses and all the original pictures and furniture just as she left it. If you are ever in Kent you should go and see it, overlooking Romney Marsh. Enchanting.

Great do for Cathleen Nesbitt at Thames Television last week. I really think she enjoyed it herself. Many charming tributes and a great gathering of friends and admirers – she took it all in her stride and made a little speech at the end, holding her son and daughter's hands, and finally made a curtsey. I dread those things but it was very well done.

To George Pitcher and Ed Cone   *28 May, Wotton Underwood*

I have agreed, after a certain amount of bribery, to come over to be in a film [*Arthur*] with Dudley Moore – my old butler image – to be made on location in New York. Martin and I will fly by Concorde and we are going to stay at the Lombardy Hotel in a suite recently occupied by Bette Davis! I am assured it is very nice and comfortable. The picture is a bit common, it seems to me, trying, but not succeeding, to be a kind of Woody Allen fantasy – but my part is rather good and *might* perhaps be funny if the director (who is also the author of the script) is clever. His name is Steve Gordon. Liza Minnelli is also to be in it. There are scenes in motorcars, Tiffany's, Bloomingdale's etc. I only pray it won't be too appallingly hot, as I am very prim and dressed up. I have a death scene in hospital wearing a cowboy hat. Keep your derision for when you see the film!

Martin in agonies at leaving the dogs – you will appreciate that – and the cockatoos. We lost both greyhound whippets and our talkative African Grey parrot earlier this year, so there are only the two shitzus left and they are very precious. Mary, our old daily from Cowley St, who still works for us several times a week, is going to live here while we are away and look after the animals, so I can only hope all will be well.

To George Pitcher   *11 October, Wotton Underwood*

Very dismayed to hear your pugilistic exploit. I'm sure it was an alarming experience, and only glad you came to no permanent harm. Gene Moore (re

---

* American actor, Ellen Terry's third husband.

Tiffany's) once got held up on the steps of his East River flat, under which a black man had been hiding. A knife was held to his chin while he handed over watch, ring, pocketbook etc. When the assailant ran off, Gene rushed up to his apartment and telephoned breathlessly to the police. 'I've been held up by a black man and am still bleeding.' A Southern sounding voice remarked, 'What a pity he didn't kill you!' and rang off. So you see!! Still, I hope the molester may yet be found, and that none of your own valuables were taken or anybody badly shaken.

On the last night in New York I had one of my periodic blackouts – as usual in a restaurant where we were dining with Marti Stevens. Very annoying and embarrassing, but I got home in a cab, sweated like mad, slept like a top and we got up in the morning and caught the Concorde. It was so maddening and terrified poor Martin, who slept on the floor all night outside my bedroom door! But I have suffered no after-effects, though he watches me like a lynx and has put me on the Scarsdale Diet (recommended in N.Y. by Coral Browne) – very boring – no butter, milk or sugar or potatoes, but fruit, steak and fish – though I don't starve it is very tedious – only one glass of wine a day, but I have already shed about 8 pounds in ten days and am really getting quite used to it, and I'm sure it's good for me. The blackout is called a syncope – a fainting fit due, presumably, to eating, drinking and talking too much when very tired – which of course I was. But I suppose it is a kind of warning and I have been sleeping enormously and keeping very quiet till I begin another silly Agatha Christie serial TV part* (of an insane Marquis) for three weeks at the end of this month.

Harold Pinter and Antonia Fraser gave an enormous party at their house – a big marquee set up in the garden – about 200 people – to celebrate their marriage after the several years old scandal of both their divorces. Now it appears they haven't been married at all yet, but hope to do so before the end of the year! The party was given to bamboozle the press! Anyway, Antonia was spectacular in white – a Boadicea Bride – and I only stayed about an hour as there was such a mob. Everyone brought wedding presents, a whole sideboard littered with them, so they didn't do so badly and I did see Peggy Ashcroft and Rebecca West, deaf but defiant, and a lot of old friends as well.

Poor old Enid Bagnold – now 90 – has been moved into a London flat, and that crazy old house at Rottingdean is being sold up next week. Alan Webb went to visit her in London, and she kissed him and then said, 'I'm reading – do you mind?' and returned to her book without further ado. Rather tragic. She lives on morphia and when Bobby Flemyng paid a call on her in Rottingdean, she upped with her skirt and gave herself an injection there and then! Oh dear, one mustn't live *too* long.

---

* *The Seven Dials Mystery.*

To Irene Worth   *16 October, Wotton Underwood*

So *The Importance* is not to be. Well, never mind, it was a nice idea, and how happy I should have been to work again with you. If we could have got the rest of the cast too, it might have been the greatest fun, but my heart already sank when Cohen began suggesting – my God – Dustin Hoffman and Robert Redford.

Tomorrow there is a literary lunch at the National Theatre for the publication of Mother's book of theatre criticism [*A Victorian Playgoer* by Kate Terry Gielgud]. Miss [Muriel] St Clair Byrne has edited it and chosen the extracts, and it is rather fascinating reading. I will send you a copy. Eleanor will be there but, alas, Val is too ill, though his wife has accepted, and of course I have to make a speech. Rather dreading it, but Mother would, I think, have been immensely gratified to see it in print – for which, of course, she never intended it. Incredible to think she wrote it 80 years ago and she has been dead for 20!

To Michael York   *17 November, Wotton Underwood*

How very like you to write about the Polish film [*The Conductor*]. I saw it yesterday at the London Film Festival, and though of course Wajda is a masterly director, I was very disappointed with it. The cutting and dubbing were both very muddling I felt, and I don't think I give a convincing performance, except at one or two effective moments. But it was fun to see it and renew my acquaintance with the cast, and remember the fascinating time I had in making it.

1981

To George Pitcher   *14 January, Wotton Underwood*

Good of you to write and tell me of Paul Morrison's death. No, alas, I did not see him last summer, but when we did meet three years ago, I suppose it was, he was as fragile as a leaf and seemed appallingly shrunk and delicate. He was a dear man, and I was always fond of him, and I believe he was a splendid teacher.

You don't say if you liked Irene in [*John Gabriel*] *Borkman*? She had a wonderful notice from Clive Barnes. I played Erhardt in my twenties and couldn't cope with it at all – the Archer translation! 'Mother, I want to live, live, live.' Peggy Ashcroft and Wendy Hiller did it two or three years ago at the Vic. Alan Webb marvellous as Foldal, but he, too, is withering away, and only played a few times. I was lucky to see him do it – and Ralph R. was awfully good as Borkman – a wonderful sigh when he was dying, like the fluttering of a bird. I must say, the play does really rather fascinate me – much more than most of Ibsen.

I imagine *Arthur* should be released soon and am very anxious to know how it has turned out. Martin is working very hard on formalising the garden, and we have bought the Yew Avenue. The avenue originally belonged to this garden and we have opened up a gateway and are hacking down the undergrowth – it will be lovely, I think, when the summer comes. Various other improvements, but six workmen are very expensive and have to be given lunch every day, an added chore for poor Martin.

I have to go in to Exeter on the 29th and read the Prospero speech at Nevill Coghill's Memorial Service. Far too many people one knows are ill or dying.

To George Pitcher and Ed Cone   *9 March, Wotton Underwood*

All thanks for sending me the obituary of dear old Arnold [Weissberger]. I'm glad I saw quite a lot of him when we were there last summer – endless invitations to lunch at the Four Seasons. I first met him in the *Hamlet* time, when he still lived with his redoubtable Mum at 86th St and one had lily cups and canapés, and of course with his hard work and success he and Milton [Goldman] have a great flat on Sutton Place, with masses of pictures – several Magrittes, quite hideous, I think, and a lot of junk – but they were great New York personalities and indefatigably thoughtful and kind. 36 years together too, pretty good record. We went to an anniversary boys' party last year. I thought Martin would die when he realised it was stag. In someone else's very grand apartment – rather mixed group – mostly elderly, natch – and a young man in a corner obliging, if you please, on the harp! I shall miss him greatly if I ever return to N.Y.

My favourite recollection was while Mum was still alive and they gave parties every summer in the suite at the Savoy. A, B and C invitations according to celebrity status – and Anna [Weissberger] got a bit squiffy about one a.m. and yelled out 'Arnold! Arnold! Come here. Mae West is leaving.' 'No, no, Mother. *Rebecca* West.'

I turned down a boring play by Simon Gray, and also *Lolita* (for N.Y.) in which I gather Ian Richardson is to be Nabokov. Clever adaptation by Albee, I thought, but I'm sure it cannot do and anyway I didn't fancy it.

But of course I do hope to be offered a play again that is really interesting. They go on suggesting *Lear* at the National, but I can't somehow face the responsibility in case I don't prove up to it, and I have done it *four* times and would perhaps show my age too plainly, now that I am really right for it.

To Irene Worth   *19 March, Wotton Underwood*

So good of you to take time to write so fully about Arnold's death. I have tentatively suggested to Milton a sort of half hour gathering in the Drury

Lane foyer one day soon, or in the summer if Milton would rather be there himself, though he may find the pain of coming over by himself this year too hard to face. Poor chap, I do feel so much for him. I rang up Elisabeth [Bergner] to tell her and said 'Did you know they had been together for 36 years?' 'Of course,' she replied, 'I was the bridesmaid!' It is a well known story (fact, too) that when they first left to live together, Elisabeth was asked to explain the situation to Anna [Weissberger], who was always demanding a grandchild – rather sweet!

My poor brother Val has senile dementia as well as sclerosis and a bit of Parkinson's and his wife has had to put him into a private nursing home at Eastbourne after many months of trying to cope with him in their own house. Terribly sad, he hardly ever speaks and she can't communicate with him any more or discover what he still remembers and whether he really minds. He is organically perfectly strong but one can only hope it cannot go on for much longer.

Peter Hall is having a mad affair with an opera singer [Maria Ewing] and has left his wife [Jackie]. He has aged considerably – no wonder, what with Glyndebourne, *The Oresteia* and *The Ring* at Bayreuth for next year, to say nothing of personal complications, children, ex-wives and money and the N[ational] Theatre on his back. But he is amazingly cheerful and philosophical, showing the new lady's photographs proudly to all and sundry while Judith Allen comforts Mrs Hall, the children and Peter's parents – well, well.

To George Pitcher and Ed Cone   *21 April, Wotton Underwood*

We had a rather tiresome week in Rome – the city is so sadly shabby, street surfaces as crumbling as Cairo, garbage uncollected, and the noise and hazard of being driven against the walls by the traffic in all the side streets. The great buildings are still lovely, of course, and wisteria blooming on the walls, but even the Piazza Navona and the Spanish Steps are ruined by the tourist crowds and vendors, and one soon tires of pasta! We had to go 50 mile drives four times to do the filming [*Marco Polo*] but they shot my few tiny scenes in a beautiful 12th century abbey at Fossa Nova, where I stood about (grossly overpaid, I'm glad to say) in the heaviest crimson velvet robe and cape with a cap and tassels, looking like a very old lady of uncertain sex and age! Crazy conglomeration of accents – me, Denholm Elliott, John Houseman and a lot of old Italian extras – the director an Italian with no English, so an interpreter was of paramount importance. Anne Bancroft and Burt Lancaster are to appear in other scenes – they have already filmed in Morocco and in Venice, where apparently they all froze to death at the Lido in a set built to resemble the Piazza San Marco in 1100 – and now off to film scenes in China and Manchuria, if you please.

No doubt it will all *look* very splendid, but I thought the script exceedingly

dull and my part quite negligibly commonplace – just a few lines of information to join episodes together. However, everyone was very gracious and
encouraging and a large birthday cake was suddenly produced from nowhere,
which was rather touching – one of the publicity men had found out the
date.

I hear Irene has a splendid *comedy* part in the film of *Deathtrap* and is
delighted about it and being very well paid. So very glad for her. All of us in
the older generation seem to be in demand for films and television, which is
very lucky for us. Far less hard work than eight times a week in the theatre,
though I think we would all rather be there if only there were some good new
scripts. The classics seem all to have been revived to death.

There is no year on this letter, but it was hard to resist the story.

To Meriel Forbes   *21 June, Wotton Underwood*

Did so enjoy that delicious dinner with you both. Were you too polite to
notice when I scooped the biggest stick of asparagus into my lap? Made me
think of the oriental potentate at Buck House who had never eaten asparagus
before and hurled the stalks over his shoulder on to the carpet – on which
royalty, never at a loss, followed his example till the floor was covered with
stalks!

Arthur *opened in New York in July 1981.*

To George Pitcher   *31 July, Wotton Underwood*

Of course I am very bucked at the success of the picture – and thank you so
much for writing and sending the clippings. The *New Yorker* was simply
wonderful for me, but all the press were equally flattering, so I hope some
new offer may come in time, perhaps to bring one back to the U.S.? They
showed me the picture in London last week, and I must say I enjoyed it pretty
well, though apprehensive as one always is in seeing one's mug so largely
offered on the screen. I thought Liza so very good, and underestimated by
the critics. Dudley screams too much at first, but gets better all through and
is very charming and co-operative in the scenes with me. We all got on so
wonderfully well together, despite that appalling heat.

I go to Stratford on Sunday for a Shakespeare reading with two other
actors. I haven't set foot in the place since the disastrous Zeffirelli *Othello* and
rather dread seeing the new Hilton Hotel glaring across from the theatre, and
the place is a bit too full of memories to be altogether appealing any more.
Those good and exciting times with you – with my darling mother staying at
the Arden – and then the ups and downs of *The Chalk Garden*. Old Enid
Bagnold, dope-ridden with morphia and quite dotty, died not long ago and

her Rottingdean house sold up. Rather a tragic end – too many of them about as one grows old.

To Elizabeth Jennings   *30 September, Wotton Underwood*

How very kind of you to write so warmly and enthusiastically and thank you so much for the gift of your delightful poems.

I thought John Hurt infinitely touching in *The Elephant Man*, almost endearing! But what a pity they messed up the end with those starry empyreans and angel voices, and I thought Miss Bancroft quite miscast. Poor Dame Madge Kendal must be turning somersaults in her grave. She was a *most* austere Lady Bracknell figure in a Victorian bonnet when I met her several times in her old age, but my Father admired her to distraction, thought her even superior as an actress to Ellen Terry (of whom she was an implacable enemy!). I believe they had extraordinary love-hate jinks when they played together with Tree in *The Merry Wives*.

To Claire Bloom   *21 October, Wotton Underwood*

Have just sent a note to your publisher, saying how much I enjoyed reading your book [*Limelight and After*], which they kindly sent me in proof. I think you show such self knowledge and sincerity and you write most gracefully and simply – all that you say is cogent and interesting as well as generous and kind. I do hope it will be a great success when it comes out.

We wait for your appearance in the next episode of *Brideshead* with ill-concealed impatience. The first two bits already shown have been enormously liked and praised though, now that it is a success, the more picky critics are complaining – Why choose such a decadent book? – Is it communist propaganda? And there are letters to *The Times* every day complaining of tiny errors in detail – army badges, railway carriage mistakes and other small faults not a bit important. Jeremy Irons, who has opened in *The French Lieutenant's Woman* at the same time, has certainly become an International Star overnight. He seemed to be a dear boy and I am delighted for him, but it is beautifully cast all round and, of course, exquisitely photographed.

I am off to Munich for 10 weeks next month to play Albert Speer's father (50–80) in a TV serial for ABC, *The Fall of the Third Reich*.

Val Gielgud died on 30 November 1981.

To Christopher Fry   *16 December, Amsterdam*

Val had a wretched long drawn out decline, and one can only be thankful he is out of it at last. He was a dear, generous, talented fellow.

This is a marvellous, clean and luxurious city. But I work only very sporadically. Ten weeks to do about 12 days' shooting, so there is too much time to eat and sleep a lot. But many lovely things to see – broad non-traffic streets with open markets, museums, galleries etc. Luckily two very clear Sundays gave me the chance to drive to the lakes and mountains and see some superb Baroque churches and Ludwig's castle – appropriate, as I am to be in a film of Wagner during Feb. in Vienna. How I do get about in me advanced years.

To John Miller   *17 December 1981, Munich*

Many thanks for your kind letter. Val was most dreadfully stricken with a long illness of gradual deterioration, and I am really thankful that the long trek is over for him at last, and his much younger wife able to remake her life after so many months of anxiety and care.

To Meriel Forbes   *30 December, Munich*

Hailed by American tourist in Venice where we had three divine days between beastly train journeys – 'Saw you in Washington' etc. Of course he thought I was Ralph, as per.

Nice moment here when I circumvented a very fat lady in the local Fortnums and murmured over my shoulder 'Bottoms up!' A few minutes later in the street, a man rushed up, stripped off his glove, removed his hat and said, 'Ah, of course, I recognised your famous voice!'

1982

To Irene Worth   *17 January, Munich*

So terribly distressed to hear about the plane disaster in Washington* which must have appalled the whole city and spread the most dreadful gloom over everyone and everything.

As if the World was not in a sorry enough condition without such unpredictable horrors as this one. It must be really awful for you all in the play, making acting suddenly seem so unimportant. I feel much the same about the actors in Poland whom I liked so much, and Wajda and his wife who are rumoured to have been arrested and later released.†

I have still not finished my comparatively small part in the *Reich* film here,

---

* A plane taking off from Washington International Airport crashed into the Potomac, killing 78 people.
† The struggle between the Polish government and Lech Walesa's independent trade union movement Solidarity had been going on for some time.

but they promise I shall do my last day's work next Friday and they expect me to start work in Vienna on the *Wagner* film the following Monday, so I shall have to go straight on from here and Martin goes home and Mavis Walker joins me in Vienna. They promise to do my scenes in 2½ weeks – twelve days shooting – and as they have both Ralph and Larry too, I imagine they will use us and send us home as soon as they can in order to save money! What an unholy three we shall turn out to be!

To Michael York   *19 February, Wotton Underwood*

Our hearts bled for you and Hugh [Wheeler] when we saw in *Variety* that you had never opened [*The Little Prince*, music by John Barry, lyrics by Don Black, book by Hugh Wheeler]. What a ghastly waste of money and effort and what a personal disappointment for you, though I am sure you must be busy considering offers. Will you try another play or go back to TV and films like me?!

The Third Reich film [*Inside the Third Reich*] dragged on over nine weeks, and my small part only involved twelve days work, so I got very frustrated. *Wagner** was much quicker, thank God. Richardson and Olivier both came for a bit, and Derek Jacobi (as Hitler in *Third Reich*), but both films had extraordinarily mixed casts. Elke Sommer, Maria Schell, a remarkable young Hungarian actor [László Gálffi] who plays Ludwig, and a Dutch star, Rutger Hauer who plays Speer, with Blythe Danner as his wife. So the dubbing department will have its work cut out in the next few months. Burton was extremely sweet, and will I think be very good as Wagner.

Martin is working indefatigably as usual, making a new workroom for himself in the former garage, and decorating the house more elegantly than ever. We do miss you both. The cruel winter has killed all the camellias and, I expect, a lot of other plants and shrubs, and it is still foggy and cold – the traffic to and from London impossibly tiresome owing to the rail strikes and awful disasters everywhere. But the snowdrops are out and daffodils begin to peer, so we begin to hope for a proper spring and summer.

To Ed Cone   *27 March, Wotton Underwood*

We are giving a party – after a long gap in any sort of entertaining – on April 14th. How I wish you could both be there. And I go up to London tomorrow for a birthday celebration of my dear old friend Gwen Ffrangcon-Davies who is 92! Too many anniversaries. Willie Walton, Flora Robson, both 80. As a maid we once had before the war in Venice remarked, 'Ah, monsieur, les années passent si vite, si vite.'

---

* A TV film written by Charles Wood and directed by Tony Palmer.

One of Martin's dogs has a slipped disc, so he is very upset. A wonderful vet, however. Mu Richardson had a beloved white rat which died recently after a week in intensive care at the London Zoo! Oh dear, our pets too. She is quite heartbroken about it.

To Emlyn Williams   *3 April, Wotton Underwood*

Saw quite a lot of Brook [Williams] on the Wagner film. He seemed well and happy and we talked much of you of course. Richard [Burton] seemed dreadfully sad and ravaged – lonely and unhappy, but acting well, though under physical troubles with his back and, I fear, too much drink after work in the evening. I only hope for everyone's sake he will stay the course. I believe the insurance is enormous and no wonder. He was sweet to me and gave me a wonderful present when I left. I suppose he is so lavish as a kind of guilt complex. All very sad.

In the 1982 Academy Awards, JG won an Oscar for Best Supporting Actor in Arthur.

To Hugh Wheeler   *Easter Sunday 1982, Wotton Underwood*

Good to hear from you – endless letters to write after the Oscar. Fancy me a bona fide athletic supporter at my advanced age.

I have to be in a remake of *The Wicked Lady* in July here with Faye Dunaway and Alan Bates, Michael Winner to direct. I hear he is a beast. We shall see.

To Elizabeth Jennings   *24 April, Wotton Underwood*

So many thanks for your most charming letter. Of course I am pleased about the Oscar. It is odd to become a popular film performer at my age after sixty years in the theatre.

But actually I was more pleased at the success of *Brideshead* in which I had such an amusing and original character to play.

Yes, wild horses would not drag me to the Award Ceremonies either in London or California. I really detest all that mutual congratulation baloney and the invidious comparisons which they evoke.

To George Pitcher   *21 August, Wotton Underwood*

Martin came with me to Rome but it was rather hellish. The hottest summer, they said, for 20 years. The night we arrived, Italy won the World Cup, so there was all night pandemonium like the French Revolution, and there were hideous enclosures all over the Piazza Navona for some tatty art exhibit, cheapjacks all over the Spanish Steps, filth and cracked pavements, hordes of tourists and appallingly alarming onslaughts of cars and motorbikes which drove us against the walls. But I quite enjoyed the filming in the Campodoglio Museum with Gregory Peck and Christopher Plummer, both very agreeable, and a quite effective short part as Pope Pacelli in a thriller for ABC [*The Scarlet and the Black*] about the Nazi occupation of Rome.

Then I was a faithful Malvolio steward in a Restoration tushery remake of *The Wicked Lady*, being smothered in bed (like Desdemona) by Faye Dunaway, who was creating havoc and mayhem, dressed as a highwayman unbeknownst to her dull husband, and blackmailed by me, when I threaten to unmask her. Great nonsense, directed by a mad nut called Michael Winner, a foul-mouthed director with a certain charm – at least very respectful to me, though *most* unpleasant to underlings – a restless maniac mixture of George Cukor, Harpo Marx and Lionel Bart. I had a great deal of standing about with trays and servicing, and two effective scenes with Miss D. who is a very Hollywood type egotistical madam with a surrounding band of satellites – husband, make-up man, wardrobe lady and so on – taking hours to change her costume and titivate between every take, so I didn't enjoy all that very much.

Now I have one more week in a comedy [*Invitation to a Wedding*] with quite an amusing script – Ralph Richardson plays a Bishop who rides a motorbike in black leather and has a pet rat, and I am an Evangelist from Texas, arriving (dressed entirely in white) with a Stetson hat and cowboy boots, in an all white helicopter. Unfortunately I have also to assume a southern accent!! Would that Ben Edwards was here to teach it to me instead of a ghastly bore who has been given the job and pursues me everywhere, looking like a chimpanzee with flowing locks and a red beard and drives me nearly mad, whispering sometimes in my ear between every take. Martin thinks I am mad to have risked attempting the part, but I thought it might be an amusing challenge, and maybe nobody will ever see it!

To Hugh Wheeler   *21 August, Wotton Underwood*

I have to officiate at *three* Memorial Services which I dread – Kenneth More, Marie Rambert and, I expect, Cathleen Nesbitt. St Paul's Covent Garden is so full of plaques to my erstwhile friends nowadays – lately joined by Noël and Leslie Hurry – that I feel it is hardly worth my while to go home!

Nice Joyce [Carey] getting her O.B.E. She was very sweet about it saying she only got it as a survival prize!

Paul and Guy have bought a derelict house and garden in Sussex and so are never free to come here, and they are moving flat again in London – extraordinary Paul's family obsession with changing addresses. But I think he revels in the essential labours of doing so.

The house and garden are looking splendid, though Martin as usual works far too hard, coughs endlessly, and is characteristically pessimistic. I do wish we might see you soon. Real friends become so increasingly scarce.

To Irene Worth   *16 December, Wotton Underwood*

I would so very much like to be of some use in helping you to get the apartment you want. There is quite a large sum of money held in New York for me by Howard Le Shaw. If you needed some would you please borrow from that account which Milton, I know, would gladly arrange, and pay it back some time to come when you could more easily afford it. I so hate to think you are deterred by expense from moving to a more attractive home if you succeeded in finding something that really appealed to you. It would be such a pleasure for me to feel I might be of some use in the matter.

1983

To Richard Bebb   *7 January, Wotton Underwood*

I really hate the idea of a biography of Binkie [Beaumont]. Richard Huggett has been pestering me for material and has approached a number of my friends for the past two years. Having briefly met him (at the Garrick) I certainly don't want him to complete his effort, but I suppose nothing can be done to prevent him.*

Binkie's successful career will not, I feel, be of great interest to this generation. His record of achievement is very easily available, but he was primarily a businessman, and his wheeling and dealing took place over a great number of years, mostly concerned with players who are already gone. His successes and failures, his friendships and influences are very difficult to sum up, and I really doubt very much would be gained by a book about him, however carefully contrived. I am sorry to be so positive, but I know you would get small encouragement or information from those of us still alive who were fond of him.

To Irene Mayer Selznick   *18 May, Wotton Underwood*

So very kind and thoughtful of you to send me your very fascinating book [*A Private View*]. I saw in some newspaper that it had just been published with good reviews, and of course I was dying to read it. It is done with such evident care and expertise and is full of perceptiveness and gives affection[ate] and charming tributes to those you have loved as well as a good deal of reasoned criticism and justifiable censure when you have felt it to be necessary to give the whole panorama balance. Your affectionate dedication makes me very happy. You must know how much I have valued your friendship over the

---

* Richard Huggett's book on Binkie Beaumont was published in 1989.

years though we have sadly only met at such long intervals. I wish for my own sake that there was a bit more about Binkie and Enid, but your pages about them (and Ingrid and Cecil) are most splendidly observed.

What a pity you gave up doing plays – your contributions were so professional and thorough, to say the least, and it is so sad to me nowadays that there are no managements left either in London or New York that one is proud and confident to work for.

I have not acted in the theatre for the last three years, but am amazed that I don't seem to miss it and am very lucky to be entering my 80th year still quite often in demand for films and television, though I hardly feel I made any worthy mark in either except for *Providence* and *Brideshead*, both of which were well worth doing. *Arthur* was just a lucky fluke, but seems to have made me better known than anything I have done over 60 years in the theatre. Very odd and unlikely. If you ever come to England again, do please let me know. I would so love to see you and show you this house and garden which are a great joy and refuge. Alas, I hate London these days – only go up on business and really love the country place. I always remember that charming weekend you once gave me at your country house with Danny. Congratulations and take care of yourself.

To Richard Burton   *26 May, Wotton Underwood*

I sat through 6½ hours of *Wagner* – very sad that all the beauty and many good performances are nullified by the length and endless abstract shots which slow everything up just as one is getting interested in the story and characters. And the sound track is abominable – overwhelming musical background, all snippets from the operas but much of them repeated far too often – and one hears heavy breathing and crackles all the time. I can't think they will ever manage to sell it. It was agony to sit through but as I was next to Tony Palmer's mother, I tried to conceal my weariness and irritation.

To Hugh Wheeler   *4 June, Wotton Underwood*

So good to hear from you at long last. I was beginning to think we were off your mailing list. I knew you always went to St Kitts in January, and we went off to India for a month – not a very interesting part in *The Far Pavilions*, sort of pukka sahib commander, killed off in an insurrection. Very exhausting trip – ghastly airport at Delhi getting in and out at ungodly hours with maddening bureaucratic inconveniences and pretty squalid ambience. Nice people on the film, though, and Martin loved the birds and landscape. We stayed at the Maharajah's ex-Palace – now Hotel – in Jaipur, which was fairly luxurious with lovely gardens, and it was not too hot. But thirty miles each day to the location – a very picturesque but run-to-seed fort. With the car horn going all the time and hairbreadth escapes from camels, bullock carts, corpses etc. was not exactly restful.

I am, to my surprise, quite without work, a nice change after last year I must say, though I hope not permanent. Lew Allen sent Ben Edwards over twice and he brought the boy wonder Peter Sellars with him both times. The idea is to make a film of *The Tempest* which, as you know, I have always been mad to do.

The wunderkind is quite a fascinating little creature, only 22 and very sure of himself, though at the same time very polite and respectful – but both Martin and I felt a bit doubtful of his ability to direct (his first) film. Then suddenly Lew rang up to say the money was no longer available, so I don't really know what to think, as I have heard no word either from Ben or Peter. Maybe it is a lucky escape, as I don't much like the accounts of *The Mikado* in Chicago or *Lear* which he directed (and played Lear himself, it seems, when the leading man got ill) with him and Cordelia emerging from a white Rolls-Royce!

Then the director of *Scandalous*, a crazy film I made before Christmas (and in which I played a con-man in about seven different disguises – Japanese businessman, Hindustani, Traffic warden and electrician) – whom I like very much, was full of plans for me to play in a remake of *The Razor's Edge* in the part Clifton Webb did in the old movie with Tyrone Power. I was much intrigued at the prospect, but now I hear that Bill Murray, who is to star in it, will not have me as a co-star and anyway wants the part cut down. I suppose it is quite flattering in a way, but obviously he fears another *Arthur*, but I am, of course, very disappointed.

I do a television series next month – six centuries of English Poetry – to be made in various beautiful spots near here. I am to read some of the poems and link it all together. Ralph, Peggy, Diana Rigg and a few younger players are to take part, so I hope it may be quite pleasant and not too strenuous. I dread the advent of my 80th birthday next year – interviews, books and articles are all threatened, but I hope to keep them down to a minimum and resolutely refuse *Time* Magazine who wants to come here and spend time with me. I can't bear the idea of strange columnists all over the house.

Have you seen *The Draughtsman's Contract*? I was so very impressed by it, though I could not really understand it and would love to hear your views.

The weather has been frightful, as with you. Today almost the first proper summer day, and I must say the garden is a dream of beauty. Martin slaves away. I weed fairly inefficiently and spend hours burning rubbish. I think I must be something of a pyromaniac.

Joyce [Carey] flourishes – had the best notices in a revival of *Man and Superman* with Peter O'Toole who, she says, treats her most charmingly. There was a dinner at the Garrick one Sunday night in her honour – she made a very delightful speech but as the room has a frightful echo and both she and Bob Morley are nearly stone deaf, it wasn't a very rewarding evening.

Nor was a ghastly do in honour of Peter Shaffer given by the Gallery First Nighters in an hotel. Fortunately I sat next to him and was glad to see him again, but you know what these occasions are like – endless speeches and a frightful entertainment after dinner – conjurors, singers etc. from which I ducked out under cover of darkness.

To George Pitcher   *19 September, Wotton Underwood*

The garden wonderfully improved by Martin and a new full-time gardener. It really is lovely now, and I bought some new pictures and sculpture with my ill-gotten gains. The Paul Masson commercials* are apparently a great success and they have picked up a further six months profitable option.

I go today to Bath for two weeks to play an old Scottish laird in a TV (for America) of Stevenson's novel *The Master of Ballantrae*, a poor cliché part (with a death scene) and very grand powdered wig and velvet suits – including a KILT! Get me!

Irene wrote very excitedly about her new play [*The Golden Age*] for the Kennedy Center – I think it opens this week – by the author of *The Dining Room* [A. R. Gurney]. She has to waltz in black satin pyjamas!

Very worried about Ralph Richardson, who has had to come out of his Italian play at the National [*Inner Voices*] and is told not to work for a month – arthritis and also some bowel trouble. I hope to God he gets over it. He is never ill, and quite unused to pain and idleness and I am so devoted to him. I fear at 81 he may be going to have a dangerous time.

Went up to see a very striking production of *Crime and Punishment* directed by a Russian [Yuri Lyubimov] who has been doing the same version for the last five years in Moscow. Wonderful use of the stage – strobe lighting and weird music and thrilling handling of the English cast and a huge success.

Ralph Richardson died on 10 October 1983.

To Meriel Richardson   *11 October, Wotton Underwood*

Darling Mu

'There's a great spirit gone.' So hard to put things into words. But you know how deeply I loved Ralph and it puts an end to a glorious chapter of my life where he touched it with his magic – and I don't know how to express how much his friendship meant to me over these long years, and whether to mourn him most as dear friend or great artist. We had such extraordinary

---

* Following the success of *Arthur* the wine producers, Paul Masson, paid JG large sums of money to advertise their wares on TV. He did so on condition that the commercials were not shown in the UK, as Olivier also specified when he made a commercial for Polaroid. The money JG received for them ensured that he had no financial worries for the rest of his life.

rapport in our work as well as in private, and his sensitivity with me, even in the sides of me that I felt must have been so distasteful to him, never seemed to affect our relationship in the slightest way. His endless striving to perfect his work was so much more important to him than the obvious pleasures of success and recognition, and I marvelled at the way he flung himself so unselfishly into the hurly-burly of the National, where his influence and example must have gratified him.

He inspired respect, affection, admiration, was adored alike by friends and fellow players. His literary and poetic taste and curiosity never failed to justify new experiments and he never groused or made excuses over his rare failures. Above all, he was such a good man, generous, honest, discriminating and, of course, divinely humorous, not least at his own expense, and so unfailingly vital.

But you know all this far better than I do and I am quite lost in admiration of your courage and sweetness which never failed him for a moment. May you find comfort as he would so greatly wish.

Dearest love to you as ever

John

To Francis King   *16 October, Wotton Underwood*

Your appreciation of Ralph [Richardson] – most perceptive and just. He would have been delighted to be compared to [Gerald] Du Maurier. He was not at home in the great classical parts in Shakespeare, as you say. Of course, he ought to have tackled Lear, but his Othello and Macbeth (he used to say 'I couldn't see the dagger myself, so of course the audience couldn't either') made him fearful of failing in it, I am sure.

To Hugh Wheeler   *12 November, Wotton Underwood*

The sun shines here though all the leaves are down and a bitterly cold wind presages winter. Depressing week as I have to read at two Memorial Services – John Gilpin tomorrow (whom I did not know, but various people begged me and I didn't like to refuse) and Ralph on Thursday at the Abbey, which will be a tremendous and painful affair with the whole profession paying tribute – a compliment to poor Mu at least, but you can imagine I don't look forward to it. Milton is coming over specially, natch! Irene is here, also Marti Stevens. (But they don't mix, unfortunately.) I'm already dreading my 80th in April. The Garrick is giving me a dinner which I couldn't gracefully get out of, but am trying to be firm about other interviews and celebrations. Ronald Harwood (who wrote *The Dresser*) has organised a book of tributes from my friends, and Richard Findlater has done a book about the four of us – Larry, Ralph, Peggy and myself, which is quite well done. But all I really want is a quiet life and the odd bit of work. I had a fortnight in Bath, very pleasant, playing the dying Dad in *The Master of Ballantrae* – lovely clothes and a nice lot of people – Michael York (Pat, of course, much in evidence) and a nice American boy who plays Michael's brother called Richard Thomas. Stayed in a really good hotel – the Royal Crescent – and we filmed in a decayed Jacobean mansion with lovely grounds, recently bought by Jane Seymour and her rich American husband who appears to be Paul Newman's agent!

I did a week on *The Shooting Party*, rather a good Edwardian novel by Isobel Colegate. Quite a small part of a rabid anti-sports crank who makes a scene at the shoot. Scofield, who was to play the leading part, was badly smashed up in an accident with an overturned carriage in which he was driving, and now James Mason is to take over and I have one good scene still to do with him.

Otherwise no news really. Lots of offers, but none I fancied – the Inquisitor in *Saint Joan* for the National – no, really – and a magician in *Poppy* – ni moi non plus. Still, it is nice to be in demand. The Paul Masson people took up another six months option but say they have no immediate plans to make new commercials – however, they paid up promptly!

Lovely new pictures and some very handsome sculpture for the garden which will really be lovely next year. We have a full-time boy to work there, which is a huge improvement, but Martin slaves as hard as ever.

To Ronald Harwood   *27 November, Wotton Underwood*

I do congratulate you on the book [*All the World's a Stage*]. What a wealth of research it must have involved to say nothing of encapsulating the result. May I point out one important mistake in case it can be rectified in the film. Helen Hayes – the photograph is not of her, but of Helen Haye, a well-known English actress who gave me my scholarship at Lady Benson's school in 1921, and acted continuously in London all through the years before the War. I think the photo represents her as the Empress in a play called *Anastasia*. The curious thing is that when they decided to film the story (with Yul Brynner and, I think, Ingrid Bergman), Helen Haye was chosen to repeat her stage performance and they muddled the names and Helen Hayes was cast for the part instead! Rather bad luck on our actress. I remember Martita Hunt complaining bitterly because she only got a lady in waiting. I met her very tipsy at a party and she said 'I am worn out by curtseying all day to that f——— Helen Hayes!'

1984

To Jane Bown   *7 February, Wotton Underwood*

I cannot write such prettily spaced – or indeed such legible handwriting as
dear Ralph – but I do want to apologise most sincerely for my reception of
you this morning, and thank you for the beautiful book of photographs which
I have been enjoying all afternoon, as well as your patience and sympathy in
putting up with my own confusion.

You managed to melt down my rather hostile and uncooperative attitude
with the greatest possible charm and good humour, and got on with the job
to my admiration. I do hope I didn't make you thoroughly miserable after
such a bad beginning and that the pictures – despite the cold sore and my
wretched forgetfulness – will turn out to your satisfaction after all. If they
don't then I shall feel wretchedly to blame.

To Richard Findlater   *11 February, Wotton Underwood*

Of course I am flattered by your suggestion, but what more is there to write
about me? Three of my own books, [Ronald] Hayman's, endless interviews
and chat shows and more, alas, to come in the next two months, not to
mention your own two books which have pretty complete accounts of my
career.

Of course I can't possibly prevent you writing such a book, to be kept in
purdah, perhaps, till after I am dead? But I do feel a bit of a back number
these days, and all the publicity I once longed for is rather cold potatoes to
me now. There are such a plethora of theatrical memoirs over the last few
years, and my own career, though I suppose fascinating as stage *history*, is
pretty well done with. The films and television fill in very adequately from
my own point of view, but I think there is little left to write about me that
would interest the public in addition to the big mass of material that has
already been collected and published at various times. All thanks, however,
for the thought and enthusiasm.*

To George Pitcher   *7 March, Wotton Underwood*

Lillian [Gish] is a marvel. I went up to see the showing in London of *Broken
Blossoms* – with a full orchestra. She appeared on the stage and attended the
party in the bar afterwards, and I gave an interview with her for the *Guardian*
at the Savoy, where she received in a bower of flowers, intrepid and most

---

* Richard Findlater started work on the book but died before he could finish it. His papers and
recordings passed to Sheridan Morley whose biography of Gielgud was published in 2001.

fluent after her long flight. This was some weeks ago. She never stops.

I have turned down some terrible offers of financial films – one called *Space Vampires*!! and a very dull Head of Information part in a film in Madrid with Donald Sutherland. Also several theatre jobs – revival of *Forty Years On* at Chichester, the Inquisitor in *Saint Joan* at the National – and even one to do *Godot* for Anthony Page, but as you know I have never been able to bear the play. I do hope something more interesting may come up soon.

I may direct a new *Importance* if we can find the ideal cast. I wanted Irene for Lady Bracknell but she is going to the National to play Volumnia with Ian McKellen, which is exciting for her.

Our house and garden are going from strength to strength. We have a full-time gardener now, and Martin has built a beautiful orangery full of lovely plants and trees – also a lot of sculpture, which he is mad about – and I have a lot of new pictures, including a rather fascinating one supposed to be a picture of Dr Arne, who wrote 'Rule Britannia', in a dressing gown with instruments lying about.

The Garrick Club is giving me a great dinner on April 8 – 150 people, including the Duke of Edinburgh. And of course I shall have to make a speech and try not to weep or drop any notable bricks.

To Irene Worth   *23 April, Harrogate*

I watched your *Coriolanus** last night with great pleasure. Thought both performances and production very impressive, [Alan] Howard [Coriolanus] and Joss Ackland [Menenius] and Mike Gwilym [Tullus Aufidius] all excellent, and you were grandly maternal and noble – loved the costumes, especially yours, and the very becoming hair style – and the sets just right. I tried to be more enthusiastic about Menenius. The part is effective, of course, in contrast to the other senators and the mob. But the man has no human body of character that I can see, just useful for the plot and an individual attitude to the proceedings, but none of the wonderful richness of Kent or Enobarbus. I don't believe I could do anything really interesting with it and shall regretfully tell Peter [Hall] so when I get back from here next week.† But you must know how sorry I am not to be going to work with you again, but it would be stupid to involve myself without real confidence and enthusiasm. I think you will understand and forgive me.

To Michael and Pat York   *13 May, Wotton Underwood*

I've turned down a lot of silly offers – now some project of a film about Katherine Mansfield in Normandy in July, to be directed by an odd young

---

* A television version directed by Elijah Moshinsky.
† Peter Hall wanted J G to play Menenius in his forthcoming National Theatre production.

man from New Zealand who has lived in Paris for the last few years. Very vague script but it might be interesting in a documentary kind of way! *Scandalous* is a shameful flop, as it was in America too. I am sorry for poor Rob Cohen who directed it and whom I liked very much. The press merely commiserated with us all for appearing in it!

To Ronald Harwood   *12 June, Wotton Underwood*

The Garrick do was really wonderfully done, but of course you were greatly missed. What with that and another celebration at the Vic – with a very pleasant lunch afterwards at the National – countless presents, cables, letters and the two books, I was really overwhelmed with affection for which I was boundlessly grateful.

I played Lord Henry Wotton in the John Osborne version of *Dorian Gray* a year or two ago – Peter Firth as Dorian, Jeremy Brett as the painter. Rather long-winded and not much of a success, though I rather enjoyed doing it at the time and made them adapt the Graham Robertson Sargent portrait at the Tate – with the long overcoat and grey poodle – for the portrait itself, which I thought came out very effectively.

Eric Salmon's book, Granville-Barker: A Secret Life, *had mentioned the possibility that Barker was homosexual. Margery Morgan wrote to JG to ask whether he had come across any such gossip among theatre people.*

To Margery M. Morgan   *24 June, Wotton Underwood*

Your letter interested me very much. No, I never heard the slightest rumour of what you suggest about Barker. I do remember being given a very romantic photograph of him gazing out of a window as a young man, taken by Shaw, and saying as a kind of joke 'I think G.B.S. must have been rather in love with him.' People used to say in connection with his divorce from Lillah McCarthy 'I don't know which of them locked the bedroom door.' But I was also told that he was madly in love with Helen Huntingdon when he met her in America, and wrote poetry to her and languished under her window.

Of course, Shaw does seem to have spiritualised his physical passions, and his acknowledged love affairs, Florence Farr, Mrs Campbell etc., appear to have been rather tame in consummation. There is the famous story of Shaw's announcing in a lecture at some university in London that Barker had sold his birthright for a mess of pottage, or something of that sort, when Barker and his second wife were both on the platform, and that the episode completely ended their long friendship. After that he turned back to Barrie (who, of course, was impotent, with a lifelong father complex).

I think the Edwardians, especially in the Art world, became intensely self-conscious after the Wilde scandal which, of course, touched very nearly everyone connected with the theatre, and only a very few flagrant homosexuals dared to allow such an implication to be suggested for fear of it affecting their livelihood and public image, and forcibly repressed their leanings and, of course, such matters were only whispered in middle class families and polite society, and hotly denied whenever possible.

I think Helen Huntingdon – whom I only met a couple of times – was a great snob, and both she and Barker detested the gossip and publicity connected with all things theatrical. Obviously she would have hated Lillah, who was very much the actress, though I once had a most fascinating afternoon with Lillah just before she died, in which she spoke of Barker with the warmest admiration and described him reciting as a boy in knickerbockers at one of his mother's poetry Recitals at Cheltenham. So no doubt he was a bit mother-ridden as well. When Lillah's autobiography was published, I believe Barker's name and talent were not even mentioned, but whether she or Barker insisted on this, I have no idea.

To Claire Bloom   *22 August, Wotton Underwood*

I am very sad about Richard [Burton], but the razzmatazz since he died is really rather embarrassingly overstated, and I can't help feeling very sorry for Elizabeth [Taylor], of whom Martin and I both became very fond when we saw a good deal of her over the American *Hamlet*. She has been so persistently pursued and harassed, and I think has behaved unexpectedly tactfully in keeping as far away as possible. We have the Memorial Service on the 30th at St Martin's, where I have to read some Shakespeare, with Emlyn to speak the address and Paul Scofield also taking part. I dread the crowds and reporters as you can imagine. I saw a good deal of Richard three years ago, when we were both making *Wagner* (which turned out a terrible mess, cost millions and no channel would touch it either in England or America). He was looking terribly ravaged – was between wives (though he married the continuity girl afterwards*) and we lunched every day together in his caravan, a nice elderly lady looking after him and a therapist-masseur coping with his back and arms, both of which were giving him trouble. He dined with me the last evening of my work in Vienna and insisted on giving me a most lavish present – *nine* silver wine-casters [*sic*]. Then almost a year later, he suddenly rang me up at the Dorchester where I was filming a short scene. He had had quite a big operation, had married the new girl, and seemed in terrific form, looking really well again – off the drink, presumably – and so *smart*, in a beautiful Palm Beach suit. Ah well!

I hope you and Philip [Roth] are well and happy and enjoying a glorious summer in your enchanting house and garden. Ours is lovely too, thanks to Martin's unfailing hard work and application. I had a month in Normandy

---

* Sally Burton.

and Paris, making a semi-documentary about Katherine Mansfield and her husband, John Middleton Murry – a strange script, lovely locations, and a most delightful time with Jane Birkin, Judy Campbell's daughter, who I expect you know. Greatly disorganised life – lovers and husbands, *three* children and several houses, but she seems wonderfully to rise above it. A strange unit of New Zealanders, struggling manfully with a French crew. No idea if it will turn out well.

To George Pitcher and Ed Cone   *9 October, Wotton Underwood*

Don't fail to get the December edition of the American *House and Garden* in which there will be pictures of the house and an article also. They took immense trouble doing it, four days running, but fortunately they couldn't have been nicer – and the photographer, Henry Clark, who lives in the S. of France, emerged to take the pictures. I think I met him years ago with David Webster. I've not seen pictures or article yet, but feel they must be good. I couldn't risk letting them do it for the English magazine, what with burglars and muggers!, but am glad to think Martin's remarkable achievements will be able to be seen by a lot of people, including you two, who have never been here.

We are completely out with silly old Elaine [Brunner]. We had a row last year when she walked out in the middle of dining here because Martin said something praising Lady Newall (her arch-enemy), so relations were already a bit strained. Then she kicked up a fearful row about our trying to obscure the light from her very ugly windows on the level of our garden, and sent me a solicitor's letter, if you please, about what she would allow to be planted as she was making an orangery and must have full light. (She has no TOP light whatever, so it is an idiotic scheme anyway.) She also sent over a note for my 80th birthday saying 'I am not sending you a present as you will remember I sent you a Stowe Catalogue last year.' So we have had no communication whatever since – and by a miracle have not run into each other anywhere. She shuts her shutters as often as possible and ostentatiously turns her back when she goes out in her garden. Well, well. How dotty can you get?

My film in Normandy was very interesting, though fairly strenuous, but not nearly as tiring as two films I have been in since – one only 3 days (in Paris) and one here of about ten days – but for both getting up at 6.30 a.m. and not getting home till 7 or 8 at night. I stayed at the Savoy for a week to save the long car drive, but it was jolly hard work, and I earned my dough.

Chanced upon disgracefully pornographic film from Holland (natch!) called *The Fourth Man.* The censor has been pretty busy but still – perhaps it will succeed in remaining even more explicit in America!

To Hugh Wheeler   *11 November, Wotton Underwood*

I did a few days on a remake of *Camille* (playing one of her impotent rich Duke lovers, but *not* Dumas Père!) also in Paris. Then I had a couple of weeks in *Plenty* (film of David Hare's play), very good script, demon Australian director (25 takes for every shot and no pick-ups). I had two very good scenes and was mad about Meryl Streep – brilliant, charming and most expert.

I also did Tiresias in a TV of *Antigone* which is due early next year, a bit in *The Shooting Party*, and a blind hermit in *Frankenstein* (American Cable TV) as well as a ridiculous Father and Son scene in something called *Romance on the Orient Express*! So you can see I have not been idle!

Now nothing at all in the offing. I turned down Menenius in the National's *Coriolanus* which Irene and Ian McKellen are rehearsing now – couldn't bear the part and find the play so cold and unattractive. I hear they are doing it in modern dress – natch – which I should also have hated. Irene is enthusiastic as always and adores working with Peter Hall.

To Irene Mayer Selznick   *30 December, Wotton Underwood*

I was so touched and charmed to receive your affectionate letter. It seems so long since I was last in New York and the offers seem to come from all other places. But perhaps one of these fine days!

I thought of you at Enid [Bagnold]'s memorial service last year, a rather dreary affair without music (though I remember she didn't much care for music so perhaps that was intentional!). Diana Cooper, still going in her nineties and sporting her yachting cap, murmured 'Don't you think they could run to a choir?' It was quite well attended but Harold Nicolson's son gave a poor address – he had obviously not seen her for twenty years or more.

I am so glad you liked the pictures of the house and the very charming article by Molly Keane. I hope to play in a film of her last book, *Time After Time* (not as good as her one before, *Good Behaviour*). I wonder if you have read either of them. She is my contemporary and wrote several plays with John Perry (rather sad and deaf these days), which I directed long ago. I think you might enjoy them.

I was in a bit of a pickle when I moved in here, but the film cameos and especially the commercials, have been wonderfully profitable these last few years and I have been able to buy some new pictures to replace the ones I had to sell and some attractive sculptures for the garden and some pretty iron gates which I found in the Place des Vosges when I was working in *Camille*.

Yes, it *was* nice to have such a fuss made last year over my birthday. *Two* books, dinners and so on. My old friends rallied round most nobly, and I found it a great pleasure to be spoilt and praised. The nasty things about me will be written when I am dead, so I shan't have to read them, shall I?

1985

To George Pitcher   *5 February, Wotton Underwood*

Good of you to send the Peggy Ashcroft article – excellent. I can't believe she is really 77 – but wonderful for her to receive world recognition after so many brilliant successes in her stage career. I am devoted to her, as of course you know, and thought her quite wonderful in the *Jewel* [*in the Crown*]. Thought the novels (*Raj Quartet*) so brilliantly cleverly abridged. Indeed I managed to get through the four novels only *after* seeing the television, which was much easier to follow. *Passage to India* does not come out here till later in the year, but she's sure to get an Oscar for the two performances. She has always avoided publicity of all kinds, but it is lovely to have shone in the other two media as well.

I can't say I grieve for that horrid Harry Rigby* – Hugh did me a very bad turn when he brought him into my life. *Irene* was one of the most wretched experiences in my career. I think I must try and write about it one day.

Wonderful mild weather after one very cold spell (which I gather you are getting now). Snowdrops and daffodils begin to peek – such a delight to see them again. We have had such a pleasantly idle winter here, seeing very few people and only going up to London when we have to.

The wine commercial people want to renew my contract again, which is a great help to the exchequer, though the sessions are exhausting and somewhat humiliating. But I hear people find them amusing and I marvel at them wanting me to go on making them. They only demand about three days work each time, with full attention to my comforts in the way of limousines, suites at the Savoy, flowers and cigarettes provided!

Peggy Ashcroft, as predicted, won her Oscar.

To Peggy Ashcroft   *27 March, Wotton Underwood*

I am sure you have cut off your telephone and don't wonder at it, as I am sure you must have been inundated with the press as well as friends to congratulate you on the Oscar so wonderfully well deserved. I was sure you would get it, but how sickening that you couldn't go yourself.

DON'T answer – your correspondence is going to be a nightmare. All that is important is that you should get really well again quickly.

---

* Producer of *Irene* who died 17 January 1985.

To George Pitcher   *2 June, Wotton Underwood*

I've just got back from five weeks in Ireland acting in a TV adaptation of Molly Keane's second successful novel *Time After Time*. Quite an amusing part of a one-eyed eccentric bachelor brother to three very odd sisters. I had to pretend to cook!! Also had a scene with 13 cats, which I managed to survive, and the sisters have three dogs, so the animal interest complicated the shooting a good deal, also a baby pig wrapped in a towel and put to keep warm in a slow oven!

The ladies were old dears and very well cast, but five weeks is rather a long time to be so gregarious, and the older men got drunk every evening (except me), which was rather a bore. Also, perfectly vile weather – only two fine days. However, I managed to drive around and see some fine houses and gardens and went a few times to Dublin, which is very shabby and run down. Also saw *Amadeus* (too glossy), *Killing Fields* (too gruesome) and *Passage to India* which I loved, except for the miscasting of Alec Guinness and a muddled and ineffective ending.

It is lovely to be home again and the garden is simply ravishing. Also the fine weather is with us at last, but for how long, I wonder? The television regales us with an unusually hideous gallimaufry of horrors, but Martin taped *Dallas* and *Dynasty* for me in my absence, which was something of a relief, I feel rather ashamed to admit. I also have a penchant for a soap called *Cheers* shown here on Friday nights. I wonder if Ed would appreciate the leading young man who, in some very strange way, reminds me a little of you!!

To George Pitcher and Ed Cone   *30 June, Wotton Underwood*

Glad to hear Ed had such a splendid send-off. He will find the leisure unexpectedly spacious, but so long as you are both well and happy, you will both enjoy the newfound freedom. I'm beginning to feel a bit ancient, but stagger along regardless. Our two dogs are also in the 12–13 age, which worries me a bit, for Martin refuses to get another. One of them has only one eye and arthritis in his back and limps around having to be carried up and down stairs, but the other is well and frisky.

I am offered a huge part by Columbia in a sequel to *Winds of War* – Herman Wouk's novel. They are to make a second huge series [*War and Remembrance*] and offer me the part John Houseman played in the first film. Odd weeks and days shooting all over Europe – Yugoslavia, Berlin, Elba, Corsica, Seine, Paris etc., which would be pretty strenuous and it is rather a beastly script, full of horrors – Belsen, Auschwitz etc. – with me ending as I go naked into the gas chamber!! But it will be a tremendous epic and I suppose a big success as the other one was, and in its way it's a fine part and huge money. I do like working, but can't help wishing it was a bit more of a congenial subject. This endless appetite to go on plugging the Nazi horrors – wildly pro-Jewish American, of course.

Yesterday I saw *Pravda* [by Howard Brenton and David Hare] at the National – a very political piece ridiculing the Press and press barons. Wonderfully staged with Anthony Hopkins giving a superb and funny performance.

The garden is looking wonderful, though we still have no real summer and the spring didn't happen at all. But we have an excellent young full-time gardener now, which has made an enormous difference. We had 30 people for lunch last week. Irene, Milton Goldman and Mu Richardson and others, and the sun actually condescended to come out and it was a great success. London is so beastly now and I go up as little as possible.

To George Pitcher and Ed Cone   *18 November, Wotton Underwood*

How odd that you should see *Chimes* [*at Midnight*] so pat on Orson's death. I always think of him with great affection and regret that I never had the chance to work with him again, though the film was very clumsily put together and half the actors (the Spanish ones) were very badly dubbed. Money was always running out and endless difficulties arose, which he managed to rise above with remarkable blandness, and he was always very kind and amusing. Oddly enough, I wrote him a long letter a few months ago enclosing my everlasting *Tempest* project and asking him if he might be interested in directing me in it if the backing should materialise, and he sent me back an enthusiastic and affectionate answer. But I knew he was busy trying to get his own film *Lear* under way and felt sure nothing would come of it.

I've just finished being bumped off by Michael Caine in a double agent thriller [*The Whistle Blower*] – rather run of the mill spy nonsense, and I caught a foul cold hanging about in a charming Cheyne Walk house, very like dear old Cowley St, where we filmed. So draughty and huddled among furniture, crew and cameras. For some mysterious reason, they never seem to film in studios any more and one spends one's time lurking in corners or dashing off to a caravan parked two streets away. Very distracting and uncomfortable, but never mind.

We lost one of our two darling dogs – he had a stroke and now the only one left is very delicate with liver trouble. I have been begging Martin to get another, but he is very reluctant. The one left is about 13 so it cannot be long before it is time for him to go, and I do bleed for Martin who so adores him and carries him round all the time. The days are closing in fast and there is not a flower left in the garden or leaf on the trees, so one is apt to get a bit melancholy one way and another. I wish we could stir our stumps and hop over for Christmas to your side, but it is too complicated to trust leaving the dog and the birds and the house empty.

I have said I will do the Wouk TV, *War and Remembrance* next year. They have at last come up with a proper offer (and the same money) for only 28 weeks work instead of 10 months, which is a bit less daunting. Have to go to Zagreb, Poland, Paris, Rome, Florence, Yugoslavia, and learn to speak some lines in Hebrew and Yiddish into the bargain. Well, there's nothing like a new experience. Only trust I manage to stay the course.

To Irene Worth   *9 December, Wotton Underwood*

London is hell, with impossible crowds thronging to stop and see the silly Christmas lights, but I have to go up quite often for various chores.

Did Alec [Guinness] send you his book [*Blessings in Disguise*]? I like it so very much – sly and amusing as well as serious, not burdened with lists and excerpts from notices and awfully well written.

Endless Gala at the Dominion last night at which I was given an Award* and was much flattered to get a standing ovation. The award was given by Larry, but though he appeared in a box to huge applause, he didn't stay to give it to me and Anthony Hopkins substituted for him!

To Laurence Olivier   *16 December, Wotton Underwood*

Your most sweet letter touched me so very much. It was wonderful of you to take the trouble to write. You must know how greatly I marvel at your endless courage and resilience despite the wretched inconveniences and setbacks you have endured these last years. Everyone who works with you is lost with admiration and the way you cope with every trouble is a real example to us all. Even in those few days in Vienna you found the time and energy to give that splendid dinner party and to play host as delightfully as you have always done.

I know your children must be a continual blessing, and Joan – whom I thought remarkable as Lady Wishfort – seems to go from strength to strength – everyone in ecstasies over her Mrs Warren, too.†

What a long life we have both had, and so many wonderful triumphs for you, as well as a mass of glorious memories, and the television and film successes, though they can be exhausting and frustrating too, will keep your acting always as thrilling reminders over the long years. More power to your indomitable elbow.

---

* The Laurence Olivier Awards given by the Society of West End Theatre. JG was given a Special Award.
† Joan Plowright played Lady Wishfort in the 1984 Chichester Festival Theatre production of *The Way of the World* and Mrs Warren in the 1985 National Theatre production of *Mrs Warren's Profession*.

1986

To James Lees-Milne   *4 February, Wotton Underwood*

How good of you to write and of course I am delighted to hear you enjoyed the Irish frolic. I can happily reciprocate by telling you how enormously I have enjoyed your books, though I don't think Wotton – the big house of which this one is part of the complex – comes under your eagle and discriminating eye? Mrs Brunner, who owns it, is rather a tiresome prima donna, though she did save the house when it was on the verge of being pulled down, and we are barely on speaking terms, which is rather a pity with such a near neighbour. However –

How many moons away are the War days when we used to meet. I don't think you were present on the occasion at the Dorchester during the V2s, when Emerald [Cunard] reproved the head waiter.

'Where is the butter?'

'No butter I'm afraid, my lady.'

'No butter? One must have butter. What is the Merchant Navy doing?'

At which point a V2 flew over and burst noisily a few miles off, fortunately. And Emerald never turned a hair.

To Hugh Wheeler   *17 March, Wotton Underwood*

I'm having a mad time. *War and Remembrance.* Just finished a month in Yugoslavia (where I had one of Tito's hunting lodges to stay in – huge suite, antlers on the wall and wonderfully quiet in the midst of a deep forest, completely snowed in) but the work was pretty gruelling. Huge unit with hundreds of Jews and natives flown in for crowd scenes, and hideous gas chamber scenes with 350 men, women and children all stark naked, followed by a day in the gas chamber itself when I had to lie prone on a mat, while four naked men fell on top of me one after the other – a real gang-bang crematorium!! I might have enjoyed it more in younger and happier days. Now I have a break, and go to Bristol later this week to make a TV of *The Canterville Ghost* which might be quite fun and a welcome change from all the horrors. Poor Martin all alone here but spent the time washing all the walls of the gallery room on a scaffolding – incredible energy and lovely result, of course. But the cold was ghastly here though I think not quite as bad as we had in the East.

The director, Dan Curtis, is quite an amiable Hollywood Teddy Bear, but has no idea of time, and we work sometimes till 9 or 10 at night and I usually have to get up at 6.30 to be in time for 8.15 call on location. The extras, make-up girls and ADs have a terrible time and the electricians strike from time to time, but Jane Seymour (who plays the part Ali McGraw did in *Winds of War*) is a great dear, and very easy to work with. There is also a nice set designer from Canada, Guy Comtois, who is agreeable company for occasional meals, and Mavis Walker is at hand under strict orders from Martin to protect me and fetch and carry. So all things considered I have kept well – and sane – and it is a fascinating experience in its way – a 90 million budget, they say, and I can well believe it. The whole thing, 27 hours viewing, can't be finished before spring next year, and I can't help wondering if I shall be lucky enough to be alive still when it is finally shown!

To Howard Turner   *22 November, Wotton Underwood*

So you are only 68, a mere child. I am dismayed to have to admit to a slightly tottering 82, which is hard for me to believe, but I thank God I have a wonderful chum who has been with me now for 23 years, and we have a most lovely 18th century house here with dogs and birds and a lovely countryside round us. I am doing a TV play *Quartermaine's Terms*, which was done in N.Y. a few years ago – an amusing, not too long part, though I do have to write out my lines and jab them into my memory these days.

Do please let me know if you are in England. I would so love to see you again, and we needn't stare at each other too closely to see how much we have both altered.

To Gwen Ffrangcon-Davies   *15 December, Wotton Underwood*

I wish you could have been at the National Film Theatre last Sunday to see the clip of our *Romeo* Balcony Scene, though it only lasted one minute! Taken apparently by Pathé News. It was very clever of them to find it. I looked horrendous but you were so graceful and yearning as you leaned down and dropped the long scarf for me to seize. A real curiosity and strange nostalgia after 60 years. Heavens above – and you were heaven, too.

1987

To Irene Worth   *31 January, Wotton Underwood*

I went finally to *Les Liaisons Dangereuses* (by Christopher Hampton from the novel by Choderlos de Laclos] and was bitterly disappointed. Having not been to the theatre all year, except for your two plays, I was agog with pleasurable expectation but, alas, I could *hear* nobody in the 4th row at the Ambassadors – no diction or style, they all moved like clodhoppers and hung red hands in their laps. Clever lighting and direction and the very explicit seduction scenes had the audience spellbound – mostly American middle aged Lady Tourists, it seemed to me. The leading lady, Lindsay Duncan, who has had raving notices and awards, seemed to me utterly without interest or accomplishment. It would have been a fine part for Vivien. The only bright spot was dear old Jean Anderson, in a tiny part, who had style and one could hear every word. But I had a miserable afternoon.

I have three weeks in N. Italy in May for another TV – rather a good script. All the cast, however, are to be Italian (except, God knows why, Susannah York, who is very ill cast in my opinion) and though I am to speak all my part in English, the whole thing is to be dubbed into Italian, French and German, but not released in English! All very odd. They are also paying me a ridiculous fee to do Pickering in a record of bits from *My Fair Lady* with Kiri te Kinawa (can't possibly spell it) [Kanawa], Ustinov as Doolittle,* Jeremy Irons as Higgins, only two days work – most peculiar.

To George Pitcher   *4 April, Wotton Underwood*

We have had a fairly quiet winter. Now it is trying to be spring, but the rain pours down, and a horrific gale blew half a big chestnut tree and a big lump of lead off, so we have scaffolding for repairs and are lucky not to have the top floor rooms soaked. Daffodils begin to peer, but the crocuses and snowdrops all blown or withered. Martin has a bad back and goes for acupuncture and laser beam treatment when he finds the time. Refuses to lie up as he ought to do, and the enchanting new dogs and many new birds, as well as feeding me, keeps him everlastingly hard worked and occupied. I begin to ache a good deal and watch my balance, hoping I am not going to succumb to the necessary decrepitude.

The TV production of a Simon Gray play, *Quartermaine's Terms* was shown last week and I am a dotty old headmaster in it. Had a lot of nice letters about it, and thought it very well acted all round, and extremely funny as well as moving – so that was nice. They also ran *Arthur* again and *The Canterville Ghost* comes out on Easter Sunday, so I am much in evidence on the box again.

Larry Olivier is 80 on May 22nd, and Peggy Ashcroft 80 in November. Oh dear, the tributes and interviews which I shall try and avoid as much as possible.

In June I go to Israel – a few days in Tel Aviv at the beginning of June – home for a fortnight, then another two weeks in Jerusalem. A studio part in an Agatha Christie film [*Appointment with Death*] with Ustinov and Lauren Bacall – very grand cast but really no character. However, I rather reluctantly accepted it and turned down a very big but revolting part in a TV film to be shot in Pasadena in July – an old man who is spotted by a 16 year old boy as

---

* For some reason, Peter Ustinov pulled out and was replaced by Warren Mitchell.

having been a Nazi monster and then becomes psychopathic – murders a cat and subsequently two muggers whom he has brought home, and the boy goes mad after the old man's death and goes round shooting everybody within sight. I really couldn't bring myself to do it. Quite enough of concentration camps and Nazis last year and besides, though it isn't meant quite like that, I feel it would look as if I had seduced the boy! So I said firmly no, despite vigorous attempts to persuade me.

Do you hear anything of Hugh? He never writes or telephones any more, and I rather tremble to think what has become of him. One's circle of friends gets ever shorter – so sad. But Ben Edwards and Rouben still keep in touch.

Did I tell you I was asked to go to Yale in July to get an Honorary Degree and also to Washington for some do at the Folger Library, but I can't face either and have pleaded work, which is more or less true.

To Irene Worth   *13 May, Wotton Underwood*

I have had a quiet week or two before going to Israel for June to do a rather absurd part in an Agatha Christie – yes, still another film [*Appointment with Death*]. Peter Ustinov and Betty Bacall are to be in it and possibly Michael York, so it might be fun, even with that very vulgar but quite funny director, Michael Winner, whom I worked with in the remake of *The Wicked Lady* three years ago. My television film in Italy was rather delightful, working in a villa next door to the hotel (rather crumby) where I stayed in Lake Como. Most of my scenes lying down or reclining on sofas, not long hours, no make-up, and a lovely little town beside the glorious lake.

The Derek Jacobi play [*Breaking the Code* by Hugh Whitemore] was patchy and only just effective, I thought, and as for *Henry IV Part 1* which I had to sit through at the Vic, really abysmal, I thought. Appalling stunt rock-and-roll production by Michael Bogdanov. Am I too old now to get any pleasure from going to the theatre? Have tickets for the Peter Hall *Antony* [*and Cleopatra*] on June 4th which has won universal praise – everyone says Judi Dench is brilliant, [Anthony] Hopkins less so. I shall be fascinated to judge for myself.

We miss you, as always, very much. Martin refuses to discuss his bad back which I think is a continual irritation for him, and I have had a lot of muscular rheumatism and lumbago, swollen ankles etc. which is a bit of a bore, but at my time of life how lucky there seems to be nothing else wrong. Larry's 80th on the 22nd – endless press columns and celebrations. I shall contribute as little as I decently can!

To George Pitcher and Ed Cone   *3 June, Wotton Underwood*

Delighted you saw *Quartermaine* and liked it. I was pleased with it myself, I must say – so well cast and acted all round. I had turned it down when they originally offered it me for the London production, not (stupidly) understanding that there are schools in Cambridge for teaching English to foreign students (I mixed the characters up thinking they were undergraduates!) and missing the whole point – that the offstage people talked about so much, never appeared. It was singularly stupid of me.

Glad to hear of Ed's successful birthday celebrations. Larry Olivier had his 80th last week, but I kept clear, contenting myself with writing a tribute for the Gala Programme, though I didn't go to it myself. Martin detests him, and my friendship with him has always been a bit dicey as I adored Vivien, who was also very fond of me, which I think Larry resented, though I do appreciate, of course, what a tricky time he had with her.

Yes, all the deaths are very depressing, and illnesses as well. Did you ever meet [Hermione] Gingold with me? She was a mad old character, but witty and fun for a short period. In the War she played brilliantly in intimate revues, and her dressing room always packed with glamorous Americans in pink trousers, many of whom I believe she managed to entice into her bed, though she was always very dirty and untidy in a series of wigs which looked as if she had slept in them, too. She had a wonderful moment when she did a skit on *Medea* which I made such a hash of when I directed it – with Judith Anderson in New York and Eileen Herlie in London. Gingold marched up to a minor character leaning against a pillar and nudged her out of the way, withering her with the remark 'This is my personal column.'

The summer refuses to come properly (not to put too fine a point on it). Rain drenching the flowers just as they are coming out, and quite cold again. Lillian [Gish] actually got to the Cannes Festival and her film [*The Whales of August*] was shown to the Royals. She wrote me an enthusiastic letter and Alec Guinness told me she was wheeled about, graciously accepting champagne from beneath copious mufflings. The film got quite good reviews, but is very slight. (I was asked to play Vincent Price's part in it but was fortunately busy) and I am glad I turned it down as it was apparently something of a nightmare. Bette Davis impossibly temperamental and spiteful, resenting Lillian's co-starring and sweetness, and L. herself couldn't remember more than a few lines at a time. 'Eheu fugaces Postume, Postume', as I once had to quote in some long-forgotten play I acted in!

To Lady Susana Walton   *7 July, Wotton Underwood*

Of course I shall be very glad to subscribe to the Fund* and hope you will succeed in raising the necessary sum to achieve such a splendid project.

I well remember the beauty of your lovely house and garden when I visited it with Binkie so long ago, and also have the most grateful and charming memories of William, not only when he so kindly did the music for my

---

* Lady Walton wanted to build a concert hall in memory of her husband, Sir William Walton.

Macbeth production in 1942. And do you remember Binkie's dinner at Lord North St to celebrate William's 70th birthday – was it – and how Marlene Dietrich burst in and made a ridiculous scene and embarrassed us all mightily.

Hugh Wheeler died on 26 July 1987.

To George Pitcher and Ed Cone   *10 August, Wotton Underwood*

Ben Edwards rang yesterday and told me that there will be a small gathering at Sardi's tomorrow to commemorate Hugh, organised by Hal Prince, so I am glad to think he will have friends to think of him there and sorry I cannot be among them. We have no answering service here, so I don't know who Johnny can have left the message with. I suddenly saw the obituary in the London *Times* and was, of course, greatly shocked and saddened. The newspapers, both here and in New York, gave him a remarkably honourable send-off. I only wish he could have achieved the same kind of interest in his last years, which were, I fear, pretty desperate, with half-completed projects and increasingly bad health.

The circle of friends does grow depressingly smaller every year, and I am incredibly lucky to be working and compos mentis as the months go so quickly by.

Thank you for sending me the Margot Peters review of the Ellen Terry book. I think it marvellously perceptive and well researched, but of course you would not find it as fascinating as I do. Strange, as I wrote them both, that two American college ladies should manage to write so vividly about Mrs Pat and Ellen, neither of whom either of them ever saw or met, far better than the English books about them both – except, of course, for Ellen's own memoirs which are really strikingly good.

Having a quiet, restful time here after my exhausting month in Israel. A couple of indifferent films offered for the autumn and a very fascinating play which sorely tempted me, but the part just not good enough to warrant my return to the live theatre, which would involve my going to live in London again and also a lot of publicity and possible disappointment.

Peter Hall has done a really fine production of *Antony and Cleopatra* at the National, which I greatly enjoyed last week – a great joy to enjoy Shakespeare again after so many stunt productions and directors' tricks.

We've had hardly any summer here at all – still no sunshine and the garden drenched. We have an adorable new Tibetan terrier puppy called Arthur to go with Simon and Aaron, the other two both a year older. He broke a leg in two places a week ago, but leaps about with a bandaged limb as bright as a button. We think of you both, as always, with love and fondest thoughts – from Martin too, of course.

John Russell Thompson, who had been an extra in JG's Macbeth, *wrote to say that he had a set of records of William Walton's incidental music for the production.*

To John Russell Thompson   *27 August, Wotton Underwood*

I was none too pleased when I heard the *Macbeth* records again, used in the Tennent production of Wilder's *The Skin of Our Teeth* a good many years later! But I suppose they were finally swallowed up or thrown away when the firm broke up soon after Binkie Beaumont's death. I am sure Lady Walton would be glad to have them left to her at your death. She is still living in Ischia, and engaged in planning a memorial Concert Hall there in her husband's memory, to which I have just subscribed.

You don't say what profession you turned to when you left the stage. I hope it has brought you good luck.

To Clive Francis   *24 September, Wotton Underwood*

All congratulations on your splendid personal notices in *Earnest*.* I felt a pang of jealousy when Donald [Sinden] spoke to me about the production at the Garrick Club.

I always hoped to direct the play again myself. The Haymarket people proposed it for Derek Jacobi a couple of years ago and I was very keen to take it on, but Derek went off to New York with Benedick and Cyrano, so it never happened. I'm sure you are much better as Jack than Derek would have been and the whole thing seems to have gone well, especially where you are concerned. I am so glad for you.

To George Pitcher   *12 October, Wotton Underwood*

I have news for you – they are doing a sequel, if you please, to *Arthur* and my butler character is brought back from the dead for two short scenes! Dudley [Moore] and Liza [Minnelli] playing their original parts, too. So I hope to be in New York for about a week and shall long to see you and Ed, of course. I'm still trying to persuade Martin to come, but at present he firmly refuses to leave the house and animals.

In addition I have, after much hesitation, agreed to go back to the stage in February!! I like the play [*The Best of Friends* by Hugh Whitemore] very much. It is a kind of three-handed life – letters between Bernard Shaw, Dame Laurentia McClachan, Abbess of Stanbrook, and Sydney Cockerell (my part), who was a friend of both of them and curator of the Fitzwilliam Museum at Cambridge for some years. Only six performances a week and no Monday

---

* Clive Francis played Jack Worthing in *The Importance of Being Earnest* at the Royalty Theatre, directed by Donald Sinden.

nights. I am only signing for an eight week run, with eleven previews and a month's rehearsals. Rather alarming prospect. I shall have to live in London during the week, but I am really rather thrilled at the prospect. I hope I shan't have to eat my words – and be able to remember them too!

Irene is playing Mrs Clandon in Shaw's *You Never Can Tell* at a theatre in Wales. Expects to come in to London later on, but of course is dying to play the Abbess in my play. But I think they hope to get Rosemary Harris, who is a splendid actress and nice person. Shaw to be played by an Irish actor whom I don't yet know.*

To George Pitcher and Ed Cone   *October? 1987, Wotton Underwood*

Alas, I can't persuade Martin to come. Birds and dogs and the house – all impossible to leave – such a shame. So I shall come with Mavis Walker, who has nannied me in all my films for the last year (and threatens to concoct a book about our trips together). Warners are putting us into the Regency Hotel, and we are to fly by Concorde. The filming is only due to take 3 days (two short scenes), but as one of them is in the Bowery (or some such dive) they say they may take longer and only work me half days to keep me from standing about too long in the cold. I shall hope to have two days before and two days after, so there won't be time, alas, to come to Princeton. I'll telephone you when I arrive and we can fix a day, perhaps for lunch. I long to see you both, of course.

I have to do a 3-day long documentary on my whole career. They are going to shoot it here in the big room and some bits outside too, if it isn't too wet and cold – and they will bring lights and generators etc., a great upheaval which we rather dread. I hope it may not prove too daunting an experience, and also not too much of an In Memoriam!

The exhibition† is rather well done, though limited. The new Theatre Museum in Covent Garden where they show it is a clumsy building and has rather dark underground showrooms in fairly limited space, but it has some lovely blown-up photographs, slides, models etc., and some acrid correspondence (which I had quite forgotten) with the designer of the scenery [Michael Ayrton] for the *Macbeth* production in 1942! I hope it will be seen by students and theatre buffs who are interested.

Foggy and dreary weather here and Martin is very edgy about my exhausting myself with all the work ahead. I am very busy learning my long part in the play, and seem to manage about a page a day.

---

* Shaw was played by Ray McAnally.
† The Theatre Museum mounted an exhibition on Gielgud's life and work.

To Lillian Gish   *15 October, Wotton Underwood*

I tried to telephone you yesterday but was told your number had been disconnected, probably to avoid the press and well-wishers for your birthday, which I am sure would have brought you many intruders on your privacy.

This is just to send you my ever affectionate love and greetings, and to tell you I am due to come to New York in the first week of December to do three days filming in the sequel to *Arthur,* in which they have written me a couple of quite funny scenes in my original part. Dudley Moore and Liza Minnelli are also in it again.

So don't be surprised if I ring you up and shall so hope to get a glimpse of you.

To Peggy Ashcroft   *18 December, Wotton Underwood*

Darling Peg

I do so hope you can wear these, but am slightly afraid your ears are not pierced! And they are too small for screws! If you can't wear them (or would never want to) will you *please* go to the shop in Beauchamp Place where I bought them and choose a pin or brooch instead.

I do so want you to have some trifle that you can *wear* occasionally, though I know most jewellery is not in your line, but this is such a special occasion and we have been friends for *such* a long and happy time.

Still hoping to make it on Sunday, but know you will understand if I can't. So maddening.

Ever devotedly, John.

To Elisabeth Welch   *23 December, Wotton Underwood*

Your programme last night was such a delight. So amusing, dignified and elegant, just the right mixture and how splendid you looked in the red dress. I feel very privileged to have seen Piaf and Elena Gerhardt when she was in her later years, to say nothing of Mabel Mercer, whom I knew a little, and always went to see when I was in New York. I expect you knew her too. So lovely that you have repeated your earlier triumphs and gained, I am sure, a whole new audience of youngsters – and something of the sort has happened to me too. So the TV and cinema are certainly not to be despised! May our health and memory long hold out!

To Irene Worth   *23 December, Wotton Underwood*

Here is the *Independent* notice* – rather mild, I'm afraid, but you really must not allow yourself to mind about Sheridan Morley after all the raves, especially for you in all the other really important papers which everyone reads in New York as well. So disappointing for you, I know, but you simply mustn't let it ruin your Christmas.

1988

To George Pitcher and Ed Cone   *28 February, Wotton Underwood*

It is really very exciting for me to have this big success – all the ovations, packed houses and many visitors afterwards – all the playwrights, Stoppard, Simon Gray, John Osborne etc., crowding in – so perhaps one of them will write me a nice wheelchair part in a year or two. The stage door crowds with cameras and programmes to sign, people of all ages, very young and quite old! So it has all been worthwhile. I live at the Ritz during the week and come down on Saturday nights – we don't play Monday nights and only one matinée each Saturday. I am supposed to finish on April 2nd, but may give them three weeks more. New York is a tempting prospect for the autumn, but much as I should love it in a way, I feel the play is itself too scrappy and élitist for Broadway, and regretfully don't think I shall risk it. Sufficient unto the day!

Poor Paul [Anstee] is having a wretched time. His Canadian chum of about 15 years is stricken with leukaemia – (everyone thinks it is Aids but he strongly denies it) – but he has to take him into hospital for transfusions almost every week and cope with pills, meals etc. when he is at their flat. He is extraordinarily philosophical and refuses to be sympathised with. Their house in Sussex was devastated by the big gales a month ago and they lost 58 trees in their garden. I really do admire his devotion and care so very much – he seems to keep cheerful and is still working hard in his shop.

Martin is wonderfully pleased at the success and spends hours answering my sudden onslaught of fan mail. I get very tired and sleep every afternoon with occasional film going at lunchtimes. London is fearfully noisy and cluttered with road repairs and terrifyingly increased traffic and inconvenience, but I have lovely rooms looking on to the Green Park and manage to see quite a lot of (increasingly) old friends for short suppers and lunches, so one way and another, I have so very much to be thankful for. I am sure you are having a sad time with your beloved dog. Our three are such a joy.

* Irene Worth was playing Mrs Lanfrey Clandon in Shaw's *You Never Can Tell* at the Haymarket Theatre.

The youngest, Arthur, has become quite devoted to me, and they all sit up to wait for my return at midnight on Saturdays.

*To Robert Back**   *18 April, Wotton Underwood*

My Father had an uncle Henry whom I knew quite well as a boy. He and his wife, Aunt Kitty, were a nice old couple living, I remember, in Oriental Place, Brighton, but he died very tragically. I well remember my parents' distress at the time, for he walked into an empty lift-shaft in his London Club and died immediately. I suppose the gate had been accidentally left open or did not work properly. Very sad.

To George Pitcher and Ed Cone   *17 May, Wotton Underwood*

Martin has trouble with his back – ought not to garden or lift things, but of course he insists on doing so. He had some treatment at Stoke Mandeville – laser beams and acupuncture – but now he won't go to *any* doctor and creeps about defiantly. Very tiresome of (and for) him, but he won't even be asked how he is!

I'm glad George Rose got his excellent career obituaries before the real news broke.† Quite a lot in the *Telegraph* here and no doubt the American scandal sheets had a good time. It's a tragic end to such a fine acting career. One is only hopeful that there are no relatives still alive to be upset. I saw him with Marti Stevens just before Christmas, little thinking it was the last time. I shall miss him as I do Hugh.

My wretched handwriting seems to get worse with my old age. Hope you can still decipher it.

Glorious weather – the garden is heavenly and the dogs exceedingly frisky. No other news really. Wonderful ovation on the last night of the play – everyone standing up! But I am quite glad to be quiet for a bit – the extra three weeks were very exhausting.

To Cecil Lewis   *18 May, Wotton Underwood*

I only met [Charles] Ricketts once when he did some costumes for a one-act play (called, I remember, *The High Constable's Wife*) which I acted in for a special performance opposite Barbara Morley Holder and directed by Lewis Casson, who terrified me rather with his insistence on phrasing and rhythm

---

* Robert Back, a local historian, came across the name Henry Gielgud while researching the Bedford Park Club in west London.
† George Rose had a second home in the Dominican Republic. He intended making his lover his heir. When his affection shifted, so the story goes, he was beaten to death in case he was tempted to change his will.

inherited, no doubt, from Poel and Granville-Barker. He used to make strange explanatory noises himself.

How very fascinating that you knew Ricketts so well. Of course I greatly admired his décor in *Saint Joan* and *Henry the Eighth* – but *not* the Casson *Macbeth* which was clumsy and over-pictorial, with Sybil like an overdressed parrot! And disastrous battle tableaux.

To Cecil Lewis   *2 June, Wotton Underwood*

Well, I did hit the nail on the head, didn't I? I can't think how the name of the play and that of Barbara Morley Holder suddenly came so clearly out of the blue into my memory. And to think you were the author – somewhere in a private theatre in St John's Wood,* wasn't it?

I dined the other night to celebrate Athene Seyler's 90th birthday and she suddenly burst into song with 'Oh, Mr Porter' and some other early Edwardian ballads, so I suppose as one gets older the very strong recollections of one's youth spring inevitably to one's mind. A bit comforting really, but also a bit sad. Of course I should simply love to have the Ricketts book if you should chance to find it.

To George Pitcher   *14 July, Wotton Underwood*

All thanks for your letter and the clipping. I feared when I read the script that the film† was too full of continual drunkenness, and sequels are seldom a success, so the failure of this one doesn't surprise me.

I am not surprised to hear you are giving up your holiday. Poor Martin has not been away from here since India three years ago, as he says he can't leave the dogs, birds and the house, and it would be impossible to find anyone to cope with them. I do regret so much that he is a kind of prisoner, and only hope the continued effort and isolation doesn't tire him out.

We used to have six dogs at Cowley St and when we moved here. All of them have died at intervals, of course, and now we have three divine Tibetan Terriers who are a continual joy and anxiety too! Their names are Simon, Aaron and Arthur. The latter has taken a real fancy to me, which is flattering. He is a year younger than the other two, as Martin thought three the best number, in case anything should happen to one of them. He also has three big macaws, about 8 cockatoos, 4 tortoises and a number of small birds – and looking after them takes about 1½ hours every day, but he doesn't seem to mind that.

I am having a quiet time – for me – a few days as Wolsey in *Man for All*

---

* Garden Theatre, 40 Hamilton Terrace.
† *Arthur 2: On the Rocks.*

Seasons with Charlton Heston (both of us rather unsuitable).

Do you remember a friend of mine, Jimmie Morcom, who was once working as scene designer at Radio City Music Hall? He jumped out of a window the other day and killed himself, God knows why. I saw him last Christmas when I came over. Oh dear – Hugh gone too!

War and Remembrance *was shown in the USA in November 1988.*

To George Pitcher   *21 November, Wotton Underwood*

All thanks for your sweet and thoughtful sending of the cuttings. Was hoping to hear from the few N.Y. friends I have left – Marti Stevens, Ben Edwards, Rouben – but no word from any of them so far. *Variety* says I am the best in the cast – hope it may be true. I still can't quite get used to having work I did two years ago shown so many years later. I really wondered if I should live till it was released – and it won't be shown here till the autumn of *next* year – so! It was six months of my life's toil, so I only hope it was worth it!

Yes, of course I know what you mean about Irene [Worth], lack of humour, occasional folie de grandeur, etc., but she has been a wonderful friend to me ever since *Day by the Sea*, when I first met and worked with her, and behaved quite splendidly over my trouble, which happened the same year – 1953 – and ever since.

A man called Kenton Coe, who was a friend of mine, and particularly of Martin, may be coming to Princeton one of these days, and I took the liberty of giving him your names and address when he cropped up here the other day. He is a struggling modern opera composer with a commission from the Baton Rouge Symphony Orchestra for next year. He is quite agreeable and I thought he would be very interested to talk to Ed. I hope you won't both find him a bore and won't mind my having suggested it. His opera is called *Rachel.*

I've no work on hand at the moment, and the leaves are falling fast, but I have had some interesting talks with Peter Greenaway, a brilliant youngish film director, who made *The Draughtsman's Contract.* I have recently done some days with him on a version of Dante's *Inferno*, which, of course, I've never read! I spoke yards of rather well written blank verse, fortunately on autocue, so I didn't have to learn it. He now has some most exciting ideas about a possible fantasy version of *The Tempest* which, of course, I've always longed to do – especially if it is not a theatre version of the whole play which would, I think, be rather a bore. Greatly hope something may come of it for next year.

To George Pitcher   *4 December, Wotton Underwood*

Glad you approved of me in *W and R.* But I don't think from the accounts I have seen so far that they will get much of their 110 million dollars back, especially as the second half is not to be shown till May – a long time for it to grow cold, and all my best scenes are in the last half, which is very painful and horrific.

1989

To Irene Worth   *8 January, Wotton Underwood*

Your spacious table napkins are in daily use, most handy with my increasingly untidy table habits, which I hope you have not noticed as often as poor Martin does! And my handwriting simply refuses to get any bigger, though I do try. Trust I shall not become a slobberer as well as a cripple as time goes by.

To George Pitcher and Ed Cone   *9 January, Wotton Underwood*

Thank you for your very kind invitation. The house certainly sounds most attractive, and of course I should love to come, but July seems a long way off, and I'm very much hoping a TV version of *The Tempest* may materialise for June and July, which might mean I couldn't get away. I never like to make commitments far ahead, for fear of sudden offers.

To Dadie Rylands   *28 January, Wotton Underwood*

I know you must be greatly saddened at dear Arthur [Marshall]'s death, though I heard from John Perry, who is also most upset, that he died in his sleep, as we all hope to. I had not seen him – except on the box – for a number of years. The last occasion was when Lynn Fontanne gave a somewhat macabre though gallant dinner party in the Oliver Messel suite at the Dorchester on the last occasion when she was in England. Jamie Hamilton and others – all men – were also guests and the most colossal joint of beef was served, which I felt sure most of us would hardly be able to chew, let alone digest. Our joint ages around the table must have been Methuselan. I felt like saying, as the lady did in the Bobby Helpmann story when the customs man wanted her to pay duty on some tennis balls she was bringing as a present for her son. She split open the box, rolled the balls down the counter and snapped out 'Oh, give them to the poor of Dover!'

To Pat and Michael York   *24 April, Wotton Underwood*

I am rehearsing the John Mortimer novel for TV [*Summer's Lease*] and we do some shooting here in London and at Shepperton beginning next week, and then we are off to Tuscany, which should be pleasant, though I rather hate leaving Martin and the garden during what one hopes will be the best of the summer.

I have a very amusing part to play, which I hope I may do justice to, and the other principal parts are played by Susan Fleetwood, Rosemary Leach and Michael Pennington.

Filming was interrupted by a recurrence of JG's prostate problem, and he returned briefly to London for treatment.

To Meriel Richardson   *18 June, Tuscany*

Feeling much better and the shooting seems to be going well. Everyone appears glad to have me back and they look after me very solicitously. Susan Fleetwood is splendid to work with and speaks so lovingly of Ralph when they were together on *The Cherry Orchard.*

To Irene Worth   *2 July, Tuscany*

They are filming the Palio today in Siena, but thank God I am not wanted! 'The crowds – and the people!' as Ernest Thesiger remarked when he came back from serving as a private in the 1914 War!

Laurence Olivier died on 11 July 1989.

To Joan Plowright, Lady Olivier   *11 July, Siena*

Dear Joan

I find it almost impossible to write you anything adequate about Larry's death. The whole profession will be mourning with you and you will be overwhelmed with messages of sympathy from all over the world.

It is difficult for me to believe that he is gone – but what a rich legacy he leaves behind – not only of his brilliant talents and extraordinary range of achievement, but the memory of his own vital, courageous personality, his determination and power as performer, manager, director and defier of the lightning, the originality of his approach to every new and challenging venture, his physical bravery, not only on the stage but in the valiant way in which he faced his few failures and defeats, above all his refusal to give up when he had become so ill.

As you know, we were never intimate friends over these long years. He only spoke to me on one very memorable day – I think it was just about the time when he had fallen in love with you. We talked at the Algonquin for about an hour and he told me of some of his tortured times with Vivien and a few other personal problems, a confidence which touched me very much.

I was, I confess, always a bit afraid of him, for he had a certain remoteness and spiritual authority which I imagine Irving also had? Perhaps it was a fitting part of his own acting genius and his gift for leadership.

His meeting with you and the blessing you brought him in giving him the children he always longed for must, to some extent at least have given him a great reward, despite all the miseries and complications of the South Bank. How he contrived to go on giving such fine acting performances over those appallingly difficult years was an amazing triumph of concentration and devotion.

I am sad not to have seen him these last years, but I hesitated to intrude on the family life he had so richly deserved and I felt it might distress him to find me still lucky and well enough to go on working while he himself was so sadly disabled.

Please don't dream of writing – my affectionate thanks for all you gave him and always my fondest wishes and admiration.

To Irene Worth   *26 October, Wotton Underwood*

The great memorial service for Larry* was a tremendous affair, extremely well organised to the minute and hugely attended, of course. Alec [Guinness] made a memorably clever and appropriate speech, and Peggy [Ashcroft] and I recited our little poems. Patrick Garland had done a fine job and Joan [Plowright, Lady Olivier] behaved most dignifiedly and hosted a huge party at the National, where one knew everyone but found it rather difficult to get around in a narrow bar upstairs. Poor Jill Esmond in a wheelchair and Lord Goodman dreadfully infirm on two sticks. Eleanor, who watched it all on television, said it should have been held in Drury Lane rather than the Abbey. I know what she meant.

Then, on the same evening, came news of Tony Quayle's death from cancer. With Milton [Goldman] and Larry that makes the usual prophetic three. Let's hope that is enough for the present.

I believe Laurie [Evans] is to organise a tribute for Milton next month at the Haymarket which I rather hope may not materialise. We shall see.

What other news? Jeffrey Archer's play [*Exclusive*] about the newspapers with [Paul] Scofield, Alec McCowen and Eileen Atkins got thoroughly roasted by the critics, but I believe had enormous advance bookings, so will probably run quite profitably. [Albert] Finney and [Janet] Suzman have a success in a new Ronald Harwood play [*Another Time*] about S. Africa, and Peter O'Toole has had superb notices for his near monologue [*Jeffrey Bernard is Unwell* by Keith Waterhouse] about Jeffrey Bernard, a Soho drunk who writes for the *Spectator*. I have never heard of him!

Judi Dench has wonderful notices for her Ranevskaya in what reads like a

---

* Held in Westminster Abbey on 20 October 1989.

new, rather tricksy production of *The Cherry Orchard* in a new version by Michael Frayn, directed by a man called [Sam] Mendes, of whom also I have never heard! One feels so out of touch with so many new young talents.

I am doing a lot of recordings of various kinds which keeps me out of boredom, and the plans with Peter Greenaway seem to be progressing slowly. I saw his new film *The Cook, the Thief and the Lover* [*sic*]* – quite spectacularly brilliant, but perhaps rather too strong meat for you, though his excuse for its many disgusting moments is its echoes of Jacobean tragedy. I know he will be fascinating to work with anyway.

---

* *The Cook, the Thief, His Wife and Her Lover.*

THE NINETIES

1990

To Irene Worth   *27 February, Wotton Underwood*

Very wintry here, tremendous storms and gales. Our roof lost tiles etc. and we had a great hole which flooded part of the gallery room. Scaffolding up, but too windy for the men to climb up! Very tiresome, but far worse in the North.

I am to spend Sunday night staying at Royal Lodge to read some poetry to the Queen Mother. There's Glory for you, as Humpty Dumpty said. Ted Hughes, Gowrie and the Strongs* are to be of the party! Hope I shan't lose my head.

The *Tempest* film is supposed to start on March 27th. A month in Amsterdam (studios) then three weeks off and two more in May in Holland. Thrilling script, I think. Cross your fingers for me.

To George Pitcher and Ed Cone   *4 June, Wotton Underwood*

I finished the film work [*Prospero's Books*] last week, after a very arduous but fascinating two months. Have seen nothing yet, but Greenaway promises to show me some sequences on a big screen in London fairly soon. He goes to Japan to edit it and develop all the magic tricks and so on, and hopes to finish it later this year and show it next year at the Cannes Festival. Rather a long time to wait. I had a thrilling experience making it – weighed down by enormous cloaks and costumes which were very exhausting to walk and stand in. But the sets are superb, also the lighting. I think it will be like a sort of moving ballet with me speaking all the text from the play which I am writing in my cell! Amazing assortment of players of both sexes, mythological crowds, animals, Dutch clowns, children, Negroes etc., most of them stark naked, but one grows quickly accustomed to that! I tried not to stare too obviously at the tremendous display of genitalia and even had to play naked myself in a pool in which I am reading from a huge book, with a tiny model galleon in the other hand, with Ariel peeing in a huge arc above me and between us we conjure up the storm! I have a sort of Doge's headdress in the other scenes and two huge cloaks – made in Japan – with a microphone hidden in their folds – one red, one blue, but incredibly heavy to move about in – and, at the end, when I break my staff and hurl the books into the sea, a black velvet suit,

---

* Ted Hughes, Poet Laureate; Grey Gowrie, 2nd Earl of Gowrie; Sir Roy Strong, former Director of the Victoria and Albert Museum and his wife Julia Trevelyan Oman, designer and photographer.

high-heeled shoes, a gigantic ruff and huge hat with black and white feathers – no mean feat, I can assure you.

I fell quite in love with Amsterdam – the Van Gogh show and the Rijks-museum superb, and the drives I went [on], enchanting with the waterways, windmills and spring flowers and little lambs. Trams and bicycles a bit of a menace in the town, but very good restaurants and everyone speaking English. I had an ex-nurse as my companion who guided me through the traffic and was extremely efficient and agreeable, and although the studio was dreadfully cold (an aeroplane hangar) the crew and everyone worked with the utmost kindness and consideration. Altogether a great experience.*

To Clive Francis   *4 November, Wotton Underwood*

I had some bad luck with my health while we were doing *Summer's Lease* in Tuscany last year, and one or two minor ailments lately, but have kept very quiet about them. If the Press once gets hold of any illness at my time of life, they will be sure to bury me prematurely, which is an idea I do not relish yet awhile. But I do feel a bit out of things, especially, of course, the pleasures of rehearsal and discipline I have so long enjoyed in the live theatre. Ah well!

Oddly enough, I was once approached about playing in the Orton play.† Ralph agreed, as you may remember, with disastrous results. I have never seen it myself – missed it at the Whitehall when Lindsay did it. Feel very ambivalent about all his plays. Loathed [*Entertaining*] *Mr Sloane* the first time, but was converted by Beryl Reid, hated *Loot* when I read it. Anyway, all good wishes for your production.

1991

To Irene Worth   *28 January, Wotton Underwood*

The gala for Gwen [Ffrangcon-Davies] was a huge success – 100 people and of course a host of familiar faces, many of them not seen for twenty years or more! Your absence was much sadly emphasised when your message was read out. Peggy and I both made speeches and finally Gwen herself, who amazed us all by speaking extempore for seven or eight minutes, ending with quite a long excerpt from Lilith's speech in *Back to Methuselah*! She looks tiny and frail and something of a skeleton when I put my arms round her, but I think she took everything in, ate quite a good dinner and certainly rose magnificently

---

* Note from Clive Francis: 'I tried very hard with Robert Fox to make a film of *The Tempest* with JG and approached Peter Greenaway to direct; he declined. Interestingly enough when our project collapsed, Greenaway re-emerged with *Prospero's Books*!'

† Clive Francis had just opened in Joe Orton's *What the Butler Saw* at Wyndham's Theatre. Ralph Richardson played Dr Rance in the first production at the Queen's Theatre in 1969.

to the occasion. She says her post has been unceasing and she even spoke some poetry on radio the other night, her voice still clear and resonant.

To Irene Worth   *3 February, Wotton Underwood*

I finished my idiotic part in the Michael Douglas film [*Shining Through*], a wretchedly unsatisfactory job which took three months to complete, ten days work and meant chugging off to Berlin, Leipzig and Klagenfurt where I spent three weeks sitting in hotels waiting to be called for one or two close-ups. Dreadful waste of time, though absurdly overpaid. Also I have turned down a part in a film of [Michael] Frayn's play *Noises Off*. I think nothing of the part and it would mean 10 weeks in April and May in L.A. or Florida. But [Peter] Bogdanovich, who is to direct it and whom I did like very much when I met him, keeps telephoning to try and persuade me. But I don't think I will give in unless they offer me enough money to enable me to retire afterwards. We shall see.

To James Roose-Evans   *10 March, Wotton Underwood*

I always hated *Tiny Alice*, and thought I was anyway far too old for the part. I accepted it rashly after reading only the first two acts, thinking the first two scenes very exciting. But oh dear, the rest, and that impossible death monologue which Albee absolutely refused to cut or change. The seduction scene was pretty embarrassing though Irene was wonderfully good. I never want to see it in London. Can't think why you should want to resuscitate it.

To George Pitcher   *16 March, Wotton Underwood*

You may like to know that I had a prostate operation back in 1977 (brilliantly done from outside so that I didn't have to be cut open). But unfortunately it got bad again last year when I was in Tuscany doing *Summer's Lease* and I worked most painfully for a week and then came back to have another operation, after which I was able to come back to Italy and finish the work. But it was a wretchedly uncomfortable time. Then I got something called cellulitis which made my feet and legs swell up, and I coped with that all through *The Tempest* film, in which I had to stand and walk in enormously heavy robes down long corridors, which didn't help. Having got rid of that, I fell a couple of times, and have since been full of rheumatism and awkwardness of balance. So you see my sins are at last beginning to find me out! But I plough on as best I can. We made a radio version of *The Best of Friends* six weeks ago and are now rehearsing a television version of the same play with Wendy Hiller and Patrick McGoohan, both very good. We shoot it next week, then I have to receive a BAFTA award for my film career!, and also spend another evening at Windsor reading some prose and poetry to the

Queen Mother. I did a similar reading last year and it evidently went off well, as I have been asked again. Lunch, dinner as well as the reading, and the Queen as another guest! So you see I am still mobile, though not as nimble as of yore. Thank God the memory seems to hold up.

By the way, please don't mention my illnesses to anybody. We had much ado to keep them out of the newspapers who heard rumours and tried to use them, Martin as usual a tower of strength in keeping them quiet.

To George Pitcher and Ed Cone   *29 May, Wotton Underwood*

Prospero's Books was not finished in time to be shown at the Cannes Festival, but Greenaway did give a private showing of the first reel only to an invited audience, who were apparently enraptured. I am to be shown it in a few weeks time, and it is to go to the Venice Festival in August before opening in London. They want me to go to Venice to receive an award, but I don't think I have the stamina for all that razzmatazz – interviews, photographs, crowds etc.

No news really. I am having acupuncture for my hips and back which continue to ache a good deal – so boring. We've had a few lovely days and the garden is a dream of beauty, peonies, lilacs and laburnums etc., all blooming – but now it is cold and windy again and we have a fire and heating on. Oh, this wretched climate.

Peggy Ashcroft has had a stroke and is in a coma since last Thursday – so sad. One doesn't know what to wish for, and dreads paralysis or speechlessness if she comes out of it. Such a dear and affectionate friend and partner for sixty years, as well as such a superb actress.

Peggy Ashcroft died on 14 June 1991.
  Eva Le Gallienne died on 3 June, 1991.

To Irene Worth   *16 June, Wotton Underwood*

Here is *The Times* on Eva. I only suddenly remembered that I first met her in 1926, I think, when I was understudying Noël in *The Vortex*. She took me to supper at the Gargoyle Club in Dean Street. With her was a red-haired girl called, I think, Josephine Hutchinson. To my great surprise she invited me to act with her in New York in a number of parts – Romeo and Liliom were mentioned – and she would act and direct in all of them. I said rather rudely 'But suppose we don't get on,' and turned down the offer flat. I can't imagine now why I was so quick to refuse! Many years later I had a charming lunch with her and Peggy Webster in their country house and she was awfully nice. Of course I knew Mercedes De Acosta too, and Gwen and I acted in a play she wrote [*Prejudice*] at the Arts Theatre in about 1930, I think. You probably heard that she, Mercedes, Gladys Calthrop and another (perhaps Cheryl

Crawford) were once referred to as the Four Horsewomen of the Algonquin at the time when they ran the 14th Street Repertory Theatre together.

She and Peggy were acting in a rather good stage version of *Alice* [*in Wonderland*] when we were in the theatre next door with *The Lady's Not for Burning*, and we would suddenly see one of them in full costume, having slipped in to watch us from the wings!

Far too many deaths, but Gwen, Helen [Hayes], Lillian [Gish] – yes, and Marlene too seem to defy the years. Wonder if we shall do the same – not *too* long, I hope.

To Dadie Rylands   *23 June, Wotton Underwood*

I thought you were so gallant to agree to read the verses, and so beautifully too. It must have been a great emotional strain and I didn't trust my own self-control well enough to speak myself.

I found myself strangely detached until the coffin was carried past. I think Peggy would have liked the elegant church [St Mary's Paddington] and I imagine the readings and music were very much what she would have liked.

It does seem extraordinary that both you and I should have outlived her. I always imagined she would easily see us out, but I can't help being thankful she did not recover from the coma. One cannot bear the thought of her being paralysed and speechless.

I know how dearly she loved you and how much she would have appreciated your brave contribution to her passing. Of course we shall both miss her always and remember the wonderful past times we both had, both in the theatre and away from it. What a good person she was – so rare and special.

To Irene Worth   *8 July, Wotton Underwood*

I think it was you who first introduced me to Patrick White, and we got on together very well, rather to my surprise as I quickly realised what a complicated creature he was. I lunched with him at his country house when I was in Australia and remember he had no use at all for *Ages of Man*, did not like recitations and longed to be successful as a playwright himself. Several of his plays were done in Australia but made little impact. I gather Ralph was a great fan of his and made me read *Riders to* [*in*] *the Chariot* and later on I read three or four of his other novels which I found very striking and powerful.

Bernard Miles had a very sad end. His wife [Josephine Wilson] died last year and he had a stroke some months ago, was put into Denville Hall but had to be transferred to a mental home where he finally died. No money at all. I gather the children will be helped by kind Dickie Attenborough and [illegible]. Oh dear. What a sad ending to an eccentric but adventurous career. I always thought the Mermaid was a considerable achievement, really well designed and the best of the newly built theatres.

To Pat and Michael York   *24 July, Wotton Underwood*

Prospero's Books was shown to me last week, and there was a special showing of it at BAFTA on Sunday, to which I invited three friends, all of whom seemed greatly impressed. It goes to the Venice Festival in September and will also be released in London and New York, so I have great hopes for its reception.

I am also recording the Book of Genesis (in short ten minute doses) for Radio, which will be quite difficult but keep me out of mischief for a few days.

Ronald Harwood was instrumental in putting forward the proposal to change the name of the Globe Theatre to the Gielgud.

To Ronald Harwood   *31 August, Wotton Underwood*

What a delightful idea. But could you not also persuade the owners of the Comedy Theatre to change its name to the Richardson at the same time. It was the last house Ralph acted in and I would feel less presumptuous if his name could be honoured at the same time as mine.

To Bryan Forbes   *8 September, Wotton Underwood*

Do you suppose your publishers might offer to engage you to do a biography of Gwen [Ffrangcon-Davies]? She is an incredible survivor. Rang me last week to tell me she had just done two days in a new Sherlock Holmes TV with Jeremy Brett. She played a four minute scene on location (having never filmed before except in studios) and though in a wheelchair, she was full of delight and excitement over the experience. Of course everyone had made a great fuss of her, and she sounded incredibly youthful and enthusiastic, though her sight and hearing are both very bad. A great advertisement for Christian Science, which seems to have succeeded in seeing her through all her difficulties. She still lives alone in her Essex cottage, where all her neighbours vie in looking after her.

To Howard Turner   *11 October, Wotton Underwood*

Of course I was simply delighted to hear from you again, and to know how much you had enjoyed the film [*Prospero's Books*]. It was a great experience taking part in it, and a long unsatisfied wish to do the play on screen, and I feel very lucky to have lived long enough to achieve it and to be given the opportunity when I am so senior!

To Alistair Bannerman   *11 October, Wotton Underwood*

How delightful to have your letter. I do remember our brief reunion that day at Stourbridge, and it is very pleasant to think our short time together in the theatre* has stayed in your memory with such good effects.

The Shakespeare book [*Shakespeare – Hit or Miss?*] is rather a frivolous little effort, hastily concocted to come out at the same time as the film, which certainly seems to have created enormous, though sometimes controversial criticism. I think you will find it most original and fascinating, if a bit over elaborate. So glad the book amused you.

To George Pitcher and Ed Cone   *17 October, Wotton Underwood*

Little news to give you. I won an EMMY award for *Summer's Lease* and *The Tempest* film has made a great stir everywhere, though we won no prizes at the Festivals when it was shown, and the press is greatly divided for and against, though I have been greatly praised for my own performance. I think it is pictorially stunning, wonderfully imaginative, a superb conception – only the last scenes are over-elaborate and a bit indigestible after so much splendour in the first half. Martin, Irene and (wait for it) Lindsay Anderson, who is usually bitterly destructive of other people's work, all most enthusiastic, and the film did huge business for six weeks in London. I have to give an interview to the *N.Y. Times* tomorrow. It was shown at the N.Y. Film Festival and will be released all over America shortly. Anyhow, I am quite proud of having lived to see it, and know that after I am gone there will be this last example of my Shakespearean work.

We see very few people, but I am very glad to enjoy the house and garden. There are too many memorial services at which I have to speak – one for Peggy Ashcroft next month at Westminster Abbey, where I had to unveil a plaque to Olivier in Poets' Corner under the Bard's statue and next to David Garrick! Great scandal about a new life of L.O. [by Donald Spoto] in which he is said to have had a long affair with Danny Kaye! Quite unexpected news to me, but I suddenly remembered that he (Danny) had entertained me lavishly in Hollywood for *Caesar*! Perhaps he conceived making a pass at me and thought better of it when he actually met me. He certainly did make me very drunk on rum punches! So you never know – and I never shall.

To Hume Cronyn   *7 December, Wotton Underwood*

I had a whale of a time reading your charming book [*A Terrible Liar: a memoir*] – so full of good things both theatrical and domestic, and infused with your energetic enthusiasm and generosity. I'm sure it will have a great success. You have certainly enjoyed an extraordinarily varied and colourful life and have obviously managed to enjoy it even in its ups and downs.

---

* Alistair Bannerman played small parts in JG's 1937–8 season at the Queen's Theatre.

I don't quite know why, I always see you and Bob Whitehead sitting at table with your pipes demurely ranged next to the knives and forks! Pipes were so very popular in England up till the Second War, but since then they seem to have been relegated to be the privilege of the older generation. I had to smoke one in plays during the twenties and they always rather daunted me! I remember Joe Mankiewicz was also a devotee, probably still is. I never knew you were such a friend of Hitchcock. I only worked for him once, and I don't think he fancied me much. I admired his films but only for their ingenuity and expertise. He never seemed very interested, I thought, in his actors and I was rather shocked when he made jokes about Madeleine Carroll having an affair with Robert Donat in front of the whole unit! Long before we all became impervious to the modern scatological fashion of conversation.

1992

To Irene Worth   *2 January, Wotton Underwood*

Gwen appears on the TV tonight in her cameo with Jeremy Brett's *Sherlock Holmes* episode. Marvellous that she should be seen acting again, and she appears to have loved the outing with everyone courting and pampering her.

Wendy Hiller has survived quite a bad operation and managed to finish a TV part. 'Two sticks offstage and one on,' she boasted to me. What a professional example to us all.

I am recording the Ghost in *Hamlet* with Kenneth Branagh next week with [Derek] Jacobi and a fine young cast. His *Henry V* film was shown last week and impressed me very much – a terrific feat of direction which he has evidently taken to like a duck to water. I have never cared much for the play, and he has really done wonders with it and it compares very favourably even with Larry's fine film version.

To James Roose-Evans   *29 February, Wotton Underwood*

As to a studio master class, I really don't feel I could do it. I have written four or five books now about the theatre and Esmé [Percy] never wrote one, so he was much fresher and always so ebullient. My stories and jokes are now so often repeated and out of date. I never go to the theatre or movies any more – watch a lot of television, yes, but I am so very out of touch during the last ten years or so, I'm sure I would not be of any use on such a panel.

Peter Barkworth and that good actress Maria Aitken begged me to do a master class on TV but I really don't want to. Those programmes can be so embarrassing, though I think the musicians – Solti, Tortelier, Schwarzkopf etc. – are better at it than actors. I think Dirk Bogarde's interviews are quite unworthy of him, for instance.

To George Pitcher   *1 April, Wotton Underwood*

What splendid news that you will be here after the summer. Hope you won't find everything in England so much changed for the worse, and that we shall all be still alive and kicking.

I've had a lot of minor ailments this last year and now seem to be gradually growing deaf – a great bore for everyone including myself. I am about to experiment with a hearing aid which, I am assured, will be almost invisible. I hope so.

Don't go near *Shining Through* – an idiotic script and wretched part, which was only four days work, but forced me to waste three long months on travel to Berlin, Leipzig and Klagenfurt, sitting in my hotel rooms most of the time. Seem to have had a success on radio, reading the Book of Genesis – rather odd. Quite difficult managing pages of repetition and pronunciation of names, tribes, places etc. I was given five pages of how to speak them just before having to go on the air!

The garden is blossoming and the animals all doing well. So glad Irene is to play her part in [*Lost in*] *Yonkers* for the screen. She thought she had lost it to Joan Plowright, and is very delighted they have finally engaged her.

To George Pitcher   *1 June, Wotton Underwood*

I am doing *Swan Song* next week with young [Kenneth] Branagh. He is a nice fellow with enormous energy and ambition with a most charming wife [Emma Thompson] who is splendid in the Forster film, *Howards End*.

I am reading Evelyn Waugh's *Decline and Fall* for a cassette later this month.

To Alec Guinness   *20 June, Wotton Underwood*

You are always such a kind and generous host and I did enjoy that delicious lunch. It is always a great joy to see you, even on a melancholy occasion which you helped to mitigate so charmingly. I still live in hopes we may work together in a film or television before my old bones and memory begin to disintegrate for ever.

To George Pitcher and Ed Cone   *4 November, Wotton Underwood*

I went to a great do at Buckingham Palace – a fine concert in honour of [Georg] Solti's 80th birthday and the Prince [of Wales] gave a suitable speech and his wife looked lovely as usual. A glamorous if somewhat exhausting evening. I'm supposed to be taping a narration for a TV version of *Christmas Carol* (Jack Palance as Scrooge). Nothing else on the back burner at the moment except the dreaded Christmas season. I gather *The Best of Friends* TV shown last week was very successful in the U.S. and Canada.

1993

To George Pitcher and Ed Cone   *9 January, Wotton Underwood*

Just received the splendid book of caricatures you so kindly sent. I always used to go to see Dolly [Haas] and Al Hirschfeld when I was in New York, ever since Dolly played in *Crime and Punishment* with me and Lillian Gish. They are very sweet, both of them, and he is amazingly talented and versatile, obviously still as indomitable as I am!

We have had an extremely quiet Christmas and New Year. There doesn't [seem] to be too much to be cheerful about, one way and another. I stagger up to London to get my hair cut and lunch with Paul. John Perry was here for a few days, dreadfully deaf and gaga, his energy, wit and memory quite gone – most painful to see. However, the snowdrops are peeking up so can spring be far behind.

To Alec Guinness   *1 February, Wotton Underwood*

Thank you so much for coming last night. It was a strange and uneven occasion, wasn't it?* I hear Dirk [Bogarde] and John Mills are long-time enemies who were somewhat dismayed at their close – or brief – encounter. How lucky that Johnnie couldn't see him. I hope it didn't bore you to death, and that we can stumble on together for a while.

To George Pitcher and Ed Cone   *22 February, Wotton Underwood*

So very sweet of you to invite us to your summer residence, which does sound ideally pleasant, but I fear I won't be able to manage it. I think my travelling days are over at last. I've had rather a depressing winter with two separate weeks in bed with my wretched foot trouble recurring – cellulitis, whatever that is – some kind of uric acid weakness – and apart from that, I seem to get tired dreadfully easily and frightened of losing my balance. I force myself to totter round the garden a couple of times every day and am going to have a complete check-up in Oxford one day soon.

I hope you will understand my reluctance. It would have been just lovely to be able to accept, but I am sure I must be content to stay put and perhaps do some recording or a few days of filming here and there. I have been trying to read the whole new edition of Proust, which I must say is quite fascinating, though I have to skip some of the most lengthy elaborations of style and snobbery. But the descriptions of places and the vividness of the main characters are well worth the effort.

---

* The British Association of Film and Television Arts (BAFTA) gave a tribute to JG.

To Irene Worth   *4 October, Wotton Underwood*

I have two new pictures, wonderful present from Martin. One a portrait by Lawrence of John Philip Kemble (Mrs Siddons' brother) as Hamlet, the other an enchanting William Nicholson of a grey street in France with cats and lighted windows. Such a marvellous surprise.

To George Pitcher and Ed Cone   *9 November, Wotton Underwood*

I fear this 90th is going to be a big bore, and I am already refusing various offers to celebrate it, though of course it is pleasant that the occasion still interests people, especially in America.

I am just going into rehearsal of a little-known play by Priestley written in 1945!* Rather interesting, but a long part to learn, which I rather dread. For television, of course.

1994

The actress Gwen Watford died on 6 February 1994.

To Richard Bebb   *7 February, Wotton Underwood*

Dear Richard

When I rang up only a few days ago to inquire for Gwen, I was much surprised and delighted when she answered herself, which I hoped to mean she was really looking forward to success with the new treatment. Alas, what a tragic disappointment. She was such a splendid actress and sweet woman and the whole profession will be grieving with you today. She obviously fought the wretched disease with the utmost gallantry and determination, and one can only remember her with the greatest admiration and affection.

You will have many letters, so please don't dream of answering these few inadequate lines of sympathy. It is extraordinary to think I knew her even before you did when she came with her rather formidable headmistress (Miss Catt, was it?) to lunch at Mrs Jefferson's, after which I saw her act in St Leonards in *Mädchen in Uniform*, and first admired her talent.

I will telephone in a few weeks to see if you feel like lunch with me at the Club one day.

With love as ever
John.

---

* *Summer Day's Dream*, directed by Christopher Morahan.

To George Pitcher   *25 February, Wotton Underwood*

So sorry to hear of Ed's wretched accident. I do a good deal of slipping and tottering myself these days, and find everything more hard work, dressing and undressing, writing letters and keeping appointments, trying not to be infuriated by delays and traffic hold-ups etc., etc. The dreaded ninetieth is all too threatening and I am trying to forestall all the publicity and refusing photographers and interviews as much as I possibly can.

I start one week's work next Tuesday playing Scarlett O'Hara's grandfather (aged 94) in a stupid mammoth sequel to *Gone with the Wind* [*Scarlett*] with a French accent, so I try to remember Charles Boyer!

To Alec Guinness   *16 March, Wotton Underwood*

It is really very sweet of you to want to give a party for me.

Martin is very sorry not to come. He says he can't leave the house empty with the birds and dogs, and I think he feels he sees too much of me already. We only have intermittent help these days which makes it very difficult to get away. I enclose a tentative list, too many I am sure, but some will be sure not to be free to accept.

Much love and grateful thanks to you both, and have a lovely Italian holiday. I shall so look forward to your party and I do so much appreciate the most kind thought.

To Lillian Gish   *15 April, Wotton Underwood*

Darling Lillian

So happy and grateful for all the affection and wonderful tributes to me and especially yours, and the beautiful souvenir with all the splendid photographs.

Fondest love as ever, John.

To George Pitcher and Ed Cone   *13 June, Wotton Underwood*

I have been awarded a very distinguished prize by the Japanese, and am to be given it later on at the Japanese Embassy in London, including a *very* big cheque! There's a story for you, as Humpty Dumpty remarked.

To George Pitcher   *16 October, Wotton Underwood*

I am doing a few completely insignificant parts in various films and TV which suffice to pass the time and keep my hand in. Received the very glamorous award from the Japanese at the Embassy here – very nice that they still gave it me without insisting on my going to Tokyo. A huge gold medal and a *very* handsome cheque (yen-yen). But it meant rather an exhausting ceremony with speeches, interviews and photographers etc.

Now on the 2nd of November, another do in London, when the Globe Theatre in Shaftesbury Avenue is to be renamed the Gielgud. Another speech, I fear, and a large gathering which I rather dread, though very flattering of course.

Sad to read of Jessica Tandy and Dolly Haas both gone – Toby Rowland here too. Dreadful for poor Hume [Cronyn] to be left alone. Elaine [Brunner] bade me to tea last week. I had not seen her for about five years! Very crippled, one of her dogs dead and the other badly disabled. She was tearful but indomitable, asking fondly about you and Ed.

1995

To George Pitcher and Ed Cone   *20 February, Wotton Underwood*

Thought the enclosed would interest you. It was a great to-do* – huge congregation and beautiful singing by the boys' choir, but rather heavy occasion. I read very badly and Judi Dench, whom I usually admire, was shockingly bad as Lady Bracknell.

John Perry died last week. He had had several bad falls and become completely disorientated – lingered wretchedly for about two months in hospital and nursing home. Keith Baxter and I visited him in a nursing home a week or two ago, but he didn't appear to recognise us, and was hopelessly deaf and confused. One cannot help being glad that it is over for him.

He was my first great love and we lived together from 1936 up till the beginning of the War in 1940. I rather neglected him in these last years as he became so deaf and forgetful, and I never quite forgave him for becoming Binkie's lover in 1938 and only admitting it (silly me!) in 1942! He also sold the enchanting cottage we had in Essex in the '30s while I was in America! He was a bit of a ruthless adventurer, but so handsome and amusing, and now, of course, I regret his death, though I could not wish him to live on in that bemused state.

No work at the moment except for some odd recording jobs. Frightful gales and storms. I can't help being riveted by the [O. J.] Simpson trial. Martin gave me Sky where it is to be seen nightly, though he says I should be ashamed of myself for following it!

---

* To celebrate the centenary of Oscar Wilde's imprisonment, a plaque was unveiled in Westminster Abbey.

To George Pitcher and Ed Cone   *15 July, Wotton Underwood*

Very delighted to receive the handsome photograph and to see you both looking so well despite the ravages of old [age] which you both seem able to dispel. How wonderfully things have turned out both for you and me – such partnerships are surely rare and to be greatly cherished.

Little news to tell you. John Lahr has written of the new *Richard the Second* directed at the Cottesloe Theatre by a woman, Deborah Warner, and Richard is played by an actress, Fiona Shaw! I would rather love to see it, judging by his review, but dread being spotted and cornered to give my opinion. It does sound intriguing.

1996

To George Pitcher and Ed Cone   *18 February, Wotton Underwood*

The winter has seemed very long, and though the crocuses and snowdrops are coming up well, there is a freezing cold wind and more snow promised for the next few days. Martin and I have both had flu colds. I have no work in prospect almost, I think, for the first time in my life. So we are both a bit depressed. Our small circle of friends get fewer every month, and London seems more disagreeable every time I have to go up.

Well, one must cheer up and get on with things.

To Miller Lide   *21 February, Wotton Underwood*

So good to hear from you again. I have lost nearly all the friends I once had in New York and it is a great pleasure to hear from the few that are left, yourself especially. Please give my fondest love to Kate Hepburn.

Old age is no picnic, I'm afraid. But I do have wonderful companionship in this beautiful house and garden and the few odd days working at films and TV keep me going.

To George Pitcher   *4 March, Wotton Underwood*

No news here. I am rather depressed. No work on the horizon, only invitations to anniversaries and award celebrations, which I detest, and I never seem to stop sending congratulatory cables for birthdays and ceremonies of various kinds, both here and in America. Irene is due back here and will give a week of Recitals in London in April. Don't know which of the many she seems to have up her sleeve. Marti Stevens also threatening a short visit.

Snowdrops and crocuses coming up and daffodils begin to peer, but it is still unpleasantly cold. I have skipped at least four memorial services. Do hope they won't give one for me. Ireland and Bosnia (to say nothing of the Royal Divorce*) compete with your election fears. Not much to be cheerful about, is there?

To George Pitcher and Ed Cone   *5 September, Wotton Underwood*

All thanks for your letter. Like you I suffer from various minor troubles – sciatica – or is it arthritis – my hips hurt and I worry about balance and am wary of stairs and uneven surfaces. Shall have to get used to using a stick, I suppose.

A few odd jobs to keep me out of mischief. They are going to make a cassette with extracts of my 50 years on radio which I will eventually send you a copy of, and I have a few days next month in a TV serial by Anthony Powell [*Dance to the Music of Time*], whose books I have never read.

To Miller Lide   *9 September, Wotton Underwood*

Nice to hear from you again, and I rejoice to see your handwriting is almost as minute as mine. I keep on trying to make it more easy to read but it only seems to get smaller and smaller as I get older and older. You must use a magnifying glass I fear!

Of course I well remember Young Island and our blissful days there until Vivien suddenly had one of her attacks and we had to smuggle her from reporters shrouded in dark glasses when we left.

In those days there were only half a dozen huts and a well stocked bar. I have never learned to swim properly and nearly managed to drown myself till Vivien kindly swam out to rescue me!

Good to hear of dear Kate Hepburn. I have just finished reading an excellent biography of her [by Barbara Leaming]. I have always adored her. Is the faithful Phyllis [Wilbourn], who she inherited from Constance Collier, still alive, I wonder. I always liked her so much.

Sorry to hear that the Fry play [*The Lady's Not for Burning*] seemed difficult for your audiences. I had great difficulty in directing and acting in it, but we had a perfect cast – all dead now, alas, alas. I do miss New York, but have very few dear friends left there nowadays.

To Irene Worth   *20 October, Wotton Underwood*

I can hardly believe you are already in Australia. Wonder whether you have already opened with your recitals and how well have they gone? Your delightful

---

* The Duke and Duchess of York were divorced earlier in the year.

cards are so welcome, but of course you do seem very far away, and is it not a great strain remembering all the new people's names and where you met them. I find large gatherings of strangers impossible to cope with any more, but of course there are many good times to look back on and I'm amazed to get on with life without going to the theatre, movies and concerts any more.

No interesting news to give you. *Borkman** has had very mixed reviews and Finney and Tom Courtenay have had a big success with a French play called *Art* [by Yasmina Reza] translated by Christopher Hampton.

Don Bachardy is here for the opening of his portrait exhibition at the National Portrait Gallery and the publication of Isherwood's diaries. I have not yet seen them. Claire [Bloom]'s book [*Leaving a Doll's House*] about her lovers and marriages has created something of a sensation. Very painful reading but no doubt she needs the money badly. All the name dropping will sell it well, I'm sure. But sad.

Michael Billington's life of Pinter [*The Life and Work of Harold Pinter*] is a bit over-adulatory but full of interest about the days before he was a success, and I have just finished a terrifying account of the wretched Romanov family, consisting entirely of personal letters and diaries.† The love letters between the Tsar and Tsarina are so childishly touching and the killing of Rasputin as well as the final ghastly murders of the family are quite devastating to read.

I do apologise for my wretched little handwriting. I keep trying to make it bigger and more legible but it seems to be a hopeless struggle. Hope you have a microscope handy.

To Julie Kavanagh‡   *2 November, Wotton Underwood*

I do hope you enjoyed the research on Freddie's book. I was so touched that you should send it to me, and I am quite enthralled in rushing to read it, though I have only got to the 20s so far!

Memories came flooding back. I was an avid fan of the Ballet. Arnold Haskell and I were both at Westminster School, and we used to escape on half-holidays and climb to the gallery of the Coliseum, ignoring the sniggers of the other occupants at our rubbed [?] top hats and jam pot collars. I used to haunt Cyril Beaumont's shop in the Charing Cross Road and spent much pocket money buying some of his Diaghilev cutout figures, especially those of Tchernicheva, who was my especial favourite.

I was in the audience at the first night of *The Sleeping Princess*, when the magic forest refused to grow despite Lopokhova's persuasive wand. Nothing happened except alarming creaking of reluctant saplings, and in her third act

---

* The National Theatre production of *John Gabriel Borkman* with Paul Scofield in the title role had opened in July.
† *A Lifelong Passion* by Andrei Mayhunas and Sergei Mironenko.
‡ Julie Kavanagh, a neighbour of Gielgud's, had written *Secret Muse*, a biography of Frederick Ashton.

she slipped and fell on her behind! But how glamorous it all was, though of course I never saw Nijinsky. I remember sitting next to Irene Dean Paul at [the] White Tower restaurant and she said 'Do feel my hair, it's just like a fur muff!'

Brenda's [Dean Paul] brother Napper married Beatrice Lillie's sister Muriel, did you know? And when Elizabeth Ponsonby died and was cremated, two girl friends afterwards in a bar are supposed to have said, 'It was wonderful dear, she frizzled up like a crepe suzette!' I never knew Fred very well, but I have enchanting memories of him too.

Hope you can read this wretched scribble. I recommend a magnifying glass! All thanks and sincere congratulations.

1997

To Jennifer Aylmer   *9 February, Wotton Underwood*

Can it really be more than seventy years ago that I stood beside your Father [Felix Aylmer] on the Regent stage, when he played Robert E. Lee? It was my second ever professional engagement as an actor, given me by dear Nigel Playfair, and I was greatly in awe of your illustrious parent, sweltering in a heavy greatcoat and trying not to get entangled in my sword as we gazed through field glasses at an imaginary distant battle, but actually surveyed a good many empty seats.

Little did I think I would one day have the privilege of directing him and would watch him manoeuvring his scenes with Edith Evans, who was apt to be somewhat disdainful of his tempo, though they were also so splendid acting together in *Daphne Laureola* – one of his very finest performances, I thought.

To Lady Solti   *10 February, Wotton Underwood*

I have sent a cheque to your fund for Sadler's Wells. I always hated the present building and hope they will manage great improvements.

To George Pitcher   *11 February, Wotton Underwood*

So glad about *Shine* and its phenomenal success, as great here as with you. I never met Mr [Geoffrey] Rush. I have been nominated for an award by the Screen Actors Guild, but I think the man who plays the father [Armin Mueller-Stahl] is likely to get it as he well deserves.

I go the Palace on the 28th for ten minutes with Her Majesty to receive the prize [the Order of Merit]. All sorts of instructions by letter, including a demand that I insure the medal for £5000 and *return* it after my death! Rather amusing precautions. I remember Lillian Gish saying, 'Don't examine your Oscar too closely – only silver gilt!'

To Kevin Brownlow   *18 February, Wotton Underwood*

Yes, I well remember Maurice Bradell [Braddell]. We were both playing small parts at the Regent Theatre in the early twenties and I think he understudied me on one occasion.

Many years later in New York he suddenly confronted me in the street, looking dreadfully down at heels and ravaged and we exchanged a few vague remarks. I was greatly embarrassed and hurried away and was so ashamed afterwards that I never thought of offering money – or even a drink – but the meeting was so surprising that I was completely taken aback.

1998

To Jenny Graveson [Arnold Bennett Society]   *21 January, Wotton Underwood*

I knew Arnold Bennett very well, but only by sight. I think he stammered a bit, and looked very unusual with a quiff of hair combed upwards and frilly shirts. I seem to remember a bunch of seals hanging out of his waistcoat pocket. He was Sir Nigel Playfair's business partner and was one of the three directors of the Lyric Theatre Hammersmith which, under Playfair's skill and daring experiments became so hugely successful during the twenties.

Bennett's first marriage was a failure, a French lady [Marguerite Soulié] who sang at parties and the Sitwells mocked her. He fell violently in love, after his divorce, to [*sic*] an ambitious and eager young actress whom he finally married and they had a very much loved child and she changed her name from Dorothy Cheston to Dorothy Cheston Bennett. Though I very often saw him both at Hammersmith and the Regent Theatre (where he backed several seasons with little success), I don't think I ever had a chance of talking to him. But I was enormously impressed with the *Old Wives' Tale* and *Hotel Imperial* as well as several other of his novels.

He had a huge public, was a workaholic, and mentions every detail of his output in his diaries, noting down all his expenses, even his tips and bus-fares!

To George Pitcher and Ed Cone   *1 July, Wotton Underwood*

It was lovely to see you both, if only so very briefly, and of course it was good to hear your trip was such a great success and that you enjoyed the change and got back safely. I bet your hound was glad to greet you on your return. I fear foreign travels no longer seem to appeal to me.

The garden is looking so beautiful now that the roses are in full bloom, but we have stormy weather and only occasional bursts of sunshine. I've been recording the Chorus in *Pericles* for a new Shakespeare anthology, and also some letters from Rachmaninoff to his daughter, lamenting his banishment from Russia.

To George Pitcher and Ed Cone   *11 October, Wotton Underwood*

Good to hear from you again. We are very low at the moment. Martin and I both stricken with feverish autumn colds and the papers full of depressing news in the press and television. I have no work of any kind and begin to think I have been around too long. Perhaps the light may shine again one of these days.

To George Pitcher and Ed Cone   *24 November, Wotton Underwood*

Martin is suffering from [some] sort of blood ailment called LYMPH NODE. So good of you both to worry about him. Thank God it isn't cancer. He goes for treatment every week, but insists on going to shop and feeding me three times a day. Very fractious and unhappy, as of course I am too. They say it will take seven months to get better.

We only have a cleaning girl three times a week and have no visitors or excitement, and I keep mislaying my hearing aid, which makes me very dull company. My handwriting gets so small that I can hardly read it myself without a magnifying glass! Well, well, one must try not to grumble.

I think the Shakespeare book you kindly sent me a review of, sounds a bit pretentious, don't you? Sorry to write so drearily but I always hate Xmas anyway.

Martin Hensler died in December 1998.
   This letter was written on Martin's birthday, but no year is given.

To Martin Hensler   *19 April. What a lucky day for me.*

My dearest Martin

I gave you my heart long ago. Wish I had something more worthy to give you now. You have given me your life, and I only pray you do not feel you have wasted it. May the sun shine again for us soon.

Devotedly

Grandad.

1999

To George Pitcher   *10 April, Wotton Underwood*

Dearest George

Thank you so much for your sweet letter. I have broken a bone in my ankle and am crawling about on two sticks – an added complication. Thankfully I am well looked after by the chauffeur [Peter Heard-White] and gardener [Vincent Flood-Powell], both amazingly watch[ful]? and attentive, though inconvenient for domestic schedules.

The end was really horrendous. Weeks in and out of hospital – we were both laid up for several weeks, then I was able to bring him back home, which he begged me to do. Then I had to watch him delirious and imploring him [*sic*] to let him go. He just stood up in his bed one morning and fell forward suddenly on his face.

He wanted no funeral or ceremony of any kind, so I just sprinkled his ashes on the garden and am trying to face up to the future without him – very hard, as you can imagine. May you be spared such horrors when the dreaded time comes.

Irene has had a slight stroke and her understudy in appearance [*sic*], but she sounds cheerful and undismayed. She hopes to [be] back in a fortnight's time.

What a ghastly month. M.'s black tabby died the other day. My sister died suddenly of a heart attack, mercifully short. Everyone tries to be kind and helpful but to what avail? M. was suffering from Hodgkin's Disease, a form of cancer I believe.

To George Pitcher   *7 September, Wotton Underwood*

Everything is such an effort and I have to be helped around still on my two wretched sticks, and not seem to be getting better. My friends come down from time to time and help to cheer me up – not very successfully, I fear. I suppose it is inevitable after seven long months. I crawl about from one room to another and try not to let me down [*sic*].

I think of the past with nostalgia and, as ever, much affection.

Love, John.

John Gielgud died, at the age of ninety-six, on 21 May 2000.

Appendix
The Golden Quill

In October 1993 John F. Andrews, editor of William Shakespeare: his World, His Work, His Influence *and President of The Shakespeare Guild, wrote to John Gielgud asking if he would be the honoree of The Shakespeare Guild's inaugural gala the following year, which happened to be Sir John's ninetieth birthday.*

JG did not reply, so JFA wrote again some six weeks later in similar terms. The gala was now to include a black tie 'variety special' at Washington's National Theatre, a White House Reception hosted by President and Mrs Clinton, a dinner at the Folger Shakespeare Library and possibly another dinner at the National Building Museum. JG would be presented with a commemorative sculpture and the inaugural Sir John Gielgud Award would be bestowed on a theatre professional who had achieved distinction in the classical repertory.

To John F. Andrews   *27 November, Wotton Underwood*

I very much appreciate your two cordial letters, but I fear I must persist in refusing to take part in any official celebration of my birthday. I have written already, both to the Haymarket management and the Garrick Club, begging them to make no plans for the occasion. I know how the younger generation have respect and affection for my work and I need no public recognition after so many years of happy association both in England and America.

The deaths of so many of my most distinguished colleagues has greatly saddened me, and I shall never forget what I owe them in fellowship and working harmony. I am very much aware of having to reserve my energy so as to go on working in films and television, though no longer, alas, in the living theatre, and I really dread large gatherings, compliments, interviews and publicity of all kinds which tire and embarrass me.

I cannot hope to avoid all this completely but I do intend to make every effort to reduce the kindness of my well-wishers to the minimum. I hope you will not think me very discourteous but I really feel most strongly my honest wish to keep my birthday as private as I possibly can.

As to the Prize you suggest, of course I should be delighted to have it given in my name but I'm afraid I cannot offer to come over to present it myself.

In his letter of 1 March 1994, JFA kept JG informed about plans for the gala and the award, offering first class air fare and accommodation and 'a much more stellar roster of activities' if JG would travel. Failing that, would he send a letter, or could JFA send an interviewer and TV crew to Wotton to record an interview?

To John F. Andrews   *16 March, Wotton Underwood*

I need hardly say how grateful and flattered I am to know that I am so happily remembered by so many American friends.

It is a great blessing to me to know that my work has brought me so many dear friends over these long years, and that I am still able to keep on acting, even though I fear my appearances in the live theatre are over now.

Please give my love and greetings to all who are at the celebration you are so kindly sponsoring, and I only wish I could have been able to join you myself and respond in person to your great warmth and kindness.

My times in America have brought me so many cherished memories, and I always feel it is my second country.

JFA wrote on 20 May and sent a programme and pictures of the event at which Tony Randall spoke of JG's influence on twentieth century classical acting. The five foot acrylic prototype of The Golden Quill (the name for the Gielgud Award) was unveiled; future recipients would receive an eighteen-inch bronze replica. The inaugural award was not made on this occasion, but plans were now afoot for this to happen in 1995 in England.

To John F. Andrews   *31 May, Wotton Underwood*

I need hardly saw how delighted I was to receive your very charming letter and the splendid photographs.

It is such an enormous pleasure to know that I still have so many enthusiasts for my work, and I always look back so very happily in remembering so many wonderful visits to America and the great number of friends and colleagues I met there. Among the hosts of well wishers I was lucky enough to receive on the occasion of my birthday, none was more greatly appreciated than yours. How sad that I could not be with you for the Folger celebration. It all sounds to have been such a warm and overwhelmingly flattering occasion, and I was so touched that Tony Randall should have spoken so eloquently about me.

Your idea of having the London Award next year at the Old Vic is a most happy one, and I shall be eager to attend it next year.

JFA wrote again in August 1994 suggesting that the 1995 Award might now take place at the newly named Gielgud Theatre. There was a distinct possibility that Marvin Hamlisch, who had just completed a 60 city tour with Barbra Streisand, would be the musical director.

However, JFA wrote in March 1995 to say that it had 'taken longer than we anticipated to find a sponsor to endow the citation with a suitable stipend and an underwriter to support the costs for a theatre gala that will be worthy of so august a ceremony'. It was now hoped that the inaugural Golden Quill might be bestowed on JG's ninety-second birthday in 1996, perhaps at the new Shakespeare's Globe Theatre on Bankside which Sam Wanamaker had caused to be built.

To John F. Andrews   *9 April, Wotton Underwood*

Of course I was delighted to receive your very charming letter, but April of next year is still a long way off and I am very wary of committing myself so far ahead. Maybe it might be best to wait and see if Wanamaker's Bankside Theatre is really ready to open in the summer of 1996 and try to arrange the giving of the prize to me at the same time.

I really feel I have had my career appreciated so fully in many ways and do not seek further rewards at all, except for the wonderful good fortune in still being alive and able to go on working, even in a small way, while my faculties allow me.

No, I have not received *The Tempest Everyman* and would be very glad if you would kindly send it to me.

In November, JFA wrote to say that the 1996 inaugural Award would now take place at the Folger Library 'under the gracious patronage of Sir John Kerr, her Britannic Majesty's Ambassador to the United States, and Lady Kerr'. In addition to the first class flight, JG was now offered accomodation with the ambassador. The format of the gala would be 'Ages of Man' when a number of 'eminent colleagues' would recite some of those speeches that JG had been doing for 40 years. An additional lure was that 'the Library's original reading room features a handsome stained glass window with the Seven Ages of Man as its pictorial sub-ject. We intend to use that window, or a large reproduction of it, as backdrop for at least a segment of the award gala. And we expect to entitle the event "All the World's his Stage" a theme that applies both to you and to the playwright whose poetic drama you've done so much to keep vital for twentieth century audiences.'

To John F. Andrew   *9 November, Wotton Underwood*

Greatly as I appreciate your immense kindness in wishing to honour me with such a prestigious compliment, I must very regretfully refuse your kindness in inviting me to come to the Folger next year.

For the last two years I have begun to feel my age too much to face all invitations away from home, and try to reserve all my remaining energies to be able to go on playing small parts for films and television which, as well as sound recordings, only require engagements for a very few days at a time.

Of course I am greatly touched and pleased to be invited, and would be very honoured to stay with the Ambassador in Washington.

But I know I am no longer limber enough to face the long journey or capable of meeting a large gathering, however welcoming, and I must very regretfully say no to your most gracious invitation.

I do hope you will understand and pass on my grateful thanks to all concerned.

JFA was naturally disappointed but assured JG that he could change his mind right up to the last moment. Perhaps he would consider a television interview 'in the manner of the David Frost dialogue that enraptured television viewers a decade or so ago'.

The Golden Quill was finally presented to Sir Ian McKellen on 20 May 1996; JG was unable to be present but sent a videotaped message. JFA wrote to tell him that all had gone well and promised to send a programme and a recording of the event.

To John F. Andrews   *20 July, Wotton Underwood*

I was so delighted to hear and read of the celebration at the Folger. It sounds such a very successful and exciting event and obviously carried out with much care and good will by everyone concerned.

There is a possibility that I may be playing a part in a film project taken from a Joseph Conrad story in which I understand Ian McKellen is also hoping to appear. Of course I should like that very much. We are supposed to be shooting it in September if all goes well in preparation.

Kindest regards and very grateful thanks.

JFA wrote in August with plans for the 1997 Award which was planned to take place in England at the Garrick Club or the Theatre Royal Drury Lane or any one of half a dozen other theatres. JG was asked if there were anyone he would like to see as the next 'awardee'.

To John F. Andrews   *8 September, Wotton Underwood*

Please forgive me for not writing before but I have been away from home for several weeks, and only got back yesterday to find your very charming letter and the splendid tapes of the Gala evening which I enjoyed very much indeed.

Of course I am sad at having to miss such a prestigious occasion, though I should have blushed to hear the nice things said about me.

I hope you will use a magnifying glass in order to decipher this letter. I keep trying to make it bigger and easier to read, but it seems to get smaller and smaller as I get older and older!

My grateful thanks as ever and I shall look forward to hearing of your future plans for next year's award.

The 1997 Award took place at the Folger which happened to be having its 65th birthday celebration. A White House reception was offered again to encourage JG's presence, but JFA seemed to realise that JG was unlikely to travel. He therefore proposed an event in England – 'a relatively intimate affair – a Sunday afternoon lunch, for example, or an early evening reception, with a few brief tributes and a bit of entertainment – at which a select company of your friends and associates would assemble to congratulate you for your investiture in the Order of Merit. As we envisage it, the gathering could take place in Middle Temple Hall. The audience would be an invited one and the guest list (which would have to be limited to around 250, including partners and a few representatives of the press and electronic media) would be compiled by people who are well acquainted with you and your closest professional colleagues.'

As a footnote, this event would also announce the establishment of the Gielgud Charitable Trust (a subsidiary of The Shakespeare Guild) 'a fund to assist aspiring actors with the education and training they require to gain a foothold in the profession you've done so much to ennoble'.

To John F. Andrews   *18 December, Wotton Underwood*

Though I much appreciate your kind suggestion of a ceremony next April, I must tell you that I am totally opposed to such a project.

I am refusing all invitations of such a kind except the occasion of my investiture at Windsor in February. I can no longer enjoy or cope with gatherings of more than a very few people, and feel that there has already been quite enough kindness and appreciation from friends and colleagues in messages and letters. Of course, it is all very pleasant and flattering, but I do have to limit my resources these days and continue living here in the country as quietly as I possibly can.

Your idea of a new Charitable Trust would, of course, please me greatly if it could be organised without publicity.

The Golden Quill Award for 1997 was to be presented to Sir Derek Jacobi. JFA hoped that JG might send another videotaped message, or, if he would prefer, 'we'll arrange a small dinner party or a quiet reception in London – at the Berkeley, say, or the Garrick Club, unless you'd be more comfortable in a theatrical setting like the Gielgud, the Haymarket or the Old Vic – so that you can convey your regards to the honoree in person'.

By the beginning of April, JG had obviously not done much about his message, so JFA wrote with a few suggestions. 'It would be kind to acknowledge': the 65th anniversary of the Library, the 'honorary benefactions' of the British Ambassador and Lady Kerr, the President and the First Lady, the benefit chairman Mrs Samia Farouki, Dame Diana Rigg who would be presenting the Quill and, of course, Sir Derek the recipient.

To Sir Derek Jacobi   *28 April, Wotton Underwood*

I need hardly say how pleased I am to congratulate you on the Golden Quill Award in recognition of your distinguished record of success both in the live theatre and films and television.

I have such happy memories of working with you several times in the theatre, both as partner and delighted audience, and I am very sorry not to be able to be with you at the presentation which I know will be a most prestigious occasion. I remember my own several visits to the Folger with its Globe Theatre and wonderful collection of theatrical memorabilia.

I gather this is the 65th anniversary of the Library, and I envy the participation of a number of eminent people gathered to honour the occasion and I would like to salute the honorary benefactions of the British Ambassador and his Lady as well as the gracious patronage of the President and First Lady. A word of appreciation, too, for Mrs Samia Farouki and the kind appearance of Dame Diana Rigg.

I have such vivid and enthusiastic memories of many of your performances; your remarkably effective Hitler in *The Third Reich*, Claudius, of course, both the stammering Emperor, the equally striking man in *Breaking the Code* and Shakespeare's Claudius in Kenneth Branagh's great film, to say nothing of Richard the Second and many other triumphs.

It was always such a pleasure to be with you and to enjoy our times in working with you, to observe your modesty and [illegible]. May you live long and prosper.

With every possible good wish and congratulations.

JFA wrote to JG after the ceremony. 'Owing to a modesty that endeared him to everyone who met him, Derek elected not to share with the audience the lovely note you'd written to congratulate him. He did permit us to make copies of it however, and we've conveyed them to the luminaries you were so kind to mention in your beautifully phrased message.'

Plans were afoot for the 1998 event, but JFA's efforts at persuasion seem to have finally recognised defeat. He wrote to JG in May to thank him for the message he had sent to Zoë Caldwell, the recipient of the Quill for that year.

By 1999, the ceremony had moved to the Barrymore Theatre, New York, possibly because that was where the recipient (or 'laureate' as the 'honorees' or 'awardees' were now known), Dame Judi Dench, was performing in Amy's View.

Once more JG sent his good wishes, though sadly his message to Dame Judi was dictated and no record of it seems to have survived. However, JFA assured him that it would 'be immensely meaningful both to the honoree and to the audience assembled at the Barrymore Theatre to salute her and her many accomplishments'.

Regrettably, that appears to have been JG's last involvement with the Golden Quill. In January 2000 Kenneth Branagh received the award in Middle Temple Hall.

For some reason, no Quill was awarded in 2001 but in 2002 Kevin Kline became the first American recipient, but by 2003 the Quill was back in the safe British (though resident in America) hands of Lynn Redgrave.

Acknowledgements

I am indebted to many people and institutions all over the world for their help in tracing and finding letters. A number of them went above and beyond the call of duty on my behalf; they know who they are, but I hope they will understand that I have space here only to print their names. My sincere thanks to all of them, even though in some instances I have not, in the end, used the material they so kindly lent me. Thanks also to those who were unable to help, but were gracious in their responses.

John Andrews, The Shakespeare Guild; Paul Anstee; Jennifer Aylmer.

Robert Back; Keith Baxter; Richard Bebb; S. N. Behrman Papers, Manuscripts and Archives Division, The New York Public Library, Astor, Lenox and Tilden Foundations; Professor Jean-Norman Benedetti; Alan Bennett; Barry Sterndale Bennett; Michael Billington; Kitty Black; Stephen Bourne; Ben Brewster and Dorinda Hartmann, Wisconsin Center for Film & Theatre Research, University of Wisconsin at Madison; Alan Brodie; Sally Burton.

James Cairncross; Simon Callow; Ruth Carruth, Beinecke Rare Book and Manuscript Library, Yale University; Don Chapman; Lynda Claassen, Mandeville Special Collections Library, University of California; Michael Coveney; Jonathan Croall.

Geoff Davidson, Society for Theatre Research; Barry Day; Dame Judi Dench; David Diamond.

Brian Eagles, Howard Kennedy Solicitors; Jo Elsworth, University of Bristol Theatre Collection; the late Laurence Evans.

Mrs Suzanne Farrington; Fredric W. Wilson and Annette Fern, Harvard Theatre Collection; Richard Finkelstein; Christopher Fitz-Simon; Bryan Forbes; Clive Francis; David Franklin and Jim Harvey; Christopher Fry CBE.

Marian Gallagher, Public Record Office of Northern Ireland; Judy Gielgud; Maina Gielgud; the Howard Gotlieb Archival Research Center at Boston University; Jenny Graveson; Matthew Guinness.

Sir Peter Hall; G. Laurence Harbottle; Kitty Carlisle Hart; Ann Harvey; Ronald Harwood; Bryan J. Hewitt; staff at the Houghton Library, Harvard University; Oliver House, Colin Harris and staff at the Bodleian Library, Oxford; Frances Hughes; The Huntington Library, San Marino, California; Lord Hutchinson QC of Lullington.

Elizabeth Jennings Papers, Special Collections, Lauinger Library, Georgetown

University, Washington D.C.; Kathryn Johnson and staff at the British Library; Lona Jones and the staff at the National Library of Wales.

John Knowles

The late Basil C. Langton; Barbara Leaming; Frances Lewis Miller Lide; Eliza Loizeau-Hutchinson.

The Raymond Mander and Joe Mitchenson Theatre Collection; staff at the Mandeville Special Collections Library, University of California, San Diego; Giordana Mecagni, Dorothy Feiner Rodgers Papers, Schlesinger Library, Radcliffe Institute, Harvard University; John Miller; Sir Jonathan Miller; Sir John Mills; Rosalind Moad, Archivist, King's College Library and Archive Centre, Cambridge; Margery M. Morgan; Sheridan Morley; Maureen Murray.

Dr Mark Nicholls and Jonathan Harris, St John's College Library, Cambridge.

The Trustees of the Estate of the late Lord Olivier OM; Bill Orth.

Tony Palmer; Robert Parks, Pierpont Morgan Library, New York; Professor George Pitcher and Professor Edward T. Cone.

Louise Ray, National Theatre Archive; Piers Paul Read; James Roose-Evans; Colin Rose; Ruth Rosen.

Roger Sansom; Bob Schanke; Paul Scofield CH; Dr Laurence Senelick; Shakespeare Institute Library, University of Birmingham; Sir Donald Sinden; Marc Sinden; Lord Snowdon; Lady Solti; Richard L. Sterne; Alan Strachan.

Bob Taylor and Mark Maniak, New York Public Library for the Performing Arts; Dr Harold Tedford; Claire Hudson and staff at the Theatre Museum, London; Dr Richard Thompson; Howard Turner.

Department of Rare Books and Special Collections, University of Rochester Library; The Harry Ransom Humanities Research Center, The University of Texas at Austin.

Van Volkenburg-Browne Papers, Special Collections Library, University of Michigan; Hugo Vickers; Mrs George Voskovec.

Lady Susana Walton MBE, D.Mus.; Raymond Wemmlinger, Hampden-Booth Theatre Library, New York; Ted Wilkinson; Clifford Williams-Gentle; Don B. Wilmeth; Joan Winterkorn, Bernard Quaritch Ltd; Mary Wolfskill, Library of Congress Manuscript Division; the late Irene Worth.

Michael and Pat York.

Cast List

There are certainly omissions in the following list. The editor and publishers would be glad to receive any additions or corrections for future editions. Titles are not given; theatres should be assumed as London unless otherwise stated; biographical information usually relates to the links with John Gielgud (JG).

ACKERLEY, J. R. (Joe) 1896–1967, British writer and editor.

ACKLAND, JOSS b. 1928, British actor; appeared with JG at a memorial service for Michael Redgrave in 1985.

ACKLAND, RODNEY 1908–91, British playwright; JG's first association with him was in 1932 when he appeared in Ackland's play, *Strange Orchestra*.

ACTON, HAROLD 1904–94, British aesthete and writer.

ADDINSELL, RICHARD 1904–77, British composer, accompanist to Joyce Grenfell; partner of Victor Stiebel, fashion designer.

ADLER, STELLA 1901–92, American actress and teacher.

ADRIAN, MAX 1903–73, Irish-born actor, partner of the actor and director, Laurier Lister. JG first worked with him in *Love for Love* in 1943.

AGATE, JAMES 1877–1947, British drama critic and diarist.

AHERNE, BRIAN 1902–86, British-born actor.

AINLEY, HENRY 1879–1945, British actor; JG played Iago to his Othello in a radio production by Val Gielgud in 1932.

AINLEY, PATSY, daughter of Henry Ainley; stage manager for JG's US tour of *Ages of Man* in 1958.

AINLEY, RICHARD 1910–67, British actor, son of Henry Ainley; first appeared with JG in *Richard of Bordeaux* in 1933.

AITKEN, MARIA b. 1945, British actress.

AKED, MURIEL 1875–1955, British actress; first appeared with JG in *Prejudice* in 1928.

ALBEE, EDWARD b. 1928, American playwright; JG appeared in his *Tiny Alice* in 1964 and directed *All Over* in 1971.

ALBERY, BRONSON (Bronnie) 1881–1971, British theatre owner (Wyndham's etc.) and producer.

ALBERY, DONALD 1914–88, British theatre owner and producer, son of Bronson Albery.

ALDOUS, LUCETTE b. 1938, Australian ballerina.

ALDRIDGE, MICHAEL 1920–94, British actor; appeared with JG in *Caesar and Cleopatra* (1971).

ALEXANDER, TERENCE b. 1923, appeared in JG's production of *Macbeth* in 1942.

ALLEN, ADRIANNE 1907–93, British actress, married to Raymond Massey, mother of Anna and Daniel Massey; first worked with JG when she played Mrs Frail on the 1947 US tour of *Love for Love*.

ALLEN, LEW b. 1922, American producer.

ALLGOOD, SARA 1883–1950, Irish actress and the creator of Sean O'Casey's Juno in *Juno and the Paycock*. JG appeared with her in a charity show in 1935.

ALLIO, RENÉ 1924–95, French designer; designed *Tartuffe* for the National Theatre in 1967, in which JG played Orgon.

ANDERSON, JEAN 1907–2001, British actress; appeared in JG's 1958 production of *Variation on a Theme*.

ANDERSON, JUDITH 1898–1992, Australian actress; played Gertrude in *Hamlet* in 1936 and Medea in 1947.

ANDERSON, LINDSAY 1923–94, British film and theatre director who directed JG in *Home* in 1970.

ANDERSON, MARIAN 1897–1993, American singer.

ANDERSON, MARY 1859–1940, American-born actress.

ANDERSON, MAXWELL 1888–1959, American playwright.

ANDREU, MARIANO 1888–1977, Spanish artist and stage designer; designed JG's 1949 production of *Much Ado about Nothing*.

ANDREWS, HARRY 1911–89, British actor who first appeared with JG in *Noah* in 1935.

ANDREWS, JULIE b. 1935, British actress.

ANSTEE, PAUL, British interior decorator and designer; partner, friend and executor of JG.

ARIS, DOREEN, British actress who played Miranda in *The Tempest* in 1957.

ARLEN, HAROLD 1905–86, American composer.

ARLISS, GEORGE 1868–1946, British-born actor.

ARMSTRONG, WILLIAM (Willie) 1882–1952, Scottish-born director who directed JG in *The Circle* in 1944.

ARNAUD, YVONNE 1892–1958, French actress who appeared with JG in *Love for Love* and *The Circle* in 1944.

ASHCROFT, PEGGY 1907–91, British actress who appeared with JG many times, the first when he directed her as Juliet in the OUDS production of *Romeo and Juliet* in 1932.

ASHMORE, PETER 1916–1997, British theatre director.

ASHTON, FREDERICK 1904–88, British dancer and choreographer.

ASHTON, WINIFRED – see Clemence Dane.

ASQUITH, ANTHONY (Puffin) 1902–68, British director, mainly of films.

ATKINS, EILEEN b. 1934, British actress; appeared as an extra in *The Tempest* (1957), in which JG played Prospero.

ATKINSON, BROOKS 1894–1984, American journalist, theatre critic and author.

ATKINSON, ROSALIND 1900–77, British actress who first appeared with JG in *Crime and Punishment* in 1946.

ATTENBOROUGH, RICHARD b. 1923, British film director, actor and producer; JG played a cameo part in his *Oh! What a Lovely War* (1969).

AUDEN, W. H. (Wystan Hugh) 1907–73, British poet.

AUDLEY, MAXINE 1923–92, British actress who appeared with JG in the 1950 Stratford-upon-Avon season.

AUMONT, JEAN-PIERRE 1911–2001, French actor.

AVEDON, RICHARD b. 1923, American photographer.

AYLMER, FELIX 1889–1979, British actor; JG first worked with him in *Robert E. Lee* at the Regent Theatre in 1923.

AYRTON, MICHAEL 1921–75, British painter, sculptor, illustrator and writer who designed JG's 1942 *Macbeth*.

BACALL, LAUREN (Betty) b. 1924, American actress, married to Humphrey Bogart and subsequently to Jason Robards Jr.

BACHARDY, DON b. 1934, American artist, partner of Christopher Isherwood.

BACHAUER, GINA 1913–76, Greek pianist.

BADDELEY, ANGELA 1904–76, British actress, married to Glen Byam Shaw; worked with JG several times over forty years, first of all in *The Insect Play* in 1923.

BADEL, ALAN 1923–82, British actor who first worked with JG in his 1942 *Macbeth* and played the Fool to JG's King Lear at Stratford-upon-Avon in 1950.

BAGNOLD, ENID 1889–1981, British novelist and dramatist; JG directed her play *The Chalk Garden* in 1956 and appeared in *The Last Joke* in 1960.

BAILEY, JAMES 1922–80, British set and costume designer for *The Way of the World* in 1953 when JG played Mirabell.

BALDWIN, WILLIAM (Billy) 1903–83, American interior decorator.

BALL, LUCILLE 1911–82, American actress and comedienne.

BALL, WILLIAM (Bill) 1931–91, American director.

BANBURY, FRITH b. 1912, British actor, director and manager; appeared with JG in his 1934 *Hamlet*.

BANCROFT, ANNE b. 1931, American actress.

BANKHEAD, TALLULAH 1902–68, American actress.

BANKS, LESLIE 1890–1952, British actor; directed JG in *Prejudice* in 1928 and appeared in several of his productions in the 1940s.

BANNEN, IAN 1928–99, Scottish actor who first worked with JG as Third Murderer in *Macbeth* in 1952.

BANNERMAN, ALISTAIR, British actor in JG's 1937–8 season at the Queen's Theatre.

BANNERMAN, MARGARET 1896–1976, Canadian-born actress.

BARKWORTH, PETER b. 1929, British actor who played Sir Benjamin Backbite in JG's 1962 production of *The School for Scandal*.

BARNES, BINNIE 1905–98, British actress.

BARNES, CLIVE b. 1927, latterly American-based British journalist, critic and writer.

BARNES, MAE 1907–96, American dancer and singer.

BARR, RICHARD b. 1917, American producer.

BARRAULT, JEAN-LOUIS 1910–94, French actor and director.

BARRIE, J. M. 1860–1937, Scottish playwright and novelist; JG played Mr Dearth in his *Dear Brutus* in 1941.

BARRON, MARCUS 1869–1944, British actor who first appeared with JG in the 1926 production of *The Constant Nymph*.

BARRY, HILDA b. 1884?, British actress who appeared with JG in *Bingo* in 1974.

BARRYMORE, ETHEL 1879–1959, American actress.

BARRYMORE, JOHN 1882–1942, American actor whose Hamlet J G admired greatly.

BARTLEY, ANTHONY, first husband of Deborah Kerr.

BARTON, JOHN b. 1928, British academic and director.

BATES, ALAN 1934–2003, British actor who appeared with J G in the remake of *The Wicked Lady* in 1983.

BAX, CLIFFORD 1886–1962, British author and playwright.

BAXTER, JANE 1909–96, British actress; first appeared with J G in *The Importance of Being Earnest* in New York in 1947.

BAXTER, KEITH b. 1933, Welsh actor; a long-time friend; with J G in the Orson Welles film *Chimes at Midnight* (1964).

BAYES, NORA 1880–1928, American vaudeville artiste.

BAYLIS, LILIAN 1874–1937, South African-born manager of the Old Vic Theatre from 1912 until her death. J G made his first appearance as a walk-on at the Old Vic in 1921, and returned in 1929 as Miss Baylis's leading man.

BEATON, CECIL 1904–98, British designer, photographer and author. His first professional association with J G was when he designed the sets and costumes for *Crisis in Heaven* in 1944.

BEATON, NORMAN 1934–94, Guyanan-born actor.

BEAUMONT, HUGH 'BINKIE' 1934–94, managing director of H. M. Tennent Ltd; produced many plays which J G directed and in which he appeared.

BEBB, RICHARD b. 1927, British actor, husband of Gwen Watford and friend of J G's in latter years.

BEDFORD, BRIAN b. 1935, British actor who first appeared with J G as Ariel in *The Tempest* in 1957.

BEECHAM, THOMAS 1879–1961, British conductor and impresario.

BEERBOHM, MAX 1872–1956, British caricaturist and writer.

BEESLEY, ALEC 1903–87, husband of the playwright Dodie Smith.

BEHAN, BRENDAN 1923–64, Irish playwright.

BEHRMAN, S. N. (Sam) 1893–1973, American playwright.

BEL GEDDES, BARBARA b. 1922, American actress.

BEL GEDDES, NORMAN 1893–1958, American designer and producer.

BELL, JAMES CLEVELAND b. 1910, partner of David Webster.

BELL, MARIE 1900–85, French actress.

BENNETT, ALAN b. 1934, British playwright and author.

BENNETT, ARNOLD 1867–1931, British novelist and playwright.

BENNETT, JILL 1931–90, British actress who appeared as an extra in J G's 1949 production of *Much Ado about Nothing*.

BENNY, JACK 1894–1974, American comedian.

BENSON, FRANK 1858–1939, British actor-manager.

BENTHALL, MICHAEL 1919–74, British director of theatre, opera and ballet; directed J G as Cardinal Wolsey in the 1958 production of *Henry VIII* at the Old Vic.

BENTLEY, ERIC b. 1916, British-born critic, editor, translator and playwright.

BERENSON, BERNARD 1865–1959, art historian and connoisseur.

BERG, GERTRUDE 1899–1966, American actress.

BERGMAN, INGMAR b. 1918, Swedish stage and film director.

BERGMAN, INGRID 1915–1982, Swedish actress who first worked with JG in 1973 when he directed her in *The Constant Wife*.

BERGNER, ELISABETH 1897–1986, Austrian-born actress who appeared with JG in the TV version of *In Good King Charles's Golden Days* (1970).

BERIOSOVA, SVETLANA 1932–98, Lithuanian-born ballerina.

BERLE, MILTON 1908–2002, American actor and comedian.

BERNARD, JAMES (Jimmy) 1925–2001, British composer, partner of Paul Dehn.

BERNHARDT, SARAH 1844–1923, French actress.

BERNSTEIN, SIDNEY 1899–1993, film and TV executive, head of the Granada empire.

BERRY, NEAL, American actor; a member of the ensemble in the 1936 US production of *Hamlet*.

BEST, EDNA 1900–74, British actress married to Herbert Marshall; JG appeared with her in *The Constant Nymph* in 1926.

BETTI, UGO 1892–1953, Italian playwright and poet.

BING, RUDOLPH 1902–97, General Manager of the Metropolitan Opera, New York.

BIRKIN, JANE b. 1946, British actress, daughter of Judy Campbell.

BLACK, KITTY, administrator and translator, secretary at H. M. Tennent Ltd; ran the Company of Four for Tennents.

BLACKWELL, BLANCHE b. 1912, neighbour and friend of Noël Coward in Jamaica.

BLAKELY, COLIN 1930–87, Northern Irish actor who appeared with JG in *Oedipus* in 1968.

BLATCHLEY, JOHN 1922–94, British actor and director; played in JG's 1944–5 season at the Theatre Royal, Haymarket.

BLOOM, CLAIRE b. 1931, British actress; first appeared with JG as Alizon Eliot in *The Lady's Not for Burning* in 1949.

BOGARDE, DIRK 1921–99, British actor and writer who appeared with JG in the film *Providence* (1970).

BOGART, HUMPHREY 1899–1957, American actor, married to Lauren Bacall.

BOGDANOV, MICHAEL b. 1938, British director.

BOGDANOVICH, PETER b. 1939, American film director.

BOLT, ROBERT 1924–95, British playwright; married to Sarah Miles.

BOND, EDWARD b. 1934, British playwright; JG appeared in his play *Bingo* in 1974.

BOOTH, EDWIN 1833–93, American actor.

BOOTH, JAMES b. 1933, British actor.

BOOTH, SHIRLEY 1898–1992, American actress.

BORGE, VICTOR 1909–2000, Danish pianist and comedian.

BOURCHIER, ARTHUR 1863–1927, British actor.

BOWERS, LALLY 1917–84, British actress whom JG directed in *The Last of Summer* in 1944.

BOWN, JANE, British photographer, notably for the *Observer*.

BOYD, STEPHEN 1931–77, Irish-born actor; mainly in films.

BOYER, CHARLES 1897–1978, French actor.

BRADDELL, MAURICE 1900–90, British actor; first appeared with JG in *The Insect Play* in 1923.

BRAITHWAITE, LILIAN 1873–1948, British actress; mother of Joyce Carey. JG appeared with her first in *The Vortex* in 1925 taking over the part of Nicky Lancaster from Noël Coward.

BRANAGH, KENNETH b. 1960, Northern Irish-born actor and director who appeared with JG on film and radio.

BRANDO, MARLON b. 1924, American actor who appeared with JG in the 1953 film of *Julius Caesar*.

BRETT, JEREMY 1933–95, British actor; first worked with JG when the latter directed him in *Variation on a Theme* in 1958.

BRICUSSE, LESLIE b. 1931, British composer.

BRIDIE, JAMES 1888–1951, Scottish playwright.

BRIEN, ALAN b. 1925, theatre and film critic.

BRISSON, FREDERICK 1915–84, American producer who worked with JG on *Five Finger Exercise* in the USA in 1959.

BRITTEN, BENJAMIN 1913–76, British composer.

BROOK, PETER b. 1925, British theatre and film director with whom JG first worked in 1950 playing Angelo in *Measure for Measure*.

BROWN, IVOR 1891–1974, British theatre critic for the *Observer*.

BROWN, PAMELA 1917–75, British actress; first worked with JG on the 1947 US tour of *The Importance of Being Earnest*.

BROWN, TEDDY 1900–46, American xylophone player.

BROWNE, CORAL 1913–1991, Australian actress.

BROWNE, E. MARTIN 1900–80, British writer and director closely associated with the work of T. S. Eliot.

BROWNE, IRENE 1896–1975, British actress, singer and dancer; first appeared with JG in *The Return of the Prodigal* in 1947.

BROWNE, MAURICE 1881–1955, British actor-manager who presented JG's Hamlet at the Queen's Theatre in 1930.

BRUNNER, ELAINE, JG's neighbour in the large house at Wotton Underwood.

BRYAN, DORA b. 1924, British actress.

BRYANT, MICHAEL 1928–2002, British actor, played Walter Langer in JG's 1958 production of *Five Finger Exercise*.

BRYNNER, YUL 1920–85, Russian-born actor.

BUCHHOLZ, HORST 1933–2003, German actor.

BUCKMASTER, JOHN 1915–83, British actor, Gladys Cooper's stepson.

BUDBERG, MOURA 1892?–1974, Russian translator, former mistress of Maxim Gorky and H. G. Wells.

BULL, PETER 1912–84, British actor who played Edward Tappercoom in JG's 1949 production of *The Lady's Not for Burning*.

BURNS, GEORGE 1896–1996, American comedian.

BURR, RAYMOND 1917–93, Canadian actor, best known for his portrayal of Perry Mason in the TV series.

BURR, ROBERT 1922–2000, American actor. He appeared in JG's 1964 US production of *Hamlet* and may have understudied Richard Burton.

BURRELL, JOHN 1910–72, British director who, with Laurence Olivier and Ralph Richardson, ran the Old Vic Company's post-war seasons at the New Theatre.

BURRILL, ENA b. 1908, British actress who appeared with JG in *Noah* in 1935.

BURSTYN, ELLEN b. 1932, American actress.

BURTON, RICHARD 1925–84, Welsh actor; first worked with JG in 1949 as Richard in *The Lady's Not for Burning*.

BURTON, SALLY, widow of Richard Burton.

BURTON, SYBIL, first wife of Richard Burton.

BURY, JOHN 1925?–2000, British stage designer who designed the sets for a number of plays in which JG appeared.

BUTLER, BILL, British? theatre director.

BUTLER, JOHN 1918–93, American choreographer.

BYERLEY, VIVIENNE 1906–95, press agent for H. M. Tennent Ltd.

BYRON, ARTHUR 1870–1943, American actor who played Polonius in the 1936 US production of *Hamlet*.

CADELL, JEAN 1884–1967, British actress who first worked with JG in 1930 when she played Miss Prism in *The Importance of Being Earnest*.

CAINE, MICHAEL b. 1933, British actor who appeared with JG in the film *The Whistle Blower* (1986).

CALDER-MARSHALL, ANNA b. 1947, British actress; played Cleopatra to JG's Caesar in the 1971 Chichester Festival Theatre production of *Caesar and Cleopatra*.

CALDWELL, ZOË b. 1933, Australian actress.

CALHERN, LOUIS 1895–1956, American actor who played the title role in the 1953 film of *Julius Caesar*.

CALLAS, MARIA 1923–77, Greek soprano.

CALTHROP, GLADYS 1894–1980, British artist and stage designer.

CALVERT, PHYLLIS 1915–2002, British actress; JG directed her in *The Complaisant Lover* in 1959.

CAMPBELL, JUDY b. 1916, British actress who appeared in JG's 1941 production of *Ducks and Drakes*.

CAMPBELL, MRS PATRICK 1865–1940, British actress; JG played Oswald to her Mrs Alving in a 1928 production of *Ghosts*.

CANNAN, DENNIS b. 1919, British playwright and translator.

CANTOR, ARTHUR 1920–2001, American producer who took over H. M. Tennent Ltd after 'Binkie' Beaumont's death in 1973.

CAPALBO, CARMEN, American director and producer.

CAPOTE, TRUMAN 1924–84, American novelist and journalist.

CAREY, JOYCE 1898–1993, British actress; daughter of Lilian Braithwaite; JG worked with her on several occasions, the first being a charity show in 1934.

CARLISLE, KITTY b. 1914; American actress; married American playwright Moss Hart.

CARON, LESLIE b. 1931; French actress, first wife of Peter Hall.

CARROLL, MADELEINE 1906–87, British actress.

CASADESUS, ROBERT 1899–1972, French pianist.

CASSON, LEWIS 1875–1969, Welsh-born actor and director, husband of Sybil Thorndike. First worked with JG in 1925 when he directed him in *The High Constable's Wife*.

CASTLE, CHARLES b. 1939, South African born author, playwright and TV producer.

CHAMBERLAIN, RICHARD b. 1934, American actor; appeared with JG in Peter Wood's 1971 TV production of *Hamlet*.

CHAMPION, GOWER, 1910–80, American choreographer and director.

CHANNING, CAROL b. 1925, American comedienne; JG appeared in a TV show with her in 1959.

CHANNON, HENRY 'CHIPS' 1897–1958, American-born Member of Parliament and diarist.

CHAPLIN, CHARLIE (Charles) 1889–1977, British film actor and director.

CHAPMAN, EDWARD 1910–77, British actor; first appeared with JG in an amateur production of *I'll Leave It to You* in 1922.

CHAPPELL, WILLIAM 1908–94, British dancer, actor, designer and choreographer; first worked with JG in 1950 when he designed sets and costumes for *The Boy with a Cart*.

CHARON, JACQUES 1919–75, French actor and theatre director.

CHATTERTON, RUTH 1893–1961, American actress.

CHAUVIRÉ, YVETTE b. 1917, French ballerina.

CHERRY, HELEN 1915–2001, British actress, married to Trevor Howard; worked with JG in the 1955 season at the Palace Theatre.

CHEVALIER, ALBERT 1861–1923, music-hall artist and actor.

CHEVALIER, MAURICE 1888–1972, French actor and singer.

CHURCHILL, DIANA 1913–94, British actress; JG appeared with her in a charity show in 1935.

CHURCHILL, SARAH 1914–82, British actress, daughter of Winston Churchill.

CILENTO, DIANE b. 1933, Australian actress.

CLAIRE, INA 1892–1985, American actress.

CLARENCE, O. B. 1870–1955, British actor; JG first worked with him in the 1925 production of *The Cherry Orchard*.

CLARK, KENNETH 1903–83, British gallery director, art historian and critic.

CLARKE, WARREN b. 1947, British actor; first appeared with JG in *Home* in 1970.

CLEMENTS, JOHN 1910–88, British actor; JG only appeared with him in the 1974 *Tribute to the Lady*, celebrating the centenary of Lilian Baylis's birth.

CLIBURN, VAN b. 1934, American pianist.

CLIFT, MONTGOMERY 1920–66, American actor.

CLOWES, RICHARD, British journalist and press agent.

CLUNES, ALEC 1912–70, British actor who played Caliban to JG's Prospero in the 1957 production of *The Tempest*.

COATS, PETER 1910–90, British garden designer, known as 'Petticoats', an intimate friend of Henry 'Chips' Channon.

COCHRAN, CHARLES B. 1872–1951, British impresario.

COCO, JAMES 1930–87, American actor.

CODRON, MICHAEL b. 1930, British theatre producer.

COE, KENTON b. 1932, American composer.

COGHILL, NEVILL 1899–1980, Fellow of Exeter College, Oxford; directed the 1945 production of *A Midsummer Night's Dream* when JG played Oberon.

COHEN, ALEXANDER 1920–2000, American producer.

COHEN, ROB b. 1949, American film director.

COHN, JOAN 1911–96, wife of Harry Cohn, head of Columbia pictures; second wife of Laurence Harvey.

COLBERT, CLAUDETTE 1903–96, American actress.

COLE, GEORGE b. 1925, British actor, adopted son of Alastair Sim.

COLE, JACK 1914–74, American choreographer.

COLEFAX, SIBYL 1874–1950, interior designer and society hostess.

COLLIER, CONSTANCE 1878–1955, British actress.

COLLIER, PATIENCE 1910–87, British actress; JG first worked with her when he directed *The Cherry Orchard* in 1954.

COLLINS, JOAN b. 1933, British actress who worked with JG on a film in the TV series *Tales of the Unexpected* (1978).

COLVIL, ALISON, Scottish stage manager who worked with JG on many productions, firstly on *The Cradle Song* in 1944.

COMPTON, FAY 1894–1978, British actress who played Ophelia to JG's Hamlet in 1939.

COMTOIS, GUY, Canadian set designer.

CONE, EDWARD T. (Ed) b. 1917, American composer and former Professor of Music at Princeton University; partner of George Pitcher.

COOKMAN, A. V. (Victor), British theatre critic, mainly for *The Times*.

COOPER, DIANA 1892–1986, British actress and socialite who appeared with great success in Max Reinhardt's *The Miracle* in 1911.

COOPER, GLADYS 1888–1971, British actress who appeared with JG in *L'École des Cocottes* in 1925.

CORNELL, KATHERINE (Kit) 1898–1974, American actress, wife of Guthrie McClintic.

COTTEN, JOSEPH 1905–94, American actor.

COURTENAY, TOM b. 1937, British actor.

COWARD, NOËL 1899–1973, British actor, playwright, composer and director; JG first appeared in a Coward play in 1922 when he played Bobbie in *I'll Leave It to You*.

COX, BRIAN b. 1946, Scottish actor who appeared with JG in *Julius Caesar* in 1977.

CRAIG, EDITH (Edy) 1869–1947, British actress and director, daughter of Ellen Terry.

CRAIG, EDWARD GORDON 1872–1966, British designer and actor, son of Ellen Terry.

CRAWFORD, CHERYL 1902–86, American theatre producer.

CROFT-COOKE, RUPERT 1903–79, British novelist and biographer.

CROMWELL, JOHN 1887–1979, American actor and film director who played Rosencrantz in the 1936 US production of *Hamlet*.

CROMWELL, RICHARD 1910–60, American actor.

CRONYN, HUME 1911–2003, Canadian actor; JG first directed him in *Big Fish, Little Fish* in New York in 1961.

CROSBIE, ANNETTE b. 1934, British actress.

CROSS, BEVERLEY 1931–98, British actor and playwright; appeared with JG in his season at the Palace Theatre in 1955.

CUKOR, GEORGE 1899–1983, American film director.

CULSHAW, EILEEN, made the costumes for JG's 1942 production of *Macbeth*.

CULVER, ROLAND 1900–84, British actor who first worked with JG in a charity performance of *Drake* in 1939.

CUNARD, 'EMERALD' (Maud) 1872–1948, society hostess.

CURRIE, FINLAY 1878–1968, Scottish actor who appeared with JG in *Musical Chairs* in 1931.

CURTIS, DAN b. 1928, American director of the 1986 TV film *War and Remembrance* in which JG appeared.

CUSACK, CYRIL 1910–93, Irish actor; appeared with JG in *The Tempest* with the National Theatre at the Old Vic in 1974.

CZINNER, PAUL 1890–1972, Hungarian-born film director, married to Elisabeth Bergner.

DANE, CLEMENCE 1888–1965, pen name of Winifred Ashton, British novelist, artist and playwright; JG appeared in a radio version of her play *Will Shakespeare* in 1931.

DANNER, BLYTHE b. 194?, American actress who appeared with JG in the 1982 TV film *Inside the Third Reich*.

DARE, ZENA 1887–1975, British actress who first worked with JG when he directed her in *Spring Meeting* in 1938.

DAVENPORT, A. BROMLEY 1867–1946, British actor who appeared with JG in *The Insect Play* in 1923.

DAVIOT, GORDON 1896–1952, pseudonym of Elizabeth Mackintosh who also wrote historical novels under the nom de plume of Josephine Tey. She wrote *Richard of Bordeaux* specifically for JG.

DAVIS, ALLAN 1913–2001, British theatre and film director.

DAVIS, BETTE 1908–89, American actress.

DAVIS, DONALD 1928–88, Canadian actor.

DAVIS, JOE 1912–84, British lighting designer who lit several shows which JG directed.

DAVIS JR, SAMMY 1925–90, American entertainer.

DAWSON, BEATRICE (Bumble) 1912–76, British costume designer who worked on a number of shows that JG directed.

DE ACOSTA, MERCEDES 1893–1968, American poet, novelist and playwright; JG appeared in her play *Prejudice* at the Arts Theatre in 1928.

DE BANZIE, BRENDA 1915–81, British actress.

DE CASALIS, JEANNE 1897–1966, South African actress and writer; JG first appeared with her in a charity show in 1935.

DE HAVILLAND, OLIVIA b. 1916, American actress of British parentage.

DEHN, PAUL 1912–76, British writer and critic, partner of James Bernard.

DELFONT, BERNARD 1900–94, Russian-born British theatre and film impresario.

DELYSIA, ALICE 1899–1979, French actress and singer.

DENCH, JUDI b. 1934, British actress who first worked with JG when she was an extra in *Henry VIII* at the Old Vic in 1958.

DE NOBILI, LILA 1916–2002, Swiss born stage designer.

DENT, ALAN 'JOCK' b. 1905, theatre critic, secretary to James Agate.

DESMOND, FLORENCE 1907–93, British actress and impersonator.

DE VALOIS, NINETTE (Edris Stannus) 1898–2001, Irish-born dancer, choreographer and director, founder of the Royal Ballet.

DEVINE, GEORGE 1910–66, British actor, director and manager, notably at the Royal Court; a student at Oxford when he appeared in JG's production of *Romeo and Juliet* in 1932.

DEWHURST, COLLEEN 1924–91, American actress; JG directed her in *All Over* in New York in 1971.

DE WILDE, BRANDON 1942–72, American child actor who graduated to adult roles.

DE WOLFE, BILLY 1907–74, American actor whom JG directed in *Irene* (1972).

DEWS, PETER 1929–97, British theatre and television director.

DEXTER, JOHN 1925–90, British theatre and opera director, associate director of the National Theatre under Laurence Olivier.

DIAGHILEV, SERGEI 1872–1929, Russian ballet impresario.

DIETRICH, MARLENE 1910–92, German actress and singer.

DIFFEN, RAY, American costumier; worked on the 1959 US production of *Much Ado about Nothing*.

DIGNAM, MARK 1909–89, British actor who first appeared with JG in *The Tempest* in 1957.

DI VERDURA, FULCO 1899–1978, Sicilian duke and jewellery designer.

DODGE, BERNARD (Bernie) d. 1964; JG's American manservant, sometimes nicknamed 'Niobe'.

DONALD, JAMES 1917–93, British actor; first appeared with JG playing a small part in the 1940 production of *King Lear*.

DONAT, ROBERT 1905–58, British actor whose career was cut short by ill health.

DONATI, DANILO b. 1926, Italian set and costume designer who worked on the film of *Caligula* (1979) in which JG appeared.

DORN, MARION 1896–1964, British textile designer.

DOUGLAS, LORD ALFRED 1870–1945, poet and lover of Oscar Wilde.

DOUGLAS, MICHAEL b. 1944, American actor who appeared with JG in the 1991 film *Shining Through*.

DOWN, LESLEY-ANNE b. 1954, appeared with JG in the 1977 TV version of *Heartbreak House*.

DRAKE, ALFRED 1914–92, American actor and singer who played Claudius in JG's 1964 US production of *Hamlet*.

DRAKE, FABIA 1904–90, British actress.

DRAPER, RUTH 1884–1956, American actress and *diseuse*.

DRINKWATER, JOHN 1882–1937; poet and playwright; JG appeared in his play *Robert E. Lee* in 1923.

DU MAURIER, GERALD 1873–1934, British actor-manager.

DUFF, LADY JULIET 1881–1985, society hostess.

DUKE, PATTY b. 1946, American actress.

DUNAWAY, FAYE b. 1941, American actress who appeared with JG in the remake of *The Wicked Lady* (1983).

DUNCAN, LINDSAY b. 1950, British actress.

DUNHAM, KATHERINE b. 1912, American dancer and choreographer.

DUNLOP, FRANK b. 1927, British theatre director.

DUNN, GEOFFREY 1903–81, British actor; JG directed him in *Nude with Violin* when he took over from David Horne.

DUSE, ELEANORA 1858–1924, Italian actress.

DYALL, FRANKLIN 1874–1950, British actor who took over from Frank Vosper as Claudius in JG's 1934 *Hamlet*.

EASON, MYLES 1915–77, Australian-born actor.

EASTON, RICHARD b. 1933, Canadian-born actor; first worked with JG when he played Claudio in the 1955 production of *Much Ado about Nothing*.

EDDISON, ROBERT 1908–91, British actor; first worked with JG when he played Epihodoff in *The Cherry Orchard* in 1954.

EDGEWORTH, JANE, British Council Drama Department.

EDWARDS, BEN 1916–99, American scene and lighting designer who worked on several of JG's US productions.

EGAN, PETER b. 1946, British actor who appeared with JG in *Caesar and Cleopatra* in 1971.

ELDRIDGE, FLORENCE 1901–88, American actress.

ELIOT, T. S. (Thomas Stearns) 1888–1965, American-born poet and playwright.

ELLIOTT, DENHOLM 1922–92, British actor.

ELLIOTT, GERTRUDE 1874–1950, British actress who played Emilia when JG played Cassio in the 1927 production of *Othello*.

ELLIOTT, MADGE 1898–1955, British actress, wife of Cyril Ritchard.

ELLIS, MARY 1897–2003, American-born actress and musical comedy performer; appeared with JG in a charity show in 1935.

ENGEL, SUSAN b. 1935, Austrian-born British actress.

ENTHOVEN, GABRIELLE 1868–1950, collector and theatre archivist.

ESMOND, ANNE 1873–1945, British actress; appeared with JG in several productions, first in *The Great God Brown* in 1927.

ESMOND, JILL 1908–90, British actress, first wife of Laurence Olivier.

EVANS, DAVID 1893–1966, British actor who first appeared with JG in *The Lady's Not for Burning* in 1949.

EVANS, EDITH 1888–1976, British actress; first appeared with JG in *The Lady with a Lamp* in 1929.

EVANS, JESSIE 1918–83, Welsh actress who appeared with JG in *Crime and Punishment* in 1947.

EVANS, LAURENCE 1912–2002, JG's agent.

EVANS, MARY, wife of Laurence Evans.

EVANS, MAURICE 1901–89, British actor; appeared with JG in a charity show in 1935.

EVANS, REX 1903–69, British actor.

EWING, MARIA b. 1950, American soprano, Peter Hall's third wife.

EYRE, RONALD 1929–92, British director and writer who directed JG in *Veterans* in 1972.

FABER, LESLIE 1879–1929, British actor and director; first appeared with JG in *L'École des Cocottes* in 1925.

FAGAN, J. B. (James Bernard) 1873–1933, Irish-born actor, director and writer; director of the Oxford Playhouse where JG worked in 1924.

FAIRBANKS JR., DOUGLAS 1909–2000, American actor.

FAITHFULL, MARIANNE b. 1946, British singer and actress.

FARINGDON, GAVIN 1902–77, 2nd Lord Faringdon.

FARR, FLORENCE 1860–1917, British actress.

FARRELL, M. J. (nom de plume of Molly Keane) 1904–96, Irish novelist and play-wright; JG directed four of her plays, three of which were written with John Perry.

FAULKNER, TRADER b. 1930, Australian actor; worked with JG when he took over from Richard Burton in *The Lady's Not for Burning* in New York, 1951.

FEAST, MICHAEL b. 1946, British actor; appeared with JG in the National Theatre productions of *The Tempest* (1974) and *No Man's Land* (1976).

FEDOROVITCH, SOPHIE 1893–1953, Russian stage designer who designed the sets and costumes for Peter Brook's production of *The Winter's Tale* in 1951.

FERBER, EDNA 1885–1968, American novelist and playwright.

FERRER, JOSÉ 1912–92, American actor.

FERRIS, BARBARA b. 1942, British actress whom JG directed in *The Constant Wife* in 1973.

FEUILLÈRE, EDWIGE 1907–98, French actress.

FFRANGCON-DAVIES, GWEN 1891–1992, British actress and singer; JG first appeared with her when he played Romeo to her Juliet in 1924.

FIELD, BETTY 1913–73, American actress; JG directed her in *All Over* in New York in 1971.

FIELDS, GRACIE 1898–1979, British singer and entertainer.

FILDES, AUDREY b. 1922, British actress who first worked with JG in *Crime and Punishment* in 1946.

FINCH, PETER 1916–77, Australian actor who appeared with JG in the remake of *Lost Horizon* (1972).

FINDLATER, RICHARD 1921–87, British theatre critic and author; JG's official biographer, but died before he could complete the book.

FINLAY, FRANK b. 1926, British actor.

FINNEY, ALBERT b. 1936, British actor.

FIRTH, PETER b. 1953, British actor who appeared with JG in a TV version of *The Picture of Dorian Gray*.

FLEETWOOD, SUSAN 1944–95, British actress who appeared with JG in the TV serial *Summer's Lease* (1989).

FLEMING, ANNE 1913–81, wife of Ian Fleming.

FLEMING, IAN 1909–64, British journalist and novelist, creator of James Bond; married to Anne Fleming.

FLEMING, TOM b. 1927, Scottish actor.

FLEMYNG, ROBERT (Bobby or Bobbie) 1912–95, British actor; first worked with JG when he took over the part of Tony Fox-Collier in *Spring Meeting* in 1938.

FONDA, HENRY 1905–82, American actor.

FONTANNE, LYNN 1887–1983, British-born American actress, wife of Alfred Lunt.

FONTEYN, MARGOT (Peggy Hookham) 1919–91, British ballerina.

FORBES, BRYAN b. 1926, British actor, director and author.

FORBES, MERIEL (Mu, Lady Richardson) 1913–2000, British actress, second wife of Ralph Richardson; appeared with JG in *The School for Scandal* in 1962.

FORBES-ROBERTSON, JOHNSTON 1853–1937, British actor-manager.

FORSTER, E. M. 1879–1970, British novelist.

FORWOOD, TONY d. 1988, British actor, partner of Dirk Bogarde.

FOSSE, BOB 1927–87, American director and choreographer.

FOX, JAMES b. 1939, British actor.

FRANCIS, ARLENE 1907–2001, American TV interviewer.

FRANCIS, CLIVE b. 1946, British actor and caricaturist.

FRANKAU, PAMELA 1908–67, British novelist.

FRANKENHEIMER, JOHN 1930–2002, American film and TV director; directed JG in *The Browning Version* for American TV (1959).

FRANKLIN, MICHAEL, Terence Rattigan's partner.

FRASER, ANTONIA b. 1932, British historical biographer, second wife of Harold Pinter.

FRAYN, MICHAEL b. 1933, English novelist and playwright.

FROSCH, AARON, American lawyer.

FRY, CHRISTOPHER b. 1907, British playwright; JG directed and played in his *The Lady's Not for Burning* (1949).

FURSE, ROGER 1903–72, British designer; first worked with JG when he designed the sets and costumes for *King Lear* in 1940.

GABOR, EVA 1919–95, Hungarian-born actress, sister of Magda and Zsa Zsa.

GÁLFFI, LÁSZLÓ b. 1952, Hungarian actor who worked with JG in the TV film *Wagner* in 1982.

GALLI-CURCI, AMELITA 1882–1963, Italian soprano.

GARBO, GRETA 1905–90, Swedish-born actress.

GARDINER, REGGIE 1903–80, British actor; he and JG were at RADA together.

GARLAND, PATRICK b. 1935, British director who directed JG in *Forty Years On* (1968).

GARNETT, DAVID 1892–1981, British novelist and critic.

GARSON, GREER 1904–96, British actress.

GASKILL, WILLIAM b. 1930, British theatre director and teacher.

GÉLIN, DANIEL 1921–2002, French actor.

GENET, JEAN 1910–86, French novelist and playwright.

GENNARO, PETER 1919–2000, American choreographer who staged the musical numbers in *Irene* (1972).

GERHARDT, ELENA 1883–1961, German lieder singer.

GHERARDI, PIERO 1909–71, Italian stage and film designer.

GIELGUD, ELEANOR (Mrs Ducker), JG's sister. Her husband, Frank Ducker, died after only a year of their marriage.

GIELGUD, FRANK 1860–1949, JG's father.

GIELGUD, LEWIS 1894–1953, JG's eldest brother.

GIELGUD, KATE TERRY 1868–1958, JG's mother.

GIELGUD, MAINA b. 1945, ballerina and choreographer, JG's niece.

GIELGUD, MIMI DE, French actress, first wife of Lewis Gielgud.

GIELGUD, VAL 1900–81, JG's elder brother.

GIELGUD, ZITA GORDON b. 1911?, Hungarian actress. Second wife of Lewis Gielgud.

GILDER, ROSAMOND 1891–?, American author and theatre historian.

GILL, ERIC 1882–1940, British artist, engraver, sculptor and typographer.

GILL, PETER b. 1939, British theatre director and playwright.

GILLMORE, MARGALO 1897–1986, British-born actress.

GILPIN, JOHN 1930–83, British ballet dancer.

GINGOLD, HERMIONE 1897–1987, British actress.

GIRAUDOUX, JEAN 1882–1944, French diplomat, novelist and playwright.

GISH, DOROTHY, 1898–1968, American actress and sister of Lillian Gish.

GISH, LILLIAN 1893–1993, American actress who played Ophelia to his Hamlet in the 1936 US production and Katerina in the 1946 US production of *Crime and Punishment*.

GLENVILLE, PETER 1913–96, British actor and director who directed JG in *The Return of the Prodigal* in 1948.

GOBBI, TITO 1913–84, Italian baritone.

GODDEN, RUMER 1907–98, British novelist.

GOETZ, RUTH (1912–2001) and AUGUSTUS (1901–57), adapted *The Heiress*, which JG directed in 1949.

GOETZ, WILLIAM 1903–69, American film producer.

GOLDMAN, MILTON d. 1989?, American agent, partner of Arnold Weissberger.

GOODNER, CAROL 1904–2001, American actress who first appeared with JG in *Musical Chairs* in 1931.

GOORNEY, HOWARD b. 1921, who appeared in JG's 1962 production of *The School for Scandal.*

GOPAL, RAM 1912–2003, Indian dancer.

GORDON, RUTH 1896–1985, American actress.

GORDON, STEVE 1938–82, American film director who directed the *Arthur* films (1981, 1988).

GORHAM, KATHLEEN 1932–83, Australian dancer and teacher.

GORING, MARIUS 1912–98, British actor who first appeared with JG in *The Merchant of Venice* in 1932.

GRADE, LEW 1907–98, Russian-born agent, TV and film producer.

GRAHAM, MARTHA 1894–1991, American dancer and choreographer.

GRANGER, STEWART (James Stewart) 1913–93, British actor; married to Jean Simmons.

GRANT, CARY 1904–86, British-born actor.

GRANVILLE-BARKER, HARLEY 1877–1946, British actor, dramatist, director and author; an influential figure in JG's life through his writing and especially his contribution to the production of *King Lear* in 1940.

GRAY, SIMON b. 1936, British playwright.

GREENAWAY, PETER b. 1942, British film director who directed JG in *Prospero's Books* (1990).

GREENE, GRAHAM 1904–91, British novelist and playwright. JG appeared in his play *The Potting Shed* in 1958 and directed *The Complaisant Lover* in 1959.

GREET, PHILIP BEN 1857–1936, British actor-manager and director.

GREGORY, PAUL b. 1920, American film producer.

GREIF, STEPHEN b. 1944, British actor.

GRENFELL, JOYCE 1910–79, British actress, singer and *diseuse.*

GREY, JOEL b. 1932, American actor.

GRIFFIES, ETHEL 1878–1975, American actress who played Avdotya in the US production of *Ivanov* in 1965.

GRIFFITH, HUGH 1912–80, Welsh actor.

GRIMES, FRANK, Irish actor.

GRIMES, TAMMY b. 1934, American actress.

GROCK (ADRIAN WETTACH) 1880–1959, Swiss clown.

GRUNDGENS, GUSTAV 1899–1963, German actor and director.

GUINNESS, ALEC 1914–2000, British actor; first worked with JG as the Third Player and Osric in his 1934 *Hamlet.*

GUINNESS, MATTHEW b. 1940, British actor, son of Alec and Merula Guinness.

GUINNESS, MERULA (Merry) 1914–2000, British actress, wife of Alec. As Merula Salaman she played the Tiger in the 1935 production of *Noah.*

GUTHRIE, TYRONE (Tony) 1900–71, British theatre director; first worked with JG at the Oxford Playhouse when Guthrie was an actor and assistant stage manager.

GWILYM, MIKE b. 1949, Welsh actor.

GWYNN, MICHAEL 1916–76, British actor who played Antonio in JG's 1949 production of *Much Ado about Nothing*.

HAAS, DOLLY 1910–94, German-born American actress married to the cartoonist Al Hirschfeld; played Sonya in the 1947 US production of *Crime and Punishment*.

HAGEN UTA b. 1919, German born American actress.

HAGGARD, STEPHEN 1911–43; first appeared with JG in *The Maitlands* in 1943 and played the Fool to his Lear in 1940.

HAIGH, KENNETH b. 1931, British actor, the original Jimmy Porter in *Look Back in Anger* in 1956; appeared with JG in the 1970 film *Eagle in a Cage*.

HALL, PETER b. 1930, British theatre, opera and film director, second Director of the National Theatre. He first directed JG in *The Battle of Shrivings* in 1970.

HALL, STANLEY 1917–94, British wigmaker, perfumier and make-up artist.

HAMILTON, HAMISH (Jamie) 1900–1987, American-born British publisher under his own name.

HAMILTON, NANCY 1908–85, American actress, writer and director.

HAMPDEN, WALTER 1879–1955, American actor.

HANDL, IRENE 1901–87, British actress and novelist.

HANKIN, ST JOHN 1869–1909, British playwright; JG appeared in his play *The Return of the Prodigal* in 1948.

HANNEN, NICHOLAS ('Beau') 1881–1972, British actor married to Athene Seyler; first appeared with JG in *Red Sunday* in 1929.

HARDING, LYN 1876–1952, Welsh actor who first appeared with JG in *Henry IV Part 1* at the Old Vic in 1930.

HARDWICK, PAUL 1918–84, British actor who played the Gardener in JG's 1952 production of *Richard II*.

HARDWICKE, CEDRIC 1893–1964, British actor; in the 1926 *Hamlet* at the Royal Court, JG played Rosencrantz and Hardwicke the First Gravedigger.

HARDWICKE, EDWARD b. 1932, British actor, son of Cedric Hardwicke and Helena Pickard.

HARE, DAVID b. 1947, British playwright, screenwriter and director; JG appeared in the film of his play *Plenty*.

HARRIS, JULIE b. 1925, American actress.

HARRIS, MARGARET ('Percy') 1904–2000, one of the three women designers working as Motley.

HARRIS, RADIE 1905–2001, American journalist and gossip columnist.

HARRIS, ROBERT (Bobby) 1900–95, British actor who first appeared with JG in *Richard of Bordeaux* in 1932.

HARRIS, ROSEMARY b. 1927, British actress who appeared with JG in his last stage play, *The Best of Friends* in 1989.

HARRIS, SOPHIA 1901–66, one of the three women designers working as Motley.

HARRISON, REX 1908–90, British actor.

HART, MOSS 1904–61, American playwright and theatre director.

HARTNOLL, PHYLLIS 1907–90, British theatre historian.

HARVEY, LAURENCE 1928–73, Lithuanian-born actor; played Malcolm in JG's 1952 production of *Macbeth* at Stratford-upon-Avon.

HARWOOD, RONALD b. 1934, South African-born novelist, playwright and biographer.

HASKELL, ARNOLD 1903–80, British ballet critic, boyhood friend of JG.

HASSALL, CHRISTOPHER 1912–63, British actor, author and poet; played Romeo in JG's 1930 OUDS production.

HAUER, RUTGER b. 1944, Dutch actor who appeared with JG in the TV film *Inside the Third Reich*.

HAWKINS, JACK 1910–73, British actor who first appeared with JG in a 1933 charity performance of *A Kiss for Cinderella*.

HAWTREY, CHARLES 1858–1923, British actor-manager.

HAY, IAN 1876–1952, Scottish novelist and playwright.

HAYE, HELEN 1874–1957, British actress; JG appeared with her once in a charity show in 1935.

HAYES, GEORGE 1888–1967, British actor; worked with JG several times, the first being a charity performance in 1927.

HAYES, HELEN 1900–93, American actress whom JG directed in *The Glass Menagerie* in London in 1948.

HAYMAN, RONALD, British author who wrote a biography of JG in 1971.

HAYWARD, JOHN 1905–65, British anthologist and bibliophile who attended Hillside School with JG.

HEBERT, FRED, American producer, formerly production stage manager.

HELBURN, THERESA 1887–1959, joint Administrative Director of the Theatre Guild.

HELLMAN, LILLIAN 1905–84, American playwright.

HELPMANN, ROBERT 1909–86, Australian ballet dancer and actor; JG directed him when he took over from Michael Wilding in *Nude with Violin*.

HEMMINGS, DAVID 1941–2003, British actor who appeared with JG in *The Charge of the Light Brigade* (1968).

HENDERSON, FLORENCE b. 1934, American actress.

HENSLER, MARTIN d. 1999, Hungarian, JG's partner for almost forty years.

HEPBURN, AUDREY 1929–93, British film actress.

HEPBURN, KATHARINE 1907–2003, American actress.

HERBERT, A. P. 1890–1971, British writer.

HERBERT, JOCELYN 1917–2003, British designer, notably at the Royal Court; designed set and costumes for *Home* (1970).

HERLIE, EILEEN b. 1920, Scottish actress; JG first directed her as Medea in 1948.

HERRING, REED, American actor who played Fortinbras in the 1936 New York *Hamlet*.

HESTON, CHARLTON b. 1924, American actor; he appeared with JG in the 1970 film version of *Julius Caesar* directed by Stuart Burge.

HICKMAN, CHARLES 1876–1938, British actor and director; JG directed him in *The Merchant of Venice* in 1932.

HICKS, DAVID 1928?–98, British interior designer.

HIGNETT, H. R. 1870–1959, British actor who first appeared with JG in 1925 in *Doctor Faustus*.

HILLER, WENDY 1912–2003, British actress; first worked with JG when he directed her in *The Cradle Song* in 1944.

HIRSCHFELD, AL 1903–2003, American cartoonist.

HITCHCOCK, ALFRED 1899–1980, British-born film director who directed JG in the 1936 film *The Secret Agent.*

HOBSON, HAROLD 1904–92, British theatre critic, mainly for the *Sunday Times.*

HOCKNEY, DAVID b. 1937, British painter, printmaker and designer.

HOFFMAN, DUSTIN b. 1937, American actor.

HOLDER, BARBARA MORLEY, British actress who appeared with JG in *The High Constable's Wife* in 1925.

HOLLAND, ANTHONY b. 1912, British stage designer.

HOLLIDAY, JUDY 1921–65, American actress.

HOLLOWAY, BALIOL 1883–1967, British actor who appeared with JG at the Old Vic in 1930 in *As You Like It.*

HOLLOWAY, STANLEY 1890–1982, British actor and singer.

HOLM, CELESTE b. 1919, American actress.

HOLMES, MARTIN, historian with a strong interest in Shakespeare.

HOPE-WALLACE, PHILIP, British theatre critic, notably for the *(Manchester) Guardian.*

HOPKINS, ANTHONY, b. 1937, Welsh actor.

HORNE, DAVID 1898–1970, British actor; first worked with JG in his 1939 production of *The Importance of Being Earnest.*

HORNE, LENA b. 1917, American singer and actress.

HOUSEMAN, JOHN 1902–88, Rumanian-born American actor, director and producer of the 1953 film of *Julius Caesar.*

HOUSTON, BILLIE 1906–72, Scottish variety artiste.

HOUSTON, RENEE, 1902–80, Scottish variety artiste, sister of Billie.

HOWARD, ALAN b. 1937, British actor.

HOWARD, LESLIE 1893–1943, British actor. He and JG worked together briefly early in their careers at the Oxford Playhouse in 1924–5.

HOWARD, TREVOR 1913–88, British actor who played Lopakhin in JG's 1954 production of *The Cherry Orchard.*

HOWARTH, DONALD b. 1931, British playwright.

HOWE, GEORGE 1900–86, British actor. After training together at RADA, JG worked with him more than any other actor.

HOWELL, JANE, British director; co-director of *Bingo* at the Royal Court in 1974.

HUDSON, ROCK 1925–85, American actor.

HUGGETT, RICHARD, Irish born actor and author, biographer of 'Binkie' Beaumont.

HULBERT, JACK 1892–1978, British actor, director and manager.

HUNT, MARTITA 1900–69, British actress; first worked with JG in *Holding out the Apple* in 1928.

HUNTER, N. C. 1908–71, British playwright; JG directed and appeared in his play *A Day by the Sea.*

HUNTER, ROSS 1920–96, American film producer responsible for the remake of *Lost Horizon* (1972).

HUNTINGDON, HELEN 1867–1950, American poet and novelist, second wife of Harley Granville-Barker.

HURRY, LESLIE 1909–78, British artist and designer who first worked with JG when he designed the décor for the British production of *Medea* in 1948.

HURT, JOHN b. 1940, British actor.

HUSSEIN, WARIS b. 1938, Indian-born stage, film and television director. He directed JG in *Half-Life* in 1977.

HUSSEY, OLIVIA b. 1951, Argentinean born British actress who appeared with JG in the 1972 remake of *Lost Horizon* in 1972.

HUSTON, WALTER 1884–1950, American actor, father of director John Huston.

HUTCHINSON, JEREMY b. 1915, third husband of Peggy Ashcroft.

HUTCHINSON, JOSEPHINE 1903–98, American actress.

HUXLEY, ALDOUS 1894–1963, British writer.

HUXLEY, MARGARET 1899–?, sister of Aldous.

HYDE-WHITE, WILFRID 1903–91, British actor.

HYSON, DOROTHY 1914–96, British actress whom JG directed in *Lady Windermere's Fan* in 1945; married Anthony Quayle.

IDEN, ROSALIND 1908–90, British actress, third wife of Donald Wolfit.

INGE, WILLIAM 1913–73, American playwright.

INGHAM, BARRIE b. 1934, British actor who first appeared with JG in *Henry VIII* in 1958.

IRELAND, ANTHONY 1902–57, British actor who first appeared with JG in *Three Sisters* at Barnes in 1926.

IRONS, JEREMY b. 1948, British actor; appeared with JG in the TV adaptation of *Brideshead Revisited* (1981).

IRVING, GEORGE S. b. 1922, American actor and singer who replaced Billy de Wolfe in *Irene*.

IRVING, HENRY 1838–1905, British actor, the first actor to be knighted.

ISHAM, VIRGINIA, British actress, sister of Gyles Isham, boyhood friends of JG.

ISHERWOOD, CHRISTOPHER 1904–86, British novelist.

JACKSON, EDITH d. 1996, secretary to Rex Harrison.

JACKSON, GLENDA b. 1936, British actress and politician.

JACOBI, DEREK b. 1938, British actor who appeared with JG in *Tartuffe* in 1967.

JAMESON, PAULINE b. 1920, British actress who first worked with JG when he directed her in *The Heiress* in 1949.

JANVRINE, JOHN, 'Binkie' Beaumont's doctor, Daphne Rye's second husband.

JARVIS, MARTIN b. 1941, British actor who appeared with JG in a reading of *Paradise Lost* in 1974.

JEANS, ISABEL 1891–1985, British actress; JG directed her twice, the first time in *Spring 1600* in 1934.

JEFFERS, ROBINSON 1887–1962, American playwright; JG directed his *Medea* in New York in 1947 and in London in 1948.

JEFFREY, PETER 1929–99, British actor who appeared with JG in the reading of *Paradise Lost* in 1974.

JENKINS, MEGS 1917–98, British actress whom JG directed in *A Day by the Sea* in 1953.

JENNINGS, ELIZABETH 1926–2001, British poet.

JERROLD, MARY 1877–1955, British actress; worked with JG several times, the first being when he directed her in *The Old Ladies* in 1935.

JOHN, AUGUSTUS 1878–1961, Welsh painter.

JOHNS, GLYNIS b. 1923, British actress.

JOHNSON, CELIA 1908–82, British actress; JG directed her in a charity show in 1934.

JOHNSON, PHILIP b. 1906, American architect.

JOHNSON, RICHARD b. 1927, British actor who first worked with JG in his 1944–5 season at the Theatre Royal, Haymarket.

JOHNSTONE, PINKIE, British actress who first worked with JG in *The School for Scandal* in 1962.

JONES, EMRYS 1915–72, Welsh actor who played Malcolm in JG's 1942 *Macbeth*.

JONES, JENNIFER b. 1919, American actress, married to David Selznick; appeared with JG in the film of *The Barretts of Wimpole Street* (1957).

JONES, RODERICK 1877–1962, head of Reuters, husband of Enid Bagnold.

JOURDAN, LOUIS b. 1919, French actor.

KAHN, ADDIE, MRS OTTO 1896–1956?, widow of the banker and philanthropist.

KAINZ, JOSEF 1858–1910, Austrian actor.

KANIN, GARSON 1912–99, American playwright and director, married to Ruth Gordon.

KANN, LILLI 1898–1978, German actress whom JG directed in *The Cradle Song* in 1944.

KAUFFER, E. McKNIGHT 1890–1959, American artist who designed the sets for JG's production of *Queen of Scots* in 1934.

KAUFMAN, GEORGE S. 1889–1961, American playwright, director and play doctor.

KAYE, DANNY 1913–87, American actor, comedian and singer.

KAYE, NORA 1920–87, American ballet dancer.

KAZAN, ELIA 1909–2003, Turkish-born American actor and director.

KEANE, DORIS 1881–1946, American actress.

KEANE, MOLLY (Mary Nesta Skrine) – see M. J. Farrell.

KEEN, MALCOLM 1888–1970, British actor who worked with JG for the first time when he played Shylock in the 1932 Old Vic production of *The Merchant of Venice*.

KELLERMAN, SALLY b. 1936, American actress who appeared with JG in the 1972 film *Lost Horizon*.

KELLY, FELIX 1914–94, British artist and designer who first worked with JG on *A Day by the Sea* in 1953.

KELLY, PATSY 1910–81, American actress; played Mrs O'Dare in *Irene*, the 1972 American musical from which JG was sacked.

KEMPSON, RACHEL 1910–2003, British actress, wife of Michael Redgrave; first worked with JG in *The School for Scandal* in 1937.

KENDAL, MADGE 1840–1935, British actress.

KENDALL, HENRY (Harry) 1897–1962, British actor.

KENDALL, KAY 1926–1959, British actress married to Rex Harrison.

KERR, DEBORAH b. 1921, British actress who appeared with JG in the 1952 film of *Julius Caesar*. Married (1) Anthony Bartley; (2) Peter Viertel.

KERR, JEAN 1923–2003, American playwright married to Walter Kerr.

KERR, WALTER 1913–96, American theatre critic of the *New York Herald Tribune* and later the *New York Times*.

KILTY, JEROME b. 1922, American actor and playwright. JG appeared in his adaptation of Thornton Wilder's *The Ides of March* in 1963, which he also directed.

KING, DENNIS 1897–1971, British-born actor who followed JG as Jason in *Medea*, 1947.

KING, FRANCIS b. 1923, British novelist and critic.

KINGSLEY, SIDNEY 1906–95, American playwright.

KIRSTEIN, LINCOLN 1907–96, dance impresario, founder of New York City Ballet.

KITCHEN, MICHAEL b. 1948, British actor who appeared with JG in *No Man's Land* 1976.

KITT, EARTHA b. 1927, American singer and actress.

KOMISARJEVSKY, THEODORE 1882–1954, Russian director and designer; he and JG first worked together when Komis directed JG in *Three Sisters* in 1926.

KORDA, ALEXANDER 1893–1956, Hungarian-born film producer and director.

KRAMER, STANLEY 1913–2001, American film director.

KUBELIK, RAFAEL 1914–66, Czech conductor and composer.

LACEY, CATHERINE 1904–79, British actress who appeared with JG in *The Maitlands* in 1934.

LAHR, JOHN b. 1941, American critic, son of Bert Lahr.

LAINE, CLEO b. 1927, British singer and actress, married to John Dankworth.

LANCASTER, BURT 1913–94, American actor.

LANCHESTER, ELSA 1902–86, British actress, wife of Charles Laughton.

LANE, DOROTHY 1890–1984, British actress who first worked with JG in his 1944–5 season at the Theatre Royal, Haymarket.

LANG, HAROLD 1923–70, British actor, director and teacher; appeared with JG in *Much Ado about Nothing* and *King Lear* in 1955.

LANG, ROBERT b. 1934, British actor.

LANGHAM, MICHAEL b. 1919, British director who acted as assistant to Anthony Quayle on the 1950 Stratford-upon-Avon production of *Julius Caesar*.

LANGNER, LAWRENCE 1890–1962, joint Administrative Director of the Theatre Guild.

LANGTON, BASIL C. 1912–2003, British actor and manager.

LAUGHTON, CHARLES 1899–1962, British actor; married to Elsa Lanchester.

LAURENCE, PAULA b. 1916, American actress; took over the part of Zinaida for the US production of *Ivanov*.

LAURIE, JOHN 1897–1980, Scottish actor who appeared with JG in the 1925 production of *Two Gentlemen of Verona*.

LAWRENCE, GERTRUDE 1898–1952, British actress and singer; JG directed her in a charity performance in 1934.

LAWSON, WILFRID 1900–66, British actor.

LAYE, EVELYN 1900–96, British actress and musical comedy star; JG appeared with her in a charity show in 1935.

LEACH, ROSEMARY b. 1925, British actress; appeared with JG in the TV series *Summer's Lease* (1989).

LEAN, DAVID 1908–91, British film director.

LEE, CANADA, 1907–52, American actor.

LEES-MILNE, JAMES 1908–97, British architectural historian, biographer and diarist.

LE GALLIENNE, EVA 1899–1991, British-born actress and director.

LEHMANN, JOHN 1907–87, British poet, publisher and editor.

LEHMANN, LOTTE 1888–1976, German soprano.

LEIDER, JERRY, American producer who co-produced J G's US tour of *Ages of Man* in 1958.

LEIGH, VIVIEN 1913–67, British actress, second wife of Laurence Olivier; first worked with JG as the Queen in his OUDS production of *Richard II* in 1936.

LEIGHTON, MARGARET 1922–76, British actress; first worked with JG when he directed her as Lady Macbeth to Ralph Richardson's Macbeth at Stratford-upon-Avon in 1952.

LENYA, LOTTE 1898–1991, Austrian-born actress and singer, and wife of Kurt Weill.

LESLEY, COLE 1909–80, Noël Coward's personal assistant and biographer.

LEVIN, BERNARD b. 1928, dramatic critic and journalist.

LEVINE, SOL d. 1996, American film producer.

LEWIS, CECIL 1898–1997, author and broadcaster.

LEWIS, ROBERT (Bobby) 1909–97, American director.

LIBERACE (Wladzin Valentino) 1919–87, American pianist and entertainer who also appeared in *The Loved One* (1965).

LIDE, MILLER, American actor who appeared with JG in the US production of *Ivanov* in 1966.

LIEBERSON, BRIGITTA 1917–2003, German-born actress and ballerina Vera Zorina, wife of Goddard Lieberson and formerly married to George Balanchine, choreographer.

LIEBERSON, GODDARD 1911–77, composer, record producer and president of Columbia Records.

LILLIE, BEATRICE (Lady Peel) 1894–1989, Canadian-born revue artist; appeared with JG in *Hands Across the Sea* in 1940 and on his wartime ENSA tour.

LINKLATER, ERIC 1899–1974, British novelist and writer for radio; JG directed his *Crisis in Heaven* in 1944.

LION, LEON M. 1879–1947, British actor and manager.

LISTER, FRANCIS 1899–1951, British actor who first appeared with JG in *Richard of Bordeaux* in 1933.

LISTER, MOIRA b. 1923, British actress; appeared with JG in his 1955 season at the Palace Theatre.

LITTLEWOOD, JOAN 1914–2002, British theatre director and joint founder of Theatre Workshop.

LIVESEY, ROGER 1906–76, British actor who first appeared with JG in *Musical Chairs* in 1931.

LLOYD, FREDERICK 1880–1949, British actor; appeared with JG on a number of occasions, the first being in 1929 when he played Jacob Engstrand in *Ghosts*.

LLOYD, MARIE 1870–1922, British music-hall artiste.

LOCKE, PHILIP b. 1928, British actor who appeared with JG in *Oedipus* in 1968.

LOCKWOOD, MARGARET 1916–90, British actress.

LÖHR, MARIE 1890–1975, British actress; first worked with JG in a charity show in 1939.

LOMAS, HERBERT 1887–1961, British actor who first worked with JG in *Richard II* in 1952.

LONSDALE, MICHEL b. 1931, French actor.

LOOS, ANITA 1888–1981, American writer of *Gentlemen Prefer Blondes* amongst other things.

LOSEY, JOSEPH 1909–84, American film director, long resident in Britain.

LOWE, ARTHUR 1915–82, British actor who first worked with JG as Stephano in the 1974 National Theatre production of *The Tempest*.

LUMET, SIDNEY b. 1924, American film director.

LUNT, ALFRED 1892–1977, American actor; husband of Lynn Fontanne.

LYMAN, DOROTHY b. 1947, American actress who appeared with JG in *The Battle of Shrivings* in 1970.

LYNN, RALPH 1882–1962, British actor best known for the Aldwych farces of the 1920s.

LYUBIMOV, YURI b. 1917, Russian director.

MAC LIAMMÓIR, MICHEÁL 1899–1978, British-born actor; appeared with JG in the 1959 US tour of *Much Ado about Nothing*.

MacGRATH, LEUEEN 1914–92, British-born actress.

MacGRAW, ALI b. 1938, American actress.

MacINNES, COLIN 1914–76, British novelist.

MACKAY, ANGUS, British actor married to Dorothy Reynolds.

MACKENZIE, RONALD 1903–32, British playwright; JG appeared in his plays *Musical Chairs* (1931) and *The Maitlands* (1934).

MACKINLAY, JEAN STERLING 1882–1958, Scottish singer, wife of Harcourt Williams.

MacLAINE, SHIRLEY b. 1934, American actress.

MacMAHON, ALINE 1899–1991, American actress engaged to play the Nurse in JG's 1947 production of *Medea* but replaced by Florence Reed.

MacOWAN, MICHAEL b. 1906, British director.

MACRAE, ARTHUR 1908–62, British actor and playwright.

MACREADY, W. C. (William Charles) 1793–1873, British actor-manager.

McANALLY, RAY 1926–89, Irish actor who appeared with JG in *The Best of Friends* in 1988.

McCARTHY, DESMOND 1877–1952, British critic, notably the *Sunday Times*.

McCLINTIC, GUTHRIE 1893–1961, American director, married to Katherine Cornell; directed JG in the 1936 US production of *Hamlet*.

McCOWEN, ALEC b. 1925, British actor.

McDOWALL, RODDY 1928–98, British-born actor and photographer.

McDOWELL, MALCOLM b. 1943, British actor who played the title role in the 1979 film *Caligula*.

McEWAN, GERALDINE b. 1932, British actress; took over as Lady Teazle for the US tour of *The School for Scandal* in 1963.

McGOOHAN, PATRICK b. 1928, American-born actor who appeared with JG in the TV version of *The Best of Friends* (1991).

McHUGH, HARRY ('Mac') 1887–1974, JG's dresser.

McKELLEN, IAN b. 1939, British actor.

McKENNA, SIOBHAN 1922–86, Irish actress who played Lady Macduff in JG's 1952 production of *Macbeth* at Stratford-upon-Avon.

McKENNA, VIRGINIA b. 1931, British actress; first worked with JG when she played Perdita in the 1951 production of *The Winter's Tale*.

McMANUS, MARK 1935–94, Scottish actor who played Mark Antony in the 1977 production of *Julius Caesar*.

MAGEE, PATRICK 1924–82, Irish actor who appeared with JG in *The Battle of Shrivings* (1970).

MAGNANI, ANNA 1908–73, Italian actress.

MALLESON, MILES 1888–1969, British actor and playwright; first appeared with JG in his 1943 production of *Love for Love*.

MANDER, RAYMOND 1911–1983, British theatre historian.

MANGO, ALEC, British actor who played Ross in JG's 1942 production of *Macbeth*.

MANKIEWICZ, JOSEPH 1909–93, American film director who directed the 1953 film of *Julius Caesar* in which JG played Cassius.

MANSFIELD, KATHERINE 1888–1923, New Zealand short story writer.

MARAIS, JEAN 1913–98, French actor, lover of Jean Cocteau.

MARCH, FREDRIC 1897–1975, American actor.

MAGARSHACK, DAVID, Translator of Russian novels and plays.

MARKHAM, MONTE b. 1938, American actor; leading man in *Irene*, which JG directed in 1972.

MARSH, EDWARD 1872–1953, British civil servant, classicist, translator, patron of the arts and supporter of JG in early years.

MARSH, LINDA, American actress who played Ophelia in JG's 1964 US production of *Hamlet*.

MARSHALL, ARTHUR 1910–89?, British writer and humorist.

MARSHALL, HERBERT 1890–1966, British actor, husband of Edna Best.

MARTIN, MARY 1913–90, American actress and singer.

MARTIN, MILLICENT b. 1934, British actress and singer.

MASEFIELD, JOHN 1878–1967, Poet Laureate, novelist, playwright and critic.

MASON, BREWSTER 1922–87, British actor who first worked with JG in *The Winter's Tale* in 1951.

MASON, JAMES 1909–84, British actor; first worked with JG in the latter's production of *Queen of Scots* in 1934.

MASSEY, ANNA b. 1937, British actress; first appeared with JG in *The Last Joke* in 1960.

MASSEY, DANIEL 1933–98, British actor; first appeared with JG in his 1962 production of *The School for Scandal*.

MASSEY, RAYMOND 1896–1983, Canadian actor, father of Anna and Daniel Massey; married to Adrianne Allen.

MATHIS, JOHNNY b. 1935, American singer.

MATTHEWS, A. E. (Alfred Edward) 1869–1960, British actor; took over as Sir Richard Furze in JG's 1938 production of *Spring Meeting*.

MAUGHAM, W. SOMERSET 1874–1965, British novelist, short story writer and play-wright; JG appeared in, and directed, a number of his plays.

MAXWELL, ELSA 1881–1963, American socialite and party-giver.

MAYNE, FERDY 1916–98, German-born actor who appeared with JG in the 1946 production of *Crime and Punishment*.

MENDES, SAM b. 1956, British theatre and film director.

MENOTTI, GIAN-CARLO, b. 1911, Italian-born composer.

MERCER, MABEL 1900–84, American singer.

MERCHANT, VIVIEN 1929–82, British actress, first wife of Harold Pinter.

MEREDITH, BURGESS 1907–97, American actor.

MERIVALE, JOHN (Jack) 1917–90, Canadian-born actor, companion of Vivien Leigh in her later years; took over as Lvov for the US tour of *Ivanov* in 1966.

MERMAN, ETHEL 1908–84, American musical comedy actress.

MERRALL, MARY 1890–1973, British actress.

MERRICK, DAVID 1911–2000, American producer.

MERRICK, JIM 1924?–99, American casting director?

MESSEL, LEONARD d. 1953, stockbroker and grandfather of Oliver Messel.

MESSEL, OLIVER 1904–78, British stage designer; worked with JG several times, notably on *The Lady's Not for Burning.*

MESSINA, CEDRIC d. 1993, British producer director who made the TV version of *Heartbreak House* (1977) in which JG played Captain Shotover.

MICHAEL, RALPH 1907–94, British actor who played Jason in JG's 1948 London production of *Medea.*

MIELZINER, JO 1901–76, American stage designer, including the 1936 US production of *Hamlet.*

MILES, BERNARD 1907–91, British actor, director and producer; founder of the Mermaid Theatre.

MILES, SARAH b. 1941, British actress who appeared in JG's 1961 production of *Dazzling Prospect*; married to Robert Bolt.

MILLER, GILBERT 1884–1969, American producer, including *The Patriot* in New York in 1927, JG's first American appearance.

MILLER, JOHN, b. 1937, British journalist, biographer and critic.

MILLER, JONATHAN b. 1934, British theatre and television director who directed JG in the TV version of *Alice in Wonderland* (1966) and in *From Chekhov with Love* (1968).

MILLS, GRACE 1883–1972, American actress who appeared in JG's 1947 New York production of *Medea.*

MILLS, HAYLEY b. 1946, British actress, daughter of John Mills.

MILLS, JOHN b. 1908, British actor whom JG directed in *Charley's Aunt* in 1954.

MILNE, A. A. 1882–1956, British author, dramatist and lyricist.

MILTON, ERNEST 1890–1974, American-born actor who first appeared with JG in *Katerina* in 1926 at Barnes Theatre.

MINNELLI, LIZA b. 1946, American actress and singer; appeared with JG in the *Arthur* films (1981, 1988).

MINOTIS, ALEXIS 1900–90, Greek actor; cast as Porfiry in the New York production of *Crime and Punishment* but replaced before opening by Vladimir Sokolow.

MIRREN, HELEN b. 1945, British actress.

MISTINGUETT 1872–1956, French music-hall and cabaret performer.

MITCHELL, JULIAN b. 1935, British playwright; JG appeared in his play *Half-Life* in 1977.

MITCHELL, WARREN b. 1926, British actor.

MITCHELL, YVONNE 1925–79, British actress who first worked with JG in his 1944 production of *The Cradle Song.*

MITCHENSON, JOE 1911–92, British theatre historian.

MOISSI, ALEXANDER 1879–1935, Italian-born Albanian actor.

MOLYNEUX, EDWARD 1891–1974, British couturier.

MONTAND, YVES 1921–91, French actor.

MONTGOMERY, BERNARD LAW 1887–1976, British World War II soldier.

MONTGOMERY, ELIZABETH 1902–93, with sisters Margaret and Sophia Harris, a designer who worked as Motley.

MOORE, DUDLEY 1935–2002, British actor and pianist; appeared with JG in the *Arthur* films (1981, 1988).

MOORE, GENE 1910–98, window designer for Tiffany's.

MOOREHEAD, AGNES 1900–74, American actress.

MOOREHEAD, ALAN 1910–83, British writer and journalist.

MORCOM, JIMMIE d. 1988?, American scenic designer.

MORE, KENNETH 1914–82, British actor.

MORGAN, CHARLES 1894–1958, theatre critic of *The Times*, 1926–39, and playwright.

MORGAN, MARGERY M., Lecturer in English, author of *A Drama of Political Man*.

MORLEY, ROBERT 1908–92, British actor and playwright; directed by JG in Peter Ustinov's *Halfway up the Tree* in 1967.

MORLEY, SHERIDAN b. 1941. Biographer, including JG's official life (2000).

MORRISON, PAUL 1906–80, American lighting designer; worked as JG's assistant on the 1947 New York production of *Medea*.

MORSE, BARRY b. 1918, British-born actor who appeared in JG's 1944 production of *Crisis in Heaven*.

MORSE, BEN, American stage manager and secretary to JG.

MORSE, ROBERT b. 1931, American actor who appeared with JG in the film of *The Loved One* (1964).

MORTIMER, JOHN b. 1923, British barrister, novelist and playwright; JG appeared in his TV adaptation of Evelyn Waugh's *Brideshead Revisited* (1981) and in his own *Summer's Lease* (1989).

MOSTEL, ZERO 1915–77, American actor.

MOTLEY, name under which the sisters Margaret and Sophia Harris worked with Elizabeth Montgomery.

MUNDAY, PENELOPE b. 1926, British actress; first worked with JG when she played Margaret in his 1952 production of *Much Ado about Nothing*.

MURDOCH, IRIS 1919–99, British novelist.

MURPHY, GERALD 1888–1964, American artist, the inspiration for Dick Diver in F. Scott Fitzgerald's *The Great Gatsby*.

MURRAY, BARBARA b. 1929, British actress who appeared with JG in the TV version of *Heartbreak House* (1977).

MURRAY, BILL b. 1950, American actor.

MURRAY, BRIAN b. 1937, South African-born actor who played Cassio in the 1961 production of *Othello* at Stratford-upon-Avon.

MURRY, JOHN MIDDLETON 1889–1957, critic and editor, married to Katherine Mansfield.

MYERS, RICHARD 1888–1958, American businessman and arts lover.

NAISMITH, LAURENCE 1908–92, British actor who played Sir Oliver Surface in JG's 1962 production of *The School for Scandal*.

NARES, OWEN 1888–1943, British actor.

NASH, GEORGE 1873–1945, American actor who played the First Gravedigger in the 1936 US production of *Hamlet.*

NATWICK, MILDRED 1905–94, American actress.

NEILSON-TERRY, PHYLLIS 1892–1977, British actress and JG's second cousin; he first worked with her on her tour of *The Wheel* in 1922.

NELSON, BARRY b. 1920, American actor.

NESBITT, CATHLEEN 1888–1982, British actress with whom JG first worked in 1926 in *Confession.*

NESBITT, ROBERT 1906–95, British theatre producer, notably of variety spectaculars.

NEVILLE, JOHN b. 1925, British actor; JG directed him as Joseph Surface in his 1962 production of *The School for Scandal,* and later took over the part himself.

NEVINSON, NANCY b. 1918, British actress who appeared with JG on the ENSA tour in 1945.

NEWLEY, ANTHONY 1931–98, British actor and writer.

NEWMAN, ERNEST 1868–1959, British music critic.

NEWMAN, PAUL b. 1925, American actor.

NICHOLLS, ANTHONY 1902–77, British actor who appeared with JG in his 1955 season at the Palace Theatre.

NICHOLS, BEVERLEY 1898–1983, British novelist, journalist and playwright.

NICHOLS, DANDY 1907–86, British actress who played Marjorie in the 1970 production of *Home.*

NICHOLS, MIKE b. 1931, American actor and director.

NICHOLSON, NORA 1892–1973, British actress who appeared with JG for the first time in the 1925 production of *The Cherry Orchard.*

NIKOLAEFF, ARIADNE, Russian translator.

NILSSON, BIRGIT b. 1922, Swedish soprano.

NOGUCHI, ISAMU 1904–88, Japanese artist who designed the 1955 production of *King Lear.*

NOVELLO, IVOR 1893–1951, Welsh actor-manager and composer; one of the many who appeared with JG in *The Players' Masque for Marie Tempest* in 1935.

NUNN, TREVOR b. 1940, British theatre and film director, formerly Director of the Royal Shakespeare Company and, later, the National Theatre; married (1) to Janet Suzman.

NUREYEV, RUDOLF 1938–93, Russian ballet dancer and choreographer.

NYE, PAT 1908–94, British actress who appeared with JG in *Caesar and Cleopatra* in 1971, at Chichester Festival Theatre.

OBEY, ANDRÉ 1892–1975, French playwright. JG played Noah in the 1935 production of Obey's play of the same name.

O'BRIEN, EDMOND 1915–85, American actor who played Casca in the 1953 film of *Julius Caesar.*

ODETS, CLIFFORD 1906–63, American playwright.

OLIVER, EDNA MAY 1883–1942, American actress.

OLIVER, VIC 1898–1964, Austrian-born comedian, married to Sarah Churchill.

OLIVIER, LAURENCE 1907–89, British actor, manager and director, first Director of the National Theatre. He and JG appeared only once in a play together when

JG directed him in *Romeo and Juliet* in 1934, but later they appeared together in films.

O'NEILL, EUGENE 1888–1953, American playwright.

OSBORNE, JOHN 1929–94, British playwright.

O'SHEA, TESSIE 1913–95, Welsh entertainer and actress.

O'TOOLE, PETER b. 1932, Irish-born actor who appeared with JG in the film *Caligula* (1979); married to Siân Phillips.

PAGE, ANTHONY b. 1935, British director.

PAGE, GERALDINE 1924–87, American actress.

PAGETT, NICOLA b. 1945, British actress.

PALANCE, JACK b. 1919, American actor.

PALMER, LILLI 1914–86, German actress, married to (1) Rex Harrison, (2) Carlos Thompson. She appeared with JG in the 1936 film *The Secret Agent*.

PALMER, TONY, British film and TV director; directed the film *Wagner* (1983) in which JG played Pfistermeister.

PAPAS, IRENE b. 1928, Greek actress.

PARKER, CECIL 1897–1971, British actor who first appeared with JG in *The Constant Nymph* in 1926.

PARKER, DOROTHY 1893–1967, American critic and writer.

PARKINSON, NORMAN 1913–90, British fashion and portrait photographer.

PARRY, NATASHA b. 1930, British actress, married to Peter Brook; JG directed her in his 1954 production of *Charley's Aunt*.

PASCAL, GABRIEL 1894–1954, Hungarian born film producer and director.

PASCO, RICHARD b. 1926, British actor who played Lvov in JG's 1965 production of *Ivanov*.

PATRICK, ROBERT b. 1937, American playwright.

PAXINOU, KATINA 1900–73, Greek actress.

PAYN, GRAHAM b. 1918, South African-born actor and singer, partner of Noël Coward.

PEARSON, RICHARD b. 1918, British actor who appeared with JG in *Half-Life* in 1977.

PECK, GREGORY 1916–2003, American actor.

PEMBERTON, REECE, British designer, first worked with JG when he designed the set for *Indian Summer* in 1951.

PENNA, TARVER OR TARVA, British actor who played Lennox in JG's 1942 production of *Macbeth*.

PENNINGTON, MICHAEL b. 1943, British actor who appeared with JG in the TV series *Summer's Lease* in 1989.

PERCY, ESMÉ 1887–1957, British actor who first appeared with JG in *Douaumont* in 1929.

PERKINS, ANTHONY 1932–92, American actor.

PERRY, JOHN 1906–95, Irish-born actor, manager and co-author of several plays with the Irish writer Molly Keane; lover of JG in the 1920s and 30s.

PETTINGELL, FRANK 1891–1966, British actor who first appeared with JG in *The Good Companions* in 1931.

PHILIPPE, GÉRARD 1922–59, French actor.

PHILLIPS, ROBIN b. 1941, British actor and director who worked with JG on *Caesar and Cleopatra* in 1971.

PHILLIPS, SIÂN b. 1934, Welsh actress whom JG directed in *The Gay Lord Quex* in 1975; married (1) to Peter O'Toole.

PIAF, EDITH 1915–63, French cabaret singer and songwriter.

PICKUP, RONALD b. 1940, British actor who appeared with JG in *Oedipus* in 1968.

PINTER, HAROLD b. 1930, British playwright and poet; JG played Spooner in his *No Man's Land* in 1975.

PIPER, JOHN 1903–92, British painter, printmaker and designer.

PIRANDELLO, LUIGI 1867–1936, Italian novelist and playwright; JG twice appeared in his play *The Man with a Flower in his Mouth*.

PITCHER, GEORGE b. 1925, Princeton professor of philosophy, partner of Edward (Ed) T. Cone, composer and professor of music.

PLAYFAIR, NIGEL 1874–1934, British actor-manager who directed JG in *The Insect Play* in 1923.

PLEASENCE, ANGELA, British actress.

PLOWRIGHT, JOAN b. 1929, British actress, third wife of Laurence Olivier; appeared with JG in *Tartuffe* in 1967.

PLUMMER, CHRISTOPHER b. 1927, Canadian actor who appeared with JG in the film *Murder by Decree* (1978).

POEL, WILLIAM 1852–1934, British director.

PORTER, ERIC 1928–95, British actor who appeared in JG's 1952–3 season at the Lyric Theatre, Hammersmith.

PORTMAN, ERIC 1903–69, British actor.

POWELL, ANTHONY 1905–2000, British novelist.

POWELL, MICHAEL 1905–90, British film producer and director.

POWER, TYRONE 1913–58, American actor.

PREMINGER, OTTO 1906–86, Austrian-born film producer, director and actor.

PRESTON, KERRISON 1884–1974, British solicitor and art historian.

PRICE, LEONTYNE b. 1927, American soprano.

PRICE, VINCENT 1911–96, American actor, married to Coral Browne.

PRIESTLEY, J. B. 1894–1984, novelist, playwright and essayist; JG appeared in the stage adaptation of his *The Good Companions* in 1931.

PRINCE, HAROLD (Hal) b. 1928, American director, particularly of musicals.

PROCKTOR, PATRICK 1936–2003, British artist.

QUARTERMAINE, LEON 1876–1967, British actor; first appeared with JG when he took over as Mercutio from Laurence Olivier in JG's 1935 production of *Romeo and Juliet*.

QUAYLE, ANTHONY 1913–89, British actor and director; first worked with JG in 1932 when he appeared in *Richard of Bordeaux*; married to Dorothy Hyson.

QUINN, ANTHONY 1915–2001, Mexican-born actor.

QUINTERO, JOSÉ 1924–99, Panamanian-born director.

RABB, ELLIS 1903–98, American actor.

RAINS, CLAUDE 1889–1967, British actor; taught JG at RADA and appeared with him in *The Insect Play* in 1923.

RAMBERT, MARIE 1888–1982, Polish-born British ballet dancer and teacher.

RANALOW, FREDERICK 1873–1953, British actor and singer who appeared with JG in a charity performance in 1935.

RANDALL, JULIAN 1916–98, British actor who appeared with JG in his 1945 ENSA tour of *Hamlet* and *Blithe Spirit*.

RANDALL, TONY b. 1920, American actor.

RATHBONE, BASIL 1892–1967, South African-born actor.

RATTIGAN, TERENCE 1911–77, British playwright; JG directed his *Variation on a Theme* in 1958 and appeared in an American TV production of *The Browning Version.*

RAWLINGS, MARGARET 1906–96, British actress who played Mrs Dearth in JG's production of *Dear Brutus* in 1941.

REA, OLIVER, American producer.

REDFIELD, WILLIAM 1927–76, American actor who played Guildenstern in JG's 1964 US production of *Hamlet.*

REDFORD, ROBERT b. 1937, American actor, film director and producer.

REDGRAVE, LYNN b. 1943, British actress, younger daughter of Michael Redgrave.

REDGRAVE, MICHAEL 1908–85, British actor, married to Rachel Kempson, father of Corin, Lynn and Vanessa; appeared with JG in his 1937–8 season at the Queen's Theatre.

REDGRAVE, VANESSA b. 1937, British actress who appeared with JG in the film *The Charge of the Light Brigade* (1968); married to Tony Richardson.

REDMAN, JOYCE b. 1918, Irish-born actress.

REED, FLORENCE 1883–1967, American actress who played the Nurse in JG's 1947 New York production of *Medea.*

REED, JOE, American producer.

REED, REX b. 1940, American journalist, critic and actor.

REEVE, ADA 1874–1966, British actress and music hall artist who played Dotey Cregan in JG's 1944 production of *The Last of Summer.*

REID, BERYL 1920–96, British actress.

REID, KATE 1930–93, Canadian-born actress.

REINHARDT, MAX 1873–1943, Austrian theatre and film director.

RESNAIS, ALAIN b. 1922, French film director who made *Providence* in which JG played Clive Langham (1976).

REYNOLDS, DEBBIE b. 1932, American actress who played Irene in the show of that name from which JG was sacked as director in the US in 1972.

REYNOLDS, DOROTHY 1913–77, British actress, co-author of *Salad Days;* she first appeared with JG as the Matron in *Forty Years On* in 1968.

RHODES, MARJORIE 1903–79, British actress.

RICHARDSON, IAN b. 1934, Scottish actor.

RICHARDSON, RALPH 1902–83, British actor; the first of many occasions on which he worked with JG was in a play called *Prejudice* in 1928.

RICHARDSON, TONY 1928–91, British theatre and film director; made two films in which JG appeared, *The Loved One* (1964) and *The Charge of the Light Brigade* (1968); married to Vanessa Redgrave.

RICKETTS, CHARLES 1866–1931, British costume designer.

RIGBY, HARRY C. 1925–85, American producer of *Irene* (1972).

RIGG, DIANA b. 1938, British actress.

RITCHARD, CYRIL 1897–1977, Australian actor and musical comedy performer, played Algernon in JG's 1942 production of *The Importance of Being Earnest.*

RITMAN, WILLIAM, American designer, including the 1964 New York production of *Tiny Alice* in which JG played Julian.

RIVERA, CHITA b. 1933, American actress and singer.

ROBARDS JR., JASON 1922–2000, American actor; JG directed him in *Big Fish, Little Fish*, New York, 1961, married to Lauren Bacall.

ROBBINS, JEROME 1918–98, American dancer, choreographer and director.

ROBERTS, RACHEL 1927–80, Welsh actress, married to Rex Harrison.

ROBERTSON, W. GRAHAM 1866–1948, painter and illustrator.

ROBESON, PAUL 1898–1976, American singer and actor.

ROBEY, EDWARD, London magistrate, son of George Robey.

ROBEY, GEORGE 1869–1954, British music-hall performer and actor; who appeared with JG in *The Players' Masque for Marie Tempest* in 1935.

ROBSON, FLORA 1902–84, British actress; she and JG first worked together at the Oxford Playhouse in 1924.

ROEHRICK, WILLIAM 1911–95, American actor who played Guildenstern in the 1936 US production of *Hamlet.*

ROGERS, PAUL b. 1917, British actor who appeared with JG in *Volpone* and *Half-Life* in 1977.

ROOSE-EVANS, JAMES b. 1927, British theatre director; directed *The Best of Friends* in 1988, JG's last stage play.

ROSE, GEORGE 1920–88, British actor who first worked with JG when he played Dogberry in the 1949 production of *Much Ado about Nothing.*

ROSENTHAL, JEAN 1912–69, American lighting designer; lit JG's US productions of *Hamlet* (1962) and *Ivanov* (1966).

ROSMER, MILTON 1881–1971, British actor; JG was directed by him at RADA and worked with him on several occasions subsequently.

ROTH, PHILIP b. 1933, American novelist married to Claire Bloom.

ROTHSCHILD, VICTOR 1910–90, British zoologist, bibliophile and first head of the government 'think tank' from 1970–4.

ROUTLEDGE, PATRICIA b. 1929, British actress.

ROWLAND, TOBY 1916–94, American-born impresario who worked for H. M. Tennent Ltd before becoming an independent producer.

RUDKIN, DAVID b. 1936, British playwright.

RUDMAN, MICHAEL, American theatre director.

RUSH, GEOFFREY b. 1951, Australian actor.

RUSSELL, KEN b. 1927, British film and television director.

RUTHERFORD, MARGARET 1892–1972, British actress who first worked with JG when he directed her in *Spring Meeting* in 1938.

RYE, DAPHNE, casting director for H. M. Tennent Ltd.

RYLANDS, GEORGE ('Dadie') 1902–99, Fellow of King's College, Cambridge and noted commentator on Shakespeare; directed the 1944 production of *Hamlet.*

SACKVILLE-WEST, EDWARD 1901–56, musicologist and BBC features producer of *Pilgrim's Progress* with JG in 1940.

SAINT-DENIS, MICHEL 1897–1971, French-born theatre director and teacher; directed JG on three occasions, the first being *Noah* in 1935.

SAINT-DENIS (NEE MAGITO), SURIA 1903–88, French actress and teacher, wife of Michel Saint-Denis; assisted JG with music and mime on several productions.

SALVINI, TOMMASO 1829–1915, Italian actor.

SARRUF, VALERIE b. 1940, British actress who appeared with JG in *The Ides of March* in 1963.

SASSOON, SIEGFRIED 1886–1967, British poet and autobiographer.

SAVILLE, VICTOR 1897–1970, British film producer and director.

SCALES, PRUNELLA b. 1932, British actress who appeared with JG in poetry readings.

SCHAEFER, GEORGE 1920–97, American film and television director.

SCHEAR, ROBERT (Bob), American stage manager, who first worked with JG as assistant to the producer on *Ages of Man* in 1958.

SCHELL, MARIA b. 1926, Austrian actress who appeared with JG in the TV film *Inside the Third Reich*.

SCHLESINGER, JOHN 1926–2003, British theatre and film director; directed JG in *Julius Caesar* at the National Theatre in 1977.

SCHLESINGER, PETER, friend of David Hockney.

SCHNEIDER, ALAN 1917–84, Russian born American theatre director.

SCHNEIDER, MARIA b. 1952, French actress, who appeares with JG in the 1976 film *Caligula*.

SCOFIELD, PAUL b. 1922, British actor who first appeared with JG in 1952 when he played Don Pedro in *Much Ado about Nothing*.

SCOTT, GEORGE C. 1927–99, American actor.

SEARLE, ALAN, Somerset Maugham's secretary.

SEELEY, TIM b. 1936, British actor; directed by JG in *Variation on a Theme* in 1952 but was replaced before the West End by Jeremy Brett.

SEIDMANN, PAUL-EMILE DR, husband of Ginette Spanier.

SELLARS, PETER b. 1957, American theatre and opera director.

SELLERS, PETER 1925–80, British actor.

SELZNICK, IRENE MAYER 1907–90, American producer, daughter of Louis B. Mayer (of MGM), ex-wife of David Selznick; co-producer of *The Chalk Garden* in 1956.

SERAFIN, TULLIO (1878–1968), Italian conductor.

SERVOSS, MARY 1881–1968, American actress.

SEYLER, ATHENE 1889–1990, British actress; she first worked with JG when she played the Czarina in *Red Sunday* in 1929.

SEYMOUR, JANE b. 1951, British actress who appeared with JG in the TV serial *War and Remembrance* (1987).

SHAFFER, ANTHONY 1926–2001, British playwright best known for *Sleuth*.

SHAFFER, PETER b. 1926, British playwright; JG directed his first stage play *Five Finger Exercise* in 1958 and appeared in *The Battle of Shrivings* in 1970.

SHARAFF, IRENE 1910–93, American costume designer.

SHAW, FIONA b. 1958, Irish actress.

SHAW, GEORGE BERNARD 1856–1950, Irish playwright; JG played in eight of Shaw's plays, the first being *Captain Brassbound's Conversion* at the Oxford Playhouse in 1924.

SHAW, GLEN BYAM 1904–86, British actor and director; worked with J G for the first time in *Queen of Scots* in 1934; married to Angela Baddeley.

SHAW, MARTIN b. 1945, British actor who appeared with J G in *The Battle of Shrivings* in 1970.

SHEARER, NORMA 1902–83, American actress.

SHELDON, EDWARD 1886–1946, American playwright and dramaturg.

SHERWOOD, MADELEINE b. 1922, Canadian-born actress; J G directed her in *All Over* in 1971.

SHERWOOD, ROBERT 1896–1955, American playwright.

SHUARD, AMY 1924–75, British soprano who sang Cassandra in J G's 1957 production of *The Trojans*.

SIGNORET, SIMONE 1921–85, French actress.

SIMMONS, JEAN b. 1929, British actress; married to Stewart Granger.

SIMPSON, MAY, Noël Coward's Jamaican housekeeper.

SINDEN, DONALD b. 1923, British actor whom J G directed in *The Heiress* in 1949.

SITWELL, EDITH 1887–1964, British poet.

SKINNER, OTIS 1858–1942, American actor, producer, writer and director.

SMITH, DODIE 1896–1990, British novelist and playwright; J G played Nicholas in her *Dear Octopus* in 1938; married to Alec Beesley.

SMITH, MAGGIE b. 1934, British actress; J G directed her and her then husband Robert Stephens in *Private Lives* in 1972.

SMITH, OLIVER 1918–94, American producer.

SMITH, REGINALD, British actor who first worked with J G at the Oxford Playhouse in 1924 in *Captain Brassbound's Conversion*.

SMYTH, DAME ETHEL 1858–1944, British composer.

SOFAER, ABRAHAM 1896–1988, British actor who appeared with J G in *Gloriana* in 1925.

SOKOLOW, VLADIMIR 1889–1962, Russian actor who played Porfiry in the 1947 New York production of *Crime and Punishment*.

SOLTI, GEORG 1912–97, Hungarian-born conductor; conducted Benjamin Britten's *A Midsummer Night's Dream*, which J G directed in 1961.

SOMMER, ELKE b. 1940, German actress who appeared with J G in the TV film *Inside the Third Reich*.

SONNING, NOËLLE 1895–1986, British actress who became better known as the children's author Noël Streatfeild. She appeared with J G in *The Insect Play* in 1923.

SPAIN, NANCY 1917–64, British novelist, broadcaster and journalist.

SPANIER, GINETTE, directrice of the fashion house of Balmain.

SPEAIGHT, ROBERT 1904–76, British actor and writer. A fellow student at RADA, he and J G first appeared together professionally in *King Lear* at the Old Vic in 1931.

SPENCER, MARIAN b. 1905, British actress who first worked with J G in 1943 when she played Mrs Foresight in *Love for Love*.

SPIEGEL, SAM 1903–85, American film producer.

SQUIRE, RONALD 1886–1958, British actor; J G directed him in *Ducks and Drakes* in 1941.

ST JOHN, CHRISTOPHER d. 1960, British writer and friend of Ellen Terry, partner of Edy Craig.

STAMP, TERENCE b. 1938, British actor and writer.

STANDING, JOHN b. 1934, British actor; JG directed him when he took over from Robert Stephens in *Private Lives* in New York, 1974.

STANISLAVSKY, KONSTANTIN 1863–1938, Russian actor, director and teacher.

STANLEY, KIM 1925–2001, American actress.

STEELE, TOMMY b. 1936, British singer and actor.

STEIGER, ROD 1925–2002, American actor.

STEIN, JOSEPH (Jo) b. 1912, American writer and producer.

STEPHENS, ROBERT 1931–95, British actor who first worked with JG in *Tartuffe* at the Old Vic (National Theatre) in 1967; married to Maggie Smith.

STERNE, RICHARD b. 1942, American actor and author of *John Gielgud Directs Richard Burton in Hamlet.* He appeared in JG's 1964 US production of *Hamlet.*

STEVENS, MARTI, American actress and singer.

STEVENS, ROGER 1910–98, American producer.

STEWART, SOPHIE 1908–77, Scottish actress; appeared with JG when she played Joan Clareville in *The Maitlands* in 1934.

STIRLING, PAMELA, British actress.

STOKOWSKI, LEOPOLD 1882–1977, British-born conductor.

STONE, ALIX (Lixie), British stage designer.

STOPPARD, TOM b. 1937, Czech-born British playwright.

STOREY, DAVID b. 1933, British novelist and playwright; JG played Harry in his play *Home* in 1970.

STOTT, JUDITH b. 1929, British actress who first worked with JG in *Much Ado about Nothing* in 1955.

STRASBERG, PAULA 1911–66, American drama coach and wife of Lee Strasberg, director and teacher.

STRASBERG, SUSAN 1938–99, American actress, daughter of Paula and Lee Strasberg.

STRAVINSKY, IGOR 1882–1971, Russian composer.

STREEP, MERYL b. 1949, American actress who appeared with JG in the film of David Hare's *Plenty* (1985).

STREHLER, GIORGIO 1921–97, Italian director.

STREATFEILD, NOËL – see Sonning, Noëlle.

STREISAND, BARBRA b. 1942, American singer and actress.

STRICK, JOSEPH b. 1923, American film producer.

STRIDE, JOHN b. 1936, British actor who played Valerius Catullus in *The Ides of March* in 1963.

STRITCH, ELAINE b. 1925, American actress and singer.

STUART, OTHO 1865–1930, British actor and manager.

STYNE, JULE 1905–94, British-born composer of musicals including *Gypsy* and *Funny Girl.*

SULLAVAN, MARGARET 1911–60, American actress.

SUSSKIND, DAVID 1920–87, American television producer.

SUTHERLAND, DONALD b. 1934, Canadian actor.

SUTHERLAND, JOAN b. 1926, Australian soprano.

SUZMAN, JANET b. 1939, South African-born actress; married to Trevor Nunn.

SWANSON, GLORIA 1898–1983, American actress.

SWINLEY, ION 1891–1937, British actor who first appeared with JG in the tour of *The Wheel* in 1922.

SYKES, CHRISTOPHER 1907–86, British novelist, biographer and BBC radio producer.

TAGG, ALAN 1928–2002, British stage designer; first worked with JG when he designed the sets and costumes for *Halfway up the Tree* in 1967.

TANDY, JESSICA 1909–94, British-born actress who first appeared with JG in *Musical Chairs* in 1931.

TATE, HARRY 1872–1940, British music-hall artiste best known for his *Motoring* sketch.

TAYLOR, ELIZABETH b. 1932, British-born American actress, married (twice) to Richard Burton.

TAYLOR, LILY, wardrobe mistress for H. M. Tennent Ltd.

TE KANAWA, KIRI b. 1944, New Zealand soprano.

TEMPEST, MARIE 1864–1942, British actress. She and JG appeared together in *Dear Octopus* in 1938.

TENNENT H. M. (Harry) 1879–1941, theatrical manager.

TER-ARUTUNIAN, ROUBEN 1920–92, Armenian-born stage and film designer who designed JG's productions of *Ivanov* (1965) and *All Over* (1971).

TERRY, ELLEN 1847–1928, British actress, JG's great-aunt.

TERRY, HAZEL 1918–74, British actress, JG's cousin. She first worked with JG when he directed her in *The Last of Summer* in 1944.

TERRY, KATE 1844–1924, British actress, JG's grandmother.

TERRY, MARION 1852–1930, JG's great-aunt.

TERRY-LEWIS, MABEL 1872–1957, British actress, JG's aunt.

THEBOM, BLANCHE b. 1918, American mezzo-soprano who sang Dido in JG's 1957 production of *The Trojans*.

THESIGER, ERNEST 1879–1961, British actor; first appeared with JG in *Doctor Faustus* at the New Oxford Theatre, London, in 1925.

THOMAS, RICHARD, American actor who appeared with JG in TV adaptation of *The Master of Ballantrae* (1984).

THOMPSON, CARLOS (Juan Carlos Mundin Schaffter) 1923–90, Argentinian actor who was married to Lilli Palmer from 1958 until her death in 1986.

THOMPSON, EMMA b. 1959, British actress; married to (1) Kenneth Branagh.

THOMPSON, ERIC 1929–82, British actor and director.

THOMPSON, JOHN RUSSELL, British actor.

THORNDIKE, SYBIL 1882–1976, British actress, married to Lewis Casson. Apart from charity shows, she and JG first worked together in 1948 in *The Return of the Prodigal*.

THRING, FRANK 1926–94, Australian actor.

TILLEY, VESTA 1864–1952, British music-hall artist.

TITHERADGE, MADGE 1887–1961, Australian actress.

TOMS, CARL 1927–99, British designer of the sets for JG's 1959 production of *The Complaisant Lover*.

TOSCANINI, ARTURO 1867–1957, Italian conductor.

TRACY, SPENCER 1900–67, American actor.

TRAVERS, BILL 1922–94, British actor, married to Virginia McKenna. He appeared with JG in the film of *The Barretts of Wimpole Street* (1957).

TREE, HERBERT BEERBOHM 1853–1917, British actor-manager.

TREE, MAUD 1863–1937, British actress, married to Herbert Beerbohm Tree.

TREE, VIOLA 188?–1938, British actress, daughter of Herbert Beerbohm Tree; she appeared with JG in a charity show in 1935.

TREVOR, AUSTIN 1897–1978, Irish-born actor who worked with JG on a number of occasions, including at the Old Vic in 1921 when JG made his first appearance on the professional stage.

TUCKER, SOPHIE 1884–1966, American vaudeville and cabaret artist.

TURNER, HOWARD b. 1928, American actor and writer.

TUTIN, DOROTHY 1930–2001, British actress who worked with JG for the first time in 1952 when she played Hero in *Much Ado about Nothing*.

TWIGGY (Lesley Hornby) b. 1949, British model and actress.

TYNAN, KENNETH 1927–80, British theatre critic and writer.

ULANOVA, GALINA 1910–98, Russian ballerina.

ULLMANN, LIV b. 1938, Norwegian actress who appeared with JG in the film *Lost Horizon* (1972).

URE, MARY 1933–75, Scots-born actress, married to John Osborne, later Robert Shaw.

USTINOV, PETER b. 1921, British actor, director, writer and raconteur; played Porfiry in the 1946 production of *Crime and Punishment*; JG directed his play *Halfway up the Tree*.

VALENTINA (Valentina Schlee) 1904–89, Russian couturier.

VALLEE, RUDY 1901–86, American singer and actor.

VANBRUGH, IRENE 1872–1948, British actress; worked with JG in a number of charity shows, the first being *A Kiss for Cinderella* in 1933.

VAN DRUTEN, JOHN 1901–57, British playwright.

VANNE, MARDA d. 1970, South African-born actress, partner of Gwen Ffrangcon-Davies.

VAN PRAAGH, PEGGY 1910–90, Australian ballerina.

VARRERE, JEAN, American theatre director?

VERDON, GWEN 1925–2000, American musical comedy actress married to Bob Fosse.

VERSOIS, ODILE 1930–80, French actress.

VIDAL, GORE b. 1925, American writer and critic who wrote the film script of *Caligula*.

VILAR, JEAN 1912–71, French actor, director and founder of Théâtre National Populaire.

VINAVER, STEVEN, British theatre director.

VISCONTI, LUCHINO 1906–76, Italian theatre, opera and film director.

VOSKOVEC, GEORGE 1905–81, Czech-born actor who first worked with JG on *Big Fish, Little Fish* in 1961.

VOSPER, FRANK 1899–1937, British actor and playwright. He and JG first worked together in *Musical Chairs* in 1931.

WAJDA, ANDRZEJ b. 1926, Polish film director.

WALKER, MAVIS, JG's travelling companion and chaperone in later years.

WALKER, RUDOLPH b. 1939, Trinidadian-born actor.

WALLER, DAVID 1920–97, British actor who first appeared with JG in *Henry VIII* at the Old Vic in 1958.

WALLS, TOM 1883–1949, British actor, best known for the Aldwych farces in the 1920s.

WALPOLE, HUGH 1884–1941, British novelist. JG directed the adaptation of his novel, *The Old Ladies*, in 1935.

WALSH, KAY b. 1914, British actress.

WALTON, SUSANA, married to William Walton.

WALTON, TONY b. 1934, British stage designer.

WALTON, WILLIAM 1902–83, British composer who wrote the music for JG's 1942 production of *Macbeth*.

WANAMAKER, SAM 1919–93, American actor and director, founder of the reconstructed Globe Theatre in London.

WARD, PENELOPE DUDLEY 1919–82, British actress.

WARFIELD, DAVID 1866–1951, American actor.

WARNER, CHARLES 1846–1909, British actor.

WARNER, DAVID b. 1941, British actor.

WARNER, DEBORAH, British theatre director.

WARNER, JOHN 1924–2001, South African-born actor.

WARREN JR., WHITNEY 1898–1986, American philanthropist, son of the famous architect.

WARRICK, RUTH b. 1925, American actress directed by JG in *Irene* in 1972.

WASHBOURNE, MONA, 1903–88, British actress who played Kathleen in the 1970 production of *Home*.

WATERS, ETHEL 1896–1977, American actress and jazz singer.

WATFORD, GWEN 1927–94, British actress, married to Richard Bebb.

WATLING, PETER d. 1961, British playwright.

WEBB, ALAN 1906–82, British actor who first worked with JG in *Out of the Sea* in 1928.

WEBB, CLIFTON 1889–1966, American actor.

WEBSTER, BEN 1864–1947, British actor-manager who first worked with JG in *Gloriana* in 1925.

WEBSTER, DAVID ('The Margrave') 1903–71, General Administrator of the Royal Opera House, Covent Garden.

WEBSTER, MARGARET (Peggy) 1905–72, British actress and director, daughter of Ben Webster and May Whitty.

WEIGEL, HELENE 1900–71, German actress, wife of Bertolt Brecht.

WEILL, KURT 1900–50, German composer, married to Lotte Lenya.

WEISSBERGER, ARNOLD 1906–81, American lawyer and agent, partner of Milton Goldman.

WELCH, DENTON 1915–48, British-American writer.

WELCH, ELISABETH 1904–2003, American singer and actress, a member of JG's troupe to Gibraltar in 1942 to entertain the troops.

WELCH, GARTH b. 1936, Australian dancer and choreographer.

WELD, TUESDAY (Susan Ker) b. 1943, American actress.

WELLES, ORSON 1915–85, American actor and film and theatre director. JG played Henry IV in his film *Chimes at Midnight*.

WERFEL, FRANZ 1890–1945, Czech playwright, novelist and poet.

WEST, REBECCA (Cicely Isabel Fairfield) 1892–1983, novelist and journalist.

WHEELER, HUGH 1912–87, British-born writer and lyricist. JG directed his play *Big Fish, Little Fish* in New York in 1961.

WHIGHAM, MARGARET, Duchess of Argyll 1912–93, society hostess.

WHISTLER, REX 1905–44, British artist and designer.

WHITE, PATRICK 1912–90, Australian novelist and playwright.

WHITEHEAD, ROBERT 1916–2002, American producer.

WHITTY, MAY 1865–1948, British actress married to Ben Webster.

WILBOURN, PHYLLIS, companion of Constance Collier and later Katharine Hepburn.

WILDER, CLINTON, American producer.

WILDER, ISABEL 1900–95, sister of Thornton Wilder.

WILDER, THORNTON 1897–1975, American playwright and novelist. In 1963 JG appeared in *The Ides of March*, a play by Jerome Kilty adapted from Wilder's novel of the same name.

WILDING, MICHAEL 1912–79, British actor. JG directed him in *Nude with Violin* when he took over JG's part of Sebastian.

WILLIAMS, BROOK, Welsh actor, son of Emlyn Williams.

WILLIAMS, EMLYN 1905–87, Welsh actor and playwright; JG directed his play *Spring 1600* in 1934 and appeared in *He Was Born Gay* in 1937.

WILLIAMS, HARCOURT (Billy or Billee) 1880–1957, British actor and director. He was resident director at the Old Vic when JG joined the company in 1929.

WILLIAMS, MICHAEL 1935–2001, British actor, married to Judi Dench; appeared with JG in the 1970 film *Eagle in a Cage*.

WILLIAMS (née O'SHANN), MOLLY d. 1970, wife of Emlyn Williams.

WILLIAMS, TENNESSEE 1911–83, American playwright; JG directed his play *The Glass Menagerie* in London in 1948.

WILLIAMSON, NICOL b. 1938, Scottish actor.

WILSON, JACK (John C.) 1899–1961, American theatre manager and producer, friend and associate of Noël Coward.

WILSON, JOHN DOVER 1881–1969, Shakespearean scholar and editor.

WILSON, SANDY b. 1924, British composer.

WINNER, MICHAEL b. 1935, British film director; JG appeared in his remake of *The Wicked Lady* in 1983 and in *Appointment with Death* in 1988.

WINTERS, JONATHAN b. 1925, American actor and comedian; appeared with JG in the film of *The Loved One* (1964).

WINTERS, SHELLEY b. 1922, American actress.

WITHERS, GOOGIE b. 1917, Australian actress.

WOLFIT, DONALD 1902–68, British actor and manager. He first appeared with JG in 1926 in *The Lady of the Camellias*.

WOOD, AUDREY 1905–85, American literary agent.

WOOD, CHARLES b. 1932, British playwright; JG appeared in his screenplay, *The Charge of the Light Brigade* and his play *Veterans* in 1972.

WOOD, JACK master carpenter for H. M. Tennent Ltd.

WOOD, JOHN b. 1930, British actor.

WOOD, PETER b. 1928, British theatre director.

WOODBRIDGE, GEORGE 1907–73, British actor who first appeared with JG in his 1942 production of *Macbeth*.

WOODCOCK, PATRICK 1920–2002, medical practitioner and socialite, JG's doctor.

WOOLLCOTT, ALEXANDER 1887–1943, American dramatic critic and humorist.

WOOLLEY, MONTY 1888–1963, American actor.

WORTH, IRENE 1916–2002, American-born actress, who often worked in Britain. She and JG appeared together for the first time in *A Day by the Sea* in 1953.

WREFORD, EDGAR, b. 1923, British actor.

WRIGHT, HAIDEE 1868–1943, British actress.

WYMAN, JANE b. 1914, American actress.

WYNYARD, DIANA 1906–64, British actress who first worked with JG when she played Beatrice to his Benedick in *Much Ado about Nothing* in 1949.

YARNALL, AGNES 1904–89, American sculptor.

YORK, MICHAEL b. 1942, British actor who appeared with JG in the remake of *Lost Horizon* (1972).

YORK, SUSANNAH b. 1941, British actress who appeared with JG in *Summer's Lease* (1989).

YOUNG, STARK 1881–1963, American critic and writer.

ZEFFIRELLI, FRANCO b. 1923, Italian theatre, opera and film director who directed JG in *Othello* in 1961.

ZINNEMANN, FRED 1907–97, American film director.

Index

John Gielgud is referred to as JG.
Numbers in *italics* indicate letters sent by JG. Titles in *italics* refer to stage productions unless stated otherwise.
Also, theatres are in London unless stated otherwise.